SEEDTIME ON THE CUMBERLAND

SEEDTIME

on the

CUMBERLAND

Harriette Simpson Arnow

With a Foreword by
WILMA DYKEMAN

THE UNIVERSITY PRESS OF KENTUCKY

103449

ISBN: 0-8131-1487-X, cloth; -0146-8, paper
Library of Congress Catalog Card Number: 82-40464

Scholarly publisher for the Commonwealth,
serving Bellarmine College, Berea College, Centre
College of Kentucky, Eastern Kentucky University,
The Filson Club, Georgetown College, Kentucky
Historical Society, Kentucky State University,
Morehead State University, Murray State University,
Northern Kentucky University, Transylvania University,
University of Kentucky, University of Louisville,
and Western Kentucky University.

Editorial and Sales Offices: Lexington, Kentucky 40506-0024

To my parents,
Mollie Jane Denney and Elias Thomas Simpson

CONTENTS

MAPS

The line maps in the text were made especially for this book by Everett Dudley Weldon, and are based on wide research among many authoritative sources too extensive to enumerate.

FOREWORD

WILMA DYKEMAN

WHEN *Seedtime on the Cumberland* was published in 1960 its author had already won critical and popular acclaim as a novelist, particularly for her long and tragic story of an uprooted Appalachian family in *The Dollmaker*. There were those historians who looked with some doubt, perhaps dismay, on the entrance into their discipline of a storyteller with no formal academic degree in the field of history. At the other extreme were critics and fellow novelists who wondered why so gifted a weaver of fiction should withdraw to the dry and dusty archives of the past.

Seedtime on the Cumberland soon dispelled both condescension and misgivings. In her reconstruction of the years of early exploration and settlement from 1780 to 1803 in the Cumberland River country of southern Kentucky and middle Tennessee Harriette Simpson Arnow combined the historian's dedication to thorough research and factual authenticity with the novelist's sensitivity to nuance and irony, human foibles and ingenuity in the service of survival and eventual shaping of a society.

In the concluding chapter of *The Structures of Everyday Life,* Volume One of his monumental study, *Civilization and Capitalism,* Fernand Braudel evokes a vivid personal memory. "A very old bell used to strike the hour in the little village in Lorraine where I grew up as a child; the village pond drove an old mill wheel; a stony path, as old as the world, plunged down like a torrent in front of my house; the house itself had been rebuilt in 1806, the year of Jena, and hemp used to be retted in the stream at the bottom of the meadows. I only have to think of these things and this book opens out for me afresh. Every reader, prompted by a chance memory or journey or a passage in a book, can do the same."

In the opening pages of *Seedtime on the Cumberland* Harriette Simpson Arnow recalls the moment of her initial conscious inspiration and research in local history. "It was not until I was eighteen years old, away from home in a remote place, that I made my first note—a description of a shot bag of ground hog hide, realizing as I looked at the old, worn thing that when the great storytellers died and mice and rats and time had their way, many little things of the ordinary people would be lost."

Arnow shares Braudel's sense of the specific and the personal: "Times and places were mingled in my head"; she writes, "the past was part of the present, close as the red cedar water bucket in the kitchen, or the big cherry press put together with pegs, or the parched corn a grandmother now and then made for us." And she says, "My people loved the past more than their present lives, I think, but it cannot be said we lived in the past. Two things tied all time together; these had run through most of the old stories to shape the lives of men, and so did they shape our lives and the lives of the people about us. These were the land and the Cumberland."

I do not consider it inappropriate to associate the Frenchman Braudel, acknowledged by many of his peers to be "the greatest living historian," with the work of Kentuckian Harriette Simpson Arnow. On a smaller canvas, within a more limited time frame, Arnow fulfills the vindication set forth by Braudel: "It remains for me to justify one last choice: that of introducing everyday life, no more no less, into the domain of history. Was this useful? Or necessary? Everyday life consists of the little things one hardly notices in time and space. The more we reduce the focus of vision, the more likely we are to find ourselves in the environment of material life: the broad sweep usually corresponds to History with a capital letter, to distant trade routes, and the networks of national or urban economies. If we reduce the length of time observed, we either have the event or the everyday happening. The event is, or is taken to be, unique: the everyday happening is repeated, and the more often it is repeated the more likely it is to become a generality or rather a structure. It pervades society at all levels, and characterises ways of being and behaving which are perpetuated through endless ages."

Details of "the environment of material life" are precisely what Arnow has searched out so diligently and recorded so imaginatively in *Seedtime on the Cumberland*. Over a long period of years she gleaned data from family journals, court records, and personal inventories, gathered minutiae from regional, state and local archives, obscure as well as familiar documents and monographs and other traditional sources. Above all, she held fast to that oral history which was a rich and remarkable part of her own family and regional experience. Like the midden at some ancient archaeological site these accumulated items became a treasure awaiting the insight and organization of an interpreter. Shaped by Arnow the material became more than an exemplary document of local history. It grew into a classic study of the Old Southwest, the opening of the Appalachian frontier, the confrontation and adaptation of European and native Indian and the land to which each laid claim.

From beds of limestone laid down in the dim mists of Ordovician ages to the pioneer's gun and cedar washtub and search for salt, from networks of Indian trails lacing the landscape to the settlers' log cabins, rendering of lard and making of soap, shaping of ballads and herbal medicines, scarcely a daily activity or everyday necessity escapes Arnow's full attention. Gradually we begin to comprehend the challenges of a transplanted people responding to an unfamiliar landscape and an understandably hostile host resisting the intrusion of acquisitive strangers. Steadily we respond to the fullness of Arnow's knowledge and its elaboration from the individual and the particular to the general and the community empiricism. And consistently the writing is sharp, exact, sensory, thought-provoking.

There is, for example, a paragraph on the lowly rural skill of whittling: "All farmers gouged, and scutched, and chopped, and rived, and drew, and bored, but more than anything they whittled, and like generations of borderers before them they never got caught up with their whittling. The first things whittled would have been handles for the extra axes, hoes, mattocks, broadaxes and other tools brought. Night in and night out while the wife and daughters spun or carded or sewed by the fire the settler and his older sons must whittle—pegs of many sizes, a button for the barn door, gears of some good hardwood, oak or beech for the horse mill, dasher for the churn, spinning stick, powder funnel, or some intricate thing such as a wooden door lock, complete with turning key. . . . He could never stop whittling; he worked with knife and wood while sitting up with the sick or the dead, or waiting for a turn of corn to be ground or his horse to be shod, or the auction to begin. And always he chose his wood with care; beech wood for the plane stock, but dogwood for the weaving shuttle with bobbin."

Describing the crucial choice each settler made regarding location of home and barn, Arnow draws upon her personal knowledge of place, seasons, and a farmer's needs to create this sharply rendered passage: "The hill and valley farm, still much a part of life on the Cumberland, had other certain things; but these could not be eaten, sold, or worn—an ever-changing variety of shadow and sunlight not found in flat lands or among great mountains. Each farm is different, yet roughly most follow a pattern. Few settlers or their descendants wanted to live low in a valley, but high on the hill where they would like to be, took them too far from the corn, tobacco, wheat, and other crops in the valley as well as the road that usually followed the creek, and so they compromised and settled halfway up the hill.

"Crops and barns lie below them; above are pasture fields, below or around is the orchard with beehives, and even now an occasional bee gum under the trees, and a rich and level spot near the house for a garden. Each thing suited to its particular location. Such a farm has a quality unknown in any other for it feels the changing shape of hill shadow; the winter afternoons when all below lies cold and blue and the creek pools slowly skim with ice, the upper slopes are warm and bright; or on another farm the child coming home from school on the southern side of a hill steps from a snowless world of sunshine into a snowy waste of limestone crag and undripping icicles that lie above his northwardly sloping home. Each had its advantages."

Arnow concludes that those first settlers in the Cumberland River country were basically still English colonials. She says, "The successful pioneer was a master hand at adapting old learnings to a new environment; we see this not only in the physical aspects of his life—log house learned from the Swede; whiskey from the Scotch; corn, moccasins, poplar dugout, from the Indians, but also in the pattern of agriculture, trade, industry, education, speech, and all other aspects of his life."

When we have finished reading the last well-wrought page of *Seedtime on the Cumberland* we know those aspects of life at that place and in that time in full and flavorful detail. We have experienced, for a brief and memorable moment, part of that frontier life in transition from its European past to its American future.

AUTHOR'S ACKNOWLEDGMENTS

THIS work is not a history, nor is it concerned with the lives of famous men and women, nor does it pretend to be an exhaustive study of the pioneer. I have tried to re-create a few of the more important aspects of pioneer life as it was lived on the Cumberland by ordinary men and women. I owe the bit of knowledge gleaned entirely to all the other people, those now dead who took the time and trouble to save a store account or write their memoirs, and the living who furnished material, told me where it could be located, or answered questions. I can't remember my first question about the past; there was for many years no conscious hunting. I took the tales and songs that came my way with half a listening for many of the voices belonged to the very old and I was very young. I cannot even acknowledge them, not knowing exactly who told what.

It was not until I was eighteen years old, away from home in a remote place, that I made my first note—a description of a shot bag of ground hog hide, realizing as I looked at the old, worn thing that when the great storytellers died and mice and rats and time had their way, many little things of the ordinary people would be lost.

I wrote in time of younger days, but through all the writing there were the reminders of a way of life long dead for most—a word or phrase, a song, a game, a plant used for medicine. Notes for a work on the past went on and the background reading. I at first hoped to write of the old days and old ways of our world in Kentucky—the country of the Big South Fork and the Cumberland below it down to Tennessee. Readers of my fiction sometimes suggested I try such a work; one of the most interested was Mr. Marcellus B. Frost in Nashville, a sender of notes and clippings.

Ten years or so ago the hunt quickened, and all reading became centered on the past, but soon I realized that we in Kentucky south of the Cumberland with neither roads nor railroads, only the river, had had no world of our own. The past and the future for the old had been in Tennessee—all things went down the Cumberland, all goods up. Nashville was their town.

Thus it was that my searching centered in the Tennessee archives at Nashville. Mrs. Gertrude Morton Parsley, Reference Librarian, State Library Division, Tennessee State Library and Archives, was for many years an unfailing source of information on where to find what and sometimes on what, both in person during my several trips to the Library and in the furnishing of photostats, sketches, and microfilm, with many letters to clear up doubtful points. Mr. Robert T. Quarles, Jr., in his dual role of President of the Tennessee Historical Society and Director of the Archives of the State of Tennessee, gave me in conversation some of the history of early settlers he carries in his head, and guided me to many helpful manuscripts. I, in time, approached Dr. Henry Lee Swint, Professor of History, Vanderbilt University, to ask the very great favor—would he read the manuscript? He not only agreed but in the course of conversations through the years gave many helpful suggestions on possible source materials.

Another most helpful in suggesting sources and furnishing photostatic material was Dr. Josephine L. Harper, Manuscript Librarian, State Historical Society, The State of Wisconsin. Help came also from members of the staff of the Joint University Library of Nashville, Homer Chance and staff of the Ann Arbor Public Library, Dr. Jacqueline Bull, Archivist of the University of Kentucky Libraries, the New York Public Library, and, of course, the Detroit Public Library where the work began. I am particularly indebted to Chief James M. Babcock and staff of the Burton Historical Collection, and to Mrs. Frances Brewer of the Rare Book Room, both in Detroit.

The work could not have been completed without the use of the libraries of the University of Michigan, and for permission to use them I am deeply indebted to Dr. Frederick H. Wagman, Director of the University Library. Particularly helpful were Miss Margaret I. Smith and staff of the Reference Department and Miss Ella Hymans of the Rare Book Room, though I at one time or another got much help from the Transportation Library, the Natural Resources Library, the Medical Library, and the General Library where most published materials cited in the work—state records, historical magazines, biographies, collections of correspondence—were to be had. Material and help came also from the staff of the William L. Clements Library; particularly helpful in pointing out early and rare maps and furnishing photostats for study was Dr. Christian Brun, Map and Print Librarian.

Furnishing photostats and giving time in correspondence were R. N. Williams, 2nd, Director of The Historical Society of Pennsylvania, and Dr. Roy W. Drier, Professor, Michigan College of Mining and Technology. The U.S. Army Engineers of the Nashville District have through the years answered a very great many questions relative to the pre-locks-and-dams history of the Cumberland, and furnished much helpful material unobtainable elsewhere. Help came also from the Department of Ethnology, Smithsonian Institution; the late Anna Liza Wilson of Keno, Kentucky; and Louis D. Wallace, Editor, Department of Agriculture, State of Tennessee, who furnished much material and answered many questions relative to early agriculture.

I am particularly indebted to Mrs. A. S. Frye, Somerset, Kentucky; she not only found many hard to get and privately printed source materials but did a great deal of the research and typed early court records from the Kentucky counties on the Cumberland. I am grateful for the time given by the staffs of the various museums mentioned in this work, and particularly so to the late Mr. Russell Dyche of London, Kentucky, who answered many questions relative to the tools of the pioneer; and Mr. Massey of the Mountain Life Museum, Levi Jackson Wilderness Road State Park in Kentucky, who spent a great deal of time bringing all manner of objects from spinning sticks to drawing knives outside for photographing. A deep debt is owed also to the many families with heirlooms who invited us into their homes, gave permission for photographing, and explained and told histories; sometimes a calf yoke such as that of Mr. Kemmer at Kemmer's Stand in Tennessee; other times an especially fine example of set ware, like the churn made without metal, belonging to Loretta Rogers of Monticello, Kentucky. Especially helpful were Mr. and Mrs. Henry Hail, Mr. and Mrs. Grover Foster, and Mr. and Mrs. Norman I. Taylor, all of Pulaski County, Kentucky, and Mr. and Mrs. Fanillen Bell, Mr. and Mrs. Jackson Denney, Mr. and Mrs. James Simpson, and Mr. and Mrs. John C. Burton, all of Wayne County, Kentucky, and Mr. Ed McMurtry of Castalian Springs, Tennessee.

As usual in any piece of writing the neighbors did their share. Dr. Eugene Leslie not only loaned contour maps and materials and told me much of the region's geology, but also read and criticized the chapter on geology.

I am deeply grateful to Dr. Madeline Kneberg, Professor of Anthropology, University of Tennessee, for reading and criticizing the chapter on the prehistory of the region.

I wish also to express my gratitude to the many individuals and institutions who gave permission to quote a publication or manuscript; without such the work could not have been accomplished.

In time the giant manuscript reached Dr. Swint who read, commented, and offered suggestions. Many of these were incorporated in this much smaller work, but such opinions, expressed or implied, contradictions, conclusions, or mistakes are the sole property of the author. They cannot be blamed on Dr. Swint or any of the others who read the material for accuracy; they did not see the final manuscript carved from the original.

My husband, as usual, corrected and edited, and daughter Marcella typed bibliography, reference cards, sketched reference maps and artifacts, while all, including son Tommy, bore with me on the many trips up and down and all around the basin of the Cumberland.

EXPLANATION OF BIBLIOGRAPHICAL REFERENCES

UNPUBLISHED RECORDS

The county records of Tennessee are from the typescripts prepared under the supervision of Mrs. John Trotwood Moore, and housed in the State Library Division of the Tennessee State Library and Archives, Nashville, and used by permission of Gertrude Morton Parsley, Reference Librarian. I have followed the original page numberings for convenience in referring to the originals. The original early Sumner County Records are the property of the Archives Division, Tennessee State Library and Archives, Nashville; the others named are owned by their respective counties and housed in the county courthouses.

There was among the early court clerks no standard method of labeling or enumerating records. Smith County, Tennessee, Court Minutes Books are quite typical; listed by letter—A, B, etc.; and in the same county one set of records was referred to as *Inventories and Appraisements*, with the first wills in another volume, while the Minutes of the county courts were often labeled *Order Book*. I have, to avoid confusion, followed the system of Mrs. Moore; all volumes are listed by Roman numerals, thus A is now I. I have also adopted a standardized title, thusly:

DC, I	*Davidson County Court Minutes, 1783–1790.*
DW, I	*Davidson County Wills and Inventories, 1784–1794.*
DW, II	*Ibid., 1794–1805.*
MW, I	*Montgomery County Wills and Inventories, 1797–1810.*

SC, I	*Sumner County Court Minutes, 1787–1791.*
SC, II	*Ibid., 1791–1796.*
Smith C, I	*Smith County Court Minutes, 1799–1804.*
Smith W, V	*Smith County Wills, 1814–1826.*
SW, I	*Sumner County Wills and Inventories, 1789–1822.*

All the above county records are now a part of the Records of the State of Tennessee, but prior to 1790 Davidson and Sumner counties were a part of North Carolina; the same counties were a part of the Territory South of the River Ohio, 1790–1796; it was not until the creation of the State of Tennessee in 1796 that any county was officially part of Tennessee.

The Kentucky counties studied were first a part of Virginia, and beginning in 1780 a part of Lincoln County.

LC, I, thus refers to *Lincoln County Court Order Book*, microfilm edition, housed in the Margaret I. King Library, University of Kentucky, and used by permission of Archivist Dr. Jacqueline Bull.

As counties were created on the Cumberland, the records of each were listed under the name of the county, and housed in the various courthouses. Kentucky has made no record of the originals, and all references are to the manuscripts, though I have taken the same liberty as with those of Tennessee in volume numberings, and have, in so far as possible, adopted standardized titles, thusly:

CW, II	*Cumberland County Will Book* (inventories and sales are also included) B, *1815–1825.*
PC, I	*Pulaski County, Court Minutes, 1799–1803.*
PD, I	*Pulaski County, Deed Book, 1799–1805.*
PD, IV	*Ibid., 1819–1821.*
PW, I	*Pulaski County, Wills and Inventories, 1801–1818.*
PW, II	*Ibid., 1818–1829.*
WC, I	*Wayne County Court Minutes, 1801–1824.*
WD, I	*Wayne County, Deed Book, 1801–1821.*
WM, I	*Wayne County, Mortgage Book, A, 1832–1837.*
WW, II	*Wayne County Wills and Inventories, 1827–1848.*

PUBLISHED RECORDS AND COLLECTIONS

AMS	American State Papers, Washington, 1832–1861.
I	Illinois Historical Collections.
I, V	Clarence W. Alvord, ed., *Kaskaskia Records, 1778–1790*, Springfield, 1909.

I, VIII   James Alton James, ed., *George Rogers Clark Papers, 1771–1781,* Springfield, 1912.

I, XVI   (III British Series) Clarence W. Alvord and C. E. Carter, *Trade and Politics in the Illinois Country, 1767–1769,* Springfield, 1921.

Material from the volumes listed above is reprinted by permission of the publishers and copyright holders, the Illinois State Historical Library, Springfield, Illinois.

M   Archives of Maryland, published by authority of the State under direction of the Maryland Historical Society, and edited by William Hand Browne.

M, VIII   *Proceedings of the Council of Maryland, 1687–1688,* Baltimore, 1890.

M, XXIII *Ibid., 1696/97–1698,* Baltimore, 1903.

NCR   *The Records of North Carolina,* published by order of the General Assembly under the supervision of the trustees of the Public Libraries, I, IX and X collected and edited by William L. Saunders.

NCR, I   *The Colonial Records of North Carolina, 1662–1712,* Goldsboro, 1886.

NCR, IX   *Ibid., 1771–1775,* Raleigh, 1890.

NCR, X   *Ibid., 1775–1776,* Raleigh, 1890.

The following were collected and edited by Walter Clark.

NCR, XII   *The State Records of North Carolina, 1777–1778,* Winston, 1895.

NCR, XIII *Ibid., 1778–1779,* Goldsboro, 1896.

NCR, XVI   *Ibid., 1782–1783,* Goldsboro, 1899.

NCR, XVII *Ibid., 1781–1785,* Goldsboro, 1899.

NCR, XVIII *Ibid., 1786, with a supplement from 1779,* Goldsboro, 1900.

NCR, XIX   *Ibid., 1782–1784, with a supplement from 1771–1782,* Goldsboro, 1901.

NCR, XX   *Ibid., 1781–1785,* Goldsboro, 1902.

NCR, XXI   *Ibid., 1788–1790,* Goldsboro, 1903.

NCR, XXII *Miscellaneous Records of the State of North Carolina,* Goldsboro, 1895.

NCR, XXIV *Laws of the State of North Carolina, 1777–1788,* Goldsboro, 1895.

TP   The Territorial Papers of the United States.

TP, IV   Clarence Edwin Carter, ed., *The Territory South of the River Ohio, 1790–1796*, Washington, 1936.

VS   Virginia *Calender of State Papers and Other Manuscripts;* published under authority of the Library Committee, and edited by William P. Palmer.

VS, I   *Ibid., 1652–1781*, Richmond, 1875.

VS, II   *Ibid., 1781*, Richmond, 1881.

VS, III   *Ibid., 1782–1784*, Richmond, 1883.

VS, IV   *Ibid., 1785–1789*, Richmond, 1884.

MANUSCRIPT

W   Manuscript originals in the possession of the State Historical Society of Wisconsin, Madison, Wisconsin.

My heavy use of this material, collected by Lyman C. Draper, takes two forms. Many journals and other source materials cited have reprinted portions of the Draper Manuscripts; original source of such materials is indicated by W, followed by series, volume number, and page when given.

Heaviest use was made of the microfilm edition of the Draper Manuscripts, issued by the State Historical Society of Wisconsin.

MAGAZINES

A   American *Historical Magazine and Tennessee Historical Society Quarterly*, pub., Tennessee Historical Society, Nashville, 1896–1904.

FP   Publication of the Filson Club, 1–32, Louisville, 1884–1922.

FQ   *The Filson Club History Quarterly*, 1926—. Material used by permission of the publisher and copyright owner, the Filson Club, Louisville, Kentucky.

RK   *Register* Kentucky *State Historical Society*, 1902—. Material reprinted by permission of the publisher and copyright holder, the Kentucky Historical Society, Frankfort, Kentucky.

THM   Tennessee *Historical Magazine*, Series I and II, 1915–1937. Material reprinted by permission of the publisher and copyright holder, Tennessee Historical Society, Nashville, Tennessee.

VM   Virginia *Magazine of History and Biography*, 1893—. Material reprinted by permission of the publisher and copyright holder, Virginia Historical Society, Richmond, Virginia.

SEEDTIME ON THE CUMBERLAND

CHAPTER I

THE OLD BOOT

I COULD see Granpa in spite of the pitch dark. His hat was dark felt, low-crowned, wide-brimmed, and his clothes were blue and faded; around him was none of the bright trappings of war, neither silver sword, nor waving flag; the long eight-sided gun barrel was dull; only the gunstock of close-grained, well oiled maple made a faint shine like a half-smothered star. The powder horn high up around his neck was old and yellowed; a fit mate for the shot bag of ground hog hide. Still, in the black foggy dark I could see everything, even the little charger of whittled bone, swinging and jingling on the powder horn string.

The only brightness was in the horse, sorrel, bright as red clay in the rain, but so wet I couldn't tell if the mat of bubbles on his chest was sweat lather or river foam. I could only crouch shivering and watch. A few seconds ago the water had been to the horse's knees; now it rolled by the saddle girth; and while I watched, a ripple lapped against a saddle bag; but Granpa came on, the bridle held lightly in his right hand, the gun high in his left, the butt not touching the water.

Granpa never looked in my direction, but I was conscious of his face —pale blue eyes, dark brown skin with furrows down the thin cheeks, and lank black hair, combed back and tied with a careless whang that had let strands loosen and fall across his forehead. I searched his face for fear or trouble, but couldn't find any. A long riffle of foam came whirling down and the water coiled like yellow snakes. I wanted to cry out, but did not. Granpa's life depended upon silence as well as on the horse.

I couldn't bear to watch; the horse was going under; Granpa's left arm was trembling like a tree in the breaking stillness before a storm, for al-

1

ways he must hold the gun higher to keep water out of the breeching. I buried my face on my knees, but peeped just as the horse's nose bobbed under. I waited, breath held, until he flung it up, snorting and blowing and flinging his head about as if he would see the sky—but there was no sky— only the rainy dark and the Brandywine rolling down.

The horse rolled part way over, lifeless as a log; I saw the glint of his right front shoe as the main current of the river took its will of him, turning his head downstream away from me, but Granpa stayed with him and kept gun and powder dry.

I wanted to comfort myself with thought of a young river maple I had watched fight a high June tide on the Cumberland. The water would roll over it, and it would bow its head all the way under; but when the slim trunk seemed broken or bended for-ever, the top would spring up, and with a great gurgling leap free itself from the flood. Over and over the sapling had done that, fighting the river all through the hours of the tide, and winning, for when I went back to see, it had been straight with no memory of the flood save for the stalks of young corn, uprooted and caught in its branches.

The memory was no help. I watched a horse, not a tree; only the green cornstalks were the same; these from somebody's late roasting ear patch up the Brandywine were whirling down, entangling the man and the horse. I squinted, unable either to hope or despair. I couldn't tell if what I saw were the roily bottom of a wave or the horse's withers. The water surged again, but just as I started to squinch my eyes, I saw the horse's neck, all of it down to his chest, and then I saw the shoulder muscles ripple. The horse was over the hog back of the current, and he was swimming, strong and sure.

There was more to the story, but the rest never mattered. Granpa was all right. We heard his horse's shoes soft on wet leaves as he rode away through the rain and the dark to join the Americans and Count Pulaski. Now that the terrible need for secrecy and silence was over, we shifted, straightened, and eased our cramped muscles. The Tories couldn't get Granpa now as they could have done while he slipped through their lines and crossed the river.

Which Granpa? How many greats back? I never asked. In time I learned his name was Thomas Merritt. He was only one of many grandfathers and grandmothers, uncles and aunts, their kith, kin, and enemies, as well as many animals, both wild and domestic, who came to our house, often as now in winter when the lamps were lighted, and the black and ugly wood-burning stove a sister had named Hirschevogel filled the room with heat and a pleasant roaring.

I remember my father's eyes were blue in the lamplight and his hair was black, and these I gave our grandsire; but of my father's voice and the other voices around me I remember nothing. Grandfather Merritt like all other people and things the voices brought to life, blotted out the world around me while I listened; even the songs are unconnected now with the tone of the singer. Our father sang much, not just the hymns and ballads common to our household, but sinful dance tunes such as *Buffalo.* He and our mother recited much poetry; I think they remembered everything learned as children or taught as teachers, but whether story, song, or poem, there were visions in their voices. Hard-hearted Barbara Allen was tall and fair with reddish hair, but Shady Grove was little and dark with a straight black bang.

Isaac Watts was dead before the Revolution, but his hymns, sung often and many with more of the militant air of a march than submissive resignation unto God, always brought fresh and many-colored visions of God's awful throne, the land of Canaan, the river Jordan, and quite often Satan. Our father's stories and songs came mostly of evenings, but the songs and the stories of our mother and grandmothers came and went effortlessly, unceasingly as the wind on our hill. There was at first, for me at least, no conscious act of listening; the human voice was a part of life taken for granted since everybody sang or talked while he or she worked; even the woman who came at times to wash the clothes and scrub the bare kitchen floor, she also told stories and sang.

I shivered at the tickety-tack of a death warning, or watched in silent awe as the cattle knelt at midnight on Old Christmas; my heart leaped up with dreams of hidden riches as the blind man groped in vain for the lost pots of silver. I heard the panther answer when the woman down on New River called her eaten child. I shivered at the pretty woman with a basket who could change herself into a doe; and all life left me while I watched the wild hogs, the woman, and her baby.

Most of the stories were of true things from the borderless land of long ago. This was a place in time unmeasured by years; the days on the other side of the mountains when some of our people had read the Bible in German and nailed geese to boards for fattening seemed no further away than the time a great-grandmother attending a house party helped her girl friend engineer a late-houred dance in a religious home—no word of rebuke was spoken; young hostess and guests were aroused at four o'clock and made spin all day with the slaves. Even the dim time beyond the ocean when others of us were bloodied but proud under the word Covenanter seemed no further back than when the chimneys fell in the earthquake of 1811.

Early, I knew death in many forms; the guerrillas alone in The War had used all manner of means in killing men of all ages. I tasted the bitterness of political battles and religious schisms, attended many schools both as pupil and teacher, wandered through the tanbark woods, the stave woods, the log woods, watched the burning creeks in the early oil fields, smelled the saltpeter caves, and the wool that had to be pulled from sheep dead of the wildcats if a body wanted linsey-woolsey. I saw the Cherokee in Georgia when I went on trips with the cattle, horse, and hog drovers. I knew floods, drouths, fires, storms, and the disaster of May snow on full-leafed timber. I, too, felt the blood on my feet and staggered with weakness when I watched the struggles of Granpa Dick to catch a bird as weak and chilled as he somewhere in the bitter weather of the north in the War of 1812; and so great was my hunger I never gagged as I swallowed the warm blood and cold feet of the still-trembling bird.

Times and places were mingled in my head; the past was part of the present, close as the red cedar water bucket in the kitchen, or the big cherry press put together with pegs, or the parched corn a grandmother now and then made for us. This was the same as the parched corn from the old days, or the cornmeal mush we sometimes ate, no different at all from the mush in the stories. An old shirt in a trunk upstairs, square-armholed, stitched by hand, of cotton grown and woven and spun on the Big South Fork of the Cumberland, could have been the same as that worn by some old granpa with many greats before his name. My people loved the past more than their present lives, I think, but it cannot be said we lived in the past. Two things tied all time together; these had run through most of the old stories to shape the lives of men, and so did they shape our lives and the lives of the people about us. These were the land and the Cumberland.

There was at the head of our stairs a window; and always at night, no matter what the weather, I pulled the curtain; and if I carried a lamp, I pushed my face close against the glass to shut out the light in order the better to see. Many times during the day just passed I would have seen the same thing, but still I looked. Our house rose gaunt and white and high on the western side of a hill above the Cumberland; east were the hills and from our eastern windows we could see nothing save our own hill rising, but west past the river lay a wide sweep of hilly to gently rolling country. The Highland Rim it is called in Tennessee, Pennyrile in Kentucky, and a kind of no man's land between the Bluegrass and the Cumberland Plateau or hills.

Living so at the meeting place of Highland Rim and hill was like having a prize seat in some vast amphitheatre. We could, on fair days or on the white moonlit nights of winter, see for miles and miles across the old high valley of the Cumberland, and past this rows of low hills until earth and sky met in a dark nothingness. Northward we could see at night the lights from the county seat town of Somerset; nearby was Ferguson with its railroad shops and roundhouse where the big double headers were hooked up for the long pull over the mountains and into Tennessee. South and west all set about in the dark, so dim at times there was wonder if it be light or low star, were the lighted windows of farm homes, many at that time yellow-gleaming from coal oil lamps, for electric lights like many other things, including roads, were slow in coming to our part of the country.

Closer, were the brighter lights of Burnside that, after pausing on a narrow bench of level land at the point where the Big South Fork met the Cumberland, rose step-like over limestone bluffs and ledges to a hilly bench of higher land where the churches, the school and most of the homes, all painted white, were gathered. Even in its boom days during my early childhood when all the business life of the town was gathered in the lowland by the river, the place had hardly more than a thousand people; but in it were five churches, five lumber mills, several stores, a Masonic Temple, the brick building housing both elementary and high schools, a bank, and a frame hotel with more than seven gables.

I remember the mules pulling the heavily loaded wagons up from the ferry or the steamboat landing. I remember the stagecoach that ran between Burnside and Monticello until 1915; and all about me were people like my grandmothers and Cousin Dora Taylor who remembered well the days before the coming of the railroad in '78 when the Cumberland was the only highway, and most things from pianos to candy came from Nashville.

There was a varied life in the town, though many now would make of us all one, for all of us were native born, white, and Protestant when we got religion. I do recall that once I heard talk of a foreigner. He dealt in meat, and his speech was strange; worse, nobody had so much as seen his father, or even knew where he had been born—Cincinnati some said. In any case he was not one of our people. There were others not of us exactly—some of the mill owners and managers, but they had been there many years; every one knew from where they came and they had relatives.

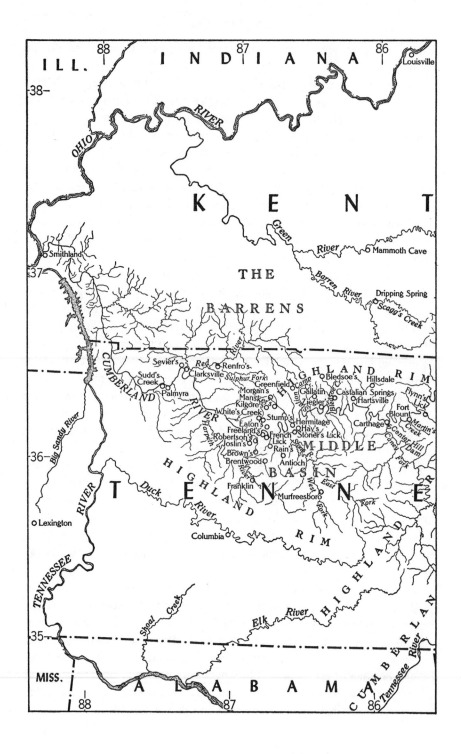

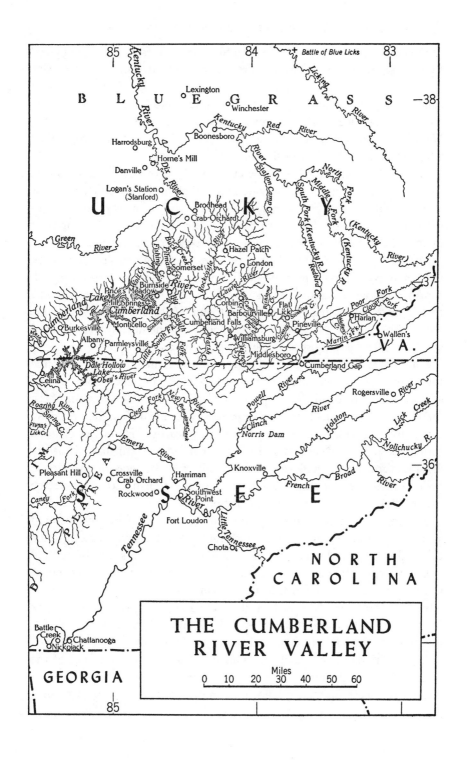

THE CUMBERLAND
RIVER VALLEY

Miles
0   10   20   30   40   50   60

The scarcity of nearby relatives troubled me at times as a child, and often I felt a stranger there, though I can recall no one unknown to me as I went about the innumerable family errands. There was in the town a good handful of people, including teachers in school and Sunday school, to be cousined. Still, we were strangers; many of our classmates such as the Newells and the Richardsons lived on land heired down from first settlers who had come at the close of the Revolution.

I could not from the window see even the lights of our country—a part of the adjoining county of Wayne, hidden behind hills to the south; for we were hill people. I had been born there, the fifth of most of my generations, and it was from Wayne that most of the stories came. No horses of my childhood could ever be so fine as the five-gaited saddle horses that took prizes at the Wayne County Fair, nor mules so strong and sleek and black and big, hickories so straight and tall, nor Teachers' Institutes so filled with romance and leg o' mutton sleeves. I knew the big hickories were gone like the chestnut oak, skinned for its tanbark and left to die; the big chestnuts were dying with blight, oxen were seldom seen, metheglin never brewed at all any more, and most of our kin were gone away.

Still, it was there, a place in the geography of time, built on the same things that shaped our lives—the land and the river. Everybody owned at least a little land, and the expression "land poor" was common. Many families of the town had at least a vegetable garden and a family cow, daily twice-driven to and from some pasture field nearby. "He comes of good farming stock," was enough said of the birthright of a man, and earthly dreams were not of mink coats and Cadillacs or of vice-presidencies in great industrial establishments, but to own a good farm with a big stretch of bottom land and a fair boundary of timber.

Farming was not just an occupation. It was a way of life that colored all our days from birth till death with family food coming directly from the land or the products of the land converted into milk and butter and meat and eggs. In the old days all through our country of the upper Cumberland the bigger farms had been worlds more sufficient unto themselves than farms would ever be today. The land had given cotton or flax for a sheet, wool for a coat, saltpeter for gunpowder, or white oak for barrel staves. The family farm had place for the family graveyard as well as blacksmith shop and distillery. This was true to a lesser extent of the rolling, wondrously fertile lands of the Cumberland Country in Middle Tennessee where practically all crops known to the American Colonies, save rice and possibly indigo,[1] were grown in the early days. Cotton had once been the most important cash crop around Nashville, but never king as in the deeper south, for the Cumberland would never have a king, not even Andrew Jackson.

The land itself could not have been called king; we loved it too well, even more if possible, since there was less of it, than did the farmers southwest of us in the Tennessee Bluegrass. Seldom I think, if ever, were we envious when a letter or a relative visiting back home reminded us that in distant places—Texas, Missouri, Canada, or Oregon—for the people like most other products of our country had to go away—there were vast stretches of level, rock-free land.

Land without rocks and flat for miles like a river bottom was hard to imagine. In no place save in the bottoms could one get very far from the rock. If rocks are the bones of the earth, our hill is a skeleton; it was no uncommon thing to dig post holes with dynamite. Even in the Tennessee Bluegrass the old stone walls attest to the number of rocks once on now smooth fields; and though Nashville has borne many proud titles such as "Athens of the West," the finest phrase of all, I think, is "splendid City of the Rocks looks down." [2]

Land, land, no matter what it was—cedar bluff, sheep skull rock, creek meadow, sage grass field, or pine ridge—we loved it all. Our love was not untouched with materialism. All land was good for something. The steepest and rockiest of limestone hillsides would grow cedar; and hanging over all of Burnside as in many places in the Cumberland Country was the smell of cedar, some from the pencil factory and some from Mr. French's works which, among other things, made faucets for the wine barrels of France.

Timber, coal, stone quarry, or oil field could bring money from the land. Our household was for a time brightened by oil checks from Wayne, small and divided among many heirs, but a pleasant income from some mineral rights heired by our father; sweeter because unearned; often we children heard, "Even a mule can work," but we also heard, "An idle mind is the devil's workshop."

[1] Daniel Smith, *A short description of the State of Tennessee, lately called the Territory of the United States south of the river Ohio*, Philadelphia, 1796 (cited hereafter as Smith, *Description*), mentioned, 24, rice and indigo among the crops "to be most important," but I can find neither record nor tradition of either having been grown on the Cumberland.

[2] John M. Gray, *The Life of Joseph Bishop*, Nashville, 1858 (cited hereafter as Gray, *Bishop*), 218. Joseph Bishop, "the little shooting Bishop," was a mighty hunter, Indian scout, and bailiff who settled in Middle Tennessee in 1791.

Much of the family talk and many of the stories centered on the land, but the land could never stand alone. Running through it all was some creek or spring or branch or river that drained into the Cumberland, if not the river itself. This was a heritage from Virginia where the boundaries of land were marked by the water courses. As early as 1769 fifty-six Virginians had petitioned for "60,000 acres of land in the upper valley of the Cumberland River," with the boundaries to begin at the "Falls of Cumberland." [3] Once started, such a system could not be stopped— "Thence up the creek sixteen poles from the third fallover of Little Indian Creek," so runs a call, typical of many others, defining a boundary of land bought several years ago on the Big South Fork of the Cumberland.

North Carolina, owning all the middle Cumberland, attempted a system of square corners for her lands beyond the mountains, but never quite succeeded. Today most farms in the Cumberland Country have a bit of hill and a bit of hollow, and many roads such as Shake Rag Creek and Sugar Creek in Tennessee bear the names of creeks they followed in the days when creek bed and road were often one.

Thus, the land and consequently the scenes of most of the stories were pin-pointed by running water: "the little mare from the Elk Spring Valley," "the year your mama taught Big Sinking," or "the buggy that got washed away at Fishing Creek Ford." Men were born and were buried, not in the half-remembered names of non-existent places that were names only, thought up to make the exchange of mail possible, but on creeks and branches. George Rogers Clark had owned land down around Meadow Creek in Wayne; [4] Andrew Jackson had had a store on Stone's River, not far from the Cumberland; the Long Hunters and Daniel Boone had spent much time down around Mill Springs; Davie Crockett lived a while down on Obey's River, not so far from Wolf River where the father of Mark Twain, Marshall Clemens, lived; he had used to visit relatives over in Kentucky, and had a store and a "great boundary" of land. Later, there were other names: Sergeant Alvin C. York was also from the Wolf River Country and Cordell Hull had grown up by the Cumberland, and no different from many other farm boys, had ridden log rafts down to Nashville.

No one of our people was a riverman, but many stories centered on the river itself, often a baptizing, for until quite recently baptism, the most sacred rite for many of us, was performed in creek or river. In other tales running water was the villain instead of the background; these almost al-

[3] VS, I, 262.
[4] WD, I, 1.

ways began, "The creek was up, and . . ." Sometimes it was a story of how the water gaps got washed out and the cows and horse stock all ran away, or the spring branch carried the milk and butter and clabbered cream right out of the milk house; but more often than these came the stories of weddings, births, deaths, funerals, the news, and the mail, all hedged about by the risen creeks with overturned buggies and swimming horses.

And just as it ran through the stories, so did the Cumberland, though far below us in the valley, run through the days of our lives. We watched it, frozen or flooded, or in pool, daily from our front yard; played in it; swam in it; and groped through its fog. Many sounds drifted up from the valley that held Burnside and the river: train and mill whistles, church and school bells, sometimes music and singing, and now and then on a summer's evening the tantalizing music of a calliope in some traveling carnival we were never allowed to attend. Around us were the sounds of the woods and the fields; mockingbirds and rain crows I remember, and a wood thrush that would flit behind me to and from the spring, forever singing; and always through the summer twilights and into darkness the whippoorwills and katydids. There were in spring and early summer the gees and haws of plowmen as in autumn. All days brought the barking of dogs and more faintly the cowbells, and often at night the cries of hunting hounds to bring visions of a fox I'd always known; he ran forever through a field of ripened wheat with a red rose in his mouth.

There was among all these sounds only one that never stopped, constant, yet forever changing—that of the Cumberland racing down Smith Shoals just over the hill from our home. Sometimes the water cried out with a deep wild roar when the river was high and the wind from the north; but when the wind came out of the southwest the sound was thin and faint; then, sometimes within the very hour, it would strengthen, entering even the house with a high clear note. And always we noted the change, for the sound of Smith Shoals was, especially for our mother, a better forecast of the weather than a sunset. "Listen to the shoals. Rain," she would say. It would rain, and in the truthfulness of her forecast we would find no cause for wonder. I have known women hemmed in valleys, too narrow for a sunrise or a sunset or even a morning star, who could forecast the weather well by the sound of distant train whistles.

There was another sound from the river, more dramatic, but less enduring. Usually it came on foggy nights of fall or winter when the river was at steamboat tide. I would half awaken, listening, or maybe hear it before

I fell asleep, a long-drawn crying like a faraway hound or the horn of a hunter in some low valley calling his hounds home. More fully awakening, I would know the sound for that of a little steamboat, most likely the *Rowena* that ran until 1936, battling her way up from Nashville through the foggy bends of the Cumberland. Downstairs, our elders reading late, might stop to listen, and the talk would turn to the steamboats, for Burnside ever remembered its title—Head of Navigation of the Cumberland River. Smith Shoals marked the beginning of white water, through which not even a canoe could go upstream. Upriver was another world. Harlan in Kentucky was much further away than Nashville in Tennessee.

The steamboat whistles would bring ponderings on the little river towns, known only from much talk—Burkesville, Celina, Carthage. Past these was glamorous Nashville, still visited by many from our section of the country by steamboat even in my childhood. Nashville seemed brighter and finer than New Orleans. That great place was too far away, but brought closer through one of our mother's great-uncles who had in the course of his business as storekeeper been many times to New Orleans in the old days before The War.

Talk on the steamboats and Smith Shoals made only a little of the conversation centered on the Cumberland. There were two ferries in the town, and consequently much talk of what went on in the traffic jams of buggies, mule-drawn wagons, droves of hogs and geese and turkeys, and herds of cattle, all waiting for the ferries or struggling up the steep and muddy riverbanks. There was even more talk of the bridges that were to come and solve all problems and make of Burnside a metropolis. In time the bridges came; the talk only increased; one bridge was carried away on a tide, and the other was a toll bridge for many years. Everything was changed for the coming of Wolf Creek Dam below us, but the larger the bridges grew, the smaller did Burnside become.

Much talk concerned the state of the river itself. It seems now in thinking back that the Cumberland was either too low for steamboats or about to flood the town; or else the Big South Fork alone was rolling down, wild and flecked with foam and red with the earth of Tennessee. In times of high tide there was always the added threat of a breaking log boom with millions of board feet of cedar, hickory, poplar, oak, walnut, and ash rushing off downriver. The great logs would make an uneasy flooring, completely covering all the muddy river between the boom chains and the turn of the next bend. Sometimes a big boom on a high tide would break; but there were rivermen like Bunk Hardwick [5] who could go out, even in the dark, and standing as firmly on the shifting logs as other men on the ground, take the long pike poles and bring the logs home again behind the groaning boom chains.

Floods were times of great excitement, less dreaded I think than the dreary stretches of weeks or months when the river was too low for steamboats, the booms stood empty, and men were idle because the mills couldn't run without logs. Suffering still more, were the farmers down-river with neither roads nor railroads, dependent upon the steamboats to take their wheat, chickens, eggs, and other produce to market and bring all bought goods.

This is not the story of the river, but neither the land nor the people who lived in our world could be entirely separated from the Cumberland; and just as a creek or a valley gave place to a story, so did the Cumberland in time give me a place of my own on the schoolroom map. The easiest way to find it is to use a map showing physical features only, though on any map it is easily lost. Near the mouth of the Ohio are two rivers entering from the southeast. The southernmost is the Tennessee, big sister of the Cumberland, famous as the home of TVA and honored with two volumes in the "Rivers of America" series. Only a few miles above the mouth of the Tennessee, and not a great many below the mouth of the Wabash on the other side, the Cumberland enters the Ohio. Smaller than the Tennessee, the Cumberland still runs more than seven hundred miles from its headwaters of Poor and Clover forks above Harlan Town on the western flanks of the Appalachians to Smithland at the mouth. Its easternmost streams are separated from the waters of the Tennessee by Cumberland Mountain, and throughout it runs roughly parallel to the larger river as it swings southward and westward out of the coal country and pine woods, across the Highland Rim, down into the Tennessee Bluegrass, then out and into the Kentucky Pennyroyal or Barrens. A crooked river, it travels less than half its length, entering the Ohio about 325 miles due west of where it started.

The drainage basin forms a curious, shoe-like shape, something like an old-time buskin, badly worn and wrinkled, with a gob of mud caught in the instep, blurring the heel, yet with all the parts of a foot covering. The long and narrow toe, lifted as if for kicking, touches the Ohio, the wrinkled

[5] Used by permission of the publishers, Stearns Coal and Lumber Company, from *The Gum Tree Story*, by W. A. Kinnie (cited hereafter as *The Gum Tree*), 10–11.

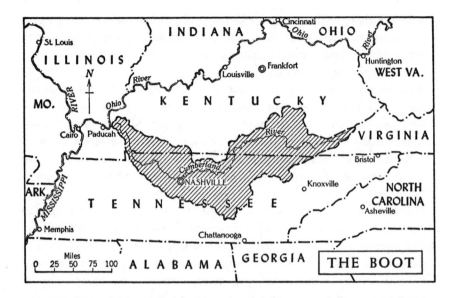

THE BOOT

heel goes southward onto the high tableland of the Cumberland Plateau and is shaped by the Caney Fork and its tributaries. The top of the shoe is formed by the Rockcastle and its many crooked creeks, a rough country the old ones found it as they went through it on their way to the Kentucky Bluegrass. The Rockcastle region is still less rough and wild than the country of the upper Cumberland; here, the river flows for sixty miles or so in the narrow valley, often scarcely ten miles wide, between Pine and Cumberland mountains.

Drawn out and colored the old boot looks small on a map of the United States; it is. The drainage basin, though around 325 miles from east to west, averages less than sixty miles from north to south,[6] the whole about 17,720 square miles, or an area near the size of Connecticut, Delaware, and Maryland combined. Proportionately as to population it is even smaller; the three states named have a population of over five million; the estimated population of the whole Cumberland Country today is only 1,330,000;[7] for it is not a country of cities, but primarily of county seat towns, farm

[6] Used by permission of the author, S. A. Weakley, from *Cumberland River Floods Since the Settlement of the Basin with Special Reference to Nashville, Tennessee.* Submitted to the Faculty of Vanderbilt University in fulfillment of the requirements for the degree of Civil Engineer, 1935, and housed in Joint University Libraries, Nashville, 1–9.

[7] Population figures are based on the 1958 estimate of the Nashville District, Corps of Engineers, U.S. Army.

14

and forest lands. Nashville, the largest city, has less than 200,000 people, and is only fifty-sixth in rank in the United States; and even Nashville, home of the State Capitol, seventeen universities and colleges, two large publishing houses, and numerous other industries, still remembers the two things upon which all its life once rested—the fertile farm lands and the Cumberland. River tonnage is higher than it has ever been. Stories of the best sorghum molasses, the fastest horse, or the hound with the sharpest nose still make the front pages of the two Nashville daily papers.

It cannot be said we ever thought of the whole of the country drained by the Cumberland as our own. The long toe of the boot in West Kentucky, often flat, and sometimes marshy, was another world as was the Harlan coal country at the other end, or for the matter of that any place above Smith Shoals where the boats couldn't go. On the other hand all of the Big South Fork deep into Tennessee was our world and had always been as was the main river flowing down to Nashville.

Even this small place never had a way of life entirely its own, different from that in the rest of the world; nor is it safe to make any generalization on the lives of its people. Still, there was a time before the coming of the army engineers and behind them the railroads, and even behind the steamboats and the memories of my grandparents, when the way of life in the wide or narrow valleys of the Cumberland in our part of Kentucky had a good deal in common with that of the settlers in Middle Tennessee, differing in degree rather than in kind—Nashville was the metropolis for all, the river the common highway. Men high up on tributaries of the Big South Fork built flatboats and shipped down whiskey, tobacco, hemp, and other farm products and manufactured goods to be sold in Nashville, New Orleans, or even Amsterdam.[8] Middle Tennessee, far wealthier, more devoted to cotton, still produced much the same crops, though on a larger scale.

Another bond lay in the nature of the people. None of the Cumberland Country, save the far western portion, got, as did northern and central Kentucky, any appreciable number of early settlers from New England and the Middle Colonies. Both Virginia and North Carolina contributed heavily in settlers for the middle river, and both set aside lands on the Cumberland as payment for the veterans of the Revolution; and though

[8] PD, IV, 227. "Messrs. James Old & Co.—You will please pay over to Mr. John Hughes all proceeds arising from the sale of one hundred four thousand and thirty pounds of tobacco that I consigned to you which was shipped to Amsterdam—C. Stewart, March 20, 1820."

most Revolutionary soldiers sold their warrants to land speculators, many did come to the Cumberland from Virginia and North Carolina. Not all of us have as many Revolutionary ancestors as has Mrs. Henry Hail of Somerset with nine, but most of us can with no scratching find two or three. East Tennessee was another bond in common, furnishing settlers for Middle Tennessee as well as our part of Kentucky, and most of us had more kin southward in all directions than north or east in Kentucky; even the ministers often drew congregations from both Kentucky and Tennessee; the Cumberland Presbytery, for example, was organized according to the river, not state boundaries.

Yet early I learned that not all people, even those around us, had the same things in their lives we and many others had—a love of books, animals, earth, rocks, plants, the sound of the human voice, politics and religion, green beans cooked with bacon in an iron pot all day, every day, all summer long; pomegranates in the garden, tansy by the doorstep, hot toddy for any ill or woe of life, turnip greens, cornbread baked in iron, and the brightest smiles and happiest talk for kin and memories.

The old ones lived on memories; but for me they were not enough. Sometimes I changed them to my liking; foggy times were good for this; and we had in fall and winter many still gray days when the sky was lower than our hill. Wraiths of fog wandered about all day long, and even when the rain was stopped, the woods dripped still as from a heavy dew; and all sounds came clearly up from the hidden world below us like sound heard through water. At such times the cows did not stray far from the barn, and I was denied my favorite occupation—the hunting of our cows through the steep acres of the hill pasture above the house. Still, there was the walk home from school; first, down a lane that went past the graveyard where through the shifting fog any fresh grave glowed a bright brick red, for our land was a bright land of gray or white limestone and red earth, brighter yet when washed by the rain and contrasted with the dark green of cedar boughs that in fog or rain were darkened instead of brightened. There was a creek to cross, and then the road up the hill under the great cedars and over limestone ledges, some step-like, others higher, craggy and gray.

It was in the gray stillness with the smell of cedar, of wet earth, and the fainter smell of decaying limestone all about me, that I remade the memories as I wanted them to be. True, there was confusion; the past, present, and the stories I was beginning to read were all mingled in my head. The Lost State of Franklin of which I had heard my elders speak floated somewhere with the Lost Atlantis, and in it Sevier rode with Galahad. There was Zollicoffer, too, but as a rule I could never think too long on The War. Middle-aged I am now, and so cannot remember a time when there was peace in the world, but for me there will ever be only one "The War." None of my ancestors was in it, only collateral relatives on either side. It was no easy thing for a man to stay home in our country and keep alive in the borderland that was the upper Cumberland; but worse than the soldiers of either the North or the South who invaded it turn by turn were the horse thieves and the guerrillas.

Who were the guerrillas? "Oh, it all depended . . ." There were some who claimed Tinker Beatty was a guerrilla; others said the same of "Champ" Ferguson.[9] My grandmothers had suffered from all—horse thieves, the North, the South, the guerrillas. The stories they told were worse than the simple shedding of one man's blood by another man. In some counties there was neither court nor church for five years. War was total, undeclared, and without rules.

Above our house could still be traced the embankments where the cannon had stood to watch for gunboats on the Cumberland. I wasn't fond of going there. Nor did I like to think on General Zollicoffer, dead in the Cumberland River fog, nor did I like to be reminded of the agony of the man—a relative—who had lost his mind in thinking he had killed Zollicoffer, "a great fine man, too fine to die," he had used to say.[10] I had

[9] Tinker Beatty, partisan leader of Union forces that harried our part of the Cumberland, testified that he and his men had killed, by bushwhacking—shooting from ambush—at least twenty-five men. He took only one prisoner and that one was wounded. Nothing happened to him, but "Champ" Ferguson, guerrilla for the South, was tried for his military crimes by a U.S. Army Court during the Occupation of Nashville, and after a trial of more than two months was hanged Sept. 26, 1865. Thurman Sensing, *"Champ" Ferguson—Confederate Guerilla*, copyright Vanderbilt University Press, Nashville, 1942, quotes much testimony concerning the activities of both men. Omitted is that of one of my grandmothers—she was a young bride out with her in-laws trying to make sorghum molasses—the plant new at that time and untried by most in our region until The War cut off sugar—when "Champ" Ferguson came with a band of men; they amused themselves by leaping their horses back and forth across the big sugar-water kettles used for lack of an evaporator; on this round "Champ" killed only one—a young boy—shot so they said in the road— and left for the hogs.

[10] General Felix Kirk Zollicoffer, 1812–1862, was killed at the Battle of Logan's Cross Roads, erroneously referred to as the Battle of Mill Springs by a marker on the wrong side of the Cumberland. Jan. 19, 1862, was a rainy, foggy time, and Isaac Chrisman, son of innumerable Isaac Chrismans, thought he had killed Zollicoffer. Soon, he brought his rifle to a Wayne County, Ky., blacksmith shop, and insisted it be forged into a pruning hook. Col. Speed S. Frye of the Union Army was said to have boasted of killing Zollicoffer, and the story was told that southern-sympathizing relatives dropped the *e* from their name so as to show they were no longer kin of the northern branch.

no feeling of glory when I thought of Champion Ferguson—Forguson, we said—captured, tried for his war crimes, and hanged by the Union Army.

I could only shiver at The War, but all the others—the old dead, the wronged, the maimed, and the disappointed—came into gay life. The woman saved her baby from the wild hogs, and another fed her husband apples from her apron. In the story she had been cold in worn linsey-woolsey and a thin shawl, hurrying to the jail with an apron full of apples, all she had as a treat for her husband, accused of burning a barn. He never ate the apples for "down the road a little piece, they'd strung him up, but not so high but she could reach his feet; and they'd not done such a good job, slow it was, for he'd kicked that little cedar tree all to pieces." But in the fog there were no swinging feet and all were happy endings.

I wearied in time of happy endings, and wanted instead the actual life behind the memories, the life I could not see. I could see Granpa at the Brandywine; I could see another Granpa, named Andrew Jackson Denney in 1817, our mother gave us his childhood. I could see the soldiers in the War of 1812 and old Granpa Gholson out of the Revolution meeting them by the Cumberland, but in between I could not see, not even in the fog.

How was it then, life on the Cumberland before 1803 when "We" bought the Louisiana Country, before men were split by The War with Middle Tennessee one world and our part of the river three. I wondered but never found a book. A very great deal has been written—histories, the lives of famous men associated with the region—Andrew Jackson, Sam Houston, Davy Crockett, Sergeant York, Cordell Hull, President Polk, famous jurists and lawyers, generals and admirals, and of course the most notorious of all criminals, the Harpes. Other writers have dealt in detail with the famous roads that crossed the river—the Natchez Trace and the Wilderness Road—and many works of fiction have used some segment of the country as background, but almost nothing has been written of the actual life of the first settlers, the why and the how of the ordinary people who came first to the Bluegrass and the limestone valleys.

CHAPTER II

ROCKS AND EARTH

THERE WAS another thing much further away than Granpa Merritt, but not so far but it, too, could live again in the fog. This was the old sea, and when the fog was thick below us, hiding the town and the river, it seemed only the old sea come again, for all about were the traces of life that had been there.

There were the shells, more delicately fluted and daintier than either the mussels or periwinkles we found in the Cumberland; some smaller than my little fingernail, others of the size and roundness of large hickory nuts, but all stone, sometimes fast in a limestone ledge, but often alone in a gullied bank. There were corals, too, of many shapes and sizes; some like leafless but stemmed flowers, others shaped like little horns, pretty things that could have belonged to the nimble, black-footed goats of the old witch tales.

All these were but the more noticeable reminders of seas, dry these many millions of years, for all the land and the life of the Cumberland Country were shaped by long-gone seas. The nature of the seas determined the nature of the rocks, and the decaying rocks made the soil, for practically all the soil of the Cumberland basin is formed from rocks once the floors of many different seas.[1] Glaciers never came bringing earth and rock from

[1] Used by permission of the Division of Geology, Department of Conservation, State of Tennessee, Nashville, from *The Stratigraphy of the Central Basin of Tennessee* by R. S. Bassler, copyright Division of Geology, Nashville, 1932 (cited hereafter as Bassler, *Tennessee*), 12–18. See also W. H. Twenhofel, *The Building of Kentucky,* copyright Kentucky Geological Survey, Frankfort, 1931 (cited hereafter as Twenhofel, *Kentucky*), 106–107.

elsewhere, nor did winds blowing through centuries lay down great beds of loess, nor is any part a newly risen flood plain or ocean shore.

Movements deep within the earth, the lives and deaths and slow decay of billions of animals and plants, and the Cumberland working with the weather through the million and more of centuries, all these produced from the old sea floors a land of many streams, rich in soils, minerals, and scenery. Most sought after by the first settlers were the wide bottoms and the rolling lands of Middle Tennessee in the Big Bend Country of the Cumberland where the rich black loam "fine as flour" [2] was fifty feet deep and more by the river with the low hills fit for cultivation to "the very top." The cane grew "thirty feet tall and three inches thick," [3] and the corn yield was a hundred bushels to the acre. There were cedars "four feet through and forty feet to the first limb," [4] and walnuts eleven feet in diameter.[5]

There was big timber, too, on the upper river, though in many spots the land was as Dr. Thomas Walker described it in 1750: "The Mountains very Steep and on some of them is Laurel & Ivy." [6] He was in the region of the Rockcastle, one branch so crooked the Kentucky Trace crossed it eleven times within twenty-eight miles, and the roads continued for generations to be "very stoney and knobby for anybody or horse." [7] The Cumberland must also cross, both before and after reaching Middle Tennessee, the Pennyroyal or Highland Rim, a country of great sinkholes and caves, red clay and underground streams.

Much of the Highland Rim was a treeless land, known as the Barrens, but all over were river and creek bottoms as well as hillsides and ridge

[2] John Haywood of the County of Davidson, *The Natural and Aboriginal History of Tennessee up to the First Settlement therein by the White People in the Year 1768*, Nashville, 1823 (cited hereafter as Haywood, *N & A*), 3.
[3] Reprinted by permission of the publishers, The Arthur H. Clark Company, Glendale, California, from *Early Western Travels 1748–1846* edited by Reuben Gold Thwaites, copyright by the Arthur H. Clark Company, Cleveland, 1904–1907 (cited hereafter as Thwaites, *Travels*), III; "André Michaux's Travels into Kentucky, 1793–1796" (cited hereafter as Michaux, "Journal"), 95.
[4] Smith, *Description*, 12.
[5] Gray, *Bishop*, 41.
[6] FP, 13. J. Stoddard Johnston, *First Explorations of Kentucky*, Louisville, 1898. "Journal of Dr. Thomas Walker," May 9, 1750 (cited hereafter as Walker, "Journal"), 58. The term "Laurel & Ivy" as used by Dr. Walker referred to rhododendron and mountain laurel; the older names are still used in the Southern Appalachians.
[7] Reprinted by permission of Mesdames Gertrude Williams Miller and Martha Williams Jan De Beur from *Early Travels in the Tennessee Country, 1540–1800*, edited and compiled by Judge Samuel Cole Williams, copyright by the author, Johnson City, Tenn., 1928 (cited hereafter as Williams, *Travels*); "John Lipscomb's Journal of 1784," (cited hereafter as Lipscomb, "Journal"), 274.

coves where the soil, black with humus, supported a mighty growth of timber, especially poplar that was often "seven feet in diameter and eighty feet to the first limb." [8] There was much game, big game, even on the upper river, though never so plentiful as in the Tennessee Bluegrass. Dr. Walker found in 1750 a herd of buffalo, "and I believe there were a hundred." [9]

It was the varied plant life that attracted the first scientists, the André Michauxs, father and son, interested in all manner of things, but chiefly botany. They also, beginning with the elder in 1795, took notes on what were to them more unusual natural phenomena than the plants—the rocks and fossils. Most visitors and many early settlers commented on the rocks, particularly those of the Central Basin and the Highland Rim, formations that underlie younger rocks and soils of much of the United States, but in few places can they be so easily seen as on the Cumberland.

Simple viewing of sinkholes, caves, and fossils was not enough for some. Judge Haywood, "Father of Tennessee History," was among the first to do more than take notes. How deep was a sinkhole when the bottom could not be plumbed by "three bed ropes tied together, and fifty feet of hickory bark added with a heavy piece of lead, the whole totaling 380 feet"? Geology was at this time, 1823, an infant science, but Judge Haywood published a book devoted chiefly to the prehistoric peoples and natural history of Middle Tennessee. He was the first to attempt to explain the formation of the Tennessee Bluegrass; almost entirely surrounded as it is by the walls of the Highland Rim, he concluded that, "billows once rolled over this large plain, it is too evident to admit of denial." [10]

Many wondered on many things, but the real foundations for the hundreds of scientific studies made of the soils and rocks and fossils of the Cumberland were laid by Dr. Gerard Troost who in 1831 was appointed by the General Assembly of Tennessee to make a Geological Survey of the State.[11] This was one of the first plans for such a survey made in the United States. Dr. Troost at the time was earning five hundred dollars a year as Professor of Chemistry, Mineralogy and Geology at the then University of Nashville. He continued in his various capacities [12]

[8] *The Gum Tree*, 33.
[9] Walker, "Journal," 57.
[10] Haywood, *N & A*, 5, 10.
[11] THM, Series II, Vol. III, Henry G. Rooker, "A Sketch of the Life and Work of Dr. Gerard Troost," 3-19.
[12] George William Featherstonhaugh, *Excursion in The Slave States from Washington on the Potomac to the frontier of Mexico with sketches of popular manners and geological observances*, London, 1844 (cited hereafter as Featherstonhaugh, *Excur-*

for many years, and as State Geologist made nine reports of what he found, his work clarified by many sketches and diagrams. He was contemporaneous with other local great men such as Sam Houston, Davy Crockett, and Andrew Jackson so that his greatness as an early scientist was smothered under the fame of his neighbors. Yet, Dr. Troost as he went on horseback across flooded rivers, through rattlesnake and bear infested country, or up and down the rough trails of the unsettled Plateau and mountains gathering material for his reports endured more hardships than a Davy Crockett.

The study of the Cumberland Country's rocks and fossils has continued constantly since the days of Dr. Troost. During my girlhood it was no uncommon thing to meet on our hill a group of young men busied with surveying instruments or tapping rocks with little hammers. These were members of the Summer School of Geology of the University of Michigan which for many years maintained a camp on the Cumberland near Mill Springs.

The young men wandering in strange places caused little wonderment, for by then even the old-timers could not remember when geologists had not been studying our rocks. Dr. David Dale Owen and his chemist Dr. Peter had before The War gone into every county in Kentucky while preparing their geological survey of the state; [13] and down in Tennessee Dr. James M. Safford not only continued the work begun by Dr. Troost, but also made a survey of much of our part of the country for a large iron and timber company.[14]

In between and since have been the others; some pure intellectuals hunting information from the rocks, others checking the possibilities of oil or coal. Always and all over were the surveyors; some making contour maps, others locating tunnels, bridges, cuts and fills for the highways that did not

sion), I, 192–199, gives an intimate account of Dr. Troost and his museum, little appreciated at that date.

[13] David Dale Owen and Dr. Robert Peter, M.D., Chemical Assistant, *Report of the Geological Survey in Kentucky made During the years 1854–1855 in Conjunction with the Third Chemical Report of the Soils, Marls, Ores, Rocks, Coals, and Mineral Waters of Kentucky*, Louisville, 1857. A similar report for the years 1856–57 was also published.

[14] J. M. Safford, *A Geological reconnaissance of the State of Tennessee*, Nashville, 1856. Safford also compiled a *Geological Report of the Coal and Oil Lands in Pulaski, Whitley, and Wayne Counties* (Ky.) *belonging to the Cumberland River Coal Company of Kentucky*, Louisville, 1865. These early geological reports, like those of Dr. Troost, have been superseded by more learned works, but they do give reliable information, unobtainable elsewhere, concerning little-known aspects of life in Kentucky and Tennessee before The War.

come until the 1930's; still more came for the AAA, National Forest, State Parks, and at last the Corps of Engineers who in time brought dams, and for each dam all roads had to be relocated and this meant more surveyors.

The multitude of rocky hills, steep bluffs, and crooked creeks made all such work difficult, but at the same time the many splendid exposures of rock made for a geologist's paradise. There were many riddles in the rocks. One of the more noticeable was the position of the oldest fossils. It is reasonable to think the deeper a river cuts, the older the fossils it brings to light. This is not true of the Cumberland nor of various other rivers, particularly the Tennessee, the Kentucky, and the Ohio. In places all these rivers flow upward in geologic time; on the Cumberland the oldest fossils and hence rock formations are not found near the mouth in Kentucky, or even on the main river, but near Murfreesboro on the West Fork of Stone's River.[15]

In order to understand a little of the why of the Cumberland Country let us look at one of the oldest things brought to light by the cutting down of the river. This is the fossil of a shellfish, so small it can be covered with my little finger.[16] Many seas had come and gone over future Kentucky and Tennessee and most of what is now the United States by the time of our bivalve, close to half a billion years ago. Somewhere in the long reach of time behind this smallish shellfish—not flattened like an oyster, but roundish like a hazelnut—the first forms of life had appeared in the sea water.[17]

All things must have a name, and to the eon that has elapsed since the first life forms appeared scientists have given the name phanerozoic, or "time when life was revealed." This eon has in turn been divided into three eras. The first or oldest of these is the Paleozoic; and it was during this era that all the rocks exposed in the basin of the Cumberland were laid down, though neither the oldest nor youngest rocks of this era are represented.[18]

It was in the second from the bottom up of the six periods into which the Paleozoic has been divided that our fossil was found. This was the Ordovician, estimated by some to have lasted as long as 60,000,000 years. The rich farm lands of Middle Tennessee are formed from limestones laid down by the many different Ordovician seas,[19] and in the bottom of the

[15] Bassler, *Tennessee*, 16, Fig. 2.
[16] *Ibid.*, 51, 193, Plate 5.
[17] Used by permission of the publisher, McGraw-Hill, from *Geology* by O. D. von Engeln and Kenneth E. Caster, copyright McGraw-Hill, New York, 1952 (cited hereafter as von Engeln and Caster, *Geology*), 419.
[18] Bassler, *Tennessee*, 13-17, 19-23, 50-51. See also Twenhofel, *Kentucky*, 106-108.
[19] Bassler, *Tennessee*, 12-18.

oldest brought to light by the river was our fossil, an exact reproduction of the living animal, even to the tiny flutings of the shell.

The long name—brachiopoda Pia nodema subaequata (Conrad) Murfreesboro—for this small thing is more than a name, almost a life history. Brachiopoda refers to the family, the first successful shellfish, and the most dominant life form of the entire Paleozoic Era. Pia was only one of a great many species, and was, one might say, but an elderly cousin of the "old sea shells" we children used to find in the rocks further up the Cumberland. The last word, Murfreesboro, refers to the rock formation in which it was found, the oldest rock brought to light by the Cumberland, and named for Murfreesboro, Tennessee, where it outcrops. Our fossil, not peculiar to that one formation, is found in younger beds of Ordovician stones, but gradually disappears. Conrad refers to the person who found and classified it. The remaining words are descriptive, and henceforth we shall refer to it only as Pia.

Scientists have in some measure reconstructed for us the world that Pia knew, though exact agreement is rare and black and white statements are dangerous. Practically all are agreed, however, that Pia's sea was fairly shallow. Sometimes the Ordovician seas were small, sometimes larger, with the general trend toward enlargement so that by middle and late Ordovician most of the continent of North America was alternately a shallow quiet sea or a waste of monotonously level lands, newly risen. There was a more permanent land mass centered on the Laurentian Mountains in Canada, another in the far west, and still another eastward.[20] This was Old Appalachia, east of today's Appalachian Mountains, and hardly an ancestor, a semi-permanent but changing land mass, worn at times into a low and rolling plain, but always rising again, and always pushing westward,[21] yet always far from the seas that made the limestone rocks of Middle Tennessee.

We can imagine this part of the sea, or Pia's world, far from the mouths of rivers, as a silent sunlit place, undarkened by shadow of bird or insect wing, and undisturbed by splashing fish. No pollen of flower, nor black earth rich with humus, nor scale of snake sifted down into the quiet water. The world's life through all of Ordovician time was centered in the sea.[22] Old Appalachia is thought to have been low at this time, but not necessarily

[20] Von Engeln and Caster, *Geology,* 626–637.
[21] *Ibid.,* 236–237.
[22] *Ibid.,* 636–643.

quiet; there are, found in the stones around Pia, indications of three different ash fall outs from the east.[23]

Pia had for company several other species of brachiopods, some larger, a few smaller. Still other families of shellfish, particularly the gastropods, were represented by many species whose convoluted shells remind one sometimes of snails, sometimes of periwinkles. Also common was a little stick-shaped creature, long, slender, but with a finely grooved shell. Another was the trilobite, a curious pillbug-like animal, even then with a long ancestry, but it also was destined to disappear. There were sponges, varieties of coral, and great colonies of minute animals called bryozoa.[24] Contrasted with the rich life of the sea, the earth was still barren rock or sun-cracked wastes of newly risen sea floor.

Pia died, and his shell along with billions of other shells and limey fragments settled into the ooze of the sea; above him the millions of years of Ordovician time went by while the great beds of limestones that underlie a good part of the world were put down. Sometimes the seas withdrew and many forces, both physical and chemical, began the work of bringing the level of the land down to that of the sea. Marine waters would cover it again, and thus the layers of limestone exposed in Middle Tennessee, though belonging to the one period, represent the work of many seas of varying depths, shapes, and sizes.

The earth did not passively sit while the seas built and the atmosphere, running water, and weather destroyed; through all the changes of seas, lands, climates, and seasonless spaces of time while the rocks of the Cumberland basin were being built, the base rock of the earth was seldom still. These earth movements affected the lives of the people who were to live there millions of years later quite as much as the things left by the seas.

One of the oldest movements to affect the Cumberland began millions of years before Pia lived. This was the formation of a great trough which extended in a narrow belt from the St. Lawrence to Alabama.[25] Much later, but sometime after living things were well represented in the seas, this trough filled with sea water. Thus, in the time of Pia it lay there, a long and narrow valley in the sea, its eastern border near the foot of Old

[23] Used by permission of the Division of Geology, Department of Conservation, State of Tennessee, Nashville, from *The Geology of Nashville, Tennessee* by Charles W. Wilson, copyright Division of Geology, Nashville, 1948 (cited hereafter as Wilson, *Nashville*), 61.

[24] Von Engeln and Caster, *Geology*, 636–643. Bassler, *Tennessee*, 51.

[25] Von Engeln and Caster, *Geology*, 645–647, Fig. 354.

Appalachia, that had through the centuries tried to fill the trough with the sediment of its rivers. Thick beds would be deposited until the levels of land mass and trough sediment were close, but as has been said Appalachia never stayed low. Each time she arose and crept westward, the trough, instead of being completely overridden, would also creep westward with a wave-like motion. Rocks on the eastern rim, formed in the sea, might be uplifted to become a part of Appalachia, but the westward-creeping trough, forever filling, forever deepening, was always there.[26] This story of strain and stress, movement and countermovement is one of great complexity, but in the main it made for deeper seas over what is now the Appalachians, and hence, East Tennessee.[27]

Other deep-seated movements within the earth bulged up the layers of rock and ooze below the surface of the sea, so that here and there some millions of years after Pia died, and thought to have been in mid-Ordovician times, low domes began to rise—slowly. The best known of these was a giant bulge southward from Canada across Ohio, Kentucky, Tennessee, and into Alabama. This is now known as the Cincinnati Arch or locally in Tennessee the Cincinnati-Nashville Dome, though its two areas of greatest uplift were not centered on the future sites of these cities; in Tennessee, Nashville is on the northwestern flank with Murfreesboro near the crest. This dome persisted through all future seas that were to come and go over what is now the central part of the United States.[28] Sometimes the dome was no more than a low wave-washed island; at other times it was covered by the sea, but regardless of its height as compared to the surfaces of the seas, it was always higher than the surrounding sea floors, so that younger formations could never be deposited so thickly on its sides and top.

Deposits of two long periods, the Silurian and Devonian, are but scantily represented in the Nashville Basin, which, during this time, is thought to have been mostly above the sea. Little of the area drained by the Cumberland owes its surface features to rocks put down during these periods, though several of their formations underlie most of the Cumberland Country outside the Nashville Basin, and can often be seen in creek or river bluff, especially the Devonian shales.[29]

The world Pia had known passed away. Chlorophyl-manufacturing plants and air-breathing animals began to inhabit the land, and along with this change came another in the geography of the world. Appalachia with

[26] Von Engeln and Caster, *Geology*, 236–237.
[27] Wilson, *Nashville*, 61.
[28] Von Engeln and Caster, *Geology*, 629. Twenhofel, *Kentucky*, 108–109.
[29] Bassler, *Tennessee*, 120, 133. Twenhofel, *Kentucky*, 106, 108, Fig. 20.

the trough on her western flank pushed westward, and for the first time
in its long history the trough began to disappear, and in New England was
cut completely by a land mass.[30]

There came a time known as the Mississippian Period; during it, as in the
time of Pia, warm shallow seas covered most of what is now the Mississippi
Valley as well as much of the West. Though fish now swam in the seas, the
brachiopods were still well represented as were the corals. These were the
old stone flowers and sea shells of my childhood, for it was during this time
the great beds of limestone so characteristic of much of the Highland Rim
were laid down. Limestone was not the sole deposit; most of the Pennyroyal in Kentucky and the Highland Rim in Tennessee with their varied
rocks and surface features are a part of the Mississippian Plateau, the work
of many seas through many millions of years.[31]

Long as the Mississippian period was, some thirty million years or so,
it was but part of a great stretch of time comprising three geologic periods,
and collectively known as the Carboniferous. It was during these times of
warm moist climate and seasonless years when all things grew without
check or hindrance, and particularly through the Pennsylvanian, that most
of the earth's coal, including that of the Cumberland, was formed.

The formation of coal went on for many millions of years. Sometimes
the plant-filled swamp flourished but briefly, and only a thin layer of the
vegetable matter that would in time make coal could accumulate before
the land sank and the seas came in. This process might be repeated over
and over so that many layers of thin coal separated by shales, slates, sandstones, and other formations would be the result. Other times the swamp
lasted for many thousands of years to leave a seam thick enough for mining.[32] In general there is in all the Cumberland coal country—that is chiefly
on the upper river above the mouth of the Rockcastle and the Plateau in
Tennessee—at least one seam of coal thick enough for mining, and often
two.

Source lands were closer while the coal was being formed so that most of
it was buried under thick layers of sandstones and pebble-filled conglomerates; thus these, rather than limestones, make the surface rocks of the
Plateau and hills.

The warm time of luxuriant growth gave way at last to a climate something like our own today. Deserts covered much of the earth and geologists

[30] Von Engeln and Caster, *Geology*, 590–591.
[31] Twenhofel, *Kentucky*, 108, Fig. 20.
[32] Von Engeln and Caster, *Geology*, 561–565.

have found evidence of great glaciers that today seem strange places for glaciers—South Africa, India, Madagascar—and stranger still the glaciers moved toward what are now the poles instead of away from them.[33]

Hand in hand with this change in climate went a change in the geography of what was to be the United States. Much of this was brought about by a series of complex earth movements, collectively known as the Appalachian Revolution. Old Appalachia that had been pushing slowly westward for many millions of years, at last pushed over the trough on her western flank. The layers of sedimentary rocks in the trough were first folded, then bent upon themselves as the great land mass pressed forward. The original Appalachia has long since been eroded away, though parts of the upturned bottom of the old trough made up of ancient sediments and lava flows may still be seen in the Blue Ridge Mountains and the Great Smokies.[34] The folding and faulting extended as far as Pine and Cumberland mountains in Kentucky which are the eroded remains of old earth wrinkles.

The Appalachian Revolution was not a quick changing of the face of the earth, but a slow and intermittent thing; yet used as a landmark in time for it marks the end of an era, that of the Paleozoic. Save in the far western portion in that narrow strip of land known as "Between the Rivers," and during a much later period, the Cretaceous, the Old Boot was never again covered by the sea.[35] The building of rocks elsewhere in the world continued for 185,000,000 years or so; the Sierra Nevadas, the Alps, as well as the Rock of Gibraltar, are all younger than the rocks of the Cumberland.[36]

The work of the seas—the building—was finished. This had been no single job, but consisted of millions of complex operations, chemical as well as physical, that would, for their unraveling, need most of the "ologies" of science. The story of a rock, even that of a sedimentary limestone unchanged by heat or pressure, is a great deal more than the mere physical process of particles of lime from animal shells falling onto the bottom of the sea and then emerging as stone. There were complex questions of sea water temperature, rate and direction of withdrawal of the sea, chemical content of the water, the air, nature and distance of the nearest land mass, all of which had a direct bearing on the life and content of the sea water, and hence on the composition of stones built under its ooze. Tides, winds, earth

[33] Von Engeln and Caster, *Geology*, 533–534.
[34] *Ibid.*, 504–531, Fig. 272.
[35] Twenhofel, *Kentucky*, 107.
[36] Bassler, *Tennessee*, 1–6. Von Engeln and Caster, *Geology*, 439, 490–491.

movements, climates, and seasons all helped shape the rocks that would rise
from the sea.

Some of these would decay into the wondrously fertile soil of the Bluegrass. Other regions such as those of the Barrens were less fortunate. Ancient rivers, their beds now filled with layers of younger stone, carried
materials that through a complex chemical process became nodules and
often great masses of chert or flint that never decayed.[37] This was useful
to the Indian, but made for a poor and rocky land where in places little but
scrub oak would grow. Other rivers carried oxides of iron. Sometimes there
was hardly enough to color the rock, but often the iron deposits, such as
those put down during the Mississippian Period all around the flanks of the
old dome, and particularly rich along the Harpeth River, made iron mining
an important early industry.

There would be salt and oil and building stone; gypsum, marl, alum,
limestones rich in nitrates, others with thick deposits of phosphate, saltpeter
in the caves, and here and there small amounts of other minerals as well as
the coal. However, before many of these along with the soil could be ready
for man's use, other forces must work for many millions of years on the old
sea floors. Some weathering processes consisted of complex chemical reac-
tions like those taking place in the leaching of limestone or the formation of
Pia's fossil.

Others such as the cutting action of running water were physical. There
had been rivers on Old Appalachia, and as she pushed westward and slowly
overrode the trough there were rivers still. In time rivers ran down and
across the Appalachian Plateau, some draining into the Atlantic; others
sending their waters to the sea by way of the Mississippi. The more northerly of these, notably the Ohio and her upper tributaries, were changed by
the glaciers.[38]

The Cumberland was not, but it was affected by earth movements that
went on for millions of years after the seas withdrew and the river was
born. Cumberland Gap, for example, is a notch almost a thousand feet deep
in Cumberland Mountain. Geologists always agreed that once a river
flowed there. At one time it was thought to have been the Cumberland,
which, as the land rose, got cut off, so that waters once flowing north
into it, now flow south into the Tennessee. The hypothesis now is that

[37] Bassler, *Tennessee,* 154–155.
[38] Used by permission of the University of Kentucky from *Geology of Kentucky*
by Arthur C. McFarlan, copyright University of Kentucky, Lexington, 1943 (cited
hereafter as McFarlan, *Kentucky*), 162, Fig. 18.

Cumberland Gap was cut by a northern tributary of the Tennessee; later, in some time of slow uplift the stream, no longer able to cross the rising mountain, was stolen by the Cumberland.[39]

Once out of its narrow valley between Pine and Cumberland mountains, the only part of the Cumberland drainage basin greatly affected by the Appalachian Revolution, the river had still greater earth forces to struggle against on her way to the sea. This was the intermittent pushing up of the Nashville Dome that had begun in Ordovician times, and continued at intervals long after the seas had permanently withdrawn. The last uplift is thought to have taken place in the present or Recent geologic age.[40] Since the doming up of the layers of rock was not a localized thing, but a widespread movement, most of the drainage basin of the Cumberland was affected.

At more than one time in its history the dome knew a long stillness. The Cumberland and many of her tributaries would become old and sluggish streams winding tiredly to the sea, so little below their level that in order to flow at all they must meander back and forth like streams caught in marshy meadows. The dome would rise again, forcing the Cumberland into a swifter downward cutting. The old wide valley where once it had meandered would be left high above, sometimes as a bench of land on the side of a hill as on many tributaries of the Caney Fork and other streams; other times there would be a wide and rolling plain such as those of the Middle Basin, with the river set much lower between steep limestone bluffs. Seldom could the river straighten its course, no matter what the hurry. At Burnside the old meanders almost touched; they were so close that Bunker Hill, now an island in Lake Cumberland, was almost an island with the Big South Fork bending round it; when the cutting quickened, the stream broke through the narrow neck of land between the meanders, but as it had to hurry down, the old channel was left as a high, and dry, river valley. As a rule the river could only follow its course, and so we have the Cumberland and many of her streams following tired-seeming meanders, but running with shoals and riffles below sheer bluffs like young and spritely rivers.

The old high wide valleys such as those of Wolf River, the Big South Fork, Stone's River, and the Caney Fork remained to make good farming land of dark red earth and limestone rocks, for even far up the Cumberland the dome pushed the limestone high enough the river found it under the sandstone and shales. This uplift of the dome was neither regular, nor even,

[29] McFarlan, *Kentucky*, 216–217.
[40] Bassler, *Tennessee*, 17. McFarlan, *Kentucky*, 155–158.

but an intermittent, widespreading sort of thing; nor was it the only one; there was, for example, another bulging up known as the Rockcastle Uplift which affected much of the upper Rockcastle.

Nothing was neatly or quickly done, and the results of the earth movements depended not only on the extent of uplift, but on the kind of rock uplifted. Had the Cincinnati-Nashville Dome been of sandstones and conglomerates, the whole history, not only of the river, but of the states that in time occupied the land, would have been another story. Though seemingly hard to the touch, limestone is one of the poorest of all fighters; it yields more readily to heat, running water, pushing roots, and most aspects of the weather than do the sandstones and conglomerates, and also has an enemy, all its own, that eats within the stone, year in and year out. This is the circulating ground water that gradually dissolves and leaches the rock away.

If the limestone be of a certain kind and pure and thickly bedded, little holes and narrow crevices in time become great caverns, drained by underground streams and studded with stalactites and stalagmites. Mammoth Cave, though not in the Cumberland drainage system, was produced in the same formations that occur in much of the Highland Rim and Pennyroyal. As a child I early learned our world was still in the process of formation when a neighbor, plowing his garden, saw his mules plunge downward, taking the plow; another sinkhole had just been born.

One could almost think of the Tennessee Bluegrass as a very large, and very special sinkhole, formed in the domed-up layers of limestone, and so very old that instead of rock debris on the bottom there are many feet of the most wonderful dirt on earth for the growing of the bone, hide, hair, teeth, and muscle of animals. The dirt got that way because above it there were once layers of limestone rich in phosphates and other minerals. Millions of generations of plants have grown, died, decayed, and left their humus, but the decaying plant could add no minerals not found in the soil formed from the disintegrating limestone, or the air, or produced by some one of the many chemical changes brought about by weathering. Fortunately for future dwellers on the Cumberland, the rocks productive of the best soils decayed most quickly.

The dome, while the rocks were being built, had been like an irregular hill in the sea, and around it fell deposits different from itself. These in time formed rocks, sometimes hard, sometimes soft, but in general harder and yielding less readily to all the forces of weathering, so that the Nashville Basin is almost surrounded by the stone walls of the Highland Rim.

Throughout the Cumberland the most noticeable features of the scenery came about in the same fashion—soft rock next to hard rock, though as a rule, instead of side by side, the soft limestone or shale is under a very hard limestone or conglomerate. The river or some one of its tributaries would first cut a gorge, slowly through the hard layers, more quickly through the soft; all the multiple agencies of weathering would begin work on the bluff exposed by the running water. The softer shales and limestones under the harder rock would yield more quickly to form a great hole in the side of the bluff, roofed with hard sandstone or conglomerate. These rockhouses, as they were known, are common on the upper river, particularly along the Rockcastle where, over and over, the river and its creeks built them, for in time the overhanging roof of hard rock would fall, another hole begin, while the stream bed below grew cluttered with the great blocks and chunks of stone, so hard the running water affected them but little. Other times the sides of a narrow ridge would weather and decay more quickly than the harder top; this would be left high in the air to form a natural bridge such as the large one in McCreary County, now a tourist attraction.[41]

Sometimes soft rock came below hard in a stream bed, and a waterfall would be the result. There was, for example, long ago, though the time is short as compared to the age of Pia's fossil, a high falls near Burnside, Kentucky, in the main body of the Cumberland. The water could do little with the hard rock over which it ran, but underneath was a softer rock. This yielded quickly to the backlash of the plunging water, so that in time the water flowed, not over a bluff, but over a great shelf of stone with a rockhouse beneath. Soon, there was so little holding up the shelf a part of it fell, and the edge of the waterfall went upriver. This was repeated for a very great many centuries until the near seventy-foot drop known as Cumberland Falls traveled [42] to its present site forty miles upriver. There are on most of the tributaries of the Cumberland many falls and rapids. The headwaters of the Caney Fork on the Plateau are especially noted for their falls; Fall Creek Falls in Bledsoe County, Tennessee, drops in one sheer swoop 256 feet into Cane Creek Gulch.

This is the highest of all, but the whole of the river might be thought of as a stream coming downstairs. The branches that join to form the upper Cumberland—Poor, Martin, and Clover—are partly fed by the Big Black Mountain with an elevation of more than 4,000 feet. The river as it crosses

[41] This is not to be confused with Natural Bridge State Park, a good many miles north in Wolfe and Powell counties of Kentucky.
[42] McFarlan, *Kentucky*, 238.

Pine Mountain near Harlan is still a thousand feet above the sea. Caney Fork and Obey's in their upper reaches on the Plateau in Tennessee are often around 2,500 feet, but by the time the river reaches Nashville it is only about 370 feet above sea level, and yet to go down, though long ago smoothed out by lock and dam, are the shoals and riffles near the mouth of the Harpeth.

There is no one place where one can see all the rocks and soils of the Cumberland. One can, however, see a good deal just below Pleasant Hill, Tennessee on U.S. 70 South. As the road drops down from the Plateau where the elevation averages more than 2,000 feet, one can see the rolling hills and valleys of the Highland Rim, only a thousand feet or less above the sea, more fertile near the Plateau than westward where it flattens out into the gray- or brown-soiled land often strewn with flint, and known as the Barrens. Past this, misty and blue, as if it were indeed the lake Haywood thought had been there, is the Middle Basin, never entirely flat save by the river, but equally good on the high and low places, a roughly shaped north-south oval, between five and seven hundred feet above sea level, containing about 5,500 square miles, most of it drained by the Cumberland.

Turning away, one looks eastward and up to the towering bluffs of the Plateau, dark-streaked with coal, layered with sandstone and pebble-filled conglomerate, a place where pine trees, huckleberries, ivy, and laurel grow. In Tennessee a rather flat region, but in Kentucky deeply cut with streams and lower. Much of it is still in timber both privately and publicly owned; in Kentucky's McCreary County, for example, only seventeen per cent of the land is in farms; the rest is held by the federal government as forest with minor holdings by coal and timber companies.

The heavy rainfall, the wide diversity of soils and elevations, and its climate, partaking of the characteristics of both north and south, made it possible for most of the plants and animals native to the eastern half of the United States to have flourished there. Long before the parrakeet and the buffalo there were mammoths and ground sloths.[43]

The first settlers were primarily interested in good land; the Plateau was for many years after settlement owned by the Cherokee as was the Harlan coal country, and, at least on paper, all the southern drainage basin of the

---

[43] W, 6XX, 137, quoting the Carolina *Gazette*, Feb. 22, 1798, describes 60-lb. teeth and a "paunch holding 20 wagon loads," found at a lick on Richland Creek, a few miles south of present-day Nashville. Dr. Troost in time had quite a collection in his museum.

Cumberland forty miles above Nashville.[44] The tip of the boot with its narrow strip of marshy land attracted few settlers for many years, while those who settled above Smith Shoals, north of the Cumberland in what are now Whitley, Knox, and Laurel counties in Kentucky, belonged to another world; they could not use the Cumberland as a highway, and Nashville was not their town.

The pioneers, even the first ones, needed a town, a place in which to buy and sell, but many little limestone valleys high up on Pittman or Meshack or some other creek of the Cumberland were settled before Nashville was a place, even on paper. Men risked their lives and those of their children to hold narrow strips of creek bottom and steeply rising timbered hills. In driving over the rich farm country in Sumner County and other parts of Middle Tennessee, it is easy to understand why people would risk, much and endure all for the land; no country on earth is more bountiful or more beautiful. As one travels east through Smith County or down into the region of the Caney Fork or even upriver into the wide bottoms of Cumberland County or to Meadow Creek in Wayne, the understanding is still easy; there is after 175 years of farming an air of peace and plenty— good homes, big barns, fat cattle, tall corn and tobacco, set mostly in wide valleys between low hills.

There were before the building of the dams wide bottoms along most of the Cumberland below Burnside, with, as one travels downriver, the bottom lands along the lower reaches of the creeks and branches growing wider. Up the river, in land now owned by the Cumberland National Forest on creeks long forgotten, Brush, Cooper, Cedar Thicket and their small branches—names now found only on long-ago recorded deeds—the bottom lands are narrow, the valleys small. Forest trees and undergrowth cover most of these narrow little valleys, but the traveler if he follow long enough on foot some deeply rutted road grown up in poplar saplings or pine thicket, can find remains of a long since rotted-down rail fence, traceable chiefly by the heavier growth that was once a fence row. Sometimes there are the decaying trunks of ancient apple trees, and often a little search-

<hr />

[44] W, 1XX, 65, is a remembered account of the Treaty of Nashville with the Chickasaw in 1783. This formed the basis for future Indian treaties, including that with the Cherokee at Hopewell in 1785, *ibid.*, 3XX, 11. The Cherokee by this treaty held all land south of the Cumberland, east of a point "40 miles above Nashville," but this boundary went unobserved by the white man. See in the Clements Library "Map of the Tennassee Government, formerly part of North Carolina taken chiefly from Surveys By Gen'l D. (Daniel) Smith & Others," Carey's General Atlas, 1795 (cited hereafter as Smith, Tennessee Map), which shows all of the land drained by the Big South Fork as well as most of what is now Wayne County along with all of the Plateau in Tennessee as belonging to the Cherokee at this date.

ing will bring to light a smoothly cut stone or so, embedded in the earth and buried under leaves and mold. Nearby can be found other cut stones until slowly the pattern takes shape—the large stone was once part of a hearth, others belonged to chimney, spring house, foundation, or family graveyard; all this in places now so remote the nearest road fit for any automobile is many miles away. Stockton's Valley, a flourishing community by 1795, cannot today be reached by an automobile.[45] Why did people settle in these narrow creek valleys?

Not long ago we took our children when we went to look over and check up on two old family graveyards in the Big South Fork Country. As the graveled road roughened and outliers from the Cumberland Plateau thickened, becoming at last crooked ridges, the children asked, "Why did they come here? What was there for them here?" We could not take the car all the way to Denney's Creek on Sinking Creek of the Big South Fork of the Cumberland, but we did reach Denney's Gap, a lonesome spot today, but long ago a busy place with store and post office. Most of the surrounding land is now deserted, roadless; and the big log houses, and much later when the sawmills came, the bigger frame houses with double porches front and back, were all burned long ago. Some of it we walked through, visited two graveyards—Matthew, born in 1772, under a proper stone, but Matthew's parents under great cairns of unmarked rocks, for when they died panthers troubled the dead.

As the children pestered with their "Why in the world did they want to live in such a place," I tried to see it with the eyes of around 1785 when they are thought to have come. Different from others, there was no tradition of their having been Tories and forced to hide in the hills, nor were they Baptist fleeing persecution. Had they wished to hide they would not have gone to this particular place; though now so remote, it was in the 1780's about as close to the civilized world to the east as any place nearby, and there were, less than half a day's horseback journey away, at least three other settlements.[46] A major Indian trail as good as any road west of the

[45] Used by permission of the Standard Publishing Foundation, Cincinnati, Ohio, from *Life of Elder John Smith* by John Augustus Williams, second edition copyright by the Standard Publishing Foundation, 1904 (cited hereafter as Williams, *Smith*), 22-24. The subject of this biography, later prominent as a minister in the newly organized Christian Church and sometimes known as Raccoon John Smith, was born in East Tennessee in 1784, and in 1795 settled in the still rather new community of Stockton's Valley near Wolf Creek of the Big South Fork in what is now the southwestern part of McCreary County.

[46] THM, Series I, I, 40-65, "The Journal of General Daniel Smith, one of the Commissioners to Extend the Boundary Line between the Commonwealths of Virginia and North Carolina, August 1779 to July 1780," edit. from W, 46J, 118, by St. George L. Sioussat (cited hereafter as Smith, "Journal").

mountains and better than most [47] was only a few miles away, with a criss-cross of smaller trails all around.

More important to the settler who would sell tobacco or tar or barrel staves was a stream that at high tide would take a flatboat or a hollowed log canoe. This settlement offered not only the creek, but also the Big South Fork a few miles away, navigable by fairly large craft, a highway important enough that years later a neighbor had a boat yard.[48] Even in Middle Tennessee the settler wanted to be, if not on, at least near the Cumberland or a large tributary, for anything that couldn't walk to market, had to go down the river.

Land on creek or river was even more important away from the Middle Basin, for in the rougher country the only fairly level land was bottom land, and usually it was the best land, but hillsides and coves far up the river, black with humus from millions of generations of plants, were also rich, supporting a mighty growth of timber. Thousands of valleys like that of Denney's Creek which today seem so rough when judged against the backdrop of Iowa, Ohio, the Great Plains, or the deeper south, were not in 1780 considered so. Rougher lands on the Yadkin, New River, the Holston, and even in the upper reaches of the Shenandoah Valley had been sought out and settled by earlier generations.

There was then no feeling against even quite steep slopes as there is today when farm machinery is widely used, and the general public is aware of soil erosion solely as being done by water running down hill. Some even felt that crops did better on a hillside, and Landon Carter,[49] a Virginia planter, once complained his lazy help had planted the corn in the low land instead of the hillside as he had directed. Everything indicates the pioneers wanted at least a bit of roll to their land. The first pamphlet describing Middle Tennessee, written in 1795 by Daniel Smith, land speculator wanting settlers, was careful to point out that only the bottoms along the river were perfectly flat; the rest was rolling.[50]

Enough rich land for corn and hemp and tobacco with a stream to carry goods to market was only part of the advantages the little valley offered the first settler. He also wanted "everlasting water," in the form of a spring.

[47] This was a prong of the Great Lakes Trail. See Chap. III, n. 33.
[48] WD, V, 389.
[49] Used by permission of the Carnegie Institution of Washington from *History of Agriculture in the Southern United States to 1860* by Lewis Cecil Gray, copyright Carnegie Institution of Washington, 1933 (cited hereafter as Gray, *Agriculture*), I, 174.
[50] Smith, *Description*, 34.

One might almost say the least use of a spring was as a water supply for drinking and cooking; these required little water. A good spring, over which a stone spring house would in time be built, was refrigerator, pantry, cellar, and milk house in summer; in the periods of sharp cold, common even around Nashville, it kept the kraut from freezing and warmed the farm animals on bitter mornings. In the old days when much manufacturing was done on the family-size farm, good spring water was a must. The water rotting of hemp was usually done in a pool below the spring, and such activities as distilling, hog killing, hominy making, ash and saltpeter leaching, dairying, dyeing, and of course laundry, all called for large amounts of water. The forted farm, the fort a must in the early years, was always built either enclosing a spring or adjacent to one.

The hill and valley farm, common along the Cumberland, even on the outer edges of the Middle Basin, had in pioneer days many other advantages of no import today. Far up the river, the old dome lifted the limestone high enough, river and creek at last cut into it, and thus the settler had in addition to a small strip of good land, other things only limestone could give. Limestone made the building of stone fences easy, could be burned into lime needed for the tan vat or the chimney mortar, and for any who would make a little iron, limestone in some form was a must for flux; lime also could be sold downriver. Higher than the creek valleys, but still in the limestone were the saltpeter caves, rich enough to supply the needs for gunpowder of the farmer and his sons, and sometimes a surplus readily sold downriver. In the coves upriver there were often high on the ridge sides, rockhouses, handy things, welcomed by the pioneer before he could build a house; finished with camping in one, he could still use it as a stable; a bluff up on Sinking Creek got its name of Tobacco Cliff because the farmer in the valley below used it for the curing of tobacco.

The sandstone itself, or freestone as the easily worked varieties were then known, was needed for chimney rocks and gravestones. Grindstones were often cut from the harder sandstones, while a particularly hard, but not too coarse, conglomerate found above or between layers of sandstone could be shaped into millstones.

The variety of formations on the hill and valley farm also made for a variety of soils, mantled with a rich and diverse plant life. These woods resources had an important place in the first settler's scheme of things. The Wolf River or creek farm often has, high above and mesa-like, an uninhabited world of piney woods and beggar lice, thin-soiled and sandy, but good land for sheep or cattle, and with plenty of pine knots for tar.

Tar was an important item to the pioneer, especially for the hempen rope made in the old rope walks; the posts of one, far up in the now deserted Denney Country, were still standing when my mother was a girl.

The variety of soils on one farm, from the limestone low by the creek to the piney woods above, furnished in addition to tar practically all woods products known at that time in America. All woods settlers used a wide variety of plants from white oak for whiskey barrels to walink for the newborn baby's tea. The woods upriver continued for generations to serve as pasture part of the year for most farm animals; cows grazing in the canebrake and on the pea vine were ever a part of pioneer life, while hogs could not only subsist but in the fall fatten after a fashion on the abundant oak, beech, and chestnut mast.

The hill and valley farm was in general a place of abundance until The War; if land got scarce or things seemed crowded the young ones would move on—Mississippi Territory, Indiana, Texas, Missouri—the earliest will books show heirs in distant places, almost always south or west. It was The War that made of this land, neither North nor South, a kind of Marching-Through-Georgia that lasted four years. The last time they came to what had been a great-grandfather's place, they at first could find nothing not stolen, destroyed, or hidden. At last they saw the bees, still making honey in the bee gums under the apple trees; and so they took a pinch of sulphur, put it under each gum, set it on fire, and never rode away until the bees were dead.

There was in these now lonesome valleys no loneliness; even well before 1800 there was with the Denneys another Scotch family from Virginia, the Smalls, and soon came Dicks, Moodys, Dodsons, and many others to settle on the tributaries of Big Sinking Creek. They built a community, not only with substantial log houses for themselves, but by 1800 they were organizing and soon building a house for Big Sinking Baptist Church. Such communities flourished in many long since forgotten valleys of the Cumberland; as early as 1785 so great was the fame of this land that offered everything, a group came from New York to settle in the vicinity of Albany, Kentucky, and hence the name. The people could not compare in wealth with those who settled the Middle Basin, but neither did they know poverty. Hogs and cattle in the woods, plenty of horses, a few slaves, big log houses, an abundance of food, and good health.[51] Their relative prosperity

---

[51] Samuel R. Brown, *The Western Gazetteer or Emigrant's Directory*, Auburn, New York, 1817, declared, 97, Wayne County "the most healthy part of state," and found "fevers few in Tennessee."

rested almost entirely upon the varied gifts of the old seas. Only a part of their livelihood came from farming; they sold all manner of produce from lard to saltpeter and ginseng, and in return bought many things from copper kettles to books, but basically they lived from the land.

The hill and valley farm, still much a part of life on the Cumberland, had other certain things; but these could not be eaten, sold, or worn—an ever-changing variety of shadow and sunlight not found in flat lands or among great mountains. Each farm is different, yet roughly most follow a pattern. Few settlers or their descendants wanted to live low in a valley, but high on the hill where they would like to be, took them too far from the corn, tobacco, wheat, and other crops in the valley as well as the road that usually followed the creek, and so they compromised and settled halfway up the hill.

Crops and barns lie below them; above are pasture fields, below or around is the orchard with beehives, and even now an occasional bee gum under the trees, and a rich and level spot near the house for a garden. Each thing suited to its particular location. Such a farm has a quality unknown in any other for it feels the changing shape of hill shadow; the winter after-noons when all below lies cold and blue and the creek pools slowly skim with ice, the upper slopes are warm and bright; or on another farm the child coming home from school on the southern side of a hill steps from a snowless world of sunshine into a snowy waste of limestone crag and undripping icicles that lie above his northwardly sloping home.

Each had its advantages; fruit on the northern slope would survive the early frosts that killed flowers of the forward-spring-expecting trees on the southern, and though the woman on an eastern hillside might never see a sunset she could do her bean-stringing and churning in the coolness of long shady afternoons. The advantages and disadvantages of each, like everything else in life, all depended; but for most firstcomers to the Cum-berland, farming was a way of life. Such a people, different from those who today see farming as purely a capitalistic enterprise, welcomed this land that offered so much in addition to rich soil; they were blind to nothing; a small waterfall up a rocky creek could mean a mill; and a scantily soiled limestone ledge, unfit for any cultivated crop, was a thing every settlement needed; such places were almost invariably thick with red cedar, and cedar was a must for churns, pails, and piggens.

CHAPTER III

THE FIRST SETTLERS

ONCE I HAD a garden on a bench of land on the side of a narrow valley, a valley so narrow with the hill across the way so high that, though the hillside faced west, the hill shadow would creep across my garden long before suppertime. It was then, while my husband did the barn chores and the long shadow merged into twilight, I did my gardening.

Gardening went slowly at times, for my hoe was always turning up things other than dirt, and I would kneel, clean the just-found thing and study it, or even take it into the house. The place had then been farmed for more than one hundred and fifty years, and all around were the reminders of other farm wives; I smelled the tansy they had set, cared for the hop vine, cut back the honeysuckle, and rescued the burning bush from brush and saplings, for the place had long been abandoned with the Cumberland National Forest taking the fields of neighboring farms.

My hoe found many things—square nails, fragments of broken dolls and dishes, small chunks of iron rusted into shapelessness, now and then an ox shoe crumbling with rust, bone buttons, or small fragments of cane splints once part of a weaving sleigh. Side by side with such things I often found reminders of those others who had known and loved the valley and maybe used the spring, long before a white woman came with tansy and hop vines and demands for a good stone spring house that in time got built, only some generations later to be scattered by tenants, the blocks used for stepping stones. Those others had been master hands at working in stone, and I found only stone reminders, usually arrowheads of flint, other times some larger shapes, flaked but seemingly unfinished and over which I could only wonder.

I had, like many gardeners on the Cumberland, been finding such since childhood; as a teacher I often from my pupils had little gifts of arrowheads and larger objects of stone, smooth, with a groove around the middle. Other times we would, when exploring some shallow and dry cave, find flint-flakings under the blown-in leaves and thin layer of rock dust; clearly men of long ago had sat in the shelter and worked enough to replenish their supply of arrowheads, or so we thought.

The spring plowing of most any garden plot or field I ever knew usually yielded some reminder of these people who disappeared before white men were around to write their history. Once, while walking over the country some years ago I came among a crew of men building a road in one of those high, wide limestone valleys up on Big Sinking. They had dug into a clay and gravel bank some distance back from the stream, and found a lot of skeletons. I selected from the scattered bones two quite good skulls and took them home to show my mother.

One came all to pieces on the trip and only a part of the other was left, chiefly, the lower jawbone with the teeth sound-looking still, but sadly worn and little higher than their sockets. I had envisioned some old chief, dying ripe and filled with years, but when I took the skull to an anthropologist at the University of Cincinnati, I learned it was that of a young woman. Years later I learned from another anthropologist [1] down in Tennessee that the young teeth had been worn down by gritty food; seeds, nuts, and other fare that pounded by a stone pestle in a stone mortar had got particles of grit from the stone tools, and so the teeth had suffered.

When did the woman live, and of what group or tribe or nation, are all questions that cannot be exactly answered. Some of the artifacts found could have been used by modern tribes of Indians, for many hunted over the region, but for none was any part of the river basin more than a temporary home. The Cumberland from the time the French first learned of it was a no man's land. It is doubtful, too, if much hunting was done with bow and arrow or stone club by modern Indians. The Cherokee were, by 1673, and for how much earlier we do not know, getting guns from the Spanish.[2] Less than twenty years later a band of the forever-hounded,

[1] Correspondence, Dr. Madeline Kneberg, Professor, Department of Anthropology, University of Tennessee, Knoxville.

[2] Used by permission of the publishers, The Arthur H. Clark Company, from *The First Explorations of the Trans-Alleghany Region by the Virginians* by Charles W. Alvord and Lee Bidgood, copyright The Arthur H. Clark Company, Cleveland, 1912 (cited hereafter as Alvord & Bidgood, *Explorations*), 214. The Cherokee in addition to Spanish muskets had also "brass potts and kettles from three gallons to thirty," quoting Abraham Wood, a trader, to John Richards, Aug. 22, 1674.

forever-wandering Shawnee coming into Anne Arundel County, Maryland, had ten guns among them, though many were armed with bows and arrows.[3] Other tribes of Algonkian and most of the Iroquois, who also visited the Cumberland at times, were being supplied with guns by the French and Dutch at an even earlier date.

Lack of any knowledge of the former owner never kept the searching for worked flint and other artifacts from being a pleasant pastime and there are numerous private collections all up and down the Cumberland. Many farm homes have somewhere around a few good arrowheads, now and then a stone ax, and less often a piece of pottery. These finds have also, like the fossils, attracted scientists, so that many objects found in the basin of the Cumberland can now be seen, labeled and explained, in some museum. The largest collection is at the University of Tennessee in Knoxville.

Many of the most important remains were destroyed before scientists could come upon the scene. This was particularly true of human bones. The finding of these all up and down the Cumberland by such early visitors as the Long Hunters appears, judging from the many accounts that have come down to us, to have been of almost constant occurrence. Sometimes the bones were found in caves, sometimes in mounds, but usually in stone-lined graves.

Judge Haywood, who in addition to the riddle of the rocks, also tried to solve the mysteries of the vanished peoples, pointed out that the graves were found in large collections near every lasting spring, often in conjunction with ancient walls of rock and earth, enclosing up to a hundred acres of land, "the whole covered with a stratum of mold and dirt eight to ten inches deep." [4] Most of the hills and ridges in the vicinity of Nashville were studded with stone-lined graves, and a large cemetery occupied the side of the hill that was in time crowned with Fort Zollicoffer.[5]

Constantine Rafinesque, scientist and teacher at Transylvania College in Lexington, attempted in 1822 to list all sites and monuments in Kentucky. He found earth walls, village sites, and mounds in every Kentucky county drained by the Cumberland. These were especially numerous in the west-

[3] M, VIII, 342.

[4] John Haywood, *The civil and political history of the state of Tennessee from its earliest settlement up to the year 1796: including the boundaries of the state*, Knoxville, 1823 (cited hereafter as Haywood, *C & P*), 96.

[5] *Annual Report of the Board of Regents of the Smithsonian Institution for the year 1877* (cited hereafter as *Report of Smithsonian for 1877*) contains a number of reports on excavations into southern mounds and graves. See in particular R. S. Robertson, "Antiquities of Nashville, Tennessee," 276–278.

ern end of the basin with twenty-four monuments and five sites in Trigg County alone. He also listed many sites in the narrow valleys high up the river, even what appeared to him to have been a fortified town above Williamsburg.[6] Still further up the river near the Three Forks there was for many years a place called Mount Pleasant, so named because of a large mound near the river; the name was in time changed to Harlan. One wonders if this mound were anything like that found by Dr. Thomas Walker in 1750 near what was to be Pineville, Kentucky—"a round hill made by Art about 20 feet high and 60 feet over the top." [7]

Reminders of vanished peoples were even more numerous in Middle Tennessee, and many were the conjectures as to their history. One of the most persistent of the legends grown around them was that they had been of the white race. There was a tradition among the Shawnee that all of Kentucky and Tennessee had once been settled by whites who were exterminated in a great battle at Falls of the Ohio.[8] Some early writers, including Filson of Kentucky, maintained these white people had originally come from Wales. There is a large body of literature dealing with the tradition of "Welsh speaking Indians" who were supposed to have been descendants of Modoc and his followers who sailed from Wales in 1170.[9] There were among the early settlers many Welshmen, and most of the tales were based on reports of these men having met Indians who understood their language. Rich and persistent as these stories are, there is no evidence that Welsh or other white men were ever prehistoric dwellers on the Cumberland.

The complete story of early man on the Cumberland will probably never be known. Tons of pottery, bones, flints, stone images, pipes, and other objects have been dug up by "pot hunters," plowed and hoed up, gathered from the bottoms of gullies to be kept or thrown away, but the only finds that have much scientific value are the few taken from excavations by

[6] Constantine Samuel Rafinesque, *Ancient History or Annals of Kentucky*, Frankfort, 1824. Listed in the Appendix of this work, county by county, are sites Rafinesque thought represented the remains of prehistoric peoples, but he neither described nor attempted excavation.
[7] FP, 13, Walker, "Journal," 54-55.
[8] Used by permission of the copyright owners, Mesdames Gertrude Williams Miller and Martha Williams Jan De Beur, from *Dawn of Tennessee Valley and Tennessee History* by Judge Samuel Cole Williams, copyright by Samuel Cole Williams, Johnson City, Tenn., 1937 (cited hereafter as Williams, *Dawn of Tenn.*), Appendix 441-443, quoting John Sevier, Oct. 9, 1810, to Maj. Amos Stoddard.
[9] *Ibid.*, 1-3. See also FP, 35, a facsimile reproduction of the original Wilmington 1784 edit. of John Filson's *Kentucke*, ed. Willard Rouse Jillson, Louisville, 1931, 95-97.

anthropologists and archaeologists. An effigy pipe of obsidian with jeweled eyes found near the Cumberland in Wayne County, Kentucky, was, when taken alone, about as meaningful to the archaeology of the region as it was to the child who tied a string around its neck and used it for a plaything.[10]

The answers to many questions may have been irretrievably lost when the Army Engineers dammed the Cumberland. A survey headed by Gordon R. Willey of the Bureau of American Ethnology was in 1947 conducted on what is now the bottom of the lake formed by Center Hill Dam on the Caney Fork, 26.6 miles above its mouth on the Cumberland at Carthage, Tennessee. Here, in an area of only 23,000 acres, Dr. Willey found twenty-eight open village sites, three large "temple mounds," three caves that showed evidence of prehistoric occupation and various other archaeological sites to make a total of thirty-nine.[11] Our government was asked for $24,000 to be used for the excavation of at least one of the mounds. The request was denied, and all are now buried under the lake. Various other surveys of sites to be covered by dams have been made, but funds for complete study and excavation have so far been unobtainable.

Rather fitting in its way that the graves, the temple mounds, the broken salt pans, the hoes, scrapers, beads, broken vases, charred ears of corn such as the eight-rowed flint found in Christian County, should along with the children's playthings rest forever unviolated under the waters of the Cumberland. It was a river, judging from the great diversity of objects found in its valley, known not only to many people, but also to many cultures.

The various groups who made pottery and those most in evidence were not the first to live on the Cumberland, and the prehistory of the valley cannot be entirely separated from the larger but not entirely known story of early man in North America. It is generally conceded that human beings have lived here for at least 20,000 years; some say 100,000, and that the first settlers came by way of the Bering Straits before the glaciers had withdrawn from all of what is now the United States.

In time there were possibly many groups of primitive hunters and food gatherers who neither cultivated the soil nor made pottery. The well made fluted points of one such group who lived before Folsom Man—so named because his grooved arrowheads were taken from a site near Folsom, New Mexico—have been found over much of Tennessee, particularly on the

[10] This story came from John C. Burton, collector, Monticello, Kentucky.
[11] Facts and figures used by permission of River Basin Surveys, Bureau of American Ethnology, Smithsonian Institution, from *Appraisal of the Archeological Resources of the Center Hill Reservoir, Tennessee, October 1947* (cited hereafter as *Center Hill Survey*), 1–2.

Highland Rim around the Nashville Basin. These Clovis points, as the earlier ones are known, have been found in conjunction with mammoth bones,[12] a circumstance that would indicate great antiquity.

Another group of early hunters on the Cumberland were known as the Eva People, though these are more closely identified with the Tennessee where reminders of what must have been their favorite food—mussel shells —are much more abundant. Judging from the size of the piles and the scarcity of stone hunting implements, the mainstay of their diet was mussels, abundant in most rivers of the Middle Mississippi Basin, and of easy gathering.

These early mussel eaters or Eva People must have been a rather lazy lot, not much given to the chipping of stone or the growing of food. Their hunting was done with the atlath or dart thrower, a simple contrivance of wood with an antler hook, and a polished stone weight as balance. Their bread, such as it was, consisted of nut meats and wild grain pounded into meal with a stone pestle in a shallow mortar. There is no indication they could either weave or make pottery, and their dead were buried with none of the care characteristic of later cultures, but they liked to ornament themselves with shell pendants and beads of canine teeth.[13]

The time of these people is not exactly known. Mussel shells from refuse found in Butler County, Kentucky, gave a date through carbon dating of between seven and eight thousand years, while a bit of burned bone associated with Folsom points showed an age of around ten thousand years.[14] Neither bone nor shell was from the Cumberland, but it seems reasonable to assume that men hunted mussels or bigger game there several thousands of years ago. "The mussel eaters remained until nearly the beginning of the Christian Era, and were probably displaced by new peoples with more advanced cultures." [15]

There may have been many groups that lived chiefly through hunting, some eating of one thing, some another, so that many patterns of living were represented at one time. These early wanderers and food gatherers as contrasted to those who farmed and made pottery are roughly designated as belonging to the Archaic stage. This phrase does not make a great deal of sense, but prehistoric cultures, even when their time zones are not

[12] Correspondence, Dr. Madeline Kneberg.
[13] James B. Griffin, ed. *Archeology of the Eastern United States,* copyright University of Chicago Press, Chicago, 1952, Dr. Madeline Kneberg, "The Tennessee Area," 190–198.
[14] *Ibid.,* 365–366.
[15] Correspondence, Dr. Madeline Kneberg.

exactly known, must still have some means of identification, and for this purpose, scientists, working in the basin of the Tennessee River, set up a table roughly divided into six cultural periods. The first three of these six are known as the Archaic; in the first period there was no worked flint, the second contained worked flint, and in the third, vessels of soapstone and sandstone appear along with worked flint, but during none of these periods had man yet learned to make pottery.[16]

Civilization did not advance steadily or evenly; it is possible that during the time of the Eva People who made no pottery and were but little given to the chipping of flint, some nearby group farmed, made pottery, and chipped flint. The Jesuit fathers found, for example, tribes in the north who grew no corn at all and were little more than wandering hunters, while nearby were other tribes of both Iroquois and Algonkian who had reached quite a high degree of civilization, growing much corn and living a sedentary life.

Most scientists are agreed that through the centuries many ways of life were represented along the Cumberland, for the river seems to have been a natural passageway along which many cultures traveled eastward from the Mississippi Valley, each leaving some evidence of its particular way of life.[17]

Excavations have been made on sites occupied at different times by different groups. Hines Cave near Mill Springs on the Cumberland yielded evidence of at least three different cultures. The floor of the cave was covered with many ash layers, and around the remains of ancient fires were found bone awls, needles, and flint skinning knives. The cave had also served as a cemetery, and found in one of the twenty graves opened was the skeleton of a young girl buried with an arrow in her ribs; with her was mica thought to have come from North Carolina. There was the skeleton of an old man with lesions on his skull, suggestive of syphilis. Still older, was a number of artifacts found overgrown with a stalactite nearly eight feet in diameter.[18] Judge Haywood wrote of still other forms of cave burial in which the body, wrapped in layers of deerskin and bark, was placed in a cane-lined casket.

The best known of the cultures that flourished on the Cumberland are

---

[16] Facts and figures used by permission of River Basin Surveys, Bureau of American Ethnology, Smithsonian Institution, from *An Archeological Survey of Celina Reservoir Project, Monroe County, Kentucky, September 1951* (cited hereafter as *Celina Survey*), 13–14.

[17] *Center Hill Survey*, 10–12.

[18] Material used by permission of the Kentucky Geological Survey from *Ancient Life in Kentucky* by William Snyder Webb and William D. Funkhouser, copyright Kentucky Geological Survey, Frankfort, 1928, pp. 129–134, 332.

represented by those who buried their dead in stone-lined graves. All of these groups, though their patterns of living varied, had reached a high degree of civilization as attested by the things they left behind them, especially pottery.

Pottery, unlike the softer things of animal skins, bark, or wood, was not completely destroyed by either time or fire. Fragments and whole pieces are found in varying degrees of abundance over the whole of the Mississippi Valley. Much attention has been given to a study of it, and the degree of civilization reached by a group has come roughly to be measured by the kind of pottery it made. Man in time learned that clay could be shaped and further strengthened with coarse grass or other materials, then hardened by heat. Pottery made in such fashion is known as pottery I. A more advanced culture was represented by pottery tempered with crushed limestone or some other form of grit; the still more advanced, or pottery III, was that strengthened with crushed mussel shells.[19]

The rich soil south of Nashville along the Harpeth River and its tributaries was, in the early days, almost as noted for mounds, stone graves, and remnants of fortifications as was the Middle Cumberland. Twenty-nine sites were reported from Williamson County by William M. Clark, alone, who did a good bit of excavating on the Harpeth.[20] Not all the sites belonged to one culture, but most are thought to have been representative of people who buried their dead in mounds of rocks and earth, and are sometimes referred to as the "Burial Mound People." Some of these groups on the Harpeth arranged their dead so as to make it possible to inter them in small stone-lined graves, usually hexagonal in shape, and often no more than thirty-two inches wide and eighteen inches deep. The smallness of the graves gave rise to a popular belief these early Cumberlanders had been a race of pygmies. George William Featherstonhaugh, an English geologist who visited the region in 1834, refuted this theory by measuring the bones.[21] Modern anthropologists recognize the very small skeletons found at many sites for those of children. "The tallest (based upon calculations of stature from the femur) were about five feet, nine inches, the average being considerably less." [22]

Not all who buried their dead in earth and rock mounds lived exactly

[19] *Celina Survey*, 13-14.
[20] *Report of Smithsonian for 1877*, W. M. Clark, "Antiquities of Tennessee," 269-276. See also *41st Annual Report of the Bureau of American Ethnology*, copyright Smithsonian Institution, Washington, 1919-1924 (cited hereafter as *41st Report of Bureau of Ethnology*), W. E. Myer, "The Fewkes Group," 559-605.
[21] Featherstonhaugh, *Excursion*, I, 79-97, 177-192.
[22] Correspondence, Dr. Madeline Kneberg.

alike, or even put the bodies in stone boxes, but those so often found on the Harpeth were quite representative of one of the most numerous groups of Burial Mound People on the Cumberland. They were also one of the most highly civilized. They lived in fortified villages surrounded by cornfields in which they grew squash and other vegetables. A piece of pottery "perfectly resembling a squash" was found on one of their sites, and in another the charred remains of grains of corn.

They made much pottery and many implements of bone, flint, shell, and stone. They wore beads and amulets, some carrying the likeness of a human face, and also found were "two beautiful pieces of ivory carved with a precision seldom seen among Indians." Dug from the bottom of a burial mound in association with a decayed human skeleton, indicative of "great antiquity," was a hollow, hourglass-shaped bobbin of hammered raw copper still wound with a bit of vegetable fibre, and thought to have been used by a priest in a religious rite or worn as a symbol of authority. Possibly less ancient, but showing more and finer workmanship, was a copper mask also found in a burial mound. This, oval in shape and about as large as a man's face, was made of four copper pieces beaten together; other pieces were riveted on either side to represent ears, while the eyes, eyebrows, nose, and mouth were indicated by small dots.

One of the most interesting things taken from the burial mounds was the stone images in human shape. These came from many localities and were usually referred to as "idols," though modern Indians were never known to worship idols, nor is there proof the prehistoric peoples of the Cumberland did. Some of the smaller of the stone statues of either sex were in reality effigy pipes, but those found by Clark on the Harpeth were larger and had no openings for pipe stems. "One of these idols," Clark wrote, "weighs 27½ pounds, and is cut from solid sandstone. It is remarkable for its great resemblance to the idols of India and China. The workmanship is rude, it is true, but faithful in its details." [23] He described other stone figures, two representing women in which the breasts were well developed, and the spinal column marked along the entire length of the back.

Representing a still higher cultural level, and even more common on the Cumberland were those who used mounds as sites for places of worship instead of burial. They also buried their dead in stone-lined graves, but their skeletons were arranged at full length. W. E. Myer,[24] whose careful

[23] *Report of Smithsonian for 1877*, Clark, "Antiquities of Tennessee," 275–276.
[24] W. E. Myer (1862–1923) spent most of his early life in Middle Tennessee, and later much of his research was centered there. See *42nd Report of Bureau of Ethnology*, 729, for biographical note.

and painstaking work has contributed most to our knowledge of the pre-history of the Cumberland, said of these people, named for a site he exca-vated: "Somewhere in nearly every rich bottom of the Cumberland River in Middle Tennessee traces of one or more of their homes can be found; and probably one third of known Indian remains in Middle Tennessee be-longed to the Gordon." [25]

The site chosen for excavation was a few miles from Nashville, and north-east of what is now Brentwood in Davidson County on the H. L. Gordon farm. Myer estimated that within a radius of sixty miles from the Gordon Site, there had been at least two hundred other remains of ancient villages, most long since put to the plow. Since the prehistoric peoples had the same sharp eye for good land, not subjected to flooding, as did the early Cumber-landers, their village sites were usually the first lands to be cleared and farmed.

The village studied was thought to have originally covered 11.2 acres once surrounded by walls, possibly much like that of a town of the Tunica on the lower Yazoo River described by Father Jacques Gravier in 1700. Myer conjectured that all about the town, save the land given up to the cemetery, had been the cornfields, long since grown up with big trees. He found within the town itself traces of eighty-seven house circles, though there were indications that once the town had held 125 circular houses fifteen to forty-six feet in diameter with the large temple not circular in shape. He surmised the total population had averaged about 1,250.

Everything was buried under a black mold, fourteen to thirty-one inches deep, the whole overgrown with trees—one, an elm, thirteen feet in cir-cumference, showed three hundred growth rings. The riddle of how the people left their homes or why was an unsolved one, for there was no sign of war, no fire, no sudden pestilence. The woven walls of the six dwellings and temple excavated had just fallen down and rotted. No unburied skele-tons were scattered about to indicate a sudden invasion or pestilence. Still, housewives left, scattered about on the clay floors of their homes, many objects not belonging there; enough to indicate some need for haste so overpowering there was no time for methodical packing and carrying away.

Dr. Myer learned much of the life of the people from these untidied homes, but could give no reason for what must have been an unpremedi-

[25] Facts and figures used by permission of the Smithsonian Institution, Bureau of American Ethnology, from *41st Report of Bureau of Ethnology*, "The Gordon Site," by W. E. Myer, 495–558.

tated flight. It is possible word of an invading army reached the village; and, in the manner of the modern Indian, the men went out to meet the enemy while the women and children sought places of safety in the hills. The Cherokee, in particular, would leave crops, dwellings, and all earthly goods if need be rather than risk the lives of their women and children.

The Gordon People took pride in their homes. Each was circular, made of upright posts interwoven with cane, the whole plastered with clay, strengthened with grass, and made smooth with a pottery trowel. The floors were of hard-packed clay with the polished fireplace or fire bowl found in each home of still thicker clay. The finding of metates indicated the pounding of corn into coarse meal had also been done in the home, and was not a communal activity.

The Gordon People must, like the modern southern Indians, have been great meat eaters, for they left large refuse heaps of bones; 85 per cent of those examined by Dr. Myer were of deer, 10 per cent wild turkey, with black bear, squirrel, rabbit, and other animals accounting for the remaining 5 per cent. There were no bones of the buffalo or the elk. Modern Indians lucky enough to have these animals within hunting range made liberal use of their bones and hides as well as flesh for food, so that it can only be concluded that the Gordon People lived before the elk and buffalo had migrated to Middle Tennessee.

We can be certain they had a variety of foods, even with neither elk nor buffalo. There would have been corn in most of the forms known to the modern Indian: bread or opone, the pone of the white man, roasting ears, parched corn to be eaten whole or pounded into meal, and sagamite, a dish made of corn and beans. Growing among the corn would have been peas, beans, watermelons, pumpkins, cushaws, varieties of muskmelons, and various other of the cucurbits, including gourds. There may have been peaches, plums, grapes, persimmons, blackberries, wild strawberries, as well as many nuts, particularly hickory nuts used extensively by modern southern Indians. Many tribes knew how to make maple sugar, and though wild honey before the coming of the white man with his bees was scarce, De Soto's men did find a southern tribe with honey. The Gordon People may have known the delights of poke greens and bear bacon as described by the Scotch trader James Adair who found much good eating among the Chickasaw. "It is surprising," wrote he, "to see the great variety of dishes." [26]

---

[26] James Adair, a Scotch trader, spent close to forty years among the southern Indians, chiefly the Chickasaw; out of his many experiences and observations came *History of the American Indian,* London, 1775. Pagination here follows the edition

Many of the tools and appliances used in the preparation of food or the production of clothing, were, like their pottery and stone implements, strong as well as beautiful. They may have had matchcoats of feathers or fur, robes of beaten mulberry bark, baskets of cane or grass, canoes of elm bark, or hollowed-out tree trunk; we do not know. All such would have decayed long ago.

They were expert stone chippers and pottery makers. They strengthened their clay with finely powdered mussel shells, and from it formed all manner of things from effigy vases, trowels, and toy animals for the children to great flattish bowls thirty inches in diameter used in the manufacture of salt. Much of the ware was highly polished and colored—red, black, cream, and buff.[27] The colors were had from yellow ocre, iron oxides, and possibly the smoke of burning corncobs for black as used by modern Indians.

The great temple where a ceremonial fire was kept perpetually burning in a large bowl of puddled clay, seemingly served as a center of social and political as well as religious life of the village. Here, the old men would have debated grave questions pertaining to peace and to war, or all might have gathered to begin some feast or festival such as the Green Corn Dance, for it would seem that all people who grew corn loved it and celebrated some season of its growth with songs and dancing.

The altar and the council house in general reminded Dr. Myer of the religious and political life of the Natchez. He judged that the Gordon People like many modern tribes held the sun as the giver of life. Pottery decorated with the quarter symbols of the world or the swastika and prayer bowls with four heads found in the graves would indicate such a religion. Owl effigy vases were also found, and possibly the Gordon like the Natchez venerated the owl.

They were a people who, judging from their treatment of the dead, loved their children well as did the modern Indians. All above approximately twelve years were buried in the cemetery of stone-lined graves. Younger ones were buried under the clay floors of the homes with their heads near the family hearth. The child's body was wrapped in a matting woven from the outer bark of cane, then covered with earth mixed with periwinkles such as are still found in the river. Polished and decorated burial urns that

published with notes and index and copyrighted by Judge Samuel Cole Williams, Kingsport, Tenn., 1930, and used by permission of the copyright heirs, Mesdames Martha Williams Jan De Beur and Gertrude Williams Miller (cited hereafter as Adair, *American Indian*), 437–439.

[27] W. E. Myer, "The Gordon Site," *41st Report of Bureau of Ethnology*, 520–530.

Dr. Myer conjectured had held food for the child on his long journey to the other world were often found near the small skeletons along with mussel-shell spoons. Sometimes there were pottery beads for adornment, or playthings—a toy sunfish bowl or an image vessel decorated with the likeness of a raccoon.

We know nothing of their form of government, but it must have been a stable one. Dr. Myer estimated the people occupied the site for around 450 years, living peacefully all the while, longer than any modern race of white man without a major war. It would seem to have been, at least economically, a somewhat classless society as "There was no great place on the hill, and neither was there the hovel in the hollow below."

They had on the whole better food, clothing, and shelter than many civilized peoples of the world today. They sowed and reaped and hunted, practiced their religion, made music with drums, stringed instruments, or pebble-filled gourds, and played games, among them, chunkey,[28] a game enjoyed by modern Indians. They must have been a happy, forever busy people.

Complete as were the excavations, they left many questions unanswered. Dr. Myer conjectured the village he studied had been deserted sometime before 1000 A.D., judging from the depth of the mold and the state of the forest. Not all anthropologists agree with him, but place the Gordon People, usually, at a much later date. There is, too, the problem of their place in the larger picture of the prehistory of the Mississippi Valley as a whole. Myer felt similar remains found in many places in the South and in Missouri and Arkansas were also those of the Gordon. Lately, there is a tendency to distinguish between the Gordon and similar cultures found in the Mississippi Valley.[29] In any case they were one group of Temple Mound People, all of whom had reached a high degree of civilization, lived in villages, had well developed handicrafts, grew much of their own food, and placed their houses of worship on mounds.

They must have loved the Cumberland well, and may have been masters of river navigation, but boats or temporary rafts of cane stalk would have long ago decayed. We do know, however, that they like other prehistoric peoples were great overland travelers. Practically all excavations of sites once used by the Burial and Temple Mound Peoples and even earlier cultures have brought to light materials and objects from long distances. Myer

[28] Good examples of chunkey or "chunge" stones as they are sometimes called may be seen in the Mountain Life Museum of Levi Jackson Wilderness Road State Park, London, Ky.
[29] *Center Hill Survey*, 12–15, 26.

conjectured that the Gordon People being expert flint chippers and near a supply, bartered worked flint for mica, obsidian, copper, and other materials not found locally. There are many well authenticated cases of modern Indians traveling more than a thousand miles on overland trails,[30] and the prehistoric peoples appear to have done the same.

Dr. Myer, in addition to all the work of excavation he supervised, also did a massive job of research on early Indian trails.[31] His conclusion was that the trails followed by the modern Indian, the Long Hunter, and the pioneer were the same as those used by prehistoric man in his role of traveling merchant. The buffalo and the deer would have had no small hand in their shaping, found passes and fords and salt licks, widened them here and there, but the range of these animals was too limited to have made the network of trails that tied the copper country of the far north to St. Augustine in Florida, or made it possible for a long-ago merchant on the Harpeth to trade worked flint for shells on the flintless Atlantic coast, as the shells, bored for hanging, so often found in graves, are almost always from distant places—the Gulf Coast or the Atlantic.

Copper alone would account for many long journeyings northward. All so far examined from sites on the Cumberland is unsmelted and from the copper country of the north. Dr. Roy W. Drier of Michigan College of Mining and Technology who has done extensive research on copper in Michigan's Keweenaw Peninsula is of the opinion that man mined copper there as long as seven thousand years ago.[32] It is doubtful if copper was carried to the Cumberland so long ago, but at some time men from Middle Tennessee and up the river picked their way through the network of trails that led to upper Michigan. They most probably went by way of the Great Lakes Trail that followed the ridge on the eastern side of

[30] John Lawson, *The history of Carolina; containing an exact description of the inlets, havens, corn, fruits, and other vegetables of that country together with the present state thereof. And a journal of a thousand miles, traveled thro several Nations of Indians. Giving a particular account of their customs, manners, etc.*, London, 1709 (pagination 1903 ed., Charlotte, N.C., cited hereafter as Lawson, *Carolina*), 29. See also Pierre Margry, ed. *Découvertes et établissements des français dans l'ouest et dans le sud de l'Amérique Septentrionale 1614–1714*, Paris, 1876–1886 (cited hereafter as Margry, *Découvertes*), l, 353, "*50 journées de chez . . . plus de 500 lieues*" in speaking of a band of Indians. See also John Spencer Bassett, ed. *The writings of "Colonel William Byrd of Westover in Virginia, esqr.,"* New York, 1901 (cited hereafter as Byrd, *Writings*), 158.
[31] Myer, "Indian Trails of the Southeast," *42nd Report of Bureau of Ethnology*, 727–854.
[32] Correspondence, Dr. Roy W. Drier, Michigan College of Mining and Technology, Houghton, Mich. See also *Inside Michigan*, July, 1953, Roy W. Drier, "Michigan's Most Ancient Industry," 15–16.

the Big South Fork then came down into the Cumberland valley to cross the river at Smith Shoals. It then continued northward, crossing the Ohio near the present site of Cincinnati, and on up into the northern region of the Great Lakes, intersecting on the way with many lesser trails.

One of the most famous of all Indian trails, at least to the white man, was the Great War Path through Cumberland Gap, down and across the Cumberland at the ford near present-day Pineville, then up through eastern Kentucky, splitting at Es-kip-pa-ki-thi-ki on the Red River of the Kentucky; both prongs of this trail continued north crossing the Ohio eastward of the Great Lakes Trail. It was over this trail that the dreaded Iroquois most often came into the country of the Cherokee, though when striking at enemies on the Virginia and Carolina Piedmont, they had a choice of other trails—that up the valley of the Kanawha or still further eastward, up the Valley of Virginia.[33]

Thought to have been one of the oldest trails in the Cumberland Country was another north-south trail, the Middle Chickasaw Path, worn two feet deep when the white man found it. It went south from what is now Nashville, crossing the Tennessee in what is now northwestern Alabama below the Muscle Shoals, then bearing west and south into a maze of trails that led to the Mississippi or the Gulf. This in time fathered the Natchez Trace. In going to the Atlantic Coast for shells instead of the Gulf, prehistoric man in the region of Nashville would have followed the same route eastward across the Plateau early travelers followed. This was Tollunteeskee's Trail that at Nashville intersected with the Chickasaw Path; it crossed the river here, then after going far enough north to escape the twisting bends of the Cumberland it turned eastward, crossing the river opposite the mouth of Flinn's Creek, and, following this creek, climbed onto the Highland Rim, and continuing in a southeast direction went up and over the Plateau, some miles north of present-day Crossville, then down by way of the Crab Orchard until, near present-day Rockwood it intersected with the Great Lakes Trail, that in turn led south to Chattanooga or north by way of present-day Harriman and up the valley of the Emery into Cumberland drainage. Another important trail out of Nashville, though not among the first to be used by the white man, was the Cisca or St. Augustine Trail. Leading southeast across the southern tributaries of Stone's River, it swung across the Highland Rim and the Plateau, then down into the valley of the Tennessee, crossing at Battle Creek, a few miles west of

[33] Myer, *42nd Report of Bureau of Ethnology,* Plate 15, 748, "The Trail System of the Southeastern United States."

Chattanooga; after swinging east to Chattanooga, it continued to present-day Augusta, Georgia, where it intersected with other trails, one leading to St. Augustine.[34]

These were only the major Indian trails; a traveler could reach any point in the United States by Indian trail; they formed a network covering the country with side roads and paths. We think, for example, of one trail through Cumberland Gap; there was, but Cumberland Gap could be reached from many directions; there were the Clinch River and Cumberland Gap Trail, the New River and Cumberland Gap Trail, while all other major trails mentioned intersected with trails that would eventually lead to the Gap.

It is hard to overestimate the importance of these trails in the exploration and settlement of the country by men who as a rule traveled by horseback instead of by canoe. A study of the trails will help to explain the wanderings of the Long Hunters, the routes of the first settlers, and the location of our roads of today. True, even the first roads of the white man did not exactly follow any given trail; originally made by animals and modified by men who walked, there was some change for the horseman; more change when the pack-horse trace became a wagon road, and still more when the wagon road became a highway for automobiles. Yet, at many points as at Cumberland Gap the very old and the very new know the same pass, and stranger still the white man built a very great many of his towns at the intersections of the old trails.

[34] *Ibid.*, Plate 14, 746, "Archaeological Map of the State of Tennessee."

CHAPTER IV

RIVIÈRE

DES CHAUOUANONS

FORESTS and canebrakes reclaimed the land once planted to corn, and trees grew high above the carefully buried dead. The land, empty of human inhabitants, was still no wilderness. The first white visitors to describe it found the Barrens,[1] treeless reaches of grassland where in late spring the wild strawberries reddened with juice the travelers' horses up to their knees, and at all seasons the buffalo were plentiful. This soil would grow trees; they grow there now; why it was treeless then is an unsettled point. The Indians often used rings of fire to hunt the deer and buffalo, and repeated burnings through the centuries may have caused the lack of trees, and once treeless the great herds of buffalo helped destroy the young growth.

In any case the Barrens appear to have been enlarging; the forests of Middle Tennessee and in the valleys up the Cumberland, though filled with fine tall timber, were "park like"[2] and never so dark and impenetrable as those north of the Ohio, and over much of the country the woods were so open and with so little undergrowth a traveler could see a deer for 150 paces. There were, too, along the creeks and rivers, treeless glades and valleys, sometimes filled with cane as were the bottoms of

[1] As early as 1718 Guillaume de l'Isle in his *Carte De La Louisiane Et Du Cours Du Mississippi* showed the barrens north of the Cumberland. This map was reproduced by Charles A. Hanna, *The Wilderness Trail*, copyright Charles A. Hanna, New York, 1911 (cited hereafter as Hanna, *Wilderness Trail*), and quoted by permission of the publishers, G. P. Putnam. Map facing I, 122.
[2] J. G. Ramsey, *The Annals of Tennessee to the end of the 18th century*, Philadelphia, 1853 (cited hereafter as Ramsey, *Tennessee*), 77.

the Caney Fork, or only high grass like that of Price's Meadows in Kentucky, near the mouth of Meadow Creek on the southern side of the Cumberland.[3] More rarely there were meadows of wild clovers where a man could plant corn and never cut a tree or grub a cane stalk; such a stretch of land was Clover Bottom on Stone's River, a few miles east of Nashville and now cut by U.S. 70 North.

Most of the uninhabited basin of the river that would in time be called Cumberland was a paradise for ruminants. Here, they could find everything needful—salt licks, grass in the barrens, ferns in the forest—and many varieties of wild legume, especially pea vine, flourished in any stretch of open, cane-free woods. Buffalo, elk, and deer, all abounded. The heavy mast—beech, chestnut, and acorn—fattened bear and turkey alike. Red-billed parrakeets, or Cumberland parrots as they came to be known, red and gray squirrels, raccoons, oppossums, foxes, great droves of wolves, panthers, and wildcats as well as many smaller animals and birds, all throve in the abundant land. There were in the river hundred-pound catfish and twenty-pound perch,[4] and along it many beaver, some with ponds more than a mile long.[5] Swans, wild geese, and other varieties of waterfowl were unusually plentiful.[6]

How long this hunter's paradise remained without people we do not know. The first recorded visitors mentioned no old fields or orchards to indicate previous Indian occupancy, though temporary hunters' camp sites were fairly common on the upper river.[7] The story is that because it of-

[3] WD, I, 204. This 1801 deposition of Michael Stoner concerning people and places in the neighborhood of present-day Mill Springs, Ky., in 1775, sheds much light on the region at that date when settlement was just beginning.
[4] Smith, *Description*, 10.
[5] WD, I, 211–213, deposition of Nathaniel Buckhannon. The early work of Thomas Hutchins, lieutenant in the British Army and designer of Fort Pitt, done chiefly 1763–1769, is the earliest known attempt by the British to map and describe the Middle Mississippi Valley, much of the territory newly acquired from the French by the Treaty of Paris in 1763. See in particular Thomas Hutchins, "Courses of the Shawanoe River from the Mouth Upwards." This material, part of an unprinted 1769 manuscript, studied by photostatic copy from and by permission of the Historical Society of Pennsylvania (cited hereafter as Hutchins, "Notes"), contains many references to canebrakes, licks, beaver dams—see in particular Sheet 6 (my own numbering)—soil, timber, streams, and other natural features viewed from the Hutchins boat on the Cumberland. Beaver appear to have been unusually plentiful; numerous creeks all up and down the river were named Beaver, and early records of Davidson County have many debts to be paid in beaver.
[6] Gray, *Bishop*, 52, 55. Dr. Walker in 1750 commented on the waterfowl seen in the neighborhood of present-day Pineville; FP, 13, Walker, "Journal," 6, 75.
[7] FP, 13, Walker, "Journal," 54. See also Joseph W. Wells, *History of Cumberland County, Kentucky*, copyrighted and published by Joseph W. Wells, Louisville, 1947, and used by his permission (cited hereafter as Wells, *Cumberland County*), 9, 10.

fered such good hunting and was so accessible by trail and river to many tribes in all directions, the country was set aside as a hunting ground; the land, now known as Middle Tennessee, was called the Middle Hunting Ground, and was claimed by "the four nations." [8] Four nations as claimants would have been too few; there were the Chickasaw and the Creek with smaller numbers of Alabamas to the south; the Overhill Cherokee, though living on the headwaters of the Tennessee, claimed and used the land for hunting, as did the Iroquois northward; and from between the Wabash and the Mississippi came the Miami and the Illinois. All these as well as the Shawnee hunted over the Cumberland Country after the region was known to the white man. [9]

Well known and prized as it was as a hunting ground by many tribes, the Cumberland was still rather late in coming under the full knowledge of the white man, for it had at most only temporary towns to attract traders. In 1540 members of De Soto's party may have been close to Cumberland County, Tennessee, on the Plateau, but like the legends of the Welsh-speaking Indians there is for this no authentication. Indians on what is presumed to have been the Tennessee told De Soto that "towards the north there was a province called Chisca, and that a forge was there for copper." Hoping for gold instead of copper, since he had heard "there was another metal there of the same color save that it was finer," De Soto sent "two Christians" and some Indians to Chisca, while he and his men waited at Chicaca, "a small town of twenty houses."

"In three days they that went to Chisca got back." The travelers relating that the country on the way was thinly populated and it was said there were mountains over which the beasts could not go, and finding the distance was becoming long "they agreed to return, coming from a poor little town where there was nothing of value, bringing only a cowhide (young buffalo) as delicate as a calfskin the people had given them. . . ." [10]

There has been much discussion as to exactly where De Soto went in his wanderings, and hence the location of the towns named is vague. Some

[8] A, V, "Correspondence of General James Robertson," 72–73. The author and his correspondents were at this time, 1805, treating with the Chickasaw.

[9] I, XVI, 354, 363. Charles Morgan writing, July 20, 1768, from Kaskaskia in the Illinois told of an attack on the Cumberland by the "Post St. Vincent Indians," from the Wabash; these described as consisting of Potawatamies, Piankishaws, Wiotonans, Kickapous, Miamis, and Vermillion tribes.

[10] Edward G. Bourne, ed., and Buckingham Smith, tr., *Narrative of the Career of Hernando de Soto in the conquest of Florida as told by a knight of Elvas and in a relation by Luys Hernandez de Biedma, factor of the expedition*, New York, 1904, I, 77, 80.

historians [11] place Chicaca, where he waited, at the mouth of the Hiwassee River above present-day Chattanooga; a round trip of three days northward from this point would have taken the traveler onto the Plateau in Cumberland River drainage, but we know only that De Soto waited at a point quite far north; snow fell and "there was plenty of ice," and as he marched on he soon found what must have been the Suck in the Tennessee River.

Another hundred years went by and the Cumberland ran on, but one of several prongs of the system that drained that giant, open-ended meat platter, the Mississippi Valley. Spain and France, and later, England and Holland began to plant colonies along the Atlantic Coast; and of them all, France, using the chain of the St. Lawrence and the Great Lakes as a highway, penetrated most deeply into the interior. It was a French interpreter and student of Indian languages, Jean Nicolet,[12] who discovered for the white man the water route that would eventually lead to the Cumberland.

One of the most fearless as well as curious of Frenchmen, he began to hear not long after his coming to Canada in 1618 distorted stories of the Winnebago, many sleeps distant to the north and west. At last in 1639 he had his heart's wish of being sent as ambassador to this far town near the head of Green Bay on the western side of Lake Michigan. He chose for his ambassadorial or working dress a flowing robe of rich Chinese silk embroidered with birds and flowers because he thought the Winnebago, so far west as they were, might be men of Cathay.[13]

Great must have been his disappointment to find only breech-clouted Indian men, frightened squaws, and curious children. Still, he made friends, and when the Indians spoke of a Great Water and offered to guide him there, he followed them up what is now the Fox River, a stream coming out of the southwest; past the headwaters of this they portaged across country to the Wisconsin, a tributary of the Mississippi.[14] He never reached the larger river, but later wrote he had been only three days distant from the sea. His was a mistake made by many adventurers and explorers. The Indians in speaking of the Mesha Sabi did mean a great water, but the greatness was for the Mississippi, not the sea.

Explorations had been quickened by the coming of the Jesuits in 1611.

[11] Williams, *Dawn of Tenn.*, 4–8.

[12] John Gilmary Shea, *Discovery and Exploration of the Mississippi Valley*, New York, 1853 (cited hereafter as Shea, *Mississippi*), xx–xxi.

[13] Francis Parkman, *La Salle and the Discovery of the Great West*, Boston, 1879 (cited hereafter as Parkman, *La Salle*), xxiv.

[14] Shea, *Mississippi*, quoting Fr. Vimont, xxi.

The priests in order to be effective missionaries must learn the Indian languages, and so early we find them suffering every conceivable hardship including torture and death as they lived among the various tribes. Most of the Indians around the Great Lakes and northward and to the east were members of two great groups or federations: most numerous were the Algonkians to whom belonged such tribes as the Mohicans, Pequots, and Narragansetts; and like an island among the Algonkians and roughly centered in what is now central New York State were the Iroquois, or the Five, later Six, Nations, a much more closely knit and politically astute group, though smaller.

The writings of such Jesuit missionaries as Brébeuf, Le June, Jogues, and René Goupil [15] give memorable pictures of life among these Indians, especially during the endless northern winters in the long bark houses, which, though often warm and cheerful places with corn hung on the rafters and food for all, were filled with smoke, fleas, and "unbridled and unruly children pellmell with restless dogs."

Life varied from tribe to tribe, but among most of both the Iroquois and Algonkian the people lived in long, many-familied dwellings, hunted much, but grew corn for bread. The Jesuits left stories of the doings of the medicine men, games, feasts, hunting expeditions, jokes and songs, death and hunger, grave and dignified councils among which, in the Iroquois, the women had a voice. There were tales, too, of their religions with some legends much like our own Old Testament stories. Sometimes the laughter was louder, the merriment of the often gay Indians greater than common. A prisoner or so was being burned to death, flayed alive, or slowly dismembered with dull clam shells, always with great care so that the torture might be prolonged as long as possible. Yet, often above the delighted shrieks of the women and children, rose the warrior's death song. Such brave warriors sometimes had the honor of being eaten; the Hurons were particularly fond of feeding small pieces of the raw heart of a brave victim to their small sons, hoping thereby to give them some of the dead man's courage in death.

The Indians had always fought, even at times among the tribes of the same Nation or Federation. During the time of the Jesuits the wars quickened. The Iroquois were forever on the warpath, and theirs was a double vengeance. Outnumbered and hemmed in by the Algonkians, though greater warriors, the Iroquois had for many years suffered much from their neighbors. Matters for them had been worsened by the coming of Champlain. He had first made friends with a tribe of Algonkians, and had in 1609 gone

[15] Francis Parkman, *The Jesuits in North America*, Boston, 1876.

with them against a tribe of the Iroquois, who could only run away or die helplessly from the guns of Champlain and his soldiers, their arrows for the most part useless against the armored Frenchmen.[16]

Champlain's victory was a sad day for France. The Dutch came to eastern New York, and by 1630 were supplying their Iroquois neighbors with guns. The Algonkians, though also armed with guns, and outnumbering their enemies, were usually defeated. The conquest and dispersal of the Erie were finished by around 1656. Six years later the scattering of another Algonkian tribe, the Shawnee,[17] began. It is through the Jesuit accounts of the south-ward fleeing Shawnee that we first hear of the lower Mississippi Valley and the Cumberland.

Father Lalemant wrote from Montreal in 1662: "Proceeding rather west-erly than southerly another band of Iroquois is going 400 leagues from here in pursuit of a nation whose only offence consists in its not being Iroquois. Furthermore, if we believe our Iroquois who have returned thence, and the slaves whom they have brought thence, it is a country which has none of the severity of our winter, but enjoys a climate which is always temperate—a continual spring and summer as it were. Their villages are situated along a Beautiful River, which serves to carry people down to the Great Lake (for so they call the sea). . . ." [18]

Bands of the widely scattered Shawnee were heard of from many places; around 1665 La Potherie wrote of a captive Chauouan, or Shawnee, who related he had lived near Carolina, and that "his village was only five days journey from the South Sea and was near a great river which, coming from the country of the Illinois, empties into the sea." [19]

The Jesuits represented a frontier not found among the English colonists —that of religion. Young ex-Jesuit Sieur de la Salle, coming swiftly behind and some times ahead of the Jesuits, brought with him the frontier common to all nations—that of the trader. He envisioned a vast empire to be built by France in the New World; and in the great river, Mesha Sabi, of which he, too, heard from the Indians he saw a possible connecting link between Can-ada and the South Sea.

His fruitless attempts to find the mouth of the Mississippi make some of the most tragic reading in all history,[20] but more of a tragedy for the his-

---

[16] Francis Parkman, *Pioneers of France in the New World*, Boston, 1867, 310–324.
[17] Hanna, *Wilderness Trail*, I, 158. The word *Shawnee* was spelled in many ways; the English version almost always began with *Sh* and that of the French with *Ch*.
[18] *Ibid.*, I, 120.
[19] *Ibid.*, I, 121, quoting La Potherie.
[20] Parkman, *La Salle*, 356–408.

torian is the vagueness, which seems at times to smack of pure falsehood, that clothes the account of his earlier exploration in the upper valley. There is, for example, a letter of 1667, the authorship of which both Parkman and Hanna ascribe to La Salle. The letter states that La Salle followed the Ohio to a point in the 37th degree of latitude where it fell from a great height into a vast marsh.[21] The rapids of the Ohio are closer to 38½ degrees than 37, but the falls of Cumberland are very close to that degree.

La Salle, like many of the Jesuit priests, learned something of the Iroquoian language, and in 1669, two years after his claimed exploration of the Ohio, we find him listening to a band of Senecas who had come by water to Montreal on a hunting and trading trip. "They told him that this river (the Ohio) took its rise only three days journey from Sonnontouan, and that after one month of traveling one came upon the Honniasontkernons and the Chauouanons, and that after having passed the latter and a great cataract or waterfall there is in this River, one found the Outagame and the country of the Iskousogo and that in that country, deer and buffalo were as plentiful as the trees of the woods." [22]

It is indeed passing odd that the Senecas who lived in western New York and hence were familiar with the great cataract of Niagara should have referred to the rapids of the Ohio with their total fall of twenty-seven feet in two and one half miles, and which in high water did not even need portage, as a "great cataract." Yet, the early French in writing of the rapids use the same expression as for Niagara— *"et un grand saut ou cherte d'eau."* [23] In 1699 still another band of Senecas told La Salle he might find the villages of the Honniasontkernon and the Chauouanons on the Ohio "above the falls." [24] There was only one river east of the Mississippi with a great waterfall close to the 37th degree of latitude; that was the Cumberland, and on it, "buffalo were as plentiful as the trees of the woods."

Parkman in discussing it thinks La Salle was mistaken in his latitude calculations. Hanna in his careful summaries of all known facts is most uncertain La Salle explored the Ohio at all, and points out that his writings as well as maps of his journeyings all indicate La Salle thought the Ohio and Wabash drained into the Tennessee.[25] The "great cataract or waterfall" in the 37th degree of latitude remains a tantalizing mystery.

[21] Hanna, *Wilderness Trail,* II, 87–88.
[22] *Ibid.,* II, 116–117.
[23] Margry, *Découvertes,* I, 116.
[24] Hanna, *Wilderness Trail,* I, 158.
[25] *Ibid.,* II, 92–115. Hanna also reproduces and discusses, *ibid.,* 92, Franquelin's 1684 map of La Salle's discoveries as further proof.

No historian thinks of it as being in the Cumberland, but could some wandering Frenchman have visited Cumberland Falls with a compass even before Father Marquette went down the Mississippi in 1673? Cumberland Falls, though in wild and rough country, was very close to a major Indian trail,[26] that looped, touching the river at Price's Meadows, and again near the mouth of Marsh Creek just above the Falls. The Cumberland falls into a gorge, not a marsh, but a traveler following the circular trail in springtime, could have found wide bottoms, flooded and with a marsh-like appearance. It does seem that La Salle had met some Frenchman familiar with Cumberland Falls, but we can only accept such facts as are set down in history. He may have confused one Indian's tale of Cumberland Falls with that of another who meant the rapids of the Ohio, or he may have learned all he knew of the eastern side of the Mississippi Valley from his servant and great hunter, Nitka, "one of our Shawnee Indians who constantly attended him from Canada to France and from France to Mexico." [27]

All explorers of America had to get their first ideas of the unknown from the Indians; even Father Marquette, as he prepared to descend the Mississippi wrote: "we gathered all possible information from the Indians who frequented these parts, and even from their accounts traced a map of all the new country marking down the rivers on which we were to sail, the names of the nations and places through which we were to pass, the course of the great river, and what directions we should take when we got to it." [28]

The accounts of the travels down to the mouth of the Arkansas of Father Marquette and Joliet, and their maps, particularly that of Joliet, have been discussed by many historians. Nobody credits either with having been near the Cumberland, but there is reason to believe Marquette described the Cumberland and not the Ohio when he wrote in his narrative of 1675: "We came to a river called Ouabouskigou. This river comes from the country on the east inhabited by the people called Chauouanons in such numbers that they reckon as many as 23 villages in one district, and 15 in another, lying quite near each other; they are by no means warlike, and are the people the Iroquois go far to seek in order to wage an unprovoked war upon them; and, as these poor people cannot defend themselves (because they have no firearms) they allow themselves to be taken and carried off like flocks of sheep. And innocent though they are, they never-

---

[26] The Great Lakes Trail, *supra*, III, n. 31.
[27] Shea, *Mississippi*, 197, "Narrative of Fr. Douay."
[28] *Ibid.*, 7–8, "Narrative of Fr. Marquette."

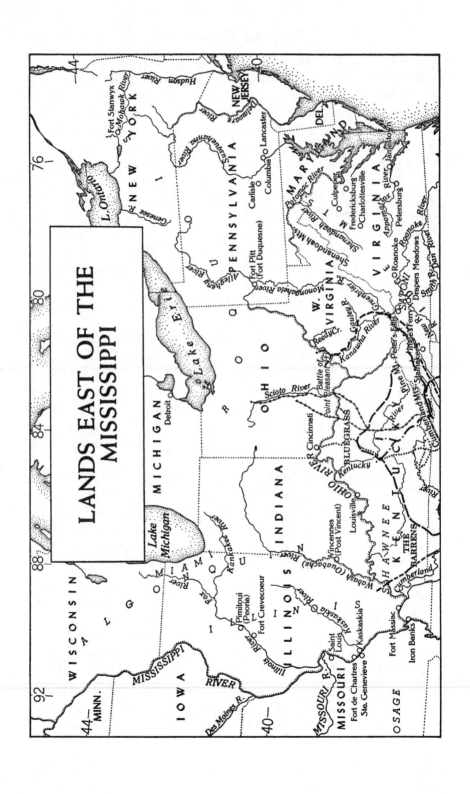

LANDS EAST OF THE MISSISSIPPI

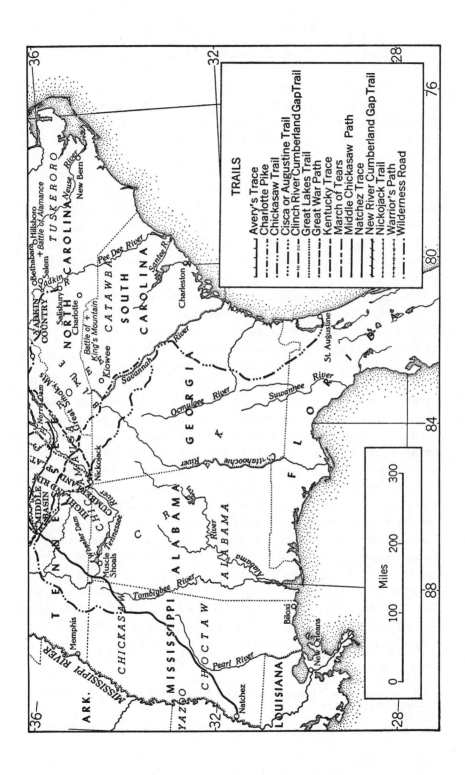

TRAILS

Avery's Trace
Charlotte Pike
Chickasaw Trail
Cisca or Augustine Trail
Clinch River Cumberland Gap Trail
Great Lakes Trail
Great War Path
Kentucky Trace
March of Tears
Middle Chickasaw Path
Natchez Trace
New River Cumberland Gap Trail
Nickojack Trail
Warrior's Path
Wilderness Road

Miles

0   100   200   300

theless sometimes experience the barbarity of the Iroquois who cruelly burn them." [29]

The early French thought of the Ohio as being a minor stream, and gave the name Ouabachi or Wabash, not only to the Wabash, but also to all the Ohio below its mouth.[30] Thus, it is possible that Father Marquette, his knowledge of the Mississippi Valley based entirely on what he had learned from the Indians, confused their description of the Cumberland with that of the Ohio. Some historians construe a river on Joliet's map of 1674 to be the Cumberland; nameless, it flows into the Ohio from the south, and near its headwaters are shown "Chauouanon" villages.[31] Marquette's map, done in the same year, is interesting when compared with La Salle's claims of five years earlier. Marquette shows the Chauouanon far east of the Mississippi, and much too far south to have been on the Ohio above the falls.[32]

Wrong as Father Marquette's ideas of the geography of the Mississippi Valley may have been, he did correctly describe the cane, catfish, and buffalo he found along the Mississippi that later travelers would find along the Cumberland, and most particularly the buffalo.

"We find," he wrote, "that turkeys have taken the place of game, and the Pisikious or wild cattle, that of other beasts. We call them wild cattle, because they are like our domesticated cattle; they are not longer, but almost as big again, and more corpulent; our men having killed one, three of us had considerable trouble in moving it. The head is very large, the forehead flat and a foot and a half broad between the horns, which are exactly like those of our cattle, except that they are black and much larger. Under the neck there is a kind of large crop hanging down, and on the back a pretty high hump. The whole head, the neck, and part of the shoulders are covered with a great mane like a horse's; it is a crest a foot long, which renders them hideous, and falling over their eyes, prevents them seeing before them. The rest of the body is covered with a coarse curly hair like the wool of our sheep, but much stronger and thicker. It falls in summer, and the skin is then soft as velvet. Indians make of them beautiful robes; the flesh and fat of the Pisikious are excellent and constitute the best dish in banquets. . . . They are scattered over the prairie like herds of cattle. I have seen a band of 400." [33]

[29] Shea, *Mississippi*, 41-42.
[30] Hanna, *Wilderness Trail*, II, 103-104, quoting Fr. Membre.
[31] Williams, *Dawn of Tenn.*, 42, believed Fr. Marquette meant the Cumberland.
[32] Shea, *Mississippi*, 238.
[33] *Ibid.*, 19.

There may have been, at the time of Father Marquette's writing, Frenchmen near the mouth of the Cumberland hunting buffalo with wandering bands of Indians, for as early as 1676 a Boston merchant, Richard Wharton, was writing, "The French are reported to be very diligent in the discovery of the lakes and land behind New England, Virginia, and Carolina. Monsrs. Brunett and Marston report that some persons that have been three years upon discovery are this year returned to Canada with a clear discovery of all the land to the south behind Carolina. . . . To give assurance of their travels they have brought home Parraketoes and other certayn signes." [34]

Coureurs de bois were much given to deserting white civilization for that of the Indian, and still others—deserted soldiers, debtors, white prisoners of war—with reasons for leaving Canada lived with the Indians and followed them in their wanderings. Still other Frenchmen at this date and for some years later hunted gold and silver over much of the Mississippi Valley and carried on mining operations in what is now Tennessee. [35] Such hunters were inclined to be secretive about their movements. All these as well as the lost and the wandering, or simply curious, may have traveled over most of the Mississippi Valley, but left neither journal nor relation.

That Frenchmen early knew at least something of major Indian trails is borne out by Franquelin's map of 1684,[36] based on La Salle's notions of the Mississippi Valley. Shown on this map is a westward flowing stream labeled Rivière Bleu or Skipaki-cipi, and construed by many historians to have been the Cumberland. One of the several Shawnee towns shown near this river is Chisca, possibly the same De Soto hunted. Leading from Chisca to the Florida coast was an approximation of the St. Augustine Trail, and labeled, "the path traveled by the Casquianampo and the Chauouanons in trading with the Spanish."

One Frenchman, familiar with many trails of the Cumberland Country, at least by 1691, was Martin Chartier, a Canadian who went south, not for furs or gold, but for love, or so it would seem, of an Indian woman. He had served a three years' apprenticeship in Canada as a house carpenter, and was thus no mere wandering *coureur de bois*, but a skilled workman

---

[34] Quoted by permission of the editors of *The Mississippi Valley Historical Review* from Vol. XXI, 256, copyright 1934.

[35] Reuben Gold Thwaites, *France in America, 1497–1763*, Harper and Brothers, New York, 1905, 77.

[36] Hanna, *Wilderness Trail*, II, 92, facing *Carte De La Louisiane ou Des Voyages Du S.- De La Salle*, by Jean Baptiste Franquelin, Paris, 1684.

and "a man of many parts," including the ability to survey.[37] We first hear of him in the winter of 1678–79 when La Salle hired him to help build a fort at Niagara. The fort finished, La Salle set his carpenters to the building of the largest sailing vessel on the Great Lakes up to that time. This was the *Griffin*, a vessel of about forty-five tons, intended for the fur trade above Niagara Falls.[38]

We can imagine Chartier wearing a red handkerchief for head covering, white shirt, red underwaistcoat, long footless waist-high hose, and Indian shoes—clothing commonly worn by other Canadian workers and *coureurs de bois*.[39] No different from many other Frenchmen in the woods, he took an Indian wife, and may have been already married while at Niagara. Less than fourteen years later [40] or in 1692, he is described as having a sixteen-year-old daughter. His wife seems to have been a Shawnee whom he could have met at Niagara, for by this date captive or scattered bands of Shawnee were to be met with in many places.

We next hear of Martin Chartier in the Illinois Country, near the site of present-day Peoria where La Salle was attempting to build a fort which, because of the many disasters that overtook him at this time, 1679–80, he named Fort Crèvecoeur. The *Griffin* upon which La Salle had built most of his dreams of a trading empire in the Great Lakes, was lost with a rich load of furs on her first journey back to Niagara. When news of this was brought to the workmen in the wintry Illinois woods, neither La Salle nor his faithful lieutenant, the Italian Tonty, "*bras de fer*," was there to reassure the men they would, in spite of the financial mishap, be paid.[41]

Some had had no pay for three years, and, on hearing the news, they began to desert, the first group leaving about "the time of Epiphany," or

[37] Quoted by permission of the North Carolina Historical Commission from *Account of the Founding of New Bern* by Christoph von Graffenried; ed. and tr. by Vincent H. Todd; pub. and copyrighted by the North Carolina Historical Commission, Raleigh, 1920 (cited hereafter as Graffenried, *New Bern*), 247, 383–384. Graffenried shortly after 1700 went up the Potomac past the site of present-day Washington, D.C., and there in the then backwoods he met Martin Chartier, by then a well-to-do trader to the Indians.

[38] Parkman, *La Salle*, 119–150. See also the translation of La Salle's letter, used by permission of James M. Babcock, Chief, Burton Historical Collection of the Detroit Public Library, from an English typescript of Margry's *Découvertes*, tr. by Miss Edith Moody, London, 1897–1907, and acquired by the Burton Historical Collection (cited hereafter as Margry, *Translation*), II, 215–270.

[39] *Ibid.*, II, 110–111, contains a description of the clothing confiscated from Chartier and his companions.

[40] M, VIII, 146.

[41] What happened at Fort Crèvecoeur depended much upon which side told the story; see Parkman, *La Salle*, 151–174, and Shea, *Mississippi*, 149–184, quoting Fr. Membre.

January 4. Still others said they left La Salle's employ because "the said Sieur de La Salle wanted them to build sleighs," to take his goods to the Indian villages of the Illinois. Moyse Hillaret's story, told at a trial in Quebec, was that the men did no more than pay themselves their long overdue wages, taking instead of money, beaver skins, guns, and ammunition from La Salle's stores at Crèvecoeur and leaving a statement of what each took.[42] La Salle was of another mind: he declared that "five or six rascals stole the value of five or six thousand livres in beaver skins and goods at the Illinois when I was absent." He was accused of mistreating his men, but insisted: "The 22 men who deserted and robbed me are not to be believed on their word, deserters and thieves as they are." [43]

Most of the accused men were captured, but Martin Chartier was one of eight who in the summer of 1680 escaped to the Dutch in New York, and lived for a time at a place "called Asoprio" between "Albany and Cannida." [44]

The strange thing is he didn't stay there. He went back to Canada where he was captured, and put into prison in irons. He again escaped, but instead of fleeing to the safety of New York, he went to the Illinois and is thought to have reached the Indian villages in the neighborhood of Fort St. Louis in 1684,[45] hardly a safe place for a man La Salle thought a criminal. Chartier went for something, and we suspect it was his wife.

His next six years were spent largely in wanderings, first south where he met a band of Shawnee, then north again with the Shawnee when they came up with some "twitteway Indians." [46] The Shawnee, homeless by this date and forever wandering, then "traveled southward for two years before they found a convenient place of settling down, having been guided by eight Catouqui [Cherokee] Indians, and there they lived three years."

Historians of the Mississippi Valley [47] are agreed this convenient place was the Cumberland; it was easily reached from the Illinois Country, and was the only river even fairly safe; the Cherokee, the Creek and the Chick· asaw made any stretch of the Tennessee impossible, while a trip up the

[42] Most of the information on Chartier in Canada and the Illinois consists of testimony given by various witnesses at the trial of the deserters; this is the story of Moyse Hillaret, ship's carpenter, as related in Margry, *Translation*, II, 112–114.

[43] *Ibid.*, I, 106–111.

[44] M, VIII, 517.

[45] M, VIII, 345. Chartier's movements in Maryland were also told in the form of testimony, often indirect quotations in letters. Some, such as the above, is Chartier's testimony "eight years hence," and the year was 1792.

[46] M, VIII, 517–518.

[47] Hanna, *Wilderness Trail*, I, 158. Williams, *Dawn of Tenn.*, 18–20. There is, however, no complete agreement on his exact movements.

Ohio to reach the Kentucky would have brought the Shawnee danger-
ously close to the Iroquois.

Once again Chartier followed the Shawnee: "It happened that about two
years since [1692] they went away; and sometime after, about August, he
resolved to follow them, and took a canoe and went after them three hundred leagues in forty days. . . . he guessed the way, and was guided by
the course of the river, and found water in all places." He had a gun, but
neither pot nor skillet, and "hunted for his victuals, which, as he got, he
roasted. . . . And when he came to them [the Shawnee] they made him
very welcome." [48]

Chartier spent about two years on the Cumberland with the Shawnee,
hunting and fishing, and they may have stayed in one place long enough
to raise a corn crop. A trip of three hundred leagues or nine hundred miles
from the Illinois would have taken Chartier far up the Cumberland, and
they possibly spent most of their time on the stretch of river between
Obey's and the Big South Fork. Game was plentiful here, and at this point
they were furthest from the enemies that surrounded them in all directions.
Hanna thought they gradually went up the river to the Warrior's Path
crossing, then overland through Cumberland Gap.[49] They could have
done this, though the chances are they went no higher than Smith Shoals
and avoided the rough upriver country; from Smith Shoals they could
have followed the Great Lakes Trail in either direction, and from it
worked their way through a network of trails going east.

Regardless of what trails they followed, the summer of 1692 found
Chartier with seventy-two Indian warriors, one hundred and twenty
women and children, and the Cherokee prisoners near the mouth of the
Susquehanna in Anne Arundel County, Maryland.[50] The group had three
hundred beaver skins; eight of the warriors were armed with guns, the
rest with bows and arrows. Chartier, later described as speaking several
languages, was able for one "good beaver skin," to hire a guide to take
him and his followers about sixteen miles to the trading post of Mr. Jacob
Lootons, a Baltimore County trader. The good people of Maryland were
frightened out of their wits by such a "parcel of strange Indians," all except "the said Lootons' wife, who came out of the store with her arms
abroad crying out, 'Hey-Ho, who are you coming to kill now,' and such
like discourse." [51]

[48] M, VIII, 145–146, 517.
[49] Hanna, *Wilderness Trail*, I, 158.
[50] M, VIII, 342–346.
[51] M, VIII, 348.

They were more hungry than bloodthirsty, exchanging one beaver skin for thirty green apples, another for thirty nubbins, still others for "four bottles and some sugar," and at last half a dozen matchcoats. Suspected of being a spy for the French, Chartier was put into St. Mary's jail and kept for some months. In spite of this, he managed to make friends, for upon his release he and some of the Shawnee were made welcome by Colonel Casparus Herman, and on his lands by the south bank of the Lower Elk River they put up their "fabrics."[52]

Chartier before the year was out had set up as an Indian trader near the mouth of the Susquehanna, and continued as a well-to-do man, wearing a coat of "rich fur" in winter, and enjoying the love and respect of the Indians who called him Father. He soon moved up the river into Pennsylvania, settling on a large tract of land near what is now Columbia. He acted at times as an interpreter, and served as an unofficial liaison between the government and the Indians.[53]

We wonder if it were Chartier or some other Frenchman of whom Governor Nicholson of Maryland wrote in August of 1698 in a long letter to the Boards of Trade in London: "For upon Inquiry I had an account from some Chaouonon Indians whose country lies to the Southwest of South Carolina & a Frenchman that came with them, and was with La Salle that journey he was killed; that the French have some settlements West Southerly not above 200 miles from the falls of the Potomack. One of the chief of these Indians I got to chalk out the way to those Settlements, & so to the River Maschipi, to the parts adjacent and down to the Bay of Mexico. I had one who with the help of the French Man made a small rude draught with a pen, which I find in some to agree with Hennepins Maps."[54]

We doubt if this Frenchman who helped the Indian draw a map of a French settlement, supposedly only two hundred miles from present-day Washington, D.C., was Chartier. It is not reasonable to think that having once escaped La Salle's wrath he would follow him to the southwest into what is now Texas. Still, he could have; he was south sometime during 1684–90 before he went away with the Shawnee.[55]

In any case, Chartier was not the only Frenchman to have wandered over much of the United States before the beginning of the eighteenth

[52] M, VIII, 350.
[53] Hanna, *Wilderness Trail*, I, 170–171.
[54] M, XXIII, 500. Williams, *Dawn of Tenn.*, 19, thought the man was Chartier; Hanna, *Wilderness Trail*, I, 135, also thought it was Chartier, but that he lied.
[55] M, VIII, 345.

century, and after settling in the east, he made several trips across the mountains and into the Mississippi Valley. Christoph von Graffenried while on an exploratory expedition up the Potomac in 1712 found near what is now Washington, D.C., a Frenchman "named Martin Chartier, who had married an Indian woman, and thereby was in great credit with the wild Indians of the nations which lived beyond Pennsylvania and Maryland. . . . This same Martin Chartier had also made the journey to Senantona to look for mines with Mr. M and contributed a good sum of money to it." Von Graffenried told of how they climbed a high hill and looked into the distance, and decided at last that the mine was "situated beyond Virginia, and not beyond Pennsylvania as the map of it had been given to us." Later, "we went to Martin Chartier's where we were lodged and treated after the Indian fashion." [56]

Senantona remains a mystery but one wonders if the furnaces found on the Clear Fork of the Cumberland by the Long Hunters and of "very ancient date" [57] could have been the work of Martin Chartier, nor would he have been the only Frenchman to have tried his hand at mining in some hidden valley. Such men are nameless now to history, and Chartier is remembered chiefly because he led the first band of Shawnee back in the general direction of their old home between the Great Lakes and the Ohio.[58] Other scattered bands trickled into Pennsylvania, and most seem to have come by way of the Cumberland. In 1739, for example, we find James Logan reminding six Shawnee chiefs assembled in Philadelphia that, "forty years ago a considerable number of families of your nation thought fit to remove from the great river that bears your name, where your principal correspondence was with the French nation, and in 1699 applied to the Indians of Susquehanna to settle amongst them." [59]

The bands of Shawnee mentioned by Logan as having come from the Shawanoe or Cumberland River before 1699 were not the last of the tribe who tried to live there. Father Jacques Gravier wrote in 1700, "It [the Ohio] has three branches, one coming from the northeast, and flowing behind the country of the Ouiamis [Miamis], is called by us, the St. Joseph, but by the savages the Ouabachie, the second comes from the country of the Iroquois and this is called the Ohio; the third on which the Chaouanoua live comes from the south-southeast. The stream formed by the junction of these flows into the Mississippi." [60]

[56] Graffenried, *New Bern*, 247, 383–384.
[57] Haywood, *C & P*, 33–34.
[58] Hanna, *Wilderness Trail*, I, 170.
[59] *Ibid.*, I, 18.
[60] *Ibid.*, II, 104.

At the time of this writing there were still enough Shawnee on the Cumberland to attract at least one French trader. An old man, name unknown, he had been there for some years before 1700. His trading post was on a prehistoric mound a few miles west of present-day Nashville. Some years later a young French Canadian, M. du Charleville, came up from New Orleans as his helper. Their Shawnee customers, however, were so constantly hounded by both the Chickasaw and the Cherokee they began to slip away in small bands. This went on for some years; at last all decided to leave. The old trader sent M. du Charleville, only nineteen years old, down to New Orleans with the winter's peltry in March of 1714. The trader and the remaining Shawnee planned to abandon the place the following summer.

The Chickasaw learned of the Shawnee plan, and when the Shawnee and the old trader started down the Cumberland, warriors were waiting in bark canoes on either side the river, just above the mouth of the Harpeth. Even the Frenchman was killed, and those who did escape with their lives were taken prisoner.[61]

The Chickasaw were not the only southern tribes to resent the attempted settlement of northern Indians in their hunting grounds. The Yazoos, Creek, and Natchez all at various times defeated stray bands of Shawnee.[62] Not the least of their enemies were the Overhill Cherokee. Judge Haywood wrote of an aged Cherokee chief who boasted in Charles Town, "What! Shall the Cherokee perish! Never! Shall the conquerors of the Shawnee perish!"[63] It took many battles to drive the widely scattered Shawnee out of the deeper south, then off the Cumberland. The Little Carpenter or Attakullakulla, a vice chief of the Cherokee prominent during the time of the Long Hunters and the settlement of East Tennessee, told a story handed down from his father of a war party sent against the Shawnee about 1714. The Cherokee were coming back home, seemingly from Middle Tennessee, and with several Shawnee scalps when they ran into another party of Cherokee warriors, who mistook them for enemies and killed several before they discovered their mistake.[64]

The Chickasaw also claimed: "We drove them out ourselves and the Cherokee had no hand in the War." One of the Chickasaw stories jibes with that of the Jesuits written between 1660–70 of the Iroquois pursuit of

[61] Ramsey, *Tennessee*, 45, 90. Haywood, *N & A*, 222–224.
[62] B. F. French, ed., *Historical Collections of Louisiana and Florida*, New York, 1846–1853, New Series, 1869 (cited hereafter as French, *Collections*), 123, quoting Fr. Penicaut.
[63] Haywood, *N & A*, 241.
[64] Williams, *Dawn of Tenn.*, 77, n. 21.

the Shawnee into the land of "perpetual spring and summer," for according to the Chickasaw version, told in 1805, some Shawnee fled far south "close to a hundred and fifty years ago," and gradually worked their way north to the Cumberland.[65]

Maps of the region, particularly those of Guillaume de l'Isle, tend to prove that even the Cumberland was no permanent haven for the Shawnee. In his 1703 map of Mexico and Florida De l'Isle locates a Shawnee village at the head of what appears to be the Cumberland, but on his 1718 *Carte De La Louisiane Et Du Cours Du Mississippi* he depicts what is undoubtedly the Cumberland, a stream running roughly parallel to the *Rivière des Casquinambaux* with *les Cheraqui* on its headwaters—the Tennessee . . . and on this map the Cumberland is called, "River of the Ancient Chaouanons so called because formerly the Chaouanons lived there." [66]

There was around 1747 another Shawnee settlement attempted on the Cumberland, also headed by a man named Chartier, but this was Peter, half-breed son of Martin, who, dissatisfied with life in the east, led a band of rebels west. His group was of course not allowed to stay, and around twenty warriors were killed in a surprise attack by the Chickasaw. The rest, estimated at around 270, made their way down the river; the women, children, and aged in canoes, the braves walking as guards along the shore.[67] They had hoped to regain their brethren, some of whom were by that date settling above the Ohio, but when Peter's band tried to go upriver their progress was so slowed by the spring flood rolling down, they gave up and stopped a few miles below the mouth of the Wabash. Here, they founded a temporary Shawnee Town.[68]

There are conflicting accounts of the movements of Peter Chartier and his band, but Thomas Hutchins, charting the Cumberland in 1769, noticed the "remains of an old Shawnee Town which was picketed in as appears by some of them still to be seen." [69] This abandoned fort, located by Hutchins about a mile from the Natchez Trace and less than a mile from a "Big Buffalo Lick" and hence near the site of future Nashville, was less significant of settlement than as a reminder that no one, either Indian or white, could live on the Cumberland.

[65] A, V, "Correspondence of General James Robertson," 67–96. See also Haywood, *N & A*, 223.
[66] *Supra*, n. 1, this chapter.
[67] Hanna, *Wilderness Trail*, I, 311–312, II, 134, 241.
[68] *Ibid.*, II, 241. See also Mann Butler, *A History of the Commonwealth of Kentucky*, Louisville, 1834 (cited hereafter as Butler, *Kentucky*), 369, quoting "Croghan's Journal of 1765," which mentions this Old Shawnee Town by then deserted.
[69] Hutchins, "Notes," Sheet 8.

The Indians of various tribes hunted there at times, but always so much blood was shed when they accidentally met, the Middle Cumberland came to be avoided as a hunting ground. The French soon learned of this lack of Indians, and Tennessee historians are agreed that from the beginning of the eighteenth century French hunters went up the Cumberland as far as the site of present-day Nashville, for the river was easily reached by water from either the Wabash or the Illinois Country. The 1718 map that showed the Cumberland abandoned by the Shawnee also designated an area north of the Cumberland as a desert and "place to which the Illinois go to hunt the beef." This desert was the treeless Barrens, the beef, the buffalo. This region, drained partly by the Cumberland but chiefly by Green River and smaller streams, would in time be a favorite of hunters from the English colonies, though in 1718 they were fifty years away, but we can be certain that with the Indians hunting buffalo there were at least a few *coureurs de bois*.

CHAPTER V

THE LONG LEARNING

". . . We were so feeble for want of nourishment we could not continue our journey. . . . Some of our men were obliged to subsist upon the sap, young leaves, and tender buds of trees." [1] This story of near starvation was written by the French priest Penicaut of a group traveling in the spring of 1700 by water up to French outposts in the Illinois. The men were well armed; many were seasoned soldiers; they suffered from neither intense heat nor cold; and traveled by canoe in a river filled with fish through a game-filled land. Yet, had food not been sent to them they would have starved.

The trouble was they had no Indians. The great French explorers never traveled without Indians to serve as guides and hunters. Martin Chartier was a rarity in that he was skilled enough in woodscraft and hunting to find his way and live for forty days alone. The English were even more helpless than the French. Most any school child is familiar with the sufferings of the Pilgrims and the "starving time" at James Town. It seems doubtful if any could have survived without help from the Indians, and as it was most died.

Seventy-nine years after the men of whom Penicaut wrote grew weak from hunger, there came a winter so cold that west of the Appalachians it was forever after known as the hard winter. On Christmas day, 1779, the Cumberland at French Lick, future Nashville, was frozen solid; and "in that hard winter cattle at French Lick would lay down and put their heads to their sides, as is their way, and thus would be found frozen stiff;

[1] French, *Collections*, New Series, 64.

76

turkies were known to freeze on their roosts and tumble off." [2] And of Kentucky: "A great country for wild turkeys and they liked to have starved to death; a heap, a heap of them died." [3]

The wild things died, but Dr. Thomas Walker, one of Adlai Stevenson's grandsires, then sixty-five years old, encamped by the Cumberland in what is now Pulaski County, Kentucky, lived warm and well fed on fresh-killed buffalo. His journalizing companion, Daniel Smith, did write "very cold," when the river froze. [4]

Nor did the weather trouble other travelers coming overland to Middle Tennessee. There were not only men, but also young children and married women, usually with babies or about to have babies, riding over rough trails through the bitter weather. They neither sickened nor starved, though by that date game was getting scarce in much of the country they came through, and in some families the corn got finished before the trip. There was in that winter much suffering and tragedy elsewhere in the new west, starvation and frostbite in Kentucky, [5] and even seasoned woodsmen had their troubles. Henry Scaggs, an experienced hunter, had, because of the hardness of the ground, to bury his young son in a hollow tree when he died in the woods. [6]

Henry Scaggs hunted on alone, undaunted by the weather, as did those others, encamped in the woods or riding on to the Cumberland. How had these people learned to live in the woods as civilized human beings, in spite of enemy Indians and bitter weather? The first settlers were not

---

[2] W, 32S, 306; this from the story of Mrs. John Donelson, III, Mary Purnell, who came as a bride to Middle Tennessee by flatboat in the winter of 1779–1780.

[3] FQ, II, 95–128, "Reverend John D. Shane's Interview with Pioneer William Clinkenbeard," edited from W, 11CC, 54–66 (cited hereafter as Clinkenbeard "Interview"), 112.

[4] THM, I, Smith, "Journal," 58. This was the second trip of Dr. Thomas Walker to the Cumberland Country; he was at this time a commissioner appointed by Thomas Jefferson, Governor of Virginia, to help extend the North Carolina–Virginia Boundary; and the line was for many years known as the Walker Line.

[5] Newton D. Mereness, *Travels in the American Colonies*, New York, 1916 (cited hereafter as Mereness, *Travels*), "The Journal of Colonel Henry Fleming," edited from the Draper Manuscripts of the Wisconsin Historical Society (cited hereafter as Fleming, "Journal"), 619–654. Colonel Fleming spent the "hard winter" in Kentucky traveling from station to station, attempting with two other commissioners to settle land disputes.

[6] Story used by permission of the Wisconsin Historical Society from *Documentary History of Dunmore's War, 1774, Compiled from the Draper Manuscripts in the Library of the Wisconsin Historical Society* by Reuben Gold Thwaites and Louise Phelps Kellogg, published and copyrighted by the Wisconsin Historical Society, Madison, 1905 (cited hereafter as Thwaites-Kellogg, *Dunmore's War*), 239, quoting W, 3B, 230–238.

adventurers or professional soldiers,[7] but basically farmers, bringing through the cold their wives and children, bound servants and slaves, domesticated animals, plow-points, the blades of hoes, axes, adzes, and seeds to plant come spring. How even had they learned of the rich land on the Cumberland, far as it was from any outpost of white civilization; and in between many steep-bluffed creeks and rivers to cross and all behind the walls of the Appalachians?

At the time of the first permanent settlements on the Cumberland there had been for many years French in the Illinois familiar with the good land along the river. Why did the French never try to settle the Cumberland?

Some answers never came at all, and none came fully blown and dated. The discovery of the Cumberland by the English colonists was a slow thing done in stages. Trader, hunter, land speculator, farmer found it, but it took the farmer to hold what he had found—and the French who came to the Cumberland were not farmers.

There were among the English on the eastern coast no Father Marquettes or La Salles. Dreamers and schemers there were, but theirs were economic dreams, chiefly of trade with England; and this to follow the usual pattern, with colonials as well as Indians supplying the raw materials, England the manufactured goods. Settlement followed trade but in 1607 about the most any Briton could say of the new world away from the coast was "that across the Apalatsi Mountaynes was no immediate sea but broad rivers." Ten years after Jean Nicolet had in 1639 found the headwaters of the Mississippi, the English colonists could only write: "The Indians of late acquainted our Governor that within five dayes journey to the westward and by south, there is a great high mountaine, and at the foot thereof, great Rivers that run into a great sea. . . ."[8]

New Englanders, preoccupied with business and shipping and with the French at their backs, showed no taste for exploration. It was for the southern colonists to lead the way into the west. It was not easy; unlike the French, they had no highway of lakes, but instead a wall of mountains. The push was slow. Settlement for generations hugged the low and sandy lands along the sea and by the mouths of rivers.

The only men concerned with the interior were those who traded with the Indians and as the Indian receded from the coast, the trader followed, but by 1646 the most western outpost of any trader was Fort Henry commanded by Colonel Abraham Wood, and it just touching the Fall

[7] *Infra*, Chap. IX, "The Travelers."
[8] Alvord & Bidgood, *Explorations*, 46, quoting an unknown author.

Line, at the Falls of the Appomattox, near the site of present-day Petersburg, Virginia. Here converged Indian trails leading to the backwoods of Virginia and what was to be the Carolinas,[9] and out from it went English and Scotch traders, their Indian burden bearers loaded down with strouds, rum, matchcoats, beads, hatchets, knives, and other articles to be exchanged with the Catawbas, Saponies, Tuskeruroes, and other eastern tribes [10] for deer and beaver skins to ship to England.

It was not until many years after going there that Colonel Wood financed and planned the explorations that were to give him a place in American history, and this done chiefly one suspects with the hope of widening trade with the Indians. His first exploring party, sent out in 1661, was headed by two white men—Robert Batts and William Fallam—who bore a commission, "for the finding out the ebbing and flowing of the waters on the other side of the Mountains in order to the discovery of the South Sea." [11] America as yet had developed no white men able to stay alive for months in the woods, carrying little but guns and ammunition. Batts and Fallam, no different from other woods travelers of the day, were guided by Indians, who also served as hunters. Even so, the journal they kept of their travels is filled with stories of hunger and hard travel.[12]

They like Father Marquette went through a nameless, unmapped land, and hence there is some uncertainty as to just exactly where they did go. Most agree they did get through the Blue Mountain, as the Blue Ridge was then called, and reach Peters' Falls in what is now Giles County, southwestern Virginia. If so they were on land drained by the Mississippi, and stood on the eastern rim of the midwest, for they had reached a tributary of New River which is in turn a tributary of the Kanawha that flows north into the Ohio.

Batts and Fallam carved initials, branded names on trees to show possession of the land by Virginia, a procedure difficult to understand since the original grant had extended to the South Sea; but like so many other "first" explorers they found already initialed trees. They set up sticks "to watch the ebbing and flowing of the tide" that is the tide of New River, high in the Appalachians. Back at the trading post of Colonel Wood they reported they had seen sails in the distance.[13] Eager for a sight of the sea

[9] See *42nd Report of Bureau of Ethnology*, Plate 15, 748, "The Trail System of the Southeastern United States."
[10] Lawson, *Carolina*, 1–33.
[11] Alvord & Bidgood, *Explorations*, 71.
[12] *Ibid.*, 183–193, "John Clayton's Transcript of the Journal of Robert Fallam."
[13] *Ibid.*, 192.

and expecting it, they had mistaken for sails the crags of distant mountains glimmering through the fog.

Another wanderer in the Southern woods was the German physician, John Lederer. During 1669–70 he spent eighteen months in the South, and made three tries at crossing the mountains, but most are agreed he got no further than the headwaters of the Yadkin, an eastward flowing river. He did speak at least one truth: "They are certainly in great error who imagine the continent of North America is but ten days journey over from the Atlantick to the Indian Ocean." [14]

No woodsman and unable to speak any Indian's language, he had much trouble in traveling, but more than any peril of the wilderness he dreaded the Indian children. He so angered the women and headmen of a village when he refused to let a child use his horse as an archery target that he almost lost his life. "These Indians," he wrote, "are so indiscreetly fond of their children, that they will not chastise them for any insolence." [15] An observation made by many a priest and trader, for all Indians seem to have believed in the modern or permissive method of raising children.

Not satisfied with the discoveries of Batts and Fallam, Abraham Wood sent out in the spring of 1673 two more explorers, James Needham, a gentleman from South Carolina, and a young man, Gabriel Arthur. He is thought to have been a servant, indentured to Colonel Wood; and unfortunately for posterity, unable to read and write.[16]

These men with eight of the ever-necessary Indians went southwest across the headwaters of the Yadkin, then up and over into the land of westward flowing streams but southward of where Batts and Fallam had been, for the streams they sometimes crossed and sometimes followed were the headwaters of the Tennessee. The exact location of the Indian town they at last found is a disputed point; most think it was Chota at the mouth of the Little Tennessee, and peopled by the Tomahitan Cherokee. No English trader had as yet been so far westward, but in the spring of 1673, these Cherokee had muskets bought from the Spanish to the south.[17]

James Needham left Gabriel with the Cherokee to learn their language while he started back to report to Abraham Wood, but on the way he was killed by an English-hating Cherokee. The murderer and his friends

[14] Alvord & Bidgood, *Explorations*, 166, quoting "The Discoveries of John Lederer in three several Marches from Virginia to the West of Carolina," Collected and Translated out of Latine from his Discourses and Writings by Sir William Talbot, Baronet, London, 1672.

[15] *Ibid.*, 158–159.

[16] *Ibid.*, 79.

[17] *Ibid.*, 214, "Letter of Abraham Wood to John Richards," Aug. 22, 1674.

rushed back to Chota determined to kill the other white man. They tied him to a stake, heaped dried cane about him: "but before ye fire was put too ye King came into ye towne with a gunn upon his shoulder and heareing of ye uprore, for some was with it and some against it. Ye King ran with great speed to ye English man. Who is it that is going to put fire to ye Englishman? A Weesock borne started up with a firebrand in his hand said that am I. Ye King forthwith cockt his gunn and shot ye Weesock dead."

This is the first story of white man among Cherokee, and somewhat typical of them all; the Cherokee were almost never of one opinion about anything, and they, particularly their chiefs, were in time to show the English many kindnesses. Young Gabriel was well treated by the man he called King, though the Cherokee had no rulers with the despotic powers of kings, not even during war. They were at this time living in peace with their neighbors and most of the long trips Gabriel took with them were pleasant hunting or foraging excursions.

Historians comment most on a journey Gabriel made with a party that went "forth with sixty men and travelled tenn days due north and then arrived at ye monyton Towne situated upon a very great river." Finished with the visit, thought to have taken place at the mouth of the Kanawha, the "very great river" the Ohio, the sixty Cherokee with Arthur then "marched three days out of theire way to give a clap to some of that great nation. where they fell on with great curage and were as curagiously repulsed by their enemies."

Gabriel was wounded by an arrow and taken prisoner but: "These Indians tooke Gabriell and scowered his skin with water and ashes, and when they perceived his skin to be white they made very much of him." [18] They are thought to have been a band of the widely scattered Shawnee, living somewhere along the Ohio, possibly in Kentucky opposite the mouth of the Scioto. In any case many miles from their old hunting grounds north of the river, for by that date they had been defeated by the Iroquois.

Whoever and wherever they were, they cured Gabriel of his wound, returned his gun, gave him rokahamony to eat, and put him on a road that led back to the Cherokee town with the friendly chief. Most agree the road young Gabriel followed was the Warrior's Path that crossed the Ohio at the mouth of the Scioto, went south across the Red River branch of the Kentucky River, then up Station Camp Creek of Kentucky River

[18] *Ibid.,* 218.

and through Ouasiota Pass into the Ouasiota Mountains or what we now call the Kentucky Mountains.[19] Past the tributaries of the Rockcastle, the road jogged sharply to reach the shallow waters of the ford in the Rivière des Chauouanons or Skipaki-cipi or Rivière Bleu,[20] later to be known as the Cumberland, then jogged up again, through the gap and down. Gabriel avoided the many diverging trails, and got back to the Cherokee in time to take a pleasant ramble down the Tennessee. He is usually considered to have been the first white man from the English colonies to penetrate the eastern half of the Mississippi Valley.[21]

This discovery of the upper Cumberland as a nameless stream hemmed in mountains had been rather quickly done, but was an accident signifying nothing. More significant was the presence of an English trader west of the mountains. Gabriel never forgot his calling; even when wounded and lost among the Shawnee he tried to make them understand through signs that their beaver could be traded for more valuable things. He was part of what was ever the first frontier in the American colonies—that of the trader. The rivalry for this trade would be bitter; as Gabriel traveled through the woods on foot, Father Marquette traveled far west of him by canoe, while somewhere south Spanish traders may have been counting deerskins.

The Scotch and English traders of Virginia and Charles Town were not long content with trade on their side of the mountains, and as early as

[19] Hanna, *Wilderness Trail*, II, 117–118, was of the opinion that "Ouasiota Pass" was the Indian name of the pass on Station Camp Creek of Red River leading to the Ouasiota Mountains in Kentucky, and not Cumberland Gap as some historians believe. Quoting Ramsey, *Tennessee*, 87, he pointed out that the Cumberland River was sometimes known as the *Wariota*, a corruption or misprint of *Wasiota*, in turn a variant spelling of *Ouasiota*. Early English maps uphold Hanna's opinion. See in Clements Library, Lewis Evans, "A General Map of the Middle British Colonies in America: Viz Virginia, Mariland, Delaware, Pensilvania, New Jersey, New York, Conecticut and Rhode Island," London, 1756. Cited hereafter as Evans, "1756 Map of the Colonies," this work labels most of what we today call the Allegheny Mountains the "Ouasiota Mountains." See also in the Clements Library, Thomas Hutchins, "A New Map of the Western Parts of Virginia Pennsylvania Maryland and North Carolina; comprehending the River Ohio and the waters that flow into it," London, 1778. This map cited hereafter as Hutchins, "1778 Map," based on Hutchins' travels into the territory won from the French, and on his many notes, gives a truer picture of the region than any previous map. He clearly shows and describes what we now know as the Kentucky Mountains, and labels them "Ouasiota."

[20] Once again there is no agreement that each of these names belonged to the Cumberland. Williams, *Dawn of Tenn.*, 44, was of that opinion as was Hanna, *Wilderness Trail*, II, 92. The most common name was some one of the many variant spellings of Shawnee; and Thomas Hutchins so designated it, and he came a hundred years after Gabriel Arthur.

[21] "Firsts" are never known. Batts and Fallam, Alvord & Bidgood, *Explorations*, 73, found in September of 1671 two trees initialed respectively MA, NI, on a branch of New River, a tributary of the Ohio.

1686 the ever-faithful Tonty was warning La Salle that the English had come down to the Mississippi by way of the Cheraqui and Chauouanon rivers. James Moore could have been on the headwaters of the Cumberland in 1690, for in that year he journeyed over the "Apalathean Mountains, and took up seven sorts of ore," and further reported that the Spaniards had been at work in mines, "within twenty miles of me." [22]

The gold fever that had so afflicted the first settlers was by this date waning, and the venturesome speculator turned instead to Indian trade. In 1692, the same year that Martin Chartier went across country from the Cumberland, a Dutch trader, Arnold Viele from Albany, led a party of twelve white traders down the Ohio to a band of Shawnee, thought to have been living near the mouth of the river at that time.[23] Two years later they got safely home again, bringing more Shawnee with them, but the bulk of trade from the eastern colonies was not to be on the Ohio, though a few of the more venturesome of the Virginia traders, roughly following the route of Batts and Fallam, went to New River,[24] and from there on down to the Ohio. Enough that in 1700 the French commandant at Detroit instructed his Indians to go to the Beautiful River and seize the goods of the English.

Well before this date the Virginia and Carolina traders had quite well established trade routes leading south and west, and by 1794 Tonty was again reporting to La Salle that "some of the English from Carolina had settled on a branch stream running with the Ohio." [25] This was undoubtedly the Tennessee, for that stream and not the Cumberland became the water route from the Southern Appalachians down to the sea, and also the eastward route for runaway Frenchmen such as Jean Couture.[26] Rough as the Tennessee was, it had nothing absolutely impassable such as Smith Shoals and Cumberland Falls, with portage made almost impossible by the unscalable bluffs along much of the upper river.

As early as 1699, James Boyd, a Frenchman, reported to the Boards of Trade in London that the Carolina traders, "had made many journeys through the country westward to above 1,000 or 1,200 miles distance," [27]

[22] Williams, *Dawn of Tenn.*, 26, quoting Moore to Edward Randolph.
[23] Hanna, *Wilderness Trail*, II, 124.
[24] New River was for many years known as Wood's River, and it was not until around 1750 that the present name was adopted. Walker, "Journal," March 13, 1750, "to the Wood's or the New River."
[25] Williams, *Dawn of Tenn.*, 26.
[26] *Ibid.*, 21–22.
[27] Used by permission of the publisher, The University of Michigan Press, from *The Southern Frontier 1670–1732* by Verner W. Crane, copyright University of Michigan Press, Ann Arbor, 1929, 1956 (cited hereafter as Crane, *Frontier*), 64, quoting from "Journal of the Board of Trade," Dec. 8 and 12, 1699.

and in the same year, Iberville was writing, "There are several Englishmen from Carolina with the Chicahas [Chickasaw] where they trade for roebuck skins and Indian slaves. They came from Carolina by a river which ends at some high mountains over which they carry everything, and from there convey their goods to the Chicahas on horses." This vague passage would indicate that though the river was used, both ends of the journey had to be done on foot or horseback. The Tennessee was never very satisfactory, particularly for the traders out of Charles Town. Soon the Carolina traders were swinging southward through what is now Alabama; this route had no mountains, and the Carolina traders thus had an advantage over those from Virginia,[28] and Charles Town became the center of Indian trade.[29]

As early as 1707 Thomas Nairne, a Scotch trader, authored an Indian act for Carolina.[30] Schedules of prices were set up, varying with the yearly demand and the distance of the tribe from Charles Town. Among the Cherokee, for example, a gun sold for thirty-five deerskins, a broadcloth coat for thirty, though a calico petticoat cost only fourteen; even one skin could buy scissors, a knife, two strings of beads, or thirty bullets.[31] In the season of 1706–07 such articles brought 121,355 deerskins into Charles Town.[32] There was also the trade in beaver, which though small compared to that in deerskins, was still no minor item. An average-sized deerskin when dried weighed about two pounds so that many could be carried long distances by horse or man power. Once at a seaport they were tightly packed into large barrels or hogsheads, holding around eight hundred skins each.[33]

The Indian trade was the most important business of the South, not connected with agriculture, and grew ever bigger and wider-ranging. The archives of Charles Town alone listed, before 1715, more than one hundred licensed traders among the Cherokee, Creeks, Chickasaw and other southern tribes. Eleazer Wiggan is thought to have been the first trader to live among the Overhill Cherokee in what came to be eastern Tennes-

---

[28] William Byrd, *Writings*, in his "History of the Dividing Line," 184–185, complained of the roundabout route of the Virginians and pointed out and described the route, 117, 236–237, the traders had used to take.

[29] Crane, *Frontier*, 23.

[30] *Ibid.*, 148.

[31] Williams, *Dawn of Tenn.*, 71. William Byrd, the son of an Indian trader, knew much of the Indian trade in early days; *Writings*, 234–235, 239, describes goods and pack-horse caravans.

[32] Crane, *Frontier*, 112.

[33] *Ibid.*, 111, 126–127. See also Gray, *Agriculture*, I, 137.

see, and had by 1716 been there so long he was able to act as interpreter.[34]

The trader usually took a temporary Indian wife, and thus early, white blood was mingled with that of the southern Indians. The half-breeds, especially the males, grew up to be loyal Indian citizens, ever foremost in all later wars against the settlers that came at last into the Cherokee country. Some of the most dreaded leaders and chiefs such as McGillivray of the Creeks and John Watts, the Bloody Fellow, of the Cherokee, had as much white blood as Indian.[35]

Still, no matter how much the trader might love the Indian way of life, even at times leading braves into battle as did James Adair, his allegiance was always to England. All the better class of Scotch and English traders served the Crown faithfully and well as interpreters and ambassadors to the Indian nations. The trader might go hundreds of miles westward from the Atlantic coast, but always the strongest of bonds tied him to England; she was both customer for skins and source of supply for manufactured goods.[36]

The trader, unlike the settler, adjusted to circumstances and saw no reason to change the pattern of life in the backwoods. It is doubtful if any trader, even James Adair who spent more than thirty years with the Cherokee and Chickasaw, could have long survived alone in the woods as did the white hunters who later came to the Cumberland. He depended upon the Indians around him for all needs not supplied by the goods he brought—everything from food to women.[37] The trader both respected and trusted the Indian, and was inclined to take his side of things. Some, such as Thomas Nairne, saw the Indian as the main defense of the west,

[34] Williams, *Dawn of Tenn.*, 70.

[35] Alexander McGillivray (1759-1793) was the son of a Scotch trader, Lachlan McGillivray and a half-French half-Creek girl; different from most of the other half-breed chiefs he never led war parties against the Cumberland settlers, but seems to have instigated many attacks: see TP, IV, 32; Ramsey, *Tennessee*, 516; Judge Williams in Adair, *American Indian*, n. 288-289, told a good bit of the man. See also John Walton Coughey, *McGillivray of the Creeks*, copyright University of Oklahoma Press, 1938. This work contains a life sketch but is devoted chiefly to his correspondence. John Watts, the Bloody Fellow, was the son of a trader and interpreter to the Cherokee, I, XVI, 417. He is often mentioned in the Draper Manuscripts, and was wounded at the siege of Buchanan's Station on Mill Creek in Middle Tennessee in 1792, Ramsey, *Tennessee*, 600.

[36] Hanna, *Wilderness Trail*, is devoted chiefly to the varied roles of traders out from Pennsylvania and the Middle Colonies. George Croghan, *ibid.*, II, 1-68, is possibly the best known of all colonial traders for his many services in fields other than trade, but most men, including those of the south such as James Adair, were considerably more than mere sellers of goods to the Indians; proof of their fidelity as a group to England was that practically all took her side in the Revolution.

[37] Adair, *American Indian*, 291, 361, 369, 439.

for even as early as 1700, many colonials were realizing that sooner or later war would come with France. "They [the Indians] are now," Nairne wrote in 1709, "our only defense in the back parts." [38]

Other colonials were inclined to see all Indians, even those tied by English trade, as potential enemies instead of allies. They saw the greatest hope for "defense in the back parts" in the settler who, pushing fenced fields ever further into Indian territory, was anathema to Indian and trader alike. As early as 1698 Governor Nicholson, alarmed by stories of French settlement brought by the Indians, was advocating the planting of colonies in the Mississippi Valley to serve as buffers against the French.[39] In the same year Dr. Daniel Coxe of London, physician to the royal family, actually did send two armed ships of Huguenot refugees with a few English gentlemen up the Mississippi to plant a colony, "Carolana," on the lower river. He also had plans for a second settlement in what is now West Tennessee, but the French put an end to his plans.[40]

A few traders were also among the first to see the Mississippi Valley as something more than a source of skins. "I have been a considerable way to the Westw. upon the branches of the Mesisip," Price Hughes, a trader, wrote in 1713, "where I saw a country as different from Carolina as the best parts of our country [Wales] are different from the fens of Lincolnshire." He wrote on of many fine navigable rivers, pleasant savannas, coal, lead, iron, lime, and freestone with several salt springs—"a thorough intermixture of Hills and Vales and as fine timber as the largest I ever saw in England." [41] He made a map of the region, appealed to Queen Anne to plant a Welsh colony there, apparently near the Chickasaw; but he was in 1715 seized and put to death by Indians.

One wonders what would have happened could any of these projected colonies have materialized. "Nothing," appears to be the most probable answer; that is, nothing but failure for the colony as a whole, and death from starvation, exposure, and Indians for most of its members. Failure would not have come from laziness or stupidity. There were, all through these years, in France, Germany, Austria, and Switzerland many Protestants undergoing all manner of persecutions from death by breaking on the wheel to economic reprisals. The Scotch-Irish, too, knew the ever-heavier hand of England.

These people looked hungrily toward the English colonies, and many

---

[38] Williams, *Dawn of Tenn.*, 64.
[39] M, XXIII, 501.
[40] Alvord & Bidgood, *Explorations*, A Memorial by Dr. Daniel Coxe, "Account of the Activities of the English in the Mississippi Valley in the Seventeenth Century," 231–249.
[41] Crane, *Frontier*, 99–103; his death, *ibid.*, 107.

did come of their own will as contrasted to felons, bound servants, and slaves who were sent. England wanted more colonists to supply raw materials and, if need be, fight the French. Many of the colonists in Virginia and Carolina would have welcomed several shiploads of refugees, capable of settling the backwoods and holding off the Indians, for as late as 1710 the oldest of Virginia plantations was uncomfortably close to the border. Scattered clearings were just coming to the neighborhood of the old trading post, established by Colonel Wood in 1646, and this only at the meeting place of Fall Line and Coastal Plain.

Land above the Fall Line was often better than that below, but it took more than a hundred years for Virginia, the most western-minded of all the colonies, to establish settlers there. The trader could measure his distance in miles; the settler who would live away from the sea had to master, not mere miles, but skills as well as attitudes.

The story of New Bern, North Carolina, is fairly typical of early attempts at settlement by people with no mastery of the woods. The settlers were chiefly German Protestants who had fled persecution in the Palatinate to England where they were given refuge by Queen Anne. She even paid the passage of several hundred of these who, together with a few Swiss, left England in 1710 to form a settlement at the mouth of the Neuse River in North Carolina, among them Jacob Zollicoffer, ancestor of General Felix Zollicoffer. The plan for the colony was paternalistic, almost feudal, but the refugees were fortunate in having an honest and sympathetic patron, Christoph von Graffenried.[42] They came with passage paid, a site for settlement chosen, tools and provisions enough to last them a while. They, like the Pilgrims close to a hundred years before, were honest, intelligent, and often educated, unafraid of hardship and willing to suffer much for their faith.

Half of them died of overcrowding and starvation on the way over, for the refugee like the slave enriched many generations of English and New England ships' captains. Others survived the crossing, only to die of starvation and sickness in the swampy lands of coastal North Carolina. Yet, many did survive both the crossing and the "seasoning" as it was known, for most who came from the cooler climates of Europe suffered at least some sickness when they came to the southern colonies. Still, after recovering from the first round of sickness, they suffered much. The help promised by men in high places failed, and the colonists could neither feed nor clothe themselves.[43]

[42] Graffenried, *New Bern*, 9-25, 43-52.
[43] *Ibid.*, 49-76.

Von Graffenried had chosen his people carefully, so that most needed skills would be represented, and many were required. There had to be carpenters, joiners, plasterers, and sawyers in order to build the only kind of home they knew to build on the rockless, clayless coastal plain— one of sawed timber. This, in addition to skilled workmen, demanded saws, hammers, nails, trowels, chisels, shingles, and lime that had to be got from the burning of oyster shells.[44] Such a house took time in the building that might have gone to clearing fields and fortifying against the Indians; and during the long weeks of its building the owner and his family had to live in some makeshift shelter such as a tent or even house of bark and boughs, thereby increasing their liability to illness through exposure to rain and cold.

The man who could with felling ax, broadax, drawing knife, auger, and froe ride into the woods and in a few days' time build an all-weather house of logs in which he could live decently, and in comfort when it was finished, was not there. The "house made of Logs Such as the Swedes very often make in America," [45] was still very much a rarity on the Carolina coast.

The New Bern settlers had brought plenty of clothing, but soon they were almost naked. They had when food got low, bartered clothes with a nearby tribe of Indians for "wild meat, leather, bacon, beans, and corn." Less than a day's journey away were game-filled woods, but there were no hunters in New Bern, and nobody to teach hunting.[46] There were in North Carolina at that time famous hunters, who could, wearing the head and skin of a deer, stalk the living animal until they could get close enough for the kill; but these were Indians.[47] The white hunter, so pro-

[44] Graffenried, *New Bern*, 377: "At first I had a good number who began to fell timber in order to build the houses. There were two carpenters, a mason, two carpenters and joiners, a locksmith, a blacksmith, one or two shoemakers, a tailor, a miller, an armourer, a butcher, a weaver, a saddler, a glazier, a potter, and tile-maker, one or two mill-wrights, a physician, a surgeon, a schoolmaster." This from the English version of the French translation of Von Graffenried's account in German. See also Lawson, *Carolina*, 50, for list of further needs.

[45] Lawson, *Carolina*, 127; the house mentioned here was only a storehouse with "barrels of pork," and belonged to Governor Southwell of North Carolina.

[46] Graffenried, *New Bern*, 223–240, English translation of the German, illustrates well both their dependence upon the Indians and their inability to get along with them; the settlers, often unwittingly, insulted the Indians in various ways, and were at last attacked.

[47] Lawson, *Carolina*, 10: The stalking Indian wore, ". . . an artificial head to hunt withal; they are made of the Head of a Buck, the back part of the Horn being scraped and hollow for lightness of carriage. The skin is left to the settling of the shoulders, which is lined all around with small hoops, and flat sort of lathes to hold it open for the arm to go in. They have a way to preserve the eyes as if Living. The Hunter Puts on a

ficient he could make money from the selling of skins, was not yet in America; the North Carolina planters paid the Indians to hunt for them.

The difference was not entirely in men, but also in the hunting weapon. There were no rifles. Shortly after 1700 John Lawson, well supplied with Indian guides and weapons, went into the wild woods above the Fall Line of North Carolina. His weapon was a fuzee. "We saw plenty of turkies," he wrote, "but perched upon such lofty oaks our guns would not kill them." [48] However, the ancestor of the gun that would send a ball into the highest of trees may have been there, for "Santee Jack an Indian shot with a single Ball, missing but 2 shots in above 40." [49] This, Lawson considered very fine shooting. The chances are it was done by a rifled-barreled gun Santee Jack had got by barter from some French or German refugee. The Germans had for many years been making short-barreled weapons with half a turn of rifling the full length of the barrel.[50] These early German Jaguers were between .70 and .75 caliber, and thus required a pound of lead for twelve to fifteen balls,[51] and around half that amount of powder, making such a weapon an expensive thing to use, and, with ammunition, a man-sized load.

Santee Jack's gun may have been a "snap-haunce" or chicken thief, the name by which early flintlocks were ridiculed, but whatever the manner of firing, the gun would have been not only clumsy, inaccurate, heavy, and expensive, but also slow and loud in the loading. The balls were molded to groove diameter to insure a tight fit, and so had to be pounded down the muzzle, a noisy business that scared any game within hearing away, while the slowness made such a gun almost useless in a hard-pressed Indian battle or even against a just-missed and still-charging buffalo. Lawson meant no ridicule of the North Carolina farmers when he told of their

Match-Coat made of Skin, with the Hair on, and a piece of the white part of the Deer's skin, that grows on the Breast, which is fasten'd to the neck end of this stalking head, so hangs down. In these Habiliments an Indian will go as near a Deer as he please, the exact motion and Behavior of a Deer being so well counterfeited by em, that several times it hath been known for two hunters to come up with a stalking head together. . . ."

[48] *Ibid.*, 23.
[49] *Ibid.*, 13. Judging from Lawson's mention of the term "flintlock," the much older wheel locks were not even at that late date entirely outmoded in the colonies.
[50] It should be emphasized that no single description of either length or rifling could apply to all early rifles; some were straight grooved, and some swirled more than others. See W. W. Greener, *The Gun and its development*, eighth edition, London, 1907.
[51] The rifle was a development, not an invention; big ones continued to be used; as late as 1792 Cumberland settlers used "a large ounce ball rifle and dropped five men by the single fire." W, 6XX, 286.

manner of killing bear, treed by dogs, "the Huntsman shoots him out of the Trees, there being, for the most part two or three with Guns, lest the first should miss or not quite kill him." [52] Less than sixty years later, Michael Stoner who spent most of his life on the Cumberland would prod a bear's den with his rifle muzzle and demand, "Who keeps da house?" [53]

Hunting had progressed, however, since the days when Captain Miles Standish floundered through the woods with his "bugle-mouthed" weapon. Not the least improvement was in the use of dogs. One wonders how the Pilgrims managed without them. Lawson took a spaniel bitch into the woods with him, and southern farmers commonly owned coon and fox hounds; some had dogs trained to follow bear by scent, and "Then bark and snap at him till he trees." [54] There were bird dogs and many other varieties, for all Europe had known and loved the dog, as had the Indian, but the American dog that would come with the first settlers to the Cumberland and could trail an Indian, spring on the back of an elk and begin chewing on its neck in search of the spinal cord,[55] catch a chicken for the pot, or kill the rattlesnake that threatened the baby, developed rather slowly. The Indians, of course, had many dogs, mangy things that never barked, and served no purpose, except in times of feast or famine to fill the pot.

The Virginia and Carolina hunters of Lawson's day were also handicapped when it came to traveling through the woods, for the horse, a must for later hunters, was at this date but little used, though they so abounded in the backwoods of Virginia that any man who could catch one could have it.[56] As long as the colonies hugged the coast and lower reaches of the rivers, travel was almost always by canoe. Plantations were tied to England by ships that often could come to their private docks; neighbors visited by canoe or shallop with even the women and girls managing their craft [57] with the same dexterity their descendants would have with horses.

Tidewater of around 1700 was but little more than a suburb of England. England was home; the language of ships' captains ruled the coast, and it

[52] Lawson, *Carolina*, 68.

[53] W, 30S, 326.

[54] Lawson, *Carolina*, 26, 66, mentions bird dogs. Robert Beverly, *The History and Present State of Virginia, in Four Parts,* by a Native and Inhabitant of the Place, London, 1705. (Pagination and quotes follow the reprint, ed. Charles Campbell, Richmond, 1855, and cited hereafter as Beverly, *Virginia*.) Page 255 describes what is possibly the first hunting, purely American and not a development of that in Europe—raccoons and possums by dogs that treed the animal.

[55] W, 30S, 260.

[56] Beverly, *Virginia*, 257–258. These horses were at times hunted with dogs.

[57] Lawson, *Carolina*, 48.

was to England the wealthier sent their sons to be educated. Nor were they self-sufficient in other matters; the great planters were cash-crop farmers, though they never saw the cash; tobacco went to England and goods came in its stead. "They have," Robert Beverly wrote with some disgust in 1705, "their Cloathing of all sorts from England; as linen, woollen, silk, hats, and leather. Yet flax and hemp grow no where in the world, better than there. Their sheep yield good increase and bear good fleeces; but they shear them only to cool them—the very furs that their hats are made, perhaps go first from thence; and most of their hides lie and rot, or are made use of, only for covering dry goods in a leaky house—nay, they are such abominable ill husbands, that though their country be over-run with wood, yet they have all their wooden ware from England; their cabinets, chairs, tables, stools, chests, boxes, cart wheels, and all other things, even so much as their bowls and birchen brooms, to the eternal reproach of their laziness." [58]

This was certainly true of many wealthy southern planters. Still, the southern colonials had, as a group, accomplished a great deal in the first hundred years of colonization. First, they had learned to produce all the staples of their diet. Beverly, no different from later commentators, found Virginia the "best poor man's country in the world—and nobody that is poor enough to beg." [59] There were in the woods great droves of hogs that "swarm like vermin" on the mast, so plentiful it was seldom necessary to feed the hogs, though some of the planters had by the throwing out of corn, trained them to come in at the sound of a horn. [60] There were plenty of cattle, herds of a thousand were common, [61] and some North Carolina planters had as many as three thousand. These were sometimes watched over by herders, even then known as cowboys, for the American cowboy has been around since about 1632. [62] There was also abundance of pullets, capons, chickens, ducks, and geese. [63] In both Virginia and the Carolinas there were beautiful gardens of shrubs and flowers, while every farmer had his kitchen garden where he grew all manner of "pot herbs." There were also sweet potatoes, large as "the thigh of a child," and many varieties of the pulse family, particularly the bushel bean, throve amaz-

[58] Beverly, *Virginia*, 239.

[59] *Ibid.*, 223.

[60] Lawson, *Carolina*, 46. See also for hogs in Carolina, Graffenried, *New Bern*, 297–298, and in Virginia, Beverly, *Virginia*, 262–263.

[61] Graffenried, *New Bern*, 308—Letter of Samuel Jacob Gabley, "Out of America or India the 9th of April, 1711."

[62] Gray, *Agriculture*, I, 147.

[63] Beverly, *Virginia*, 236–237.

ingly; [64] in fact they had varieties of most vegetables grown today, except tomatoes.

The bread in "gentlemen's houses" was usually wheaten, but by 1700, many of the "poorer sort" preferred the "pone"; [65] there was hominy and woods travelers knew how to parch corn. [66] The wealthy imported most of their beverages—chocolate, tea, coffee, and a wide variety of alcoholic drinks; but the poor man knew that tea could be made from sassafras, [67] and metheglin brewed from the honey in the pods of the honey locust tree. [68]

Corn whiskey was not yet there, but it was on the way; some of the North Carolina planters were malting corn, and using it to brew beer from the juice of the bruised stalks; others made beer of persimmons or molasses and bran. [69] Dairying was not greatly developed, but there was plenty of milk for drinking, with butter for export. [70] Some planters, notably the French along the Santee, were making cloth from home-grown flax and wool. [71]

The colonials had as a group completely mastered river navigation with the smaller craft, usually pirogues of hollowed-out cypress, [72] built on the plantation. They were better fishermen than hunters, and had even improved upon the method of making weirs, learned from the Indians. [73]

Their woods learning had progressed more slowly, but most made some use of wild leathers and meats. Different from the French, the Americans seldom depended upon wild meat, but were fond of venison, and most especially of bear. "It stands between Beef and Pork, and the young Cubs are a Dish for the Greatest Epicure living. I prefer this Flesh before any Beef, Veal, Pork, or Mutton; and they look as well as they eat, their fat being as white as snow, and the sweetest of any Creatures in the World. If a man drink a quart thereof melted, it never will rise in his stomach. We prefer it above all things to Fry Fish and other things in." [74] John

---

[64] Lawson, *Carolina*, 43–44, and Beverly, *Virginia*, 237, declared, "I don't know any English plant, grain, or fruit that miscarries in Virginia."

[65] *Ibid.*

[66] Lawson, *Carolina*, 28–29.

[67] *Ibid.*, 54. Sassafras in addition to being a substitute for tea for the poor man was also a medicine, for the bark of the "Root is a Specifick to those affected with Gripes."

[68] Lawson, *Carolina*, 55.

[69] Beverly, *Virginia*, 238.

[70] Lawson, *Carolina*, 45.

[71] *Ibid.*, 47.

[72] *Ibid.*, 55.

[73] Beverly, *Virginia*, 256.

[74] Lawson, *Carolina*, 67.

Lawson, the writer, cared little for buffalo, though he did observe, "the younger calves are cry'd up for excellent food, as very likely they may be." [75]

Americans had by this date learned a good deal of the uses of native trees and plants, but little compared to what the men who would settle on the other side of the mountains must know. They had learned to eat a wide variety of fruits and nuts, believed in the virtues of Seneca snake-root, knew cedar was good for coffins, and that beech decayed quickly.[76] Poplar and hickory, so important to later settlers away from the sea, they hardly knew at all; nor could they learn any more than they could learn how to make maple sugar—sugar maples, poplars, and hickories were rare along the coast.

We, thus, cannot blame the New Bern settlers for their failure. Their letters, always asking for things, reflect less the weaknesses of individuals than that of a society unable to live away from the sea. "I will not write much or complain," one wrote. "If one has money and property, gold and silver, he can be master here as in Europe, but I will say that for a poor man it is better there than here." [77] Another repeats this complaint, while others of the men bewail the lack of womenfolk to cook and wash for them: these men could not, like the Long Hunters, live without women for months. Most ask for things—"a dozen ready-made shirts, a few sheets, 10 ells of linen cloth;" utensils and tools of iron and brass, many of which later men would make for themselves of wood: and over and over we read, "one should not trust to supporting himself with game." [78]

However, such were the cruelties and hardships of the Old World, the persecuted and the displaced continued to come to the New. In 1715 Governor Spotswood of Virginia wrote of another group of Palatinate refugees: "I did in compassion to these poor strangers and in regard to the safety of the Country, place them together upon a piece of land, several miles without the inhabitants, where I built them habitations." [79] This settlement was Germanna, the far west of 1715 since it was above the Falls of the Rappahannock. It was true, these Germans, like the Huguenots and

---

[75] *Ibid.*

[76] *Ibid.*, 50–66. Lawson here describes and gives the uses of the wild plants known to him and even attempts, 60, to describe the manner of making maple sugar as carried on by the Indians, remarking that the "Sugar-Tree . . . is found . . . in places near the mountains." It seems clear that no white settler known to Lawson had made maple sugar, a food important to later generations of pioneers.

[77] Graffenried, *New Bern*, 309, letter of Jacob Ware.

[78] *Ibid.*, 308–309, letter of Jacob Gabley; see that of Christian Engel, *ibid.*, 314–6.

[79] *Ibid.*, 25.

the Scotch-Irish, were welcomed as buffers against the Indians, but those at Germanna were miners, selected primarily for their skills. Spotswood was opening an ironworks where he hoped to make from native ores, kettles and other things ordinarily imported from England. He kept silent on this; it would never do to tell the Lords Commanders a colonist was attempting iron manufacture.[80]

Spotswood, no different from George Washington's father, never made a fortune out of iron, but iron was only one of several things that turned his face toward the wild woods. Virginians such as he, though enjoying many privileges, were more or less at the mercy of England. Sometimes their tobacco brought good prices, other times it did not; planters must then go deeply in debt to the British merchants or learn to make the things they had to have. Loyal British subjects and good Church of England men, some such as Spotswood still saw the need for a more self-sufficient economy on their side of the sea.

Different from New England, Virginia offered little in the way of business, save the Indian trade, and though much of the Byrd and other Virginia fortunes had fattened from the trade, it was of later years not enough for Virginia gentlemen, for the Virginia aristocracy had to have money in order to continue as aristocracy, and land, even land in tobacco, did not always bring in enough. Land to subdivide and sell was more lucrative, and equally respectable. Thus, the real estate business was most tempting to men such as Spotswood, and changes in colonial policy plus rapid migration favored the land business.

At first land could be had only by paying the passage of settlers too poor to pay their own; the man who paid the transportation costs got fifty acres of land for each person brought into Virginia.[81] The transported one usually had to spend five years in working out the cost of his passage, but at the end of that time he or she also received fifty acres of land. He could then set up as a small farmer, for there was in Tidewater, along with the great planters a much larger group of middle-class farmers with the right to vote, and there continued to be until after the Revolution no Virginians "poor enough to beg." [82]

[80] Material used by permission of the publishers, Louisiana State University Press, from *Three Virginia Frontiers* by Thomas Perkins Abernethy, copyright Louisiana State University Press, Baton Rouge, 1940 (cited hereafter as Abernethy, *Three Frontiers*), 38.

[81] *Ibid.*, 39.

[82] Thomas Anburey, *Travels through the interior parts of America*, London, 1789 (cited hereafter as Anburey, *Travels*), found, II, 373–374, no poverty in Virginia during his tour, August 1776–December 1781.

Growth of the Virginia middle class was assured when the price of land dropped from twelve pounds or two passages per hundred acres to only ten shillings. Better yet the small farmer could by 1669 get it through direct purchase. Profiting even more from the new land laws were the men such as Governor Spotswood, who got the land in large grants from the crown and at extremely low prices; the price so low they could sell it for six times what it had cost,[83] and still keep it within the means of the middle-class farmer who could pay on time, usually with tobacco.

It is probable that as Governor Spotswood rode in 1716 with his Knights of the Golden Horseshoe across the Piedmont, over the Blue Ridge and on to the Shenandoah, where they enjoyed a somewhat glorified picnic,[84] he looked at the land about him, not with the wondering eyes of an explorer, but with the shrewd glance of a real estate man. Virginia was over a hundred years old, and the sandy lands below the Fall Line were old and worn from too many crops of tobacco. Rich as well as poor would soon be forced to go to the then backwoods of the Piedmont and soon behind the Blue Ridge.

Refugees of all denominations were coming in increasingly large numbers, and from the looks of things in the British Isles there would be more, especially from Scotland and the Scotch farmers settled in Northern Ireland. England demanded what the Scotchman would never give—religious conformity. The bloody battles went through kings and generations, and along with the warfare England tried economic reprisals. Laws passed in 1689, favoring English manufactured cloth over any from Ireland, be it manufactured by Scot or Irishman, practically destroyed the agriculture of the Scotch-Irish and the home industries built upon it. The Test Act of 1704 reduced most Scots in Ireland to little more than outlaws with none of the rights or privileges of citizens.[85] The Scots and the Scotch-Irish began a slow trickle to the English colonies, trying at first to live in New York and New England.

They began to leave in droves when in 1714 Queene Anne passed the Schism Act, and the doors of their churches were nailed shut.[86] Some

[83] Abernethy, *Three Frontiers*, 54-55.
[84] Joseph A. Waddell, *Annals of Augusta County, Virginia, with Reminiscences Illustrative of the Vicissitudes of its Pioneer Settlers*, Richmond, 1886 (cited hereafter as Waddell, *Annals*), 7-9, quoting from the diary of John Fontaine, member of the party.
[85] Charles Augustus Hanna, *The Scotch-Irish, or The Scot in North Britain, North Ireland and North America*, New York, 1902 (cited hereafter as Hanna, *Scotch-Irish*), I, 1.
[86] *Ibid.*, I, 57-61.

came directly from Scotland, but most from Ulster; sometimes they were known as Dissenters, though this term was in Virginia applied to members of most Protestant denominations other than the Church of England. In time these refugees from Ulster were denominated Scotch-Irish; a better title would have been the Scots-who-had-lived-in-Ireland; they had never mingled with the Irish in religion, politics, or social life.[87]

Most settlers in the new world hated the Scotch-Irish; his ideas were held to be subversive for he believed in the individual conscience, and the heresy of complete separation of Church and State, views proscribed in most of the colonies save Rhode Island, Pennsylvania, and the southern colonies. True, Virginia had an established, tax-supported church, that of England, but in 1689 the Toleration Act had given any seemingly subversive religious group the right, after first getting permission, to form a church body, though all members must continue to pay the tax, usually in tobacco, for the upkeep of the Church of England.[88] The colony of North Carolina was even more tolerant and easy-going.[89]

This in sharp contrast to New York where in 1707 Governor Cornbury had had the Presbyterian ministers Francis Makemie and John Hampton arrested merely for preaching in private homes.[90] The Reverend Thomas Craighead, ancestor of a long line of ministers of that name to be prominent in the old southwest, had in 1715 tried to settle in Massachusetts, but with little better luck than five shiploads of Scotch-Irish who came three years later. They were permitted neither to disembark in that town, nor to stay in it, but were unloaded elsewhere and sent out at once to the backwoods to serve as buffers against the Indians.[91]

The Pennsylvania government was more lenient, at least on paper, but Pennsylvania lands were expensive; nor had Rhode Island much to offer in the way of cheap lands. Governor Spotswood, and others of the Virginia landholders, must have understood that Virginia would attract all those whom no one else would have; land was cheap in the backwoods, and more important was the tolerance of the easy-going southerners com-

[87] Hanna, *Scotch-Irish*, I, 498–505.
[88] Nor were taxes all: "Until the year 1781 any couple desiring to be legally married had to send for or go to some minister of the established Church, however far off he might live." Waddell, *Annals*, 19.
[89] North Carolina did not even stipulate belief in Christ; a 1669 law merely stating that "seven or more persons agreeing on a religion were to constitute a Church." The Jewish faith was not debarred; Jews were not only admitted, NCR, I, 203, but, *ibid.*, I, 609, allowed to vote.
[90] Hanna, *Scotch-Irish*, II, 93–94.
[91] *Ibid.*, II, 16–22.

pared to most of the rest of colonial America. In any case, even before actual settlement had gone much above the Fall Line, land speculators began to "take up" thousands upon thousands of acres of land on the Piedmont. The home government wanted settlers in the backwoods, and to encourage settlement and not mere land speculation, gave all holders of a thousand acres or less, a ten-year exemption from quitrents and taxes; equally encouraging to settlement as opposed to the mere holding of the land was the law passed in 1713 by the Virginia House of Burgesses stipulating that every landowner should cultivate three acres out of every fifty of arable land.[92]

The scarcity of land below the Fall Line and the attractiveness of the south in general so quickened settlement toward the west, that by 1727 it was clear the line between Virginia and North Carolina, long in dispute, must be surveyed and extended. Virginia chose as a commissioner to oversee the running of the line Colonel William Byrd,[93] wealthy and distinguished member of a wealthy family, and like most other wealthy Virginians of his day, in the land business, owning at his death 179,440 acres of land. Yet, in keeping with the Virginia tradition, he was never all businessman, but had many interests, not the least of which was books; he had a library of four thousand volumes and was much given to the keeping of journals that today make rich reading.

In the process of running the line, Byrd took a party of around thirty men through the Dismal Swamp, and onward for two hundred miles into the backwoods. William Byrd was a Tidewater aristocrat, and compared to some of the settlers who were by that date living above the Fall Line, he was no woodsman. Yet, the journal [94] he kept of the survey shows well the great progress in learning to live in the woods,[95] made in the less than twenty years since Graffenried's settlers had starved and died at New Bern. Byrd and his men, different from John Lawson and most early travelers, lived in a world where everybody rode horseback; Byrd even complaining that Virginians were so fond of horses they would, in order to

---

[92] Abernethy, *Three Frontiers*, 42–46, 50.

[93] John Spencer Bassett, Introduction to Byrd, *Writings*, "The Byrd family of Virginia," xl–lxxxviii.

[94] Byrd, *Writings*, already cited by no means contains all of his journals and diaries; the most of it, 3–255, is given up to "History of the Dividing Line," the account of running the line from the coast to "within sight of the mountains."

[95] They had also learned to live from the woods; less than twenty years after Lawson spoke of the houses such as "the Swedes build," Byrd, *Writings*, 78–79, found most houses in North Carolina of logs covered with shingles 3 ft. long and one broad, "hung upon lathes with pegs," doors hung on wooden hinges, wooden locks, the whole built with no nail.

ride one mile, walk two to hunt a horse.[96] The colonial horse was smaller than the average English horse of that day,[97] but sure-footed and tough, able to live for weeks on cane, pea vine, brush and wild ferns, yet intelligent enough to take much training. He had to learn to graze with hobbled feet at night, unmindful of the clanging bell that all horses taken into the woods must wear, though stopped during the day while traveling. The horse must know to stand when buffalo or deer were found and the hunter sprang off,[98] and how to manage swift muddy water instead of drowning himself by bucking or rearing back. Above all, he must, like the dog, never be afraid of anything—trails so steep he sometimes fell backward, smell of blood or fresh meat, Indians, scream of panther, or howl of wolf.

Such animals with no food but woods fare, could do a hundred miles in one day, three hundred through rough country in five days, or carrying the customary pack of two hundred pounds travel steadily for days.[99] Most colonists at this date were not greatly interested in the breeding of fine horses from purebred stock brought from England, nor was the "fine breed of running woods horse" [100] developed by the Chickasaw chiefly from Spanish breeds, then so well known to the white man. A horse was to most, even Virginians, still a horse instead of a passion. Byrd and his men also had plenty of what might be denominated American dogs, for they like the average horse of the Virginia farmer were less a breed than a development, lively animals, wise and tough.

Colonel Byrd when he went into the woods did a very daring thing, never before done by white men; he brought only biscuit and trusted to "Providence for meat," when the men, each of whom had brought a ten days' ration, should have exhausted their supply. The surveying party from North Carolina consisting of only "three or four men," brought "five hundred pounds of bacon and dry'd Beef, and five hundred pounds of Bisket." [101] Byrd's trust was not entirely in Providence, for "since we could not entirely rely upon the dexterity of our own men," he hired an Indian, one of a tribe of Saponi on the Piedmont, as a hunter.[102] His party

---

[96] Byrd, *Writings*, 197.
[97] Lawson, *Carolina*, 45–46.
[98] FQ, II, Clinkenbeard "Interview," 108.
[99] Packs varied; Byrd, *Writings*, 235, gave the customary pack of the Indian traders as 150 to 200 pounds, and the rate at about 20 miles a day if "Forage happens to be plentiful." Hanna, *Wilderness Trail*, II, 222, quoting Col. Nathan Boone from Lyman C. Draper's "Life of John Finley," gives 100 half-dressed deerskins, weighing around 2½ pounds each as the customary horse load; this was close to 50 years later.
[100] Adair, *American Indian*, 205.
[101] Byrd, *Writings*, 104.
[102] *Ibid.*, 117.

fared fairly well, though on some days, "several deer came into our view but none into the Pot," [103] and there was then little to eat but bearhide soup.

Byrd's account indicates the party [104] had only smoothbore muskets, but by that date the rifle had both improved and grown more common, particularly on the borders of Pennsylvania in Lancaster County. This region, more than any other, had attracted those of non-English extraction who forever in search of cheap lands and toleration must push continually west—Scotch-Irish, German, Swiss, and French. These settlers, still east of the Susquehanna and hence the spot where Martin Chartier had had his trading post, would push west a little further, and then turn south, and following river and creek valleys push into, across, and down the Appalachians.

They brought with them many things to plant in Virginia, the Carolinas, and soon East Tennessee, and one of their most important gifts to the border was the rifle, as most are agreed that what came to be known as the American rifle was developed by German, Swiss, and French borderers in the neighborhood of what is now Lancaster, Pennsylvania.[105] The barrel would be long, usually around forty-two inches, with six to eight rifling grooves that made a complete turn in about forty-eight inches. Weighing less than a dozen pounds, light compared to the old guns, it was no burden for even the man on foot; better yet was the smallness of its bore, so small a pound of lead would be good for forty bullets, and soon guns were using even less, sixty, seventy shots to the pound of lead.

More wondrous still, this rifled-barreled gun was not only deadly accurate, but it would kill a turkey in the highest of trees, for its optimum range was around one hundred yards. Equally unbelievable was the loading; a man could do it in half a minute and never make a sound. A hickory rod had replaced the iron rod and mallet; the new thing was a shallow

[103] *Ibid.*, 131.

[104] The men, chiefly borderers and part-time Indian traders, were ordered, *ibid.*, 26, to "come armed with a Musquet and a Tomahack, or large Hatchet." Remarks such as "Goose-shot in piece," *ibid.*, 124, would indicate they had no form of rifle; the word *musket* could be applied to any small firearm, but as rifles even among 1783–1800 inventories on the Cumberland were usually denominated rifled-barreled or, as among English travelers, "rifle-barreled firelocks," "musket" in 1728 would ordinarily mean an unrifled gun, smaller than a blunderbuss.

[105] The old border from the headwaters of the Potomac, south to the upper reaches of the Yadkin, was in a sense one world, but has for the most part been dealt with colony by colony or county by county. I. Daniel Rupp, *Early History of Western Pennsylvania and of the west*, Harrisburg, 1846, contains a deal of source material relative to life in Pennsylvania prior to the French and Indian War, particularly Lancaster County from which so many migrated south and west.

hole in the stock for holding grease or round pieces of linen or deerskin already greased and cut, each about the size of a half dollar. These greased circles of material were known as patching; by putting one around each bullet the marksman could get a tight fit with bullets no larger and even smaller than the smallest diameter—that from land to opposite land—of the gun barrel, for the greased cloth patched out their size. made a snug fit, yet could still be pushed quickly and soundlessly home with the hickory rod.[106] Such a weapon was not only cheap to use, but very handy for the man who wanted to carry into the backwoods enough ammunition for several weeks or even months of hunting.

Colonel Byrd, in spite of his daring in depending on the woods for meat to feed twenty-six men,[107] no one of whom had a rifle, was still a beef- and biscuit-eating Englishman. He described with wonder many aspects of life in the woods that were by that date commonplace to backwoods settlers. He for the first time heard that the eating of bear's meat would increase the potency of a man,[108] but found the most delicate part of the animal, the foot, almost too much like a human foot in appearance, to be enjoyable.[109] The buffalo were almost gone from the Piedmont, but he had his first taste of the udder and tongue, the choice parts beloved by all hunters.

The woodsmen with Byrd knew how to take the beaver by sprinkling the trap with the essences of his "prides" mixed with sassafras.[110] They knew how to hunt the deer, both by stalking and ring hunting; at times fire was used to form the ring, and then it was pitiful to see and hear the surrounded deer, "they weep and groan like a human creature," Byrd wrote.

Byrd's hunters also knew when and where to look for wild turkeys, sometimes weighing as much as fifty pounds,[111] and so fat they "burst when they fell from the trees." They had mastered much plant lore; like

---

[106] It is generally conceded that the rifle, prominent on all southern borders after the French and Indian War, was perfected around what in time came to be Lancaster, Pa. J. Thomas Scharf and Thompson West in their *History of Philadelphia 1609–1884*, Philadelphia, 1884, state, III, 2270, that by the time of the French and Indian War small arms were being manufactured in Philadelphia. Captain G. W. Dillin, *The Kentucky Rifle*, National Rifle Association of America, Washington, 1925, is one of the best works dealing with the development and use of the rifle, though throughout the pioneer period this firearm was not referred to as the "Kentucky rifle."

[107] Byrd, *Writings*, 275–277.

[108] *Ibid.*, 190.

[109] *Ibid.*, 118.

[110] *Ibid.*, 120–121.

[111] *Ibid.*, 108.

people in Pulaski County, Kentucky, two hundred years later they knew that pennyroyal when rubbed on the body would keep off seed ticks.[112] They knew many of the forest trees, and their uses, but different from generations of later woodsmen they were unable to tell the fertility of the soil by the species of trees and plants that grew on it.[113] Nor could they build a raft of dry cane stalks tied together with pawpaw strings as could later woodsmen,[114] nor did they build a boat of elm bark laced together with the tough inner bark of the hickory as did men twenty-two years later when crossing the Cumberland.[115] Byrd and his men could only wait for a swollen stream to go down. They had in general much more trouble in getting through the woods than later hunters; their horses gave out, and they had to walk. Many, including Byrd, suffered much with their feet, for none of them save possibly the Indian, wore moccasins or "Indian shoes," commonly worn by the *coureur de bois*,[116] certainly by the time of Martin Chartier, and for how long before him we do not

[112] *Ibid.*, 213. Byrd knew many of the herbs still gathered in a few places in the hills—wild angelica, and colt's foot, *ibid.*, 129; star grass, 109; St.-Andrew's-cross, 111; Indian physic, 113; fern root, another snake-bite remedy, 116; Seneca snakeroot, 116, dittany, 205; ginseng, 210–211. This last was in later years dug only to be sold, not as a medicinal herb as Byrd used it. This was 1728 and research tends to indicate that all herbs now used in the hills were known by this date; some years ago I asked Mrs. Anna Liza Wilson, a neighbor on Little Indian Creek of the Big South Fork of the Cumberland, to send me a representation of the herbs she used for medicinal purposes. Some were classified by Dr. Rogers McVaugh, Professor of Botany, University of Michigan. Many were found in the old herbals, and still others used by Mrs. Wilson, such as Seneca snakeroot, were also mentioned by Byrd.

[113] Byrd had a fair eye for land, but mentions neither large pawpaw nor big cane, the two plants looked for by later settlers as proof of good land. André F. Michaux, *Travels to the Westward of the Allegany Mountains*, London, 1805 (cited hereafter as Michaux, *Travels, 1802*), as it was in this year he visited Kentucky and Tennessee, six years after the last visit of his father in 1796 already cited, gave, 202–207, the most complete description of methods of judging land found; he, following the custom in Kentucky of that date, divided it into three grades; that with only a scattering of scrubby oaks, post oaks, was generally considered poorest, and hence the term found often in the Draper Manuscripts, and still heard at times, "post-oak land" meaning very poor soil.

[114] Byrd, *Writings*, 201, 203. They had while waiting considered building a raft tied together with grapevines; seemingly no man among them knew how to build the raft quickly made from materials found on the banks of most streams—"cane laid cross wise in layers and tied together with paw-paw strings." This from Parson John Kirkwell's account of the Nickojack Campaign in Middle Tennessee in 1794, W, 32S, 230–271. One account states that Edmund Jennings—he helped Daniel Boone cut the road to Boonesborough in the spring of 1775—swam the Tennessee—Nickojack Town was on the other side—five times in one night, towing a raft with a pawpaw string in his teeth, *ibid.*, 6XX, 10–11.

[115] This was Dr. Thomas Walker; see his "Journal," April 20–21, though in fairness to the woodsmen in Byrd's party it should be pointed out that neither elm nor hickory will peel in the fall when Byrd and party finished the last part of the survey.

[116] Margry, *Translation*, II, 116.

know. John Lawson wore them in the North Carolina woods, but it was not until more than twenty years after Byrd that we find a party of Englishmen wearing moccasins constantly while in the woods.[117]

As cooks Byrd's men did fairly well. Like later hunters they were fond of cooking more than one kind of meat in the pot, but the pot and the kettle were about all they used. They baked no hoecakes, nor did they cook in the ground. One of their more interesting dishes was that of fat bacon fried in a skillet, then, grease and all, covered with a pint of rum; "both which being dished up together, served the Company at once for meat and Drink." [118] Still, they could not live without bread and wheaten bread at that.[119]

However, as Byrd traveled away from the sea, he found people who had no bread but cornbread, and some of them lived in homes which he rather contemptuously called pole-pens. Their logs were probably not so closely laid or carefully notched as those that were by 1728 being built on the North Carolina coast, but the log house like the rifled gun was traveling west. The houses usually held many children, and though Byrd didn't think too much of the men he met, he almost always praised the women, who, different from the English women he knew, clothed their families with cloth of their own making. He found in his journeyings only one case of hunger, and that of a lone miner,[120] with no wife and ten miles from any corn. Men with women had, in addition to corn, sweet potatoes, and the ever-present pork and "seas of milk." [121]

Not all the settlers Byrd met in even the backwoods displeased him; and often he found good food, good homes, and proper plantations with slaves and well cultivated fields. Most of those he met on the Virginia Piedmont, and, judging from their names,[122] the most of even his chain

---

[117] Dr. Walker and party stopped on Easter Monday, "Journal," April 16, and "I made a pair of Indian shoes, those I bought being bad." May 10, he dressed elkskin for another pair, and July 8, when almost home by way of the Green Bryer, "Nigh the top of the Allegheny Ridge," he made still another pair.

[118] Byrd, *Writings*, 76.

[119] *Ibid.*, 173. They carried bread bags covered with deerskins, and one of the main reasons for turning back when within sight of the mountains, *ibid.*, 178-179, was the low state of the bread supply, 1,000 pounds, *ibid.*, 105, at the beginning.

[120] *Ibid.*, 284-285.

[121] *Ibid.*, 107, 319, 322 are among the many references to dairy products, including "lean cheese."

[122] *Ibid.*, 276. This list of guards and chain carriers with few indicative of any nationality save English, is in interesting contrast to muster rolls from border counties of Virginia during the French and Indian War; VM, I, 378-390, and *ibid.*, II, 37-49, lists the origins of several hundred men; Scotland, Ireland, and Germany are well represented, as also are the more northerly colonies, particularly Pennsylvania, with a goodly number from New Jersey.

carriers and other helpers, were of English origin. In general up to the year of Byrd's survey, most Virginia settlers, even those on the Piedmont, were either descendants of Tidewater families, or had come first to some Virginia seaport, and from there gone west. This pattern of migration changed quickly. It is thought to have been in 1727, or possibly a year earlier, that the first settler came overland from Pennsylvania and into the lower Shenandoah Valley of Virginia. This was a German, Adam Miller,[123] or Müller, the first known drop in a great flood of migration that rolled up and into Virginia.

In 1730 Isaac and John Vanmeter got a grant of 100,000 acres. The next year they sold this to Joist Heidt,[124] or Heydte, in time Hite, a Hollander who had in 1710 come to New York, bringing possessions and people in three ships. He migrated into Pennsylvania and in 1732 came with a numerous company, including sons and sons-in-law, to the lower Shenandoah Valley in Virginia.[125] Hite prospered to some extent and lived well, but he suffered a misfortune that would in time be suffered by numerous pioneers in Tennessee, but above all in Kentucky. He discovered the land he had bought in good faith was, through no fault of the seller, already claimed by a land speculator, Lord Fairfax, who in 1736 was granted more than 100,000 acres of land on "the river Sherando." [126] Joist Hite sued; the action like the thousands of other such suits to come, dragged on for years. Seldom, if ever, was the settler able to outrun the land speculator.

Hard on the heels of those in the lower valley came others, chiefly from the Pennsylvania frontier. They pushed up the valley to the headsprings, not only of the Shenandoah, but of the more northerly branches of the Potomac, and soon onto New River, a southern branch of the Kanawha. Yet, practically all paid some promoter for their land.[127] In 1733 when Byrd went again into southwestern Virginia to take up a twenty thousand acre plat for himself on the Dan River in North Carolina, just south

---

[123] Abernethy, *Three Frontiers*, 55.

[124] Waddell, *Annals*, 9–10.

[125] *Ibid*. See also for early settlement and life in the valley of the Shenandoah, Lewis P. Summers, *History of Southwest Virginia*, Richmond, 1903 (cited hereafter as Summers, *Southwest Virginia*), 41–45. Samuel Kercheval, *History of the Valley of Virginia*, Woodstock, Va., 1902 (cited hereafter as Kercheval, *Virginia*), 45–55, gives a somewhat different version.

[126] Waddell, *Annals*, 14. The lawsuit beginning in 1736 ended in 1786 in favor of Hite's heirs, for he was long since dead, Kercheval, *Virginia*, 156.

[127] Early records of Augusta County established in the upper valley by Act of 1738, though the first court session was not held until 1745, show 166 deeds prior to 1755 were of land bought from Robert Beverly.

of the Virginia line, he must have smiled to himself. He and the surveyors from North Carolina, when in 1728 they had surveyed the line 169 miles from the coast, had had a mighty argument, ending with the North Carolina men going home in a tiff. Their contention was they had gone far enough, and that it would take settlement "an age or two" to reach their point, fifty miles from the most westerly inhabitants on the southern boundary.[128] Now only five years later, land, that is in amounts large enough for the real estate companies, was getting scarce east of the mountains, and the borders would soon again be in doubt, though the Virginia men, urged on by Byrd, had surveyed the line seventy-two miles past the point where the North Carolina men had quit.[129]

It had taken the English more than 125 years to settle lands hardly that many miles from the sea, and in order to do it a race of men had to be bred for the business. They were not mere suburbanites of England. Even good old English ale must by 1733 have had at times quite an American flavor, at least that brewed by Mr. Chiswell, a prosperous Virginia gentleman. "He farther told me," Byrd wrote, "that he had brewed as good ale of malt made of Indian corn as ever he tasted; all the objection was, he could neither by art or standing, ever bring it to be fine in cask. The quantity of corn he employed in brewing a cask of forty gallons was two bushels and a half, which made it very strong and pleasant." [130]

Byrd was pleased to hear of the ale, but in general he didn't like much of what he found among the backwoods settlers. He loathed, as Washington did later, the nights he sometimes had to spend in a backwoods cabin. The thing, however, that troubled him more than the physical aspects of their lives was their mental make-up. He could not quite accept the independence of the North Carolinians he met along the line; even those of English origin didn't seem to worry too much whether their babies were baptized or no. They could live in good content without priests, lawyers, or physicians, and this amazed him. Byrd realized he was meeting a new breed; a people who could with only Bibles to read, keep their self-respect and feel properly religious without ministers.[131] These North Carolinians were not only physically free of the necessity of overmuch trade with England, but psychologically free. The French along the Santee had never had an English home, but even North Carolinians whose

[128] Byrd, *Writings,* 127–128.
[129] *Ibid.,* 175.
[130] *Ibid.,* 347. This was during Byrd's second trip west when he went to learn about mining and iron manufacture, "A Progress to the Mines," *ibid.,* 333–386.
[131] *Ibid.,* 63.

fathers had been born in England, were less inclined than the Virginians to think of it as home. Some of this feeling may have come about because, what with poor harbors and silt-choked lower rivers, the North Carolina settlers saw less of English ships, and many of their exports had first to be shipped overland to some Virginia harbor. Still, lack of harbors could never entirely explain these people who lodged justice but "indifferently," the "Court-House having much the Air of a Common Tobacco-House." They had "neither Church, Chappel, Mosque, Synagogue;" were "neither guilty of hypocracy nor superstition," and paid no tribute "either to God or to Caesar," for everyone did just what seemed "good in his own eyes." [132]

William Byrd, though looking west, preferred those parts of the Virginia Piedmont, notably that in the region of the upper James, settled chiefly by Jeffersons, Randolphs, and other first families of Virginia. They, like the Byrds, were more self-sufficient than their fathers had been, their thoughts turning more and more to the west,[133] but little of the blood of these was to be represented in the first settlements of the west across the Appalachians.

There would be North Carolinians in great plenty, most, like the pioneers from Virginia, descended from settlers who had migrated up the Great Valley of Virginia from the borders of Pennsylvania. There were German, Swiss, French, Welsh, sometimes English—a Methodist or a Baptist—now and then a Pennsylvania Quaker, or a family down from New Jersey, New York, or even New England—all hunting toleration and cheap land. There were above all Scotch-Irish; few were rich, but not all were pinching poor as Andrew Jackson's people coming to the Waxhaws a few years later. Many such as the Calhouns or the Prestons [134] were well-to-do immigrants able, provided unpatented land could be found, to claim the King's Bounty for having brought themselves to the New World.

[132] *Ibid.,* 79–80. Byrd like other travelers in the southern colonies found no poverty, for, *ibid.,* 80, in North Carolina of 1728 "Nothing is dear but law, Physick, and Strong Drink." This would indicate that the North Carolinians had not yet mastered the art of making corn whiskey, in time the cheapest drink of all.

[133] FP, 13, J. Stoddard Johnston, *First Explorations of Kentucky,* "Sketch of Dr. Thomas Walker," 4–19, is a brief but clear picture of that part of the Virginia Piedmont of 1750, much on the James inhabited by Jeffersons, Dr. Walker, Madisons, and other influential Virginia families.

[134] W, 31S, 103, is a copy of the importation oath of John Preston, May 12, 1746, in which he declared he had at his own expense imported himself, his wife Elizabeth, and children William, Lettice, Margaret and Ann from Ireland, and so "prayed that he might partake of his majesty's bounty."

We cannot be certain it was entirely poverty and persecution that made the Scotch-Irish along with many Germans, push up and up into the higher lands, with some crossing the Blue Ridge, following the eastern rim west and south to settle on the Piedmont in southwestern Virginia where in 1745 Lunenburg County was created. Others such as the Boones went on into the Yadkin Country of North Carolina; [135] the Calhouns to South Carolina, with many stopping at the Waxhaws on the boundary. The Scotch and the Scotch-Irish undoubtedly loved the high valleys, snug below high hills and mountains. Swift streams between rocky hills would have reminded them of their homeland, that is if any among them had been in the habit of using such a pretty word. The land-that-had-been-home was for them as for the French or German Protestant, a place of persecution, hardly an earthly paradise on which to hang fond dreams of going home.

Most made ideal backwoodsmen, and with them from the Pennsylvania frontier they brought two things no frontier family could live without—the long rifle and the know-how of the log house. Most were much given to diversified farming, were weavers of cloth, makers of butter, and breeders of sheep, cows, horses, and of course, pigs. Trees were rather new to the Scotch-Irish, but rough lands, danger, hardship were not; neither Scotland nor northern Ireland is exactly smooth, and instead of Indians there had been English soldiers and unfriendly Irish, and always the grim business of being a Dissenter. Many of both the Germans and the Scotch-Irish had, in Pennsylvania, known the hard lot of an indentured servant.[136]

Only twenty-one years after Byrd surveyed the line seventy-two miles past what the North Carolina men considered sensible, it had to be extended again. This time Peter Jefferson, father of Thomas, and Joshua Fry, teacher of mathematics at the College of William and Mary, carried it past the outer rim of the midwest for they surveyed to Steep Rock Creek on the Holston.[137] The wilderness of the Shenandoah that Governor Spotswood had visited with so much pomp and ceremony in 1717, was

---

[135] Mereness, *Travels*, "Diary of a Journey of Moravians from Bethlehem, Pennsylvania to Bethabara in Wachovia, North Carolina, 1753" (a translation from the German), 327–356, gives a good picture of the back country and the rigors of overland travel by the most common route—up the Great Valley—that continued to be used.

[136] Waddell, *Annals*, 17, pointed out that some indentured servants were well educated, serving as clerks and teachers, while others, *ibid.*, 5, quoting from *A Cloud of Witnesses*, were escaped prisoners, seized by the English for their signings of the Covenant.

[137] Waddell, *Annals*, 467–468, and also FP, 13, Introduction, 3, 34.

now very much a part of the civilized world, and divided into two counties. Even high up on New River there was a mill, and all around were farmers, growing grain, curing bacon, making hominy,[138] and among the Scotch-Irish, whiskey, a drink so plentiful that in 1746 it sold for only a dollar a gallon in the taverns of Augusta County, as compared to $1.50 for rum, and 83½ cents per quart for wine.[139]

Settlement had by 1750 begun to push down the north fork of the Holston in Virginia. On March 24, 1750, Dr. Thomas Walker and a party of five other Virginians stopped and helped Samuel Stalnaker "to raise his house." [140] This cabin was on the Lewis Evans map of 1756 marked as the westernmost limit of settlement, though in that year Indians killed Stalnaker's wife and son, and took him prisoner.[141] He escaped and "The Old Dutchman" was still there twenty-six years later and still telling people how to get to Kentucky.[142]

I say "still" because Dr. Walker had hunted up Stalnaker, hoping to get him as a guide to a pass in the mountains. Stalnaker had business of his own and could not go, but Dr. Walker, apparently following his directions, found the Great War Path. Five weeks after leaving his home, a few miles east of present-day Charlottesville, Virginia, and still following the "plain Indian Road," Dr. Walker with his party came to the top of a ridge on which were "Laurel Trees marked with crosses, others blazed and several figures on them." [143] This was Cave Gap, later known as Cumberland Gap from the name Dr. Walker gave the river below, when he reached it a few days later.

Dr. Walker was not hunting the Cumberland; he had set out to find 800,000 acres of good land, for he was head of the Loyal Land Company. Seemingly he hunted "Kenta-ke" [144] or "place-of-fields." Dr. Walker

[138] Dr. Walker spent, "Journal," March 14–21, 1750, between the Blue Ridge and Reedy Creek of New River that flowed into the Ohio.
[139] Waddell, *Annals*, 30. The author translated the shillings and pence into dollars, and by his estimate the Virginia pound was worth, $3.33⅓, though the only dollar known in the colonies was the Spanish dollar.
[140] Stalnaker was already encamped on the Holston; he and Dr. Walker had met two years before in the Holston Country, "on his way to the Cherokee Indians," and Walker now in 1750 had expected him "to pilate me as far as he knew. . . ."
[141] Thwaites-Kellogg, *Dunmore's War*, 58, 232.
[142] Roy F. D. Smythe, *A Tour in the United State of America*, London, 1784 (cited hereafter as Smythe, *Tour*), I, 314. Smythe, a paroled prisoner of war, was then on his way to visit the Kentucky settlements.
[143] Walker, "Journal," April 13, 1750.
[144] Hanna, *Wilderness Trail*, II, 182, quoting sources from N.Y. Col. Docs., though I found no authentication for the popular belief that Kentucky meant "dark and bloody."

never found the Kentucky Bluegrass, but he did name and cross the Cumberland. Near the site of present-day Barbourville two men of his party, "built a house 8 x 12, cleared and broke up some ground and planted corn and peach stones." [145] This is usually referred to as the first white settlement on the Cumberland, or in Kentucky, but there is no evidence [146] that any one lived there after Walker and his party left, two days after it was finished.

The journal Dr. Walker kept of the travels of his party is somewhat startling when put side by side of that of John Lawson written less than fifty years before. Dr. Walker's men, always letting themselves get hurt, and often falling down, were no match for such woodsmen as Michael Stoner and others who came to the Cumberland, but still they were able to go into the woods with only hominy, meal, guns, ammunition, and a few tools and live for months with some discomfort, but no actual suffering. The woods were conquered; the long learning was finished. Yet, settlement on the Cumberland was more than twenty years away; the French and Indian War, followed by the King's Proclamation of 1763, were dams checking the flood, but not lessening the water.

In the meantime there was the rifle. Dr. Walker was never a man to boast, but he could not forbear a summary: "We killed in the journey 13 buffaloes, 8 elks, 53 bears, 20 deers, 4 wild geese, about 150 Turkeys, beside small game. We might have killed three times as much meat, if we had wanted it." [147]

Dr. Walker and his men could not only kill meat, build log houses, make bark canoes, moccasins, temporary rafts, they could, particularly Dr. Walker, take care of any emergency that arose— "But the lame horse was as bad as we left him, and another had been bit on the nose by a snake. I rubbed the wounds with Bears Oil and gave him a drench of the same and another of the decoction of Rattle Snake Root some time after." And for

---

[145] Walker, "Journal," April 28, 1750.

[146] True, it was shown and continued to be shown on British maps, possibly to prove to the French that England had colonies west of the Mountains. See in the Clements Library, John Mitchell, "Map of the British and French Dominions in North America with the Roads, Distances, Limits, and Extent of the Settlements," London, 1755 (cited hereafter as Mitchell, "Map of 1755"). This shows Walker's Settlement, but like Evans, "1756 Map of the Colonies," also shows how little was known of even the eastern half of the Middle Mississippi Valley; in both maps all of the Cumberland is shown as being in Virginia, and in general the idea of Mississippi drainage as a whole is less perfect than revealed in the De l'Isle Map of 1718. Dr. Walker again visited the region 29 years later in company with Daniel Smith, but Smith in his Journal made no mention of any previous settlement by Walker.

[147] Walker, "Journal," July 13, 1750.

Colby Chew, hurt when his horse fell, "I bled and gave him volatile drops & he soon recovered;" and for Ambrose Powell's dog Tumbler, killed by a large buck Elk, "we named the run Tumbler's Creek." They lost their "every awl," but "I made one with the Shank of an old Fishing hook, the other people made two of Horse Shoe Nailes, and with these we made our shoes or Moccosons."

CHAPTER VI

THE ILLINOIS

It is probable that as Dr. Walker explored the upper Cumberland, there were, west of him on the river, Frenchmen hunting buffalo. The Mississippi Valley from the time of Father Marquette had never been without Frenchmen, and the French settlements, particularly of the Illinois and the Wabash, played no small part in the settlement of the Cumberland.

True, the great empire to be built on trade and connected by a water route from the mouth of the Mississippi to the Gulf of St. Lawrence of which La Salle had dreamed never materialized. His forts in the Illinois fell into ruins and became no more than gathering places for wandering *coureurs de bois,* deserted soldiers, and now and then a Jesuit missionary. In 1698 Louis XIV sent Pierre Le Moyne, known to history as Iberville, to find the mouth of the Mississippi. He succeeded where La Salle had failed, and planted Biloxi on the gulf, thus beginning French colonization on the lower Mississippi.

The Illinois [1] had seemed especially favored with natural blessings, and early offered hopes of strong colonies. There was rich soil, a good climate with plenty of rain for either wheat or Indian corn. There was lead, salt, and on the Wabash, rock suitable for millstones,[2] an important item to the

---

[1] John Wesley Monette, *History of the Discovery and Settlement of the Valley of the Mississippi,* New York, 1846 (cited hereafter as Monette, *Mississippi*), I, 181–216. The term Illinois was not at first used to designate French territory south of the Great Lakes, west of the Mississippi, north of the mouth of the Tennessee, for the whole territory was denominated Louisiana, but in time Illinois was applied to a boundary of land of that general description, and still later the Wabash with Post St. Vincent (Vincennes) was spoken of, but not governed, as a place separate from the Illinois.

[2] French, *Collections, New Series,* 64–66, quoting Penicaut.

French as they had to have wheaten flour and never learned to make hominy or pound corn into meal as did the English settlers. Equally promising was the temper of the Indians, a mixed group with little of the love of war that made the eastern tribes a constant menace. Yet with all this, and large sums spent by the king, settlement was slow.

The parish records of Kaskaskia, eight miles or so south of the present site of St. Louis, Missouri, and said to be the oldest permanent settlement in the Mississippi Valley, show, for example, that between 1701 and 1713 only twenty-one infants were baptized. This output could have been equaled by any three or even two families of that date in North Carolina as described by Lawson. The fathers of these children were all Frenchmen save one, but as all the mothers were Indians except three,[3] most of these children would take the Indian way of life. As late as 1723 there were only 334 whites in all the villages of the Illinois.[4]

A high percentage of these were traders, hunters, priests, and soldiers without white wives,[5] and hence without farms. The Frenchmen who came to the Illinois were not farmers both "by head and by heart" as were most of the German and Scotch-Irish who settled on the frontiers of the English colonies. As a result the whole populace changed their food habits to some degree, and depended upon wild meat almost as much as did the Indians. Salted buffalo tongues, buffalo beef, venison hams, bear's oil were not only eaten in the Illinois, but as the French colonies on the lower Mississippi grew larger, wild meat along with peltries figured prominently in commerce down the river.

Convoys usually left New Orleans in late winter or early spring on the three-month trip by sails and oars up to the Illinois or Post St. Vincent, later Vincennes, on the Wabash. A second convoy might follow in August. The largest of the boats were the bateaux of hewed or sawed lumber; along with these were pirogues [6] of hollowed-out tree trunks, cypress in the lower south, often large enough to hold thirty men, and sometimes made still larger by splitting the hollowed log in half and inserting a keel as did the settlers along the Carolina coast.[7] There might also be a few birch bark

[3] Used by permission of the Illinois State Historical Library from *The Illinois Country, 1673–1818*, by Clarence W. Alvord, Chicago, 1922, copyrighted 1920 by the Illinois Centennial Commission (cited hereafter as Alvord, *Illinois*), 138.

[4] *Ibid.*, 202.

[5] Francis Parkman, *The Old Regime in Canada*, Boston, 1874, gives a good picture of early French-Canadian colonial life in general and of the *coureur de bois*, 310–315, 319–321.

[6] Alvord, *Illinois*, 212–214.

[7] Lawson, *Carolina*, 55, mentions pirogues made in such fashion capable of carrying "80 or 100 barrels," or more than 30,000 pounds; the hollowed log boat, however,

canoes, down from the north, where the white birch grew. On the upward journey these boats, in addition to soldiers and officials, would be loaded with rum, articles for the Indian trade such as beads, hatchets, matchcoats, guns, and ammunition. There would also be coffee, sugar, chocolate, wines, clothing, and other articles, many of a luxurious nature, and much in demand by white settlers. The downriver trip sometimes took no more than twelve days, even though the boats were heavily loaded with peltry, wild meat, and bear's oil.[8] Member of such a convoy was Dion de Artaguette, who in 1723 went from New Orleans to the upper settlements. He kept a journal of his travels, writing: "Fine weather. We set out at day-break and had not gone a league when we met seven pirogues full of traders living among the Illinois who had been hunting on the Rivière Ouabache. They are loaded with salt meat and bear oil which they are going to sell at New Orleans." [9]

These men, hunting along the lower Ohio, would have been in what are now southern Illinois and west Kentucky. The French hunter, different from the English, traveled by water, and confined his hunting to the neighborhood of streams, good places, for buffalo and deer fed much on the cane there. The French could thus follow the rivers and their tributaries, and kill enough game within carrying distance to load their boats. The Shawanoe or Cumberland soon became the favorite river; it had, save for now and then the Shawnee, no permanent dwellers, and it also had many salt licks as well as much cane.[10] The Green, long known as Buffalo River, was another favorite.

De Artaguette, on his return journey, stopped [11] and with some of his men went after a herd of more than a hundred buffaloes. The men wounded more than twenty, but killed only five, taking only the tongues. "The most worthless Frenchman can kill a buffalo in this region," De Artaguette wrote in the flush of his hunting triumph.[12]

It makes one wonder if De Artaguette had actually killed one of the

seems to have been in common use by the native inhabitants in all timbered areas of the world; the Cherokee, Alvord & Bidgood, *Explorations*, 213, had in 1673 a fleet of 120, "ye leaste of them will carry twenty men, and made sharp at both ends like a wherry for swiftness." The same type of boat was used in South America and the South Sea Islands.

[8] Alvord, *Illinois*, 212–213.

[9] Williams, *Travels*, "Journey of Dion D'Artaguette, 1723," 77.

[10] Hutchins, "Notes," have many references to cane and salt licks, while names featuring one or the other—French Lick, Big Salt Lick, Mansker's Lick, Bledsoe's Lick, Lick Creek, Caney Fork, Cane Creek, etc., are equally indicative of the nature of the land.

[11] Williams, *Travels*, "Journey of Dion D'Artaguette, 1723," 79–80.

[12] *Ibid.*, 80.

great beasts that often weighed more than a ton and a half, or merely watched. Fifty years before, Father Marquette had written of the "Pisikious or wild cattle" that "when attacked, they take a man with their horns, if they can, lift him up, and then dash him on the ground, trample on him and kill him. They are very fierce and not a year passes without their killing some Indian. When you fire at them from a distance with gun or bow, you must throw yourself on the ground as soon as you fire and hide in the grass, for, if they perceive the one who fires they rush on him and attack him." [13]

Buffalo hunting continued even after the Illinois Country had several well established communities, now more French than Indian. "We have," an inhabitant wrote of the region in the summer of 1750, "here whites, Negroes, and Indians, to say nothing of crossbreeds. There are five French villages, and three villages of the natives within a space of 21 leagues, situated between the Mississippi and another river called the Kaskaskias. In the five French villages are perhaps 1100 whites, 300 blacks and some sixty red slaves or savages. The three Illinois towns do not contain more than 800 souls all told. Most of the French till the soil; they raise wheat, cattle, pigs, and horses, and live like Princes." [14]

Everything was free from land to midwives. The populace was a deeply religious one with numerous holy days that gave opportunities for dances, feasts, and gay community gatherings. They were a polite people fond of long-drawn-out court proceedings, and all the ritual and ceremony of a life patterned as much as possible after that in France. Their main crop was wheat, and by 1746 they were able to send six hundred barrels of flour to New Orleans; but among them were few if any self-sufficient farmers such as those (by that date) in the Valley of Virginia. Their women were little given to dairying or the manufacture of cloth.[15] On the whole the French in the Illinois had a much easier, pleasanter life, and a more secure one under the paternalistic French government than did the borderer on the backside of an English colony with neither the home government nor that of the colony much caring whether he lived or died. Yet, the French neither prospered nor multiplied as did the backwoods people of the English colonies.

The French were not entirely without troubles; one of their greatest was the Indians on the eastern side of the lower Mississippi. France had with

[13] Shea, *Mississippi,* "Narrative of Father Marquette," 19.
[14] James H. Perkins, *Annals of the West,* St. Louis, 1850 (cited hereafter as Perkins, *West*), 64.
[15] Alvord, *Illinois,* 190–224.

much trouble destroyed the Natchez as a nation and scattered or killed the people, but she could never conquer the Chickasaw or Cherokee either with arms or diplomacy.[16] War parties from both nations were a constant menace to French commerce. The Chickasaw lived along the Mississippi, claiming what is now West Tennessee, and land to the south, but the Cherokee had no village within three hundred miles of the river. Still, they were just as active as the Chickasaw in harrying the French, for they were great travelers [17] and considered a vast territory their domain. The Overhill Cherokee in what came to be East Tennessee could, with only a bit of overland traveling, reach the Ohio by way of the Kanawha, or take the Great War Path through Cumberland Gap, or go northeast. Other trails led to the lower Cumberland, while travel on the Tennessee began in the front yard; and though they did not live on it they claimed and exercised jurisdiction over most of the land stretching out from the headwaters of New River down to the mouth of the Kanawha, down the Ohio to the mouth of the Tennessee, up it and home again.[18]

They took a lively interest in all who came and went in this kingdom, the French not excepted. A convoy leaving New Orleans in August of 1741, headed by the Sieur de Villers, and made up of three bateaux each with twenty-eight men, and several smaller pirogues with eight or nine men each, had the not uncommon misfortune of having a boat ambushed on the Ohio about a quarter league below the Wabash. The war party of around eighty Cherokee killed only three of the Frenchmen. They took the rest prisoners, and after distributing the goods, save for some ironware and three kegs of rum which they could not carry, started home with booty and prisoners.

---

[16] Monette, *Mississippi*, I, 245-277, gives quite a detailed account of the dispersal of the Natchez, and the efforts, *ibid.*, 277-293, of Bienville to defeat the Chickasaw. Adair after many years with the Chickasaw felt as do some historians of the South that this tribe saved the land on Cumberland and Tennessee rivers for the English by keeping back the French, and hence influencing the outcome of the French and Indian War; see his *American Indian*, 386-387.

[17] Possibly the best example of Cherokee travel is the letter of Abraham Wood describing the travels of Gabriel Arthur, Alvord & Bidgood, *Explorations*, 219-223. They ranged from a Spanish town in the south to the Kanawha on the Ohio, east to Wood's trading post and west down the Tennessee.

[18] This was a disputed region: the Iroquois or the Six Nations claimed land down to the mouth of the Tennessee as indicated by the treating at Fort Stanwix, Nov. 5, 1768; but by the Treaty of Hard Labor with the Cherokee three weeks earlier, their claim to land west of the mouth of the Kanawha through Tryon Mountain of the Blue Ridge was also recognized, and upheld, though the Iroquois relinquished their claim.

One of these was young Antoine Bonnefoy who later wrote of his adventures with the Cherokee. Captured in the early autumn, it was February before the party, after a leisurely trip, with long delays for hunting, up the Tennessee, reached Chota where Gabriel Arthur is thought to have been close to eighty years before. There were by now, "three English traders who each had a storehouse where I was and two servants of theirs. . . . I also found in the same village a son of André Crespe and also Jean Arlois of Bordeaux, who both had gone up the river in 1740 in the boat of Sieur Turpin, who was defeated five leagues from the River Ouibache with the boat of Liberge and Pettit. The same party defeated five Canadian voyageurs in the Ouibache the same year, and killed 25 out of 28, having two men killed and one wounded. . . . We found also a negro and negress who formerly belonged to the widow Sassier, and having been sold in 1739 to a Canadian, deserted when on the Ouibache, and were captured by a troop of Cheraquis. . . ." [19]

These captives, representing three separate forays on the lower Ohio by the Cherokee, were found in only one village, and though "beloved Chota" was the most important town, it would not have been the only one with captives. The young Frenchman found the Cherokee and their cosmopolitan collection of traders, captives, slaves and refugees, representing most of Europe, quite interesting. He was particularly taken with the French, German, and English speaking, Latin writing, German born, communist-plotting Pierre Albert Priber. No white government would let him live among its citizens so he had run away to the Cherokee, where he saw each new captive as a possible communist recruit, and was among the first to make friends with Antoine, who "prayed him to explain to me what was this alleged happiness which he promised us. Guillaume Potier and Jean Arlut were present. He replied that it would take time—that he thought we ought to join his society."

Later talks revealed that Priber had been working among the Cherokee four years, and had been adopted into the Nation and that "he had 100 English traders belonging to his society who had just set out for Carolina, whence they were to return the next autumn, after having got together a considerable number of recruits, men and women, of all conditions and occupations, and the things necessary for laying the first foundations of the Kingdom of Paradise."

Location and future of the Kingdom were all settled, and "there would

[19] Williams, *Travels*, 149-162, "Journal of Antoine Bonnefoy, 1741-42," 153-154.

be no superiority; all should be equal there; the lodging, furniture, and clothing should be equal and uniform as well as the life; all goods should be held in common; the women should live there with the same freedom as the men; there should be no marriage, and they should be free to change husbands every day; the children who should be born should belong to the republic and be cared for and instructed in all things. . . . The individual was to have as his only property a chest of books and paper and ink."

There was never any proof that Priber had so many interested traders, but had the Kingdom of Paradise materialized, its communistic influence might have touched the Cumberland River Basin, as it was to be "half way between them [the Cherokee] and the Alibamons," a tribe with rather vague holdings in what is now Alabama. Priber was safe with the Cherokee for they feared neither subversive opinions nor free speech, but he was lured away, and so died in "gaol" in Georgia.[20] Well before this young Bonnefoy had so gained the trust of the Cherokee he was able to escape on a cane raft down the Tennessee, but "Guillaume Potier, who was in our plot, having got drunk with the savages, was not in condition to go with us." [21]

The English heard through their traders of all such activities of the Chickasaw and Cherokee against the French. We can almost hear Governor Glen of South Carolina chortle as he wrote in 1754: "There never passes one year that the Cherokee do not take a boat or two belonging to the French on the Mississippi and destroy most of the crew; last year they killed eight people belonging to one Boat, and brought Two people alive into their Nation and this year they killed most of the Crew of another Vessel upon that River and brought in three Prisoners." [22]

The French and Indian War that was to decide ownership of the eastern half of the Mississippi Valley was in its bloody beginnings. The English soon realized that the "large extensive plains and savannahs swarming with deer and buffalo," would have to wait for colonization, and the westward thrust of settlement was completely stopped, even on the southern borders where the Cherokee, on whom Governor Glen had so depended, developed a large pro-French, anti-English faction.[23]

The English, not without much help from the farmers of the borders with their long "rifled-barreled firelocks," won the war and along with it

[20] Williams, *Dawn of Tenn.*, 101–113, gives various accounts of Priber, "a little ugly man." His death is from the relation of Ludovick Grant, a trader, *ibid.*, 105.

[21] Williams, *Travels*, 159.

[22] Williams, *Dawn of Tenn.*, 136.

[23] Judge Williams, *ibid.*, 184–271, gave in detail the story of Fort Loudoun and other aspects of the French and Indian War as it affected the Cherokee.

the Illinois. It is estimated that at this time the French population was around five thousand including five hundred Negro slaves.[24]

The first and largest British company to try merchandizing in the Illinois was that of Baynton, Wharton, and Morgan of Philadelphia. As early as 1766,[25] this firm began the great undertaking of getting merchandise in wholesale lots from Philadelphia to Kaskaskia, transportation activities that set a pattern to be followed by American merchants who later sent goods to the settlements in Kentucky and Tennessee. The first stage of the two-months or more journey of three hundred miles from Philadelphia to Fort Pitt was by wagons carrying around 2,500 pounds each and drawn by four or five horses.

Water transportation began at Fort Pitt where boats were built, at first, for lack of a sawmill, of hewed timber. The ideal boat, though most undoubtedly varied somewhat, was forty-six feet long, five feet deep and twelve broad, and with "not less than 22 men to row, two of whom should be good hunters. A Keg of salt should be put on board to cure their Meat when they come into the Buffaloe country as game is very scarce on the Mississippi. The Barrels they may have had with Beef or Flour in at leaving Fort Pitt may serve to pack it in. But I must not forget to observe that the Boats should absolutely be built of Seasoned Stuff with Square Stern & no lap or Clinch work." [26]

Five convoys of such boats made the thirteen hundred mile trip from Fort Pitt to Kaskaskia in 1766.[27] In addition to the boatmen, hunters, provisions, and kegs of salt, these carried almost every article known to the Indian or civilized white man of the day. There were kettles, milk and pudding pans, whipsaws, shoes and stockings, oakum for packing the seams of boats, tinware packed in coffee, and Castile soap. There were all forms of clothing from shoe buckles and shirt buttons to felt or castor hats, and thread hose, with a wide variety of materials—cambric, calico, or chintz.

[24] Monette, *Mississippi*, I, 410–411. In addition to the unpublished material of Thomas Hutchins and his "1778 Map" there was in connection with the map a 67-page booklet, *A topographical description of Virginia, Pennsylvania, Maryland and North Carolina*, London, 1778. This work (cited hereafter as Hutchins, *Description*) gives most space to the western portions of these colonies, St. Louis, etc.

[25] Mereness, *Travels*, 464–489, "Journal of Captain Harry Gordon, 1766." This work, beginning with embarkation at Pittsburgh, June 18, 1766, refers, 468, to George Morgan and his boats with the party, and also *ibid.*, to the company's boats that had already gone down in April.

[26] I, XVI, 140–141, Morgan to Baynton and Wharton, Dec. 16, 1767. See also Morgan to Baynton, Oct. 30, 1768, 436.

[27] Hanna, *Wilderness Trail*, II, 38, gives the names of the leaders of each convoy, for they did not travel in a body.

One could buy at the store stocked by the boats English cheese, Jesuit bark (quinine), a jew's-harp, or a black Barcelona hat. Playing cards, a garden spade and an ax, a handsaw or a mill saw, saltpeter, nails and ironmongery, mustard to go with one's bear meat, knives and forks, scythes and sickles, steel spurs, writing paper, or a tablecloth—all were to be had from Baynton, Wharton, and Morgan.[28] If one cared for neither of the two kinds of tea offered or coffee or chocolate there were eight thousand gallons of stronger potables from which to choose including Lisbon wines and Madeira, Jamaican and West Indian rum, though most of the wine reached the Illinois by way of New Orleans.

There had been since the days of Martin Chartier and even earlier, manufactured goods in the Illinois. At first chiefly articles for the Indian trade, but later the wealthier of the French settlers bought all manner of things from silk hose to musical instruments. There was thus nothing new about such a stock of goods, but as the goods were in quantity and easily accessible by water to the hunter and later the settler on the Cumberland, it did mean that nettle-bark petticoats or moss instead of stockings under the Indian shoes was a matter of the pocketbook and not of geography. The lower Ohio and often the Cumberland also knew the wandering French trader-hunter, and hunters did business with them.[29]

The new thing was the appearance in the west of large numbers of men, with a few women,[30] from the eastern colonies—boatmen, soldiers, hunters, traders, and just plain adventurers hired out as boatmen—who came out to the Illinois, going home sometimes back up the rivers, but often by way of the Mississippi and sailing vessels. It was a good opportunity to see the world, at least that part of it that could be seen from the Ohio and the Mississippi. The King's Proclamation of 1763 had forbidden settlement west of the Appalachians except at Natchez, but travelers could at least look. The first permanent settlement in Kentucky, Harrodsburg, was made by a Pennsylvanian, James Harrod, who went first to the Illinois.[31] Another Kentucky explorer who made at least one trip to the

[28] I, XVI, 293, 359–361, 391–405; see also sale by Bernard and Gratz, another English firm, *ibid.*, 642–645.

[29] Haywood, *C & P*, 80–81.

[30] English wives were rather rare, but, I, XVI, 447, Morgan to Baynton, Oct. 30, 1768, "Mrs. Murrey and her children came also at the same time" (in the boat of a Mr. Elliot); and Butricke to Barnsley, Oct. 30, 1768, *ibid.*, 449, in writing of a plague that struck Fort Chartres, "Carried out in a Cart four or five a day, at one time, men and their wives have been carried to their graves in the same Cart, and the poor Little Enfant Orphans following. . . ."

[31] Haywood, *C & P*, 75.

Illinois was John Findley, sailing down the Ohio from Fort Pitt March 8, 1766, as Captain of the *Otter*, and a speedy craft she must have been for she reached Fort Chartres, just above the Kaskaskia River, the sixth of April.[32]

Many came and went and wandered, but others of the British stayed in the Illinois for years. Among these was George Morgan, a young Welshman, junior member of the firm mentioned, for he had married the boss's daughter. He left his wife in Philadelphia when he took charge of his firm's branch at Kaskaskia, and from the long and rather homesick letters to her and his friends and business connections we learn much of life in the west. More than a year after his coming, he wrote of his arrangement with a tenant who was "to draw one half the Profits after fencing in One hundred Acres, building the house, Stables, Barn, Cow Houses, etc. which will make my place very valuable without any expense to me."

He wrote of his "Pidgeon House . . . in the Shape of Parson Smith's Folly & Full as large," that held two hundred couples so that soon he would have squabs. He had thirty-one baby chicks from three hens and eleven more hens setting, each on thirteen eggs, and he thus hoped to have fresh meat during the summer, to eat with the peas and beans from his garden. His smokehouse was bulging with "sufficient bacon" to last as long as he stayed, but the bacon like twenty hams was of the bear and not the hog; he also had one hundred venison hams and two hundred buffalo tongues plus twenty pieces of "excellent beef"—buffalo.

He missed the more civilized fare of home and wrote of the six milch cows and twenty sows he had bought: "and was it possible to get a good woman, I would pay for the Place in Butter only in less than twelve months —for the French seldom or never make any.—Although all of them are fond of it & would give a great price for it." [33]

Morgan's firm did not prosper as expected. The French, not caring for English rule, had begun to move into French territory even before the coming of the English, so there were few white customers for goods. Competition grew keener, such as that from Barnard and Gratz,[34] another Philadelphia firm that set up business in 1768.

One of the worst problems was that of not having and not being able to get the goods needed most—bread and meat for the British soldiers sta-

[32] FQ, I, Lucien Beckner, "John Findley, First Pathfinder of Kentucky," 118–119. The name of John Findley is spelled sometimes with a *d* and sometimes without; Hanna used both spellings.

[33] I, XVI, 481–482, Morgan to his wife, undated, but judging from context, autumn, 1768.

[34] I, XVI, 387. Barnard and Gratz to Mr. William Murray, Aug. 31, 1768.

tioned in the Illinois, and whom Morgan had expected to supply. He complained of the high price of flour in a country whose chief export was wheat.[35]

Meat from domesticated animals was so scarce and expensive Morgan had to do as did the French, depend upon wild meat, particularly the buffalo, plentiful on the Shawanoe as Morgan still called the Cumberland in spite of Dr. Walker's naming of it sixteen years before. The French after exhausting the supply of game along the lower Ohio had gone further and further up the Cumberland, a river particularly accessible to hunters from Fort Vincent on the Wabash. One of these hunters was to be an early settler in Nashville where he became a wealthy and respected citizen.

This was Jacques Thimote De Monbruen [36] whose great-grandfather Boucher had the distinction of being the first Canadian to be raised to the rank of nobility. De Monbruen, however, like many young Frenchmen of good family, preferred the exciting life of a hunter-trader to being a pillar of society in some small town or farm comumnity. He settled at St. Vincent while still a young man, and from there went on hunting and trading expeditions. Around 1760 when he was twenty-three years old he began to go up the Cumberland, but it was not until six years later that he found the region in which he eventually settled. He was going up the river in a "large boat with six or eight hands," when at the mouth of Lick Branch, just below where Nashville was to be, he saw muddy water and, experienced hunter that he was, knew that somewhere up the creek a herd of buffalo was crossing or stamping around a salt lick.

He found the herd at what was later called Sulphur Spring,[37] and at this

---

[35] I, XVI, 348, Morgan to Baynton and Wharton, July 11, 1768.

[36] The spelling of this name has numerous variations; official records, I, V, 355, 357, 359, etc., yield Thimote De Monbruen; see Williams, *Dawn of Tenn.*, 324-325, for life sketch.

[37] Sulphur Spring was on the Lick Branch, a small tributary on the southern side of the Cumberland, both just below and to the westward of where Nashville came to be; on this same little creek was the Big Buffalo Lick that in time came to be called French Lick, not to be confused with French Lick Station some distance away, and nearer the site of future Nashville; the lick was too low and swampy for building and was in the neighborhood of the site now occupied by the Nashville Ball Park. Thomas Hutchins, "A Sketch of the Shawanoe River," a small manuscript map in the Archives of the Historical Society of Pennsylvania, plus the Hutchins' "Notes" and his large "1778 Map" together give quite a good idea of the location of the Natchez Trace which he simply called "The Warrior's Path," as most of the well beaten Indian trails were denominated, and the Big Buffalo Lick, in time known as French Lick. Judging from all these the Indian Trail crossed the Cumberland at the mouth of the Lick Branch and followed it south for a short distance. See also in the Tennessee State Library and Archives, Nashville, the manuscript map "Nashville in 1804" made from the notes of Mrs. Temple Drake (cited hereafter as Mrs. Drake, "1804

one place was able to load his boat with hides and tallow, and so set out with "freight and boat for New Orleans." De Monbruen, though not a permanent dweller on the Cumberland until after 1788,[38] was for the next forty years closely identified with the region. Shortly after his first trip he built a hut that served as both a storehouse and hunters' station camp, and traded with most of the early settlers. He was described as a tall, "athletic, dark-skinned man, with a large head, broad shoulders and chest, small legs, a high, short foot, and an eagle eye," dressed for his first trip up the Cumberland in a blue cotton hunting shirt, deer hide leggings, a red waistcoat, once part of his uniform as a French soldier, and foxskin cap with a tail down the back.[39]

Morgan, however, hired neither De Monbruen nor any other Frenchman familiar with the Cumberland. He depended instead upon the men he had brought from Pennsylvania, many recruited in the backwoods around Carlisle,[40] where by this date most woodsmen were skilled in the use of the rifle. "In a conversation over a Bottle of Wine at Capt. Forbes (an English officer) I was much bantered about employing English hunters," Morgan wrote. "Who several insisted could neither Shoot nor hunt so well as the French or Indians. I was laughed at particularly by Col. Cole for saying I had some of the best Marksmen in the Illinois & he offered to Wager 100 pounds against any One of them whom I should choose or any five of them to shoot by turns 100 yds at a Bbl Head *without any kind of Rest whatever* —for every time They hit the Bbl he to pay me 100 pound every Time they miss'd I to pay him the like Sum."

It was Morgan's turn to laugh. "I told him he might choose the Worst Shot from amongst all the Hunters I had & on him I would Wager a Dollar each Shot for One hundred Shots Certain & as many more as he pleased. Dieverbaugh was pitched upon— Who to try his Powder set up the Head of a small Keg 100 Yds & struck it 10 times out of 11 shots as fast as he could load & fire. He then began at the Barrel & won the Whole of the One

Map"). This shows the Lick Branch and the Sulphur Spring; the actual lick, in time known as French Lick, was within sight of the Cumberland (Hutchins saw it from his boat), but not on it.

[38] De Monbruen was a traveling merchant and trapper; tradition relates that his wife was with him for much of the time, but as late as 1788, he was not yet living there, for in this year a business associate John Maxwell attempted to collect in his absence pay from the 92 men who owed him. See DC, I, 75–76.

[39] Judge Joseph Conn Guild, 1802–1883, *Old Times in Tennessee with historical, personal, and political scraps and sketches*, Nashville, 1878 (cited hereafter as Guild, *Old Times*), 311. Guild in his young manhood knew De Monbruen, but the story is traditional.

[40] I, XVI, 67, "Morgan's Journal," Sept. 30, 1767–Nov. 1, 1767.

hundred Dollars— Which before he begun I told him I would make him a present of it if he won them."

It's nice to know that Jacob Dieverbaugh, "a most excellent hunter, and a fellow whose word can be depended upon & excessively obliging," won a hundred dollars, Spanish milled, for the dollar we know today was not yet around. He was quite a man in that he was shortly after the shooting leaving the Illinois with a small boat and only three or four men for the long and lonely journey down the Mississippi, then the 1,100 mile pull up the Ohio to Fort Pitt, quite a trip in 1768.[41]

He was probably more remarkable in that he could shoot without a rest; it took a man to hold the short-butted, long-barreled, heavy—at least by today's standards—rifle steady long enough to get the fire from priming pan to barrel, and for the force of the exploding powder to rush through the long barrel. Hunters almost always shot from rests, though the gun when over a stump or a fallen tree was cushioned with moss so that the recoil might not wreck the aim; other times the rifle was rested against the side of a tree but always "as lightly as possible." [42]

We can be certain Dieverbaugh's gun was a rifle, for by this date they were so common Morgan stocked them in the store.[43] The manufacture of these early rifles was never standardized; an exact description is impossible. They were, no different from furniture, saddles, and most other manufactured goods of the day, made to order. Some liked them long, some short, and they thus ranged in length from fifty-one to seventy-seven inches with a consequent difference in weight. The weight also depended upon the gauge to some extent, and in general the rifles of 1760–70 were of larger gauge than those coming later, usually around .45 caliber, and hence using a pound of lead for each forty to forty-eight bullets.

The rifling varied less than other features and continued to be about a full turn for around forty-eight inches. We can be reasonably certain the barrel of Dieverbaugh's rifle was hexagonal, with her stock extending the full length, and in it the thimbles for holding the hickory ramrod. The stock could be of any fine-grained hardwood; Pennsylvania gunsmiths

[41] I, XVI, 349–350, Morgan to Baynton and Wharton, July 11, 1768. Morgan's brief remarks in his letter concerning the trip back to Fort Pitt to be made by Dieverbaugh, is only one of many such remarks in various sources, including the Draper Manuscripts, of trips to and from Fort Pitt before the settlement of Kentucky; taken together they indicate a good bit of travel and exploration with camping in Kentucky before Daniel Boone.

[42] Kercheval, *Virginia*, 285, quoting the Rev. Joseph Doddridge, "Notes on the settlement and Indian Wars of the western parts of Virginia and Pennsylvania" (cited hereafter as Doddridge, "Notes").

[43] I, XVI, 358, Morgan to Baynton and Wharton, July 20, 1768.

usually used rock maple, finished with soot and oil and rubbed to a high lustre. Different from later rifles, Dieverbaugh's was most probably plain with none of the elaborate inlays of silver, brass, or even gold Spanish coins so common after the Revolution. The patch or grease box would have been rather plain and of brass. There may have been on her raised cheek rest an eight-pointed, brass star, the most common ornament of the early rifles.

Dieverbaugh would have used patching, but whether of deerskin or linen we do not know. He would, in any case, have been a very busy man, shooting as "fast as he could load and fire." The American rifle with greased patching against the grooves and lands instead of pounded-in lead, and with a better grade of powder, did not have to be cleaned after every shot as had the early Jaguers, but a man out to make a showing of marksmanship might have done so. Finished with one shot, Dieverbaugh would have taken the ramrod with one hand while with the other, as one arm held the gun upright, he took from her patch box or his hunting bag a small swab, or worm, wrapped with unspun flax, commonly known as tow. He screwed the worm into the end of the ramrod, put the ramrod into the barrel, and then, holding it loosely so that the worm could turn with her rifling, he would have brought it up and down two or three times. The ramrod out, he blew down her muzzle to clear the small opening between the firing pan and barrel.[44]

He would then have taken his powder horn, pulled out the stopper with his teeth, while his left hand was bringing out the charger or device used for the measuring of a charge of powder. This was usually of whittled bone, but could be of wood, or merely the tip of a deer's antler. The powder, always expensive, was carefully measured; some hunters poured it directly into her muzzle; others used funnels; the funnel might be the end of a deer's horn with the tip cut off, or whittled of poplar or some soft wood.

Powder in, Dieverbaugh was ready for the most ticklish part of loading. He probably had his patching ready-greased and cut, but some hunters took a large piece of deerskin or linen, put a greased portion over her muzzle, and in this centered the bullet, pushed down a bit. A clean sweep of a sharp

[44] The rifle is better known than any other aspect of pioneer life; in addition to the goodly amount of printed material concerning it, many early ones can be seen in various museums of Americana: The Tennessee State Museum, Nashville, has some excellent examples, as has the Renfro Valley Museum of Mr. John Blair at Renfro Valley, Kentucky, and also the Mountain Life Museum of the Levi Jackson Wilderness Road State Park, London, Ky. There are, too, a few old-timers left, including one of my uncles, who as boys used the old rifles, though most by that date had had the original flintlocks changed to caplocks.

knife cut off the patching even with the end of her muzzle, and the ball was then forced down against the powder with the ramrod. Most, however, in later years used patching already cut and greased. Regardless of when or where it was cut, the patching must be uniform with the ball centered squarely in the middle and the patch exactly in the middle of her muzzle, else she would shoot wild.

Bullet and patching thrust down against the powder, Dieverbaugh must next look at the firing pan. If a grain or two of powder had come through, all was well; if not he had to take a little tool known as the priming wire or frizzen pin and prick her touchhole leading from firing pan to the barrel where the powder was. The frizzen pin was sometimes carried in the shot bag, often stuck in the hat brim, and other times in a place made especially for it in the cheek rest; usually it was of metal but could be a quill. Certain her touchhole was open, Dieverbaugh would then with his thumb and finger have taken a pinch of fine priming powder from a small horn kept in the hunting bag; when he had sprinkled this on the pan, closed it, he was ready to fire.[45] The double or sett-triggered rifle by which a man could adjust the pull of the trigger came later. The method of firing had been in use for many years and was not peculiar to the rifle; at the pulling of the trigger the flint struck the frizzen steel and made a spark, igniting the powder in the firing pan, that in turn exploded the powder in the barrel. Dieverbaugh would have had to change flints one or more times during his shooting for a flint was seldom good for more than fifty shots, but was cheap, costing around two cents.[46]

Dieverbaugh may have been one of the better marksmen, but there was in the Illinois, at least in 1767, a better one than he. This was Michael Stoner, later famous as a scout with Boone and defender of Boonesboro. He was a large man, speaking with a strong German accent, an indifferent hand at target practice, but against Indians or game held to be the best shot in Kentucky.[47] Hunters come overland from Virginia in 1767, met him and James Harrod,[48] both from Pennsylvania, near the mouth of Stone's River, a southern tributary of the Cumberland.

[45] Mr. John C. Burton, Monticello, Ky., was kind enough to show me not only his outstanding collection of early rifles, but also what is more rare, his very large collection of hunting bags, many with powder funnels, chargers, and turkey calls of yellowed bone.

[46] I, XVI, 392, 333, 398, Accounts of Baynton, Wharton, and Morgan, 1768. The price of flints varied with size, demand, quality, and distance from the coast, as they were usually imported from England, though fine priming powder came most often from France.

[47] W, 12CC, 43.

[48] Haywood, *C & P*, 75.

Famous for a different reason was another good marksman, and one of Morgan's hunters, though not around to see Dieverbaugh win one hundred dollars. This was Simon Girty who later sided with the Indians and stood with them in the woods of Ohio and watched Crawford as he slowly burned to death.[49] He was then in 1768 still only a lad "Who was particularly attached" to Morgan, at that time on the Shawanoe with a party of hunters.[50]

Morgan's men hunted and wandered over much of Tennessee and Kentucky in the region of Cumberland and Green rivers, but there is no record any attempted to settle, for there is no indication either Harrod or Stoner worked for Morgan. The only man from the eastern colonies who actually tried to settle on the Cumberland at this time is known only by the name of Jones. He, too, had come from Pennsylvania to the Illinois, and from there he went, in 1769, to Jones Bend,[51] in what is now Sumner County a few miles upriver from Nashville. Here, he made a clearing, planted corn, and lived until early in 1770 when he was scared away by Indian sign, but instead of going back to the Illinois he went up the Cumberland, then across country to East Tennessee where he, along with Virginia hunters by then coming to the region, spread the word of fine land on the Cumberland.[52]

Most of the English who came to the Cumberland in Middle Tennessee at this time were employees [53] of Morgan, earning about six pounds a year with food and a shelter of sorts for their work as hunters and boatmen.[54] Not a little of their time was spent as "Batteau Men" for after the long, but

[49] Kercheval, *Virginia*, Doddridge, "Notes," 219-226, gives an account of Col. Crawford's death.
[50] I, XVI, 354, Morgan to Baynton and Wharton, July 20, 1768.
[51] I am indebted to the Technical Liaison Branch, Nashville District, Corps of Engineers, U.S. Army, for a photostatic copy of "Map of the Cumberland River from the Falls to Nashville," taken from the Matthew Rheas Map of 1834. This work with bends and shoals of the river named is most helpful in understanding locations before there were political features, as all the larger tributaries, many of the smaller ones, bends, shoals, and licks, were named before settlement and continued to be referred to for many years.
[52] W, 6XX (50), 5, contains a brief account of Jones, first name not known.
[53] I, XVI, 354, Morgan to Baynton and Wharton, July 20, 1768, "There was a generous Strife between the Hunters, who should do most for me—& pleased themselves very greatly with reckoning up every Night how much money We should make by their Industry," would indicate that these, different from such Long Hunters as Michael Stoner, got only wages or a percentage.
[54] I, XVI, 330, Morgan to Baynton and Wharton, June 20, 1768. This figure, offered by Col. Cole for a man known for his "honesty and Sobriety," is very low compared to what Byrd had paid his hunters and chain carriers, forty years before—277 pounds for 2,058 man days—but still much higher than the earnings of an indentured servant who, even after the Revolution, often worked five years to pay passage money, never more than five or six pounds.

usually swift, trip down the Ohio and into the Mississippi, they had to put in at least ten days hard rowing to get a cargo up the Mississippi to Fort Chartres.[55] They then in order to hunt must go down again to the Ohio, up and into some tributary until they found game.

The herb-eating buffalo, like elk and deer, grew thin in winter when there was little to eat but cane and fern, in early spring the bulls began to fatten and by midsummer a good bull would yield as much as seventy-five pounds of tallow,[56] an important food in the butterless, and often lardless, Illinois and New Orleans. The tallow, unlike the meat, would keep in hot weather without salt, and so along with the hides was taken during the summer. Rendered in large kettles, it was then poured into white oak barrels to await shipment.

Buck running time for the buffalo was in August and September, and the bulls got so thin they were of little use for anything save hides, tongues, humps, and marrow bones, a food prized as much by the Long Hunter as by Samuel Pepys.[57] The cows after a gestation period of nine and a half months gave birth in May or early June, and, thin all summer from suckling their calves, picked up weight after being bred, and by mid-autumn would yield around sixty pounds of tallow each. The buffalo were long-lived animals with many of the cows bearing young ones yearly for thirty years, and there would thus have been in any herd many old animals fit for nothing but hides and tallow. They were, however, killed indiscriminately: a group of English hunters from August to the latter end of September in 1767 killed on the Cumberland "upwards of 700 Buffaloe & rendered their tallow." There were at the same time "twenty large Perrigoues up from New Orleans, killing buffaloe chiefly for tallow."

It was not until November when the buffalo were fat again that the hunters could begin to kill for meat; and if all the boats were the size of that commanded by Mr. Thompson, an employee of Morgan, who hunted in the winter of 1767, they could have carried away a vast quantity of meat. He took back up the river 18,000 pounds of buffalo beef, sixty venison

[55] I, XVI, 410-411, Butricke to Barnsley, Sept. 15, 1768. Fort Chartres where the soldiers were stationed was around 18 miles upriver from Kaskaskia.

[56] I, XVI, 223, Morgan to Baynton and Wharton, April 5, 1768.

[57] The Diary of Samuel Pepys, Jan. 26, 1660, "—to my Lord's lodgings where my wife had got ready a very fine dinner—viz. a dish of marrow bones; a leg of mutton; a loin of veal; a dish of fowl, three pullets, and two dozen of larks all in a dish; a great tart, a neat's tongue, a dish of anchovies, a dish of prawns and cheese." Marrow bones were of course a dish much older than Pepys or Mother Goose—still, he mentioned them first.

hams, fifty-five buffalo tongues, and a great weight of tallow, but less than Morgan needed,[58] for he hoped to get 20,000 pounds from one boat crew in the summer of 1768.[59]

Morgan liked to brag of the fine quality of his buffalo beef, lightly salted with a bushel and a peck per thousand pounds.[60] He at first had the salt brought all the way from Philadelphia, declaring that salt from the Salines in the Illinois was no good for the keeping of beef. The quality of the beef depended also upon the cooper's ability to make a good tight barrel; but Morgan, at first worried that salt buffalo would not keep a year, was able to write in June of 1768: "All ours is now as good as the day it was killed, & will keep so for seven years with proper attendance with the same kind of Coarse Salt & the same Cooper we now have." [61]

Morgan in his enthusiasm for buffalo beef and buffalo hunters, planned to send in the summer of 1768 around sixty men in four boats. At least two of these were sent and went three hundred miles up the Cumberland or close to present-day Carthage at the mouth of the Caney Fork.[62] The letter indicates one boat may have gone even further, and into what is now Cumberland County, Kentucky. As late as 1779 the stretch of river between Obey's and the Big South Fork had plenty of buffalo.[63] There were, too, all along the Cumberland, and especially above Clarksville, many salt licks within sight of the river,[64] as well as canebrakes to make for good buffalo country, and upriver the boats save for food and hunting equipment were

---

[58] I, XVI, 223-224, Morgan to Baynton and Wharton, June 20, 1768, gives the facts and figures relative to buffalo hunting. New Orleans was at this time a very small place, and undoubtedly most buffalo and bear products—oil and meat—shipped there were destined, as was much produce of later days, for the West Indies to be used as food for the slaves.

[59] I, XVI, 354.

[60] I, XVI, 361.

[61] I, XVI, 142-143, 328.

[62] I, XVI, 223-224, and 327, "Mr. Hollingshead left this the 6th Instant [June] a second Hunting Boat & intends to join the first three hundred miles up the Shawna."

[63] Daniel Smith, encamped 4 miles below the mouth of Fishing Creek in January, 1780, managed in spite of bitter weather to kill plenty of buffalo—six in one day; see THM, I, Smith, "Journal," 58-60.

[64] Thomas Hutchins, "Beginning at the Shawanoe River The 16th August, 1769 and Proceeded down the River," a photostatic copy furnished by the Pennsylvania Historical Society, owner of the unpublished manuscript, shows one of the best known of the big licks, within sight of the Cumberland across from the Blue Spring. See also in the Clements Library, James Russell, "Map of the State of Kentucky and Adjoining Territories," London, 1794. Cited hereafter as Russell, "1794 Map," this shows a Big Salt Lick at the mouth of the Caney Fork; it is possible Mr. Russell confused the location with Big Lick on the Cumberland, across from the mouth of Flinn's Creek, site of future Fort Blount, known as Big Lick Garrison as late as 1795; see Smith, *Description*, 14. All such licks were frequented by herds of buffalo.

empty as both salt and barrels remained at Kaskaskia where Morgan's cooper worked.[65]

Joseph Hollingshead, a Philadelphian, was in charge of operations. Buffalo hunting for him and his men, armed with rifles, was less dangerous than it had been in Father Marquette's day, but even so it was still a hard, bloody, and often dangerous job. The size alone of the great beasts made skinning difficult, and the rendering of the tallow in the heat of August and September, beset by chiggers, seed ticks, and gnats, was a hot and itchy job. There were skins to scrape and dry, and all the work of any hunting camp—cooking, cleaning, mending of both clothing and guns, bullets to run, skinning knife, pocketknife and hatchet, the three cutting tools most hunters had,[66] to be kept sharp and with proper handles. These hunters, like those who came overland, would have made moccasins of buffalo hide, dressed with the hair on, wearing the more easily torn deerskin only around camp. Since buffalo shoes were improved by freezing, they were on cold nights put well away from the camp fire.[67]

In the first cold weather of fall the hunter had to turn butcher and cut up and clean the carcass after first sticking the animal in the throat so that it might bleed properly. This was at times a ticklish business; a buffalo hunter in Kentucky a few years later, remembering: "My brother shot a buffalo; it laid down, and he went up towards it to stick it with his long knife. Just as he got to it, the buffalo suddenly sprang up and made after him. He dodged behind a saplin, and there they kept till he had hacked the buffalo's eyes out. It then went and lay down, but would still run after them if they went to go up to it. Buffalo would run from the smell as quick as the sight."

Even the sight of the "huge, hairy, and hideous animals," charging at forty miles an hour, was enough to startle the more timid of the hunters, for the buffalo, different from most other game, was dangerous. "I hit a buffalo in the forehead and the bullet fell off flattened it did. . . . The buffalo had been wounded several times, and lay in a creek. They stoned it till it set after them. They are very quick in their motion and it bounced up and was after Harper and Terry. I shot a buffalo once, got the bullet, and then shot a deer after chewing the bullet round.

[65] I, XVI, 142, Morgan to Baynton and Wharton, Dec. 16, 1767.
[66] Kercheval, *Virginia*, Doddridge, "Notes," 256.
[67] W, 30S, 261. This is found in a long account by Hugh F. Bell, Indian scout and hunter on the Cumberland in the late '80's; he declared, *ibid.*, 260, buffalo could in charging overtake a man on horseback; there were even at this late date a few in the Barrens where "the grass grew as high as a man's head."

"Bill Rayburn was once gored with a buffalo, in the side, about six inches in length, before he got up a honey locust tree where he got a great many thorns—my wife she picked a great many thorns out of him. Kill the leader if you could find it out, and you might kill three or four then. I never could come nigh enough to one to throw at it, without it was so poor it couldn't get out of the way." [68]

Not only could they run at top speed, following by scent instead of sight, but their complete unpredictability added still more to the sport. Times they "would rush forward with a violence and rage that upturned the very roots of the small trees which stood in their path, knowing as it were no bounds to their courage; while, under other circumstances, they were easily frightened." Whole herds could be stampeded over cliffs by the sudden appearance of a few shouting men, or "while he shot one of the cows, I captured the calf, haltered it, and at first it was much disposed to butt at us, but it soon became very docile and followed us all the day like a dog, and at night lay down by our horse." [69] "Old man Strode had one he had got in that way; followed him clear home; kept it till it was three or four years old." [70]

Some of Morgan's hunters may have had pet buffalo calves like that of old man Strode who lived about ten years later in Kentucky. We do not know the fun they had, or the danger. There were many times when, hard pressed by a charging buffalo, the hunter fought as he fought when surprised by Indians, with knife, tomahawk, or gun, loaded as he ran; grab the powder horn, dump in powder, unmeasured, bullets, two or three or even six patchless down the muzzle, the rest of the handful slammed into his mouth [71] to be kept for quicker loading in case he lived to shoot again, prime her heavy and fire away.

In July of 1768 a band of hunters on the Cumberland fought Indians instead of buffalo. The Cumberland was still a no man's land. Simon Girty hurried back to the Illinois from the "Shawana River & informed me that about 30 Indians had attacked our Boat & that nobody had made their escape but himself that he knew of—they had agreed to remove about 15 or 20 miles higher up the River that very Day." [72]

The seven scalps of Morgan's hunters and two others in time reached

[68] FQ, II, 104, Clinkenbeard "Interview."

[69] Gray, *Bishop*, 95, 106. Bishop hunted buffalo in the Illinois; by the time he reached Middle Tennessee in 1791 they were gone.

[70] FQ, II, 108, Clinkenbeard "Interview."

[71] W, 30S, 255, "two or three bullets in his mouth in readiness," one of several such references.

[72] I, XVI, 354, Morgan to Baynton and Wharton, July 20, 1768.

Post St. Vincent up the Wabash, but the tribes of Indians there were not the only ones determined to keep white hunters off the Cumberland. The Chickasaw had long claimed it from around Stone's River to the mouth, while the Cherokee continued their quarrel with the white hunters; buffalo they didn't care for, but they did object to the taking of beaver and deer.[73] It was only by exchanging peltry they could get more guns and ammunition to kill more deer and beaver, with enough left over to buy rum and a few trinkets.

Treaties were made in that year, 1768, with both the Cherokee and the Iroquois concerning the land between the Tennessee and the Ohio, but these did not automatically make things any easier or safer for Morgan's buffalo hunters. One thing that made hunting hard was the rapid dwindling of the herds, caused almost entirely by the French, or so Morgan felt. As early as December of 1767 he wrote from Kaskaskia: "They have so thinned the Buffaloe . . . that you will not now see the $\frac{1}{20}$ part of the Qty as formerly, & unless some method be taken to put a Stop to this Practice it will in a short Time be a difficult Matter to supply even Fort Chartres with Meat from thence." [74]

Morgan also accused the French, as well as the Spaniards, of instigating Indian attacks on English hunters, and trading without permits on English territory. British officials were at last aroused in the fall of 1768 to an attempt at protecting river traffic and hunters in the newly won territory by the fitting up of a boat "as a Guard for the Ohio River and to Convey a Detachment of the Regiment to Post Vincent." Colonel Wilkins bought one of Morgan's boats for two hundred dollars, put her in charge of Lieutenant Thomas Hutchins, who at once began buying the materials needed to get her in shape to carry soldiers and supplies.[75]

Lieutenant Hutchins had first visited the Ohio region in 1764, and two years later he, in company with George Morgan, Captain Harry Gordon, Chief Engineer of the Western Department of North America, and George Croghan, Pennsylvania trader and deputy Indian agent, had with a party of boatmen started down the Ohio June 18th. They stopped a time at the Falls of the Ohio and Hutchins charted the rapids, for though he did not yet

[73] I, XVI, 417, Gage to Johnson, Oct. 10, 1768, told of how the Cherokee had made themselves understood through their interpreter, "Mr. Watts," that they were annoyed by the English who instead of hunting only buffalo, had been taking bear, deer, and beaver. This probably explains why they sometimes attacked men west of the Ohio as *ibid.*, 362, "four French Men had a very narrow Escape from a Party of Cherokees about twenty Leagues from this Place" (Kaskaskia).

[74] I, XVI, 132.

[75] I, XVI, 440–441, Morgan to Baynton and Wharton, Oct. 30, 1768.

have the title of Geographer-General, he was already making maps and charting rivers. On this trip they reached Fort Chartres, August 20, stayed but a short time and went home by way of New Orleans.[76]

Hutchins on his next trip to the Illinois spent much time in Morgan's household, eating his rice pudding and drinking his wine.[77] He charted the Kaskaskia River in the fall of 1768, and was soon busied with the matter of readying the patrol boat. Caulking her required fifty pounds of oakum, for she was "a large boat with 24 oars, to carry 35 men with six months provisions &c and a Brass six pounder Mounted on her forecastle. Her Gunwales are raised so high that the men are not to be seen Rowing. This Boat is to be Commanded by a Commissioned Officer, and is also to Cruise on the Wabash and Ohio Rivers, to intercept the French and Spanish traders from New Orleans, Carrying on an Illicit trade with our Indians at O Post and on the Rivers. It is likewise to prevent them from killing Buffalo. . . ."[78]

Seldom has any crew had such a multiplicity of duties. In addition to acting as immigration officers and game wardens, a part of the crew including the Commander, charted much of Green River, then called the Buffalo, and the Cumberland from the mouth to several miles above Nashville. The compass reading and note taking were done by Hutchins, and on the Cumberland the work was done in two sections; one set of notes, undated, reads, "The Course of the Shawanoe upwards." He mentions Hollingshead,[79] leader of Morgan's hunters, as being with him for a part of this trip that ended a short distance above what is now Nashville or near the mouth of Stone's River. The second set is dated August 16, 1769, and describes the courses of the Shawanoe downward, beginning below what would seem to be the mouth of Obey's but continuing only for around forty miles. He also charted and explored the Wabash and the Tennessee still known as the Cheraqui.[80]

Judge Williams, historian of Tennessee, thought that with Lieutenant Hutchins on the Cumberland was John Connolly, mentioned by George Washington writing in 1770: "Dr. Connolly, nephew of Col. Croghan,

[76] Mereness, *Travels*, "Journal of Captain Harry Gordon," 464–489.
[77] I, XVI, 481, Morgan to his wife, fall of 1768. Hutchins on this trip reached Kaskaskia Aug. 31, 1768, *ibid.*, 410–411, Butricke to Barnsley, Sept. 15, 1768, a letter that also contains a description of the boat.
[78] I, XVI, 498, Butricke to Barnsley, Feb. 12, 1769.
[79] Hutchins, "Notes," 3 (my own numbering): "This course brings me to the end of Mr. Hollingshead's Protection."
[80] The notes Hutchins made of the courses of the Tennessee, Cheraqui, were seen in photostatic copy from the Pennsylvania Historical Society, and remain unpublished.

who has traveled a good deal over this western country, both by land and water, confirms Nicholson's account of good land on the Shawnee River, which he has been up near four hundred miles. ". . . The Climate is fine; the soil remarkably good; the lands well watered with good streams and level enough for any kind of cultivation." [81]

Washington's enthusiastic description could be taken as a generalization of the comments Lieutenant Hutchins wrote on his map of the new country, and the notes he made as he listed the poles and courses of its rivers. Different from most of the English, he praised the Illinois Country,[82] speaking of the good swine and black cattle, and a fine breed of Spanish-bred horses the farmers had got from the Indians. He visited the saltworks at the Salines near St. Genevieve, and described St. Louis as a town of around eight hundred people, many of whom had liberal educations and were polite and helpful.

He praised even more highly the land along Green and Cumberland rivers, "of luxuriant quality," he wrote, noting the big timber, salt licks, springs, and canebrakes. He showed himself, either through first-hand experience or from others, remarkably familiar with most of Kentucky and Tennessee. He described the Cuttawa or Kentucky River as being passable to the Gap where the War Path went through the Ouasiato Mountains,[83] or today's Kentucky hills. These he described as fifty or sixty miles wide and abounding in coal, lime, and freestone, their summits generally covered with good soil and a variety of timber, with the "low or interval" land rich and "remarkably well watered."

He described what we now know as Green River as navigable for barges thirty feet long, five broad, and three deep, carrying about seven tons. This apparently a designation of the boat he had bought from Morgan.

Much of the Hutchins material, including his notes on the Cumberland and Tennessee rivers, was never published. His large map with a general description of the region was published in 1778, but this in London during the Revolution, so that none of his information was available to first settlers. It would have saved many a heartbreak [84] and a deal of trouble.

[81] Williams, *Travels,* 307.
[82] Hutchins, *Description.*
[83] Hutchins, "1778 Map," has numerous comments scattered over it concerning the nature of the soil; the original purpose as designated on the face of the map was to chart and describe "All the country comprehended" both in the grant "by the Six Nations . . . at Fort Stanwix," and that newly won from the French.
[84] Hutchins, "1778 Map," was the first to show the English that all the Cumberland was not in land claimed by Virginia; several men, including George Rogers Clark,

The Cumberland and the fine land along it was by 1769 known to many both east and west, the river charted and the country mapped, yet permanent settlement was for the middle river ten years away. There were a few English settlers in the Illinois, but the most attractive settlement, and it had to be for it was the only one permitted by the King's Proclamation between the Appalachians and the Mississippi, was that of Natchez. As early as 1765 a few families from North Carolina and Virginia embarked on the Holston, not many miles from Stalnaker's cabin, and from there went on the long and dangerous voyage down the Holston, the Tennessee, the Ohio, and the Mississippi to Natchez. They continued to come from Georgia, and the Carolinas, sometimes, it is said, by way of the Cumberland.[85] England didn't mind; she needed settlers on her borders, and at Natchez Spain was more in evidence than England.

I, VIII, 303–304, bought land warrants given soldiers of the French and Indian War that stipulated no location save Virginia; land was surveyed in the neighborhood of present-day Nashville thinking it was Virginia; Clark thus lost his land.

[85] Monette, *Mississippi*, I, 405–408. Those who came by way of the Cumberland would have taken the Great Lakes Trail overland either to the crossing at Smith Shoals, just above present-day Burnside, or followed some prong of the trail to the Big South Fork; there was below Smith Shoals nothing to impede navigation in high water.

CHAPTER VII

THE SHIRTTAIL MEN

I'm far from home, far from the wife,
    Which in my bosom lay,
Far from my children, dead, which used
    Around me for to play.

This doleful circumstance cannot
    My happiness prevent
While peace of conscience I enjoy,
    Great comfort and content.

THIS SONG, usually referred to as the first poem written in Tennessee, and sung we can imagine to the tune of some hymn of Isaac Watts,[1] must have caused the deer to lift their heads in wonder and then dart away, for it is doubtful if deer in what is now Sumner County,[2] Tennessee, had heard by 1766 a singing Pennsylvanian. The composer and singer was James Smith, who late in the fall of the year before had left his home on the Pennsylvania frontier; the following June had found him in the Holston Country of Virginia where settlement was thickening in the general vicinity of Samuel Stalnaker's place.

    There, Smith had in company with Joshua Horton, William Baker,

---

[1] Isaac Watts (1674–1748) was one of the more prolific English writers of poems, hymns, Psalms arranged for singing, theological tracts, as well as poems and songs for children. His work is well represented in the inventories of the first Cumberland settlers, and extracts appeared in their textbooks, particularly in those of Dilworth, and his hymns, like those of Wesley, are still widely used.

[2] Smith never in his narrative gave an exact location, but all historians place his camp in what is now Sumner County, Tenn. See Perkins, *West*, 133–134.

Uriah Stone, for whom Stone's River was named, and another James Smith from near Carlisle in Pennsylvania, gone west. Different from Dr. Walker, Smith's group had not come through Cumberland Gap, but across Cumberland Plateau, and into Middle Tennessee. They then had "explored Cumberland and Tennessee Rivers from Stone's River down to the Ohio." [3]

Here, the party, still eager for discovery, decided to go on to the Illinois. James Smith, the ballad maker, refused, and for a reason seldom given by any of the hunters and explorers of that day: "As I had already been longer from home than what I expected, I thought my wife would be distressed, and think I was killed by the Indians." He had had so much trouble in getting his horse through the mountains he had sent him with the other men into the Illinois; they in turn gave him most of their ammunition, "about half a pound of powder and an equivalent amount of lead." [4] Joshua Horton also loaned him Jamie, an eighteen-year-old mulatto slave he had brought along.

The two men then started east on foot, but, "About eight days after I left my company at the mouth of Tennessee, on my journey eastward, I got a cane stab in my foot, which occasioned my leg to swell, and I suffered much pain. I was now in a doleful situation—far from any of the human species, excepting black Jamie, or the savages, and I knew not when I might meet with them. . . . All the surgical instruments I had was a knife, a mockason awl, and a bullit molds. . . . I struck the awl in the skin, and with the knife I cut the flesh away from around the cane and then I commanded the mulatto fellow to catch it with the bullit molds, and pull it out, which he did. When I saw it, it seemed a shocking thing to be in any person's foot; it will therefore be supposed that I was very glad to have it out.

"The black fellow attended upon me and obeyed my directions faithfully. I ordered him to search for Indian medicine, and told him to get me a quantity of bark from the root of a lynn tree, which I made him beat on a stone with a tomahawk, and boil it in a kettle, and with the ooze I

[3] John M'Clung, *Sketches of Western Adventure*, Maysville, 1832 (cited hereafter as M'Clung, *Sketches*), contains Smith's narrative, 14–47, of Indian captivity. Historians of Braddock's defeat usually mention him as he heard the burnings of various prisoners.

[4] This would have been about a pound of lead. Baynton, Wharton, and Morgan in trading with Indians, I, XVI, 391–405, Accounts of the firm, always sold half as much powder as ball or lead, though the more skillful hunters could get by with a smaller proportion of powder. This is a good example of the value of the American rifle as contrasted to the smooth-bore guns and older rifles, for Smith's powder, depending on the gauge of his rifle, was good for anywhere from forty to sixty shots.

bathed my foot and leg; what remained when I had finished bathing, I boiled to a jelly, and made poultices thereof. As I had no rags, I made use of the green moss that grows upon logs, and wrapped it round with elm bark; by this means (simple as it may seem) the swelling and inflamation abated.[5] As stormy weather appeared, I ordered Jamie to make us a shelter, which he did by erecting forks and poles, and covering them over with cane tops like a fodder house. It was about one hundred yards from a large buffalo road. As we were almost out of Provision, I commanded Jamie to take my gun, and I went along as well as I could, concealed myself near the road, and killed a buffalo. When this was done, we jirked (dried on a low scaffold over a slow fire) [6] the lean and fried the tallow out of the fat meat, which we kept to stew with our jerk as we needed it."

Thus, did the two men, equipped with only what they could carry on foot, live alone in the woods for several months. Fear of Indians made them move their camp away from the buffalo road, but Smith was not too afraid to make a noise by shooting, for in addition to the buffalo, he killed an elk, at least one bear, a deer, and a coon, or so his description of Jamie's clothing would indicate.

Meat was of course not their only fare; in late July there would have been a few late blackberries in the shadier places along the creek banks, and before civilization was reached in October, grapes, pawpaws, and after the first light frosts persimmons, beechnuts, chestnuts, and chinkapins. Jamie doubtless knew how to make a fish basket with split cane stalks, grapevines, or white oak splits, for a tomahawk and a knife in the hands of the wise brought from the woods many tools and utensils.

James Smith's story of how he got food, clothing, shelter, and medicine from the woods sounds simple, but he had spent most of his twenty-nine years in learning the arts and skills that served now to keep him alive and sane through the long weeks of his convalescence. Born in 1737 on the frontiers of Pennsylvania, Smith, early, learned the ways of Indians, and was at the time of Braddock's defeat already a captive at Fort Duquesne. There, he and another captive, Arthur Campbell, later a great Indian fighter in east Tennessee and still later a settler on the upper Cumberland, studied Smith's Bible together and discussed it. Bible studies were soon

---

[5] Both Beverly and Lawson as well as Adair praised the Indian's skill with a green wound or skin infection; their numerous poultices were at least sterile for they boiled most of their remedies. See Lawson, *Carolina*, 62. They did not, however, boil what may have been an ancestor of penicillin, "doated grains of Indian corn beaten to a powder," *ibid.*, 130.

[6] The parentheses are Mr. Smith's. Margry, *Translation*, I, 160–165, gives a fuller description of the making of jerk, the first step in the manufacture of pemmican.

interrupted by an escape from the Indians, followed shortly by activity with the Black Boys of Pennsylvania, among whom he was a leader. He was with Bouquet in 1764, and less than two years later after having heard of the land, "that lay between the Ohioe and the Cherokee River and as I knew by conversing with the Indians in their own tongue, that there was a large body of rich land there, I concluded I would take a tour westward, and explore the country."

His only complaint while crippled was that he had no Bible, only a Psalm Book, and Watts' *Upon Prayer*. Still, "I was able to while the time away by composing verses, which I then frequently sung."

He probably sang as he worked, for it would have taken a deal of time to make Jamie's outfit, as eventually the boy "had nothing on him that was ever spun." Jamie is the first and only person I have met who wore a coonskin cap prior to 1812 when, chiefly it would seem through sympathy and admiration for Russia invaded by Napoleon, the shaggy head covering came into fashion, though both the French and English colonials had long worn fur caps in winter, these, in Virginia, known as Polish caps.[7]

Jamie also wore breech clout, leggings and moccasins of buckskin, and a bearskin, "dressed with the hair on which he belted about him." The coat was probably made in the same way as later hunter-farmers on the Cumberland made bearskin coats. The skin was first slit from "jaws to tail," paws cut off low, the foreleg skin left unsplit but that on the hind legs split, and the head cut off. The pelt had then only to be peeled off, left wrong side out, and the man put his arms where once had been the front legs of the bear. Smith was somewhat handicapped in that he had no cows to help him. Later coatmakers stretched and tied the skin to a fence or stump, sprinkled it with salt, and let the cows come around; the salt-hungry cattle would, while licking the salt, take most of the fat and soften the skin.[8]

It was October before Smith, traveling slowly with his still-tender foot, had crossed the mountains and got into the Yadkin Country. He had spent eleven months in which he had seen "neither bread, money, women, nor spiritious liquors," three of these alone with Jamie. His worst trial was yet to come. The people on the Yadkin in North Carolina, frontiersmen

[7] Used by permission of the publishers, the J. B. Lippincott Company, from *Colonial Virginia, Its People and Customs* by Mary Newton Stanard, Copyright the J. B. Lippincott Company, Philadelphia, 1917, p. 155, the Will of Thomas Warnett, 1629.
[8] W, 30S, 264.

though they were, took unkindly to bearskin coats and coonskin caps, refusing to believe Smith had crossed the mountains. He and Jamie were put into jail, and held to be such dangerous characters that a guard was "set over them." He commented with some bitterness on the difference clothing made; after a friend fitted him out with a good horse and proper clothing he was received everywhere, and concluded that "a horse thief or even a robber might pass without interruption provided only he was well dressed."

He lived to lead the Black Boys again in 1769, serve as a Colonel in the Revolution, and eventually settle in Bourbon County, Kentucky, where as a Presbyterian minister he preached many sermons.[9]

James Smith is the first to leave a fairly clear record of men who went from the English colonies across country to the lower Cumberland. We cannot be certain he was the first to go so far; by that date, 1766, traders, Indian captives such as Mrs. Mary Ingles of New River, and adventurers had been over the mountains and into what was to be Kentucky and Tennessee, but most had gone through Cumberland Gap, or by way of the upper tributaries of the Ohio. The land was not unknown.

The French and Indian War followed by the King's Proclamation of 1763 checked the western push of settlers and hindered exploration west of the mountains, but the frontier from Pennsylvania southward had, in spite of war and king, been strengthened, not with forts, but by settlers with the know-how to live on the borders, and who knew they had the know-how. They had paid a high price for this learning.[10] In some areas, notably those of western Pennsylvania and the New River region in Virginia, frontier homes were for a time abandoned and the border receded eastward. In the New River and Holston settlements, grown larger since Dr. Walker's visit of 1750, the Indians between 1754–56 killed twenty-nine men, women, and children and took forty-five prisoners.[11] It was in these years that women learned to fear the calm and beautiful weather that came after frost and most of the leaves had fallen, but before the deep snows of winter, the last weather suitable for long journeys; it was then

[9] Lewis Collins, *History of Kentucky*, revised by his son, Richard H. Collins, Covington, Ky., 1882 (cited hereafter as Collins, *Kentucky, 1882*), II, 77–79. See also Williams, *Travels*, 203.

[10] Alexander S. Withers, *Chronicles of Border Warfare*, Clarksburg, Va., 1831, revised and edited by Reuben Gold Thwaites, Cincinnati, 1895 (cited hereafter as Withers, *Chronicles*), gives, as does Rupp, detailed descriptions of many border incidents during the French and Indian War; for Smith in particular see *ibid.*, n. 67 and 109–115. See also Kercheval, *Virginia*, 65–108, and Waddell, *Annals*, 119–229, for French and Indian War.

[11] Summers, *Southwest Virginia*, 58–60.

the Shawnee came for scalps and horses, and so the frontier settler called the season Indian Summer.[12]

The war had been as a college education in Indian fighting, though actual fighting was the lesser half of what they had to learn. It took more than bravery and fine marksmanship to hold the frontier; more important was the ability to go on, in spite of war, with the little day-to-day jobs of their lives. More than one backwoods farmer, his wife, or child was killed while working in the corn or hunting the family cow.[13] Next day a survivor or a neighbor would be a bit more cautious while gathering corn or going to the spring, but all the same the work got done. They put fear in its proper place and learned to live with it; side by side with this grew a great self-confidence, the same any man gets when he knows he can outfight his enemy and still carry on the business of living. The very dogs had learned to trail Indians, the cows to smell them, and the white man could write, "We skelpt them that we killed." [14] Meanwhile, cleared fields in the Valley of Virginia and south past the Yadkin grew, even in the bloodiest years, and log cabins became log houses.

The war did not check the stream of settlers rolling up the Shenandoah; it did change the course of settlement. Families that might have pushed further west came instead into southwestern Virginia and the Yadkin Country where Indian troubles were less than further north. Settlement progressed down the Holston, but did not go below the Virginia line until 1769. Meanwhile the border population increased, and the skills and learnings needed to live there became commonplace. More men learned how to use and even make the rifle, a must for every border household during the French and Indian War. Most any farmer in the backwoods could help build a log house, and more women learned to spin and weave, make soap, hominy, cook wild meat, churn butter, and all the other skills needed to live as mistress of a civilized household in the woods.

Skills alone were not enough; it is true any man who would survive on the border had to be an artist in the use of the broadax, skinning knife, scraper, hoe, froe, auger, awl, adz, and other tools, but equally important or more so was a knowledge of the woods. All borderers who lived as farmers were woodsmen. The forest was only part enemy to be pushed

[12] Kercheval, *Virginia*, 217–218. "Pawwawing days," found sometimes in the old stories, as here came in the February thaws.

[13] *Ibid.*, 231–232, 272–273, Doddridge, "Notes." A child on the borders during the Revolution, he remembered the determination of his people to farm, Indians or no.

[14] Summers, *Southwest Virginia*, 65.

aside for cleared fields. It was for the Virginia or North Carolina settler a vast and seemingly bottomless widow's barrel yielding up all manner of things from walink for the newborn baby's tea to dogwood for the weaver's shuttle. The settler had to know these offerings, where to hunt a slender hickory sapling for the corn pounder sweep, lightwood for a bit of tar, cane stalk for the weaver's sleigh, a small and crooked white oak for a sled runner, but a straight one for a splitting maul. He had to know his wood—poplar for hewing and gouging, but cedar for riving, and so for several dozen: what would sink and what would float, what would bend, and what was best for a shoe peg. He was dependent upon the woods around him not only for building materials for house, barn, fence, much of his furniture, and many of his appliances from pitchfork to gunstock, but the woods gave him fuel, drugs, dyes, and a good bit of food. All new-settled farmers, even the wealthy, had, until fence could be built, to use the open range so that meat, milk, and butter came from woods pasture.

Wild meat was still another woods product, and though the borderer on the English colonies never depended upon it as did the French, there were times, especially when Indians killed the livestock, wild meat was the only meat. The frontier farmer like untold generations behind him enjoyed hunting, some liking it so well they wanted to do little else. It was not, even with a good rifle, an easy job. It demanded to begin with a high degree of native intelligence coupled with unusually sharp senses, and other certain attributes—patience, ability to judge distance, to distinguish even minute differences in sound.

Many farmers were skilled enough to get some meat for the family table; a smaller number could earn extra money by trapping beaver and otter, or hunting deer, usually selling only the skins, though in autumn there was some sale for venison; a whole deer bringing half a crown in North Carolina in 1776.[15] Few farmers were so skillful as Henry Fry of the Valley of Virginia who paid the whole cost of his land, 250 pounds, from the profits of his hunting.[16]

Fewer still were the men who could hunt well enough to depend upon it as their chief source of income, yet it was such men who first explored the Cumberland, their long hunts taking them there when no good hunting was left east of the mountains. A man who would live in the woods for months, depending on them for all things save ammunition, clothing, and

[15] Smythe, *Tour*, I, 291.
[16] Kercheval, *Virginia*, n., 54.

transportation, had to be a better than average woodsman, so good he never let himself get hurt. This, no minor accomplishment as any one knows who has seen a group of carefully trained and tutored Boy Scouts "roughing it."

The ability went deeper than a mere training. Years ago before the days of consolidated schools and good roads, I taught in remote sections of Pulaski County, Kentucky, now part of the Cumberland National Forest. My pupils were chiefly the children of small farmers, but all around them were the woods. At that date in that community most farm animals were still on the open range so these children like earlier generations spent much time in the woods; in rounding up the forever straying animals, in going to church, school, or to a neighbor's, and in collecting herbs, fruits, nuts, fuel, and in hunting and trapping.

They had had no nature study or lessons in woodscraft, but on a Monday morning they could, with no apparent study of the either muddy or dusty road, tell all who had ridden or walked by the schoolhouse during the week end, for they knew every shoe print, mule and horse "sign" in the neighborhood. They knew the common names as well as uses of several dozens of plants,[17] and they knew them winter as well as summer. One faint clink of a distant bell and they could tell whether made by horse, cow, or sheep, who owned the animal and what it was doing, grazing or sleeping or "hid-out." They could track a strayed mule or hog or cow for miles when there were no tracks I could see.

They, no different from the young hunters of earlier generations, ranged over rough lands and were never lost or hurt. They delighted in swinging out over creek or river and dropping into a pool of water; they climbed tall trees, explored sinkholes, caves, creek pools, rockhouses, yet I never had a school child hurt by a fall or suffer a snake bite, and though many of the boys started hunting alone at ten years of age I can recall no gun accident. Bred into them was the same caution the hunter had to have; a perch in the swaying top of a "slim" fifty-foot hickory made for good safe fun in a high wind, but only a fool would on a hot summer day stick

[17] Lawson, *Carolina*, 50–66, in listing the wild plants of Virginia gives the uses of many later mentioned by Byrd. Much of this lore came from the Indians: see John R. Swanton, "Medical Practices of the Creek Indians," 639–670, *42nd Report of Bureau of Ethnology*. Many remedies given here—ashes, infusions of sassafras, red oak bark, redbud, etc., are mentioned by correspondents of Mr. Lyman C. Draper, and many are still used. I knew, for example, many hill people who used walink, more commonly known as walking-leaf—*Polypodiaceae Camptosorus rhizophyllus;* this as well as several other herbs used by Mrs. Anna Liza Wilson is mentioned by Dodd-ridge, Kercheval, *Virginia,* 278.

his hand under a rocky ledge or into any hole where he could not see—
that was a good place for a copperhead to be. They were forever cautious;
they respected the woods, the caves, and the river as one respects honorable enemies; young children were constantly watched and guarded against
the dangers there, and it was not until they were eight years old or so
they were allowed to walk the paths alone.

The understanding by the young and their cunning was little compared
to that of the old. They knew the sky and what the sunset said, and the
wind, and I think if one long dead were resurrected in the dark in one of
those now forgotten and lost graveyards he could with a smelling of the
wind and some listening from the high hills know the season, the state of
the weather, and if there were no fog or cloud between him and the stars
he would know the time, but he could never say exactly how he knew
these things, or describe the difference in sound between a moist south
wind and a dry one out of the east.

The Long Hunters of almost two hundred years ago knew all such un-
teachable things. They had to have, too, courage with the caution and the
cunning, and in addition many skills, so many that most of their childhood
play, what little there was of it, would have been spent in learning. Early,
the farm boy learned to use the clasp or whittling knife, the long knife
kept razor sharp and sheathed for skinning, and the tomahawk for innumerable jobs from splitting a marrow bone to cutting poles for a turkey
trap. These tools instead of balls and skates were his playthings.[18] There
were contests in hatchet throwing and endless games of mumbley peg;
the knife whirling from the shoulder, the knee, the nose, behind, in front,
sidewise; for if properly thrown, either a knife or a tomahawk was a
handy weapon in hunting or Indian warfare when the gun was empty.

Judging from the things that have come down to us the pioneers were
a people fond of the sound of the human voice; they sang much, whistled,
talked a very great deal, had many rhymes, riddles, and tongue twisters.
One form of amusement common to farm boys for generations was the
imitation of the sounds made by the animals around them.[19] It was fun
to rouse the family at midnight with the breaking-day crow of the rooster,
but the ability to imitate the wild things meant more than fun; the bleat
of a fawn might bring a doe or even a hungry bear to the waiting hunter,[20]

[18] Kercheval, *Virginia*, Doddridge, "Notes," 284; for importance of tomahawk, see
Smythe, *Tour*, I, 179.
[19] Summers, *Southwest Virginia*, quoting Bickley, 127. See also Kercheval, *Virginia*,
Doddridge, "Notes," 284.
[20] Gray, *Bishop*, 47, 107.

while in buck running time, October for the deer, the sound of a doe's voice might bring an amorous buck.

Most backwoods settlers had somewhere in the woods a turkey pen, baited with paths of corn and made on the same principle as the later-day fly trap, based on the foolishness of the captured thing,[21] yet turkey was not always so plentiful, and so the hunter learned to make a turkey call from the wing bone of a turkey; and he also learned to gobble so well he could often get an answering gobble. The learning to imitate was only half of it; he had to be able to distinguish the false from the true; it was a favorite trick of the Indian to pretend to be an animal and lure the white man within range, or in ambushing, each Indian would make himself known to the others by the proper sound, depending on the season, geography, and time of day, owls and wolves most commonly at night, squirrels, turkeys, cow or horse bells by day;[22] but the backwoods settler was hard to fool. A Virginia settler by the name of Hogel[23] heard his cowbell during the French and Indian War; it didn't sound as his cow made it sound; he slipped up and killed the Indian jangling the bell; likewise on the Cumberland did Kaspar Mansker kill an Indian turkey, and Benjamin Castleman an Indian owl.

Little boys then as now were fascinated by guns, and even when they were very little would slip away and make their own of hollow but strong cane stalks. These, charged with powder and bullets, were touched off by a chunk of fire, kept handy, and while one six-year-old stood hidden in a hunter's blind of green boughs, the other ran past on hands and knees as the deer. Sometimes the "deer tumbled and scringed when struck, raising a knot as large as a partridge egg."[24] Other times they played war with cane guns at thirty paces, and the pump knots raised when the enemy was hit were big ones, but less stoic than future Cumberland settlers who could keep silent while being scalped and so not betray the bit of life left them, the wounded soldier yelled.

Complete mastery of the woods, knives, and guns along with various other skills such as cooking, mending, sewing, horsemanship, were only part of the education of the Long Hunter. He had still to learn the whole

[21] Anburey, *Travels*, II, 342–343.
[22] Adair, *American Indian*, 413, describes the manner and use of a number of imitative sounds used by the Chickasaw.
[23] Kercheval, *Virginia*, 107.
[24] Gray, *Bishop*, 12–19. Bishop's brief story of his childhood play—sailing gunboats on the tanning vat—on the frontiers of Virginia is probably typical of that of most frontier children—no organized games of ball, etc.

art and science of hunting; for hunting was not a mere pastime, "devoid of skill as it now is. The hunter . . . paid particular attention to the winds, rains, snows, and frosts, for almost every change altered the location of the game. He knew the cardinal points of the compass by the thick bark and moss on the north side of a tree, so that during the darkest and most gloomy night he knew which was the north, and so the direction of his home or camp.[25]

"The natural habits of the deer were well studied; and hence he knew at what times they fed, etc. . . . If, in hunting, he found a deer at feed, he stopped, and though he might be open to it, he did not seek to obscure himself, but waited until it raised its head and looked at him. He remained motionless till the deer, satisfied that nothing was wrong, again commenced feeding. He then began to advance, if he had the wind of it, and if not, he retreated and came up another way, so as to place the deer between himself and the wind. As long as the deer's head was down he continued to advance till he saw it shake its tail. In a moment he was the same motionless object, till again it put down its head. In this way he would soon approach to within sixty yards, when his unerring rifle did the work of death. It is a curious fact that deer never put their heads to the ground, or raise it, without shaking the tail before doing so." [26]

Many times the hunter went at night to some favorite feeding ground or lick, and there he built a blind of green boughs, and waited for the deer.[27] Others, near fair-sized creeks, made clay or rock fire-bowls in the ends of pirogues, filled these with flaming pine knots, and went up and down the stream at night. The deer, curious as were other animals, would show their eyes and be shot. This was spot lighting, an old method of hunting, known to the Indians,[28] and in later days used by white men on the Cumberland, who spotlight fish, then gig them, saving both ammunition and sound for it is illegal.

Yet even with much skill, a good rifle, and complete mastery of the woods, the hunter would often come home empty-handed. "Then the important lesson of preventing spells or enchantments by enemies was studied. Frequently on leaving home, the wife would throw the axe at her husband to give him good luck. If he chanced to fail to kill game, his gun was enchanted or spelled, and some old woman was shot in effigy,

[25] Summers, *Southwest Virginia*, 128, quoting Bickley.

[26] *Ibid.*, 128–129.

[27] Hanna, *Wilderness Trail*, II, 223, quoting Lyman C. Draper's unpublished "Life of John Finley."

[28] Kercheval, *Virginia*, 388–389, quoting Mr. John Lybrock who killed 3,000 deer.

then a silver bullet would be run with a needle through it and shot at her picture. To remove these spells, they would sometimes unbreech their rifles, and lay them in a clear running stream for a certain number of days. If this failed, they would borrow patching from some other hunter, which transferred all the bad luck to the lender." [29]

These and such superstitions are said to have been most common among the Germans, but even a Scotchman coming home with neither deer nor bear might wonder on providence—that is if he had hunted in a locality noted for its game. The hunter's frontier was forever traveling west, and as time passed the rate of travel quickened. In John Lawson's world of North Carolina in 1700 hunting lands and settled lands were almost one; bears raided the cornfields and dug the potatoes. William Byrd, twenty-eight years later, found game fairly plentiful only back on the Piedmont, a good many miles from the nearest inhabitants. During these years the European demand for deerskins had increased, and the Indian who, until the coming of the white man, had killed only to supply his needs, killed for skins to exchange for all things from rum to paint. There were, too, more white settlers to hunt.

Dr. Thomas Walker, traveling through in 1750, remembered the old days when there had been elk and buffalo and deer in the place he rode through [30]—the site of present-day Roanoke. His party had no wild meat until two weeks later when they found two young buffalo, south and west of Stalnaker's cabin or near the site of what is now Bristol, Tennessee.[31]

Hunters had by this date ranged as far west as Clinch River,[32] and possibly further; there must have been somebody who didn't cut his name on a tree. Game continued for many years to be fairly plentiful on the mountainous headwaters of the Tennessee, but hunters avoided this region; it was too close to the Cherokee, and the mountains on the upper waters were rough and hard for horsemen. They turned instead to the Cumberland; thus, most hunters of whom we have any record, went in the direction of Cumberland Gap instead of up and down the tributaries of the Tennessee.

The first group actually known to have been on the Cumberland did not go out until 1761. These, chiefly from southwestern Virginia, had as

[29] Summers, *Southwest Virginia*, 127–129, quoting Bickley.
[30] Walker, "Journal," March 15, 1750.
[31] *Ibid.*, March 30.
[32] *Ibid.*, April 9, 1750. "We traveled to a river, which I suppose to be that which hunters call Clinches River from one Clinch a hunter, who first found it."

their leader Elisha Walden, "a rough backwoodsman, near six feet tall, square built, weighing about 180 pounds," and at that time around thirty years old. He had grown up on Smith River in Pittsylvania County, Virginia, and there on the frontier he had mastered a hunter's education, for he was a skillful hunter, always home from the hunt with his horses well loaded.[33] Jack Blevins, father-in-law of Walden, was along, as was his brother-in-law, William Blevins.[34]

Another was William Pittman, "six feet tall of fine personal appearance and in his early twenties." [35] There were many Pittmans and more than one William,[36] and whether it was for this Long Hunter or some other that Pittman Creek of Cumberland River got its name we do not know. Six foot three, dark-skinned, bony, bold, "enterprising and fearless," Henry Scaggs also came. He and his brother were noted hunters, and "nothing but hunters," [37] and it was from the Scaggs men that Scaggs Creek of Rockcastle, crossed and recrossed by later travelers along the Kentucky Road, got its name.[38] Other members of the party were Charles Cox, William Newman, and William Harilson, another professional hunter, and like the Scaggs men something of an exception for most hunters practiced at least one other occupation, usually farming. Many of Walden's group may at this time have been hunting land, as Charles Cox, the Blevinses, Walden, and Newman all eventually settled in East Tennessee.[39]

This group, thought to have consisted of eighteen or nineteen men, went only a little way into the backwoods and there fixed a central or Station Camp, an arrangement common to all hunters who went any distance from home. Such places served for storage of skins as well as source

[33] VM, VI, 338; *ibid.*, VII, 249, John Redd, "Reminiscences of Western Virginia," taken from the Draper Manuscripts of the Wisconsin Historical Collections, volume and page of original not given, but thought to have been written around 1849 (cited hereafter as Redd, "Reminiscences"). See also for Walden, Withers, *Chronicles,* 59–60.

[34] VM, VI, 338, Redd, "Reminiscences."

[35] VM, VI, 340.

[36] LC, I, contains numerous references to Pittmans—the name is spelled in various ways—144, William Pittman Vs. Thomas Pittman. 191, Thomas Pittman to help oversee the road from Crow's Station to Harrodsburg; and *ibid.*, 135, 79. These references in Lincoln County, Ky., of the 1780's undoubtedly refer to Pittmans then living in the neighborhood of Pittman Creek of Cumberland; but there was also, not in Lincoln County, a Pittman Creek on Green River.

[37] VM, VI, 339, Redd, "Reminiscences."

[38] Collins, *Kentucky, 1882,* II, 416. Collins shows confusion and gives this group of hunters credit for the naming of Cumberland and Clinch rivers. See also Haywood, *C & P,* 32–33, and Ramsey, *Tennessee,* 67–68. Scaggs and the creek on the western side of Rockcastle bearing his name are spelled in numerous ways in source materials, often with a *k.*

[39] Williams, *Dawn of Tenn.,* 321–322.

of supply; from them the hunters would go out in small groups of three or four, taking with them only enough supplies for a few days. Large parties on one hunting ground not only frightened the game and competed against each other, but also aroused the Indians. Two or three men could in a week or ten days hunt the area surrounding their temporary camp site, and if successful take the peltry to the station camp, reload with supplies and then go out again.[40]

The station camp for Walden's party of 1761 was on Wallen's Creek in what is now Lee County, Virginia, and from here they ranged north and west; some are said to have seen the eleven-year-old carvings of Ambrose Powell of Dr. Walker's party and so named Powell River, as well as the valley and mountain. The exact journeyings of any one man are unknown; their home away from home was the station camp, built usually of poles, sometimes only eight by ten feet, covered with puncheons, walls on only three sides, the ends of the poles kept in place by two uprights set close enough together to keep the poles from sliding down.[41] These were known as half-faced camps. Other times an extra large, already fallen log was chosen for the back, or even a rock.

Regardless of how made, the open front was always higher than the closed back, so that rain would not drip into the fire, fronting the camp in cold weather, and close enough the men could sleep under shelter, but still keep their feet warm. There were no rules; not all hunters built even a makeshift of bark roof on poles. Thomas Sharpe Spencer lived for several months in a large sycamore tree, near present-day Castalian Springs in Sumner County, Tennessee,[42] while Kaspar Mansker, hunting in the same general region, made a hut of buffalo skins.[43] Usually a small group, planning to spend only two or three days in a neighborhood, built nothing. Men could survive without blanket or bearskin, even in a sleet storm; freezing, if not discomfort, could be prevented by sleeping one on top of the other, each man taking a turn as bed covering.[44] Much of the Cumberland Country is so well stocked with caves and rockhouses, that hunters

[40] VM, VII, 248, Redd, "Reminiscences."

[41] FQ, II, 43-70, "A Sketch of the Early Adventures of William Sudduth in Kentucky," edited from 15U, 114, of the Draper Manuscripts of the Wisconsin Historical Collections by Lucian Beckner. Sudduth was an early Kentucky surveyor who left an interesting account of many aspects of frontier living, including station camps, *ibid.*, 52, 53. See, for other types and sizes, Kercheval, *Virginia*, Doddridge, "Notes," 264, and VM, VII, 402, Redd, "Reminiscences."

[42] What is said to be the remains of Spencer's sycamore is now marked by the Tenn. State Historical Commission on State Highway 25 at Castalian Springs.

[43] Haywood, *C & P*, 78.

[44] Gray, *Bishop*, 74-75.

and travelers camped often in them as did Dr. Thomas Walker in 1750.[45]

As each man usually "carried" two horses for the bringing back of the skins, hunting parties were able on the outward journeys to take large stocks of provisions and many were needed as the hunters were often in the woods for more than a year. In addition to rifle, tomahawk, and knives, musts for all woods travelers, there were traps for otter and beaver, goodly supplies of powder and lead, and for each party a small hand vise and bellows, files and screw plates for fixing the guns when they got "out of fix."[46] The miniature, long-handled saucepan with pouring lip and of heavy iron, used for the melting of lead, was needed by every outfit. Indians often bought bullets ready-molded,[47] but the Virginia hunters were more inclined to carry bars of lead. There were extra horseshoes with the necessary nails, and everybody carried awls, one of the most important tools of the day, for no leather work could be done without one, and the hunter like the frontier farmer mended and often made numerous articles of leather—saddles, breeches, bridles, all manner of thongs to be used wherever thread or rope was needed, and of course moccasins.

This foot covering, known variously as the moccasin, Mogasin, or shoepack, was modeled after that of the Indian, and continued to be worn by hunters and trappers for a hundred years, the fashion in time spreading west of the Mississippi, and in border families with little money they were sometimes worn by the whole family. Cheapness was only one of their many virtues. They were comfortable, and soundless in the woods, leaving little mark, advantages when either hunting game or eluding Indians. The manufacture of them was simple, requiring only a knife and an awl and whatever skin or leather the maker happened to have.

Deerskin in most settlements east of the mountains was more readily had than that of the tougher elk or buffalo, so that most moccasins were made of deerskin, tanned or treated in various ways. Eastern Indians had tanned their leather, "in an Hour or two; with the Bark of Trees Boiled, wherein they put the Leather whilst Hot, and let it remain a little while, thereby it becomes qualified, as to endure water and Dirt without growing Hard."[48] The white man did many things after the Indian fashion, and may have tanned moccasin leather in this way, or he could have used ashes or lime water to make the hair slip, followed by long immersion in

[45] Walker, "Journal," May 11, 12, 13, 1750.

[46] VM, VII, 248, Redd, "Reminiscences."

[47] I, XVI, 391–405, "Accounts of Baynton and Wharton." Lead, *ibid.*, 398, 402, is now and then mentioned with powder, but much the greater proportion was sold as ball; early inventories on the Cumberland mention only lead.

[48] Lawson, *Carolina*, 69. *Ibid.*, 123, tells of tanning with dried brains and smoke.

a trough filled with shredded oak bark and water, but this method was no good for the hunter in the woods in a hurry for a new pair of moccasins; and if he wore deerskin he was forever needing a new pair. Father Hennepin had, in the winter of 1680, traveled through the Illinois woods with "dressed skins to make Indian shoes, which last only a day, French shoes being of no use in the western countries." [49] A hundred years later American settlers were still complaining of deerskin moccasins, for in addition to being easily torn, the porous leather held water like a sponge so that the wearing of deerskin moccasins in wet weather was no more than a "decent way of going barefoot," while even in dry weather the mending of them was "the labor of almost every evening."

Yet, at their worst they were far better than Byrd's shoes, and were made "as Fit for the Feet as a Glove for the Hands, and are very easy to travel in when one is used to them." Heelless, they were made of one piece of leather with a "gathering seam along the top of the foot, and another from the bottom of the heel, with gaiters as high as the ankle joint or a little higher." The whole sewed together with leather thongs, "whangs as they were commonly called." More whangs kept the moccasins and their gaiters in place for they were "nicely adapted to the ankles and lower part of the legs . . . so that no dust, gravel or snow could get within." Any loose, flapping piece of footware was a hazard in the woods, and all descriptions and pictures beginning with those of John White in 1585 show the Indians as having worn a snugly tied foot covering that came well above the ankle. Some moccasins were soled, for extra wear, and another type of homemade foot covering was the shoepack, in pattern much like today's moccasin with a leather insert over the instep, a seam in back, and reinforced with an extra sole, but at least of ankle height, laced and "snugly tied." [50]

Walden and his companions would also have worn leggings, these sometimes of leather but more commonly of "coarse woolen cloth half way up the thigh," and above the leggings, leather breeches coming to just

[49] Shea, *Mississippi*, 101, quoting Father Hennepin's Journal. This was the same Fr. Louis Hennepin mentioned by Gov. Nicholson of Maryland. He published an account of his travels, chiefly in the Mississippi Valley and the Illinois, 1678-1680, broadened somewhat by Indian captivity, as *Description de la Louisiane*, Paris, 1683. The work was widely read and translated into many languages, including English; it seems safe to say that until the English went into the Illinois after the close of the French and Indian War the most they knew of the interior of America came from Hennepin.

[50] Kercheval, *Virginia*, 152, and Doddridge, "Notes," 256–257, give a description of the dress of the average borderer during the Revolution; quotes concerning moccasins, *ibid.*, 257. See also Adair, *American Indian*, 9, 57, and W, 11CC, 146–147, ". . . he then laid the sole of his moccasin on a log as a sign for them not to follow."

below the knee, an article of dress not confined to the frontiersman but worn by working men in Europe as well as America. The rest of their clothing, with one possible exception, would have been much like that of the ordinary working farmer of the day. The usual summer shirt for everyday wear was of rather coarse linen or even hemp, as cotton clothing was at that date quite a luxury to be imported; some may have worn sleeveless leather jackets, or long-skirted, plain waistcoats of homespun, these last with sleeves, for the waistcoat of that day was not the garment we now know. Most would have brought a greatcoat, full-skirted, many-pocketed, lined, and for the borderer sometimes made of homespun, with little ornamentation, buttons of brass or horn instead of silver.

The hunter needed some protection for his eyes from rain or snow or glare of sun, and almost always wore the rather shallow-crowned, broad-brimmed hat common among farmers in the English colonies, and hunters during the Revolution were described as wearing "flopped hats of reddish hue." [51]

Some of Walden's men may have worn or carried in a blanket roll along with the greatcoat, "a hunting shirt somewhat resembling a waggoner's frock." [52] Much has been written of the hunting shirt, though it did not become high style until the time of the Revolution, but it is usually identified with the hunter of this period. It was also worn by officers and men in the army as a combination of protective covering, such as the smock of the butcher and the waggoner, and shooting jacket, and was sometimes called a "rifle shirt." The hunting shirt was a commodious smock, opening in front with a wide lap, double-breasted without buttons and held together with a sash tied in back. Tomahawk, mittens, and skinning knife were stuck under the sash, while the overlap was used to hold tow, bread, and other articles needed by a waiting or stalking hunter, but too bulky for the hunting bag. [53]

These garments were almost always of linsey, or linen, though later in

---

[51] Smythe, *Tour*, I, 179–182, described the Virginia hunter and his outfit in some detail, but like other travelers said nothing of the dress of the average farm family, even those on the borders. Portraits of the day indicate that those colonials wealthy enough to afford portraits dressed much as did those of the same relative circumstances in England, though of course behind the styles for a year or so. Judging from inventories and the lack of comment the inhabitants of Virginia and the other colonies, even those on the borders, dressed as did their counterparts in England; the relatively poor farmer and his wife of the pre-Revolutionary period much akin in dress to the working people as portrayed by Hogarth. See also Lewis Collins, *History of Kentucky*, Maysville, 1847 (cited hereafter as Collins, *Kentucky, 1847*), "Sketch of Western Hunter," opposite 101, a broad-brimmed, rather shallow hat, cloth jacket.

[52] Smythe, *Tour*, I, 182.

[53] Kercheval, *Virginia*, Doddridge, "Notes," 230, 256. See also Smythe, *Tour*, I, 181.

the dry and brushless west, the shirt became a fancy affair of leather, embroidered with Indian work and trimmed with many fringes; east of the Mississippi deerskin was seldom used as in wet weather it "was cold and uncomfortable." During the Revolution hunting shirts were of many colors; white as worn by Cresap's men was a favorite as were red and yellow.[54] Major Ferguson, British leader killed at the Battle of Kings Mountain, wore a checked duster,[55] as did other British officers, partly to protect their expensive uniforms from dirt and saddle stains and also to conceal their persons from the Whig sharpshooters, always on the lookout for officers.

It is doubtful if many hunting shirts in bright colors were worn into the woods; these were most commonly worn by the gay blades at shooting matches and the soldier while traveling or on parade. Men in the woods avoided bright colors so as not to attract the attention of game or Indians.[56] Daniel Boone is painted in a rather plain hunting shirt of cloth, though he is described as having worn in the settlements of East Tennessee in 1774 a deerskin hunting shirt dyed black.[57] A few years later, soldiers on one of Clark's Ohio campaigns wore linsey hunting shirts above leggings with breech clouts substituting for trousers.[58] As a rule, however, hunters liked their legs well covered and protected from brush, briars, not to mention seed ticks and chiggers.

Equipment as well as dress of the individual hunter varied; each would have had a blanket roll or bearskin behind his saddle, and filling it and the ever-present saddle bags were a multitude of necessities. So various were the rifles that most men carried individual bullet molds, and of course material for patching—Daniel Boone is said to have used 600-thread linen—but if a man got caught in the woods without cloth he could use deerskin or his shirttail. Tow for the wiping of the gun barrel was another necessity. They would like Dr. Walker have carried soap, razors, spare

[54] Smythe, *Tour,* I, 182.

[55] Lyman C. Draper, *Kings Mountain and Its Heroes,* Cincinnati, 1881 (cited hereafter as Draper, *Kings Mountain*), 233.

[56] Kercheval, *Virginia,* 114. This was not easy for all borderers; many loved fine dress: Col. Charles Lewis, though advised against it, did wear "a georgeous scarlet waistcoat," and was killed at the Battle of Point Pleasant in 1774, as was Captain John Frogge, Waddell, *Annals,* 137, who was "gaudily dressed in bright colors and his hat was adorned with ribbons and feathers."

[57] Reuben Gold Thwaites, *Daniel Boone,* New York, 1902 (cited hereafter as Thwaites, *Boone*), 110.

[58] I, VIII, 476, describes a company of around 200 men under Col. James Harrod, but this was most probably because the men "could not git aney thing to cover their skins." See also Kercheval, *Virginia,* 257, some of the "young bucks," or the 1776 version of today's "hot-rodders," wore breechclouts but no breeches.

clothing, and tobacco as it is often mentioned, but the hunter was more inclined to chew than to smoke.[59] Some brought fishhooks,[60] while many like James Smith carried at least a few books, often Bibles, hymn books, and works of a religious nature.

A seasoned woodsman could live for months on meat alone, but no man liked to do so, and on their outward trips they brought meal, corn, and salt, with rum, flour, and coffee for those who could afford such. Cooking was done chiefly in skillet or kettle with the flintlock supplying the fire. The hunter plugged her touchhole, and into her priming pan put a wad of tow on which he sprinkled a few grains of powder, pulled the trigger, and the resulting spark made a little glowing coal.

Some form of hunting could be carried on at most any season; summer was best for taking deerskins, but no meat save that of fawns and bear cubs was much good in hot weather. Turkeys were so covered with ticks they had to be skinned. Swans were a favorite summer food as was the doe's bag stewed into soup; this last, considered by most to be a very "delicate dish," as were buffalo humps and tongues.[61] Everybody continued to love bear meat, but when a hunter wanted a real feast he ate marrow bones. He first made a bed of embers of some good fuel wood such as hickory, and then "lay one end of the bone on the coals, cooked it a few minutes, turned it and cooked the other end, then with his hatchet hacked off one side to the marrow." [62] A group in Kentucky once had "68 marrow bones in the fire roasting at once. Stephen Biles ate the Marrow of eight of them, but they were small. We ate them all for breakfast." [63]

If a man ran out of meal but still had corn brought for his horse, and wanted bread, he "cut a sapling, leveled the top at the stump, wrapped a broad band of raw bear-hide around the top and confined it, thus formed

[59] Pipes are non-existent in early inventories of first settlers on the Cumberland, though chance accounts indicate that some did smoke, but snuff was at this date little used, for, "All Americans are smokers. They also chew and sometimes they indulge in both activities. But the American of either sex who takes snuff is a rare phenomenon." Reprinted by permission of the publisher, Harvard University Press, from *This Was America*, edited and collected by Oscar Handlin, copyright Cambridge, 1947, by the President and Fellows of Harvard College, 97, quoting a translation of Moreau de Saint-Méry, "*Voyage aux Etats-Unis de l'Amérique, 1793-1798.*" Examples of the long-stemmed, small-bowled clay pipes in use during this period may be seen in Fort Necessity Museum, near Uniontown, Pennsylvania; this collection gives much insight into the weapons, tools, appliances, clothing, etc., in use during the French and Indian War.

[60] Walker, "Journal," May 14.

[61] Everybody praised buffalo humps and tongues; see Gray, *Bishop*, 95.

[62] W, 30S, 263.

[63] FQ, II, 104, Clinkenbeard "Interview."

a mortar into which I poured the corn and beat it into meal. I then took a green bear-skin from under my saddle, hollowed out a small concavity in the ground, spread it with the flesh side up, and pressing into the hole until it fitted all round, I had quite a snug little tray. I emptied my meal into it and proceeded to work it into dough." When the dough was made, a flat rock properly slanted toward the fire was used as a griddle, and so was produced a "fine Johnny cake." [64]

Not all of the men were equally skilled as woodsmen and hunters; some were hired hands who never went after game, but were camp waiters, cooking for the others and caring for the skins as they came in. Hunting was hard work, but not all work. During the hot summer days the deer fed mostly at the rising of the moon, at dawn, and at twilight, so there were long lazy noons when the hunter never tried at all, for deer were impossible to find when hidden from heat and flies in shady thickets. A sharp-eared hunter could sometimes discover a herd of buffalo when the animals were resting on a hot summer day by the contented grunts the cows gave as they suckled their young.

In late winter the pattern of life changed; bear hibernated, and other game began in January to lose weight and continued poor and thin until late spring, but winter was trapping time for beaver, and otter pelts were in their prime. There was always a little time for amusement; sometimes rough pastimes such as watching the antics of a just-skinned wolf, or practical jokes, but judging from stray bits of information a large number read or sang as did James Smith and Daniel Boone.

There was in addition to the actual hunting and the daily business of living in camp, a good deal of work to do in readying the peltry for the trip over the mountains. "Preparing deer skins for market was something of a labor. Both the hair, and the outer grain in which the hair takes root, were scraped off with a knife, as a currier dresses leather; and then, when dry, the skin was thoroughly rubbed across a straking-board until rendered quite soft and pliant, thus stripping it of all unnecessary weight and fitting it for packing more compactly. This process, in hunter's parlance, was denominated *graining*, and the skins were then pronounced half dressed.

"The skins were brought into the Station Camp, and there, they were placed upon poles—high enough to be out of reach of hungry wolves, with several layers upon each other, then weighted down with more poles suspended by tugs, and covered with elk or other outspread skins, or

[64] Gray, *Bishop,* 152.

peeled bark to protect them from the weather. When enough of these skins were thus collected to form a pack, they were nicely folded and packed into a bale, two of which, one swinging on either side, would constitute a horse load." [65]

In addition to the animals the hunter killed for meat or peltry were several others, each for a different purpose. Elk was seldom killed for food; the meat was said to taste as good as venison, though much tougher, but of all the big game elk gave the toughest leather and was much in demand for moccasins and whangs. The English colonials cared little for buffalo beef if any other meat were to be had, nor would the bulky skins pay transport by horseback across the mountains, but buffalo robes were handy around camp and everybody enjoyed tongues and humps.

The only animal killed solely to get him out of the world was the wolf; all settlers hated wolves, their howling at night, their sneaky ways of stealing, and though they never harmed man, droves would sometimes attack and kill a dog. They were taken by digging and then artfully concealing the pit,[66] or building a small log house so baited with a piece of meat that when the wolf grabbed it, a door slammed shut over him.[67] Once he had him, the hunter sometimes "skelpted" him. "Dick Piles run a ring around the neck of a wolf once with his knife, drew its skin over its eyes, and let it go. 'Twas said he skinned another alive and let it go. He came in once with one on his back, holding it by its forefeet around his neck, and its hind feet hanging loose down his back, its mouth only tied, and its head sticking out from behind his shoulder beside his own. Piles had dark skin and a big mouth, and he came grinning in, I tell you, it did look a sight." [68]

Dick Piles lived in the same Kentucky fort as old man Strode with his pet buffalo calf, but the men of Walden's party would also have seen many sights, some man-made, but most there waiting for a man to see. No land was more various than the country they hunted over, for in it all was the monotony of neither wide prairies nor great mountains, or even forests like the pine woods of Georgia all of one species of tree. Most hunters undoubtedly had a love of the outdoors and a something inside them forc-

---

[65] Hanna, *Wilderness Trail*, II, 213–219; from Draper's unpublished "Life of John Finley."

[66] Byrd, *Writings*, 78.

[67] Used by permission of the publishers, Abelard-Schuman, Ltd., from *Pioneer Life in Kentucky, 1785–1852* by Dr. Daniel Drake, edited from the original manuscript (a series of letters to Drake's children) by E. F. Horine, Copyright by Abelard-Schuman, Ltd., New York, 1948 (cited hereafter as Drake, *Letters*), 217.

[68] FQ, II, 105, Clinkenbeard "Interview."

ing them always to climb the next hill and look over, for no man ever got rich from hunting, and a little trouble from thieving wolves or Indians or a pack horse lost in a swift creek, and a hunter came home empty-handed.

Profits varied even for the lucky. Judge Haywood states that in the course of one season an industrious hunter could earn a sum equivalent to sixteen or seventeen hundred dollars—the dollars of Haywood's day in 1823. This was an "immense amount of money," for a small farmer.[69] This figure seems too high; the skins to begin with were not free; ammunition, supplies, horses all cost money. The highest figure found for deerskins was one dollar [70] each for those of average size when delivered at some town east of the mountains. As each horse load was around one hundred half-dressed skins, it would by this reckoning have taken sixteen or seventeen horses to have brought Haywood's figure—but each hunter usually took only two or three horses, thus limiting his income for several months' or a year's work to two or three hundred dollars before expenses. Beaver was worth usually about five times—by weight—what deerskins were worth so that a hunter lucky in his beaver catch could have made a great deal, but two horse loads of beaver was a lot of beaver. Prices of all exports dropped at the Revolution, and in 1778 deerskins dried or cured with the hair on "were bringing a shilling sterling a pound," [71] or the equivalent of around fifty cents for an average-size skin.

Some like Walden did make money,[72] and in 1763 he and much the

[69] Haywood, *C & P*, 26.

[70] Hanna, *Wilderness Trail*, II, 319. Baynton, Wharton and Morgan in their branch firm at Pittsburgh in 1767, did pay more—that is, in goods—2 lbs. of powder or four lbs. of lead, for a buckskin, but the firm lost a good deal of money on such transactions. Regardless of the price, the white hunter, no different from the Indian, seldom if ever got cash; mostly skins were exchanged at the local storekeepers: Feb. 27, 1765, "Two of the Herrmans brought about 80 lbs. of deer-skins. . . . They and their company have been into the Shawanoe Country this time, but have seen nothing of the Indians." Dec. 18, 1766, "It was a busy day as hunters came in with deer-skins. They reported that several parties of hunters had fought with parties of Cherokees and some were killed on both sides." Quoted by permission of the publisher, North Carolina Historical Commission, from *Records of the Moravians in North Carolina*, ed. and tr. by Adelaide L. Fries, copyright by the North Carolina Historical Commission, Department of Archives and History, Raleigh, 1922 (cited hereafter as Fries, *Records*), I, 300, 337. The Moravians, March 28, 1764, *ibid.*, 285, started to Charles Town with 2,000 lbs. of deerskins, and the next year, *ibid.*, 301, they took five wagons loaded with, 9,400 lbs. As the Moravians lived in the neighborhood of what is now Salem, N. Car., many hunters named here in addition to the Harmons doubtless traded with them.

[71] Smythe, *Tour*, I, 291. This price is reckoned on the average weight of a half-cured skin, 2½ lbs. and the value of the shilling in Virginia at this time, *ibid.*, 4 shillings 6 pence, the Spanish dollar.

[72] Any discussion of money and wages would have to be considered in historical and sociological context. A daily wage of 50 cents, or half a Spanish dollar, was high. The

same group of men who had gone out two years earlier went out again, beginning much further west, for their second station camp was on Greasy Creek, near the line between the present counties of Hawkins and Claiborne in Tennessee.[73] During these years the favorite trail of the hunters was that through Cumberland Gap; they crossed the river at the ford of the Warrior's Path by present-day Pineville, Kentucky, went on eight miles to the mouth of Stinking Creek, and from there scattered group by group in different directions, east or west or northwest into the Dix River Country.[74]

Not all men would have taken this route, known soon as the Hunters' Trail. East Tennessee was a network of ancient Indian trails, all offering the best route through any given stretch of country, twisting through fords, finding the gaps in the ridges, leading a man on to hunt forever. Sometime during these years Walden's Ridge that runs like a long hogback across the eastern side of the Plateau was named for Walden; Newman's Ridge for Newman, with most of the creeks, branches, licks and valleys named for other hunters. Some hunters were on Clear Fork,[75] a stream not reached by going through the Gap; William Harilson and the Blevins men hunted around the mouth of Obey's River,[76] and some years later

Moravians, Fries, *Records*, I, 263–264, were in 1762 paying mowers and threshers 2 shillings a day (8 North Carolina shillings were by the Moravian reckoning worth one Spanish milled dollar); a flax swingler got 2 shillings 6 pence; a bushel of dried beans could be had for 3 shillings, but a bushel of salt cost 17, a pound of loaf sugar 4, or two days' work at mowing, but cattle, *ibid.*, 111, cost the equivalent of 10 to 12 pounds of sugar or 20 to 25 days' labor, 40 to 50 shillings. Butler, *Kentucky*, 32, in discussing the financing of Richard Henderson, land speculator, pointed out that Daniel Boone, Michael Stoner, and others hired to do the hard and dangerous work of road cutting got only the equivalent of 33⅓ cents a day, but had to pay Henderson $2.66 for each pound of powder used. Most ended up in debt to him; 8 days' labor for a pound of powder was a very high price; Morgan, I, XVI, 396, much further from a source of supply, had charged only 8 shillings per pound, reckoning 20 shillings to the pound sterling.

[73] Ramsey, *Tennessee*, 68.

[74] Haywood, *C & P*, 33–34. The Indian Trail through Cumberland Gap past Flat Lick had been known and used at times by traders, certainly as early as 1753, and possibly before Dr. Walker's trip of 1750. On Jan. 26, 1753, Alexander McGinty, Indian trader of Cumberland County, Pennsylvania, was, along with five other traders from Lancaster, Pa., and one from Virginia, robbed by "French praying Indians," on the south bank of "Cantucky River," as the traders were returning from a trip to the "Cuttawas (Cherokee) an Indian nation within the territories of Carolina." Hanna, *Wilderness Trail*, II, 255, gives the deposition of trader McGinty in full. John Findley who sixteen years later guided Boone through Cumberland Gap was robbed at the same time, but escaped. *Ibid.*, 252.

[75] Haywood, *C & P*, 33–34.

[76] THM, V, "Journal of Governor John Sevier 1790–1815," ed. John H. DeWitt (cited hereafter as Sevier, "Journal"), 255. Sevier in connection with a trip to see about the location of his land warrants around the mouth of Obey's River, mentions these men as having hunted there, but does not give a date.

Robert Crockett of the same family as Davy was killed by Indians in the Roaring River Country on the Plateau,[77] all of which would indicate that at least some of the hunters went in the same general direction as had James Smith, and all may have taken Tollunteeskee's Trail up the mountain and over, we do not know.

Not all men in the woods at this time were hunters. There is the journal, heard of but never seen, of one Swift who is said to have carried on mining operations on Red Bird Fork of Kentucky River as early as 1761;[78] later, he visited in East Tennessee, where he supposedly left a journal; people read it, and seemingly from this there sprang the multitude of legends of hidden riches and veins of silver, their whereabouts known only to blind men or Indians; stories that flourished until my childhood, but different in each locality; the silver was here, there, and everywhere.[79]

The silver was to be forever lost, but the fine hunting lasted long enough to attract all manner of men, and keep others coming back. Uriah Stone, who had been with James Smith in 1766, came back to Middle Tennessee the next year. He and a Frenchman loaded a boat with furs, and went down the rivers, but the Frenchman stole the boat. In this same year five men from South Carolina led by Isaac Lindsay hunted in Kentucky and on the Rockcastle which they are said to have named. They went on down into Middle Tennessee, taking water below the mouth of the Rockcastle, and at Stone's River they met James Harrod and Michael Stoner from Fort Pitt by way of the Illinois.[80] At this time or soon afterward Stoner made improvements on a claim to "A certain place known by the name of Stoner's Lick, on the east side of Stone's River.[81]

During the middle sixties, most of what is now Middle Tennessee and much of Kentucky on Green, Cumberland, and Dix rivers was hunted over or merely explored by the curious. There were in 1768 at least three parties of English hunters in addition to Morgan's men, all hunting on Cumberland and Green rivers. One party of Virginia hunters on the "Shawanese River" was attacked and another of "Virginia men who were hunting with six horses on one of the branches of Green River" was

[77] Ramsey, *Tennessee*, 96.

[78] Haywood, *C & P*, 33-34, here pointed out that some of the furnaces found by Long Hunters on the Big South Fork of the Cumberland were, judging from ancient horn buttons and the state of the slag, made many years before Swift.

[79] Collins, *Kentucky, 1882*, II, 414-415, adds several stories and legends to those of Haywood, and in the Big South Fork Country where Haywood located some of the mines the stories are still told. See Wayne County *Outlook*, July 21, 1955, "Legend of the Lost Gold Mine."

[80] Haywood, *C & P*, 75-77.

[81] Williams, *Dawn of Tenn.*, 323, n. 21.

robbed,[82] July 3 of that year. The Indians got all their horses and peltry, killed one, took the rest prisoner, and started to Post Vincent, but all the Virginians escaped, though Joseph Blankenship was not able to do so until he had been taken across the Ohio. He found his way to Kaskaskia where Morgan "cloathed him & furnished him with a gun & ammunition to carry him home." [83] The war party reached Post Vincent with nine scalps, seven were from Morgan's hunters, one from the Green River party and the other seemingly from a hunting party of six attacked "100 miles from the Ouabache," of whom the rest escaped.[84] These attacks were made by the Miamis and remnants of other tribes living near Post Vincent. At the same time the Cherokee in addition to capturing and killing hunters and various Frenchmen, killed the whole of a party of "Eight Emigrants from Virginia near the Ohio." [85]

In spite of Indians, the next year, 1769, was a notable one in the history of Tennessee and Kentucky. In that year Hutchins finished charting the course of the Cumberland and Tennessee; Boone, having failed on the first try, succeeded at last in finding his way through Cumberland Gap, though John Findley must guide him over the Hunters' Trail. It was also in 1769 that the push of settlement down the Holston went into what was to be Tennessee, and men in Virginia first petitioned for land on the Cumberland; some, in January, asked for land on the lower river; others, for a boundary beginning at The Falls.[86]

And in 1769 one of the largest and best known groups of "Long Hunters" spent more than a year in the Cumberland Country. Judging from the several members who later settled on land seen at this time, most were hunting land as well as game, and might in truth be called the pioneers of Middle Tennessee. We think first of the Bledsoe brothers—Anthony, Abraham, and Isaac, tall men of fair complexion and of English origin.[87] Their parents had come from England to Culpeper, Virginia, and the boys might never have gone to the frontier had not their mother died, for the three of them left home because of the unkind treatment of their stepmother. They had come about 1767 to the New River Country of western

[82] I, XVI, 367, Forbes to Gage, July 28, 1768.
[83] I, XVI, 355, Morgan to Baynton and Wharton, July 20, 1768.
[84] I, XVI, 376, Wilkins to Gage, Aug. 15, 1768, and *ibid.*, 367.
[85] I, XVI, 381, Gage to Hillsborough, Aug. 17, 1768.
[86] VS, I, 260.
[87] W, 31S, 190–201, is an account of Anthony and Isaac, their wives and children, stations, etc., after settling on the Cumberland. Both are well represented in Thwaites-Kellogg, *Dunmore's War;* see in particular *ibid.*, 106, 148, 169, 221.

Virginia. Anthony, the oldest had in the same year married Mary, the oldest daughter of Thomas Ramsey, a noted Indian fighter, active in the French and Indian War.[88] Isaac also took a Scotch wife, Catharine Montgomery, daughter of another noted border family.[89]

Abraham became more or less a professional hunter, but Isaac and Anthony were more interested in land and farming, especially Anthony who never came on the long hunts at all, and in 1774 furnished beeves for the troops in the Point Pleasant campaign.[90] Both settled in Middle Tennessee around 1784. Isaac was at this time twenty-four years old, and after surviving years of border warfare in western Virginia and East Tennessee, spent two or three years in Kentucky, and when that was safe from the Indians, he came back to the pretty land on Bledsoe Creek, and there he was killed, as was his brother Anthony.

Luckier than the Bledsoes, and hence engaged in even more Indian skirmishes, was outspoken Kaspar Mansker, then only twenty years old, but already a seasoned woodsman. He had been born on shipboard of immigrating German parents, spoke with a German accent, but is sometimes described as a Dutchman. Reared on the Virginia borders in the region of the South Fork of the Potomac, he knew nothing but the life of a borderer until the border of Middle Tennessee ceased to be, for after twenty-five years of Indian warfare in which he got several wounds, he died in 1822 on the land over which he had hunted in 1769. It was to Mansker's Station about twelve miles north of what was to be Nashville, that Andrew Jackson's future wife, Rachel Donelson, fled with her kin in the Indian-troubled times of 1780.[91]

Obediah Terrell, for whom Obey's River was named, was a chunky, small-sized man with a club foot.[92] He spent several years on the Cumberland as a farmer-hunter, and before permanent settlement was made in Middle Tennessee, hunted and camped along the river in what came to be

[88] The Ramseys were a noted family of Scotch borderers in western Virginia; Josiah who settled in Middle Tennessee in 1781 was captured by Indians when a child, and not released until after the battle of Point Pleasant, 1774; see Thwaites-Kellogg, *Dunmore's War*, 168.

[89] William Martin, W, 3XX (18), 1, who settled in Middle Tennessee around 1783, wrote of his neighbor Mrs. Isaac Bledsoe, and the pride she took in being the sister of John Montgomery, one of Clark's best officers in the Illinois campaigns.

[90] Thwaites-Kellogg, *Dunmore's War*, 169, quoting W, 3QQ, 86. Anthony Bledsoe is also well represented, chiefly by letters in NCR; see XXV, Index.

[91] Kaspar Mansker—his name spelled in various ways—is met with in practically all source materials relative to Middle Tennessee, for he was hunter, settler, warrior, as well as friend of many; for his early life see in particular W, 6XX, 53–54, 85–86.

[92] W, 5S, 62.

Cumberland and Pulaski counties.[93] A lone creature, he "had no children perhaps no wife."

Another future first settler on the Cumberland was John Rains from the New River settlements from which so many other hunters and first settlers came, and he, like the Bledsoes, had come west from Culpeper County. Ever noted for his woodcraft and skill in Indian fighting, he became an officer of militia, and like Kaspar Mansker survived close to twenty-five years of Indian warfare, fifteen of these on the Cumberland, yet he lived to be ninety-one.[94]

Also along was Humphrey Hogan who was to come overland in the hard winter of 1779–80 to settle in what is now Davidson County,[95] Tennessee. There were Joseph Brown, Ned Cowan, Robert Crockett, and Joseph Drake, a noted scout under Colonel Bouquet.[96] More of an Indian scout and hunter than farmer was William Crabtree, a "real backwoodsman," tall, slender, and with slightly red hair.[97] Another noted hunter was William Carr, who, like the Scaggs men and Walden, "always came back with skins and furs," and when no one would go with him in 1775 went off alone and was never heard of again.[98] There were also John Baker, Thomas Gordon, Jacob Harmon, a professional hunter as was his friend and neighbor on New River, James Aldridge, "a dark haired, heavily built man, stoop shouldered, but with a spritely mind." [99] Castleton Brooks also came, most possibly merely to see the country for he was a man of means and six years later served as witness for the biggest land deal in all the history of the west.[100]

Uriah Stone was going out again, and there is some question if this was the first long hunt for either Isaac Bledsoe or Kaspar Mansker. These two with John Montgomery, Joseph Drake, and Michael Stoner, who had been there in 1767, are said to have had in 1768 a station camp on what is now Station Camp Creek, north of the Cumberland in Middle Tennessee.[101]

[93] Daniel Smith spent one night at his camp near the mouth of Obey's River while on a buffalo hunt—THM, I, 58, Smith, "Journal," Tues., Jan. 4, 1780. The river was by then long since named for Obey.

[94] W, 6XX, 77.

[95] W, 1S, 62–84, is an account of this 1779 trip with eight settling families.

[96] Thwaites-Kellogg, *Dunmore's War*, 78, quoting W, 3B, 251.

[97] VM, VI, 340, Redd, "Reminiscences." Crabtree was also a scout in Dunmore's War.

[98] VM, VII, 249.

[99] VM, VI, 338–340, gives a good bit of space to these men; for Jacob Harmon or "Herrman" see Thwaites-Kellogg, *Dunmore's War*, 70.

[100] This was Richard Henderson's Transylvania purchase from the Cherokee; see Williams, *Dawn of Tenn.*, n. 36, 329.

[101] W, 1S, 59. The station was said to have been west of Station Camp Creek and south of the turnpike.

They could have done so; years later De Monbruen who visited Middle Tennessee from 1766 until he settled there, said that the first two men he had met from the English colonies were Isaac Bledsoe and Kaspar Mansker.[102] Still another source [103] had Mansker on the Middle Cumberland as early as 1762, but as he would at this date have been only thirteen, it seems a shade early.

As each hunter commonly took two, and sometimes more, pack horses there would have been a long line of horsemen and pack horses, almost always single file for the foot trails of the Indians were narrow, though here and there widened by buffalo. Ranging all around, back and forth, scouting, sniffing, forever on the lookout for game or trouble were the dogs. The general-purpose dog of the American pioneer had come into his own.[104] Little was written of him until the time of the French and Indian War; during these years he began to be mentioned, though almost never by name, in numerous accounts of border warfare—trailing Indians, fighting Indians, warning of Indians, saving the lives of his owner's family. He continued to do these things for the next forty years, but never as a hero; he was ever to be "just a dog."

There are many and conflicting accounts of the travels of the hunting party that went out in 1769.[105] Much of the confusion arose because it split into several smaller parties, each going in a different direction. Everybody is pretty well agreed they went in a body over the Hunters' Trail to Flat Lick, a noted camp site for hunters, and later, travelers into Kentucky. It was near the mouth and on the east bank of Stinking Creek, about eight miles north and a little west of Cumberland Ford.

At Flat Lick a hunter could keep on the Warrior's Path and go north into tributaries of the Kentucky River and on through Ouasiota Pass, but

---

[102] W, 6XX, 371. This account states that De Monbruen first visited the Cumberland in 1760, *ibid.*, 341; another, *ibid.*, 260, states that De Monbruen first came in 1766, but did not set up a trading post until 1785. Scattered through the Draper Manuscripts, particularly in W, 6XX, are numerous references to De Monbruen, and though not exactly alike, none mention his having fallen in with a body of Long Hunters, but all are agreed he was familiar with Middle Tennessee many years before settlement.

[103] W, 29S, 72.

[104] Mr. Wolfe's dog, Kercheval, *Virginia*, 93–95, was celebrated by a two-page quotation, but his name, alas, was not given.

[105] Most historians of the old southwest gave accounts of this long hunt. Haywood, *C & P*, 75–78, was the father of them all. Collins, *Kentucky*, *1882*, II, 416–418, following his father, follows Haywood with some variation. Williams, *Dawn of Tenn.*, 329, has a somewhat different version, but the Draper Manuscripts indicate that though all of the men may have in time reached all places named, they did not after crossing the Cumberland, and possibly even before, stay in a body. See also Hanna, *Wilderness Trail*, II, 213–229.

none of them seem to have done so at this time. Others went west over hills and ridges to miss a big bend of the Cumberland, and by way of Lynn Camp Creek and passing through the vicinity of present-day Corbin, Kentucky, they reached the Rockcastle River; judging from the stories told by Judge Haywood and others this region was a favorite of hunters.[106] Easier travel was to be had by leaving the Warrior's Path a little north of Flat Lick and taking another Indian trail that went north and west into the Dix River Country, and joined the Great Lakes Trail.[107]

These north-south trails in turn intercepted east-west trails so that a man on foot or horseback could go wherever he wished. Some went into "The Bresh," but so varied were the locations of The Brush that the term seems to have been applied to most any region of heavy undergrowth matted with vines and briars. Some located it on the right side of Cumberland Gap, which to the northward-bound hunter would be in the region of present-day Harlan; another indicated The Brush was in the region of the Hazel Patch [108] several miles north of present-day London. At least several members of the party of 1769 went through still another Brush for after reaching Flat Lick, they "went down the river and crossed at a remarkable fish dam which had been made in very ancient times, thence passed a place called the Brush, near the fish dam—where briars, brush, vines, and limbs of trees were heaped up and grown together, and near by immense hills and cliffs of rock. Following for some distance and then crossing the South Fork of Cumberland, they came to Price's Meadows. . . ." [109] This last was a favorite camping spot of hunters and

---

[106] Haywood, *C & P*, 35.

[107] Myer, *42nd Report of Bureau of Ethnology*, "Indian Trails of the Southeast," in discussing, 842–844, the Great Lakes Trail, the main body of which followed in Tennessee and southern Kentucky the route almost identical with that of the Cincinnati Southern Railroad, points out there were numerous side trails, with a converging of the two main north-south trails near the site of present-day Kings Mountain. Points, no longer shown on maps and sometimes forgotten—Parmleysville, Mill Springs (site of Price's Meadows), Whitley City, Rockwood, Tenn., and numerous others—were at the time of the Long Hunters all connected by Indian trail. Helpful in studying the movements of the hunters and first settlers in Tenn. is Myer's, "Archaeological Map of the State of Tennessee," *ibid.*, Plate 14, 746. See for Kentucky, "Streams of Kentucky," Ky. Dept. of Conservation, 1956. This map shows no trails, but it does name most of the creeks mentioned here, with not enough political features to confuse the viewer.

[108] VM, VII, Redd, "Reminiscences," 249, locates The Brush on the northwest side of Cumberland Mountain, but he again, *ibid.*, 249, locates it in the opposite direction or to "the right of Cumberland Gap." FP, II, Thomas Speed, *The Wilderness Road*, Louisville, 1888 (cited hereafter as Speed, *Wilderness Road*), 37, gives still another location in "The Journal of William Calk [cited hereafter as Calk, "Journal"] March 13–May 2, 1775." Here it was near the east bank of the Rockcastle River, not far from the crossing below the mouth of Scaggs Creek.

[109] Haywood, *C & P*, 75–76, indicated still another Brush on the south side of the Cumberland.

could be reached by any one of several trails; [110] Smith Shoals where the Great Lakes Trail crossed the Cumberland was in the old deeds designated as Fish Shoals, and this seems to have been their crossing place and would place this particular Brush in the region of Antioch, Kentucky.

Price's Meadows, near present-day Mill Springs, Kentucky,[111] was in the center of a game-filled area, easily traveled because of the many trails; one crossed the Cumberland at what came to be known as Fishing Creek Ford, another at Burkesville. Hunters with their main camp at the meadows would have followed these trails in many directions with some going west into the Green River Country. One group is said to have had a station camp near the site of Mt. Gilead meeting house in what is now Monroe County; it was near here that one of many such signs found in the region was cut on a tree, "Lost 2300 deerskins, ruination by God." [112]

Another party that included Kaspar Mansker, Isaac Bledsoe, Uriah Stone, Joseph Drake, and Henry Scaggs was not at this time a part of the group at Price's Meadows. The men kept on west after reaching the Rockcastle, following a trail that was a rough approximation of today's Kentucky 80, for they left Crab Orchard "to their right or northern side." [113] The group split into still smaller parties with only Mansker and Isaac Bledsoe going on together, and bearing southwest after crossing Fishing Creek. They came at last onto the headwaters of Bledsoe Creek in what is now the western part of Sumner County, Tennessee. They went down the creek, then turned west most possibly on Tollunteeskee's Trail to Nashville, at this point a rough approximation of present-day State Highway 25 between Hartsville and Gallatin. They reached Station Camp Creek, and followed it down until about three miles from its mouth on the Cumberland, where they found a buffalo trail crossing the creek at right angles.[114]

[110] *42nd Report of Bureau of Ethnology*, "The Trail System of the Southeastern U.S.," Plate 15, helps to a better understanding of the routes of the Long Hunters in this section of the country. The Great Lakes Trail made a great loop south of the Cumberland, touching the river at the mouth of Meadow Creek near Price's Meadows as well as at Smith Shoals where the main trail crossed. See also, *ibid.*, 797–800, Dr. Myer's discussion of that portion of what in time came to be known as the Wilderness Road between Scaggs Creek and Cumberland Ford, the southern part identical with the Hunters' Trail and the Warrior's Path. Fish Shoals or Fish Dam, in time known as Smith Shoals, appears in early Pulaski County Deeds; see PD, I, 20, Conveyance of Wiatt Atkins.
[111] WD, I, 204, 213–217, 220, contain several depositions concerning trails, hunting camps, and hunters in the region of Price's Meadows in 1775.
[112] Collins, *Kentucky, 1882*, II, 418, quoting Col. James Knox.
[113] W, 6XX, 82–84.
[114] W, 6XX, 82–84. They had gone west across the head of Green River; it appears they used the old trail across Buck, Pittman, and Fishing creeks in what is now

Here, they agreed to camp for the night, but so eager were they for exploration they rode away the same evening in opposite directions. Mansker went west and Bledsoe east to the creek on which he had already been, though at a more southerly point. "Col. Bledsoe told me that when he came to Bledsoe's Creek, about two miles from the Lick, he had some difficulty in riding along the path, the Buffelowes were so crowded in the path and on each side, his horse could scarcely get through, and when he got to the bank of the creek at the Lick, the whole land surrounding the Lick of about one hundred acres was principally covered with Buffelowes in every direction—not only hundreds but thousands; the space containing the sulphur spring was about two hundred yards each way across, and the Buffelowes had licked the dirt away several feet deep in that spring. The Buffelow did not mind the sight of him and his horse, but when the wind blew from him to them and they got the scent of him they would brake and run." [115]

Bledsoe shot two deer, but with the rampaging buffalo whose bellowings resounded from the hills and forest and could be heard for miles,[116] he was afraid to get off his horse, and left the deer to be trampled in the mire by the buffalo. Meanwhile, Mansker traveling west had got onto the creek that now bears his name, and had found another lick on his end of the buffalo road. In going from his lick back to Bledsoe's he killed nineteen deer.

Much the same story came from all parts of the Middle Cumberland—big game, beaver, plenty of bear, and also good land, for most of the hunters named were working farmers and could tell [117] rich land by the kind of growth on it—the bigger the cane the richer the land, likewise a cove thick with pawpaw meant land rich enough for hemp, beech bottoms were good, but the higher "post-oak land" such as that found over much of the Barrens was poor. And land without trees they did not want at all.

There were, however, other men who saw all land on the Cumberland

Pulaski County. Daniel Smith while surveying the line in December 1779, THM, I, Smith, "Journal," 56–58, commented after crossing Buck Creek of Cumberland, "here came in a trail to the French Lick." He was then a few miles east of present-day Somerset, but a good many miles south of The Crab Orchard.

[115] W, 6XX, 83–84. Bledsoe's Lick is in what is now Sumner County at Castalian Springs, and across the road from the marker designating Spencer's Sycamore.

[116] Haywood, *C & P*, 77.

[117] No two men judged exactly alike; see Smith, *Description*, 12; and some never learned at all; Kercheval, *Virginia*, Doddridge, "Notes," 247–251, tell of the uneasiness of farmers taking up new land, but unable to tell if it would grow good crops; sixty years after this, Andrew Jackson was trying to teach, by letter, his adopted son how to judge land.

as a fine thing, these the Indians. Hunters in 1769 were luckier than those, nameless to history, killed in the Green River Country the year before, for of this large group the Robert Crockett already mentioned was the only one killed.[118] Still, for these men, most of whom had as borderers learned the unpredictability of Indian attack, caution was ever the watchword. Many times when Indian sign was so thick the hunter was afraid to betray himself by gun or fire, he slept hidden in the cane, for no footed creature, man or animal, could get through thick cane without making a sound.[119] In spite of plentiful game, most would have kept handy a little jerk to eat in case trouble came and a man couldn't betray himself by firing a gun; another handy, easily carried food that could be eaten on the run was rokahamony sweetened with maple sugar.[120]

There was a rule in the woods that when two men were out together, no matter what the temptation of game, both never shot at once, so that always, in case of lurking Indians, there would be one loaded gun. The hunter on the Cumberland slept with his moccasins tied about his knees for a quick getaway, and his gun, loaded and primed, within arm's reach on two sets of low forked sticks pushed into the ground.

In spite of Indian dangers they enjoyed themselves along the river and in the game-filled woods from which came much delicious eating. One of the hunter's favorite dishes was stew: "the choicest bits of buffalo, deer, elk, bear, and turkey were put into the kettle with the proper seasonings;" this meant sage and red pepper, carried by many hunters, and still favorite seasonings on the Cumberland as they had been for generations in England. The stew done, each hunter fished for the parts he liked best. Usually at the end of a long hunt they were without meal, flour, or corn. They would then substitute the white meat of turkey for bread, though stewed bear's liver or the roasted kidney also made a "good substitute."

Turkeys were sometimes roasted whole; for this the cook, after cleaning, made "numerous small incisions in the turkey's skin and into each put a bit of bear fat and the proper seasoning." Lacking a Dutch oven large enough, a forty-pound turkey was cooked in a pit buried under coals as was the beaver tail that made a "luxurious meal." Take a large beaver tail "eight inches broad, wrap in wetted oak leaves, then put into a bed of embers and cover up overnight." It would by morning be "ele-

---

[118] Haywood, *C & P*, 76.

[119] Adair, *American Indian*, 320, 413, when in enemy territory tried always to camp in a "cane-swamp."

[120] W, 28S, 3-5, the account of Col. John Reese tells much of surveying, hunting, and food.

gantly cooked." Another dish suitable for overnight cooking was that delicacy of all delicacies—buffalo tongue. "First scorch the tongue a little, then peel off the outside coating, then stick upon a spit made of spice brush with the lower end inserted in the ground." This was then left roasting all night before a bed of embers with the spice brush giving it an "agreeable flavor." "What rich delicious eating," one old hunter exclaimed in later days, remembering all these as well as marrow bones on the Cumberland.[121]

Members of the party of 1769 gradually worked their way into Middle Tennessee, and around the end of the year most went home, taking the peltry, dogs, and horses. However, Kaspar Mansker, John Rains, Isaac Bledsoe, Uriah Stone, and Humphrey Hogan, all of whom save Stone later settled in the region, stayed several months longer [122] and went into the meat-packing business, but of the bear instead of the buffalo.

We wonder if in closing in on a bear they carried their leggings or some article of clothing before them. There was a belief among some hunters, notably Michael Stoner, that game would not cross any article of clothing that smelled of humankind, hunters sometimes kept small game such as coons and possums treed by tying a shirt or trousers around the trunk.[123]

Kaspar Mansker also at this time killed several buffalo to get skins to make a hut and two boats. The making of a skin or leather boat sounds quite simple. Indians and some white men could take one green buffalo hide and with a few knots and cedar limbs make a craft to carry a load across any river, but when one remembers the Lewis and Clark expedition of more than thirty years later with elaborate plans and ready-made framework but the inability to get a working model, Kaspar's boats seem somewhat marvelous. Such boats were made, hair side in, double-sewed with whangs, waterproofed with pitch, which Kaspar could also have made, then stretched over a cedar framework.[124]

The men filled the two buffalo boats, two trapping canoes, and a boat they had found, all with bear meat and peltry, and started down the Cum-

---

[121] W, 30S, 262–264, contains the recipes given.

[122] Haywood, *C & P,* 77–78. See also Collins, *Kentucky, 1882,* II, 417, and Williams, *Dawn of Tenn.,* 330–331; the accounts, each quoting different handed-down stories of different parties, do not entirely jibe.

[123] W, 12CC, 58. This narrator, Andrew Tribble, was a brother-in-law of Michael Stoner.

[124] Adair, *American Indian,* 291, describes the making of a skin boat; Kaspar was an expert. More than twenty years later "Col. Mansco invented the cowhide boats," used to carry guns and ammunition across the Tennessee at Nickojack, W, 6XX, 72.

berland from somewhere around the mouth of Station Camp Creek. They found French Lick, near the future site of Nashville, and more great herds of buffalo, but there is no mention of their having seen any of the several men from the Illinois on the Cumberland in 1769.

The party in the five small boats got safely to the mouth of the Cumberland, but here they discovered their bear meat was spoiling. They went into camp and tried to save at least part of the load by rendering out the fat. It was their turn to be molested by Indians, but, luckier than Morgan's men, they suffered only theft; Cherokee Chief John Brown and his party of twenty-five braves stole all their salt, two guns, and most of their ammunition. Happily some French traders came along, and with these the hunters exchanged peltry for salt, tobacco, flour, and taffia.[125]

They eventually got to Natchez [126] that would by the winter of 1769–70 have had in its surrounding regions several English families, but there was no sale for bear's oil, so they went down to Spanish Natches. Here, Uriah Stone found his boat, stolen by a Frenchman in 1767. Kaspar got sick and could not go home with the others; well again, he went on down the Mississippi, but at some point along the way he met a Mr. Fairchild with a drove of horses,[127] bound for Georgia. Kaspar helped the trader drive his horses through the Keowee Nation and on into the civilized region of Georgia, and from there he went home to New River.

In spite of one hunter killed and camps robbed by Indians, such were the attractions of the Cumberland that in 1771 a still larger party, said to number about forty, congregated in southwestern Virginia, then headed west.[128] Their leader was James Knox,[129] a Scotchman who had emigrated from northern Ireland when he was fourteen. He had soon learned the ways of life on the border, for by that date any community west of the Blue Ridge had plenty of good teachers. Most of his life like the lives of the other Long Hunters was to be filled with battles and skirmishes with Indians and British. He rose to the rank of major, settled in Kentucky, where he married the widow of Benjamin Logan, and lived to get rich, become a Kentucky Colonel, and member of the state legislature.

[125] There is the usual disagreement as to when and exactly where all this happened; but most follow Haywood, *C & P*, 76–78, whose account is much like those found in the Draper Manuscripts, though locations of skin houses, exact time and place of building skin boats vary.

[126] Mereness, *Travels*, "Journal of Captain Harry Gordon," Oct. 6, 1766, 479–480, gives a description of Natchez as he found it a few years before the visit of the Long Hunters.

[127] Haywood, *C & P*, 78.

[128] Collins, *Kentucky, 1882*, II, 418, quoting Col. Knox. See also W, 6XX, 85.

[129] Thwaites-Kellogg, *Dunmore's War*, 82, 111, has a brief biography of James Knox.

Another Scotch hunter from northern Ireland was young John Montgomery,[130] then about twenty-three years old. He was friend and connection of the Bledsoes, marrying a younger sister of Anthony's wife, while Isaac Bledsoe married John's sister. He, too, was active in the border warfare during much of the Revolution, and went as a captain with George Rogers Clark when it came the turn of the Americans to take the Illinois. He founded Clarksville on the Cumberland, but was killed near the mouth of the river by Indians in 1794.

Still another Scotchman from Ireland was James Dysart, an orphan who had come to America when he was seventeen in 1761. He like many immigrants had come first to Philadelphia, and then gradually worked his way south and west to the Holston. He may have on this trip carried a few books; in his old age after service at Kings Mountain he moved into a remote region in the Rockcastle Country, but when a friend commented on his solitude answered, "I am never lonesome when I have a good book in my hand." He in time collected quite a library and lived to enjoy it, dying when he was seventy-four.[131]

In addition to the three Scotchmen, new to hunting on the Cumberland, most of the others who had gone out in 1769 returned. Another newcomer was "an old man by the name of Russell so dim sighted he was obliged to tie a piece of white paper at the muzzle of his gun to direct his sight." He somehow managed to kill several deer, and was probably farsighted as he got lost, but was found nineteen days later by his son who nursed him back to health.[132]

The hunters had been gone from the Tennessee Country less than a year but when they came to Bledsoe Creek, "in four or five miles of the Lick where they had previously seen thousands of Buffelowes the cane had grown up so thick in the woods they thought they had mistaken the place until they came to the Lick and saw what had been done— One could walk for several hundred yards around the Lick and in the Lick on Buffelow skulls and bones, and the whole flat around the Lick was bleached Buffelow bones, and they found out the Cause of the Canes growing up so suddenly . . . which was in consequence of so many Buffelows being killed." [133]

[130] John Montgomery is met with in numerous sources; see Thwaites-Kellogg, *Dunmore's War*, 225, quoting W, 36J, 22. See also, I, V, 497–498, 585–587, for some of his activities as officer while serving under Clark. VS, I, 382–383, concerns a trip he made to New Orleans in 1780. He is often mentioned in the Draper Manuscripts as well as in DC, I.
[131] Draper, *Kings Mountain*, 404.
[132] Haywood, *C & P*, 78.
[133] W, 6XX, 85.

Hunters from the Illinois [134] and New Orleans had done their work well, and buffalo were never again plentiful in Middle Tennessee. The hunter's frontier was headed west of the Mississippi.

Most of the men on this trip stayed on the Cumberland until February of 1772; ammunition began to run low and all went back except Isaac Bledsoe, David and William Lynch, Christopher Stoph, and William Allen. One of the Lynches came down with the shingles, and Isaac Bledsoe started with him back to New River. The three men left on the Cumberland were attacked by Indians who took Stoph and Allen prisoner. These two were never heard of again. The other Lynch escaped, and he, too, started back east, but on the way met Kaspar Mansker and other men bringing ammunition.

All went back to the deserted camp; their dogs were still there, but grown so wild they hardly knew the men, though soon they were tame again. They continued on Station Camp Creek, but during an absence in August of 1772 the Cherokee plundered their camp and destroyed five hundred skins. The white hunters then moved to Big Barren River in Kentucky.

It was at this time Kaspar Mansker heard a strange sound; fearing trouble, he cautiously advanced to the source and found "a man bare-headed, stretched flat upon his back on a deerskin, singing at the top of his voice." [135] This was Daniel Boone, who, though coming a little late, hunted over and explored most of the Cumberland at intervals between 1769 and 1775, leaving his initials in many places, particularly Cumberland County in Kentucky.

The party led by James Knox is the last known group of Long Hunters on the Cumberland, though the place was never entirely deserted. De Monbruen was there from time to time as was Mansker. He is said to have hunted in 1775 with the Bryans, in-laws of Boone, and during this time had many exciting adventures with Indians; one he pursued all night, his way lighted by cane torches; and another he killed when the Indian tried to fool him by gobbling like a turkey.[136]

The growing restlessness of the Shawnee that in 1774 erupted into Lord Dunmore's War made hunting more dangerous; and two years later the beginnings of the Revolution made any woods west of the Blue Ridge

[134] George Morgan in spite of his preference for English hunters was, after bad luck from Indians and illness, forced to use Frenchmen, paying them for the meat brought in, I, XVI, 443, Morgan to Baynton and Wharton, Oct. 30, 1768.

[135] Haywood, *C & P*, 79, gives the date of this as August 1772. See also Thwaites, *Boone*, 94.

[136] Haywood, *C & P*, 80.

unsafe for American hunters, for the Indians sided with the British. Peltry, too, dropped in price and had to be exported chiefly by way of New Orleans. Even without these hindrances the great hunting days were ended, for most of the game was gone. Deer continued fairly plentiful in outlying regions, and until the last quarter of the nineteenth century could be found on the Plateau and up the Cumberland; nor did bear disappear with the quick completeness of the buffalo. There were a few years ago many old-timers who remembered bear from childhood, and who had killed deer on some out of the way creek, but in Middle Tennessee by 1806 elk was so scarce that when one was killed in Dickson County, the hunter had a great barbecue and invited all his neighbors, for elk meat was to most either a curiosity or distant memory.[137]

The men who hunted the elk and the buffalo disappeared with less dramatic suddenness, but more completely than did the animals they hunted. They were the last of their generations, for the hunters who went west of the Mississippi were hunters, not the many-handed men who hunted, farmed, and fought the Revolution. Many of the men mentioned as hunters were officers during the Revolution and later in the Indian warfare of Tennessee as were John Montgomery, John Rains, Isaac Bledsoe, and Kaspar Mansker. Most were good officer material; the letters of many have been preserved;[138] some spelled phonetically, revealing that their speech resembled the now almost extinct speech of the hills, filled with *gits* and *whars*.

Still, the ability to keep even a properly spelled muster roll was only a fraction of what an officer on the borders had to have. It took quite a man to persuade other men to leave their families, not to mention crops, and risk their lives on some battle front hundreds of miles away, and with no promise of pay, glory, or even food for themselves or the horses they furnished. "In the old frontier wars, every man turned out at the drop of the hat and each man was his own paymaster, forage master and commissary."[139] If he got killed there was no pension for his widow and children, not for a long time. A man who could lead men under such circumstances had to have all the woodcraft, courage, and endurance of the Long Hunter, plus something one might call personality.

Yet, somehow they did it, and like George Rogers Clark got little for their pains. The long-hunting-soldier-farmer-borderer was an unloved fig-

[137] W, 28S, 5–7.
[138] Letters of many men named here, or mention of their activities, may be found in addition to the sources named in DC, I, and DW, I, and TP, IV.
[139] W, 32S, 198.

ure; Washington praised his skill with the long rifle, but found him difficult. He was; he didn't mind fighting but hated soldiering, and had an innate distaste for drills, standing armies, and all other aspects of the military life. New Yorkers and New Englanders found him uncouth and even silly with his long shirt and "rifled barreled firelock," though even Boston made him welcome as long as he was needed. The British also hated the borderers for they found the "shirt-tail men, with their cursed twisted guns, the most fatal widow-and-orphan-makers in the world."

They were; they hated war. Fighting was a business they would be done with, and the only way they knew to end it was to kill as many men as possible. They could then return to the real struggle for more and better land on which to raise their families and get ahead in the world. Their many-handedness was typical of the times when a man had to be a world within himself: make a poem; sing a song; mend a gun; preach a sermon; shoot buffalo, Indians, British; make a moccasin or a boat; teach school; but always able to live in the woods if need be. The old west could not have been settled and won without such men. Still, the physical characteristics of the Long Hunter's way of life, were, in a sense, the least of him. It wasn't so much that he was completely master of a hard world and hence fearless, but rather it was his ability to believe in himself and the world around him. Seneca snakeroot may never have cured a single case of snake bite, but a man with faith and a bit of dried Seneca was never afraid to sleep in rattlesnake country. His faith did not stop at Seneca snakeroot, but went on, encompassing himself and other men around him.

CHAPTER VIII

ATTAKULLAKULLA

LATE IN November of 1774, "Two Indian men and a woman,"[1] listened to an organ played in the Moravian town of Bethabara near present-day Salem, North Carolina. The sweet singing both entranced and troubled the listening Cherokee, and the lid had to be taken off to prove no child was trapped within, making the sounds; the Cherokee took many scalps both white and Indian and burned a prisoner now and then, but they, like all Indians, loved children, and never in their raising of them found necessary the beatings the white man used.

The smaller of the Indian men may have smiled indulgently at the worries of his wife, the listening woman. He, from long association with the white man, knew the music was not that of a singing child. He had been delighted with the music of "ye spinnet"[2] in a Virginia mansion more than twenty years before, and in the intervening years had had many opportunities to hear an organ. This was Attakullakulla or the Little Carpenter, "the most celebrated and influential Indian among all the tribes then known," a half or vice chief of the Cherokee, and though renowned as a warrior his especial field was diplomacy. "Like as a carpenter could make every notch and joint fit in wood, so he could bring all his views to fill and fit their places in the political machinery of the Nation."[3]

---

[1] Fries, *Records*, II, 835.
[2] Williams, *Dawn of Tenn.*, 127.
[3] FP, 16—*Boonesborough*, George W. Ranck, Louisville, 1901 (cited hereafter as Ranck, *Boonesborough*), Appendix, 161–168, "Felix Walker's Narrative of his trip with Boone from Long Island to Boonesborough in March 1775," 162. Attakullakulla, though mentioned more than any other Cherokee in source materials of the old southwest, was never a full chief, as was Old Hop. Under Old Hop was also Oconostota,

He weighed only around 145 pounds, a "lean and light habited man," but "vary straight and square built," of a fine personal appearance and with a gracious and cheerful smile.[4] He spoke English perfectly, and had adopted the white man's greeting of shaking hands.[5] Still, he was very much a Cherokee with two large scores on each cheek, and his ears cut and so heavily hung with silver they reached almost to his shoulders.

Attakullakulla was at this time around sixty years old. His great-grand-fathers would have been among the strong-legged braves who traveled hundreds of miles on the hunt and the warpath with Gabriel Arthur a hundred years before. Even then his people had been losing the old ways and leaning more and more on the goods of the white man. Once when traders and their goods were scarce Attakullakulla, proud chief though he was, had gone begging to Governor Glen of South Carolina: "It was not from fear that I came here. . . . the Overhills People, being very poor and in straights for Goods, compelled me to go." But, want goods as he did, Attakullakulla could not forbear to add, "Do what we may the white people will cheat us in Weights and Measures. What is it a Trader cannot do? Some of the white people borrowed my yard-stick and cut it shorter, for which I am blamed." [6]

He would have been but a papoose on his mother's back when in 1715 French traders reached Chota after many weeks of the weary labor of pushing and pulling and poling their goods-laden boats up the Tennessee. The chiefs had let them build a scaffold in the town and there they had stood to display their goods and make orations; doubtlessly they used many fine words about brothers and friendship and peace, for through friendship with the Cherokee lay France's hopes for control of the middle Mississippi Valley.

The Cherokee had listened in polite silence, for they were ever a polite people. It is not recorded that they were rude when they sprang up, cut off the heads of the French traders, and threw their bodies into the river.[7]

chief warrior, as Attakullakulla was chief diplomat; see Williams, *Dawn of Tenn.*, n. 6, 147.

[4] VM, VII, Redd, "Reminiscences," 5.

[5] William Bartram, *Travels through North and South Carolina, Georgia, East and West Florida, the Cherokee Country—,* Philadelphia, 1791 (cited hereafter as Bartram, *Travels*), 364-365. It is a strange thing but a very great many who only saw Atta-kullakulla as did Bartram who passed him on the trail and stopped only long enough to shake hands, remembered Attakullakulla. He is more often mentioned by the British who had dealt with him for many years; there is a particularly good, but scattered representation in the Lyttleton Mss., Clements Library.

[6] Williams, *Dawn of Tenn.*, 132.

[7] *Ibid.*, 74.

Very different from the treatment they had given Gabriel Arthur, and more different still from the homage paid Sir Alexander Cuming, young Scotch Baronet and businessman, who had in "one of the most strangely romantic incidents in American history," gained Cherokee loyalty for England as well as a trade agreement.

History has not dealt kindly with Sir Alexander Cuming. Early, he lost favor with men in high places, but Attakullakulla must have remembered that strange and daring man with pleasure. Cuming had as a newcomer in Charles Town learned of England's wish but seeming inability to win the Cherokee, then, in 1730, known mostly through their white traders. No one sent him to the Overhill towns on the Tennessee, or told him how to treat with the Cherokee chiefs, a ceremonious and ticklish business.

Ludovick Grant and other traders were along, and old Eleazer Wiggan served as interpreter. Now, "submission was a thing the Cherokee had never made to God or man," and the white men who saw it all declared they would not have believed such a thing possible when Sir Alexander, "made a friend of the King of Tannassy, made him do homage to King George II on his knees, returned the same Night to Great Telliquo, was particularly distinguished in the Town-House by Moytoy, where the Indians sung songs, danced and stroked his Head and Body over with Eagles Tails; after this a Consultation was held with Moytoy and Jacob the Conjurer, who determined to present him with the Crown of Tannassy.

"The Solemnity continued, Sir Alexander made some Presents, received their Crown, Eagles Tails & Scalps of their Enemies, to be laid at his majesty King George's feet; and pitched upon six chiefs to attend him over to England, if it were possible for the Chiefs to reach Charles Town on Foot by the 20th of April, which they believed could be done." [8]

Sixteen-year-old Attakullakulla as a chief's son may have taken part in the ceremonies surrounding Sir Alexander, in any case he was one of the Cherokee who went with Sir Alexander and Eleazer Wiggan, the interpreter. They had a gay old time in England, were introduced to King George II, wined and dined by the merchants of London, and entertained in high style for about four months at public expense.

One experience the Cherokee may have found somewhat tedious was that of having their portraits painted by Isaac Besire in London. The chiefs

[8] Williams, *Dawn of Tenn.*, 89–90. See also *ibid.*, *Travels*, 115–143, "Journal of Sir Alexander Cuming."

were forced to pose in breeches, an aspect of white civilization the Cherokee were slow to adopt. The picture has survived, and we can see the seven Cherokee, some armed with sword and gun and some with bow and arrow, but all fashionably dressed in the European styles of the day, though hatless. Attakullakulla, then known as Ukwaneequa, is shown as a slight boyish figure in laced coat and breeches, armed only with a sheathed knife, and holding in his right hand a pebble-filled gourd.[9]

He must have enjoyed the trip to England for many times he asked [10] to go again, but always a second trip was denied. Still, he continued as "the most steady friend of the English," [11] and he more than any other one man helped the English hold the Mississippi Valley.

Attakullakulla as he listened to the organ on the November morning possibly went over the years that had earned him the title of Little Carpenter, building, cementing, mending the relations between English and Cherokee. Now, he was on his way to see about some further business with the white man, begun weeks before when Richard Henderson had come into the Overhill Country to offer goods and money for a large boundary of land to the west, claimed by the Cherokee as a hunting ground. Wars had been fought for centuries, treaties made and broken, and made again for this land that embraced most of the territory drained by Cumberland and Kentucky rivers or most of that between the Ohio and the drainage basin of the Tennessee. The Iroquois had claimed it, but had at the Treaty of Fort Stanwix sold it to the English, but the Cherokee had in the same year at the Treaty of Hard Labor agreed only that the white man should have land east of the mouth of the Kanawha.

Nobody had said anything to the Chickasaw who claimed a good bit of the southwestern corner around the lower Cumberland, or the Miami who had long looked upon land north of the Cumberland and on Green River as their hunting grounds. Nor did either potential buyer or seller consider the King of England who also claimed it, forbidding settlement, in spite of Virginia's long-standing claim for the northern part, and that of North Carolina and one proprietor, now Lord Granville, for the rest. Such questions of ownership seem not to have troubled either Richard Henderson or the Cherokee. As usual Attakullakulla had been chosen to deal with the white man, and his wife had been sent along as an envoy of the women,

[9] This painting is reproduced in Williams, *Dawn of Tenn.*, opposite 92.
[10] *Ibid.*, 277, 290.
[11] *Ibid.*, 234, quoting William H. Lyttleton, Governor of South Carolina during the French and Indian War.

who also must be satisfied with the goods to be received for their hunting grounds.[12]

Treating and living in peace with the English was only half of Attakulla-kulla's job. He had always to satisfy his own people that what he had done was just. This was not easy. Most Indians enjoyed a high degree of civil liberty, including freedom of speech, and the right to the use of the individual conscience. The Cherokee, like most other tribes, had no word in their language to express despotic power or obedient subject.[13] They seldom acted on impulse, but only after long deliberations, with the braves allowed to listen and have a voice in council, so that the great chiefs, and vice or half chiefs such as Attakullakulla, were leaders, not totalitarian despots ruling through fear and force.

The Cherokee had often been the despair of the English who were always wanting something—trade, land, protection, warriors for battles against the French. Major Andrew Lewis[14] who had treated with the Iroquois at Fort Stanwix cried of the Cherokee, "They're like the Devil's Pigg; they will neither lead nor drive."

Some tribes of Indians could be handled by the getting of the good will of their medicine men, a powerful group who like modern men of medicine usually lived apart from other men, enjoying special privileges and great authority with no one higher than themselves to question their pronouncements or the size of their fees—high, for most Indians had been trained to believe medicine would work in proportion to what it cost. It is not recorded that the Cherokee complained of their medicine men or sought to change them; we only know they did away with them and became a "nest of apostate hornets." [15]

Even without medicine men, the Cherokee were feared and respected by all, both white and Indian. In 1758 when all manner of strings were being pulled to get more Cherokee to fight in the French and Indian War, Forbes had written to William Pitt, "all the northern Indians, mostly our enemies, are kept in awe by the presence of so many Cherokee." [16]

---

[12] Williams, *Dawn of Tenn.*, 403–404. The Cherokee, like most Indians, were rather fond of their womenfolks. Chief Moytoy turned down a coveted trip to England rather than leave his sick wife, *ibid.*, n. 5, 90.

[13] Adair, *American Indian*, 459–460. Haywood, *N & A*, 272, said of the Cherokee: "Their darling passion is liberty. To it they sacrifice everything and in the most unbounded liberty they indulge themselves through life. They are rarely chided even in infancy, and never chastise with blows. Reason, they say, will guide their children when they are come to the use of it, and before that time they cannot commit faults."

[14] Williams, *Dawn of Tenn.*, n. 12, 177.

[15] Adair, *American Indian*, 85.

[16] Williams, *Dawn of Tenn.*, n. 15, 201.

Attakullakulla doubtless thought of those days not twenty years ago with the sorrow that all people remember the lost and the broken that cannot be found or mended, though even then in the mid-fifties the Cherokee had been less powerful than in the days of Gabriel Arthur. Still, they had been a strong nation when the English begged for help; Braddock was dead, his army defeated, and the once scattered Shawnee were strong again, their towns rising on the Ohio.

The Cherokee chiefs had been none too eager to send the warriors the English wanted; their braves had gone to other English wars and suffered at the hands of the men they had tried to help. Most of the chiefs stalled and offered excuses while the white men prepared for war, each building forts near the territory of the other. The westernmost of the English forts was Fort Loudoun, built in the heart of the Overhill Cherokee country, "in the fork of the Little Tennessee and Tellico Rivers, near a small Indian town," and put there because of the repeated requests of the Cherokee who claimed they were afraid to go on the warpath, unless there was a fort nearby to guard their women and children.[17]

Some Cherokee leaned toward the French, but the Little Carpenter managed to keep a faction friendly to the English, enough that in 1758 a large body of Cherokee went to the help of Colonel Washington. Help they gave, and then started home. Unfortunately each carried on his head an Indian scalp. Virginia had raised the bounty from ten to thirty pounds per scalp; such riches were more than some of the borderers could resist. A party of unsuspecting braves was lured by a group of German borderers led by Adam Harmon into a house and there, "They scalped all and butchered several (after the Cherokee told them they were no Shawnee)." [18] The government paid the bounty for the scalps.

Attakullakulla tried, but he could not hold back the young braves. They were men who in order to keep their self-respect as Indians, must take revenge for their murdered friends and relatives. The small chief went as a peacemaker to the English, and all blameless as he was, was seized and

---

[17] *Ibid.*, 184–195, a carefully authenticated account of the building of Fort Loudoun; location, 193; DeBrahm's Profile of Ft. Loudoun from Harvard Library, opposite 192.

[18] Adair, *American Indian*, 260. John Echols, one of the party of murderers, told in time the secret the 13 men had sworn to keep: ". . . the way the Capt proposed was to Dog them till night and then ly By till the Brake of Day and then Fall upon them and Kill them . . . We followed them and overtook them at a peach orchard . . . jest as they were leaving it . . . we Skelpt them that we killed, & then followed the other . . . he bled very much. . . ." This account from VS, I, 254–257, does not jibe with that of Adair whose version came from the Indians. Adam Harmon figured in both, but this VS account may refer to still another incident.

stripped of his arms.[19] He never gave up trying to keep the peace between the English and the Cherokee, but outrage followed outrage on either side; nor were all the low acts done by drunken Cherokee or borderers; English officers and gentlemen raped the wives of several Cherokee braves away on a hunting trip.[20]

Attakullakulla could no longer reason with his outraged people. He even organized a little expedition down to Fort Massac on the Ohio from which he returned with "two French prisoners and four French scalps," but by this time most of the Cherokee preferred English scalps. Fort Loudoun fell after one of the strangest sieges in history. The English soldiers starved because they could not risk their scalps to venture out to hunt or go over the mountains for supplies. At the same time the Indian wives of the forted men and a very few of the Cherokee men, including Attakullakulla, lengthened the siege by slipping "pumpkins and Fowles, corn and hogs into the fort." [21] The English, chiefly through starvation, were forced to surrender.

The soldiers, some with wives and children, were promised safe conduct back east. They were ambushed on the way with practically all killed or taken prisoner. Among the prisoners was Captain John Stuart, friend of Attakullakulla. The chief, as soon as he heard of the breach of faith, came and gave everything he had with him, including clothes and weapons, to the warrior who claimed Stuart as his own. Later, he and his wife and others went on a hunting trip, taking Stuart along and making it possible for him to escape.[22] Attakullakulla's life was in danger from the pro-French faction.

The British avenged their dead and the broken faith. The Cherokee in turn took white scalps, but the white soldiers, many under border leaders, destroyed whole Cherokee villages. France fell, and the badly beaten Cherokee must come to terms with the victorious British.[23] Half of the five thousand warriors they had had before the war were dead, towns were in ashes, orchards and fields laid waste; English rum, French brandy,

---

[19] Williams, *Dawn of Tenn.*, 204.

[20] Adair, *American Indian*, 260–261. Adair like most other men who spent many years among the Indians—Croghan and Johnson are good examples from the northern colonies—almost invariably saw, and often took, the Indian's side.

[21] Lyttleton Mss., used by permission of the Clements Library, Captain John Stuart to Lyttleton, July 11, Nov. 22, 1760.

[22] Williams, *Dawn of Tenn.*, 253–254.

[23] The best known of the many treaties made by the Cherokee during colonial days was that after the French and Indian War—the Treaty of Hard Labor, 1768; it marked the first attempt of the British Government to deal with them directly; heretofore treaties had been handled colony by colony.

and thieving traders along with the smallpox had reduced the morale of the Cherokee as well as their numbers. They were one with the buffalo bones found by Kaspar Mansker; there were still buffalo and there were still Cherokee, but the old days could never come again.

One wonders if Attakullakulla knew this when as an ambassador he spoke in 1763, trying to get what he could for the remnants of his people: "I am come to you as a messenger of the whole nation. . . . you live at the waterside and are in the light. We are in darkness, but hope will yet be clear with us. . . . Though I am tired, yet I am come to see what can be done for my people, who are in great distress. One God is father of us all, and we hope that the past will be forgotten. There is not a day but some are coming into and others going out of the world. As we all live in one land I hope we shall all live as one people." [24]

Attakullakulla believed what he said; other men believed him. The trouble was that though he loved England, her kings, army officers, and traders, it was not these with whom he now had to deal. England planted colonies; coming over the mountains and onto his hunting lands were people who planted themselves. The end of the French and Indian War, for the borderers who helped win it, had been more in the nature of the beginning of something very big, and no ending at all.

There was less inclination on the part of many to respect either the King's Proclamation or the boundaries of the Cherokee Nation. Thousands of settlers [25] came from Maryland, Pennsylvania, and other sections of Virginia into southwestern Virginia where the land business boomed, and much of this land was high up in valleys of the Holston, Greenbrier, New and other rivers that ran into the Ohio. Boundaries were vague, surveyors not always skillful; men settled knowing only the name of the branch or creek on which their land lay, not caring overmuch if it belonged to the Cherokee.

Virginia paid the men who had served in the French and Indian War with land warrants. Many ex-soldiers and buyers of warrants came into southwest Virginia hunting land, and they, too, were careless of the claims of the Cherokee, for the military warrants did not specify location. In July of 1768 Oconostota, a large man scarred with smallpox and a vice chief of the Cherokee, had complained to John Stuart, then in charge of Indian affairs for the southern colonies: "Father, the white people pay

[24] Williams, *Dawn of Tenn.*, 269–270.
[25] Haywood, *C & P*, 36–37, describes the rapid settlement of southwestern Virginia at this time; see also Summers, *Southwest Virginia*, 93.

no attention to the talks we have had. They are in bodies hunting in the middle of our Hunting Grounds—the whole Nation is filling with hunters, and the Guns rattling every way on the path, both up and down the river. They have settled the Land a very great way this side of the line." [26]

The settlers had built homes and cleared fields in southwestern Virginia on the Cherokee side of the line, but if forced to move, they lost everything. They appealed to Attakullakulla. He yielded again: "It is but a little spot of Ground that you ask, and I am willing that your people should live upon it. I pity the White People, but the White People do not pity me. Captain Guess (Gist) comes into our country hunting with fifty men. When we tell him of it he threatens to shoot us down. The Great Being above gave us this land, but the White People seem to want to drive us from it." [27]

Settlers continued to creep into the Cherokee country like water under a door. Attakullakulla knew what went on in the far corners of his kingdom, and when to strike at the French on the Ohio; and from traders and prisoners and his own many trips into the English colonies, even New York, he knew what was happening in countries across the sea; but it is doubtful if he knew when, in 1769, a white man came and built a cabin further down the Holston than any man had yet dared settle, for the cabin, on Boone's Creek about one hundred yards from its junction with the Watauga River, was in a cunning place, above a creek fall where it could not be easily attacked, and so situated that Indians passing on the nearby trail would never see it.[28]

The builder was William Bean, one of a race of hard-working, self-respecting borderers of Pittsylvania in southwestern Virginia from which so many Long Hunters and land viewers came. Soon, there gathered about him, relatives, former neighbors, and also several families from western North Carolina. Some of these had been in North Carolina only a few years, but this colony that had in Pennsylvania seemed such a Promised Land of freedom and cheap land, so much so that in 1765 upward of a thousand wagons had gone through Salisbury in the Yadkin Country, proved a sad disappointment, especially to those who had settled on Lord Granville's claim.[29]

This was a broad strip of land which, like that of the other proprietors of North Carolina, extended to the "South Sea." It hence embraced prac-

[26] Williams, *Dawn of Tenn.*, 358.
[27] *Ibid.*, 358.
[28] Ramsey, *Tennessee*, 94.
[29] Mitchell, "Map of 1755," Clements Library, shows Granville's Claim.

tically all that part of future Tennessee drained by the Cumberland, but this great boundary, unlike the rest of North Carolina, had never been sold to the colony, but was owned by Lord Granville, heir of the original proprietor.[30] His agents exacted heavy quitrents; added to these were the excessive and illegal fines and fees of the judges, sheriffs, and clerks under Governor Tryon.

Many settlers on this land in North Carolina found living conditions worse than in their old homes. Most of the colonies had ever been lax in protecting frontier families from either the Indians or criminals of all descriptions who fled to the backwoods. There were quitrents, fees, fines, and poll taxes, but these monies were seldom spent for the welfare of the backwoodsmen. The borderers soon learned to protect themselves. They established along the frontiers from Pennsylvania southward local organizations, sometimes for protection against the Indians as in Pennsylvania, other times as law enforcement agencies.[31]

Historians have given divers opinions on the merits and demerits of such organizations as the Black Boys of Pennsylvania and the Regulators of North Carolina. These groups at times indulged in excesses and suffered from bad leadership, but all undoubtedly came into being to correct troubles that should have been corrected by the various colonial governments. The sufferings of the North Carolina small farmers on Lord Granville's claim were so great that as early as 1759 the Regulation movement was aimed primarily at correcting the abuses of government.[32] The trouble

[30] Ramsey, *Tennessee*, 98.

[31] On the Virginia borders these spontaneously organized groups were usually known as Rangers, and though all undoubtedly committed atrocities they were the only form of protection the settlers had. In South Carolina the borderers had an even harder time; county courts were non-existent in the western portions and the farmers had no protection from criminals of all descriptions; see Ramsey, *Tennessee*, 97-98. Summers, *Southwest Virginia*, 61, 66-67, names several groups and their leaders organized by order of the governor, sometimes for the avenging of a massacre; there seems to have been in Virginia a less violent split between seaboard wealth and backwoods than in Pennsylvania and the Carolinas. Withers, *Chronicles*, 109-111, though not condoning all actions of the Pennsylvania borderers does make it understandable why such groups as the Black Boys came into being.

[32] Fries, *Records*, I, 205. See also Ramsey, *Tennessee*, 98-102; and Summers, *Southwest Virginia*, 115. Husband was a leader in the movement, but different from many of his followers, he ran away. See *"Some 18th Century Tracts Concerning North Carolina,"* published and copyrighted by the North Carolina Historical Commission, Raleigh, 1927. Chap. VII, *ibid.,* Herman Husband's "Remarks on Religion," sheds some light on his thinking. Possibly the best source of information on the Regulators, and seemingly unbiased, is that in Fries, *Records*. The Moravians lived in constant fear of the Regulators, but at the same time were afraid they would be accused by Gov. Tryon's men of hiding them or of being sympathetic, if not to their cause, at least to their persons; *ibid.,* I, 450-474, contains the editor's collection of material relating to the Regulators.

culminated in the Battle of Alamance in 1771. The Regulators, poorly armed, suffered a bloody defeat at the hands of Tryon's army equipped with cannon. Many of the wounded died when he set the woods on fire in which they were hiding, others were hanged, and still others were rounded up and put in chains, with all forced to take the oath of loyalty.[33]

The North Carolina exodus quickened. Many crossed over from the Yadkin into the Holston Country, hewed timber, built flatboats, and went down to Natchez, four hundred families arriving in that vicinity between 1773 and 1775.[34] Others settled near Bean, many pushing past him down onto the Watauga, and all thinking they were in Virginia away from the troubles of North Carolina. They learned differently when the dividing line, extended by Jefferson and Fry in 1749, had in 1771 to be lengthened again. It was a short and informal survey, but good enough to show that Bean and all those below him on tributaries of the Holston were in North Carolina on Lord Granville's Claim that lay south and parallel to the Virginia line.

Lord Granville's men were on the other side of the mountains, and never attempted any activity in what was to be East Tennessee. Closer, their claims more pressing, were the Cherokee, for though much of the land settled on the Holston south of the Virginia line was free of Indian title by a previous treaty, that on the Watauga was not. Once again, when the settlers appealed, the Cherokee, led as always by Attakullakulla, took pity. The Cherokee, in 1772, agreed to lease for ten years the land settled inside their boundaries; in return the settlers of Watauga paid what is estimated to have been several thousand dollars.[35]

Attakullakulla must have realized as he took the goods in 1772 that unless he did something, the home country of the Overhill Cherokee, the place of their towns and cornfields, would soon be swamped by the westward sweep of the white man. Would it be possible, he may have wondered, to divert the flood, send it further west, force it to pass his people by and leave them an island in the sea of whites? There was fine and level land north and west of the Cherokee, claimed by the Cherokee, but seldom hunted over by their braves, because when they went there, they met hunters from other tribes and the land "ran with blood." Certainly At-

---

[33] Fries, *Records*, I, 460. This is a second-hand account by the Moravians as they heard it from Martin Armstrong; at that time a rather lukewarm Tryon man, later he took the American side in the Revolution and came out to Middle Tennessee in 1784.

[34] Monette, *Mississippi*, I, 404–406.

[35] Ramsey, *Tennessee*, 109.

takullakulla didn't think too much of Kenta-ke, for more than twenty years before he had told his friend Dr. Thomas Walker of the fine land that Walker had already tried, and failed, to find.[36]

Attakullakulla had heard since childhood of the white man's schemes to plant colonies west of the Alleghenies. All had come to nothing. But things were different—now; very different. These people planted themselves, and there was no end to their coming. In one year, 1773, Dr. Thomas Walker had sold in southwestern Virginia at the back door of the Cherokee, 980 boundaries of land totaling 201,554 acres.[37] Still closer to the Cherokee were those who continued to come down the Holston and onto the Watauga and the Nolichucky.

Settlement had not stopped here, but had jumped hundreds of miles away into the fine flat land of which Attakullakulla had told Dr. Thomas Walker. Virginia surveyors had by 1774 marked out many boundaries of land in what was to be Kentucky, and some in Tennessee, mostly as payment for soldiers of the French and Indian War. True, the surveyors had in the summer of 1774 all run home like frightened sheep when the Shawnee started giving trouble again at the outbreak of Lord Dunmore's War, but the Shawnee had been defeated in the Battle of Point Pleasant at the mouth of the Kanawha, and surveyors had gone into Kentucky again.[38]

Attakullakulla would have known from his wide-ranging braves when actual settlement, instead of mere survey, started as James Harrod and others, chiefly from western Pennsylvania, began Harrodsburg in 1774. He would have known, too, of the hunters' camps along the Cumberland. There were around him many traders, Englishmen faithful to England, and they must have told the old chief something of what was being written of America as early as 1761: "Such a country at such a distance could never remain long subject to Britain; you have taught them the art of war, and put arms into their hands—what may they not be supposed to do if the French is no longer a check upon them." [39] He may have heard of

[36] Williams, *Dawn of Tenn.*, 126, quoting a deposition of Dr. Walker.
[37] *Ibid.*, 363.
[38] Summers, *Southwest Virginia*, 146, lists 42 surveys totaling around 48,000 acres made by John Floyd, Hancock Taylor, and James Douglas in 1774-1775; also surveying at this time was Isaac Bledsoe. Thwaites-Kellogg, *Dunmore's War*, 110-133, "Hanson's Journal," April 7-Aug. 9, 1774, is an account of surveying done in Kentucky; this, too, before Henderson's Purchase, and judging from Boone's trip of 61 days in 1774, Summers, *Southwest Virginia*, 147-148, there were a great many surveyors scattered over most of what are now central Kentucky and Middle Tennessee.
[39] Williams, *Dawn of Tenn.*, 282, quoting "Reason for keeping Guadaloupe at a Peace," etc.

one, Edmund Burke, also speaking to the English of the Americans, "But if you stopped your grants, what would be the consequence? The people would occupy without grant."

There were, not many years after Burke spoke, plenty of people, all those in East Tennessee, near Attakullakulla who had settled without benefit of grant. There would be more. Get what he could for his people while the getting was good, he must have reasoned. Sell the far hunting grounds already being settled by white men; his braves never used them much any way. In any case he agreed to accept the proposal of Richard Henderson—a few wagonloads of goods for twenty million acres of land.

Soon, wagons came creaking up and over the mountains and into the Overhill towns. Word of the big deal, so big that all previous land deals looked small by comparison, spread far and wide. The actual bargaining was not to begin until the 14th of March, but the Cherokee began in January to gather at the place agreed upon, Sycamore Shoals of the Watauga.[40]

The Indians unlike later-day whites trusted all members of their tribes so that for them there were no secret councils, no classified information. It has been estimated that at least twelve hundred Indians, about half warriors, came. The Indian women would have been as interested as the men to see the six wagons loaded with guns, ammunition, rum, and other things closer to a woman's heart—brooches, shirts, wristbands, Dutch blankets, and bright cloth.[41]

Attakullakulla could look into the faces of the children racing hither and yon, and see the influence of the white man, for after four generations of traders, prisoners of war, and soldiers among the Cherokee, there were many children with white fathers, some of these with white grandfathers. Some would be Great Warriors and die fighting the white man, others would die on the March of Tears, little more than sixty years away. A Cherokee baby born that year was George Gist, a grandson of Christopher Gist, guide for young George Washington, a strange man who while pursued by French Indians in the Kentucky woods sorrowed for a dead bird. His grandson, better known as Sequoyah, is remembered, not for the scalps he took, but because he made an alphabet for his people.[42]

Many of the Indian women dressed in the manner of white women, but no sunbonnets or housecaps, and usually bare feet or moccasins. Wives

---

[40] Ramsey, *Tennessee*, 116-117.
[41] Williams, *Dawn of Tenn.*, 409-410.
[42] *Ibid.*, 429.

and mistresses of the traders would have been resplendent in silks and satins of the latest fashion; beautiful, for according to most who saw them, all of the Cherokee women had "features formed with perfect symmetry and countenances cheerful and friendly," and were "tall, slender, erect, and of a delicate frame, moving with grace and dignity." [43]

Compared to these, the wives of the men of Watauga would cut a poor figure. Many, had they been there, which is doubtful, could have walked with but little grace; those not pregnant would have been suckling a young one with a toddler or two clinging to her skirts.[44] The borderer's wife never had the time for hunting trips with her husband or jaunts to listen to a treaty as had the Indian wife. They were, different from the Indian women,[45] voiceless as a group with no female representation in the councils of their menfolk. Yet, it was women such as these who could bear anywhere from six to fourteen children and keep the farm together while the head of the house was gone hunting, or fighting, or trading or politicing, who had forced Attakullakulla to get what he could for the land. A prophecy made by the Frenchman Iberville almost seventy-five years before had come to pass: "The spaces between these mountains and the sea are occupied by settlers whose children will be obliged to cross these mountains to find room for themselves." [46]

And so they had.

[43] Bartram, *Travels*, 484; see also his well known description of the Cherokee girls picking strawberries. Haywood, *N & A*, 279: "The Cherokee women are elegantly formed, have sprightly eyes, accompanied with modesty and chastity, which renders them far from uninteresting objects."

[44] Neither the French nor Indian wife could match the strength and fecundity of the pioneer woman of British stock; and a low birth rate may have been one of the greatest weaknesses of the Indian. In all chance accounts of groups of Indians such as those who went with La Salle or Martin Chartier, there were seldom as many children as warriors. Crane, *Frontier*, n. 91, 131, gave for the year 1715 a census of a portion of the Cherokee: the Upper Settlement towns had only 400 male children to 900 warriors, 480 young females to 980 women; the Middle Settlement only 950 boys to 2,500 men with 900 girls to 2,000 women; the Lower Settlement towns 600 men, 400 boys, with 480 girls to 620 women. Contrast this with the 1795 census (a special one taken for statehood) of Tennessee, Ramsey, *Tennessee*, 648—white males above 16 years, 16,179, below 19,944; females are lumped together 29,554, but in all census figures for early Tennessee males outnumber females and children under 16, judging from the boys, account for more than half the population as compared to a third or less for the Indian. There were of course numerous other reasons; communal living in towns on the part of the Cherokee made enemy destruction relatively easy—it was impossible for one or several war parties to destroy each forted white farm or even homes scattered over a wide area. There was, too, the border's ability, peculiarly British, to carry on a war without prostituting all of life to total warfare.

[45] Among the Chickasaw "only six beloved old women" were allowed in each temple, Adair, *American Indian*, 127.

[46] Williams, *Dawn of Tenn.*, 24.

We do not know how many white men listened to the treaty making. The treating went into the morning of the fourth day, and during this time listeners would have come and gone as to a long-drawn-out trial in a county seat town. Fifty-five [47] are known to have been there, but the chances are many more came for a little while, drawn to hear the oratory and see the sights, with some hoping to settle on the great tract of land that was supposedly changing hands. All settlers on the leased lands along the Watauga were interested; if the Cherokee were willing to sell twenty million acres, they might sell outright, instead of lease, the few thousand rented by the Wataugans. A year later 111 men of East Tennessee signed the Watauga Petition for Annexation to North Carolina; [48] many of the signers may have come after the treaty, but we cannot be certain all men then living in the region signed. In any case there were a good many settlers in the neighborhood of Sycamore Shoals by March of 1775.

The average settler on the Holston at that date was not much inclined to have his portrait painted and there were then no portrait painters, in so far as we know, in the neighborhood. The few men whose likenesses have come down to us and actually known to have been at the treaty making were all much older before the picturemaker came. In general they would have looked little different from other southern and western farmers of their day; the broad-brimmed, rather shallow-crowned hat continued to be worn as were knee breeches, hose—most commonly of wool or linen for the farmer—and buckled shoes; and most men in March at Sycamore Shoals were swathed in greatcoats and mufflers.

Clean-shaven as a rule, with long hair, some wearing it plaited and clubbed up as did Daniel Boone,[49] others had only a pigtail, and some merely brushed it back and tied it with a ribbon, a leather whang or a piece of eelskin in the manner of Andrew Jackson of later years. There would have been a sprinkling of powdered wigs; [50] it is doubtful if Rich-

---

[47] Williams, *Dawn of Tenn.*, n. 16, 405–406.

[48] Ramsey, *Tennessee*, 138, lists the signers.

[49] Thwaites, *Boone*, 110.

[50] Anthony Bledsoe who then lived in East Tennessee always wore a wig, W. 32S, 358. See Summers, *Southwest Virginia*, 116–119, for a generalized discussion of the first settlers of East Tennessee. They were predominantly Scotch and Scotch-Irish, Presbyterian, readers of Bibles and stillers of whiskey, but generalizations about the border or even one segment of it should be avoided; not all Scotch were Presbyterian; some were of the Established Church, and a few were Catholic. The border varied from point to point; see Summers, *Southwest Virginia*, 808–809, for a list of around 350 landowners on Holston and Clinch rivers between March 15, 1774, and March 20, 1775, predominantly Scotch and English; see also list of Militia and Revolutionary soldiers of Washington County, *ibid.*, 853–865. Regardless of nationality there were scatterings of Quakers, Methodist, Baptist, and many with no religion at all.

ard Henderson, a judge and especial target of the Regulators, would have appeared without one. There would also have been here and there a fancy vest, a silk-clad leg, or even a pair of military boots. All stories of the old west, even those concerned with Indian warfare, have chance mentions of men in bright dress.

The man of the west was not much given to jewelry of any form.[51] Whatever love of ornament he had was reserved for "her," meaning his gun, not his wife, for by 1775 there were a few rifle stocks inlaid with silver or even gold. Dieverbaugh's feat in the Illinois of seven years before would have been considered but "indifferent marksmanship": and a proffered target of a barrelhead at one hundred paces an insult. A seven-inch target at 250 paces was not uncommon in the Revolution.[52] Following the custom of the border, "all male inhabitants carried their rifle-barreled firelocks wherever they went." She was still much like the earlier rifle with full stock and hexagonal barrel, though some by now had sett- or double-trigger guns, as these began to be used about 1770.[53]

Seen through today's eyes many of the listening white men would look small and scrawny, insignificant beside the long rifle or shaking hands with some portly Indian chief. Tradition relates of many of the leaders that they were tall and heavy or long and lank, in size a George Washington or an Andrew Jackson. A listing of the sizes of several hundred during the French and Indian War tells a different story. Many were no more than an inch or so above five feet, most were less than five six, and rare indeed were the six-footers.[54] Small, many no doubt were, but tough, the way groundhog hide or hickory is tough, and not in the present meaning of the word.

At the heels of many were from one to half a dozen dogs of all shapes and sizes and varieties, feists and coon dogs and big rough bear dogs, but all able to do in a pinch most any thing any other dog could do, and mongrels all. The horse, too, ridden by the average farmer was not a purebred

[51] Early will books yield an occasional watch, quite often silver knee and shoe buckles; lack of rings and other jewelry was not a mark of poverty; the Scotch Presbyterians were in many respects as puritanical as the early Puritans; they frowned upon jewelry, and the marriage ceremony was usually performed without a ring; a custom new in many sections of the United States as the keeping of Easter and Christmas as holy days.

[52] John Blair Linn, *Annals of Buffalo Valley*, Harrisburg, Pa., 1877 (cited hereafter as Linn, *Buffalo Valley*), 82–83, letter of Col. Thomas Thatcher, Nov. 1775; he wrote with wonder of the marksmanship of the hunters, described as wearing round hats.

[53] FQ, II, 114, Clinkenbeard "Interview," spoke of a "double triggered gun," in 1777; Thwaites-Kellogg, *Dunmore's War*, 119, "Hanson's Journal," a "double barrelled rifle." This last I would say a rather rare weapon.

[54] VM, I, 378–390; *ibid.*, II, 37–49.

in the sense the horses that had, beginning about 1730,[55] been imported from England by wealthy Virginia planters were purebred. Still, there were certain definable varieties of American horses in use in the west by 1775. One of the most outstanding was the "beautiful Chickasaw horse," [56] noted for his fleetness and stamina, and able in a pinch to carry his rider seventy miles without rest. The Chickasaw had in their migrations from the west brought Spanish horses, crossed these with breeds from the southern colonies, and the Chickasaw running woods horse had been the result.[57]

The Cherokee by this date also had "excellant horses of a good size, well made, hard hoofed, handsome, strong and fleet." [58] The horses like the men were smaller than those of the present, usually no more than thirteen- or fourteen-hands high, but could travel "incredible journies," and in the sandy lands of North Carolina were never shod,[59] hence, hard hooves were a prime asset. Still, hard hooves or no, the horses in the rocky lands of East Tennessee, like those later on the Cumberland, had to be shod.

Horses were plentiful [60] in what was to be East Tennessee, for the early settlers there, though not wealthy as were the great landowners on the Piedmont, were not poor. They had slaves, land, guns, books, feather beds, furniture, pewter, and other earmarks of middle-class farmers in comfortable circumstances. Practically all of this well-being came from the land. There was at this date little business on the Holston.[61] They would, during the long delays and recesses that ever marked Indian treating, have gathered in little groups, squatting, whittling, chewing tobacco, talking, their voices carrying echoes of other lives in other countries—Scotland, Northern Ireland, Germany, France, Wales with possibly half of English origin,

---

[55] Gray, *Agriculture*, I, 202.

[56] Adair, *American Indian*, 205.

[57] *Ibid.*, 296.

[58] *Ibid.*, 241.

[59] Used by permission of the publishers, the Trustees of the Public Libraries of North Carolina from *The Natural History of North-Carolina with an Account of the Trade, Manners, and Customs of the Christian and Indian Inhabitants*, by John Brickell, M.D., Dublin, 1737; edited by J. Bryan Grimes, reprinted and copyrighted by the Trustees of the Public Libraries of North Carolina, Raleigh, 1911, pp. 53–54.

[60] The Great Valley through Augusta and Fredrick counties of Virginia from which many then on the Holston had migrated was less famous than eastern Pennsylvania for its agriculture, but was more noted for stock raising than Tidewater; see Kercheval, *Virginia*, 54–55.

[61] John Carter's Store just below the junction of the North and South forks of the Holston was established in 1770, and here a Natchez-bound settler could buy supplies; see Thwaites-Kellogg, *Dunmore's War*, 221. Jacob Brown on Nolachucky was another early settler who sold goods, though his main business was gun- and blacksmithing.

but there were then many Englands. The speech of most was slow, easy sounding, many making two syllables where the man of Tidewater or the New Englander would make one—oald, chaance, Rockcaastle.[62]

They would have talked of many things: the battle of Point Pleasant in which many had fought the previous fall, their farms, crops, prices, hunting, politics, and religion, but most of the talk would have been of land. Land was many things to many men, and for many of the south and the old west it was a passion. All those in East Tennessee had already moved more than once in search of better land, a wider valley, a hill with fewer rocks.

They like the Indians and later generations of farmers would have drawn with twig or knife handle maps in the mud or dust of the road, marking trails, rivers, creeks, licks, or the boundaries of a piece of land. Much of their talk would have centered on land drained by the Cumberland, some of it finer than any they had ever known. Few of the men in the neighborhood had been to the Kentucky Bluegrass, but all of the hunters who had gone overland to the Cumberland lived nearby. Word of the fine land there would have scattered far and wide. Castleton Brooks, gone on the long hunt of 1769, was there that day,[63] but in and out through the crowd for the first day or two of treating were at least three other men who had seen much more than had he.

One of these was big Michael Stoner who had visited Middle Tennessee as early as 1767 and taken up land near the mouth of Stone's River. He had since spent much time in the country that was now changing hands, and the year before had gone on a long, leisurely journey with Daniel Boone to warn the surveyors in Tennessee and Kentucky that Cornstalk had taken the warpath. Now, he was going away again as one of a party [64] hired by Henderson and headed by Boone to go ahead into Kentucky, and where there was no existing trail, blaze one, to the settlement they would make, soon to be known as Boonesboro. It is doubtful if Michael

[62] Or at least the phonetic spellings as revealed in I, VIII, the Draper Manuscript, and elsewhere would so indicate.

[63] Williams, *Dawn of Tenn.*, 406, lists 55 men known to have been present. Among those who settled on the Cumberland were James Robertson and his brother Charles, Martin Armstrong, William Blevins, and Tilman Dixon whose home built around 1787 is still standing at Dixon Springs; he was a witness for the treaty; see Ranck, *Boonesborough*, 156. Jesse Benton, brother-in-law of Nathaniel Hart associated with Henderson in the land deal, was there; his son Thomas Hart "Old Bullion" Benton later settled in Middle Tennessee with his widowed mother on land Jesse bought.

[64] Thwaites, *Boone*, 117, lists all those who went with Boone. Henderson with William Calk and others came after the road was blazed.

Stoner spent much time in the crowd, for he was "never less alone than when alone in the woods." [65]

Daniel Boone, on the other hand, never wearied of talking, especially of "Kaintuck," and with him was a long lank, gray-eyed boy who loved to talk of "Kaintuck, the bars, and the pea vine" there.[66] This was Edmund Jennings, future settler in Middle Tennessee, where he was sometimes seen with a scalp at his belt. He had been with Boone "that time his son was killed," the disastrous attempt at settlement in 1773. The drawn-out dying and the bloody bodies of the young men had not phased Edmund; he spent the next twenty years in fighting Indians, fifteen of these in Middle Tennessee. Jennings, Stoner, and Boone left with their party two or three days before the treaty was signed, or as soon as Henderson was certain the deal would go through.

It was men such as these who were and had been constantly through their generations pushing into the unknown. William Bean, the first settler in what was to be Tennessee, may have been somewhere around listening as his home was just up the river; behind him in the Bean family was a long history of migrations; first into Pennsylvania, then down the Valley of Virginia and into southwestern Virginia, and at last across the divide and into the Holston Country and down. East Tennessee was a hard and bloody land until 1795, yet by 1826 a young Bean was on the Sabine River in Texas.[67] The Boones were much the same story; they, too, had come from Pennsylvania but had crossed over into the Yadkin Country.

Somewhere around may have been Samuel Newell, at least he signed the Watauga Petition the following year. He was then about twenty-five years old, a big, blue-eyed man of English origin. He and his brother had fought at Point Pleasant, six years later he would survive a serious wound at Kings Mountain where he served as colonel; he would be active in the Lost State of Franklin, and when that collapsed settle on the Cumberland some miles upriver from Price's Station.[68] He moved in his old age to Indiana, and by 1840 descendants were in California. Elisha Walden, the Long Hunter, moved from southwestern Virginia into East Tennessee, from there to Kentucky, and next to Missouri where he died in 1844.[69]

[65] W, 12CC, 56. See PC, I, 46, and WD, I, 207–213.

[66] W, 6XX (49), 1–4, this from the account of Felix Robertson, son of James, concerning the trip Edmund made with his father in 1779–1780 to settle Middle Tennessee. See also the account of Robert Weakley for Jennings, *ibid.*, 32S, 358–360.

[67] W, 6XX (49), 4.

[68] W, 32S, 115, is Col. Samuel Newell's statement of what took place at the Battle of Kings Mountain.

[69] W, 6XX, 74.

Valentine Sevier, brother of John, first governor of Tennessee, was like his brother raised in Frederick County, Virginia; he lived for a time in East Tennessee, and from there went to Middle Tennessee, and paid for his early settling with the loss of most of his family.[70]

One could go on with a long list of families or men who were active on several borders, all of whom lived at least for a time in East Tennessee, kingpin of the old west. Twice in the next five years men had to rush from the Holston to bolster the forever surrendering stations in Kentucky, and without men from East Tennessee it is doubtful if George Rogers Clark could have taken the old northwest.[71] One could give a long list of reasons and explain the why of it all, but men risking their lives and those of their wives and children to plant corn in a field where corn had never been planted cannot exactly be explained. The land was only part of it. Things were not crowded in East Tennessee and once a man got there, and if he behaved, there was nothing to push him on,[72] no more than there was any one to push Clark on to take the Illinois. He had to beg and fight for such help as he got.

The readiness with which her settlers went to war for neither pay nor glory was soon a part of Tennessee tradition and early earned her the name of Volunteer State. Soldiers and settlers for far places were only the half of it. By no means all who went into the west were third or fourth generation borderers. The Long Hunters as a group were fairly representative of border communities; several of the most noted such as Isaac Bledsoe were first generation Americans, and many such as Kaspar Mansker and James Knox were immigrants, but different from the days of Von Graffenried's starving settlers, there was a society on the borders strong and large enough to absorb and teach the unlearned newcomers. Border society taught them considerably more than how to plant corn, build a log house, and use the rifle.

They changed in some magical way, and became another seed in a great seedbed, for East Tennessee was the seedbed of the west in politics and

[70] Valentine Sevier signed the Watauga Petition, but there is no record of his having attended the treaty making; Ramsey, *Tennessee*, 619, published his letter, telling of the massacre of most of his family, and the destruction of his station near Clarksville in 1794.

[71] I, VIII, contains many letters from men of East Tennessee; written usually to Clark concerning men and supplies from the Holston for the west; see in particular, 40, 42, 497–498, 604.

[72] Early settlers in East Tennessee with no knowledge of the boundary (Jefferson and Fry in 1749 had carried the line only to Steep Rock Creek of the Holston) until run by Isaac Bledsoe in 1771. Summers, *Southwest Virginia*, 116, thought they were in Virginia, but there is no record that anybody made any attempt to abide by Virginia laws on religion.

religion as well as soldiers and settlers. In time the whole midwest as well as the newer south had more in common with the Scotch-Irish and others then gathered on the Watauga to hear Attakullakulla than with the men of Tidewater who spoke the King's English and belonged to the Established Church.

These men and others who came to the west were to be for the next forty years often at variance with leaders in Philadelphia, New York, and New England; conservative souls who didn't like the idea of war or of controlling the Mississippi or buying Louisiana or annexing Texas,[73] for the collective land passion was strong as the individual's love of land. These men were farmers hating war; they feared standing armies and the strong central government wars demanded;[74] but if it came to a choice between blood and land, they'd risk the blood.

They had fought and they would continue to fight—in Kentucky, the Illinois, Kings Mountain—and dash many times with their leader John Sevier against the Cherokee when they, led by their traders, sided with the British. Their sons would follow Jackson to New Orleans or die in the frozen Ohio swamps in the War of 1812, sons and grandsons would precede Sam Houston, who also lived a time in East Tennessee, to Texas; some would die like the celebrated Davy Crockett whose family was represented there, and some, less celebrated, would merely plant another Baptist or Methodist Church.

The long learning had gone past the mere conquering of a physical environment. The borderers could settle far places, hold the land against all comers, and breed up their own kind to do the same—and always as farmers and individuals, not as paid soldiers or members of a planted colony.

Equally important, they had learned to govern themselves. Remote settlements such as those of East Tennessee, many miles over mountains and across rivers from centers of law and order, would not degenerate into gathering places for seminomadic outlaws as had the settlements of

---

[73] It should be remembered that though the old southwest agreed on many such matters there was even before Sevier's Lost State of Franklin in 1785 great differences of opinion; as early as 1802 Michaux the younger, traveling through, thought Tennessee would become two states, and during The War it seemed at times as if it would. There was of course never a "Solid South"; the three-way battle between Clay, Calhoun, and Jackson was between three southern gentlemen of Scotch-Irish extraction.

[74] Ramsey, *Tennessee*, 323–334, "Constitution of the State of Franklin." Drawn up in East Tennessee in 1785, it is possibly the most complete expression of pioneer governmental opinion ever made, but of course not all pioneers would have agreed with it, and, too, many of its tenets were purely English in origin—distaste for large standing armies, belief in trial by jury, etc., etc.

the Illinois during their first years. The date is without authentication, but most agree it was 1772,[75] when the men of Watauga met and formed a governing body, known as the Watauga Association. Historians use this as a landmark, for it is held to be the first known attempt in America at complete self-government.

Many have paused for finely phrased eulogies. Possibly they are appropriate and no praise can be too high for the men of Watauga. Still, in a less formal way, men on the frontiers of Pennsylvania, Virginia, and North Carolina had been exercising self-government in many matters for more than forty years. Practically all settlers in southwestern Virginia, western North Carolina, the Pennsylvania border, and East Tennessee, though often of English origin, belonged to religious minorities. It was through the practice of their religions—Baptists, Presbyters, Methodists—that the first steps toward self-government were taken.[76] Steps that had not begun in America.

No tax money built their churches, no officials chose their ministers, no government prescribed prayers, or rules for worship, or told them what to believe. Acting as individuals and without coercion men had learned to work together to form the various units of society needed to supply a lack the individual was incapable of supplying. They had in addition to churches, built schools, formed parties for protection against the Indians, choosing their leaders by popular vote, disregarding colonial laws with their suffrage qualifications. They had as borderers, forever in the minority and on the losing side, learned the tyranny of the majority. Even as they were gathered there, Virginia jails held men as prisoners, sometimes under slow torture,[77] whose only sin was that of promulgating the Baptist faith. The very diversity of religions and nationality backgrounds gave the men of East Tennessee a common bond. Pride was another. Men with good opinions of themselves are inclined to have good opinions of their fellow men.

[75] Ramsey, *Tennessee*, 133–139, is an account of the Watauga Association, but few actual facts are known.

[76] Waddell, *Annals*, 49, gives extracts from church minutes revealing many activities of these bodies such as the binding of orphans, later discontinued when a county was organized. Schools, too, were often organized through the churches, particularly the Presbyterian; ministers of this faith held in many respects the same relative positions in the border communities as did ministers of the Established Church in Tidewater; each was often the best educated man in his community, though the Presbyterians of course got no tax money.

[77] Kercheval, *Virginia*, 61–62, is an account of how Mr. Ireland in Culpeper County Jail shortly before the Revolution was so smoked with burning red pepper and sulphur, that he never "entirely recovered from the great injury."

The borderer was as a rule an individualistic sort of person, and he could not always in his reasoning see the rights of others, particularly if the others happened to be Indians or suspected Tories. He hated any government that smacked of despotism or paternalism, but he would accept leadership. And by 1775 the border was supplying its own leaders. Three of the greatest men of the old west were at the treaty of Sycamore Shoals.

Acting as witness for the deed, was John Sevier,[78] Little John to the Indians, Nolichucky Jack to the men who fought with him, and "the handsomest man in Tennessee" to just about everybody. He was ever courtly in his bearing, attending balls and teas, and fond of fancy dress; he may at the treaty have worn a claret-colored or scarlet coat, silk stockings and other clothing to match; we do not know, but in later years he dressed very well indeed. He was descended from Huguenots of some means and education, a people who in their bones remembered persecution and wanted no more of it. Born in the Great Valley, he had had a borderer's childhood, and as a baby had known the forted life at Fredericksburg.

He, like Attakullakulla, was a small man of fine appearance, and about him, too, there was a winning way that made men, not ordinarily given to following, follow him. He had come to the Watauga in 1773, later than many of the others, but already he was making a name for himself; in time he would beget seventeen children, lead thirty-five attacks against the Cherokee, be successful in all and get paid for one, he would father the Lost State of Franklin, be six times governor of Tennessee, serve as a United States Senator, and when old, his goods and his life spent for Tennessee, be published as a "coward and a poltroon," [79] by upcoming young Andrew Jackson.

This was only one of many soul-trying experiences Sevier had; one of the worst was the defection of two of his men on the way to the Battle of Kings Mountain; worse, since he had never kept his plans secret from his men, the two Tories told all they knew to the enemy. Sevier stopped to hold neither a hearing nor an investigation, but rushed on, helped win the battle, and on the way home had another battle, this of ideologies, with

[78] John Sevier, 1745-1815, has been dealt with by all historians of the old west, a few biographers, and is represented in the Hall of Fame, but for me at least his "Journal," THM, V, 159-193, 232-262, and *ibid.*, VI, 18-60, gives a better idea of the great love of life in general, interest in people, places, events, and such small matters as a horse remedy, or the sowing date of celery of this many-handed man.

[79] Tennessee *Gazette*, Oct. 26, 1803, quoting from Knoxville *Gazette* of Oct. 10, 1803: "Know ye that I Andrew Jackson am authorized and do pronounce publick and declare to the world that his Excellency John Sevier Esquire, Governor, Captain General and Commander in Chief of the Land and Naval Forces of the State of Tennessee is a base coward and a poltroon," etc. etc.

his own men.[80] They had selected around thirty Tories for hanging on the spot, but Sevier with Isaac Shelby saved most of the men from such a death, including the two traitors. There is no record he was ever labeled pro-English, or that he ever in any way persecuted the relatives of these men or others merely suspected. He was a many-handed man who could take a scalp [81] or note the blooming of violets in his garden.

Men of all nations and of all ages have at one time or another shouted in battle, but Sevier is credited [82] with re-introducing the battle shout among the borderers, his an Indian war cry that survived for many years. Settlers on the Cumberland used it in various forms, the Death-Whoo-Whoop or the scalp cry was for battle, another for victory. Women listening behind fort walls more than once mistook the victorious shouts of their returning menfolks, bearing green scalps, for those of advancing Indians.[83]

This battle cry was all the backwoodsman had in the way of war trappings. The year before he had eaten of beef and flour, sung soldiering songs,[84] and heard the fife and drum, for even in the backwoods the British colonials kept up appearances. This, now, was 1775, and for the next twenty years men fought in Tennessee with neither song nor drum, nor sword nor flag, and often without rations. It is doubtful if the ordinary soldier under Sevier ever saw a United States flag, and the idea of taking an oath to one would have thrown him into a long pondering. The only flag they ever looked at much was the white flag of the British at the Battle of Kings Mountain, and not understanding what it meant, they shot down three along with the men who carried them before Sevier and Shelby knocked up their guns.[85] The proper sign of non-resistance in the Indian wars was the gun lifted butt foremost.

[80] Draper, *Kings Mountain*, 246, 254-255, are the accounts of men who were there; see also Ramsey, *Tennessee*, 221-244, and Summers, *Southwest Virginia*, 275-278, quoting Charles B. Coale and others concerning treatment of Tories in general—not always good.

[81] All white soldiers on the borders commonly took scalps, though as a rule they confined them to those of the Indian; Thwaites-Kellogg, *Dunmore's War*, 346, "seventeen scalps dressed and hung upon a pole."

[82] Ramsey, *Tennessee*, 589.

[83] W, 6XX, 704, ". . . when the Indians fled the whites raised the Indian yell, and those at the house had no doubt they were all killed and thought it was the Indians yelling." This, only one of many such comments on the Indian warfare on the Cumberland; this around 1785.

[84] Thwaites-Kellogg, *Dunmore's War*, 330, "fife and drums"; 334, beeves; 335, "flower" (flour); 361-362, British fighting song; and 433-439, a collection of American ballads concerning the event.

[85] Haywood, *C & P*, 71. See also W, 28S, 114. I found no mention of a flag or uniform in any firsthand account of border warfare. At Kings Mountain the Whigs wore papers in their hats and the Tories pine twigs in order to tell friends from enemies, Draper, *Kings Mountain*, 270.

Another upholder of law and order in the old west and at the treaty making was young Isaac Shelby.[86] He in 1770 had settled in East Tennessee with his father Evan and brothers Moses, Evan, and James all of whom were, along with himself, to be at the Battle of Kings Mountain.[87] Isaac, first generation Welsh American, was for many years to be busied with border warfare. Finished with war, he turned to politics and became Kentucky's first governor, for early he had built a forted farm in the Kentucky Bluegrass.[88] Still, the military life in which he always served as an officer, did not make him lose sight of the rights of individuals, not even in the dark years when the East was turned against the West, and French Fever was in 1793 strong in Kentucky, so strong that many Kentuckians were going downriver with their rifles—apparently to fight for a foreign power.

Washington suggested the men be arrested on suspicion. Isaac Shelby refused: "For if it is lawful for any one citizen of this state to leave it, it is equally so for any number of them to do it— And if the act is lawful in itself, there is nothing but the intention with which it is done which can make it unlawful. But I know of no law which inflicts a punishment upon intention only, or any criterion by which to decide what would be sufficient evidence of that intention. I shall also feel but little inclination to take an active part in punishing for a supposed intention." [89]

Fellow soldier with Isaac on the Point Pleasant campaign, and now at the treaty, listening, watching all that went on, was James Robertson. He was then thirty-three years old, "a man of fine appearance, about six feet high, weighing about 180 pounds, fair skinned, with blue eyes well sunk in his head." [90] No human being is typical, but James Robertson was possibly the most nearly typical of the farmer-borderer-unpaid-soldier who

[86] VS, I, 296–297, is the deposition of Isaac Shelby concerning what took place at the treaty. These depositions are the best firsthand accounts of the Treaty of Sycamore Shoals; see also that of John Reid, *ibid.*, 284–285; James Robertson, 285–287; and that of his brother Charles, 291–292.

[87] W, 31S, 202.

[88] Much has been written of Isaac Shelby, for whom Shelby County, Ky., was named; see Collins, *Kentucky, 1847*, 523–531.

[89] *Ibid.*, 49.

[90] W, 6XX, 164. All Tennessee historians gave James Robertson, 1742–1814, some space, but he has never to any extent attracted the attention of biographers. A. W. Putnam, *History of Middle Tennessee or Life and Times of General James Robertson*, Nashville, 1859 (cited hereafter as Putnam, *Tennessee*), devotes most space to a political and military history of the region, but at the time of writing the wealth of source material pertaining to Robertson, now readily available on microfilm or like NCR published in book form, could be studied only after much travel and searching through records and manuscripts, often uncatalogued.

settled the west. No politician, and not given to schemes of increasing his fortune at the expense of his neighbors, he, like Sevier, never belonged to the little crowd who got the richest plums of land and political appointments.[91] He served Tennessee in various capacities for more than forty years and was paid for little of what he did; he lived an especial target of Indians for twenty-five years, and had two sons and two brothers scalped and killed, but when he died, away from home on a poorly paid but extremely dangerous job as agent to the Chickasaw, it is doubtful if he had as much in money and property as when he went to Middle Tennessee in 1779.

His Scotch-Irish father had settled as an immigrant in Brunswick County, Virginia. There he had married an English woman, Mary Gower. Most of their lives had been spent on first one border and then another. They had for a time lived on the upper Neuse River in North Carolina, and there the elder Robertson had died, leaving a large family with James the oldest.[92]

James had grown up, too busy helping raise the rest of the family, to take time out for education. It was not until his marriage at twenty-six that he learned to read and write, taught by his wife, Charlotte Reeves, nine years younger than he. He had spent the early years of his married life in Wake County, North Carolina, a region torn with the Regulation Movement, and is thought to have been a Regulator, but at the time of the Battle of Alamance, 1771, he had already settled on the Watauga.

He had not brought his family on his first trip west to the Holston, and in going home for them had swung south through Georgia to attend to some business. This meant a long trip over little-used trails through one of the most mountainous regions east of the Mississippi. Different from a later trip to the Cumberland, he carried no compass, and when there came several foggy days all in a row, the kind of weather dreaded by every woods traveler, Robertson got lost. In the constant rain, he let his powder

[91] Robertson's first service of record was in 1770, an appointment to the County Court (Court of Quarter Sessions this was usually called in Virginia) of Botetourt County, Va., Summers, *Southwest Virginia*, 109. Forty-four years later, he died during the troubled Indian times marked by the Fort Mims massacre. He was paid for some of his service but as late as 1805, A, V, "The Correspondence of James Robertson," 79, he was still trying to collect pay for corn he had furnished at an Indian treaty in 1795. This same source, 185-253, indicates a man hard pressed for money; he had in 1804 bid for the job of cutting and improving the Natchez Trace, south of Nashville and at that time little more than a pack-horse trail. There were complaints about his first attempts, and in order to keep the job he lowered his bid to the pitifully low figure of $6.00 per mile for building a wagon road to certain specifications.
[92] W, 31S, 34-35.

get wet, and, unable to hunt, got so weakened with starvation he could scarcely walk, and would have died had he not accidentally met two hunters. He learned much from this experience, and though often in strange country, was never lost again, only at times somewhat mistaken.[93] How many years of his life he spent in the saddle on long and lonely journeys, usually on governmental business, is a figure he never reckoned. He enjoyed the woods and the hunter's life, was fond of bear meat, sweetened rockahomony, and often wore moccasins, even when not in the woods.[94]

He was by 1775 already a noted man in the west, and had since his coming in 1770 taken an active part in the life of the Holston Country, but fame did not come until the Battle of Point Pleasant in which he not only fired the opening shot, but saved the army from a surprise attack. His wife, children, and neighbors may already have been singing:

"It was by God's kind providence, that or-der-ed it so,
That Robertson that morning, a hunting he did go,
    Before that he had walk-ed far, a savage army spied
Which drove him to the camp again, 'there's Indians boys,' he cried.

    " 'Come now brave boys,' he boldly said, 'to meet them let us go,
'For fear these cruel savages, give us a fatal blow,
    'And we must ne'r give way to them, whilst we remain alive
'Or else into the River, they surely will us drive.' " [95]

Still, his part in the long and bloody battle was but a fraction of his service in Lord Dunmore's War. One of his harder jobs was to persuade men to leave their ripening grain unharvested, not to mention families unprotected, and go the hundreds of miles to the mouth of the Kanawha. He at last got some in the notion of leaving home, but it was slow, "for my Soul I could not get them to March sooner." At last he was able to write, "I have with a Great Deal of Both good words & Bad ones prevailed." Other men had still to be collected, and his, waiting on short rations and

---

[93] W, 6XX (49), 1-3, an account by Felix Robertson, born in Middle Tennessee in 1781, and *ibid*. (50), 1-19, that of his younger sister Lavinia Robertson Craighead, plus another by Felix, *ibid*. (50), 19-25, are the most comprehensive sources of Robertson's background, his early life and family, though there are in the Draper Manuscripts many others; see in particular, W, 31S, 31-54.

[94] W, 28S, 1-5. This is an account of a surveying trip made with Robertson after the settlement of Middle Tennessee.

[95] Thwaites-Kellogg, *Dunmore's War*, 438, quoting W, 3XX, 18, sent to Mr. Draper by Col. William Martin of Dixon Springs, Tenn.

with no hope of pay, were restless. "I must stay with no more than six men unless I kill part and tye the others. . . . I have a vast deal of trouble keeping them in tune," he wrote during the delay.[96]

But keep them tuned up he did, though he had to offer five pounds of his own money to the first soldier who would bring in an Indian's hand.[97] White men and Indian alike respected such a canny man. The colonial governments, paying bounties on scalps, never seemed to realize that a full scalp taken just above the ears, could be made into several smaller ones, each worth a bounty. One group of Indians manufactured nine from two.[98]

Robertson for all his Indian fighting was still basically a farmer, who liked to be in his fields before breakfast working with his slaves.[99] He had a passion for fine horseflesh, and an interest in iron manufacture, the land business, and knew how to survey, but for most of his life he neglected his personal affairs for governmental business in Middle Tennessee, done usually for nothing. Noted as an Indian fighter, he was like Sevier respected and loved by many Indian leaders. One of his last acts was to offer a reward for the arrest of the white men who had murdered the "peaceable friendly Chickasaw named Tuscan Chickamubby. . . ."[100] Previously, he had begged governmental funds for the education of two Indian boys.[101]

He, more than any other man, though he could not have succeeded without help from such ex Long Hunters as John Rains, John Montgomery, Edmund Jennings, and Kaspar Mansker, kept alive the settlements in Middle Tennessee, and as he had already helped establish East Tennessee, he is often referred to as the "father of Tennessee." One can think of no better title; in all his dealings with the men who fought with him he had to handle them after the fashion of a father. There was no law to force men to go on expeditions, no pay once they had gone, and no restrictions on their treatment of the enemy.

"Spare the women and children," was Robertson's constant command. A band of impoverished Tories came to the Cumberland settlements and asked permission to stay. Some were for driving them away, but Robert-

[96] *Ibid.*, 94, 99, quoting W, 3QQ, 67-68. See also W, 6XX, 970, for Robertson's deer-hunting trip on the morning of the battle. Yet as in most of the old stories there were contradictions; for another version see Withers, *Chronicles*, 169.
[97] Thwaites-Kellogg, *Dunmore's War*, 139, from W, 3QQ, 73.
[98] W, 29S, 125.
[99] W, 1S, 61.
[100] Nashville *Clarion*, Sept. 15, 1813.
[101] A, V, "The Correspondence of James Robertson," 166.

son objected: "This is a free country in which no man should suffer for an opinion. If they show themselves worthy I propose to let them stay. If their acts deserve it hang them to the nearest tree."[102]

Robertson as he listened to the treaty making may have had moving to the Cumberland on his mind. He had already heard much of the region from one of the most enthusiastic real estate promoters who ever lived—Daniel Boone. This famous hunter was not exactly typical of the men of Tennessee. They were in general a grimmer, more determined bunch of men, almost never taking Indian prisoners or letting themselves be taken. Boone was captured more than once, and at the Battle of Blue Licks showed his inability to lead men who knew less of Indian fighting than he did; nor could he like Dr. Thomas Walker find, without a guide, the gap he hunted. Compared to Josiah Ramsey or Joseph Drake, he, until middle age, knew next to nothing of the ways of Indians, and paid heavily for his lack of experience when on his first venture at settlement he let his party get divided.

Michael Stoner was a better marksman, and practically all hunters had more luck than Boone, but Boone talked his way into immortality. Men believed him; and one who heard him was James Robertson; on trips between the Yadkin and Kentucky, Boone stopped in the Robertson home and talked much of the pretty land on the Cumberland. Later, when he moved his family to East Tennessee, he lived a time with the Robertsons, and there, he, his wife, and seven children were all baptized by a traveling Episcopal clergyman.[103]

Robertson, of course, knew by 1775 many other men who could have told him of the Cumberland, but the only other definitely mentioned as having done so was the Jones who had tried to settle Jones Bend.

Somebody wanted the Cumberland badly, for Richard Henderson had more trouble in treating for Middle Tennessee than for all the land he bought in Kentucky. It may have been, that being closer home and more commonly used as a hunting ground, Attakullakulla and the other chiefs disliked the idea of selling it; or they may have remembered the Chickasaw, who, living much closer, had a more valid claim than any other tribe. But nobody had bothered to ask the Chickasaw what they thought of the business. The Cherokee, when pressed to sell the Cumberland, declared, "them was their hunting grounds and their children might have reason to complain." They repeatedly insisted the land below the Kentucky

[102] Ann E. Snyder, *On the Watauga and the Cumberland*, Nashville, 1895, 25.
[103] W, 6XX, 651.

River was a bloody ground, and a reading of the depositions gives the impression that the dark and bloody ground was not Kentucky but Middle Tennessee.

Henderson was insistent and at the same time offered two thousand more pounds. They yielded. The treaty making at one point was almost brought to a standstill by the impassioned speech of a young, rather fat chief, known as Dragging Canoe,[104] said to have been a son of Attakullakulla. His sad prophetic words that the Cherokee, "once so great and formidable would be compelled to seek a retreat in some far distant wilderness" then "the extinction of the whole race," have been repeated by many.

The young chief was, in spite of all the white blood he later shed, a pathetic figure. He must have been unaware of a truth, doubtless very plain to the Little Carpenter, that even without a sale these people would settle the land anyway. In trying to get what he could for his people Attakullakulla surpassed himself in eloquence that day. Pleasant Henderson, brother of Richard, declared he "was the most fluent, most graceful and eloquent orator he had ever heard." [105]

He carried the day, selling most of Kentucky, a good-sized chunk of Tennessee, a strip for a path to Kentucky, and also the land on the Watauga, already leased by the settlers.[106] He couldn't see the March of Tears, or maybe he did see, knowing that whatever he did could not stop it. Whatever the old chief saw, the deeds were signed after three days of bargaining on "St. Patrick's Day in the Morning," and the Cherokee sold land they did not entirely own to Judge Henderson who could not buy it; much of it had already been surveyed for the Virginia soldiers of the French and Indian War and all of it was claimed by Virginia or North Carolina or Lord Granville who legally owned the very land on which they stood to treat.

Henderson's purchase and the resulting overlapping claims and counter claims brought unutterable confusion, sorrow, loss, and heartbreak to many who settled in Kentucky. Still, it was a great occasion. When everything was finished rum was served, and the Cherokee divided the goods which made but a poor showing among so many. The Cherokee were not

[104] This "large and coarse-featured" chief, VM, VII, 6, Redd, "Reminiscences," was often mentioned by all who wrote of warfare on the Cumberland, but his name like many others was spelled in various ways; often "Dragon Canoe."
[105] W, 30S, 74.
[106] W, 1CC, 17, gives the Path Deed and the Great Deed; see also Ramsey, *Tennessee*, 119–122.

alone in being dissatisfied in the spring of 1775. Six days later Patrick
Henry cried, "Give me liberty or give me death," and in May of that year
some Presbyterians got together in North Carolina, and signed a declaration [107] that, "we the citizens of Mecklenburg County do hereby dissolve
the political bands . . . with that nation."

[107] Much has been written of the Mecklenburg Declaration; Ramsey, *Tennessee*,
128–130, wrote of it in relation to Tennessee settlement; many signers later settled
in Middle Tennessee. Also taking the American side of the Revolution to a man
were the land speculators; the colonial governments showed none of the leniency
of the states later; the North Carolina Assembly, IX, 1169, outlawed Henderson's
purchase in short order and with sharp words, and gave him nothing; the States
of Virginia and North Carolina not only attempted to make his purchase binding
with the Cherokee, but each gave his company a giant boundary of land. Save for
the Path Deed and the northwestern corner of the Plateau the Cherokee sold him
nothing; the Plateau was recovered to some extent at the Treaty of Hopewell; and
later the Cherokee were inclined to boast that they had sold Henderson only their
"claim." See TP, IV, 211–212, 226–234, Gov. Blount to the Secretary of War in
1792, 1793. Attakullakulla died it is thought around 1781.

CHAPTER IX

THE TRAVELERS

How MANY Kentucky settlements there were in the spring of 1775 when Richard Henderson "bought" the land from the Cherokee, no one will ever know, but certain it is there were already a good many people in Kentucky. "That afternoon I wrote the letter in Powell Valley," Henderson wrote after reaching Boonesboro, "we met about forty people returning, and in about four days the number was little short of one hundred. Every group of travelers we saw and strange bells which we heard in front was a fresh alarm."[1] Judging from William Calk, a member of Henderson's party, most of these travelers were terrified settlers on their way to the Holston.[2]

Still, Kentucky was no different from other borders beset by Indians; always somebody stayed. Benjamin Price's camp, near present-day Mill Springs in Wayne County, Kentucky, became a settlement in that year,[3] and survived even the bloody year of the three sevens, when it was one of the only three stations left in Kentucky.[4] Several miles upriver from Price's Station a hunter by the name of Gist, possibly Nathaniel, had in the same year built a camp on the southern side of the river just across from the mouth of Pittman Creek,[5] but there is nothing to indicate this was permanent.

[1] FP, 16, Ranck, *Boonesborough*, "Henderson's Journal," 171.
[2] FP, 2, Speed, *Wilderness Road*, Calk, "Journal," 36, 37.
[3] WD, I, 213, Deposition of Nathaniel Buckhannon, "I was with Price in 1775 and assisted in building this cabin." This is part of a series of depositions given 1801–1805; still, we cannot be certain this cabin built in 1775 was the first, but the context would so indicate.
[4] The other two were the well known Harrodsburg and Boonesborough.
[5] WD, I, 213; the camp is described as having been "Nearly opposite (the mouth of Pitman Creek) on the contrary side of the river." The site is now covered by Lake Cumberland.

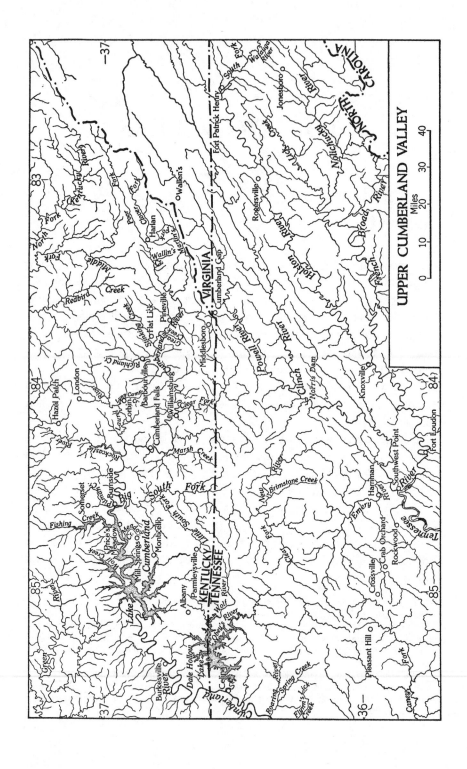

UPPER CUMBERLAND VALLEY

Miles

0   10   20   30   40

Many families in this general region, particularly up on the Big South Fork, have hand-me-down stories of Baptist ancestors who instead of stopping in East Tennessee or going down to Natchez, slipped into this part of Kentucky. Still others tell of Tories, unable to reach Canada, settled in some out of the way valley on a branch of the Cumberland. There are, too, old stories of forted farms and fights with Indians, but save for the depositions, given twenty-five to thirty years later, usually in connection with a lawsuit over land, little is known of the early history of the southeastern part of Kentucky drained by the Cumberland.[6]

In 1776 at least one other cabin was built not far from Gist's Camp, across the river on Pittman Creek in what is now Pulaski County, for: "In June 1776 as I was going down to Cumberland along with Moses Kirkpatrick, William Stewart, John Clark, Walter Brisco, John Peters, and John Robinson we stopped at a big spring on Pittman Creek and built a cabin on a 1000 acres tract for John Morgan." [7]

So many and so persistent are the traditions with now and then a deposition, it would appear there was in this general section continuous settlement from 1775 on, but first Virginia, and then Kentucky would permit no counties to be created on the Cumberland until 1799. During this twenty-five-year stretch, the county seat was never less than a day's ride away, and for those south of the Cumberland, the trip was not only longer, but complicated by the need to cross a river that had no ferry. Business went down the river or back to East Tennessee, easily reached by the Great Lakes Trail, so that few bothered to go to the Blue Grass in Kentucky to record a deed or a stock mark.

Lists of early land grants in Kentucky help not at all. First, few Kentuckians had any knowledge whatever of the southern part of the state,[8]

---

[6] Typical of the old stories is that of "Granny" Parker, dying in 1866 at the age of 106. She used to tell of coming as a young girl, around 1780, from North Carolina to Parmleysville on the Little South Fork of the Cumberland where there was a fort. See Odell Shepherd, "Little South Fork Country," Wayne County *Outlook*, July 21, 1955. Kentucky historians now and then mention this general region in connection with Indian battles; Humphrey Marshall, *The History of Kentucky*, Frankfort, 1812 (cited hereafter as Marshall, *Kentucky*), 294–300, contains brief mention of Indian skirmishes—a man killed on Fishing Creek in 1787 and the band of Indians chased across the Cumberland, and Hargrove (Hardgrove) killed in 1786 at the mouth of Buck Creek.

[7] Quoted by permission of the author from Wells, *Cumberland County*, published and copyrighted by Joseph W. Wells, Louisville, 1947, p. 12.

[8] FP, 35, Filson, *Kentucke*, the pocket map known as Filson's Map is possibly the best indication of how little was known. This map that confused untold thousands of settlers shows the headwaters of Green River as southeast of Danville, and a Pittman Creek of Green River due south or in the same location as Pittman Creek of

and secondly, land grants were almost always located by water courses, but seldom did the surveyor and almost never did those who listed his work take the trouble to name the larger body of water into which the creek or branch flowed. There was, for example, a Stinking Creek of Cumberland and a Stinking Creek of Rockcastle, numerous Indian creeks, Richland creeks, and at least two Pittmans one of these on Red River, and as a further complication there were two Red Rivers in Kentucky—one a fork of the Cumberland, the other of the Kentucky.

The name of the grantee is not always of much help. It was a small world with most of the early settlers on the Cumberland coming from a relatively small part of this world—southwestern Virginia, and North Carolina. Thus, many bore the same name. Daniel Smith was, for example, a leading citizen of middle Tennessee. Contemporaneous with him over in East Tennessee was another Daniel Smith [9] who made John Redd a pair of leather breeches. John Buchanan was a first settler on the Cumberland,[10] and his son John built a fort, while still another John Buchanan was killed in the Revolution.

Further confusion came about through the rapid Anglicization of many French and German names: Schmidt became Smith; Heidt, Hite; and Polish Sadowsky, Sandusky. Other times long names were shortened; it is possible that Holston River [11] and Michael Stoner were originally drawn from the same family name, though doubtful if from the same individual —Holstiener. The fondness of parents for giving children names used in the family for generations made for still more tangles. I had, for example, an ancestor named Isaac Chrisman; three others of the same name were living at the same time as he in East Tennessee and southwestern Virginia,

Cumberland; my feeling is it was Pittman Creek of Cumberland that many travelers passed, and hence the Pittman Station mentioned in Smith, "Journal," 58, on Pittman Creek a few miles back from the Cumberland.

[9] VM, VII, 404, Redd, "Reminiscences." There was still another Daniel Smith active in the Revolution in North Carolina, also an officer, as was this Daniel from Virginia and East Tennessee; see NCR, XXV, Index.

[10] Summers, *Southwest Virginia*, 856, lists the John Buchanan killed in the Revolution. The other John Buchanans, father and son, each lived to receive a grant of 640 acres of land as settlers in Middle Tennessee before May, 1780; NCR, XIX, 572–573. This list does not include all first settlers, but as North Carolina was somewhat stingy about giving land by "right of settlement," any person named on the list is relatively certain to have been there. Hereafter, when no authentication is given and the term "first settler" is used, it is understood the man named is listed here.

[11] Holston River, named before 1750, was so called because Stephen Holston settled on the "headsprings of the Middle Fork," some time before 1748, for in the spring of that year he sold out to James Davis, went down to Natchez, then back to Culpeper County, Va., his original home, but in time returned to the Holston, Summers, *Southwest Virginia*, 53. Holston's movings are typical of many on the borders.

all were seemingly named for a grandfather, and all had either a brother or a nephew Jacob.

However, we can be certain the cabin built on Pittman Creek in 1776 was on Pittman of Cumberland. Pittman Station on Pittman Creek of Green River was not built until late in 1779, or possibly early 1780. No one of the travelers to the Middle Cumberland in that year mentions a station on Green River, but they do mention the other.[12]

There is no record of any permanent settlement in Middle Tennessee before 1779, but the region was never completely deserted by hunters, traders, land viewers, and just plain wanderers. Sometime during these years George Rogers Clark may have visited French Lick to look over or even make improvements on land he thought he owned, for in 1767 he had bought land warrants issued by Virginia as payment for those who had fought in the French and Indian War.[13] All maps available to the Virginians still showed the Cumberland as being entirely in Virginia.

Kaspar Mansker continued to spend much time on the Cumberland and sometime, most possibly not before early 1779,[14] he built a station and planted corn close to present-day Goodlettsville on Mansker Creek, near the lick he had in 1769 found with Isaac Bledsoe, who may also have visited him from time to time as he, after going into Kentucky as a surveyor in 1774, went back to Boonesboro as a soldier-settler.[15]

Living near the lick Isaac had found was a great Paul Bunyan of a hunter, Thomas Sharpe Spencer, "the strongest man in all the west." He was not only taller than average, six foot two, but "very heavily made with

[12] THM, I, Smith, "Journal," 58. This was in December 1779; there is some question whether the other was established at this date; see Collins, *Kentucky, 1882*, II, 21.

[13] I, VIII, 304, George Rogers Clark to Patrick Henry, March 9, 1779.

[14] Most accounts of overland travel to Middle Tennessee in the winter of 1779–1780 mention Mansker's Station; but neither he nor any of his family—he had a wife and a brother George—is mentioned in any account of the several in the Draper Manuscripts as having been among the overland travelers; on the other hand his station is not heard of before this date.

[15] Isaac Bledsoe is often listed as a first settler on Cumberland; but is not so listed in NCR, XIX, 572–573, nor do Draper correspondents mention him in connection with Indian battles prior to 1783; he seems not to have come on a permanent basis until early in 1783. Isaac is fairly typical of many who settled on the Cumberland after living in Kentucky during the worst years of Indian warfare. He got no land: Anthony did get Kentucky land, though even when land was surveyed this cannot in the troubled times in Kentucky at that date be taken as proof of ownership; see FP, 33, Willard Rouse Jillson, *The Kentucky Land Grants*, Louisville, 1925, pp. 22, 149. See also FP, 34, Willard Rouse Jillson, *Old Kentucky Entries and Deeds*, Louisville, 1926, pp. 15–16. W, 31S, 193, states that Isaac lived two or three years at Boone's Station, then went back to Holston.

a mammoth foot and the strength of a lion." [16] He had come in 1776 and for some time made his home in a large hollow sycamore, broken off about twenty feet above the ground but leaning toward the south at such an angle Spencer could walk up it, crawl in—for it was about nine feet in diameter—and then go down into a hollow root large enough he could lie down. There was about the height of his head a crack just big enough he could scan the country before venturing out; the tree thus made a very fine hunter's blind, situated as it was on the south side of Bledsoe's Lick. Once, he looked out and saw half a dozen Indians. They stayed most of the day watching for game, and Spencer kept very quiet in his tree while they were there.[17]

French hunters continued to visit the region, though all the old west had grown more dangerous than ever. Practically all Indians east of the Mississippi had at the beginning of the Revolution taken the side of the British, and even more in danger on British soil than Frenchmen were Americans. De Monbruen continued to hunt on the Cumberland and sometime during these years built a hut in the vicinity of French Lick, for peltry and other produce could still be sent down the Mississippi and shipped from New Orleans. He had by the time of the Revolution been hunting and trading over the midwest for more than fifteen years, never without some danger from the Indians. Once on his way to Kaskaskia from Canada by portage and boat, he and a party of travelers that included his wife were attacked by Indians far up the Mississippi; he and his wife escaped, made a raft, held together with grapevines, and floated on down to Kaskaskia. He was attacked again while hunting on the Arkansas, but had, a short time later, a still narrower escape on the Cumberland when he was, out of sixteen men, one of the two who survived.[18]

Afraid to return to his cabin, he took refuge in a cave on the south side of the river between Mill Creek and Stone's River, several miles south of Spencer's sycamore.[19] His wife may have been nearby when the Indians attacked, for sometime during these years she is said to have borne in the cave the first known white child in the region.

Most of those who had flocked to the promised land of Kentucky were by 1777 driven back to East Tennessee or Virginia, dead, or captured. Britain seemed destined to control the Mississippi Valley, and for a time

[16] W, 6XX, 26, from Col. William Pillow's Account.
[17] W, 30S, 244–245.
[18] W, 6XX, 371.
[19] There is east of Nashville on U.S. 70 N a Tennessee Historical Commission Marker indicating the site of De Monbruen's cave a few miles from the road.

Georgia and South Carolina were with Virginia and North Carolina in doubt. Families were uprooted, torn apart by the chances of war. Whigs fled Tories as they overran Georgia and the Carolinas. Some came to East Tennessee to settle, while others stayed only long enough to build flatboats to go to Natchez.

Even the French hunters who still visited the Middle Cumberland occasionally were jittery. One, hearing the noise Spencer made as he chased a buffalo past his camp, was so frightened he jumped into the Cumberland, swam it, and went overland on foot to the Wabash. Others were frightened away by the sight of his huge footprints in the snow,[20] for Spencer during the troubled times kept himself well hidden.

He was one of the kindest and most generous of men. A hunter, Holliday, who had spent quite a while with him on Bledsoe Creek, got tired of the woods, but was afraid to try to reach East Tennessee because he had lost his knife. One day he said to Spencer "in a melancholy, whining sort of way, 'If I had a knife to cut meat, I'd go home.' Spencer drew his from his sheath, laid its ends on a couple of rocks, and with a third broke it in two pieces, and holding them towards Holliday, said, 'Take your choice,' after which Spencer went with him to show him the way and put him upon the trail." [21]

De Monbruen, living as he did near the river, saw more of such travelers as came to the region than did Spencer or Mansker. Once, when coming upriver from a trading trip down to New Orleans, he met at Deacon's Pond, near present-day Palmyra, six white men and one white woman. They had come overland from the east to some point on the Cumberland near the mouth of the Rockcastle. Here, they had made a boat, and floated down, living on buffalo.

One of the party, William Bowen, a few months later shot into a herd, wounding one, and as so often happened the buffalo charged, but "the cane being thick Bowen could not get out of the way; he was trodden down so that he could not move, nor could his companions find him; he lay there seven days; when found, the bruised parts had mortified and he died on the 18th day." [22]

These people have no historical significance, but may be taken as a sampling of the many wanderers in this country where a man with fair hunting skills and reasonable luck could live indefinitely. If there were no

[20] Ramsey, *Tennessee,* 194.
[21] W, 30S, 245.
[22] Haywood, *C & P,* 81.

traders on the Cumberland, he could get ammunition, coffee and other supplies in the Illinois. Indians were less inclined to bother the wandering ne'er-do-well than the professional hunter, or the surveyor with the land-stealer. More than anything they hated the wife and children and it was not by chance that traveling families [23] were attacked on the Kentucky Road more often than small parties of men; the woman with the baby meant that soon a cleared field and cabin would mean one more victory for the white man.

The war, as far as the southern Indians were concerned, was lost by 1778. It was the turn of the southern Tories to flee Georgia and the Carolinas. John Sevier, James Robertson, Isaac Shelby, fighting always with a few men on horseback, completely subdued the Cherokee, and settlement crept west and south. There was by 1778, no King's Proclamation to heed. The year before, North Carolina, a state at least on paper, had laid claim to all land between her present boundaries as far west as the Mississippi, and at about the same time Virginia the state had not only claimed the land owned by the colony, but had found the Henderson purchase illegal, thus paving the way for untold loss and suffering on the part of all those such as Boone who had either worked for him or bought his land.[24]

One of the men most zealous for the rights of Virginia was George Rogers Clark and when he took the Illinois Country in 1778, the future of the midwest as part of America seemed assured, but he lost Vincennes on the Wabash, and it was not until late February his victories were complete with the recapture of Vincennes and along with it Lord Henry Hamilton. Many of the men who helped do this were from the Holston, and news of the victory must have reached that region quickly, else a party of men would not have set out for the Cumberland in the late winter or early spring of 1779.

---

[23] W, 29S, 110, is an account of one of the best known, McNitt's Defeat on the Kentucky Road, the site now marked and within the confines of the Levi Jackson Wilderness Road State Park, London, Ky. See also Collins, *Kentucky, 1882*, II, 760, for Mrs. McClure and her four children.

[24] Henderson's accounts were never closed; most of those who had worked for him ended up, not only without land but in debt. See, Butler, *Kentucky,* 31–33, and Collins, *Kentucky, 1882*, II, 242; this last the letter of Daniel Boone, begging for the job of cutting the "New Rode." ". . . I first Marked out that Rode in March 1775 and Never Re'd anything for my trubel and Sepose I am no Statesman I am a Woodsman . . ." Boone to Governor Isaac Shelby, "februey 11, 1796." Boone was by then getting old; he was penniless, and had served Virginia and then Kentucky for 22 years if one counts the surveyor-warning trip of 1774 as the beginning; he did not get the job.

Men high up in narrow valleys of Holston creeks may have thought longingly of the broad lands on the Cumberland, and many during the early years of the Revolution did try settlement in Kentucky, but future settlers on the Cumberland were busy in East Tennessee. One of the busiest was James Robertson. He had helped in the bloody, bitter warfare with the Cherokee, and when they were conquered in 1777 he was given the extremely dangerous job as American agent—the first—to the same Indians he had fought. Still, Robertson like Isaac Shelby and Sevier was always respected and trusted by Indians, once a treaty was made. Rather, it was the criminal acts of a few irresponsible white men with a hatred of Indians amounting to insanity, that kept the Cherokee in a constant ferment and made Robertson's job a risky one. He had, while Indian agent, once to ride three days and three nights without stopping, and another time his life was saved by an Indian woman who told him of a plot made by Indian braves to murder him. Since agents usually lived in or near an Indian town, Robertson in 1777 moved still further down the Holston to the mouth of Big Creek.[25]

Still, busy as he was with family, job, and farming James Robertson must have spent considerable time in discussion of and planning for a trip to the Cumberland Country, for parties such as he led to Middle Tennessee early in 1779 do not spring up overnight, and as most of those who went with him later settled there, it seems clear that the whole trip was more in the nature of a first step toward settlement[26] than an exploration. Following the custom of many men who went into the woods, Robertson took with him a Negro slave. There were in addition to his young, unmarried brother Mark, six other white men: George Freeland, William Neely, Edward Swanson, Zachariah White, William Overall, and James Hanley—the only member of the party not settled in Middle Tennessee by the spring of 1780.[27]

The men went on foot to the mouth of the Holston where they crossed. From this point their route is not exactly known; they are said to have crossed Clinch River and then Cumberland Mountain at some point that caused them to reach the Cumberland high up in Kentucky, and there they

[25] W, 31S, 34-35, 46.
[26] James Robertson was somewhat at loose ends; he had lost his job as Indian agent and Joseph Martin had been appointed by Patrick Henry, W, 1XX, 29; in Jan. 1779, Robertson was paid 487 pounds for his services by the North Carolina Legislature, NCR, XIII, 909, which would indicate he did not start his exploratory journey until February or later of 1779.
[27] Ramsey, *Tennessee*, 194. Practically all sources agree on this list, though spellings vary; Freeland is often spelled Freeling.

stopped, made canoes with their hatchets, and went downriver.[28] We cannot be certain, but since they crossed at the mouth of the Holston, near the site of present-day Knoxville, their logical course would have been to take the Indian trail that went northwest from this point; they could follow it to the mouth of Obey's River, or on Brimstone Creek of the Big South Fork turn due north and follow the Great Lakes Trail to Smith Shoals, a route in use by Kentucky settlers as early as 1781,[29] and most probably the route used by Jones in coming from Middle Tennessee, for he had gone up the Cumberland as "high as he could go," and this would have meant Smith Shoals.

It was not until the party had reached Jones Bend they saw any sign of civilization, and here Robertson "knew as soon as he saw this clearing it must be the same place" of which he had heard. They went on down to French Lick where they found De Monbruen's cabin filled with buffalo tallow, but still saw no people.[30] Kaspar Mansker was by the spring of 1780 well enough established he could put up travelers,[31] and it thus seems entirely possible that while Robertson's party was exploring French Lick, Kaspar was putting in a corn crop and changing his hunter's camp into a dwelling about twelve miles north of them, while Spencer continued at Bledsoe's Lick several miles east of Mansker.

Four of the men stayed at French Lick to clear ground and put in a crop of corn. Robertson and the others went on down the river, and soon met a party of French hunters, the first men seen on the Cumberland. They described to Robertson in glowing terms the beauty of the Illinois Country, and Robertson who had among Clark's soldiers at Kaskaskia many friends and neighbors, decided to go see it for himself. The hunters had with them some handsomely made canoes in which they had sailed from St. Louis; Robertson bought one of these for a guinea and went on.[32] It was a speedy trip with the Cumberland full and swift in early spring,

[28] W, 31S, 34–35; see also *ibid.*, 6XX (50), 5.
[29] This road variously known as the Ridge Road and the Southern Wilderness Road was an adaptation of the Great Lakes Trail and fathered the well known Jacksboro Road. *The Quarterly Publication of the Historical and Philosophical Society* of Ohio, published and copyrighted University of Cincinnati Press, 1906 (cited hereafter as *Quart. Pub.* Ohio), I, "Narrative of General William Lytle" (cited hereafter as Lytle, "Narrative"), 6. General Lytle as a boy lived in pioneer Kentucky near Danville.
[30] W, 6XX (50), 3–5, the account of Robertson's daughter, Lavinia; see also that of Col. Weakley, *ibid.*, 32S, 341–342, and also *ibid.*, 31S, 33–36; many of Mr. Draper's correspondents wrote of Robertson's trip but none mentioned his having seen Jones.
[31] THM, I, Smith, "Journal," 62. Most of Smith's party stopped with Kaspar for some days.
[32] W, 6XX (50), 5. See also *ibid.*, 29S, 68.

and at the mouth of the Ohio there was the usual spring flood that often put Robertson's canoe among the trees.

Near the mouth of the Ohio, the party split again; two of the men [33] went back to French Lick, taking with them some peach stones Robertson sent to be planted there.[34] Swanson, James Robertson, and Mark went on, though it was a dangerous trip for such a small group of Americans, hated by all Indians. The party had no trouble until they stopped at the Oak Post, a trading post on the Mississippi peopled chiefly by Osage Indians, and these began to suspect Robertson as a spy when he had been there for some time buying supplies. They plotted to kill him, but he had met in the place a Spanish trader able to speak a little English, enough that he and Robertson could talk of one of Robertson's prime passions—horses. Robertson had told him he was on an exploratory journey, and also hoped to buy some Spanish horses. The trader explained all this to the Indians. They, pleased that one should come so far to buy their horses, became at once horse traders instead of enemies.[35]

Horses bought, Robertson went on to Kaskaskia, riding now instead of boating. He may, after reaching the Illinois, have seen George Rogers Clark, or Clark may have heard from others something that made him doubt the worth of the land he had bought at French Lick, where men from Robertson's party were preparing to put in a corn crop. In any case, Clark on March 9th wrote [36] Patrick Henry: "If I should be deprived of a certain tract of land on that [Cumberland] River—I shall in a manner lose my all. It is known by the name of the Great French Lick on the south or west side, containing 3,000 acres; if you can do anything for me in saving it, I shall forever remember it with gratitude." The line between Virginia and North Carolina [37] had not yet been run past the headwaters

[33] The sources already named describe this part of Robertson's trip; some mention one thing and some another, but most are agreed that Edward Swanson and Robertson's brother Mark went into the Illinois with him.

[34] Williams, *Travels*, 512, "Report of the Journey of the Brethren Abraham Steiner and Frederick D. De Schweinitz to the Cherokee and the Cumberland Settlements, 1799" (cited hereafter as Schweinitz, "Report"). The brethren visited Mrs. Frederick Stump, a first settler, and she talked of her fruit trees, some of the seed sent by Robertson from the Illinois.

[35] W, 32S, 341, and *ibid.*, 6XX (50), 8–9.

[36] I, VIII, 304. Robertson is often represented as having gone to the Illinois to buy "cabin rights" from Clark. I can find no authentication for this; the only reason given by his children and those who wrote of his trip is that "he went to explore."

[37] There seems to have been by this date a good bit of doubt that the Cumberland was entirely within Virginia; at least the matter was discussed, for in 1779, Col. Arthur Campbell, VS, IV, 365, told that the "Pilots and Hunters" thought it was in Virginia.

of the Holston but James Robertson later served as a surveyor, and carried
a compass with him on his next trip west. He may have had one at this
time, and surveyed enough to be able to tell [38] the unfortunate Clark that
the Virginia warrants he had bought were worthless, for French Lick did
not belong to Virginia.

Robertson spent some time in Clark's newly won territory, coming with
his horse stock across country to Vincennes on the Wabash, and from
there to the Falls of the Ohio, not yet known as Louisville. He came home
by the usual route, past Benjamin Logan's Station at present-day Stanford,
then home to the Holston over the Kentucky Road. He in the latter stage
of his trip would have met many bound for Kentucky, a motley crew of
Tories,[39] wealthy hoping to get more land, and poor on foot with little
but children and hope.[40] He never got home till August, and once home
found his world of the Holston stricken with moving fever; no new
disease on any border, but since Clark had won the Northwest Territory
with the result that Kentucky was safer than it had been, more prevelant
than common.

Practically all of those bound for Kentucky and many for Middle Tennessee would go overland. This meant pack horses and more pack horses;
provisions of any kind were scarce in Kentucky. In August after the corn
was laid by, young sons and slave boys would have been scouring the
woods for pack-saddle timber. The forked limb of a white oak of a certain shape and bigness made the best of pack saddles, but such was not al-

[38] It is possible that Robertson while in the Illinois did a short tour of duty for
Clark. On May 21, 1779, while this James Robertson was in the Illinois some James
Robertson, I, VIII, 323, served as quartermaster under Clark. Men from the Holston
were all over Kentucky and the Illinois; see *ibid.*, VII, 42.

[39] Treatment of Tories and suspected Tories varied from place to place, but was
often rough in East Tennessee; suspected families were denied protection of the
forts and hounded west; the prisoners taken at Kings Mountain were brutally treated
in many ways; such as forcing a man with his arms tied behind him to jump over a
rattlesnake; see W, 28S, 20-78, dealing chiefly with "Col. Campbell's Tory War."
Free use was made of "fine hickory whips . . . well prepared and toughened in the
fire," *ibid.*, 138. There is quite complete agreement, however, that most of the better
element frowned upon such and that "Robertson and Sevier did not drive them off"
W, 32S, 222. The fleeing Tories were all over the old west; FQ, II, Clinkenbeard
"Interview," 98, 100, ". . . all Tories [this in Kentucky in 1779] riding pretty high,
but you mustn't call them that."

[40] Lord Henry Hamilton as a prisoner of war gave a brief and unflattering account
of Kentucky and its hungry inhabitants in the spring of 1779. His journal used by
permission of the publisher, R. E. Banta, Banta Press, from *Henry Hamilton and
George Rogers Clark in the American Revolution*, by John D. Barnhart. Copyright
by R. E. Banta, Crawfordsville, Ind., 1951, "The Journal of Henry Hamilton, 1778-
1779," 102-205 (cited hereafter as Hamilton, "Journal"); see for descriptions of Kentucky stations, *ibid.*, 195-199.

ways easily found. "It was with a full appreciation of its value that Joseph Craig, an old pioneer preacher once stopped short in his exhortation to a large congregation in the woods, and while his eyes were still turned devoutly to heaven, suddenly pointed his finger to a branch and exclaimed, 'Brethren, behold up yonder a first rate crotch for a pack-saddle.' " [41]

Once the tree was found and felled, half the work was done; the forked limb or crotch had only to be cut the right length, the prong chipped out with hatchet and knife to fit the animal's back. A board was then fastened to each fork with wooden pins, and holes bored to receive the iron rings for carrying straps and girths. The main thing was that everything hold, for often the pack-saddle carried children, one slung on either side in a willow or split white oak hamper, or in cold weather swaddled in the feather beds and bed clothing, and all these had to stay put on trails so steep the animal sometimes pitched forward or fell on his haunches.

In other families broadaxes flew, squaring up flatboat timbers, for there was at that date no sawmill in East Tennessee. Others hunted some good hardwood, usually maple, for pegs, split and left to season as long as possible; still others were busy with mallet and froe, riving white oak shakes for the boat roof. The flatboats, though often drawing no more than two feet of water, were in regions affording a good supply of long timber, preferably poplar, as much as one hundred feet long, with space for living quarters,[42] farm animals, and supplies. Journeys were long and often slow, and the settlers lived as they went along, bore children,[43] kept school, fished, took time out for hunting either game or wild greens.[44] Each large

[41] Williams, *Smith*, 22–23.

[42] The flatboat was not standardized, but fairly typical no doubt were those used by General James Wilkinson of Kentucky. A 1787 flatboat was to be 50 x 13, "gunnels" 50 feet long . . . six inches thick and as wide as timber will admit; the sleepers for the bottom were also to be 50 feet long and six inches on all sides, the whole to be of white oak, even the pins for the one-inch holes. The usual calking of tar and oakum was called for, but the roofed section was not to be put on until she was loaded. This contract is from the Innes Papers, and is used by permission of the publisher, the Filson Club, from FP, 28, *Kentucky River Navigation* by Mary Verhoeff, copyrighted by The Filson Club, Louisville, 1917 (cited hereafter as Verhoeff, *Kentucky River*), 61.

[43] The best known trip by flatboat in the history of Tennessee was the "Journal of a Voyage, intended by God's permission, on the good boat *Adventure*, from Fort Patrick Henry on Holston River, to the French Salt Springs on Cumberland River, kept by John Donelson." First published from the Draper Manuscripts of the Wisconsin Historical Society Collections by Ramsey, *Tennessee*, 197–202 (cited hereafter as Donelson, "Voyage"). Mrs. Peyton had a child.

[44] Members of the Donelson flotilla did all such things, but there is no mention of domestic animals; these were driven overland. More typical of the usual flatboat journey, and great numbers were made, particularly on the Ohio, is the Lytle "Narrative," *Quart. Pub.* Ohio, I, 3–4.

boat had one and often more hollowed-out log canoes; [45] these were usually of poplar for it swelled when wet, was easily worked, and being lighter was less inclined to swamp. Some boat builders planned to go to Natchez, others to the Illinois, and still others to Kentucky, and long and tedious journeys these last would be, for the flatboat, little more than a civilized log raft, was almost impossible to get upstream.

James Robertson was one of around fifty in the boat-building business and though his destination was French Lick on the Cumberland he planned to cut out all the back-breaking upstream travel by meeting his family and several others at some point on the Tennessee south of Nashville, and bring them overland by pack horse. His wife with the four younger of their five children, his widowed sister Ann and her three young daughters, and the most of his slaves were to go by boat, while he with his brothers Mark and John, his oldest son Jonathan, and such hired men and slaves as were needed to drive the family stock, which was considerable, would go overland. [46]

Co-partner in Robertson's plan was big "fleshy" John Donelson, [47] then fifty-four years old, with most of his children grown and the older ones married. Son of an English trader, Donelson, different from most who came to the Cumberland in that year, was neither a seasoned Indian fighter nor borderer, but chiefly surveyor and land speculator, with good connections among some of the more important people of Virginia, [48] and he had represented Pittsylvania County in the House of Burgesses. He was not in the Revolution active in fighting either British or Indians, though in 1778 he had led a small troop of men from the Holston to Boonesboro with the intention of helping Clark win the Illinois. [49] He never got to the

---

[45] Whole families often migrated by pirogue, in Tennessee more commonly known as a dugout. John Cotton, Ramsey, *Tennessee*, Donelson, "Voyage," 199, used one.

[46] W, 6XX (50), 6–8.

[47] VM, VII, Redd, "Reminiscences," 8.

[48] W, 32S, 299–312, this, by Donelson's daughter-in-law, Mary Purnell, Mrs. Captain John, gives a sketchy account of him; see in particular, 312; his birth is here given as 1726. Helpful in understanding family relationships is "Donelson Family Chart," used by permission of G. Bowdoin Craghill, Executor of the Estate of Mrs. Pauline Wilcox Burke, from *Emily Donelson of Tennessee* by Pauline Wilcox Burke, Copyright, 1941, by Garrett and Massie, Richmond, Va. (cited hereafter as Burke, *Emily Donelson*), II, end papers.

[49] I, VIII, 42. This venture was not successful; some of the men deserted in Kentucky. Among them was a Lieutenant Hutchings, *ibid.*, 118; Donelson had a son-in-law, Thomas Hutchings, but whether the Lieutenant Hutchings who deserted while under Donelson in Kentucky was his son-in-law and hence the grandfather of Andrew Jackson's "my ward Hutchings" we cannot say. Men often bore the same names and desertion was rather common; others feigned illness when a campaign was coming up—"Pressly Anderson in Kentucky swallowed a chew of tobacco, so he

Illinois, but apparently liked what he saw in Kentucky, for he came back home his mind made up to go there. He had at one time been quite prosperous, but had of late years fallen on hard times.[50] The autumn of 1779 found him in the Holston Country where he was having a large boat, the *Adventure*, built, in which he planned to take his family to Kentucky, that, safer from Indians than it had been, was still in the turmoil of the Revolution, a haven for land speculators with friends in the right places.

Robertson persuaded him to come instead to the Cumberland as head of the flotilla in which Mrs. Robertson and others were planning to come. Robertson could meet them all, or so their plans went, with pack horses. Neither had explored the country in Middle Tennessee between Tennessee and Cumberland rivers, nor did they have any map so accurate as that of Thomas Hutchins. Robertson, knowing the mouths of the two rivers were only about twelve miles apart, judged the distance of the overland journey from the Tennessee to French Lick as about forty miles.[51]

The weather in the fall of 1779 was no good for boat building. There were in the latter part of September many rainy, cloudy days, and on the first day of October more rain.[52] This did not hold back the travelers, and the few hunters going west. Henry Scaggs was one of these. Now living on the Clinch in Tennessee, he had been hunting for close to twenty years on the other side of the mountains, and this fall in addition to a party of "upwards of 20 men" with several extra pack horses, he took his young

wouldn't have to go" (on a campaign led by George Rogers Clark), FQ, II, Clinkenbeard "Interview," 106.

[50] W, 1XX, 1–65, contains several letters by, to, or about John Donelson concerning the business of treating with the Indians and acquiring land, 1776–1783. Chief correspondents are William Blount, Joseph Martin, Indian agent; Patrick Henry, and later Benjamin Harrison. See in particular *ibid.*, 12, John Donelson writing Aug. 5, 1776; *ibid.*, 72, letter of William Blount to Donelson; *ibid.*, 50–51, Martin to Donelson. These letters, though they give little indication of Donelson's past, do indicate that he was a businessman, trying hard to make money from land, particularly land in what is known as the Big Bend of the Tennessee in present-day Alabama; they say nothing of plans for settlement on the Cumberland.

[51] W, 32S, 341. Robert Weakley like other Draper correspondents indicates that Robertson and not Donelson was the prime instigator of settlement in Middle Tennessee. Donelson to begin with was practically unknown on the borders; historians such as Summers and records of Virginia and North Carolina that yield large amounts of material on Robertson, the Bledsoes, John Montgomery, and numerous other men, usually have nothing on John Donelson.

[52] Unless otherwise indicated all references to weather are taken from THM, I, 48–65, Smith, "Journal." Daniel Smith made almost daily notes on the weather from Aug. 14, 1779, to Aug. 7, 1780. Col. Henry Fleming, up in Kentucky, kept a journal for a part of this period, Fleming, "Journal," Mereness, *Travels*, 619–643, but he, like John Donelson who also wrote a good bit of the weather surrounding his "Voyage," did not give dates of rain and snow.

son. In Powell Valley his party had the not very unusual misfortune of being attacked by Indians, who, though they killed no men, took all but eleven of the horses. All the hunters turned back except Scaggs, his son, and a man remembered only by the name of Sinclair.[53]

Another famous hunter, Zachariah Green, was also out with his brother and two other men, but these, instead of going in the direction of Green River as did Scaggs, went up the Cumberland toward the three forks to hunt and trap for beaver. The Greens were hardy souls; one was once so mangled by a bear he was left for dead by his frightened hunting companions, but survived the terrible wounds, alone in the woods save for one faithful hunting dog.[54]

Up on New River another experienced hunter, John Rains, was going over the Hunters' Trail again; but this time instead of pack horses only he took his family, two steers, nineteen cows, and seventeen horses, for he like many others had decided to settle in Kentucky.[55] Another party, much larger but it, too, made up of seasoned borderers, was on the way to Kentucky by pack horse. There was the older John Buchanan, possibly a son of the John Buchanan who had been a justice in the first court of Augusta County,[56] Virginia, almost forty years before when the border was just west of the Blue Ridge. With him was his wife and three sons—Samuel, Alexander, and John. There were John and James Mulherrin, with their families, but the Mulherrin and Buchanan men were, with Sampson Williams, Thomas Thompson, and Daniel Williams, going to Clark's Station, a mile from Danville, Kentucky, only to leave their wives and children in comparative safety while they went on down to the Middle Cumberland to start a settlement.[57]

Another party Cumberland bound and with women going along was that led by Amos Eaton, brother-in-law of Anthony Bledsoe, for he had married a younger one of the Ramsey girls. The Eatons like most others

---

[53] Thwaites-Kellogg, *Dunmore's War*, 239, quoting W, 3B, 230–238.

[54] W, 32S, 526–528.

[55] Haywood, *C & P*, 83, 85, 86.

[56] Ramsey, *Tennessee*, 196, stated the Buchanans came from South Carolina; but Buchanans usually named James or John had long been prominent on most southern borders, and a James Buchanan as a captured Covenanter from Agrennock went down on a prison ship near the Mulehead of Darness in 1679, Waddell, *Annals*, 5; still the Clan Buchanan was a large one and this does not necessarily indicate that at this time other covenanting Buchanans were trying to get to America. A John Buchanan was a member of the first court of Augusta County in 1745, *ibid.*, 26. The same John Buchanan served as deputy surveyor for Augusta in 1746, Summers, *Southwest Virginia*, 44–45.

[57] W, 32S, 296.

who came and stayed were seasoned borderers; Amos had migrated from southwestern Virginia where he had served the county as road surveyor,[58] and had lived since 1772 in a forted station seven miles above the Big Island of the Holston. Still, it is doubtful if he knew as much of woodscraft and border living as Humphrey Hogan, also of his party, for Hogan had spent much time in the west as a Long Hunter. Thomas Ramsey, brother of Mrs. Eaton, came, and around a year later, Josiah, another brother who became a major of militia[59] on the Cumberland. There were also Haydon Wells, and William and Benjamin Drake, all borderers and seasoned woodsmen.

The Eatons were neighbors of Robertson and he would have known most of those mentioned, some from the Battle of Point Pleasant, and others as land-owning families in southwest Virginia. There was among them all no family completely strange to most, save one, that of Frederick Stump, a thrifty and industrious German who had killed at least sixteen men and probably more. He had lived as a well-to-do farmer on the Pennsylvania border, until one bright moonlight night in 1768 when eleven drunken Shawnee had begun cutting down his door. He killed nine of them with a meat ax, and in the fight got twenty-seven slight wounds from their tomahawks. Two got away, but as soon as it was light next morning, he and two of his servants followed their trail, found their camp, and tomahawked them,[60] "and to add to their villany they scalped the dead which is a certain mark with Indians of a Declaration of War."[61] The Pennsylvania Quakers, forever at odds with the borderers, imprisoned Stump, but he was soon released by a mob of two thousand Paxton boys.

He had fled to Georgia where he prospered, acquiring much property, and building a gristmill. He had, during the early days of the Revolution, commanded a company under Marion. Once, after the Americans had retreated, he caught a group of British officers playing cards; he killed

[58] Summers, *Southwest Virginia*, 259, the account of the first court of Washington County, Va., meeting in Jan. 1777. There was among the first settlers on the Cumberland a large number of family relationships; Anthony Bledsoe, Amos Eaton and Col. John Montgomery all married sisters—Ramseys; Mary, wife of Anthony, was the oldest; Isaac Bledsoe and Hugh F. Bell, another early settler on the Cumberland, in turn married sisters of Col. John Montgomery—W, 30S, 81, 242.

[59] Josiah Ramsey who became an officer of militia on the Cumberland, TP, IV, 73, was a son of this same Ramsey, Josiah of Reedy Creek in Wythe County, Va. All borders, however, had Ramseys; see Thwaites-Kellogg, *Dunmore's War*, 168, for Josiah. VM, VII, Redd, "Reminiscences," 9, described Eaton's Fort on Holston.

[60] Many wrote of Frederick Stump; see in particular W, IS, 72-74, from the account of the next generation, Mrs. Thomas Eaton. *Ibid.*, 31S, 58-64, tells a good bit of Stump but is more concerned with the Eaton party in general.

[61] I, XVI, 171, 179, 209, tell something of the other side of the Stump story.

five. He was captured and imprisoned, this time at Saint Augustine in Florida. Here, no mob could rescue him, but after four months he was able to bribe his jailer with ten guineas, and escape through hostile Indian country to Georgia. The British had already burned his grist and saw mills, confiscated his property, including twenty slaves, and after his escape they offered a reward for him dead or alive.

Now, at an age then considered old, fifty-five, and with grown children, though his son John was only three years old, he traveled toward the Cumberland, poverty-stricken, but still strong in spirit as well as body.

The Eaton party, as did that of Robertson and John Rains, left in October and traveled leisurely, spending three months on the way, now and then taking several days out for hunting.[62] Not all the food would have come from the woods; like the Long Hunters they would have brought supplies of meal and salt, flour, bacon, ham, or even jerk—plain or minced into pemmican and mixed with parched corn meal and maple sugar after the fashion of the Indians.[63] We can be certain Mrs. John Rains milked one or more of the family's nineteen cows, for as game grew scarce, milk from the migrating cows was the only dependable source of fresh food for the traveling family.[64] Most would have brought some whiskey,[65] by this date taking the place of the rum that Dr. Walker and earlier travelers had carried into the woods, for the Revolution made it very hard to import either the manufactured article or the molasses from which it was made.

The Eaton party carried tents,[66] though along much of the route rockhouses were so numerous, travelers camped in these.[67] October after its rainy beginning brought a few days of pleasant weather; a time of surpassing beauty in eastern Tennessee and Kentucky. The hemlocks in the steep-walled sandstone coves of the Clinch and Holston stood dark among the yellowing poplars, and high on the ridges there were stretches of pine woods with some cedar in the limestone valleys; but mostly it was a world

[62] W, 1S, 74.

[63] Hamilton, "Journal," 123, "fat flank of Deer, dryed and lightly smoaked, this pounded small with a certain proportion of Indian-corn-meal, and maple sugar . . . They commonly mix some of this with water, a small quantity is sufficient—thus hunger and thirst are satisfied together with very little delay."

[64] Williams, *Smith*, 22. In a migration from East Tennessee to Stockton's Valley, Ky., the Smiths had little food but milk.

[65] In southwestern Virginia corn whiskey was so plentiful by 1777 it cost only 4 shillings the gallon as contrasted to 8 for rye, and rum was 16, Summers, *Southwest Virginia*, 260.

[66] W, 31S, 59.

[67] Williams, *Travels*, Lipscomb, "Journal," 272–279, mentions three caves between the neighborhood of Stanford, Ky., and the Tennessee line.

bright with leaves, clear yellow of hickory and chestnut, beech and poplar, red and gold of maple and sweet gum, blood red of black gum and dogwood, and lingering on until spring, the oaks fading from red to bronze to brown. Even the traveling children, lifting their eyes to each new hill would have known the plant life there by the color, sumac—shoemake [68] they said—was red, very red, but different from dogwood red, and cedar green was not pine green.

Green, too, was the cane that covered most of the creek and river bottoms they rode through, miserable stuff, crowding in a close wall twenty feet high and more, shutting out light and air, but forever bending enough to whip a rider in the face.[69] Peculiar stuff it was that after frost took on a strange brilliance like an artificial thing dyed green. Green, also, were the laurel and ivy leaves, abundant on the thin-soiled, sandy stretches of the Kentucky Road, pretty plants at blooming time, but sign of poor land with ivy a killer of any foolish sheep who ate it.

There was no need for any animal to eat ivy until the snows came and covered everything else. Big game was scarce [70] in most of Kentucky and Tennessee by the fall of 1780, but there were still plenty of turkeys, innumerable squirrels, hosts of waterfowl all fine and fat from the same foods that fed the hogs as they traveled along—acorns, chestnuts, beech and hickory nuts, with now and then some chinkapins, though all of these save the acorns were gathered and used by most borderers. There was still plenty of cane and wild clovers for horses and cattle, but these, like the grass in the Barrens, were not much good for grazing in the late fall.

It was not paradise, and all would have heard of how the hunting party of Henry Scaggs had been robbed by Indians, but there is no record that any of these mentioned worried overmuch about Indians or even posted guards. The men were experienced, capable, and well armed. They were, too, save for some of the unmarried guards and Stump, ruined by the Revolution, prosperous, middle-class farmers, carrying with them on their

[68] John Sevier, THM, V, 192, spelled it "shoemake."

[69] Hamilton, a half-starved, discouraged, badly treated prisoner of war, complained most, "Journal," 197, of marching through the canebrakes where the "musketoes were not idle." Calk, "Journal," 35–38, going over Boone's Road in the spring of 1775 wrote of the "turrable cane bracks."

[70] As early as the spring of 1775, Calk, "Journal," 39, saw no buffalo until after reaching Boonesboro and hunting for them. His party that included Henderson, drove beef animals, *ibid.*, 37, for food. The three journals of travel over all or part of the Kentucky Road in 1779–1780 already cited, Smith, Hamilton, and Fleming, make no mention of big game along the route, and speak instead of short rations in Kentucky. It was thirty years since Dr. Walker had visited the Cumberland when he killed all manner of game and could have killed "three times as much."

many pack horses all manner of things from extra lead and powder, black-smith tools, and plow-points to fiddles, books, crockery as well as pewter, and of course the family feather beds and "bed furniture." [71]

In dress they differed little from other farming families of the west, chiefly for the women separate skirts, long and full and since the beginning of the Revolution more commonly made of home-grown flax and wool, or the mixture later known as linsey-woolsey, with blouses or waists of thinner material, linen, wool and sometimes cotton.[72] The materials used in the dress of the men were much the same; some may have worn hunting shirts, but none was mentioned. Most men of that day dressed as did John Buchanan, Sr.,[73] in knee breeches, linen shirts, waistcoats, coats, and for cold weather the usual greatcoat, caped, many-pocketed, and commodious. Cut, materials, and ornamentation depended upon the purse, inclination, and time and place of wearing, for most first settlers had considerably more than a mere change of clothing.[74]

One of the most precious things all families carried, and immeasurable in terms of money as it could not be bought from the traveling French traders who had long visited the Cumberland, was the seed [75]—corn, oats, hemp, flax, cotton, vegetables for the garden patch, beans and pumpkin for the cornfield, tobacco, sweet potatoes for slips and Irish potatoes for seed, and possibly some grass, usually timothy, and clover, though these last were seldom grown during the first few years of any settlement. The seeds like their tools were capital goods, insuring the future; a woman could look at a gourd full of flax seed and know that in another year she would have shirt, sheet, towel, tow for the gun barrel, and fine linen for the new baby's best dress.

The settlers going through the woods to Middle Tennessee knew how to plant the seed and where; no one of them would make his sweet potato

---

[71] DW, I, 69, is the inventory of John Buchanan killed shortly after settling on the Cumberland; *ibid.*, 296, Samuel Buchanan killed a few years later.

[72] The Revolution had cut off imported fabrics, and cotton was more commonly grown than in the days of William Byrd, but cotton cloth was still a scarce and expensive article. All historians tell of the cotton grown at Clover Bottom during the first summer of settlement; see Ramsey, *Tennessee*, 450.

[73] DW, I, 29, 58, 194, 296, are inventories containing articles of clothing worn by first settlers on the Cumberland in the early 1780's. *Ibid.*, 41–43, is the 1784 inventory of the wife of a first settler. See also Kercheval, *Virginia*, Doddridge, "Notes," 250–252, for ordinary working dress of borderers.

[74] There was a good deal of variation; some had several suits with numerous waistcoats, silk, and ruffled shirts; see DW, I, 58.

[75] The carrying of seed was a common custom: Walker, "Journal," April 23, 1750, planted peach stones and corn; Calk, "Journal," 35, took "seed corn and irish tator seed."

ridges in the fat, rich, black ground of a low, wet, river bottom that would in a not too wet season grow fourteen-foot corn. They knew from the woods that most had lived in all their lives that different plants like different people needed different things. They knew, too, how to hunt what they needed from the woods without blind searching. And they knew their plants; even the five-year-old riding behind an older sister could reach out from time to time, break a twig, pick a berry or a grape, and need no watching, chewing dogwood, spice wood or some good clean-tasting shrub, everybody knowing he would never bite into a buckeye, chew poison vine, or eat a bright poison-oak berry.

They were at home in their world. It is doubtful if many of the women had traveled as much as Mrs. Stump, but moving was an old story to all save the very young children. Many came from East Tennessee and none of the settlements there was more than ten years old, and many, like the Eatons and the Robertsons, had moved more than once in the last few years. The country was new, but even to the children the life of camping out held much that was familiar; smells of leather and horse sweat, freshly killed meat, baking cornbread, wood smoke, black homemade powder with the sting of burning sulphur; sight of flickering flames, the bobbing world beyond a horse's ears that held sometimes the brightness of leaves, but on that fall much mist and fog and rain; and all the sounds familiar as some tune of Watts, rush of white water, a gun in the woods that was like a falling tree,[76] horseshoes on hard rock, and always night after night the howling of wolves and hooting of owls; all these things like the dogs that guarded them night and day had ever been parts of their lives back home in a forted station or in a lone log house.

Still, the trip to the Middle Cumberland was the longest and hardest that most of the women and children had known and most of it through wild unsettled country. Travelers from the New River Country such as John Rains would for the first two hundred miles [77] or so follow much the same route as that used by Dr. Thomas Walker thirty years before. This road had in time become the Hunters' Trail, and now it was the main road of emigrating Virginians and North Carolinians into the west.

---

[76] W, 31S, 48.

[77] Summers, *Southwest Virginia*, 281, quoting the Mss. of William Brown and Thomas Speed of 1790, gives the distance from Ingle's Ferry over New River, long a noted crossing point before there was a ferry, to Cumberland Gap as 199 miles. From Central Kentucky, the Cumberland settler had close to 200 miles more, depending on the route and the destination. The only station in Middle Tennessee mentioned by first settlers as having been passed on the way to French Lick was Mansker's.

It had been changed in places but was still basically the Great War Path that led through Cumberland Gap, down, across the river at the ford near present-day Pineville and on to the great lick on Stinking Creek, long known to the hunters as Flat Lick.

It was from this lick eight miles past the Cumberland that Daniel Boone's party had had to begin road-cutting in earnest for the trail they made to Boonesboro, though also leading north, was west of the Warrior's Path. Boone's Trace was not, however, destined to become the main road to Kentucky, for soon there were west of Boonesboro, larger and more important settlements, and already Harrodsburg, older than Boonesboro. It is doubtful if the first overland travelers to Harrodsburg from East Tennessee cut a road, using instead the old Indian trail that connected with the Great Lakes Trail south of Lexington. There was, however, by 1779 a road shown on Daniel Smith's map [78] of his travels that year as turning sharply west at Flat Lick from Boone's Road, instead of east as did the new road cut sometime in early 1780.[79] The old road continued west above a great bend of the Cumberland, and different from the newer roads came near the river again opposite the mouth of the Clear Fork, close to present-day Williamsburg.[80] It then turned north, crossing Lynn Camp Creek of Laurel River, then Laurel River, and at last after jogging down the Rockcastle, crossed it, went up again and out by way of Scaggs Creek as did the newer roads.

Logan's Station at present-day Stanford was in 1779 reckoned 113 miles from Cumberland Gap [81] and about 312 miles from Ingle's Ferry across New River in Virginia. The Kentucky Road had by the fall of 1779 known the hooves of many horses, ridden by all kinds of people—settlers bound for Kentucky, settlers rushing back east when the Indians threat-

---

[78] THM, I, opposite 54 in Smith, "Journal," is a reproduction of W, 7ZZ, 51, Daniel Smith's map, done four years before that of Filson. Though imperfect it gives a much better idea of Cumberland drainage, and hence a part of the Kentucky Road (I find nothing to indicate that either the name *Wilderness Road* or *Boone's Road* was used at this time).

[79] Mereness, *Travels*, Fleming, "Journal," 647, speaks in the spring of 1780 of the "new Road to Scaggs Creek," and in 1781 the whole road was recut by order of the Virginia Assembly; Summers, *Southwest Virginia*, 279–280. See also *The Wilderness Road*, Russell Dyche, Frankfort, Kentucky, 1946; "Early Trails and Roads Through the Wilderness of Southeastern Kentucky," map, 5, shows the Warrior's Path, Wilderness Road, and Boone's Road, but none show the same route as that of the Kentucky Road on Smith's map.

[80] THM, I, 55–58, Smith, "Journal," names the creeks crossed, and mentions points on the Kentucky Road.

[81] Mereness, *Travels*, Fleming, "Journal," 648–649, lists stopping places, and the distance between each.

ened, men rushing from the Holston to save them, then hurrying home again, fleeing Tories, fleeing Whigs, and early in the previous summer the British general, Lord Henry Hamilton, had come over the road as one of a group of prisoners. Still, the Crab Orchard in Kentucky was the first settlement reached after leaving those on the Holston near present-day Bristol, Tennessee.[82] Save for Logan's fort nearby, Crab Orchard was not a settlement, but only an orchard of ancient wild apple trees. There was another Crab Orchard on the eastern side of the Plateau in Tennessee, and two others in eastern Tennessee,[83] but wherever found, such an old orchard was a landmark for travelers.

Most of the travelers bound for Middle Tennessee followed this trail, at least as far as Flat Lick. It was over this road that Robertson had brought his Spanish horse stock, and by October he was on it again with his flocks and his herds, for it was in Powell Valley he met John Rains, and persuaded him to settle on the Cumberland instead of up in Kentucky.[84]

October that year was not too bad for travel; true, there was rain on the 12th and the 23rd brought an all day's rain, but in rainy weather most travelers lay over as they almost always did on the Sabbath unless rations were short and they hoped by moving on to find better hunting. Still, even riding through the rain was no great hardship, but rain meant risen creeks and rivers. Travelers, in swimming their horses, often got wetted; some rode on, but others, less hardy, would stop, build fires, and either change or dry their clothing—a not unexpected part of pioneer travel.

More dreaded than swimming or rafting the Cumberland and commented upon much more by later travelers were the swift-watered, rocky-bottomed creeks [85] the trails crossed and recrossed throughout the trip. Most creeks were set between high and slippery banks, sometimes so steep the rider had to dismount, no easy business for a woman on a side-saddle and clumsy with an unborn child, a toddler clinging behind, and the least one sharing the saddle in front.

[82] Hamilton, "Journal," 196–199. In this account of travel over the Kentucky Road and into East Tennessee no mention is made of Martin's Station, that was in time the last stopping place in Tennessee, 20 miles east of the Gap, nor did Colonel Fleming speak of it, but by 1784, Williams, *Travels*, Lipscomb, "Journal," 274, found a few people there.

[83] Daniel Smith's 1774 map of East Tennessee, Thwaites-Kellogg, *Dunmore's War*, 30, reproduced from W, 4XX, 62, shows the Big and Little Crab Orchards in East Tennessee.

[84] W, 31S, 34–35, one of several accounts; Robertson's daughter Lavinia, *ibid.*, 6XX (50), 8, spoke of his blazing a trail and carrying a compass, but the blazing may have been done after leaving the Kentucky Road on the other side of the Gap.

[85] Hamilton, "Journal," 197, declared the road crossed Craggs (Scaggs) Creek forty times, and complained continually of the creek crossings.

The first three weeks of November were fine for travel that year, and a good thing as most Tennessee-bound travelers would still have been in the rough country between the Crab Orchard and the Holston, though there is no proof that even at this early date all went through Cumberland Gap. Past Flat Lick, the exact route of any one party is even more obscure; there is no mention that Robertson's party went back by Logan's Station, though he had stopped there on his trip home from the Illinois. The Buchanan party, of course, went as far north as Danville,[86] in order to leave their womenfolks, while "some got lost and went as far as Lexington."

Others such as the Eatons who had with them an ex Long Hunter, Humphrey Hogan, most probably turned west away from the Kentucky Road south of Scaggs Creek and reached French Lick by much the same route as Isaac Bledsoe, late in December of that year. There was a road turning west from the Kentucky Trace just north of present-day Williamsburg; roughly following the Cumberland but keeping on the highlands and away from the bends it went on north of the Cumberland across Buck and Pittman creeks and touched the river again at present-day Burkesville, then south and west through the Barrens until it connected with trails leading to Nashville.[87]

Many travelers undoubtedly followed some approximation of this road. However they went, the trip through the Barrens to French Lick was lonely as that over the Kentucky Road; after leaving the settlements in central Kentucky, there were none for more than a hundred miles or until Mansker's was reached about twelve miles north of French Lick. Daniel Smith, traveling in the spring of 1780 from Mansker's to The Falls, rode for five days without even seeing horse sign.[88] John Lipscomb traveling in 1784 stopped at Carpenter's Station only twelve miles from the cluster now grown up in Central Kentucky on the Kentucky River; he and his party then traveled southwest and south for six days before

[86] W, 30S, 294–296. This from the account of John Carr, son of William Carr who went to Clark's Station in Kentucky in 1780—the Mulherrin and Buchanan women were there. The Carr family then came down to Middle Tennessee in 1783.

[87] David H. Burr, "Map of Kentucky and Tennessee Post offices, Post Roads, Canals, Railroads, 1839," Transportation Library, University of Michigan, shows this road, one of the most important in the early days. PC, I, 77, contains an 1801 order for the road to be worked across Pittman, Buck, and Rockcastle; not many miles past Rockcastle it connected with the road from Cumberland Gap to Stanford. Russell, "1794 Map," shows a road from Boonesboro to Price's Station on the Cumberland. My own feeling is that many overland travelers turned due west after getting into the Rockcastle Country and followed some approximation of this road, as did Isaac Bledsoe when he took the horses to French Lick; THM, I, Smith, "Journal," 56–58, 59.

[88] THM, I, Smith, "Journal," 63.

reaching a settlement, and that Mansker's.[89] Settlers, traveling entirely by horseback and with livestock in need of grazing grounds, avoided when possible the well beaten trails, already grazed and hunted over by earlier travelers.

There is among the several accounts of the first overland immigrants to the Middle Cumberland, no mention of Indians or even fear of them. The dogs were ever watchful, and men such as Robertson and John Rains would have in their sleeping been awakened by any noise not in the proper pattern, though the pattern was the ever-changing one of many weathers and always different camp sites; one camp site low in a canebrake by a creek meant a night of comparative stillness save for owls and wolves and the wind moaning like a sea in pines high on the ridges; the next night might bring the stiff rustlings of dry oak leaves, or again the leaden sound of cold November rain, for the last week in November brought all weathers but sun. Along with the rain came short-lived wet snows, and many misty "glowering" days of low skies common to the Cumberland in fall and winter.

Yet the only complaints on the weather among future settlers on the Cumberland came from a group of men. These had just cause for complaint; unlike other travelers they could not follow the trails nor did they like to work in cloudy or rainy weather, for they were surveyors. Once again the line along 36° 30″ was being extended; this time to the Mississippi, and Daniel Smith,[90] along with Dr. Thomas Walker, working as surveyor and commissioner for Virginia, liked to take a reckoning every few miles by the sun and again by the polestar.

[89] Williams, *Travels*, Lipscomb, "Journal," 275–278; on his return journey later in the same year, 1784, Lipscomb followed a more westerly route by Red River where he stopped at the station built in this year; for this Red River route see also, W, 32S, 547, as described by Gen. William Hall up Station Camp Creek. *Ibid.*, 29S, 73, gives another account that declared, "no inhabitants between Red River and the Settlements at and near Danville." The Red River settlement was not established on a permanent basis until 1784, and from there—Kilgore's—it was 18 miles to Mansker's.

[90] THM, I, 45–46, St. George L. Sioussat, "Introduction to Smith's Journal." See also W, 32S, 476, a brief life sketch by his son George. Daniel Smith (1748–1818) had been a Captain in Lord Dunmore's War, see Thwaites-Kellogg, *Dunmore's War*, 3–4, for life sketch. In 1776 he had captained a company that had gone against the Cherokee, and hence knew many of the first settlers on the Cumberland; serving in this same company, many of them as officers, were John Montgomery, Isaac Bledsoe, Anthony Bledsoe, Amos Eaton, Benjamin Drake, and others; see Summers, *Southwest Virginia*, 237–240. In 1776 Smith had been commissioned a major of militia by Patrick Henry, *ibid.*, 255, and in 1777 he was appointed a member of the court of Washington County, *ibid.*, 285. After settling on the Cumberland in 1784 he served in all manner of ways from Justice of the Peace to Secretary of the Territory South of the River Ohio.

Thirty-one-year-old Daniel Smith was what one might call a shirttail man for he could do anything the occasion demanded; draw a map, write a geography, distill a fine peach brandy, help make a constitution hailed by Jefferson as the most liberal in the United States, mend a gun, kill and butcher buffalo, treat with and fight Indians, or survey as he was doing now. He had learned much from his five-year association with Dr. Thomas Walker.

Dr. Walker,[91] already "below the ordinary size" of men, had grown stooped and gray-headed in the twenty-nine years since he had named Cumberland River. He had had a narrow escape at Braddock's defeat, but was luckier than his friend Joshua Fry who had died after being thrown from his horse at Wills Creek in 1754. Friend and neighbor of the two men, Peter Jefferson, who had helped Fry run the line in 1749, was also dead, and Dr. Walker had in 1757 been appointed guardian of the boy Thomas; now young Thomas Jefferson had succeeded Patrick Henry as Governor of Virginia. Land, the buying and selling and ownership of it, had continued to fascinate Dr. Walker; only the year before he had paid the trader George Croghan five thousand Spanish dollars for 125,000 acres; but land for himself and heirs was not enough. He had been active in pushing George Rogers Clark's plan of winning the northwest, and how much his influence counted in Jefferson's purchase of Louisiana we cannot know; Walker was, by 1803, dead, but as a man forever looking west and guardian of the boy Jefferson for seven years, his influence would have counted for something.

In addition to guards, chain carriers, and other helpers, including a surgeon, there were Isaac and Anthony Bledsoe—the first trip west for Anthony,[92] but Isaac had by 1779 spent much time in the country west of the mountains. Richard Henderson was also in the woods; his land purchase from the Cherokee had not yet been outlawed by North Carolina, for North Carolina didn't, until the line was run, know exactly what she owned, and had appointed Henderson as commissioner to oversee the North Carolina interests in the running of the boundary. Henderson's interests and those of North Carolina for the moment were one, for Henderson planned to "sell" Middle Tennessee to all those coming out to set-

[91] FP, 13, J. Stoddard Johnston, *First Explorations of Kentucky*, 4-27, "Sketch of Dr. Thomas Walker."

[92] Anthony Bledsoe was active in the civil and military life of western Virginia and East Tennessee; see Thwaites-Kellogg, *Dunmore's War*, life sketch, 106; and letters concerning his efforts to raise troops and provisions, *ibid.*, 169, 260-261. See also Summers, *Southwest Virginia*, 103, 109, 110, 116, 135, and life sketch, 748-749.

tle. He ran his own line with his own party only occasionally meeting Daniel Smith and Dr. Walker.

Surveying had for the Virginians gone badly from the beginning when they failed to find a line said to have been run by John Donelson. They had had to go back to the Holston and begin where Jefferson and Fry had stopped. Mid-autumn found them still in the rough, gameless country of the Clear Fork. They debated turning back, but as they had already spent a good deal of time and money, they decided to quit surveying in the rough country that still belonged to the Cherokee, and go on and try to find the point where the Cumberland crossed the Virginia–North Carolina line, and from there carry the survey to the Mississippi.[93]

The party turned north, crossing the Cumberland at the mouth of the Clear Fork, and soon reached the Kentucky Road, and then at Lynn Camp Creek of Laurel River the leaders paid off and discharged most of the helpers. The remaining fifteen helpers and two commissioners turned due west, crossing the Rockcastle near the mouth of Scaggs Creek, and then following a rough approximation of today's Kentucky Highway 80 and constantly hampered by flooded creeks, they reached the neighborhood of Pittman's Station which Daniel Smith visited.[94]

This relatively short trip had taken almost three weeks; heavy rains interspersed with snows, mists, and bitter winds flinging showers of snow made travel almost impossible. The worst problem, however, was the condition of the horses, long suffering from scant forage, for there was little cane along the route they had followed. It was decided to send them to French Lick, for they were on a trail leading to French Lick across present-day Pulaski County. Isaac Bledsoe left with the horses, and the rest of the party turned south after crossing Fishing Creek. The "excessive cold began" the 14th of December while they were still six days' travel on foot from the Cumberland. They went into camp on the 20th, four miles below the mouth of Fishing Creek, in present-day Pulaski County, choosing the site because of the abundance of "good canoe timber" for now it was either walk or go by boat.[95]

Meanwhile the other groups, no two together, struggled toward their destination. Both the Eatons and the Buchanans were ahead of Robertson,

---

[93] Smith sent to the Virginia Assembly a report of the year's work he and Dr. Walker performed on the border; in addition to running the line they went up and down the Ohio hunting George Rogers Clark. See Summers, *Southwest Virginia*, 699–702.

[94] THM, I, Smith, "Journal," 55–57.

[95] *Ibid.,* 56–58.

for example, yet he used a compass, and acted as trail blazer for his party. There was among hunters and Indian scouts a saying that in water it was safer to be behind, but in the woods the safest place was in front.[96] Robertson as pilot would have had to spend much time in front, and we can be certain that the rear or post of greatest danger was held by twenty-five-year-old Edmund Jennings where he could also keep an eye on the flocks and herds of his father who with the rest of the family was coming by boat in the flotilla headed by John Donelson. Edmund was still spare, six foot, large boned, with keen gray eyes set under shaggy brows above a large Roman nose and a large ugly mouth, fitting features for his long lank face. He had, since helping Boone cut Henderson's road in 1775, lived through some bloody times at Boonesboro, returned to East Tennessee and helped fight Indians in 1777 under Colonel Anthony Bledsoe. He would survive the bloody defeat of the Kentuckians at Blue Licks in 1782, go with Clark against the Indians north of the Ohio, fight at Coldwater under Robertson in '87, at Nickojack in '94 with minor skirmishes in between, serve under Jackson in the Creek War, and die in bed in 1840 when he was eighty-five years old.[97]

One reason he may have survived was that he always slept with his knife within reach and never went through an outside door without first peeping out to look for Indians; added to this he said his prayers night and morning, though in only one prayer was he ever known to ask a favor of God; this was when he ate the whole of a roasted possum, got indigestion, and thinking he was going to die, asked God as a favor to spare him, explaining that he didn't often ask favors, and promising that if he would grant this one, he, Edmund, would never ask another.[98] It is not recorded that he ever did.

Robertson's brothers Mark and John were along as was his oldest son, eleven-year-old Jonathan. His job was to drive the sheep, for his father rode at the head of a numerous company. Directly behind came his horse stock, including thirty or forty brood mares, next the hogs, cattle next, and last the sheep with Jonathan behind.

The boy's herding would go well enough until one old ram would

[96] Gray, *Bishop*, 79.

[97] In addition to the accounts of the Robertson children in W, 6XX, already mentioned, Edmund Jennings, 1751–1833, was remembered by many who wrote to or talked with Mr. Draper. See in particular *ibid.*, 3XX, 37, and *ibid.*, 32S, 358, in which it is stated he was with Boone "that time his son was killed," or 1773.

[98] W, 32S, 516–520.

grow tired of the driving and run away over the hills and hollows, down steep bluffs where no horse could follow. Then, must Jonathan dismount and go after the ram on foot, but the ram like the boy had a mind of his own, and time and time again would butt his herder down. The boy always got up, and always eventually got his sheep together, though this meant coming late to camp long after the others had eaten, for his father camped at sundown, and Jonathan was usually three or four hours after dark.[99] A heavy dark it would have been; as fall went down to winter the days increased in cloudiness, and after the first snow on November 25th, the travelers saw little of the sun for weeks.

Still, there were the camp fires; Robertson we can be certain had a good one; he was a good woodsman and so was Edmund Jennings. If the younger man built it, nobody indulged in that disease that afflicts so many around an open fire—constant rearrangement. Jennings hated people who kicked his fires, just as he disliked men who wore broadcloth or rode in carriages; his chief love continued to be Kentucky, but he never got any land there.[100]

The hard winter settled down. Ever deepening snows and the continuing cold made the last stage of the journey a bitter time for all. Creeks in spite of being swift and swollen carried chunks of ice; minutes after fording ice glazed stirrup leathers and saddle bags, and many rode in creaking suits of icy mail. However, it is only from travelers to the Kentucky settlements that one hears hardships of that winter: frozen cattle, sheep killed from eating ivy when it alone held green leaves above the snow; a father drowned and mother and children frozen on the Kentucky Road, and even young men sick from exposure or suffering from frostbite.[101]

In contrast to all this, the most talked of incident among Cumberland-bound travelers had nothing to do with the weather. Frederick Stump of the Eaton party went out one morning to hunt. He must have been a splendid marksman, but on that particular morning he could kill nothing, though he got within shooting range of game several times. He came back to camp, blazing with anger, sought out Hopper, a young man of the party, and declared, "I'll shoot you—you spell my gun." He had his gun cocked and aimed before several quick-handed men about could grab it.

---

[99] W, 6XX (50), 8.
[100] W, 32S, 516–520.
[101] Mereness, *Travels*, Fleming, "Journal," 619–643, has many references to sickness, hunger, and the suffering in general of Kentucky in 1779–1780. Col. Floyd of Kentucky lost most of his sheep that winter because they ate ivy, W, 33S, 139.

It is not recorded what Stump did to unspell his gun; maybe nothing as he grew prosperous through farming. His belief that if he could see an Indian first the Indian could not shoot him seemingly went through the years unshaken; once they chased him three miles, but saw him first.[102]

All members of the Eaton party got safely through and on the 24th of December halted on the northern side of the Cumberland about four miles from French Lick and a mile back from the river. They set up their tents, built some open-faced camps, elected officers, and settled down for the winter.[103] Next day, Christmas, John Rains, just arriving, drove steers, horses, and cattle across the frozen Cumberland. Meanwhile the Mulherrin and Buchanan men were already building a station above the big lick, or French Lick as it had come to be known, while on the other side of the lick and downriver, George Freeland was building another.[104]

Robertson's party got through around the last of December. He had on leaving the Holston in the fall, doubtlessly expected to find a finished station and cribbed corn. Somewhere on the way he must have learned that the men he had left at French Lick had had an Indian scare and gone to Kentucky. Buffalo had torn down the brush fence and destroyed the corn, and until the last of February Robertson left his livestock at Mansker's where the grazing was good.[105]

Robertson's hardest and most dangerous trip was still ahead. Sometime during the season of hard cold and deep snows he rode one hundred and sixty miles in a vain attempt to find a place on the Tennessee where he could meet his family and the Donelsons as agreed. He went too far west and struck Elk River, then rode still more miles before he discovered the Elk was not the Tennessee, and turned back.[106]

Three hundred miles up the crooked Cumberland from French Lick, the surveying party worked at building canoes. It was the first of January before they were able to launch one of the three they had made. The next day was Sunday, but meat was getting scarce. Daniel Smith and two other men went downriver in the new canoe and in spite of snow the previous night and the bitter cold, they camped out. Next day the three men killed,

---

[102] W, 31S, 74.

[103] W, 31S, 69, locates this temporary camp; it was not either the first or second Eaton's Station.

[104] The Buchanan party built the station later called by some Draper correspondents French Lick Station, the first built near the Cumberland, at least according to William Martin, W, 3XX (11), 2; the Buchanans got there before Robertson. He did not at this time build a station but helped build Freeland's, *ibid.*, 6XX (50), 9, also south of the Cumberland but on the western side of Lick Branch; see *ibid.*, 29S, 75.

[105] W, 31S, 35.

[106] W, 32S, 341.

cleaned, and butchered six buffalo, and once again camped out, the night "clear and very cold."

And cold it was, for in spite of high water, the chunks of ice were coming down so thickly the hunters could not get the heavily loaded canoe up the river, and had to spend the night with the little Long Hunter Obediah Terrell who had a camp on the river about ten miles below the mouth of Fishing Creek. This stretch of country was far from uninhabited. In addition to the several families at Pittman's Station and Gist's Station Camp on the other side of Cumberland, there was a settlement or at least travelers thirty miles downriver where cattle were wintering in a canebrake. Canoe Camp, as Daniel Smith called it, was near an Indian trail that crossed the Cumberland at Fishing Creek Ford, and one day a traveler passed by, William Young, apparently on his way to some settlement downriver, or even to East Tennessee by a shorter, safer route than that through Cumberland Gap. Across the Cumberland was Price's Station, and from it Jerry Pearce came one day visiting, and as soon as the river froze Anthony Bledsoe walked over and repaid the call.

Daniel Smith didn't go, but stayed home to mend his gun, for he had broken her "britch" when bringing the buffalo meat upriver. Next day after breaking the gun he could write, "I fixed up my gun Barr[el] in another Stock & lock." It is doubtful if the party carried extra stocks, though locks they may have had; he most probably whittled a stock, with raised cheek rest and cavity for the patch box, then took the metal parts from the old stock and put them on the new. Like the Long Hunters, these men would have carried a vise and bellows for mending the metal parts of their guns. They could have made a little charcoal, but lacking this, oak bark for the forge fire made a good substitute.[107]

They spent almost six weeks at Canoe Camp, held by the "excessive hard frost." Daniel Smith and two others made two more trips downriver hunting buffalo, and with the river frozen and no pack horses they had to go on foot. The only hint of short provisions came about the middle of January, and Daniel wrote: "Went down the river a hunting in order that less provision might serve at our Station Camp." There was no mention of discomfort from the weather, no illness, only a little complaining now and then of the ice that kept them from travel. One wishes Daniel Smith had told a little of the life in camp; the long evenings when the winter dark of cloudy days fell early on the camp low in the river valley,

[107] THM, I, Smith, "Journal," 58–59. VM, VII, 250, Redd, "Reminiscences," 250, tells of the use of oak bark in a hand forge; it was pounded fine.

they must have many times heard the hungry howlings of starving wolves, trees cracking in the cold, and the creak of ice in the never completely soundless river.

Better yet would have been their conversation. Daniel Smith, young as he was, had been a captain in the Point Pleasant campaign five years before, had lived in Baltimore, studied physics with Dr. Thomas Walker, and of late years had spent most of his time on the border in what is now Russell County, Virginia. Dr. Walker, then sixty-five, had seen the making of his country. He was a year-old baby when Spotswood led his Knights of the Golden Horseshoe up to the then unknown land behind the Blue Ridge. He was a teen-age boy when Byrd ran the line that he was running now, and getting on to manhood when Richmond was founded. He had fought or treated with Indians for much of his adult life, and was a long-time friend of Attakullakulla. He had dined with Benjamin Franklin, fought with Washington at Braddock's defeat, and knew the families of three future presidents—Jefferson, Madison, and Monroe, for they were all his neighbors. His children were marrying well; Lucy who had married George Gilmer would bear two governors, and from Elizabeth who married the Reverend Matthew Maury would come Matthew F. Maury of Tennessee who mapped the oceans.[108]

Daniel Smith, scarcely seven years married, had only a baby son, who would in time find a wife among the Donelsons, still at the commencement of their river journey. His yet-to-be-born daughter would also find a spouse among the Donelsons, and their son would serve in the White House as secretary to Andrew Jackson. Isaac Bledsoe was gone with the horses, but Anthony may have thought and talked of his children; they, too, would find spouses among those then settling on the Cumberland, and leave numerous descendants to help people, not only Tennessee, but the south and the west as well.

One who listened more than he talked for he was only a guard, and somewhat of a stranger, was Hugh Rogan. He was then thirty-two years old, a short, chunky, fair-skinned, blue-eyed man, speaking with a strong Scotch accent, for he was only four years out of northern Ireland. He and his brother-in-law had come as traders into the upper Yadkin Country, planning to investigate the new world, and if they liked it, send for their wives. Their plans were ruined by the Revolution; Hugh's wife and child

---

[108] FP, 13, 20–25. See also Collins, *Kentucky, 1882*, II, 418. A county up the Cumberland was named for one of Dr. Walker's descendants; long known as Josh Bell County, it is now Bell County.

were still in northern Ireland, and so they remained for close to twenty years.[109]

Hugh became a famous scout and Indian fighter, at one time helping save Bledsoe's Station. His brother-in-law married again, but Hugh, always declaring his marriage could be dissolved only "by his Maker," at last managed to go back in 1794 for his wife when the Indian wars were almost over and the country safer. Luckier than many guards and Indian fighters, he was granted a large boundary of rich land, and built his home on Bledsoe Creek in present-day Sumner County.[110]

Not all out in that hard winter had such happy endings. Henry Scaggs over in the Green River Country, lost first his only adult companion, Sinclair, and then his young son sickened and died. The Green brothers had better luck; hunting far up the Cumberland, they probably heeded the weather but little. During the winter they heard of the Donelson party bound for French Lick, and decided it would be nice to pay them a little visit. They made the usual poplar dugout and when the ice went out—February 12th at Canoe Camp—they started on their swift journey down the swollen Cumberland. At Cumberland Falls all except one got out of the boat and climbed down the craggy bluffs and waited by the river below the full fury of the falls; the one above took the canoe out into the middle of the current and left it to go over the falls; a man below swam out and brought the canoe to shore. The boat was reloaded and they went on their way.[111] Smith Shoals that in later years wrecked so many coal boats would, in full water, give such men as the Greens no trouble.

The Greens when they got to French Lick never saw any of the Donelson party, for none was there. John Donelson's boat, the *Adventure*, that carried thirty blacks and fifteen whites, had stayed at Fort Patrick Henry on the Holston until the 22nd of December. Why, we do not know, for the heavy fall rains had made even small streams navigable for a flatboat. When Donelson did start it was so late that he was held for two months at the mouth of Reedy Creek of Holston, "by the fall of water and the most excessive hard frost." He finally shoved off again, but went only as far as Cloud's Creek and stopped for another week, so that it was almost March, "when we took our departure with sundry other vessels bound for the same voyage." [112]

[109] W, 6XX, 110-111, is a brief life sketch, but only one of many references to him, for everybody respected and loved him.
[110] W, 6XX, 43, 525.
[111] W, 32S, 527-528.
[112] Ramsey, *Tennessee*, Donelson, "Voyage," 197.

John Donelson was neither a James Robertson nor a Daniel Smith. His multifarious misadventures began before he was down the Holston, for only one day after starting his boat got stuck on the Poor Valley Shoal, two days later another boat was completely lost and "the whole cargo much damaged."

They had by March 5th reached only the mouth of the Clinch where "Clinch River Company" headed by John Blackmore joined them. Various estimates have been given of the number of people and craft on the trip; the most common belief is there were around thirty flatboats with several pirogues, the whole bringing around fifty families which with guards and slaves made about three hundred people. Mrs. John (Mary Purnell) Donelson, Jr., for whom the trip was a bridal journey, remembered sixty-four years later the camp fires glowing in a long line beside the river, and how the Indian squaws and children screamed by the Chickamauga towns, "Brothers, how do ye do-o-o-o; come ashore." Donelson foolishly granted their request, giving them ribbons, vermillion, and tobacco, but while he was treating with them a heedless young fellow shot at a swan, and the Indians commenced firing.[113]

This was only one of many disasters the inept and unseasoned Donelson had. There were in the party at least fifty men strong enough to manage a boat; there were plenty of courageous women like teen-aged Nancy Gower who guided a boat with a bullet wound in her thigh when the men ran off. Donelson's boat had a four-pounder, and there was no shortage of ammunition.

Still, their sufferings from Indians, hunger, and hardship in general have been the theme of practically every historian of the old west. The boat of Jonathan Jennings, father of Edmund, fell behind. The Indians attacked, killed a slave, while two young white men on the boat, one a brother of Edmund, ran away, leaving the women to manage as best they could in the face of Indian fire that cut their clothes and wounded Nancy Gower.[114] The Indians caught the young men; the Jennings boy was saved by an ancestor of Will Rogers, but the other was killed. In the struggle to get away, Mrs. Peyton accidentally threw her day-old first born into the river while trying to lighten the boat.

Just above Muscle Shoals Donelson risked further trouble from Indians by tying up to "search for the signs Captain James Robertson was to make

---

[113] W, 32S, 299–301.
[114] Ramsey, *Tennessee*, Donelson, "Voyage," 197–202.

for us at that place." Robertson, ignorant of the lay of the land, had been unable to find the place, so the party moved on more discouraged than ever, and into ever-mounting disaster. The Stuarts had developed small-pox in the early stages of the journey, and in order not to spread the disease had stayed behind. Soon, Donelson could only write, "Gone is poor Stuart, his family and friends to the number of 28 persons." A Negro man had died, "being much frosted in his feet and legs," and young Mr. Payne was mortally wounded.

Actual travel gave little trouble, for once started, the trip down the swollen Tennessee was a speedy one. The fleet navigated the formidable suck and the shoals with little trouble, though judging from Donelson's journal, few of the party had even known they were there. The hungry, badly disorganized, and discouraged group reached the Ohio, March 24th. There the fleet separated, some went down the Ohio bound for the Illinois Country or Natchez, while the Cumberland and Kentucky settlers turned upstream. Added to the trials of two hundred miles of upriver travel by flatboat was the weather, for the spring of 1780 was a fitting end to the hard winter—cold rains, mist, and little sun. Different from travelers down the Ohio and many down the Tennessee, no family appears to have brought any domesticated animal, and this handy source of food was lacking. The Jennings and Robertson cattle and hogs were coming overland, but the Donelsons, who from the beginning showed much indecision, left their cattle, watched over by son William and one slave, in Powell's Valley to winter on the cane. Thus, food of all kinds including game was scarce. More than half a century later Mary Purnell Donelson remembered with pleasure the catfish caught by "old, gray-headed Mr. Harrison," a swan that was killed, and the lamb's-quarters picked for wild greens.

The Renfroes and a few other families, about forty in all, left the flotilla at the mouth of Red River, and went up it some miles to build Renfroe's Station.[115] The rest went on up the Cumberland. It was April 24th before James Robertson and Edmund Jennings could welcome their families and friends at French Lick, or the Big Salt Lick as it was sometimes called. The Donelsons went eight more miles up to the mouth of Stone's River, and then three miles up the smaller stream to Clover Bottom, and did not disembark until May first. Here, on the land Michael Stoner had claimed

[115] This station should not be confused with the station built in 1784 where the Kentucky Road crossed Red River, for this first one was destroyed a few months after being started. William Martin, W, 3XX, 32, said it was where "Port Royal now is in Montgomery County."

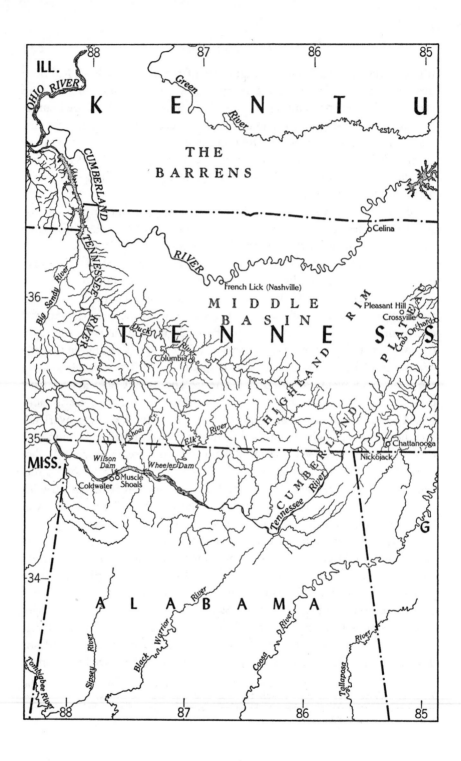

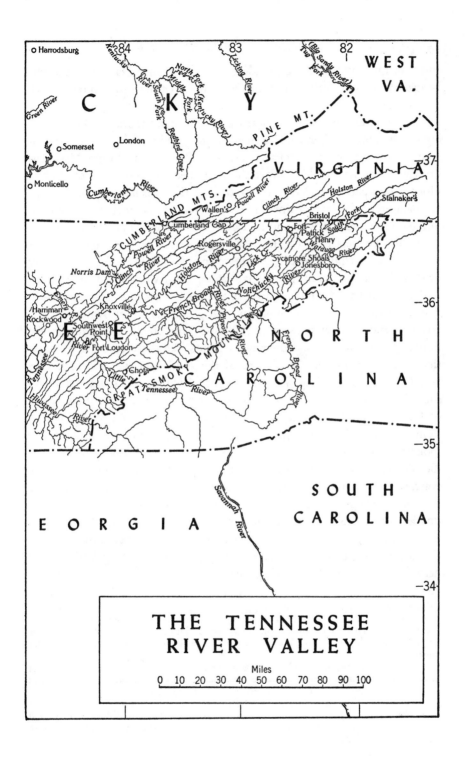

THE TENNESSEE
RIVER VALLEY

Miles

0 10 20 30 40 50 60 70 80 90 100

and later improved, Richard Henderson and Nathaniel Hart had had their Negroes build some cabins, but the Donelsons went instead into temporary quarters of open-faced camps.[116]

The Donelsons left a few months later [117] when the Indians began giving trouble, but later returned to make history. The youngest daughter of John Donelson, Sr., was thirteen-year-old Rachel, the future Mrs. Andrew Jackson. Rachel died before she could become mistress of the White House; for a part of Jackson's terms, this position was filled by the youngest daughter of Mary Purnell Donelson who remembered the lamb's-quarters; she was the wife and first cousin of Daniel Smith's grandson.[118]

Middle Tennessee was born; Mrs. Peyton had other babies, two of whom became United States Congressmen; Mrs. James Robertson's baby died within a few months, and two young sons were killed by Indians, but the children remaining and those to be born became or were the ancestors of generals, jurists, ministers, and great plantation owners, or the wives of such. Robertson's widowed sister Ann found a husband in the flotilla, John Cockrill, and their descendants like those of other first settlers became prominent in the life of the south and the old west. One could go on with a long list of who begat whom, and point out many such things as that Dr. James White coming in 1784 was the grandfather of Edward Douglass White, a Chief Justice of the United States, or that William Polk coming in 1783 was grandfather of a President. All that is looking back. In the early spring of 1780, there was no looking back; Middle Tennessee was still ahead, across a tough stretch of constant Indian warfare that even for the lucky often meant loss of all possessions. There were other troubles, so many, that in looking ahead the populace might be divided into those who stayed and those who ran away. The flotilla down the Tennessee, adventurous as it was and colorful, carried only a few of the men who actually did the hard and ugly work of making Middle Tennessee.[119] It was the few coming overland who built stations, fought In-

[116] Mrs. Donelson, W, 32S, 306, said they lived in tents; other sources say the Donelson party built open-faced camps, but none said they built a fortified station.

[117] Flood waters first drove them off the low ground to the northern side of Stone's River, and in August they moved again, this time to Mansker's Station, W, 32S, 305–306.

[118] Burke, *Emily Donelson*, II, "Family Chart," end papers clarifies all these relationships.

[119] Important as members and descendants of the flotilla came to be, they have at the expense of those who came overland been overemphasized in their role as pioneers. I can find no record that any family on the flotilla built and maintained a station in the first hard years; most left; best known of those who stayed were John Montgomery, John Cockrill, John Boyd, John Blackmore, William Neely, and David Maxwell, the last three dead of Indians a few months after settling, as were most of the Renfroes.

dians, and made the world if not safe at least possible for the Donelsons, Polks, and others including Andrew Jackson who never fought an Indian until 1813 after he became a general.

There was for a few months a small trickle of other immigrants to the region. One small flotilla from the Illinois reached French Lick only after a costly battle with Indians; yet it was more fortunate than a lone boat in which all passengers were killed.[120] Still others, such as the German-speaking Shor brothers of whom little is known, are thought to have come overland. The Cumberland settlements were fortunate in that they attracted several seasoned borderers from Kentucky; these included Philip Conrad, Nicholas and Philip Tramel, Hugh and James Leeper, all friends or at least acquaintances of the Drakes who came with the Eatons, for all had been members of Captain Benjamin Logan's Company up in Kentucky in 1779.[121]

Well equipped to wrestle with any disaster or situation that might befall were several families who had made the long trip down the Tennessee, the Ohio, and the Mississippi to Natchez, lived there a time, some for several years, and then decided to settle on the Cumberland. These included Christopher Gais and his grown son,[122] and a group who had tried, without success, a little revolution led by Phineas Lyman against Spain; among this last group was John Turnbull who came with pack-horse loads of goods to sell.[123]

There seems little doubt but that Kaspar Mansker was the first actual settler in Middle Tennessee; by early spring of 1780 he was well enough established that Daniel Smith [124] boarded with him for a few days, paying thirty dollars board and eleven dollars more for the making of a hunting shirt. The statement of the sums means little; the half-born, struggling United States behind the settlers had many troubles, and the flood of paper currency issued by states as well as by authority of the Continental Congress

[120] Mereness, *Travels,* Fleming, "Journal," 645. It is interesting how in the bitter weather and sparsely settled world of the old west in 1779–1780, news traveled. Col. Fleming, *ibid.,* 642, heard of the disaster of the Stuarts with the flotilla, on April 10, weeks before Donelson reached French Lick; Daniel Smith got a communication from Virginia, brought by Richard Henderson, whom Smith had started out with, met again on the Kentucky Road, Smith, "Journal," 57, 59, and Henderson in March met the Donelson party far down the Cumberland, and the Greens far up around Harlan heard of Donelson.
[121] Collins, *Kentucky, 1882,* I, 12.
[122] DC, I, 19, an account of the Gais property near Natchez.
[123] Haywood, *C & P,* 130, gives the date of Turnbull's coming as 1783, but he got a grant of land as a first settler, though among the group named as having come a little later.
[124] THM, I, Smith, "Journal," 62.

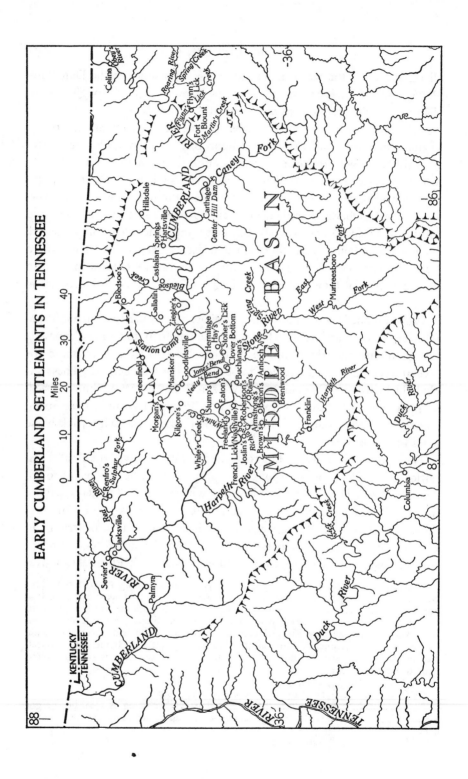

EARLY CUMBERLAND SETTLEMENTS IN TENNESSEE

Miles

0   10   20   30   40

KENTUCKY
TENNESSEE

CUMBERLAND RIVER

Sevier's
Clarksville
Palmyra
Red River
Renfro's
Sulphur Fork

Greenfield
Morgan's
Kilgore's
White's Creek
Freeland's
French Lick
Nashville
Joslin's
Brown's
Rich Armstrong's
Robertson's
Rain's
O'Baron's

Harpeth River

Franklin
Brentwood
Antioch

MIDDLE BASIN

Duck River

Duck River

Lick Creek
Columbia

Harpeth River

West Fork
Murfreesboro
East Fork

Spring Creek
Stone's River

Stump's
Eaton's
Buchanan's
Jones Bend
Neely's Bend
Clover Bottom
Stoner's Lick
Hay's
Hermitage
Ziegler's

Station Camp Cr.
Mansker's
Goodlettsville

Gallatin
Castalian Springs
Bledsoe's
Bledsoe Creek

Hartsville
Hillsdale

Carthage
Center Hill Dam
Caney Fork

CUMBERLAND RIVER

Fort Blount
Martin's Creek
Flynn's
Fort Lick
Spring Creek
Roaring River
Celina
Obey River

TENNESSEE RIVER

was only one, though even to my childhood many said of the worthless, "not worth a Continental."

There is no record of all first settlers in Middle Tennessee; possibly the closest thing is a list of 263 signatures affixed to a paper drawn up by Richard Henderson in the spring of 1780, and known as the Cumberland Compact,[125] concerned chiefly with the cost and method of buying land. This list did not, however, have the names of all who came, and by no means all those on the list stayed. The borderers were, as a group, much inclined to travel, living first here and then there, as family records and the depositions of Revolutionary soldiers asking for pensions show.

Too little is known of the early settlers on the Cumberland to permit any sweeping generalizations. It has been said that most came from North Carolina with Virginia and South Carolina represented. This is true, but such statements mean little. The southern colonies, particularly the western portions, were the homes of people with widely divergent economic, religious, and political backgrounds, as well as national origins, with no two communities exactly alike in make-up.[126] The Middle Cumberland, though drawing from many, was like no single one. In general it seems safe to say that the first settlers on the Cumberland were predominantly of Scotch and English origins, heavily seasoned with German, and smaller amounts of French, Dutch, Welsh, with a very few Irish. Practically all were Protestants when they belonged to any church.[127] There were a few of the Church of England, and still fewer Catholics such as De Monbruen.

[125] Putnam, *Tennessee*, 100–102. This includes many such as Samuel Newell and Michael Stoner, known to have settled elsewhere. Equally interesting is the number of known first settlers who did not sign; these include John Buchanan, Jr. and Sr., Edward Swanson, William and Isaac Neely; these five were granted land which would indicate they stayed; neither John Rains nor Edmund Jennings signed, but they got no land as first settlers. Only a small part of the Cumberland Compact, *ibid.*, 94–100, was devoted to government; it was in large measure a land-buying contract, with each signer agreeing to abide by the rules laid down for price, etc. The high price, 26 pounds, thirteen and four for each 100 acres may have discouraged many, though no monies were to be paid until Henderson was certain of his title. Those who had already made improvements had to enter their land with the entry taker, but the Compact did not stipulate the improver should have his land free.

[126] Interesting to compare the signers of the Cumberland Compact with those who signed the Watauga Petition, Ramsey, *Tennessee*, 138, and with such lists as the troops led by William Christian, Summer, *Southwest Virginia*, 236–240, and with the size rolls of twenty years before. Christian's list is overwhelmingly Scotch; the Cumberland Compact in general shows a greater mingling, though in all Irish are little represented.

[127] Inventories yield numerous Bibles and theological works, but religion as an institution with buildings and ministers developed more slowly in Middle Tennessee than on any other border. See Williams, *Travels*, Schweinitz, "Report," 508–515, the state of organized religion in Middle Tennessee 20 years after settlement.

The upriver counties in Kentucky drained by the Cumberland below the Rockcastle drew settlers from much the same sources as did Middle Tennessee, and had more in common with East and Middle Tennessee than with the rest of Kentucky. Much of this section is part of the Highland Rim or Barrens, but it is usually referred to as the "Kentucky Mountains," while we, the populace, are generally denominated "pure-blooded Anglo-Saxon." It is doubtful if there was a pure-blooded Anglo-Saxon in the world when any part of the Cumberland was settled, and certain it was he never came to the hills.

I cannot of course speak for the whole of the Southern Appalachians or even for all of the hills in Kentucky; the coal region on the upper Cumberland, for example, attracted in later years many nationality strains practically non-existent in colonial America, while that portion along the Ohio also received more directly from the old world as well as from the middle and northern states. My own ancestry is fairly typical in that at least some part of it is shared by most now living in Wayne County, Kentucky, and how many not living there would be a problem in higher mathematics.

We had little industry to attract and none to hold outsiders, so that most of us born there were descended of people who settled at least by 1800, and many before. All whose wills were probated were farmers as contrasted to planters; the most affluent had around twenty slaves, many none, though some used white tenants. Most in addition to farming had some other occupation—teacher, stonemason, silversmith, inspector of hemp, tavern keeper, smallish political jobs or offices of various kinds. The majority of first-settling ancestors had served at one time or another, occasionally as officers but more often as privates, in the armed forces.

A goodly number came from Virginia, but they represented many Virginias. There was for example Joseph Collins, Gent., who as Captain of a Troop of Horse joined Culpeper April 26, 1756, to go with others of the Spotsylvania militia "against Ye Indians above Winchester." Captain Joseph is said to have been a grandson of William Collins who came to the Isle of Wight County, Virginia, in 1635. Neither the date nor the Virginia ancestry is anything to get excited about; bond servants were imported at very early dates, and by far the majority of Virginians were middle-class farmers, good people but far from blue-blooded.

Susanna, daughter of Captain Joseph, married William Gholston, or Gholson or Gohalston, whose father, Anthony, had in 1728 taken up a thousand acres in Spotsylvania County. Susanna Collins Gholston named her second child for him—Anthony born in 1733. He served in the Revolution and eventually settled west of the mountains. One of his daughters married Isaac Chrisman, from still another section of Virginia, the lower Shenandoah where old Joist Heydte or Heidt or Hite had settled around sixty years before. His descendants and neighbors and in-laws—McDowells, Bowmans, Fromans, Fryes—were well represented in the old west, with grandsons serving under George Rogers Clark, and still others settling at various localities on the Cumberland.

One could go on and on; tell of English Dodson marrying Scotch Dick, with here and there some descendant of a Huguenot settled early on the Santee in South Carolina or in Virginia, for the English gentleman of Tidewater and the German farmer from the Shenandoah were only two of the many strains that were in most of us. There were several—in our community, Saunders, Mercers, Reynolds—who bore the surnames and knew they were descended from Tidewater families, settled three hundred years before, but it is doubtful if they were as purely English or Anglo-Saxon, if you will, as the average New Englander in colonial days. Practically every one had at least one Scotch ancestor, and during the early years Scotch names predominated in East Tennessee and up the river as they did on the Virginia border; in Middle Tennessee there appear to have been heavier migrations of English and German.

The French were also quite well represented, but of two basic types— those such as John Sevier of Huguenot descent and of English colonial background and the French Catholic, sometimes of Canadian background, and later come directly from France such as those who settled in the neighborhood of Harrodsburg, Kentucky, and Louisville. The Cumberland got few of these, but in going over lists of ships' passengers who were French refugees, some as early as 1660, and known to have settled on the Rapahannock and elsewhere in Virginia Tidewater, one is struck by the large number of names found on the Cumberland now, and even more common in the early days; Sublett, Chadowin—that became Shadoan—Hatcher, Dibrell, Le-Grand, Maury, Lanier, Trabue, Sallie, and many others including some such as Baillow that became Ballou.[128]

Still, these diverse people had, in settling the Cumberland, more than one common denominator. The first was their ability to live on the border, not as mere on-lookers but as workers, for even in Middle Tennessee there was, during pioneer days, no leisure class. Everybody worked.

[128] I am indebted to Mrs. A. S. Frye, Genealogist, Somerset, for a large amount of family-history material based on court minutes, and inventories from North Carolina and Virginia counties, ships' lists, and family Bibles.

They were, in common with most of the rest of the United States, literate. Only two of the 111 men who signed the Watauga Petition could not sign their names, and of the 250 signatures on the Cumberland Compact only one was a mark. Various estimates have been made of the degree of illiteracy, some as low as three per cent, not as high as that of New York State today.

They had one other thing in common—pride. Most, regardless of national origin or religion or economic status, had a feeling of worth, an abiding self-respect that months of life in an open-faced camp, or hunger, or loss of property could not destroy. In Virginia even "the peasants felt good as large land owners," an English traveler commented, while another found the North Carolina hunters with a good opinion of themselves.[129] Michaux the younger, visiting Middle Tennessee twenty-five years later, found a people proud of themselves. It took a high-headed people to do what the pioneer had to do. The most important part of the world to him was that part in which he happened to be, and so he shaped that world to his will.

[129] All historians of and travelers in the southern colonies found until the end of the Revolution, not only no poverty, but practically nothing of a "low class." See Smythe, *Tour*, I, 68–72, 182. Anburey, *Travels*, II, 370–374, after commenting on the lack of poverty, found "very few [Virginians] deficient in intellectual qualities . . . lower class less disagreeable than those of New England . . . finest lower class of any place in the world." Yet he found most southerners the "most unaccountable combination— rude, ferocious, haughty—but even low class generous, kind, helpful."

CHAPTER X

THE WOODSMEN

THE MEN and women who took the hard winter as a matter of course and once on the Cumberland, set to work to change woods and canebrake to farms, were not a race of supermen. They stood in relation to the woods as the Nantucket sailors did to the sea; not all of them together could have caught a whale, yet not even the most courageous of sea captains would have been able to throw up a half-faced camp, move in, and survive zero weather.

It had taken generations of living in the woods for the white American to learn to do such things; the tall timber that frightened many was his friend. It is doubtful if any could have survived six months in a treeless world, not even Kaspar Mansker or Thomas Sharpe Spencer. Joseph Bishop, a mighty hunter, skilled and courageous woodsman, fainted in trying to ride across a strip of treeless grassland on a hot summer day while visiting the Illinois.[1]

Still, pioneering was more than a matter of mere skill or even knowledge of the woods. There are bloodcurdling accounts of men and boys, grown up on the borders, who unfitted for loneliness among the trees, got lost and so lost their reason.[2] Others could never take the combination of

---

[1] Gray, *Bishop*, 110–111.

[2] W, 29S, 108, is an account of a lost boy in Kentucky who went "wild." Getting lost was not necessarily the mark of a poor woodsman. Many such as James Robertson did, and time and again Dr. Thomas Walker in 1750 had to climb a mountain or a tree to get an idea of where he was; whole parties of travelers got lost on the way to French Lick, but none of these got into the peculiar state of not believing even the direction of the sun. This, as described by tradition and *ibid.*, was a form of mental illness.

woods and lurking Indians. One of the few men killed in the Nickojack campaign that went out from Middle Tennessee against the Cherokee in 1794 was Gallie La Mar. Many wrote of this young man, who, safely returning from the successful expedition, was afraid to sleep on the ground as did the other men, most of whom had at one time or another—hunting, surveying, or traveling—spent many nights in the woods. Gallie La Mar climbed a tree for greater safety, but during the night had a nightmare of being attacked by Indians, fell out, and died a few days later of the injuries.[3]

Gallie La Mar, dead of wounds caused by fear, may have been an expert rifleman and a master hand at building log houses. We do not know. Such skills only made it possible for the pioneer to survive; they did not make a pioneer. Thus, though I can describe his tools and the manner of his life, I cannot explain the Cumberland pioneer. I cannot even explain why all risked, and many lost, their lives to settle Middle Tennessee. Certain it is they were not in search of the two goals most men want today—security and survival. They had as a group a great flair for living, and a love of life too great to want to live like a turnip in a tightly picketed garden—safe.

True, all frontiers attracted to some extent the failure, the misfit, and less often the criminal; but in the thinly settled farming community of any border where men had often to work together, at farming as well as fighting, cowards, criminals, and the generally no-good were less tolerated than in any fair-sized city.[4] Some, good men but economic failures, looked to the border to retrieve their fortunes, and many young single men with nothing but their lives to lose and everything to gain went as guards, cattle drovers, boatmen, but the lure for many of these was most probably love of adventure, with a wish to travel and see new country. Daniel Boone and most of those who went to Kentucky for Henderson in 1775 are good examples of such men: Boone was deeply in debt; he ever had an eye for good land, and certainly hoped and expected to get some, but along with these things was a love of the woods and of hunting.

Andrew Jackson was typical of another group that, entirely different from Boone, was attracted to the newly established border settlements because they offered more opportunity to the unestablished professional man with not too many friends and mediocre qualifications, than did the more

[3] W, 1S, 76. See also *ibid.*, 32S, 271.
[4] VM, VI, Redd, "Reminiscences," 251, told of Jacob Lewis who, suspected of wrongdoing, was denied the protection of an East Tennessee fort; forced out, Lewis, his wife, and seven children were killed by Indians.

competitive world of the eastern towns. Jackson, no more than a penniless
hog drover, had anything to lose, but much to gain, for he had at least the
hope of a job.[5] There were others on the order of Frederick Stump who,
ruined by the Revolution, went west to recover fortunes that, had they not
been lost, the losers would never have gone to the frontier. Still, hope of
riches seems not to have been the prime cause of any actual pioneering. As
a rule, those who gained greatest riches from the expanding borders, the
land speculators, never came at all, or like John Donelson left when things
got dangerous.

Bitter, grinding poverty that sent waves upon waves of immigrants to
America, such as the Irish, was not a factor in the settlement of any early
border. Poverty to the point of not having enough to eat was non-existent
in the southern colonies until the Revolution. Religious persecution did
push people out of Virginia, and unjust fines and fees that roused the
Regulators in North Carolina hastened emigration from that colony, but
neither was a part of life in East Tennessee, more attractive than ever by
1779; the Cherokee in the Chickamauga towns down the Tennessee would
continue to give trouble, but the world of East Tennessee was getting safer
as well as wider.

Look where I will I can find no reason why affluent families with position and not a little prestige in their communities should uproot themselves,
risk all to settle on the Cumberland. Yet it was families such as the Robertsons, Buchanans, Eatons, and Freelands who did just this; all had at least a
few slaves, money for provisions, ammunition, guards, and other paid
workmen.[6] Hand in hand with these possessions they had in addition to
the indefinable attributes pioneering demanded, all the needed skills. They
were not helpless without slaves and guards. Different from the Tidewater
leader, any of these men could do field work side by side with their slaves,
their self-esteem suffering not one bit.[7]

Such a man as Amos Eaton had to be hunter, warrior, horseman, farmer,
carpenter, and at times toolmaker and hence blacksmith, for the pioneer's

[5] Jackson's appointment as Prosecuting Attorney of the Superior Court by the
North Carolina Assembly came only after he had worked more than a year without
pay; NCR, XXI, 293, Jackson's memorial concerning his services was read, and he was
at last appointed with back pay agreed, *ibid.*, 717. He had during this time earned a
good bit as lawyer in the county court of Davidson.
[6] DW, I, 69, 166, 283, the inventories of John Buchanan, William Neely, and William
Overall who came on the exploratory trip with Robertson in 1779.
[7] There are in the Draper Manuscripts numerous references to men working in the
fields with their slaves: W, 1S, 61, is one of several concerning Robertson, and *ibid.*,
32S, 309, is an account of the Donelson men and those of other families gathering
cotton with their slaves at Clover Bottom in 1780.

life depended upon iron and steel quite as much as does our own today, and more directly. He would in his whole life get along with less than we buy in one automobile; but we can live without the automobile; he could have had nothing without his few iron tools and appliances. His gun is the most obvious, and used the most iron, and at times it saved his life. It could not be called his most important tool; there was in pioneer life no "most important" anything.

The Eatons traveling along, setting up tents each night, could have had neither tents nor fire without an ax, but the ax like the gun had to have a handle, and woe to the man in the woods who broke his gunstock, tomahawk, or ax handle and found himself alone and far from civilization without a whittling knife. It was not without reason that Holliday, who must have been a brave man to travel from the Middle Cumberland to East Tennessee alone, was afraid to start without a knife. Had Daniel Smith been alone and without a knife when he broke his gunstock in the hard winter, he could have starved, had there been no nearby settlements.

Much has been written of the tomahawk, "hatchet" the pioneer more commonly called it, and a visiting Englishman in writing of the Virginia hunters during the Revolution remarked that next to their rifle-barreled firelocks the tomahawk was the most indispensable.[8] This little tool, requiring a pound or less of iron, was constantly used in all manner of ways from cutting through bones in a buffalo carcass that would have ruined the edge of the skinning knife, always carried in a sheath, to making a canoe as Robertson used it. There were other times when a man without moccasins would have traded his hatchet for an awl, but he could in leather work substitute the tip of his whittling knife.

All these tools, particularly the whittling knife and the ax, were in constant use in such families as the Eatons and Buchanans. There were by the spring of 1780 several hundred acres of land cleared of cane and timber, at least enough to plant corn, much of this done in the summer of 1779 by Kaspar Mansker and the men who went with Robertson and stayed behind to put in corn.[9] Clover Bottom was a natural meadow, but Michael Stoner had made improvements there, and George Rogers Clark's letter indicates he had had some clearing done at French Lick.

---

[8] Smythe, *Tour*, I, 179.

[9] DW, I, 166, in listing William Neely's possessions, names a debt owed by James Robertson, sum unspecified, for the clearing of 1,280 acres of land. Most of this work would have been done during the summer of 1779, for Neely went back to East Tennessee and returned with the flotilla in April; he was dead and his daughter taken prisoner by midsummer of 1780; see Ramsey, *Tennessee*, 447.

Kaspar Mansker's Station [10] was in good enough shape to put up travelers by the early spring of 1780; Frederick Stump was making a permanent settlement on White's [11] Creek where his family, the Eatons, Drakes, and a number of others had spent the winter in tents and half-faced camps. The Eatons and several other families had moved east and south about three miles and built a station near the Cumberland above the Old French Landing,[12] across from the mouth of the Lick Branch up which De Monbruen had gone in 1766. On the other side of the river from Eaton's, George Freeland,[13] who had been one of the Robertson party to stay behind and clear land and plant corn, was with the help of others—Zachariah White and James Robertson among them—building a forted station with several cabins.

Destined to be the most famous and enduring of all, though its inhabitants were constantly changing, was that built largely by the Buchanan party, also on the southern side of the Cumberland. This station, soon to be known as French Lick,[14] was about a mile upriver from Eaton's; between the two in low and swampy ground was the big lick, known by some as the Big Salt Lick, by others as the French Lick, for by that time numer-

[10] There is in Goodlettsville a plaque directing one to Mansker's grave, and the general location of his station, described, W, 29S, 73, as being on the east side of Mansker's Creek, three miles from the mouth. This location is for his second station put up in 1783 after the Indians burned the first; it was in the same general neighborhood, but we cannot be certain it was on the same site.

[11] W, 31S, 59, gives the location of the first stopping place of the Eaton party and Stumps as the ford on White's Creek, one mile north of the Cumberland, and four miles northwest of where Nashville was laid out on the other side. *Ibid.*, 1S, 75, states that this was where Stump later lived. He was in 1800 still living where the road west to Clarksville forded White's Creek, Williams, *Travels*, Schweinitz, "Report," 509.

[12] W, 31S, 80-81, states that Eaton's or Heatonsburg as it came to be known was about two miles from future Nashville; this, too, was a temporary station, for around 1786 the Eatons moved and built further down the river near the mouth of White's Creek. DC, I, 54, refers to the "ferry opposite the old French Landing below Heaton's Station," but *ibid.*, 76, refers to Eaton's old Station. Helpful in understanding the location of the stations at this time before any roads were cut is Myer's Map of Tennessee Trails. See also Hutchins, "1778 Map" and "Notes"; sheet 7, my own numbering, locates the Big Buffalo Lick, later known as French Lick, "¾ mile from river bank and by the Indian trail." This Indian trail crossed the Cumberland below Eaton's Station and led north past Mansker's Station.

[13] Freeland's on the downriver or western side of the Lick was about a mile from French Lick Station, W, 29S, 75.

[14] The site of this station begun by the Mulherrin and Buchanan men is a disputed point. W, 1S, 62, states that it was between "Nashville Fort and Freelings," for there is little to indicate that it occupied any of the ground from which young Nashville was formed in 1784, though *ibid.*, 30S, 252, states that French Lick was in the upper part of what came to be Nashville, on the riverbank by a fine spring. The first station in which the Buchanans lived was never known as Buchanan's, but everything indicates that in late 1779 they began what was later known as French Lick Station.

ous big salt licks had been found. Here, too, was the Sulphur Spring on the side of the lick closest to Buchanan's. Nothing was standardized and names varied; Freeland's below the lick was often called the "lower station," and French Lick Station, "not at that time called the Bluff," was called the "upper station." [15]

These three settlements near the Cumberland and Mansker's twelve miles north were finished, at least enough to give shelter and protection, by midsummer of 1780.[16] Most of the work had been done since the breaking up of the hard cold in mid-March, but the Cumberlander, no different from any other pioneer, could never give himself completely to any one thing; even while he cut firewood he was part warrior, rifle leaned against a tree, or if able to afford him, a man hired to scour the woods and look for trouble. Mid-April meant corn-planting time, followed soon by cotton; the ax must yield to plow, grubbing hoe, and hoe. Yet, under all the ringing axes, sweating men and horses, deadened trees, planted seed, smell of new wood, or fresh-killed venison steak broiling on the coals, was the forge fire and the man handy enough with crude or even makeshift blacksmithing tools to mend the broken grubbing hoe, make a badly needed log chain from strips of iron cut with a cold chisel, reshape and sharpen the worn down plow-point, and mend the ever-needed guns as did the Long Hunters.

The skills and tools needed to do at least the rudiments of blacksmithing were not peculiar to the pioneer farmer. The iron of the day, laboriously cut and wrought by charcoal fire and water-driven hammers, was sold in long bars of a thickness suitable to the making of tenpenny nails. The farmer, who wished to save a blacksmith bill, would, using the fireplace as a forge and a block of wood covered with a thick piece of iron as an anvil, cut his own nails in the evening with chisel and hammer. Most farmers, save those in sandy Tidewater, had to have at least enough iron for horse-

---

[15] Possibly the best description of the geography of the first settlements south of the Cumberland came from Felix Robertson, though he knew it only by hearsay, for he was not born until 1781 at Freeland's. See Nashville *Journal of Medicine and Surgery*, VIII, 447; here in writing of pioneer medicine and physicians he describes the location of the two stations south of the Cumberland. He also talked with Featherstonhaugh; see *Excursion*, I, 211; both sources indicate that French Lick Station was not in Nashville.

[16] These stations and Stump's plantation were in early 1780 by no means all the attempted settlements in Middle Tennessee. Putnam, *Tennessee*, "The Cumberland Compact," 94–100, mentions 8 stations, but at the same time speaks of the large number of men who had come without "implements of husbandry," and would be obliged to return to the settlements and move out the next fall; stations mentioned, such as Bledsoe's and Asher's, were merely planned stations.

and ox-shoe nails, and the thrifty New Englander could earn a bit of money by buying iron and selling or exchanging nails.[17]

The well-to-do farmer on the Piedmont or in the Great Valley was more inclined to have his own blacksmith shop with anvil and small forge. Here, he could make nails, sharpen plow-points, mend wagon tires and remedy the many accidents common to the ironware of that day, for much of it was badly made, impure, and more brittle than our own. Seldom did the average farmer have the skill and tools to shape a horseshoe and put it on, or make a grubbing hoe, and as a result the blacksmith was one of the most important men in any community.[18]

Still, the farmer kept his tools, and when he moved he took them with him, and when going to a far frontier took several pounds of extra iron.[19] Fairly typical of the blacksmithing outfit of the average farmer were the tools of William Ramsey. He and his family came overland from western Virginia in the fall of 1781,[20] and when he was killed by Indians a few years later his blacksmith tools along with the rest of his possessions were sold.

He had a bellows, vise, three hammers, a sledge, a shoeing hammer, a horseshoe punch, a broken sledge, two pairs of tongs, two hand vises, seven files and a rasp, a wedge, cold chisel, and ax-eye punch.[21] The whole could have been carried on one pack horse with weight to spare, but with such an outfit and an anvil which was not mentioned, a man could shoe a horse, mend or even make most tools used in farming and woodworking.

Given a perfectly round steel rod and a piece of iron the skillful worker could, after shaping the iron into a long rectangle, weld it inch by inch around the rod, withdrawing the rod each time, cooling it, reheating the iron, until he had a gun barrel. If skillful enough he could then make a rifling tool,[22] and this, save for the small cutting edge, entirely of wood.

[17] Material on early iron manufacture used by permission of the publishers, the Carnegie Institution of Washington, from *History of Manufacturers in the United States* by Victor S. Clark, copyrighted and published by Carnegie Institution of Washington, Washington, 1926 (cited hereafter as Clark, *Manufacturers*), 510–517.

[18] THM, V, Sevier, "Journal," 194, 240, recounting the writer's many transactions with the blacksmith are quite typical of most journals and account books of the day; fair samples, "paid Hickey the BlackSmith 3 dollars for a grubbing hoe," Jan. 1797—"got a horse shod," Aug. 22.

[19] DW, I, 109, the inventory of John Donelson who left more iron than any other found—"230 lbs of iron—60 weight old iron."

[20] W, 5S, 61. Inventory, DW, I, 169.

[21] The ax-eye punch would indicate that the broadax was made like those still found in the hills. Good examples of an earlier pattern may be seen at the Fort Necessity Museum, near Uniontown, Pa.; these, used during the French and Indian War, were made without a punch; the metal curved around the handle as in the older battle axes.

[22] This from a traditional account told by Mr. John C. Burton, gun collector of

The most-often-mentioned blacksmith in the Cumberland settlements was Mr. Snyder, but he did not come until around 1783, and soon his business was so brisk he took an apprentice boy, and mended the guns of the Chickasaw and did all other jobs until killed by the Chickamauga in 1794.[23]

Blacksmith tools when compared to most others such as those of a cooper or shoemaker were always expensive, for anything made of iron was costly when measured in terms of cattle or day's wages. Dr. John Sappington who came in 1788 sold in that year "a set of blacksmith tools and other things" for the very large sum of 280 pounds,[24] or the equivalent of 2,800 acres of land at the price set by the North Carolina Assembly. A few years later Joseph Conrad's [25] blacksmith tools sold for ninety dollars or the price of his best horse. This was cheaper than in the early 80's when even a "cutting knife" as opposed to the larger and still more expensive "butcher knife" sold for a dollar or two days' wages.[26]

Any frontier community would have been helpless without blacksmith tools and a man able to use them. Still, we cannot say the blacksmith was the foundation of all pioneer life. So complex and interlocking was the world about the stockade walls that each skill or tool depended upon another. The blacksmith, for example, in order to function had to have cooling tubs; too heavy and unhandy to bring by pack horse. William Ramsey had his made by some neighbor, most probably William Overall, an early settler with a set of cooper's tools.[27]

The blacksmith also needed a hot fire; he could use seasoned hickory, or even oak bark, but the pioneer blacksmith like generations before him worked best with charcoal. One of the first things made around any forted station would have been some form of charcoal kiln, usually nothing more than a carefully arranged stack of split wood, cunningly laid so that it

---

Monticello, Ky. Renfro Valley Museum, Renfro Valley, Ky., has a good example of a rifling tool.

[23] Mr. Snider or Snyder settled at Clarksville but: "Mr. Snider, Betsy his wife, his son John and my son Joseph, were killed in Snider's house. . . . shot and tomahawked him in a barbarous manner." Valentine Sevier to his brother John, Dec. 18, 1794. Quoted from Ramsey, *Tennessee*, 619. Benjamin Lindsay a 15-year-old apprentice boy at work with the bellows escaped; see W, 32S, 205–207.

[24] DC, I, 82.

[25] MW, I, 3. Jacob Castleman, Sr., who settled around 1783, but was killed cutting oats a few years later also had a "parcel of Smith tools," DW, I, 194.

[26] DW, I, 107.

[27] DW, I, 283. Ramsey, *Tennessee*, 460, gave the date of Overall's death as 1783, but this seems a shade early as his inventory was not recorded until the July term of court in 1793. There were often long delays between death and appraisement, but ten years is rather long.

would burn slowly.[28] Charcoal, like cooling tubs and a great many other things from house wall to cornfield, depended upon the felling ax,[29] a simple tool but just as necessary to survival as the rifle.

The ax was part of the average pioneer farmer's life from the time he was big enough to toddle about and pick up chips for kindling until he died. The woodcutting could never stop; felling trees for clearing land or building houses was only the beginning. As settlement thickened and the woods disappeared, hundreds of men in the outlying regions earned their living by cutting wood for fuel, cook-wood, or charcoal.

The narrow or felling ax runs through all the early wills; William Neely,[30] William Overall, and Nicholas Gentry,[31] all had one or more axes. Prices varied with size and quality and demand, bringing usually about a pound or around a week's wages without keep.

A Kentucky settler of 1788 later wrote at some length of the importance of the family ax, giving the handle or helve, as two feet six inches, made of shellbark hickory, set into a head weighing between three and four and a half pounds.[32] In thinking of axes or anything else, a description should be accepted as true and exact for the one thing only. Nothing was standardized. Tools varied to fit the materials at hand as well as the user. Joseph Bishop, "the little shooting Bishop," used a shorter-handled ax than did mighty Thomas Sharpe Spencer who left his sycamore tree to live with the settlers. Sometimes he stayed at Eaton's, and sometimes at French Lick, for he was "Welcome everywhere, kind and friendly," and was especially helpful in building rail fences for he could carry a "ten rail cut." [33]

I know a few men still living in Pulaski County, Kentucky, who are masters of the whole cunning art of helving an ax: they can go to the woods, select the hickory, cut and split it and stack it for seasoning; and from the seasoned pile select a proper piece, whittle it into shape, smooth it with a piece of broken glass, then wedge it into the ax-eye so that it will stay. The pioneer ax was tenderly kept, warmed on frosty mornings to lessen

[28] This traditional method of making charcoal was still in use a few years ago down at the Jack Daniels Distilleries in Tennessee.

[29] This meant a single-bladed or pole ax, though the pioneer never used the term "single-bladed"; I found no mention at all of the double-bitted ax later woodsmen used to fell trees.

[30] DW, I, 166. William Neely was killed while trying to make salt.

[31] DW, I, 7. His was one of the first inventories recorded in new Davidson County, for he was on the list of dead entitled to land, NCR, XIX, 572.

[32] Drake, *Letters*, 44.

[33] W, 30S, 245. Thomas Sharpe Spencer was not killed until 1794 and then on the way to East Tennessee, ambushed east of the Crab Orchard on what is now Spencer's Hill; *ibid.*, 29S, 70, tells of his burial by Sampson Williams.

the danger of breaking, used only on wood, and woe to the clumsy boy who nicked the blade by letting it bounce from wood to rocky ground, or the wife who used it to cut the bone in a gammon of bacon.

The ax, like knives, hoes, and many other tools, had to be kept sharp, and one of the first things set up in the beginning station was the grindstone. William Ramsey who had the blacksmith tools also had a grindstone as did William Gower. These, like blacksmith tools, were not universally owned as were axes, but each station seems to have had one; there was one out at Clarksville, not established until 1783, owned by Valentine Sevier,[34] brother of John, and all were probably little different from those still occasionally seen, fallen into disuse and forgotten around abandoned farms. Many settlers carried whetstones in their pockets when working, and sometimes the more affluent had with his "cutting knife" a sharpening steel.[35]

The slow, shivering sigh, the trembling, then the crash of a great tree falling was a sound that went on continually in the neighborhood of French Lick, both north and south of the river during March and April of 1780. It was a sound familiar to all the settlers, and one they would hear often the rest of their lives.

Young John Buchanan, out with his felling ax, was, as he brought down a cedar four feet through and forty feet to the first limb, doing three things: preparing a field for planting, clearing an area around the fort free of trees and hence making it safer from hiding Indians, and getting timber for house wall, piggen, or firewood. Underbrush and many of the trees were good only for makeshift fence, firewood, and sometimes they were merely dragged into piles and burned.[36] But usually the felling of a tree was more than an act of destruction, done solely to be rid of the tree.

The first tree cut by any settler beginning his station was undoubtedly a hardwood; maple, one good one enough for a whole settlement, for peg wood; and oak, cedar, or some easily split wood for roof boards, doors, table tops or any other thing calling for rived planks. These were best made of seasoned wood or, better yet, made, carefully stacked, and then allowed to season, but a man with a million things to do and Indians at his back sometimes had to get on with his house walls.

---

[34] MW, I, 117. Valentine Sevier was not killed by Indians but survived until 1800.
[35] MW, I, 3.
[36] I found no mention of piles of logs burned and the ashes made into lye to be sold as in the early years in Ohio where some settlers it is said paid for their lands with lye. Ashes were needed for the manufacture of gunpowder, though in later days Nashville papers, in their "Prices current at Nashville," carried quotations for lye. The *Impartial Review* of Jan. 17, 1807, for example, listed lye, but different from other articles; neither price nor amount was given.

Judging from the many old log houses still in the Cumberland Country, as well as chance descriptions, size of the log for the house wall was more important than species. Oak, heavy and inclined to split, was avoided as were beech and hickory which rotted when exposed to damp, though all of these, especially oak, were used at times. Pine was avoided; [37] it decayed easily, fried and smelled eternally, and was when seasoned highly inflammable. Tradition has it that the first homes on the Middle Cumberland were built of hewed cedar, for the bluff below French Lick was covered with it, but all the old barns and houses I have examined were built of more than one kind of wood. Poplar was ever a favorite, soft as it was and easily worked, but it was not as abundant in the Middle Basin as further up the river. Cedar, chestnut, and ash were all quite commonly used, and in general it might be said the kind of soil dictated the kind of log the settler used.

The main thing was the log be perfectly straight and of the proper size. Hewed timbers in most of the old dwellings studied are usually no more than ten or twelve inches on their long sides, for as a rule the wall log was rectangular instead of square; most buildings have no more than six logs from doorsill to door top, and many less. I know an ancient barn built of huge timbers all between eighteen and twenty inches square,[38] and the walls of the Tilman Dixon home, the log part put up about 1787,[39] are of equally large timbers. At the other extreme is Michaux's description of the log buildings in the west of 1802; he wrote they were of tree trunks twenty to thirty feet long, but only five inches in diameter.[40] William Byrd, seventy-five years earlier, wrote of pole pens on the Piedmont, but of log houses near the Carolina coast. The poor farmer with little help and no time would certainly have used timbers no bigger than he, with what little

[37] Pines were to begin with practically non-existent in the Middle Basin where the first stations were built; and such was the constant need for tar that any pines found would more likely than not have been deadened for light wood.

[38] This barn on the Jack Denney farm of Cedar Sinking Creek of Big Sinking of the Big South Fork is known only to have been built "sometime back before The War," but it does indicate how men built when they had big timber and plenty of help—80-ft. log lengths; inner timbers large enough that only four abut on the facing of each stable door, high enough to admit with ease a 16-hand mule.

[39] This home at Dixon Springs, though later enlarged with brick, still has the log part intact. Tilman Dixon kept a store and as his home was on the main road from Nashville to East Tennessee many travelers stopped there, including in 1797 the Princes of the House of Bourbon, sometimes referred to as the Dukes of Orleans. I am indebted to Mrs. William Martin Young for half a day of her time in showing us the house and furnishings, many of these dating from pioneer years.

[40] Michaux, *Travels, 1802*, 36–37. This was a generalized discussion of the homes of the west, and he did not give a specific instance.

help he could get, could manage, while a man like Tilman Dixon with plenty of slaves, able to throw up a temporary dwelling, could afford a log house solidly built of big timber.

It might be said that as a rule, the builder avoided trees more than two feet in diameter; this size after being hewed into the proper shape with sapwood removed still made when cut to a twenty- or thirty-foot length, a timber about as big as could be conveniently managed. Once the tree was down with the proper log length cut, it then had to be "scalped" or barked, a job usually done as a part of the hewing, sometimes not at all as for a half-faced camp. Other times homes were made of "round green logs thrown up in a day," as was a schoolhouse in Stockton's Valley of 1799.[41]

In general logs for the good home were hewed square and true as if sawed. The hewing was done with the broadax, an old, old tool long known in Britain where previous generations had used it as a weapon. Most of the men already mentioned as having felling axes also had broadaxes, and men with slaves like John Buchanan had more than one. Shorter-handled, broader-bladed than the felling ax, the broadax used more iron and was consequently more expensive, selling for $5.50 as late as 1797,[42] though this could have been an unusually well made and large one. In looking at the log walls or the great hewn rafters of such a home as that of Tilman Dixon, one is struck by their smoothness, scarcely an ax mark showing.

The more affluent first settlers such as James Robertson may have hired their hewing and much of their other building done. John Coffee [43] around twenty years later paid two cents a foot, four sides, for the hewing of wall logs about a foot square when finished, or approximately $15.00 for enough logs to build a one-storied house thirty by thirty. Cheap, yet this sum represented a month's wages without keep for a hard-working, semi-skilled laborer.[44]

[41] Williams, *Smith*, 27.

[42] MW, I, 27-28. This, from the inventory of Charles Feas, a prosperous middle-class farmer was an unusually high price, though in 1790 the broadax of William Gower, DW, I, 175-176, brought 2 pounds, 11 shillings.

[43] Facts used by permission of Mr. Robert T. Quarles, Jr., President of the Tennessee Historical Society, owner of the Robert Dyas Collection of John Coffee, Donelson Family and Jackson papers (cited hereafter as Coffee Papers) housed in the Archives Division of the Tennessee State Library and Archives, Nashville. Coffee Papers, 1803.

[44] Wages were higher in the pioneering west than in the east, but it was not until past 1795 that the American dollar was much used as a basis of reckoning and pounds and pence figured in many journals and accounts until 1812 or so. Sevier, "Journal," is particularly rich in references to wages: THM, V, 233, March 11, 1797, "$11.00 for to hire a hand one month." This with keep of course, but Sevier demanded and seemingly got, also with keep, fifty cents a day for the hire of one of his slaves, *ibid.*, 242, Oct. 2. He in common with other employers paid for work done instead of

The working farmer, pressed by time and Indians, seldom bothered to hew four sides of the log before building, but squared up only the two sides that lay one above the other and left the rest until the roof was on and he and his help had more time. An expert broadax man like the man expert with the felling ax could work from many positions, though the short handle of the broadax prevented his standing upright when working on a small log on the ground.

Once in shape for raising, the log was brought to the building site; this may at times have been done by manpower, but judging from the large number who owned drawing chains along with harness and horses, most of the work of snaking timber was done by horses. The traces were often of hempen rope and sometimes leather, but the drawing or logging chains as mentioned in many inventories were made of iron and consequently always expensive. Samuel Buchanan's logging chain brought $4.00 as compared to $6.00 for a cow and calf, while as late as 1796 a logging chain sold for $11.00 as compared to a handsaw, always rather scarce, for only $3.50. Any ironware connected with harness was always expensive, seemingly scarcer and more in demand during the first years than the ever-plentiful guns. Samuel Buchanan was killed before he got his doubletrees [45] finished, but the hangings and two clevises brought $14.00.

Finished with getting out his timber, the builder had next to turn to the house foundation, and this, like everything else, depended on time, help, and inclination. In the case of the blockhouse that never served as a dwelling, the bottom logs, like those for a barn, were laid on a carefully leveled bit of ground. I found no inventory with a carpenter's level, but the builder knew to pour water on a log, or make a level with a bottle [46] so filled with

by the day or month, as: *ibid.*, VI, 47, July 1801, "paid bricklayer $3.00 for laying brick" (no. of bricks not specified); *ibid.*, V, 233, March 6, 1797, "paid Mr. Price twelve dollars for Grubing my four lots of ground" (acreage not given). In 1796, *ibid.*, 193, "Reuben Rains set in to be overseer at 40 lbs per annum." This with keep.

[45] DW, I, 296, the sale of Samuel Buchanan's inventory. The pioneer of course did not abide by Webster's *International,* for Mr. Webster, his work not yet published when most of these men died, was of New England. A great many terms used by southerners are found in no dictionary or when found are wrong. This double-tree was not part of a carriage as Mr. Webster states (Samuel Buchanan had no carriage) but in this case belonged to a plow but could be part of a wagon—a crosspiece to which the swingle trees were fastened. Mitford M. Mathews, *Dictionary of American-isms,* copyright University of Chicago Press, Chicago, 1951, is helpful at times in farming terms of pioneer days in the old southwest, but the Cumberland pioneer was basically a British colonial, not an American, and used many terms from an older language not found in any American dictionary; the best work for most aspects of his language save terms used in agriculture and some industries is Oxford Unabridged.

[46] Bottles were fairly common, and cheap. Samuel Buchanan's case and bottles with a fiddle brought only $8 in 1794, DW, I, 296. Dates given are those on which the

water as to leave only one good-sized bubble when turned on its side. Most dwellings had foundations of various kinds on which joists were laid for the floor. Commonly built during the years of Indian warfare was the rather high foundation of posts or rocks; a few puncheons were left loose in the floor so that in case of an Indian attack the besieged could lift a puncheon, slip through, and though his house might be ringed with Indians he still had a better chance of escape than when forced to go through the door when the burning roof fell in.[47]

The better homes, safe behind picketed walls, usually had a basement, or cellar as such was commonly known. One of the oldest homes on the upper Cumberland is the John Beatty place on the high lands above where Gist's Camp stood in 1775. Built sometime before 1800, it has a great basement of stone with an unusually large fireplace where in the early unsafe years the family food was cooked. The Beattys like the Sloans and the Lees whose homes built around 1800 are still in use in Pulaski County, were well-to-do with slaves. However, less prosperous pioneers with no slaves usually built quite a good home with some form of cellar beneath. The simplest type was that found in such a home as the John Smith[48] place on the Little South Fork of the Big South Fork of Cumberland, near Parmleysville, Kentucky, and put up around 1805. Built like most early homes in this region, of good-sized logs on a rock foundation, it had near the fireplace a cellar of sorts, reached by lifting a wide floor board. Here were stored Irish potatoes, cabbage, turnips, and other foods unsuited for the smokehouse or a warm loft.

Some of the poorer homes or temporary dwellings may have been floorless and with no foundation as was the cabin in which Abraham Lincoln is said to have been born, but no traveler actually saw one.[49] The Eatons had at least by Christmas of 1781 a floor fit for dancing, as did the other families in their station, but there was seemingly no cabin big enough for all the company as there was dancing in several cabins.[50]

sale was recorded in court and not necessarily the date of sale. S. Buchanan was killed in 1787.
[47] W, 30S, 256–257.
[48] This 150-year-old home, though with porches and additions of later date, is still in good condition, and I am indebted to Mr. and Mrs. Fanillen Bell, owners of the valley, for dropping their work, taking the tractor and spending half a day in taking us to the site and showing us around.
[49] James Parton, *Life of Andrew Jackson*, New York, 1861 (cited hereafter as Parton, *Jackson*), I, 177–185, an excerpt from the "Tour of Francis Baily, 1797" (cited hereafter as Baily, "Tour 1797"), 185, found loose floor boards with holes between in various homes, and stated that some homes were floorless but never gave a concrete example.
[50] W, 5S, 61.

Once the logs were hewed on at least two sides, the foundation ready, the raising began, and much of the worth of the completed building depended on the corner men who did the clinch work. Those able to dovetail the logs of a house evenly and tightly were rated as skilled workers, and in 1803 were earning a dollar a day compared to fifty cents for unskilled labor.[51] When one considers that an uneven notch or one too shallow could lift one corner higher than the other to throw the whole thing out of kilter, one can see the why of their wages. The interlocking logs were often the only thing that held the whole together, made the roof ride straight and square, and kept the corners from sagging.

Not long ago in Somerset, Kentucky, the old Dodson house built sometime before 1799 was torn down and found to have the logs, not only notched, but also pinned at each corner; this method was not unusual in the better log house. There was no one way of making a notch; those for the poles of a corncrib were flat and shallow as were the notches of a hastily built barn, while those for the better home were deeply cut at a rather steep angle, and so fitted on all sides there was little space between.

Much of the notching was done with ax and hatchet, but many men had chisels both for working in wood and metal. There is the question, too, of how much of even the very early building was done by the owner and his slaves. There was at least one carpenter in young Davidson County, Tennessee, of 1784, and his business so flourishing he took in that year an apprentice boy,[52] and from then on carpenters and cabinetmakers are quite often mentioned.

House walls went up, with door, window, and chimney openings sawed out as needed. Handsaws, though little used compared to axes, were owned by most firstcomers.[53] John Donelson had both a crosscut and the longer and heavier whipsaw, designed for sawing planks. As such saws went up and down the user had either to build a saw pit or a scaffold onto which the logs could be skidded. Next to blacksmith tools, the whipsaw was the most expensive, one bringing $31 in 1794. Other varieties of saws were more plentiful and much cheaper; the handsaw selling usually for more than the felling ax, but less than the broadax, or between three and four dollars.

Carpenters when used were called in to frame door and window openings with thick hewn facings kept in place partly by their skillful fit, but

---

[51] Coffee Papers, 1803.

[52] DC, I, 9; "Articles of Binding," for John Pierce, aged 13 years, to William Gallapsy.

[53] Beginning with Nicholas Gentry, DW, I, 7, practically all settlers with tools had at least a handsaw, many had both crosscut and handsaws as had Samuel Vernor, *ibid.*, 46, and some such as Lawrence Lollar, *ibid.*, 291, had also a whipsaw.

chiefly by pegs—one large peg, sometimes several inches long, for each log abutting on the facing. Even the first windows in the Freeland or Buchanan homes or those of Robertson's would have had a few small panes of glass. Glass was relatively plentiful, not by this date overly expensive, and many settlers could have brought a few of the small panes by pack horse. At least one Nashville merchant was stocking glass by 1787,[54] and the earliest visitors say nothing of oiled paper or shaved skins. Up the river in Pulaski County, a region more remote and with little wealth compared to Middle Tennessee, glass was so plentiful that by 1801 John James, a country store-keeper, had more than a hundred panes in stock, and for how many years before this we do not know. Forty panes brought fourteen shillings or less than five cents each.[55]

Glass was for most something that, if not had at once, was still for the future. I know of one log house, said to be more than a hundred years old, in which the people just never "got around to glass" until 1944. I visited there many times in its glassless state. Doors, following an old custom in many homes with glass, were kept open winter as well as summer, so there was always some light, and any work on dark winter days was brightened by firelight. There were, as in the pioneer cabins, shutters by the windows, and a shutter on the door, for the door was not a swinging thing but the opening through which one walked, and was closed by a door shutter.

Once the doors, windows, and fireplace openings were sawed out and secured by facings the builder was inclined to get on with the roof before finishing these or the interior. Cabins, especially those that formed a part of a fort wall, were often built on "the shanty order," that is, with only one slope to the roof, and in the fort, the slope inward, but by far the most common roof for the log house was that with a comb and a triangular-shaped gable at either end. Some accounts [56] say the top of the building was formed simply by making the logs on the gable ends shorter and shorter until the logs on the long sides met at the top, the whole topped off with a log that served for a comb. Some were undoubtedly built in this fashion, but all the older ones I have studied had rafters of hewed timbers, fitted and braced, and pegged. The best extant example of such work can be seen in the rafters and trusses of the Cragfont roof, put up around 1802.[57]

[54] DW, I, 34, 63; the inventory of the goods James Leneer sold to his brother Henry in 1787, 1788.

[55] PW, I, 3–4.

[56] Kercheval, *Virginia*, Doddridge, "Notes," 270–271, goes somewhat into detail on methods of building.

[57] Cragfont, home of Gen. James Winchester (1752–1826), active in the Revolution, the political and military life of Middle Tennessee as well as the War of 1812, is un-

This, however, is not typical of the average pioneer dwelling, for Cragfont was, judging from the comments of travelers, about the finest home in all the old west, those of Kentucky not excepted, made of stone with paneling and other interior woodwork done by skilled carpenters from Baltimore. The rafters and beams of the Tilman Dixon home, put up around 1787, are more typical of the good log house of the substantial farmer.

Regardless of how the framework was made, the roof of the settler's home was almost always covered with boards instead of the more time-consuming shingles. These roof boards, still to be found on barns upriver and now and then a dwelling, were from four to six feet long, laid in over-lapping rows, and held in place by long straight saplings known as butting poles. These were pegged at the ends, for a whole forted station could be built "without nail or screw." [58]

We used to some years ago walk in the woods with our neighbor Mr. Richmond Casada, an older man who lived by the old ways handed down. He knew every tree in his 524 acres of timber, and he would at times stop and look at a fine, straight white oak and say, "That's a good board tree." His barn and other outbuildings were roofed with boards or shakes, made in the same manner as those used by the pioneer, though fastened with nails instead of butting poles. In early 1780 we can be certain Amos Eaton and other seasoned woodsmen were out hunting board trees, and they could, like Mr. Casada, avoid the wind-shaken tree, and tell by the lay of the bark whether or no the wood would split straight and true. The board tree, different from those for the walls, needed to be of a good size; a length of white oak or cedar log, three or even four feet in diameter would when split and rived yield a number of boards, wide if need be almost as the radius of the tree, and of quite uniform thickness.

The boards like the peg wood were allowed to season as long as possible; a green peg would shrink in the seasoning and so loosen, while green roof boards were inclined to curl. The length of board timber was first quar-tered, or bolted, the same procedure as for making rails. The split could be started with an ax and iron wedges, and many men had wedges,[59] for rail fence no more than boards could be made without one, and preferably

---

doubtedly the best extant example of what one might call a "pioneer mansion" for it shows none of the influence of the oversized white columns soon to be popular in both the Tennessee and Kentucky bluegrasses, or what might be denominated Jeffersonian influence. As it stood near the main road from Nashville to Knoxville, many travelers commented on it; this was of course not Gen. Winchester's first home, for when Michaux, *Travels, 1802,* 254–255, saw it, the building was not finished.

[58] Smythe, *Tour,* I, 281.

[59] John Buchanan, Sr., killed around 1785, had for example practically all the tools named, including wedges, DW, I, 69.

two. The iron wedges were tapped in far enough to make a crack big enough to get in the gluts and wedges, triangular pieces of wood made of beech or dogwood when possible, and longer and bigger than the expensive ones of iron.[60]

The gluts were driven deep with a maul, a heavy, man-killing tool made almost always of a length of white oak, eight to ten inches in diameter, one end left whole for from six to twelve inches, the rest whittled away to form a handle. The head was often strengthened by iron bands called maul rings. John Buchanan had a pair when killed.[61]

Once the board log was bolted, heart and sap wood taken off, and the quarters split to size, eight to ten inches square, for roof boards, it was time for the froe. This was a short-handled, dull-bladed tool, designed for riving wood so as to get as much flat surface as possible, and so, driven in by a light wooden mallet, was used to make roof, door, and shutter boards as well as staves for barrels and setware such as churns. A skillful worker [62] could do amazing things with a froe; he could, from each quarter of a big log, get a few wide boards of quite uniform thickness, and many smaller ones. The wide boards were reserved for doors or table tops, while those six to eight inches wide could serve for roof boards, and even if he were unskillful and made several too small, he could always find a use for them —pickets in his garden fence or cut to the proper length, drawn, and grooved, some might serve for barrel staves.[63]

Boards intended for shutters or furniture could be smoothed with a plane, and many men had planes, but judging from the many killed before they got a stock whittled for their plane bits,[64] it is doubtful if planes were

[60] Drake, *Letters*, 67, speaks of gluts and wedges, appliances still known to many old-timers upriver who not too many years ago split rails.

[61] DW, I, 69, 283. Ring mauls appear to have been but little used; these inventories of John Buchanan and William Overall had only the rather uncommon rings, and these not yet on mauls.

[62] I used to watch "old Uncle George Wilson," of Keno, Ky., make roof boards for barns, and a few back-hill farmers can still rive, chiefly pickets for garden fence.

[63] The barrel, pipe, tun, etc., staves that entered into commerce were early standardized by law in all the colonies, but for the riving of roof boards, table tops, window frames, or anything about the house there were no rules as to size or method. In riving staves for cedar set ware, for example, they were made small and enough of the light sapwood left for a stripe, but as a rule unless trying to get a wide board out of a smallish tree, a thing the pioneer seldom had to do, the worker never rived toward the center, but split his quarters into squares of the desired size, before proceeding, for white oak or cedar will split in any direction. The heartwood was almost always discarded and the "billets were used for chunking between the logs," Kercheval, *Virginia*, Doddridge, "Notes," 271.

[64] DW, I, 7, 46, Nicholas Gentry and Samuel Vernor were both killed before they got stocks for their plane bits, but practically all the men mentioned had drawing knives.

often used on the very early homes. Much more common in inventories and more commonly known by tradition was the drawing knife. This was little more than a long knife blade, curved on both ends, and with a handle on either end. It was used in a great variety of ways from smoothing rived boards for a table top to taking the sapwood off a roof board or shaping up or "drawing" a shingle or barrel stave.

Both hands were needed to use this tool, the worker grasping a handle in either hand and pulling toward him, but as many of the pieces he worked were small, they needed a firm holding, and so he made a shaving horse.[65] This also was made entirely of wood, braced and pegged together; and like the cobbler's bench, was designed with a seat for the worker, and clamps for holding the material. On the shaving horse the clamps were usually adjustable to at least two thicknesses of wood, and were worked with a foot treadle, so that while the user's hands were busy with the knife he held the board in place with foot pressure. The shaving horse cost only the labor, while the drawing knife was usually between one and two dollars, for it required little iron.[66]

The shutter boards like the facings and roof poles were held in place by pegs, with the most common type of door [67] or window shutter made of three long rived boards and three rather narrow but thicker crosspieces. This was the simplest kind of door; ordinarily there were braces between the crosspieces, and better doors were not only braced but also made of two thicknesses of boards; even the simplest required nine pegs, and at the very least nine double holes. Thus, the small gimlet and the larger auger were among the pioneer's most necessary tools, and it is not surprising to find the same Davidson County merchant who in 1787 was selling glass, also stocked with a gross of gimlets.

Each builder needed several sizes. My ancient corner cupboard has pegs in the door facings one-fourth inch in diameter; those in the press are

[65] I found no shaving horse, known often as a shingling horse, until 1795, DW, II, 177, and that owned by well-to-do Mr. Patterson who had a violin, music books, and many books, and snuff bottles, but as not everybody was killed we could not say this was the first shaving horse in the region of Nashville. I found no shingles until around 1800, *ibid.*, 310, "6,000—$20.00." Most builders of better homes at least aspired to shingles; the stone home Daniel Smith had built in what is now Sumner County, Tenn., south of present-day Hendersonville, was finished most possibly in late 1793, and some idea of the difficulty in getting shingles and sawed lumber—she had had to let them use "split stuff" for the window frames—may be gained from Mrs. Smith's letter of 1793, A, V, 293-294.
[66] I am indebted to Mr. Henry Hail, Somerset, Ky., for a demonstration of his shaving horse, and work with the drawing knife in general.
[67] The outside door of Robertson's first home on the Cumberland, his cabin at Freeland's, had in early 1781 a door of rived boards; W, 6XX (50), 10.

three-eighths, while the facing pegs of an uncle's barn doorway are almost two inches across and several inches long; the truss pegs of Cragfont's roof are even longer, but smaller in diameter. The boring of holes for the thousands of such pegs was not the easy job it is today with a ratchet drill or even the out-curved brace to give leverage; each bit had its own handle, short and straight with a short crosspiece for better grasping; nor was the auger the strong sharp steel of today, designed like a screw. During pioneer years holes were bored with the old flat or pod augers, clumsy things of only half a twist.

The woodworker did not go to all the trouble of boring holes and fitting in pegs, sometimes wedged, and sometimes square for tighter fits, just because he was too poor or unable to get nails and screws. Bolts, window latches, chest locks, screws, horseshoe and shingling nails were never entirely lacking in the pioneer community, and were being stocked in Nashville well before 1790,[68] while John James of Somerset who in 1801 had window glass in stock, also carried a wide assortment of iron fittings from horse mill bolts to window latches. The peg or pin continued to be used for many years because the builder felt it was the best thing for his purpose. A peg would never split the wood, it held more firmly, never rusted, nor made an ugly blemish as did a nail or screw. The belief was slow in dying; my mother as late as her young womanhood once watched an old man make tiny maple pegs for shoes, though tacks were by then quite cheap.

Walls up, roof on, door and window shutters hung, often but not always with wooden or leather hinges, the log house was in shape to give pretty good protection from the weather, and some from Indians, though the most of this protection depended on the skill and courage of the owner. The interior, including the floor puncheons, often had to wait while its forever busy owner rushed with his slaves to fit land for corn, cotton, and garden stuff, and as the spring of 1780 went into summer, more and more must the Buchanans, Eatons, and Freelands look to their picketing. William Neely who had come on the exploratory trip with Robertson was dead of Indians as was Jonathan Jennings, father of Edmund, and more than one hunter was found, his head carried away to some Creek or Cherokee town.[69]

---

[68] John Rice who in 1786, DW, I, 47, took over the stock of his dead partner, James Moore, continued in business until his death in 1792; the inventory of his store, *ibid.*, 249, 255, lists all manner of things for the home and building. See also *ibid.*, II, 133, the inventory of Henry Wiggins—among many other items 41 window latches.

[69] Ramsey, *Tennessee*, 446–447. The custom of putting the head of a victim on a pole and carrying it home is quite often mentioned; two of Robertson's young sons were said to have been so treated.

Felling axes only flew a little faster as trees came down and pickets went up. Twelve- to sixteen-foot lengths of tree trunk were split, sharpened on one end and the other sunk deeply and firmly in the ground, the whole strengthened with cross braces. Rarely was a station enclosed entirely by pickets; some had cabins at the corners as had that Robertson built on Richland Creek in 1784,[70] and a few had a blockhouse at each corner as had Buchanan's second station begun in the same year,[71] this type the safest of all. The picketed fort or farm had been a feature of all western borders since the outbreak of the French and Indian War; no step in its construction was unfamiliar to the Robertsons or Eatons; both families had in East Tennessee lived through Indian attacks on picketed walls.

The area enclosed by pickets and buildings was known as the fort yard,[72] and could be entered usually by only one gate. Some of these gates were made on the order of the double farm gate, that is, fastening in the middle with each half swung on its own set of hinges. Another type was built like a water gate,[73] fastened at the top so that when the creek rose it would float up with the water. The fort gate thus built swung on pivots and had to be propped or held up when a team or rider went through, but it had the advantage of falling shut of its own weight and so, unless propped, could never be forgotten and left open; and if propped, one quick-handed boy could, on an Indian alarm, jerk out the props and let it fall shut with a bang.

Such a gate, like the cabin floor, was usually made of puncheons; for these a ten-foot length of log was split, then each side hewed down to some manageable thickness, commonly about two inches; the great plank thus formed not only required a deal of work, but "it was much as a man could do to lift one." [74] Split logs laid flat surface up are mentioned by Dr. Doddridge [75] writing of western Virginia, but I never found mention of a split-log floor

[70] W, 31S, 34, "In 1784 he [Robertson] removed to his land on Richland Creek 5 miles west of Nashville." This is only one of several references to his station. See also *ibid.*, 1S, 60, for pencil sketch showing fields, the four cabins, and Robertson's home. *Ibid.*, 29S, 67, names the families.

[71] W, 30S, 251. Buchanan's Station was mentioned by many but there are contradictions concerning the date of its building: *ibid.*, 29S, 74, locates it, as does everyone else, "4 miles East of Nashville," but adds, "timber got out in July of 1785." Most agree it had four blockhouses. See also *ibid.*, 30S, 255, Bell's Station, "seven or eight cabins joined together on three sides—fourth stockaded and a large gate." Hickman's, "ten miles below Nashville, five miles below White's Creek, on Sulphur Creek, one mile from north side of Cumberland," *ibid.*, 457, 471.

[72] W, 30S, 252, gives the fort yard of French Lick Station as an acre and a half, unusually large.

[73] FQ, II, Clinkenbeard "Interview," 99.

[74] *Ibid.*, 100.

[75] Kercheval, *Virginia*, Doddridge, "Notes," 270, states a puncheon was "half a tree."

on the Cumberland; that doesn't mean they were not there, but it does indicate rarity.

The work of building, rebuilding, enlarging, and fortifying the home and farm buildings went on constantly,[76] and few were entirely finished before 1785 or so. A family like the Eatons living a time in a half-faced camp, moving to an uncleared boundary of land and beginning from scratch with corn-planting time close at hand, had to be constantly jumping from one job to the next. Most were happy to move into a half-roofed,[77] one-roomed house with floor sills and door and window shutters, but neither floor boards nor windows. There might be nothing between the baby and the earth below the sills but a bearskin, and the wife as she went about her household duties had to trip carefully from floor sill to floor sill, and cook in a temporary fireplace of round green sticks well daubed and lined with clay.

Still, it was a beginning. The farmer and his help would, in time snatched from farming and fortifying, borrow a trowel [78] and replace the temporary mud daubing between the logs with proper plaster of lime and gypsum.[79] He could rive boards, make pegs, and build his shutters one by one, or he might hire them made and hung for about $1.25 each, provided he supplied the material, while the facing and casing of each opening cost around $1.35.[80]

A man in a hurry could lay his floor puncheons, splintery as they might be, and then at his leisure smooth them, though he had to use one of the most miserable tools, by tradition, ever invented by man. This was the

[76] All first stations mentioned were temporary affairs; Mansker and Stump are the only two first settlers found of whom I can say with any degree of certainty they continued to live on land settled in 1779–1780; Mansker's first station was burned by Indians and he built again in 1783. Stump farmed and made improvements on White's Creek, but during the early years he seems to have spent at least his nights at Eaton's. I have found no reference to a Stump's Station; there is quite complete agreement that by early 1784 there were only French Lick, Freeland's, Mansker's rebuilt station, Eaton's, and the new station being built on Red River; see W, 29S, 73–75, and *ibid.*, 30S, 251.

[77] Dr. Daniel Drake remembered living in a half-finished log house, *Letters*, 15; Brother Schweinitz, Williams, *Travels*, "Report," 519, slept in an unfinished inn without a floor, and Freeland's Station was, when the Indians attacked in January of 1781, still unfinished, W, 6XX (50), 12.

[78] Trowels were much less common than drawing knives and other tools, but several first settlers had them, including James Harrod, DW, I, 16.

[79] Mud was used as a temporary daubing on inside walls where there was less danger of bullets. Freeland's still had temporary daubing on inside walls when attacked, but good plastering for outside walls, judging from the remarks here, W, 6XX (50), 12, was one of the first things attended to; they were master hands at making mortar; much of the original mortar still holds at Cragfont, and numerous chimneys, 150 years old, have never been repointed.

[80] Coffee Papers, 1801.

foot adz, in shape and size and handle length and set of blade, not unlike a grubbing hoe, though broader-bladed and sharper, so sharp that if a man let his feet get in the way they were liable to get badly cut, and since he used the foot adz with both hands, working with bowed back on a length of wood between his outspread feet, his feet did get in the way, and hence the name foot adz. This tool was not only used to smooth the puncheons, but also in the making of sugar and meat troughs and tree-trunk canoes.

William Gower, an early settler well supplied with tools, had a foot adz that sold for more than either his grindstone or drawing knife, or one pound, fourteen shillings, almost twice as much as his hatchet that brought only eighteen shillings, though his froe was not far behind, selling for one pound, ten shillings.[81] Some first settlers had hand adzes, much like foot adzes save they were smaller and could be used with one hand to smooth the walls after the logs were lifted into place, though this could be done with the broadax or even felling ax.[82]

The chimney with fireplace was sometimes one of the last things to be finished. It might go on for some months as a "cats and cradle" affair, said by most historians to have been common throughout the old west. I never saw or heard of one by tradition, but did meet with one traveler, Brother Schweinitz, who encountered one at Mr. Shaw's house, "the last before the great wilderness." [83] Brother Schweinitz said nothing of hearths and chimneys until he got to Mr. Shaw's where everything was in the "first beginnings," not even a finished floor. The chimney caught fire "four or five times without, however, causing any particular disturbance." Each time it was put out with snowballs. Judging from the space he gave it, this was the first such chimney Brother Schweinitz, who had just traveled over most of the old southwest, had seen. Earlier travelers made no mention of wooden chimneys; these like the glassless window and the floorless cabin seem to have been more common in later years when numbers of very poor came to the borders.[84]

<hr>

[81] DW, I, 175-176. Two other Gowers, Russell and Abel, came as first settlers and one lived to get his land; there is the possibility that all these were cousins of James Robertson, as his mother was Mary Gower.

[82] Good examples of hand adzes, like the other tools named, can be found in most of the museums already mentioned; a particularly good representation of hand-forged tools can be seen in the Mountain Life Museum, though by no means all go back to pioneer days. Most of the tools named were used in out-of-the-way places until the last decade or so; and until World War II the hewing of crossties, done often with an ordinary pole ax, was a common occupation in the hills.

[83] Williams, *Travels*, Schweinitz, "Report," 519-520.

[84] Floorless cabins there no doubt were, but no traveler stopped in one. The tools of such a man as William Neely, DW, I, 166—wedges, augers, chisels, planes, files,

The art of stone-cutting was a much more common one than today, and many European immigrants, particularly those from treeless Scotland or northern Ireland, were as a group much more familiar with tools for working in stone than with ax and froe. Many settlers would have been able to cut their own chimney rocks, just as somewhat later brick for the new home was made on the plantation by the slaves, though stone dwellings [85] came before brick in the old southwest, and at least one was being put up in Middle Tennessee by 1792.

The chances are the average farmer built as much of the chimney as he possibly could; stone masons were expensive; in 1790 a Nashville mason was offered the large sum of "two hundred hard dollars with keep," [86] for only nine months' work, or more than twice as much as a worker in the early New England cotton mills would earn in a year without keep. Good chimney rock was rather scarce in the Middle Basin; the same limestone that had only to be burned to get lime for mortar was of course no good for chimneys, though some limestone was more fire resistant than others. Fine-grained sandstone was the preferred rock and most of the old chimneys in the Highland Rim and up the river were made of it.

The chimney and fireplace were, of course, like everything else, of many different patterns, but as a rule all were large, and so skillfully made that smoke from embers drawn out to bake the bread would go up the chimney instead of into the room. Most of those I have seen were of blocks of stone so huge that skids and horses were needed to get them into place.[87] Many were made with a rounded opening above the hearth with the customary keystone rock, but by no means all. I know one put up around 1805 without help of a professional mason, in which there are at the top of the fireplace two large blocks of stone, wide as the chimney in total width, but a shade wider at the top than the bottom, so that instead of a keystone rock in the middle there are only the two halves meeting; firmly

square, in addition to the others mentioned, would indicate plans for considerably more than a floorless home; Neely was not a carpenter and judging from his possessions he was less well off than most of the first settlers.

[85] Save for the log part of the Tilman Dixon home, the earliest good homes left in the old west are of stone—Daniel Smith's stonework was finished in 1793, and Cragfont was being finished in 1802, but up in Kentucky one of the oldest of the better homes, that of William Whitley, is of brick. I found no reference to brick or brickmaking on the Cumberland until around 1800.

[86] DW, I, 205.

[87] Good examples of early chimneys put up between 1785–1802 may be found in the Daniel Smith and Tilman Dixon homes as well as Cragfont, but all these were undoubtedly better than the average farmer could afford, though the John Smith home has an excellent chimney.

pressed against each other at the top, the end of each held by all the weight of rock above, these rocks could fall no more than a keystone.

The chimney of our log house on Little Indian Creek of the Big South Fork of the Cumberland had a square opening, the top of the fireplace surmounted by one massive block of stone, about six by two by one, the whole, like many other old chimneys, so carefully fitted together that long ago when the mortar fell out, the chimney not only continued to stand up, but also functioned with good draft. This chimney had by tradition been one of the earliest in the region, the stone quarried and put up sometime before 1800; around fifty or sixty years later the place had burned. The chimney rocks were then moved to a new location, and rebuilt to serve a new log house.

There were no rules for chimneys, any more than for log houses or forted stations. Possibly the most standardized thing was the blockhouse on which most descriptions agree. The beauty of this building was that it could be thrown up in a hurry, for it had neither chimney, foundation, window nor door shutter, and was built of scalped logs, hewed usually on only two sides, but on these a good job must be done, for nobody wanted big cracks in the blockhouse wall, the only thing between a man and the Indians.

A blockhouse built about 1790 at Ridley's fort [88] had a lower story of six twenty-one-foot logs, "laid one upon the other," and fastened at the corners with the usual notches. On top of these, like a flat roof, were laid a number of twenty-four-foot logs, with their longer ends jutting out to form what in its half-finished condition would have looked like a flat and overhanging eave. These longer logs were the foundation of the upper part of the blockhouse, that jutted over the lower. This made it possible for the defender to climb up between wide-spaced middle logs and direct his fire downward, and see besiegers against the walls.

Time and time again on all borders the blockhouse and fort walls saved the lives of whole stations, but many families on the Cumberland like those on other borders, in their eagerness to build homes and widen fields, depended for protection solely on their cabins and usually in Middle Tennessee with tragic results. Homes were not the only things the first settlers

<hr>

[88] Colonel Daniel Ridley, second father-in-law of John Buchanan, Jr., had been in Braddock's Defeat and served in the Revolution. He did not settle until about 1790, building in the Mill Creek Country, about two miles from Buchanan's Station a forted farm with a double log house, set in a fort yard of about an acre and a half, and defended by three blockhouses. Featherstonhaugh, *Excursion*, I, 202-203, visited him in 1834 and described and sketched one of the blockhouses, still standing, *ibid.*, I, 205.

built; by 1784 mills, stables, and outhouses are mentioned, and these followed soon by the multitude of buildings ever part of even the middle-size farm—separate kitchen, still house,[89] smokehouse, spring house, loom house, corncrib, stables and various barns, most of these, save the spring house, built of logs, though mills, still houses, and even barns were sometimes built of stone on the more affluent plantations.

There was no one way of frontier life, and though all at first lived in homes of logs, there is nothing to indicate that families such as the Robertsons, Stumps, Manskers, and other first settlers mentioned by travelers ever knew the floorless cabin with glassless windows and makeshift beds. Nobody beginning with Daniel Smith early in 1780 ever complained of the bed and board at Manskers; all chance accounts of Indian warfare indicate floors, and by 1784 there was at least one house, that of Jonathan Drake,[90] good and big enough county court with all the men required to administer justice—no small number—could meet in it.

Even in remote regions upriver where men had little help from skilled workers and often no slaves, the remaining early homes are good log houses. One of the oldest is the William Young home in Stockton's Valley, thought to have been built around 1794. It is two-storied with stone chimneys, and though much less commodious than the log "mansions" built by such men as John Donelson, it is far better than many homes of today.

The settler with help enough to manage big timbers was inclined to build a double log house like that of Tilman Dixon, still in use. Colonel Anthony Bledsoe who settled in 1784 on Greenfield's grant north of the Cumberland lived in an "old fashioned, double, or Virginia log house." [91] Francis Baily, a young Englishman, traveling thirteen years later, spent the night in a double log house on a plantation south of Nashville, where he found the whole family living in one room, the rest of the space reserved for "lumber." [92] West of Nashville he stopped with Major George D. Blackmore, a prosperous and influential citizen with several slaves, but remarked, "His house remained the same as when it was first built—and of course cut no very striking figure; but as it was like all the rest of the country, its un-

---

[89] These buildings are only mentioned incidental to some Indian tale or court record as DC, I, 21, 78, stables and stabling; *ibid.*, 19, loom house; *ibid.*, 78, "Little spring above Boyd's still house." Mayfield's lease with his tenant, John Campbell, though later, Oct. 29, 1792, provides stabling even for the tenant's horses, A, V, 206.

[90] DC, I, 12. Drake by that date, April 12, 1784, had moved away.

[91] W, 31S, 193.

[92] Parton, *Jackson*, I, Baily, "Tour 1797," 180. Baily seems here to use the expression *lumber* in the older sense, when lumber meant odds and ends stored; when they spoke of "lumber room" they meant the same as did we speaking of "plunder room." Sawed lumber was in 1797 still very scarce.

couth appearance and rough accommodations escape particular attention. None of the houses in this part of the world are built higher than the ground floor."

He was far from right; Daniel Smith's two-storied stone home was finished by that date, as was the William Young home upriver, and there would certainly have been others by then, like that of Captain John Donelson [93] who lived near the south side of Cumberland a few miles west of the present-day Hermitage. The double log house, sometimes of two stories, sometimes of one, with a ten- or fifteen-foot passway, porches front and back, and a stone chimney at either end, continued to be built even by prosperous farmers in Middle Tennessee, and it is hard to think of such a home as "uncouth." The Moravian missionaries who visited Middle Tennessee in 1799 saw the country with the approving eyes of good German farmers, and wrote of the beautiful plantations and comfortable log houses.[94] A good log dwelling set amid a cluster of outbuildings such as kitchen, smokehouse, and barns with often a mill and blacksmith shop was no mark of poverty.

Elegance came quickly to Middle Tennessee and by 1797 some were able to ride around in coaches fitted up "in all the style of New York or Philadelphia." [95] Fashions from many sources influenced home building. Daniel Smith's rather plain stone home with dormer windows, and neither columns, porticos, nor verandas, is more akin to the true colonial of English inspiration, built for generations in Virginia.[96] Larger Cragfont shows an even greater love of absolute simplicity. These patterns, especially that of the Daniel Smith home with dormer windows, were repeated over and over in frame, and sometimes brick, all with big rooms, wide central halls, and at least two chimneys.

Still other planters were inspired by the wealthy French and Spanish sugar growers in the neighborhood of New Orleans; they, too, had wide halls both front and back, but their double verandas were decorated with much ironwork, often ornate, with more ornateness in interior trim and furnishings. The Hermitage with its ostentatiously simple white columns, curving stairway, and wide hall was only one of many such plantation

[93] Burke, *Emily Donelson*, I, opposite 42, gives the floor plan of this home, not Captain John's first, but thought to have been built between 1800–1810. This should not be confused with the log home of Mrs. John, Rachel Stockley, Donelson, II, where Andrew Jackson boarded; this was on the other side of the Cumberland, near the road to Mansker's Station.

[94] Williams, *Travels*, Schweinitz, "Report," 507, 509.

[95] Parton, *Jackson*, I, Baily, "Tour 1797," 180.

[96] Kercheval, *Virginia*, 50.

seats, and compared to some is small and simple for it has no ballroom. The man with less money, but not caring for a log house, might build a single-story dwelling with steeply sloping roof, wide front porch, and double chimneys like that in which Cordell Hull was born,[97] little different from the homes being built in the Illinois by 1750.[98]

All these styles, however, were, as long as timber was to be had, of minor importance compared to that of the log house that continued to be built, even by the wealthy, for many years.

Anthony Foster,[99] an early settler and merchant of Nashville, owned a seven-hundred-acre plantation near the Cumberland, on Sudd's Creek, three miles from Palmyra; by 1804 he had only a hundred and fifty acres cleared, but had for a dwelling a "new, two-story, hewed log house, chinked and pointed, with a tongue and grooved floor, planed doors, window sashes made and put up, and a brick chimney with fireplaces above and below." There was also a kitchen, spring house, and "other convenient buildings." [100]

South of the Cumberland on the Big Harpeth there was by 1811 on seventy acres of cleared land "a comfortable dwelling thirty-six by twenty feet, and two stories high." Much larger, but also of logs, was the plantation seat Richard Orton wished to sell for cash or Negroes; this was sixty by twenty-four feet with two rooms below and four above. Each room had a fireplace; there was a "piazay," the usual separate kitchen, but of brick, a smokehouse, a dairy with a pool of water, and a stable with water.

Out on the Middle Fork of Station Camp Creek, not many miles from where Mansker and Isaac Bledsoe had found the thousands of buffalo in 1769, there was by 1811 a five-hundred-acre plantation with a hundred and fifty to two hundred cleared that had an "elegant brick house and stone outhouses such as kitchen, work and smokehouse, and a large three-story still house." There was also a "good two-story log house," the home we can imagine of the plantation miller for nearby was a three-story, stone mill house with two pair of stones.[101]

[97] On Tennessee State Road 53, a few miles from Byrdstown in present-day Pickett County.
[98] Alvord, *The Illinois*, illustration opposite 216; description, 215.
[99] Anthony Foster, though not a first settler, was a prominent Nashville merchant, in business at least by 1792; see W, 30S, 526; see also AMS, I, class V, 174; he and a number of other prominent Cumberlanders, including Daniel Smith and Andrew Jackson, were active in the championship of Gen. Butler's right to wear his queue.
[100] Tenn. *Gazette*, Feb. 1, 1804.
[101] Nashville *Clarion*, Feb. 22, 1811.

Practically all homes of even average farmers, upriver as well as down, had separate kitchens,[102] sometimes connected to the house by a covered passway, and sometimes not. Even when the mistress of the household had no slave to do the cooking, she liked a separate kitchen; it gave extra room for storage, and in the long hot summers kept the cooking heat and odors out of the main house, for in such homes the big kitchen would also serve as dining room. The Cumberlander, no different from farmers elsewhere, liked to build his house foursquare with the world, with the main entrance on the southern side, sunny in winter, cool in summer, and where the hard-driving rains and snows that most often came from the northwest could never beat in. One can still find in old log houses upriver the noon-notch in the kitchen door, though not all of these houses are old even as The War.

Log houses continued to be built in remoter regions of the Highland Rim and upriver until the 1930's when roads were built and timber, inaccessible by water, could be reached by logging road, and the farmer with not too much money found it more worthwhile to sell his timber and buy cheap building materials.

First and early settlers had no sawmills, and sawed lumber was almost prohibitive in price, and sawyers hard to find, though a few such as Andrew Jackson did put up frame dwellings,[103] even before the Indian wars were ended. Such a home was a mark of affluence, but many of the wealthiest early settlers in Middle Tennessee continued all their days in log houses. Among them were the Donelsons. John Donelson, Sr., who headed the flotilla in the winter 1779–80 was no poor man, but shortly after his death in 1785 his widow, Rachel Stockley Donelson, came back from Kentucky and on the land her husband had got north and east of Nashville at the mouth of Neely's Bend, she had a log house with needed outbuildings put up. Here, young Andrew Jackson came in 1788 to live as a boarder in a log guest house or "office," as such was called.[104]

[102] Traditionally the first log house, smallish, but well built and with a good big fireplace, put up by the middle-class farmer, became when the new big log house was built, the family kitchen or "cookhouse."

[103] This home, Hunter's Hill, was according to Parton, *Jackson*, I, 243, about 13 miles from Nashville and 2 from the site of the present-day Hermitage. Jackson's homes—he had at least six—were all in the same general neighborhood, south of the Cumberland, east of Nashville, in and about Jones Bend, but the present-day Hermitage is at least the third building of that name; and between the Hermitage and the frame was another log house.

[104] The custom of letting the young unmarried sons sleep in buildings apart from the main dwelling seems to have been brought upriver from the French and Spanish planters, but the name *office* had long been used in Virginia and was applied to any

Her son, Captain John, was even wealthier than his father, acquiring thousands of acres of the best land in Middle Tennessee. John's sisters who married wealthy and prominent men, among them Andrew Jackson, were among the first ladies of Tennessee, some with "great establishments." John and his wife, Mary Purnell, moved in the best of society; their children married well, and their youngest daughter Emily went to boarding school attended by her personal maid, for the family had many slaves and the customary coach with coachman in top hat. Yet, fashionable as they were, Captain John and his wife lived and died in a large log house. Plastered it no doubt was and possibly papered in French paper with much of the furniture imported and brought from New Orleans by keelboat, in truth a log mansion.

There was about a log house, even a very old one such as ours on Little Indian Creek, some quality not entirely measurable by such yardsticks as thrift or comfort. A few prosperous farmers still live in log houses; most weatherboarded long ago, so that one finds no hint of logs until the step over a wide doorway, or the glance out a wide-silled, but often small, window. Such homes usually have "old parts" and "new parts" with steps up and steps down when another "house" was built and connected without quite jibing, for the ease with which it could be enlarged by simply building another house by it was one of the beauties of the log house. My own experience of several years spent in a rather dilapidated one would indicate that when well floored with the walls properly chinked and sealed, such a home was warm in winter, cool in summer, and safe as a rockhouse in a high wind, and always curiously alive with a way all its own.

Frederick Stump, the Eatons, Freelands, and other first settlers fighting for time and life in 1780 had no choice, for the building of the log house with outhouses, set in a picketed fort yard of around an acre, represented only a part of their work in wood, and many times each had to put down the ax or adz or froe and pick up the whittling knife, or build an appliance or a piece of furniture the family had to have. There was, for example, the ash hopper, just as badly needed as the fort pickets. Lye water was needed for soap, but shaving soap and Castile [105] could be bought, and a

separate building as: "All their drudgeries of cookery, Washing, dairies, etc., are performed in offices detached from the dwelling houses, which by this means are kept more cool and sweet," Beverly, *Virginia*, Chap. XVI, "The Dwellings of Virginia," 235.

[105] I, XVI, 163; George Morgan in 1769 mentions it and once declared, "you cannot send me too great a quantity," and "Castell" soap is sometimes mentioned in inventories on the Cumberland, though I did not find it till 1795—DW, II, 178.

dirty face when a man was faced with loss of his scalp was not for the moment of prime importance. Powder was, and lye water was needed to make powder [106] and was also used in the preparation of hominy.

The ash hopper "like a house roof turned upside down" was made entirely of forked sticks and rived boards with a hollowed log at the bottom to catch the drippings, all fitted together with neither peg nor nail, the whole lined with grass or wheat straw, the lining no small art, for the leachings must drip down into the log instead of out between the boards.

The ash hopper was only the beginning; settling housewives needed all the woodenware they had had to leave behind. Piggens, pails, churns,[107] wash tubs, and sugar boxes were commonly of rived cedar, made with the froe, shaped with the drawing knife, set into grooved circles, and held usually with oak or hickory ties. There had to be a big keeler for washing dishes, but the bread tray, sometimes as big as a baby's cradle and shaped like a shallow trough, was made usually of gouged buckeye.

The length of hollowed-out wood assumed an almost endless variety of sizes and uses.[108] Up-ended and of oak, hollowed against the grain with the other end sharpened and stuck into the ground, it became the corn pounder, more commonly known as the hominy block.[109] Hogs were scalded, rain and sugar water collected in smaller versions of the poplar dugout when barrels were not to be had, and meat was put to soak in much the same kind of trough, though shorter and wider, when possible, and with bungholes in the bottom so that the meat might drain.[110]

I never found one in a Cumberland inventory, but some families did use wooden platters and bowls for tableware,[111] but there were around all

[106] Gray, *Bishop*, 81, is an account of burning hickory logs for ashes for powder lye in Middle Tennessee in 1792; records have references to saltpeter and brimstone, indicating that powder was made; see MW, I, 12; DW, II, 207, and PW, I, 2–3.

[107] All families had woodenware; Jacob Castleman, DW, I, 194, had an especially good representation—pails, washing tubs, churns, coolers or keelers; there were fat tubs, butter tubs, and numerous piggens. Wood for these last when specified at all was cedar: MW, I, 3, "cedar pale"; DW, II, 32, two cedar piggens. Others gave the wood of which the furniture was made; see in particular, *ibid.*, 17, and *ibid.*, 294.

[108] The Mountain Life Museum has an excellent collection of woodenware for use in the kitchen, the barn, and the field. Many families have good representations. John C. Burton of Monticello has many good examples; noteworthy is a set ware sugar box made without metal. Scattered over Wayne and Pulaski counties are many good examples of gouged feed boxes, and a few years ago there was on the Blankenship farm at Hargis an unusually large and fine example of a dugout water trough.

[109] I, VIII, 478, this type used by Clark's soldiers on an Ohio campaign was only one of several varieties. Kercheval, *Virginia*, Doddridge, "Notes," 274–275, and Williams, *Smith*, 46, describe others.

[110] The smokehouse of the Hermitage has an excellent example of a meat trough.

[111] FQ, II, Clinkenbeard "Interview," 98.

homes innumerable devices of wood from the length of sapling, halved and gouged out to make a gutter to carry rain water into the trough to the forked stick used to tighten the bed cords.[112] The first harvest of flax or wool or cotton would have kept the farmer or his help busy making a flax brake and others of the large wooden pieces needed in the preparation of cloth that could not be handily carried by pack horse. William Gower [113] was killed owning three sleighs, these most probably brought on the trip for they were easily carried but took much work in the making; had William Gower lived he would in time have had the rest of the heavy loom that like the frame for the spinning wheel could be made entirely of wood by a man fairly skillful with a few tools, as could a warping frame or a roller cotton gin.

Hand mill and horse mill stones were owned by several first settlers, and corn hard enough to grind meant that somebody must make frames for these.[114] Farm life could not be lived without baskets, much more important then than now, for they were used in a variety of ways, sometimes as sifters,[115] and the Cumberland basket, descendant of the Scotch creel instead of the Indian basket of cane splints or grass, was made usually of white oak splits; the same material with which the pioneer bottomed his chairs, though in spring when it could be peeled he often used hickory bark.

One could go on with a long list of home needs such as brooms and brushes, made from material taken from the woods, but supplying the needs of his home was only a small part of what the farmer had to do. Stables were one of the first things built, and a stable needed all manner of "barn furniture" from feed boxes and water troughs that were longer or shorter versions of the hollowed-out trough, to wooden latches for the stable doors and poplar shovels for moving manure.

Farming demanded continual working in wood, for many men shaped their own hames, swingle and doubletrees, and the expensive plow-points, never left behind, had to be fitted onto wooden frames; the settler's first

---

[112] One of my bed-cord turners is only the fork of a tree branch, bored to insert a handle; the pioneer when possible used, as in the case of the pack-saddle, something ready-made by nature.

[113] DW, I, 175–176.

[114] Hickman's horse mill, W, 30S, 464; Bell's, *ibid.*, 255. These lived to use their millstones but James Freeland, DW, I, 16, still had only the stones when killed, as had Thomas Brown, *ibid.*, 207.

[115] Williams, *Smith*, 46, used a basket as a sifter; the family of Dr. Doddridge, Kercheval, *Virginia*, "Notes," 275, used deerskin punched with a hot needle for a sifter bottom.

harrow might be nothing more than a length of brush, but when he got time he might make one with spike teeth but this, too, all of wood, as were his rakes and pitchforks.

A few had the stretchers for wagons, but most had to make do with a cart as did William Gower; [116] the better carts had iron tires, but many were made entirely of wood with hickory withe tires. Regardless of how affluent he might be, every farmer needed a sled or so, and for the not-too-wealthy first settler it might for a time be his only horse-drawn vehicle. The Halls who settled a short distance east of Bledsoe's Lick, around 1786, were quite affluent with a clock, yet when most of them were killed by Indians they were trying to escape with a few possessions on a horse-drawn sled.

Many of these things could be made with the tools already mentioned, and some like the bread tray or any small thing with a concave surface were finished with the gouge. A small tool used with one hand, it did the work of a combination hand adz, drawing knife, and knife, and runs through most early wills, for it was only a small sickle-shaped blade, the two ends curved into a single handle.[117]

All farmers gouged, and scutched, and chopped, and rived, and drew, and bored, but more than anything they whittled, and like generations of borderers before them they never got caught up with their whittling. The first things whittled would have been handles for the extra axes, hoes, mattocks, broadaxes and other tools brought. Night in and night out while the wife and daughters spun or carded or sewed by the fire the settler and his older sons must whittle—pegs of many sizes, a button for the barn door, gears of some good hardwood, oak or beech for the horse mill, dasher for the churn, spinning stick, powder funnel, or some intricate thing such as a wooden door lock, complete with turning key, at least one of which is still in use in Pulaski County, Kentucky.

He could never stop whittling; he worked with knife and wood while sitting up with the sick or the dead, or waiting for a turn of corn to be ground or his horse to be shod, or the auction to begin. And always he chose his wood with care; beech wood for the plane stock, but dogwood for the weaving shuttle with bobbin. Walnut soon supplanted tiger maple as gunstock wood on the Cumberland, most probably because it was

[116] DW, I, 175. Sleds and carts and wagon gears, though less commonly owned than woodworking tools, were plentiful among first settlers, *ibid.*, 54, 57.

[117] Gouges may be seen in many of the museums mentioned, especially Mountain Life Museum of Levi Jackson Wilderness Road State Park.

more plentiful. A corncob with a cane handle was fine for a pipe; the mash stirrer ought to be of poplar; oak was best for the bow of an ox yoke but the lighter poplar would do for the neckpiece.

There were no rules and no absolutes; a man in Indian-filled country had to make do with what he could get, nor could he in his use of wood always abide by the signs of the Zodiac and the moon. There were throughout the United States of that day an almost endless number of do's and don't's concerning wood; a few learned from the Indian, many brought from different countries of Europe. Some were governed by the moon such as: a roof board rived on a waning moon would curl; and others by the sign—a cedar post would rot if set when the sign was in the feet; and still others by the season—timber cut when the sap was down would last longer, which was more truth than superstition as was the belief that brush cut during dog days would die more quickly. Dry weather usually followed, and after that frost, so that enough new growth to carry through the winter never had a chance.

The sayings and superstitions, like the moon lore of planting time or distilling, varied with the locality, the especial almanac the region used, and also national origins, and even among any group German or Scotch-Irish there was never entire agreement, so that on the Cumberland it might be said each man was his own almanac.[118]

There are a few older men living on the Cumberland today, especially in the upper region, who know many of the old sayings and still understand the use of the old tools, growing rusty in their barns, some hand forged by long-gone blacksmiths.

First settlers to the Cumberland didn't always get to use their tools. James Harrod had a handsaw, broadax, auger, iron wedges, drawing knife, gouge, two chisels and of course a felling ax, but was killed before he got his whittling done for he had three sleighs without a loom, and a rifled gun barrel without a stock. Samuel Vernor was well supplied for the small farmer; he had a crosscut and two handsaws, three felling axes, broadax, foot adz, chisels, wedges, and a froe, but he was killed while his maul rings still waited for the maul. John Buchanan, Sr., survived many battles, but he like so many others was killed with two sets of plow irons waiting for plows, and clevises and hangings for doubletrees yet without

---

[118] Belief in such things was confined to neither the borderer nor the unsophisticated. Jedidiah Morse, *The American Geography*, Elizabethtown, N.J., 1789 (cited hereafter as Morse, *Geography*), devoted the first part of his text to the signs of the Zodiac with their Latin names, and most publications of the day took cognizance of the moon when advising farm families on their work.

the wood. John's son Samuel, killed a few years later, was one of the few whose plane bits were set in stocks and he had the three all ready—jack, jointer, and plow; but Nicholas Gentry was killed, his plane bits waiting for handles. William Overall [119] was a forehanded man, bringing in addition to the usual woodworking tools, a set of cooper's tools, and fifty pounds of iron, which had he lived would have gone into other tools or possibly horseshoes.

Tools and appliances continued for many years to be well worth carrying over the mountains. Years later, up the river in Pulaski County, John Turley's [120] bald-faced, bay filly brought only $20.00, his muley cow and her calf but nine, while a whetstone and a gimlet brought $3.51.

[119] The first five men named were first settlers receiving land, but killed by Indians; their inventories in order, DW, I, 16, 24, 7, 69, 296, 283.
[120] PW, I, 68.

CHAPTER XI

INDIANS

IF ON the evening of January 15, 1781, one could, by some magic, have been lifted high above the Mississippi Valley, and through some still greater magic have been able to see the whole sweep of country, it would, at first glance, have seemed an uninhabited stretch of grass or forest land, cut by rivers glittering in the moonlight, for the moon was bright that night, at least by the Cumberland in Middle Tennessee.[1] Given the microscopically seeing, many-faceted eye of some peculiar fly, unable to see the Indian's cabin or long bark house, but only the white man's dwelling and the lights that marked it, one could, on looking closer, have seen here and there a few flickering lights from flames of hearth fire, candle, pine knot, or grease lamp.

These pin-points of light would have made a little glow down by New Orleans and Natchez. Nearby, one would have seen fields, many old and stumpless, long cleared for sugar cane or corn. Almost due north, between two of the Great Lakes, there were a few more lights and several fields, some old enough for apple orchards. These were around Detroit, which, though getting on toward a hundred years old, was still little more than a fort on the frontier. South and west on the Wabash, the Kaskaskia, and the upper Mississippi were other old fields, and a few frame houses, but there was about these an air of neglect, almost of desolation, for the settlements in the Illinois were less flourishing than fifteen years ago, before first the British, and then the Americans came.

[1] Lavinia Robertson Craighead, W, 6XX (50), 11, mentions the weather, and Col. Robert Weakley, *ibid.*, 32S, 344, gives the date, as does Felix Robertson, Nashville *Journal of Medicine and Surgery*, VIII, 452–453.

Eastward on the western flanks of the Appalachians the scattered fields were newer, resembling less neat squares of snow-covered earth than the forest itself, for many were filled with deadened but still-standing trees. The white man's home and fields had come to Fort Pitt, and there were scattering settlements along the upper tributaries of the Ohio, but north of the river the villages were of the Indian instead of the white man. Cabins and clearings on the Holston had pushed south and west. The Blue Grass of Kentucky was dotted with cabins and girdled trees, spread thinly to The Falls.

The Cumberland was another story; the upper river including the Rock-castle region and everything down to the mouth of the Big South Fork lay uncleared and tenantless as when Dr. Walker visited it in 1750. Only the roads had widened and along them were signs of many travelers' camp fires with here and there a fresh grave, marking the hasty burial of some scalped traveler. Clearings had spread along the Big South Fork, and those on Pittmans Creek, Price's Meadows and down the river were still there, with the trail that crossed the Cumberland at Smith Shoals showing more sign of use. The settlements in this region, remote as they were, stood less than a hundred miles or so from others in East Tennessee; those in Central Kentucky were even closer, but across the Cumberland, over the hills, and in another world.[2]

More than three hundred miles down the crooked Cumberland, were the loneliest of all outposts in the young west, four little stations, three near the river, and all more than a hundred miles overland from any other white settlement. The casual observer glancing down through the moon-light would at first have thought that once again the Indians had made it plain no man should live on the Cumberland, for the region as a whole spoke more of death and failure than of life.

The Red River settlements where the Renfroes and others had built the previous spring were no more than embers among weed- and brush-choked fields with here and there a grave, sixteen dead,[3] but not neces-sarily that many graves. Clover Bottom where Hugh Rogan had worked in the corn, Mary Purnell Donelson had borne her first baby, and Na-thaniel Hart's Negroes had built cabins, stood weed-grown and deserted, as were the clearings and cabins of most other settlers, such as John Rains and William Neely.

[2] Crow's Station, Collins, *Kentucky, 1882,* II, 18, and Hall's south of Danville were both less than fifty miles from Pittman's and Price's stations.
[3] There are numerous accounts of this disaster in the late summer of 1780; see W, 32S, 307.

However, the stations built in 1779–80 by those who came overland were still standing. Eaton's, like the other three, held more people than before, for all those not dead or gone away had had to take refuge in a station. Mansker's, twelve miles north of Eaton's now held about a dozen families, including that of John Donelson. These settlements were the only ones left north of the river, though following the custom on other borders, men would during the day go out to work at clearing fields, fencing, or farming and come home again of nights.

South of the river, French Lick stood on high ground above the lick and back from the Cumberland. A road, worn now by people's feet, and those of farm animals, especially horses, a sled or so and a few carts, led from this, the upper station that by now held several families, down past the Sulphur Spring, by the Big Lick, and across the Lick Branch to Free-land's Station [4] where the Robertsons and several other families lived behind picketed walls.

In the bright moonlight and to the Indians creeping through the shadows, the place, small and unfinished, with no blockhouse, only cabins at the corners, looked peaceful and defenseless as any farm. So did all forts in the backwoods look, for they had "neither ramparts, nor ditch, nor parapet, no outpost, nor out sentry." [5] Freeland's Station had even less of a warlike air than most, for on the southern side, but outside the fort walls were the cribbed corn and the fodder,[6] which, following the custom of the day, had been pulled blade by blade, tied into bundles, stacked in piles, covered with the tops, and protected from the cows and sheep by a rail pen.

Nearby were the calf pens, and near these the milk cows, contentedly chewing their cuds with now and then the bell of one giving a faint and sleepy tinkle. The most precious farm animals, Robertson's fine horses, were inside the fort wall, and it was these the slowly creeping Indians wanted first. High up, past the upper station, the craggy gray limestone bluffs of the knob that now holds the State Capitol, shone in the moonlight, bright against the dark cedars that still stood all about on land too

[4] Felix Robertson, Nashville *Journal of Medicine and Surgery*, VIII, 452–453, in his account of the scalping of David Hood incidentally gives a good idea of the road. Mrs. Drake's 1804 map of Nashville shows the location of the Lick Branch and the Sulphur Spring, and some approximation of this path that had by that date become a road of sorts; I can find nothing to indicate there was in 1781 any road to or ferry across the Cumberland where Nashville was later located; it was not ordered cut until early 1784; meanwhile settlers used the old trail crossing near the mouth of the Lick Branch, downriver from future Nashville.

[5] Smythe, *Tour*, I, 281.

[6] W, 6XX (50), 11.

rough and rocky to clear for cultivation. On northern slopes and shady spots, patches of the recent snow [7] still lingered, but this night was clear and cold, cow's breath white in the moonlight and all the smells—horse manure, newly hewed cedar, rived oak in the door, wood smoke—sharp in the clean air. The ring of Indians tightened about the fort walls, but behind these in the cabins all seemed to be asleep. Only the dogs barked, "running back and forth," for "it was the custom of the men to place their dogs outside the fort to give warning of the approach of the Indians."

No one came to the barking dogs, and the Indians crept closer, taking care to keep hidden in the shadows. They did not know that in one of the cabins James Robertson and his wife, though in bed, talked in low voices. We don't know what they said. I imagine it was less a simple conversation than an attempt of each to supply the other with the accumulated news of a long absence, for their lives, no different from those of many other couples of that day, were for much of the time spent apart.

Early in December Robertson had heard there were up at The Falls some settlers planning to come to the Cumberland as Middle Tennessee was then known.[8] Needing men now, more than ever, he had gone there, but persuading settlers was not his sole business. His small community needed salt, for "the settlers had no salt except a little they made from the Sulphur Spring with their cooking utensils." [9] The Sulphur Spring, between French Lick and Freeland's, was handy enough, but a poor source of salt.

Salt was, for all settlers away from the sea, an important item, and almost always hard to get and expensive. Little was required for cooking, and the Long Hunters could live for months without it, but any farmer west of the Fall Line needed at least some salt to keep his farm animals healthy. Salt, too, could serve as a substitute for fence, until the settler got time to build it. Grazing was good in one canebrake as the next, but a bit of salt fed by the fort walls was one way to keep horses and beef cattle from wandering out of the country, for the cow with her suckling calf penned by the fort walls was the only animal with any reason for

[7] Most accounts that mention David Hood, including Ramsey, *Tennessee*, 455, speak of snow.

[8] There are contradictions here concerning Robertson's travels. His daughter, W, 6XX (50), 10–11, and another, *ibid.*, 31S, 46, state that he went to The Falls, "and was gone seven weeks." Those who say he had just returned from North Carolina are I think mistaken. He left for North Carolina in August of 1781, *ibid.*, 43.

[9] W, 6XX (50), 10. Salt was in the first years of any frontier settlement a problem; particularly so during the Revolution, for most had been imported. Anburey, *Travels*, II, 326, tells how the salt-hungry horses on the Piedmont would lick the sweat from each other.

coming home. There was little or no feed; for "the settlers during the first year suffered much for want of provisions, having no bread, but few vegetables of any kind, and no meat but wild animals." [10] The first year was gone, and there was by now cribbed corn and stacked fodder, but it is doubtful, harassed as they had been by Indians, if Robertson had more than enough corn for bread, nubbins and fodder for the milk cow, with some for the saddle and work horses.

The Cumberland settlers needed more salt for their own food, than did the average settler. The old days when a hunter on the Middle Cumberland could shoot a deer or a buffalo or a bear when he got hungry, as had James Smith fifteen years before, were gone. Game was so scarce that in the previous fall, a group of twenty men had gone in canoes up the Cumberland to the mouth of the Caney Fork. They had brought back the meat of five bear, seventy-five buffalo, and more than eighty deer.[11]

The keeping of this meat demanded salt unless they made it all into jerk, and stewed jerk was but a poor food. Robertson had brought home salt, by now being made near The Falls,[12] but no people. The prospective settlers "had heard the place was abandoned," [13] and so had gone elsewhere.

He had come riding home the night before, and though he had seen and heard much of the wider world, much had happened at home, for his sixth child, Felix, was hardly three days old.[14] He and his wife, Charlotte Reeves, may have talked of the baby and wondered on his future, though Charlotte who had married at seventeen, and now had her sixth baby before she was thirty, may not have talked at all. Her married life had ever been marred by the long separations, the wonderings; months her husband had been gone that time he went to the Holston and then home by way of Georgia, and they less than two years married. Dunmore's War had taken him for many long weeks in 1774; and all in between, before, and since had been the surveying, Indian treating, and short battles; these had never kept him so long, but with them the wonder had been sharper, the uneasiness quickened. In 1772 he had ridden away to placate the enraged Cherokee, and no one had expected to see him home again.

---

[10] W, 31S, 36.

[11] W, 6XX (50), 10. See also Ramsey, *Tennessee*, 450.

[12] Mereness, *Travels*, Fleming, "Journal," 620, writing in late 1779 described the salt works near The Falls. The importance of salt is further attested to by the trouble taken to get a road to the saltworks in Kentucky. See LC, 79, the August Court of 1783 order Samuel Davis, William Montgomery, and William Pittman to survey the road from John Hall's to the saltworks—this road intersecting with that from Crab Orchard.

[13] W, 31S, 46.

[14] W, 6XX (50), 11.

His first trip to the Cumberland and home by way of the Illinois had kept them separated eight months or so in 1779, and then when he did get home in August, it was only to be gone again in October, and she not seeing him again until late the next April.

So Charlotte Reeves Robertson may have said nothing, glad only to have him home and alive after the seven weeks' absence, and all the family for a little while together; that is as much as it could ever be again. Her baby one, a girl, had died during the summer, and his youngest brother John, and like a child to Robertson for he had raised him, was only a few weeks dead, killed by the Indians while picking cotton at Clover Bottom.[15] She could have thought of the dead children or the look of one D. Larriman when the Indians had, within sight of the station, cut off his head and put it on a pole.[16] The chances are she did not think too much on such; mostly those who settled the Cumberland were people with no time for looking back; the world for them was here and now; not theirs to remember or adjust to, but theirs to shape. She was undoubtedly happy lying there amid all her blessings; a son born, husband home, salt for the meat, and nearby the cribbed corn,[17] giving promise of bread to go with the meat.

Robertson, fresh from a wider world, may have talked worriedly of the policies of North Carolina and the half-born, struggling nation. Money was mostly paper and worthless; the Whigs were winning the south but they still had a long way to go, and meanwhile the Cumberland settlers could look to North Carolina for nothing, that is until the war was ended. But it would be ended soon; the Cherokee, strongest ally of the British in the south, had been defeated, some of it done by Robertson; the Battle of Kings Mountain, the preceding October, had shown that Tories could never take the old west; George Rogers Clark could hold Vincennes and Kaskaskia, and push England and her northern Indian allies clean through the Ohio woods and into the Great Lakes. A man who could then stay on the Cumberland surrounded by the deserted clearings and the dead with close to fifteen thousand warriors [18]—Cherokee, Chickamauga, Creek, Chickasaw, and Choctaw—at his back door had to believe such things.

---

[15] Ramsey, *Tennessee*, 450, gives space to the Clover Bottom incident, but lists John Robertson as the son of James. The sons of James—Peyton and Randal—were killed later; he had a nephew John and a brother John; see W, 31S, 43-53.

[16] Ramsey, *Tennessee*, 446.

[17] W, 31S, 58. Some, such as the Donelsons who didn't know better, planted in low ground and their corn crop suffered in a late flood, but the Indians did not begin a systematic destruction of crops before the summer of 1781.

[18] This figure, Ramsey, *Tennessee*, 497, is based on "The Report of the Commissioners, to Congress," by Richard Henry Lee in 1777, and did not include the

The dogs barked more wildly still. Charlotte asked James to go see why they barked so. She may have thought of Indians, forever on the prowl. The day Felix was born, a young man, David Hood, had been on the way from Freeland's to the upper station, but just as he passed the Sulphur Spring, he had been ambushed by Indians. He had fallen from three bullets, and the Indians, certain he was dead, had not bothered to split his skull before they scalped him. He had lain there for some hours, and when it seemed they were gone, he had cautiously got up. He had walked but a few steps, only to see Indians watching, laughing at his scalpless condition. He was too close to the upper station for them to risk getting close, so they only shot at him, and two more balls had entered his body.

He lay so, scalped, five times wounded, all night in the cold. Next morning men came out from the upper or French Lick Station, found the blood on the snow and trailed him to a brush pile. They, thinking him dead or dying, carried him to an outhouse. Late that night Robertson got home to Freeland's. Hearing of David Hood, he came up to French Lick the next morning. There, with a shoemaker's awl, he performed on David Hood's scalpless head the operation he had often seen done in East Tennessee, and learned from a now forgotten French surgeon; that is, he made with the awl perforations over the whole of the "outer table of the skull, pretty close together," so that the oozings from each little hole would form a scab-like covering.[19] David Hood, like a brother of Edmund Jennings,[20] survived many years, and in time all the forts on the Cumberland had at least one person able to peg a scalped head.

James Robertson may have talked of David Hood; in any case in spite of the barking dogs he kept on talking. The Indians, careful to keep in the shadows, snaked closer and closer, until several lay by the stockade gate, peeping, hunting out the horses. Others waited, guns at the ready.

Robertson most likely talked of Indians, and he may have blamed some of the settlement's troubles on the foolishness of building Fort Jefferson last spring at the Iron Banks on the Mississippi only five miles below the

Seminoles and others of the deeper south. A "Report to the Secretary of War," by the Rev. J. Morse in 1822, estimated the southern Indian population as 65,122.

[19] Ramsey, *Tennessee*, 455–456, gives the date of David Hood's scalping as 1782. Felix Robertson, Nashville *Journal of Medicine and Surgery*, VIII, 452–453, not only describes the way of treating a scalped skull, but also said his father did it and gave the date a year earlier.

[20] Scalped victims often lived for many years, but seem to have been more or less invalids. Edmund's father, mortally wounded, made his will, DW, I, 11, with a special provision for his son "who was scalped by the Indians, and so rendered incapable of making a living . . . a Negro girl named Milla and her increase . . . a choice rifle gun and horse and saddle."

mouth of the Ohio, in Chickasaw territory, with no by-your-leave from the Chickasaw.[21] The enraged Chickasaw instead of turning against the useless fort attacked the Red River settlements, and then lay in ambush to kill all who escaped. True, the Chickasaw was only one small tribe among many, but the friendship of one was better than none, for in all the tribes around there was no friend of the white settler. All history indicates that a captured Tory spoke the truth when he said: "It is the white natives of America that the Indians have the greatest aversion to." [22] The hatred had, among all tribes, sharpened at the westward push of the Americans, and with the British and the Spanish to arm and encourage, their harassment knew no end. Attakullakulla who had held the Cherokee to their word was dead, and Dragging Canoe, opposed to the treaty in the first place, had moved down to the region of present-day Chattanooga, a strategic spot. Here, he could in one swift march reach the Cumberland or a settler's cabin in East Tennessee and simply by staying at home keep reinforcements from arriving by water.

There is no record of what tribe or tribes—for by now many Indian towns held mixtures, not only of Indians but of white men [23]—were represented by the braves who ringed Freeland's Station. The barking of the dogs, sounding first here and then there as they ran round and round the walls, must have reached a wild crescendo as one Indian, standing on the shoulders of another, sprang over the high gate, swiftly unbarred it, so that more Indians, soundless and swift as water over smooth rock, could rush in and seize horses. Charlotte once again asked James to go see why the dogs barked so. This time he got out of bed, opened the nearby door, looked into the fort enclosure, and in the moonlight saw Indians trying to get horses through the gate.[24]

His yell of "Indians" rang through all the cabins. The seeming pandemonium, but smoothly running operation of a just-attacked station, sprang into action. Robertson grabbed a gun. In other cabins men seized readyloaded muskets or rifles, flung bullets into mouths, powder horn straps over heads, leaped to walls and unplugged portholes. They fought with whatever happened to be handy; a large musket "loaded with several

[21] I, VIII, "Preface," cxxiv. See also Ramsey, *Tennessee,* 446.
[22] Smythe, *Tour,* I, 345.
[23] Joseph Brown as a young boy started down the Tennessee with his family to the Cumberland settlements. Most of his family was killed, but he was adopted and taken to the Nickojack and Running Water towns. His account of his life there, Ramsey, *Tennessee,* 509–515, is one of the best to show the many European nationalities as well as Indian nations represented in any one town in 1788.
[24] W, 6XX (50), 12.

rifle bullets," [25] "Dikard rifle," [26] blunderbuss, "rifle that shot a large ounce ball," [27] and "a British musket loaded with rifle balls." [28]

The bullets sang out, heavily charged but mostly patchless, for when the fighting was close as now, a musket with half a dozen unpatched balls was better than a rifle. There were plenty of guns, for with so many dead, the Cumberland had by now almost twice as many guns as men.[29] This meant that behind each man a woman crouched, a ready-loaded gun lifted, waiting to be exchanged for the one emptied.

And a tricky job it was loading guns in the pitch dark, for Robertson, as soon as he gave the alarm, had commanded a Negro woman sleeping on the floor to get the children under the beds and throw a pail of water on the blazing fire.[30] In any night attack all lights were at once put out.[31] So unfinished were many of the cabins that light of fire or candle flame would betray figures behind the walls, and clearly show the position of the portholes; and so they fought in darkness, a smoky, stinging darkness it was, strong with smells—blood, burning powder, scorched patching from the first fire, the burning grease of a hot gun barrel, and sweat of many busy people crowded into one small space.

Young children might lie motionless and curled into smallness under the beds, but the men of twelve years old and up manned portholes. Twelve-year-old Jonathan, rapidly earning the reputation of being as "good a soldier as ever pulled a trigger," [32] was right there with the other men. The fight was close and hot with Indians on both sides the cabin. Zachariah White got splinters in his eyes, and Major Lucas and a Negro man asleep in an unfinished cabin were mortally wounded at the first fire.[33]

One wonders what the three-day-old baby did, rifles and muskets roaring round him; outside the barking dogs, screams and neighs of wounded

[25] W, 32S, 498.
[26] W, 28S, 127. This is undoubtedly a variant spelling of Dechard. The word *musket* as used on the Cumberland designated a smooth-bore gun, but larger than a "smooth-bore," smaller than a blunderbuss.
[27] W, 6XX, 286.
[28] W, 32S, 345.
[29] At French Lick in April of 1781 there were 40 guns and 21 men, W, 32S, 313. At Hickman's, *ibid.*, 30S, 458, there were in 1790 eight guards and 17 guns; many men, however, owned more than one gun.
[30] W, 6XX (50), 11.
[31] Most narrators of the hair-raising disaster at Zeigler's, in 1792, north of the Cumberland, near "where Cairo now stands," blame the fact that the family and neighbors were sitting up with the corpse of a man killed by Indians that day, and so had a blazing fire and candles to betray every crack. See W, 6XX, 86–88, and also Gray, *Bishop*, 56–59; Bishop was at that time in Middle Tennessee but was not at Zeigler's.
[32] W, 1S, 61.
[33] W, 6XX (50), 12.

horses, bellowings of frightened cows as amid much jangling of bells they ran away, and over it all the wild roars of the yelling men, both white and Indian.

The Cumberlander always yelled in battle; his war whoop [34] was his drum, fife, uniform, and flag; it not only gave him heart but it sometimes tricked the Indian, for many yells betokened many men, and so they must have yelled that night, at least the men; women and children would have kept silent as quail in cover, though different from the men, they screamed sometimes when being tomahawked or scalped. The women would have had little time or mind for anything save the loading of the guns; working quick and certain in the dark,[35] a timid one maybe wondering if the heat of the gun, almost too hot to handle, would explode the powder as she rammed the bullet down, but most concerned solely with making certain the pinch of priming hit the pan and that the touchhole was open and the flint sharp.

Charlotte Robertson could not ease her mind with activity. Her bed, for safety had sometime before been placed with the head against the inner wall as Indians were expected to attack on the outside. Worse, in all the haste and work the inner wall had been given only a temporary mud daubing. The moment needed to lift enough to crawl or roll off the bed, taking Felix with her, could have been the very one that brought a bullet. She could only lie flat and still while bullets whistled through a crack "eight inches above her head." [36]

Robertson, Zachariah White, George Freeland, Jonathan, and Mark at last got the Indians out of the station and the gate latched; but this was only the first round. The battle went on for four or five hours, the tumult unabating; the Indians "howled like wolves," [37] and tried to fire the station. They never succeeded. Many accounts are given of women putting out fires blazing on roofs while their men manned portholes below. Who did it here we do not know, but it was done.

All, however, could only stand and watch, while the Indians, enraged

[34] There are in the Draper Manuscripts numerous brief references to yells; typical, W, 32S, 352—"The Indians raised the whoop the whites raised the yell." W, 6XX, 704, is a reference to what was commonly known as the "green scalp cry." The trader James Adair had an unusually complete mastery of the Chickasaw whoops and could give many; his *American Indian*, 295, "shrill whoop of friendship"; 296, "shrill whoop of defiance"; 347, the "death whoop-whoop." Which of these fathered the Rebel yell I do not know, possibly a combination.

[35] The borderers had to develop great skill at loading; Louis Wetzel, a noted borderer in western Virginia, could load even while running, Kercheval, *Virginia*, 238–239.

[36] W, 6XX (50), 12.

[37] W, 30S, 256, a common practice of the Indians.

by their failure, went round to the south side, set the corn and fodder on fire, and killed what cattle had not run away.[38] The smell of burning corn meant hunger as did the dead cows and the destroyed fodder; but it had happened before and it would happen again.

They were happy when dawn came, just looking at each other and finding all but two alive. Robertson's blue eyes were bright, we can imagine, in his smoke-blackened face, for the old muzzle-loader often blacked the user's face, particularly when it flashed in the pan as often happened. And as after any battle they were a smelly, dirty crew, even the women would have smelled of powder from the many loadings. Up the hill at French Lick there must have been a deal of unrest during the night with men by portholes and women fingering powder chargers in the dark, for next morning as soon as it was light, and in spite of lurking Indians, men came from there.[39]

It was decided to abandon Freeland's, at least temporarily.[40] What belongings could be taken by pack horse were collected, women and children, including the four-day-old Felix who grew up to be a doctor, were put on horseback. Armed men galloped through the fort gate, women on side saddles, some like Mrs. Robertson with babies in arms and toddlers on behind, galloped after, and at a gallop they went, horsemen behind, in front, and beside them, dogs circling the horsemen. Mrs. Robertson had a little Negro clinging behind her. He fell off, but was rescued by another woman, and though Indians were firing at them from the hill, all got safely up to French Lick.[41]

French Lick, built by the Mulherrins and Buchanans, now taking all refugees who, like the Robertsons, could for the moment bring little but their lives, was still unfinished. Once again all faced months of little or no bread, and wild meat scarce in woods forever filled with Indians. Nor could they give much time to the preparing of ground for planting. There were at most no more than twenty-five men south of the river; some had

---

[38] W, 6XX (50), 12. Ramsey, *Tennessee*, 451, differs somewhat from the account of Robertson's daughter, but does describe a terrific battle with "not less than 500 shots" fired into the house.

[39] W, 6XX (50), 13.

[40] W, 6XX (50), 13. This decision seems to have been confined to Robertson, Zachariah White, and a few others. True, Mrs. Craighead wrote, *ibid.*, 17, that "only Nashville and Eatons remained." There was at this time no Nashville, and all other accounts give three stations during the darkest years after Mansker's was burned; French Lick, Eaton's, and Freeland's; see W, 29S, 75, this locates a "Freelings" a mile downriver from French Lick Station with Eaton's on opposite side. See also W, 1S, 62; 31S, 80–81; and 32S, 318.

[41] W, 6XX (50), 13.

to work at finishing the station; others had to hunt wild meat, and always some must be deployed as spies and guards; for when a woman milked a cow or wrestled with the calf, or a slave went for wood, or girdled a tree, or grubbed out cane for a garden patch, or tapped a tree for maple sugar, hunted hogs or horses, cut cedar for roof boards, peeled hickory in the early spring for a chair bottom, he or she had to be guarded, usually by two men who, when they opened their "budgets" to eat, stood back to back, eyes sweeping the country, eating with one hand, the other cradling the rifle against his body.[42]

Fighting the Indian was never on the Cumberland an end in itself. The supreme goal of all endeavor was to get on with the business of living, and this in the summer of 1781 was not easy. The first job was to strengthen stations. George Freeland and a few other men held Freeland's, while Robertson and his family continued at Buchanan's or French Lick.

The struggle for food, fuel, and housing meant work for everybody. Their pattern of life was not that of the southern planter or "gentleman of rank" who arose at nine, walked as far as his stable to see his horses, and breakfasted between nine and ten.[43]

Their days were those of middle-class farmers who, with no overseer, went early to their fields, though breakfast was late, coming after some hours of work.[44] It is doubtful if many of the settlers at French Lick had, at sunrise on April 2, 1781, eaten breakfast, but all were busy; men out hunting, women at the milking, and Zachariah White in the schoolhouse hearing his scholars recite their lessons, for "some would go by daylight to say first." Lessons were in progress with laggards running across the fort yard when the Indians attacked. Zachariah White, the teacher, picked up his ever-handy gun, "ran out the south side of the fort," but "got but a few steps and was wounded."

Old Mr. Buchanan had better luck; he ran into a rail pen and "killed ten Indians."[45] We can be sure women ran to the cabins, leaving calves to finish the milking as the cows ran away, while everybody grabbed bullet bags, powder horns, and extra guns. How many men were out hunting we don't know, possibly no more than two or three. French Lick, though

[42] Gray, *Bishop*, 125.
[43] Anburey, *Travels*, II, 329–330, and Smythe, *Tour*, I, 41–42, described the pattern of rest, meals, and work of the middle- and upper-class planters of Virginia.
[44] W, 32S, 346, and *ibid.*, 1S, 61, refer to an Indian attack at Robertson's Station on Richland Creek when "the horn had just blown for breakfast," and Robertson and his sons were out hoeing corn with the slaves.
[45] W, 32S, 313–316. This was John Buchanan, Sr., who was killed not long after moving to Mill Creek, *ibid.*, 361, and not Major John, his son.

the blockhouse and several cabins were unchinked, was better fortified than most, for it had the little four-pounder, a swivel gun brought by John Donelson on the boat *Adventure;* and now they loaded it with pieces of pots and rocks and fired it.

The battle was brief. The Indians appeared to have contented themselves with the usual stealing of what horses were outside the fort walls. At this time of day and year there would have been several hitched nearby, being fed, or harnessed for the day's work in the woods and fields It looked as if the whites had won a victory.

Less than a year before a small party of Indians had swooped down on Freeland's and stolen several horses. James Robertson and a handful of other men had ridden in pursuit.[46] They got no scalps, but had so frightened the Indians they galloped off leaving some riderless horses. A parley was now held to discuss the taking of another such trip. Some say Robertson was for it, and some say against; in any case by ten o'clock they were decided, and the horsemen paraded in the fort yard,[47] then rode through the fort and away, while once again women such as Mrs. Robertson watched their retreating backs and wondered, probably without too much worry. Danger was so little expected the women had with them only one man, and that the mortally wounded Mr. White.

This time the wonder of the women concerning the fate of their men was short; for "just as their hats were seen disappearing over the hill, they were fired upon by a large party of Indians." [48] The quick disappearance of the Indians had been a decoy, not a retreat; the creek bluff [49] swarmed with Indians; some say as many as five hundred. They were roughly divided into two parties; one up near the fort walls waiting to seize the station, the other hidden in the brush and cedars "down by the branch." It was these who first attacked the little army. At the first scalp cry of the Indians the white men sprang from their saddles, "took tree," fired, and then tried to reload with Indians firing at them from every direction.

Up at the fort the watching women and whining dogs, shut up when

[46] Ramsey, *Tennessee*, 448.
[47] W, 6XX (50), 17.
[48] W, 6XX (50), 17.
[49] The Draper correspondents here agree quite well, and though there is disagreement in several points with Ramsey's account, *Tennessee*, 452–453, all indicate that The Bluff on which the fighting took place was above and by a branch. Descriptions of the location of French Lick Station, W, 32S, 252–253, for example, as being above the Sulphur Spring near the Lick Branch fit early accounts of the battle. Later writers have at times represented The Bluff and hence the Battle as being along the Cumberland. The fighting was not within sight of the fort, but over the hill and down.

the men rode away, could only listen to the shots, the white man's yell, and the Indian's whoop. Some may have reloaded the swivel, and some may have stood by portholes with loaded guns. We don't know. I have never found an account of a pioneer woman on the Cumberland firing a gun, but they may have done so. They fought when being scalped or killed with whatever happened to be handy, and usually this meant nothing. Years later, Miss Steel,[50] riding out to visit a neighbor, was attacked by Indians; her dead hands, all cut with the knives she had grabbed at, were filled with Indian hair. Mrs. Castell of East Tennessee fought so it took two braves, two knives broken and a tomahawk to kill her,[51] but usually the women were like those at Zeigler's, so burdened down with babies and young children they were trying to protect, they had no hands free for fighting.

The battle down by the branch in the cedars and the cane was something like a woman's battle; the bloody hand-to-hand encounters of men too hard-pressed to reload, and so forced to fight with hatchets, clubbed guns, and more rarely knives. Unlike the British soldier, the American never whittled the handle of his big sheathed knife to fit his gun barrel so it could be used as a bayonet. A hatchet was better; a bayonet wouldn't split a skull; if it went through bone at all it was inclined to stick; the stuck man might run away, the knife going with him, or worse yet he might use his own knife or hatchet while the other was trying to free his. A man with strong teeth and long thumbs and fingernails hardened in candle flames was not helpless, even without any weapon. He could in an instant gouge out a man's eyeballs with his thumbnails, meanwhile ripping off ears with his forefingers and taking off the nose with his teeth.[52]

The white men down by the branch got help from unexpected quarters; the dogs, "hearing the shouting made their way to it, being trained to fight Indians."[53] Tradition credits Mrs. Robertson with having turned them loose; they are honored with the credit for having saved the fort and possibly Middle Tennessee. The Indians, once their guns were empty, were hard put to reload with dogs chewing them to pieces. These dogs were

---

[50] W, 32S, 485, from Mrs. General James Winchester's account.

[51] Ramsey, *Tennessee*, 292-293. She had two scalp locks taken, indicating it had taken two braves to kill her.

[52] Anburey, *Travels*, II, 348-349. Morse, *Geography*, 418, also gives biting and gouging but neither writer actually saw such a fight, and the only time I found anything like it was in DC, I, 48, "pliant's nose was bit."

[53] W, 6XX (50), 17. In addition to this account by Lavinia, Robertson's daughter, see *ibid.*, 32S, 313-340—the story of Andrew Castleman.

the fierce general-purpose, bear-baiting, Indian-trailing-hunting dogs kept by most settlers. Some families, even as late as 1800, had between twelve and fifteen.[54]

The other help came from the riderless horses, freed when the men treed. They dashed back toward the safety of the fort, but unable to get in, ran round and round the walls. Many of the Indians, more horse conscious than bloodthirsty, began to catch horses instead of attempting to scale the fort walls. The troubles of the other party down by the branch may also have checked them, for what they had planned as an easy surprise attack from ambush, had turned into a bloody battle. The white men were, with the help of the dogs, able in a few minutes to begin a gradual movement back to the fort.

It was a slow and bloody business that took more than an hour, each step marked with heroism: "Amongst those who escaped towards the fort, was Edward Swanson, who was so closely pursued by an Indian warrior as to be overtaken by him. The Indian punched him with the muzzle of his gun, and pulled trigger, when the gun snapped. Swanson laid hold of the muzzle, and wringing the lock to one side, spilled the priming from the pan. The Indian looked into the pan, and finding no powder in it, struck him with the gun barrel, the muzzle foremost; the stroke not bringing him to the ground, the Indian clubbed his gun, and striking Swanson with it near the lock, knocked him down. At this moment John Buchanan . . ."[55] And so on with the rest of the story, only one of many in which one man risked his life to save another.

Not all were saved; some say as many as seven were killed on the spot, and at least four of the wounded died; Zachariah White died that night, Alexander Buchanan died later, and Isaac Lucas, who managed to get back to the fort, died some days later, and of James Leeper it was said, "could he have had a good surgeon he would have recovered."[56]

The loss of life in this, referred to as The Battle of the Bluff, was much less than that already suffered at other places on the Cumberland, notably on Red River, but "after this battle a sudden panic seized the people. Most —despairing of being able to accomplish the enterprise of settling the country—determined to remove to Kentucky as a place of comparative safety."[57]

[54] Williams, *Travels*, Schweinitz, "Report," 518. See also W, 12CC, 44, and *ibid.*, 32S, 243, 260, for feats of hunting and Indian-fighting dogs.
[55] Ramsey, *Tennessee*, 453.
[56] W, 32S, 314.
[57] W, 6XX (50), 17.

Robertson always considered [58] the year 1781 as the worst of the fifteen years of Indian warfare on the Cumberland. That year, as in the previous year, crops on the northern side of the river grew without much destruction from the Indians, but little was grown around French Lick but cotton and garden stuff, "for the women could not milk the cows or the men go and get a little wood but what they would be shot at," [59] and "that year having no bread and having to hunt their meat they suffered a great deal."

Big game was scarce and usually miles away, but the river and the woods were still filled with food. There were squirrel, turkey, and bear which continued quite plentiful on the borders of the settlements in Middle Tennessee until past 1800, also fish, and a good variety of fruits and nuts —a few bushels of chestnuts would fend off starvation for several people during lean weeks when there was no corn for bread. However, all these were for the most part useless. Years later, an old-timer remembered how three soldiers were once sent to pick wild strawberries; one or possibly two would have watched while the other picked. Matthew Turpin [60] was killed picking mulberries, one of the young Ramseys badly wounded as he gathered pawpaws, and wild cherries and grapes brought death to others.

Few ventured to do such things, or got back to the fort if they did venture. Most ran away as did the Donelsons who left Mansker's Station for the comparative safety of Kentucky sometime in the spring of 1781, and are said to have lived at Davis's Station near Colonel William Whitley's place at present-day Brodhead.[61] Mansker's Station withstood a siege, then all decided to leave. Kaspar, his wife—he had no children—and his brother George with the other relatives and neighbors lived at French Lick for more than a year.[62] Kaspar was forced to stop farming, but he never stopped fighting; mostly he used a British musket, and though he was once wounded in the back while in the woods, he could always say, "I gave the vile creatures a pounce," [63] and he did—many pounces. Shortly after

[58] NCR, XXII, 790–791, Robertson to Daniel Smith, July 7, 1789. Robertson had by this date been twice wounded, lost two sons, two brothers, and numerous kin and neighbors but he could still comment that the Indians were the worst they had been since 1781.

[59] W, 6XX (50), 17.

[60] W, 32S, 307.

[61] Mary Purnell (Mrs. John III or Capt. John) Donelson stated, W, 32S, 309–310, the family lived there until 1785.

[62] W, 6XX (50), 19. There is agreement that Mansker left French Lick Station in 1783 and rebuilt his old fort, but the date of the burning of the first is a disputed point; it happened after the Donelsons left for Kentucky.

[63] W, 32S, 345.

he left it, Kaspar's Station was ransacked and burned, leaving only three forted stations in all of Middle Tennessee.

Frederick Stump managed to keep on farming. His place was not completely destroyed, but the Indians killed his oldest son, once chased him three miles, and from time to time burned various of his outbuildings, but he hung on.[64] Stump, like the Mulherrin and Buchanan men, who had brought their wives and children down from Kentucky in the fall of 1780,[65] had made up his mind to stay, and so he stayed though this meant living most of the time at Eaton's.

On Christmas night of 1781 William Ramsey from Culpeper County, Virginia, came with family, slaves, and pack horses, bringing blacksmith tools and other possessions, arriving at Eaton's when "frolicking and dancing were going on in the different cabins." [66] Some may have danced with not overfull stomachs; food continued scarce. Many were killed while hunting, but men, prodded by the hunger of their children, repeatedly risked their lives to do it. John Cockrill, who had come in the Donelson flotilla and shortly afterward married Robertson's widowed sister, Ann Johnston, later wrote of how he fed his family—his wife and her three little daughters—Mary, Elizabeth, and Charity.[67]

"It had been three days that we had very little to eat," he wrote. "As it was, the children were following their mother about the cabin and saying, 'Mother, I'm hungry.' I said, 'I can't stand that; I must have meat or die.' So I took my gun and started. My wife said, 'You better come back; you'll never see the fort again.' I said, 'The children are starving: I must go. I can see as good as the Indians and I will not follow any path; so they can't waylay me.' I went out and killed a bear and cut off his skin and, with most of his meat wrapped up in the skin, took it on my back and carried it home. The children came around as my wife was helping to cut it up. They said, 'Give me a little; I've had nothing for three or four days,' and others said, 'Divide it out; only save me some for tomorrow.' Others said, 'My children are starving.' I said, 'I will go out again tomorrow. Divide it out.' " [68]

[64] W, 31S, 59. It was not, according to this account, until the fall of 1781 that Stump and others in the neighborhood had to "collect at Eatons," that had "35 guns." Stump's increasing prosperity is attested to by early court records: DC, I, 69, permission granted for an ordinary, though he had been putting up travelers since 1780; and *ibid.*, 107, permission to erect a mill on White's Creek.

[65] W, 30S, 296.

[66] W, 5S, 61.

[67] These children are mentioned in the 1784 will of their Uncle Mark, killed without issue, though married, DW, I, 53.

[68] Reprinted by permission of the copyright owners, Mesdames Gertrude Williams Miller and Martha Williams Jan De Beur, from *Tennessee During the Revolutionary*

Time and again such men as Robertson, Cockrill, the old Long Hunters Kaspar Mansker and Thomas Sharpe Spencer, the Drakes, Ramseys and others risked their lives, not in fighting Indians, but merely in doing a thing that had to be done—hunting a cow that had calved,[69] or escorting a widow to visit her son dying as her husband had died, of Indian wounds and away from home.[70]

These things for some went on for fifteen years. The long warfare in Middle Tennessee was vastly different from that in Kentucky where station after station surrendered with large numbers of men going meekly away as prisoners. Nor was the warfare in the Kentucky Bluegrass of long duration; the last fairly large invasion was in 1782,[71] only seven years after the first settlement, and for much of this time Clark's soldiers were in the Illinois or at The Falls, now and then making forays north of the Ohio.

The Cumberlanders struggled along with no help from any source, save for a few men sent out around 1790, and these never got paid; scouts and guards, when paid at all, were paid by the settlers. Yet, no station ever surrendered and in all the scalpings, wounds, and deaths only two white men were ever taken alive by the Indians. One of these escaped and came home; the other, Samuel Martin, stayed ten or eleven months, and in 1782 came back "elegantly dressed including silver spurs," [72] and with two valuable horses; and since he was the first and only man who "had profited by Indian captivity," it was only natural he should "be whispered about."

The southern Indians knew how to treat a brave warrior from the opposing side; they stuck him full of fat pine splinters until he bristled like a porcupine, and amid many other refinements of torture featuring red-hot gun barrels they set these on fire, though he of course lived for many hours after the splints had burned into his body.[73]

Martin's fate is not recorded; and we know only of one Dulain who left a wounded man in the woods that he was ridden out of the settlement on a

---

War by Judge Samuel Cole Williams, published and copyrighted by the author, Nashville, 1944, p. 177.

[69] This was Samuel Barton, first settler and member of the first court of Davidson County, and probably the man for whom Barton's Creek was named; for his cow see W, 32S, 318–319; according to this account he also was saved by his dogs.

[70] W, 31S, 196, is the account of how in 1794 Thomas Sharpe Spencer saved the life of Mrs. Anthony Bledsoe, riding out to visit her mortally wounded son, Thomas, engaged to be married; her husband had already been killed.

[71] This was the Battle of Blue Licks, and though there were after this date many small-scale forays and a good many deaths, Central Kentucky or the Bluegrass was quite safe.

[72] Haywood, *C & P*, 122.

[73] Byrd, *Writings*, 161.

rail,[74] for they had a little saying, "It's a bad man who brings home bad news." [75] All in all the warfare in the Cumberland settlements was shaped to some extent by experiences on other borders, notably East Tennessee, for the Robertsons, Eatons, and several others who held the settlement together had spent several years there. East Tennessee men did not surrender.

Years later one wrote of how he felt about the business. During this period he and a companion got separated while hunting; the other man was killed by a party of Chickamauga before either man knew there were Indians about. The living man whom the Indians had not seen stood behind a tree and debated. He could stay there, safe, for the Indians had with them no dogs trained to trail white men, and from their careless actions they showed they thought the dead man had been alone. The young man thought a time, then walked over and gave himself up. "I couldn't face the women," he wrote. He was a coward not to go back when men were needed so, but still he knew, standing there thinking, that he no longer had a home, or a place in his own world as a man among other men. It cost him a deal of suffering and around three years' captivity but he was eventually able to return as a man.[76]

This hard code of Tennessee was in sharp contrast to Kentucky where one fruitless campaign above the Ohio followed another, and earlier the surrendering stations. Boone's surrender of the salt makers made Boone a hero to more than one historian; but we can almost hear the angry scratching of Bailey Smith's pen and his hard angry breathing as he wrote from the Holston to Clark in the Illinois: "a few days ago there Came an Express from kentuckey and informed me of captain Daniel Boone with Twenty Eight men being taken prisoners from the Salt Licks on licking creek without Sheding one drop of blood." [77]

Still, the Cumberland warfare, different as it was from that in Kentucky, was not like that of East Tennessee where time and again bands of well trained, well horsed men, led usually by Sevier, made a quick dash against an Indian town, and always returned—triumphant. There were not on the Cumberland, men enough for dashes, had anybody wanted to dash. John Rains and the younger Castlemans who came down from Kentucky around

[74] W, 32S, 435.
[75] Kercheval, *Virginia*, 88. Possibly the best example of the truth of this is the time Simon Girty went to Morgan with the news that everybody save himself was dead of Indians on the "Shawanoe."
[76] W, 28S, 18.
[77] I, VIII, 40, March 7, 1778.

1783 [78] sometimes went on forays into Indian territory, but this was forbidden, both by the weak federal government that feared to antagonize Spain, and by Robertson who tried to be law-abiding. There were in all the fifteen years only two offensive actions; Coldwater in 1787 and Nickojack in 1794, both organized by Robertson,[79] both successful, and in both the men went unpaid, but not unfed. This was done by the Cumberlanders.

In spite of the almost constant warfare, with practically all first settlers who managed to survive having more than one close relative killed, the Cumberlanders never forgot their real business, and this to settle the land. And for all the dead, wounded, captured, and scalped children, homes burned, livestock destroyed and stolen, they feared the Indian far less and consequently hated him less than we today fear and hate our enemies.

Indian warfare colored all physical aspects of their lives, but morally the pioneers were but little degraded. Take scalps they did, but the cry for mass extermination and mass removal of the Indians did not come from the pioneers. There was then among men on the frontier, a greater respect for human beings in general than we know today. A man was always a man even though an enemy. "I hated to see him take the oath," a Whig in East Tennessee wrote of a Tory who, blindfolded, a rope around his neck, hands tied behind him, could still have life and liberty if he would pledge allegiance to the American cause. The Tory, as did unnumbered and forgotten others, swore allegiance to King George, and then sprang off the tail gate of the wagon so his fellow prisoners would not be forced to hang him.[80]

These same men who admired the ability of the Tories to stand up and die like men with no sniveling, knew what it was to do just that, for many were Scotch or Scotch-Irish. There was behind them a long tradition of

[78] The Castlemans came originally from the same region as did Kaspar Mansker, the South Fork of the Potomac; and "old Jacob" lived for a time at Red Stone, Old Fort in Pennsylvania, from there went to Harrodsburg, and then at "Robertson's solicitation," came down to Middle Tennessee in 1783 where he lived in a cabin "between the fort and the spring." This from W, 1S, 59–60, is only one of numerous references to the Castlemans. See also *ibid.*, 31S, 325. Old Jacob was a brother of Benjamin, though neither was the only one of that name; sons and nephews were often named after uncles and fathers. In January of 1783 they applied to Lincoln County for the 400 acres of land they had been told they could get; the request was of course denied; see LC, I, 8, 13; they remained in Kentucky sometime longer, for at the June Court, *ibid.*, 18, Jacob was appointed constable for the district of Harrodsburg.

[79] There are in the Draper Manuscripts numerous accounts of these expeditions, each gives details known to one man, and none is so comprehensive as those of Ramsey; see his *Tennessee*, 464–474, for Coldwater, and *ibid.*, 608–616, for Nickojack.

[80] W, 28S, 34–36. This was only one of many such incidents in Col. Campbell's Tory War.

men, and women too, who had died, often horrible deaths, worse than those inflicted by the Indians, because they would not say the right words. It was natural for such men to admire many of the Indian leaders.

There was often much to admire, but in thinking of the Creek, Chickasaw, Cherokee, and Chickamauga one should not envision Stone Age men with feathers in their hair, slipping through the woods and armed with bow and arrow. These tribes [81] were to begin with an agricultural people, growing much corn; they had known better homes, food, clothing, and shelter than did many of their contemporaries in Europe or for the matter of that, better than many white homes that today occupy their old lands.

They had suffered much from the white man, but along with smallpox, rum, and other offerings of white civilization, they had adopted many of its ways. The Cherokee, Creek, and Chickasaw were rapidly becoming nations of farmers with many fine horses and cattle. Some southern Indians now built their homes of logs as did the white man, used many of his tools and weapons, and quite often wore his clothing. Their leaders could usually understand if not speak English, and several were at least half white. One reads of "Tom Tunbridge's step son," John Walker, George Field, "John Watts, the bloody fellow," and after 1783 "McGillivray of the Creeks."

John Watts was described as a large portly, noble-looking Indian, a "generous honorable enemy." [82] Dragging Canoe killed a very great many whites, but one of his enemies wrote in admiration of how the disgruntled chief shot one of his own men dead as soon as he discovered the warrior was trying to molest a captured white woman.[83] Hard pressed as the Cum-

---

[81] Bartram, *Travels*, Part IV, 483–522, is a generalized discussion of the southeastern tribes as Bartram found them in 1775–1776, though throughout his work there are other descriptions such as that of his visit to the Cherokee, where in a trader's home the Indian wife gave him for breakfast, venison, hot corn cakes, "excellent butter and cheese." In his summing up of dress he found "sometimes a ruffled shirt of fine linen." Williams, *Travels*, 259–265, "Brother Martin Schneider's Report of His Journey to the Upper Cherokee Towns, 1783–1784," is an intimate glimpse of the Cherokee at home. Another, *ibid.*, 459–492, is contained in Schweinitz, "Report," who in 1799 visited the Overhill Cherokee with the hope of establishing a mission. See also, *ibid.*, Baily, "Tour 1797," 380–390, for a 1797 account. Adair, *American Indian*, written before the Revolution, tells much of the influence of European cultures; about the only things in addition to food the Chickasaw rejected were trousers and mills. The Cherokee were particularly interested in improving their agriculture; when in 1776 they captured Mrs. Bean of East Tennessee they told her they were taking her so she could teach their womenfolks how to make butter and cheese, Ramsey, *Tennessee*, 157.

[82] W, 30S, 320–321.

[83] W, 30S, 321. Doublehead was another described as "large, ferocious, wiley."

berlanders were, few became so brutalized as to see the Indian as no more than a fellow brute, to be exterminated on sight. An Indian was still a man. He was never outlawed. An enemy could come with a flag of truce to Robertson on some business such as returning captive children, and need no guard, knowing he would neither be jeered nor shot at,[84] nor did the old ones in their many accounts of Indian warfare ever stoop to epithets. Chickasaw were, after the treaty of 1783, often in and out of the settlements, and two young Seviers, cousins, were killed because they mistook a group of enemy Indians for friends.[85]

There was still, even after the United States was born, a lingering sense of chivalry, a feeling for fair play, even in Indian warfare. The paid informer was unknown, and the turncoat never idolized or even respected. One of the pilots who led the troops to Nickojack in 1794 was Dick Findlestone, a half-breed trader, who, weary of the continuing murders of the whites, came and told Robertson of further plots and offered his services as guide. He had married into the tribe, and though his wife and children were unhurt in the attack, Parson John Kirkwell, a member of the expedition, wrote, "a wicked man for thus destroying his own people." [86]

Most men were killed while going about their business, this, to farm and build a forted station and stout log house; without these their guns would have been useless, and sources indicate it was the musket and the blunderbuss that saved the forts on the Cumberland. The long range and accuracy of the rifle were useless when hundreds of Indians rushed the fort walls, but a big musket loaded willy-nilly with pewter spoons, broken teakettles, and rifle balls was, at close range, effective as today's sawed-off shotgun.

Most of the men who owned anything at all, for some came as hired men with little save their clothing, had at least one gun and usually two, a rifle and a musket. Like the rifles, the muskets were of various shapes and sizes; some cannon-like such as Valentine Sevier's big brass blunderbuss [87] which, because of its powerful kick, he kept fastened to a block of wood; others used the British musket as did Mansker, loaded sometimes with a whole handful of rifle balls, other times with buckshot.

[84] There are many references to Indian visits to James Robertson; see in particular NCR, XIX, 739, and *ibid.*, XVII, 91–92.
[85] Ramsey, *Tennessee*, 596–597.
[86] W, 32S, 270–271.
[87] The time most often mentioned was the siege of Valentine Sevier's Station in 1794, W, 32S, 206. He filled his "big brass blunderbuss" with spoons, etc., anything he could grab, for the Indians were killing his children; the kick of the gun knocked out two of his teeth.

Rifles, too, were of all shapes and sizes; even the Dechard, mentioned more than once, meant only that the rifle had been made by a man of that name who, during the time of the Revolution, manufactured rifles in Lancaster, Pennsylvania. The custom of buying the rifled barrel, then stocking and locking it, was fairly common. Jacob Castleman had, when he was killed, two rifles, two rifle barrels, four shot bags, "some powder and a piece of lead." [88]

Some of these things may have belonged to Jacob's dead sons or grandsons; the Castlemans were noted Indian fighters and many were killed; one of the greatest as well as the luckiest was Abraham,[89] who went on so many Indian-fighting forays, often with John Rains, the Indians nicknamed him "The Fool Warrior." [90] Still, death by Indians was so common that when one heard a man or woman had died they did not ask of what disease, but, "How did he get killed?"

Quite often a dead man meant two or three extra guns, and this may account for the comparative cheapness of guns; even "a rifled gun with silver mountings and the finest inlaid stock" sold in 1799 for only eighty dollars or less than a good horse.[91] Most cost between a fourth or a fifth of this amount, though the mere statement of a sum does not always mean a great deal. Many were the forms of currency used, but as a rule the county courts specified "hard money," when goods were sold to satisfy a debt or settle an estate. The shilling at this time was usually credited [92] at six to the dollar or nineteen to the pound which was valued at three and one-third dollars, but as few articles were standardized and those sold at auction, sometimes badly worn, the price means little. Edward Larrimore's [93] "rifle-gun" that sold sometime before 1784 brought four pounds ten shillings, or only four shillings more than his coat and waistcoat of hemp linen. The gun may have been old and worn, the coat and waistcoat new, but it is also possible that among the small circle of bidders, clothing was more in demand than guns. Most guns brought between ten and fifteen dollars or

[88] DW, I, 194. See also W, 32S, 320; he was the father of Abraham and Andrew. Typical of first settlers are James Freeland, DW, I, 16, "two riffle guns." James Harrod, *ibid.*, 16, "musket gun, smooth bore gun, rifle gun."
[89] W, 31S, 145.
[90] Ramsey, *Tennessee*, 599–603.
[91] Williams, *Travels*, Schweinitz, "Report," 495.
[92] Thwaites, *Travels*, III, Michaux, "Journal," 86. This was in 1796, and as the value of pound and shilling had varied colony by colony so did they in the early years vary on the Cumberland. Fries, *Records*, I, 263, gives several of these values in 1762. In North Carolina for example 8 shillings were worth one Spanish dollar, in neighboring Virginia only 5 shillings 8 pence equaled one Spanish dollar.
[93] DW, I, 6.

three to five pounds;[94] more than the average milk cow with calf, but considerably less than a good feather bed.

Another important item in Indian warfare was the bullet mold; these of course varied in size and quality; many men had small, single-pattern molds to match their rifles, while others were multiple-patterned, suitable for the guns of a whole station. Both types can still be seen in museums and often in private homes, and all, usually of brass, were expensive, for they were one of the few things the average blacksmith could not in a pinch make with ordinary blacksmithing tools. Nicholas Gentry's[95] set most probably had several molds for different calibers. It sold for the large sum of two pounds six shillings, or if measured in whiskey, eleven gallons at the price set by Davidson County Court in 1784.[96]

Bullets were growing longer, but most used on the Cumberland during the years of Indian warfare were, judging from the old molds, round. There were a few homemade cartridges in use during the Revolution,[97] and many merchants stocked ball, but early Cumberland inventories indicate that each man bought lead and used running powder, which he also made at times. Jacob Castleman was only one of many who left powder and lead; David Lucas[98] had two pounds of lead when killed, Thomas Brown[99] had twenty-five, and William Gower,[100] killed in the summer of 1780, left six pounds of powder and eight pounds of lead. The whole sold for six pounds; a good bit of money for a cow and calf at the same sale brought only six pounds, ten shillings. Still, this was considerably cheaper when measured in terms of day's wages than Henderson had got from Boone and others for powder in 1775—eight days' work for one pound.[101]

Many rifles from this period have survived; one can see in the Tennessee State Museum at Nashville John Buchanan's long rifle with full stock and hexagonal barrel, and also that of Robert Cartwright with its hickory ramrod. More famous than either, is that of William Whitley, now on display in his home. Colonel Whitley often chased and sometimes captured the

[94] AMS, I, Class V, Military Affairs, 45-75, has references to prices and parts for small arms during 1794-1795.
[95] DW, I, 7.
[96] DC, I, 26—4 shillings per gallon.
[97] NCR, XII, 470. Cartridges had long been known; *Regulations For the Prussian Infantry*, tr., London, 1754, contains in its directions for loading, references to cartridges, 31-33.
[98] DW, I, 45.
[99] DW, I, 308.
[100] DW, I, 175.
[101] Butler, *Kentucky*, 32.

parties of Indians that were forever killing and scalping travelers along the Kentucky Road, and in 1794 he and a large body of men "just happened" [102] to be around at the time of the Nickojack campaign and they all went with the Cumberlanders.

A man with a gun, a woman to load it, and a stockade wall in front of him could keep off Indians, but the gun was useless against the greatest threat to the settlers on the Cumberland and in Kentucky—the higher powers, sometimes a State Legislature, sometimes a land speculator, and often the two together. In August of 1781, James Robertson risked his life day in and day out by riding the more than six hundred miles, most of it through Indian infested country, to Salem, North Carolina. He hoped to find the Assembly in session, and place before this body a Petition [103] of the Cumberland Settlers, asking they be allowed to keep their land. The previous summer the North Carolina Assembly had granted the land that Zachariah White, William Neely, Edward Larrimore and dozens of others had lost their lives to keep, to the Revolutionary soldiers, and hence to any man with money enough to buy a soldier's land warrant.

James Robertson and a few others waited several weeks, but in all the turmoil of the Revolution the Assembly did not meet during the winter. He could not at this stage, when all were threatened with the loss of everything, afford to ask for help; instead he told the members he did meet that those on the Cumberland could hold the land against the Indians; and though he could not have been certain when he started home in January of 1782 that any white settler there was still alive he suggested that a county be created on the Cumberland.

[102] This expedition like that at Coldwater was against Federal orders, and great care had to be taken not to implicate Colonel Whitley. Ramsey, *Tennessee*, 609, tells how Sampson Williams went to Kentucky and persuaded Col. Whitley to come with a group of volunteers; Col. Whitley "arrived at the rendezvous," 610, but in Robertson's letter of explanation to William Blount, Governor of the Territory, we learn, 618, ". . . Col. Whitley arrived with about one hundred men . . . from Kentucky . . . saying they had followed a party of Indians . . . that they were determined to pursue to the Lower Town."

[103] NCR, XVI, 524-526, Martin Armstrong to General Sumner, Feb. 26, 1782.

CHAPTER XII

THE BARE ESSENTIALS

It was October 7, 1783,[1] and Haydon Wells who, in the winter of 1779–80, had come overland with the Stumps and Eatons, had so far lost only an eye to the Indians.[2] We know little of Haydon Wells, except that he was a good and respectable man,[3] living north of the Cumberland and at least sleeping at Eaton's Station, for it along with Freeland's and French Lick still hung on. There were by now several more men in the settlements than back in 1781. In the June just passed there had been 124 in the three stations named,[4] and more up at Mansker's, for he had returned to his old place, and was now rebuilding his station that would "remain strong." The only newcomers who had gone to the trouble and expense of putting up a station were the Mauldins and a few others, building over on Red River near the trail that went up to The Falls.[5]

Haydon Wells as he crossed the Cumberland at the old French Landing [6]

[1] DC, I, 2.

[2] W. 31S, 63.

[3] Haydon Wells had been a member of the elected "Committee of Notables" governing Middle Tennessee, at least for the first nine months of 1783, under the terms of the Cumberland Compact; see Putnam, *Tennessee*, 183.

[4] *Ibid.*, 182–200, gives this number as having voted in Eaton's, Freeland's, and Nashborough; nothing is said of a French Lick Station. My own feeling is that Nashborough was the more formal name of French Lick Station; Draper correspondents spoke of French Lick but not Nashborough.

[5] *Ibid.*, 182–200. W, 29S, 73, describes the station as having been on the road to Danville 18 miles from Mansker's, begun by Henry Rutherford, but completed by "Old Ambrose Mauldin and son moses" in 1784. Draper correspondents indicate there were in 1783 only three stations until Mansker rebuilt his.

[6] There is nothing in the official record to indicate that any road save those blazed out by the settlers on the way, had been cut by late 1783.

below Eaton's Station, then climbed the hill past Freeland's, and on up in the direction of French Lick Station, may, glancing now and then at a face new to him, have thought on all the great happenings in the wider world. Even hunters in far-off places knew by now the Revolution was ended, for back in corn-planting time the Continental Congress had ratified the provisional Treaty of Paris.

Fodder pulling and topping time were past, and soon would come corn gathering, but such fine words as peace and victory were not for the first settlers on the Cumberland, save in the business Haydon Wells was now on his way to attend to. The Continental Army was disbanded, and already some of the ex-soldiers were among the newcomers to the settlements. They had come to view the bounty promised by the State of North Carolina to her soldiers.

It had on paper sounded fine and noble—land for the soldiers. North Carolina of all the thirteen colonies had the most concern for what we today refer to as the "common man." A state of affairs that had somewhat worried William Byrd, but in North Carolina a man had continued to be very much a man, allowed to worship as he wished, welcomed as a settler regardless of religion or nationality. The abuses of Tryon's men on Lord Granville's Claim had been something of an exception, and were not a part of the overall policy of North Carolina. Those most hated by the Regulators such as Richard Henderson had taken the American side of the cause, and like other land speculators prospered more under Whig leadership than under that of the Tories.[7]

During the Revolution, most of the Whig leaders and particularly the officers had held the soldier of the line in high esteem. Running through the North Carolina records are the letters of officers, begging, forever begging for their men, occasionally explaining, "as the weather is bad and wet I ordered a gill of rum for each man immediately," and rum was scarce; or, "nothing can be more comfortable to the army than vegetables." [8] The North Carolina soldier of the Revolution, though suffering much, had never reached the sorry state of the Virginia private.

Colonel Davie had by hook and by crook got supplies for him; levies for beeves, hogs, and corn were laid on North Carolina counties, and they in turn levied farmers and merchants, who were paid in certificates. These were merely promises to pay, but all the bankrupt North Carolina Treas-

---

[7] It was for this reason that many Regulators took the Tory side in the Revolution; Smythe, *Tour*, I, 227–228, and many also felt bound by the oaths they had taken.

[8] NCR, XII, 456.

ury could offer. Horses, food, and anything else obtainable were confiscated from Tories, and these goods went to the soldiers.

It is doubtful if Haydon Wells, John Cockrill, Amos Eaton, and others on the Cumberland who knew what it was to fight on an empty belly, were angered when they in 1780 heard that the newly formed State of North Carolina planned to pay her soldiers, and those who had supplied them, with land, and the land might be on the Cumberland.[9] All little men of the old west, some from bitter firsthand experience, knew what had by 1780 happened to the fine land in the Kentucky Bluegrass. It was by that date pretty well gone to the land speculators, and men such as the Castlemans, John Kennedy, John Costillo,[10] and John Montgomery who had kept it from falling into the hands of the British, had got nothing,[11] nor did Virginia attempt to give even her officers any of the good land west of the mountains; hills and Barrens they might have, but not Bluegrass.

North Carolina, on the other hand, saved, at least on paper, the best for her officers and soldiers of the Continental Army, but the first settlers, though soldiers themselves or the widows of soldiers, were to get nothing. It was then that Robertson got up the Petition of the Inhabitants of Cumberland, and went in a vain attempt to place it before the North Carolina Assembly. In April of 1782 when the Assembly did meet, Robertson's friend, Martin Armstrong,[12] brought the Petition to the attention of the lawmakers; members of the House read it, referred it to a committee for study, and sent it to the Senate.[13]

Back on the Cumberland during the bloody, bitter summer of 1782 when the Indians destroyed the crops of those they could not kill, the settlers could only work and wonder while back east the North Carolina Assembly decreed what should be done with the land they had cleared and fenced. The lawmakers worked further on the Act for the Relief of the Officers and Soldiers, stipulating the amount of land each should get. Even a private

[9] NCR, XXIV, 338, Sect. V. This was but a preliminary bill for a boundary of land in East Tennessee, but judging from Martin Armstrong's letter, *ibid.*, XVI, 524-526, a few months later all eyes were turned on Middle Tennessee land.

[10] The Castlemans had served at Harrodsburg, the other two under Logan, Collins, *Kentucky, 1882*, II, 12.

[11] As early as 1779 Virginia set aside land for her soldiers; the strip included most of the Cumberland drainage in Kentucky, but what was not owned by the Cherokee and Chickasaw was Barrens or hilly. See for the Kentucky land mess in general, Marshall, *Kentucky*, 172-177, 185-187.

[12] NCR, XVI, 524-526, Martin Armstrong to Gen. Sumner, Feb. 26, 1782; the bill, *ibid.*, XXIV, 419-422, setting aside Middle Tennessee was passed the following spring; no copy of the petition Robertson took to North Carolina at this time has been found; we know of it only through this letter and Draper correspondents.

[13] NCR, XVI, 103-104.

who had served only a short term was to get one square mile—640 acres—that is at least on paper; a brigadier general got 12,000.[14]

Three men—Absolem Tatum, Isaac Shelby, and Anthony Bledsoe—good men, but no one of whom then lived on the Cumberland—were to lay off the great boundary of land set aside for the soldiers, and for their services each was to get 5,000 acres. Each surveyor who helped run the outside lines was to get 2,500, and though there were then surveyors on the Cumberland, notably James Robertson and James Mulherrin, the surveyors were not chosen from among the first settlers. Their work would not be dangerous, for they would be surrounded by chain carriers, markers, guards, and hunters, each of whom was to be paid in land; good jobs for the amount of work each demanded, and they would go to the man on the spot, and the spot was over the mountains in North Carolina. Even the hundred men who did nothing but guard [15] the others as they walked round the boundaries were to get 320 acres each.

Nor were Richard Henderson and company forgotten. Henderson's claim [16] had in North Carolina been declared illegal as it had been in Virginia, but both states rewarded him most liberally; from Virginia he got a giant tract of good land in the Green River Country, and from North Carolina 200,000 acres of as good land as there was in East Tennessee, wide bottoms with well timbered hills, some of it now covered with the lake formed by Norris Dam.

It was all a strange business, and stranger still were the matters concerning land that did not come before the North Carolina Assembly. Plans [17] were in 1782 being made to treat with the Chickasaw, and though most of the land the Chickasaw claimed and the settlers wanted belonged to North Carolina, it was men from Virginia, most eager for the treating, and it was in Virginia [18] by Patrick Henry that Joseph Martin, agent to the Cherokee in North Carolina, had been appointed.

Soldiers, Indians, land speculators, and officials were by 1782 reasonably certain of getting at least the promise of a piece of the giant political plum that had been made of Middle Tennessee and the western

[14] NCR, XXIV, 420.
[15] NCR, XXIV, 421.
[16] NCR, XVI, 151–152.
[17] The possibility of a Chickasaw Treaty was the subject of many letters from Benjamin Harrison to Joseph Martin, John Donelson, and Isaac Shelby; see in particular, W, 1XX, 53, 54, and 50, John Bowman's copy of a talk the Chickasaw gave Simon Burney, July 9, 1782, and NCR, XVI, 441–442, Benjamin Harrison of Virginia to Alexander Martin of North Carolina.
[18] W, 1XX, 29. Joseph Martin superseded Robertson.

lands. Only those who had actually settled the Cumberland, built stations and during the Revolution kept it from falling into the hands of Spain or England, were certain of nothing. Their petition had not been wholly rejected, but it had gained little support.[19]

Each man over twenty-one who had settled on the land before June 1, 1780, could have the right of preemption. This meant only he had the right to buy the land on which he lived, paying ten pounds per hundred acres.[20] Such a law was worse than useless. There were in the summer of 1782 only three stations in all of Middle Tennessee; even Kaspar was completely broken up and living at French Lick, and Stump was at least sleeping at Eaton's Station. The only bright spot in 1782 was that the first step had been taken toward the creation of a county on the Cumberland.

Every settler needed and wanted a county, less as a law enforcement agency than as a means of keeping his business straight. The Middle Cumberland was during its first three years of settlement, a part of Washington County, a giant sweep of land embracing most of what is now Tennessee, created in 1777 at the request of the settlers of East Tennessee, who soon had their own county seat at Jonesborough, but few men on the Cumberland could afford to travel the hundreds of miles through dangerous country just to record a stock mark, a mortgage, or a work contract.[21]

Seventeen eighty-two moved through death and hunger into 1783, and once more the Cumberland settlers must plant gardens, corn, cotton, flax, and tobacco, less and less certain the land they'd cleared and fenced would ever be their own. The North Carolina Assembly met again, but instead of doing anything for the settlers it created a land office,[22] not in Middle Tennessee as Robertson and the others had requested in their petition, but hundreds of miles away at Hillsborough. The land wasn't there, but the influence was, and for more than a year men in high places had had surveyors who would take their pay in land, searching out fine land for them. Thus, men who had never seen the Cumberland, slept by a camp fire, fought either the British or the Indians, were already planning to get great tracts of land west of the mountains.[23] Buying was easy. They had only to collect

---

[19] NCR, XIX, 633. See also for action in house, *ibid.*, XVI, 68.

[20] NCR, XXIV, 421. There was no separate law concerning the settlers, only a paragraph in the land bill for the soldiers.

[21] Washington County, Tenn., had been organized in 1778; Robertson was a member of the court, Ramsey, *Tennessee*, 181.

[22] NCR, XXIV, 478–482.

[23] In addition to the correspondence in W, IX, see NCR, XVI, 958–960. This long letter between ex-Gov. John Caswell—who following the fashion must have sworn "on the Holy Evangels of Almighty God" to fulfill his duties—and his son concern-

the warrants of soldiers, too poor to settle, and so much in need of all things
—food for their families or a horse for the spring plowing—they would dis-
pose of the useless warrant for whatever they could get. The merchant,
bankrupt from supplying the army, was another good source, but if a man
had influence enough, nobody questioned overmuch the source of his warrants.

Most tempting of all was the fine land in Middle Tennessee, all ready and
waiting with hundreds of acres cleared and even a few well fortified stations; rough, but a man could put up with such a life for a few weeks or
whatever time was needed to make certain of his land. He could then go
home again and live safe and snug, either moving out when the land was
safer from the Indians, or merely holding on to sell. Most of the men who
got rich out of Kentucky Bluegrass land never had to fight an Indian.[24]
The North Carolina lawmakers stipulated that only certain individuals—
notably the settlers—should be allowed preemptions or the privilege of
buying [25] a warrant in the boundary set aside for soldiers. The big loophole
was there was no law saying a settler with a preemption or a soldier with
an outright grant could not sell it.

The Assembly set aside a tract embracing all of what is now Middle
Tennessee with some left over, and in so doing quite accidentally granted
one part of the Petition of the Inhabitants of Cumberland, for they made it
into a county, Davidson, the first on the Cumberland. Such was the need
for this form of local government that County Court was functioning before the boundaries of the county were surveyed, or even the bill creating
it had been passed by the Senate of the North Carolina Assembly.[26] Thus
it happened that Haydon Wells, landless still but one-eyed, was on his way
to a home near French Lick; court was meeting there and Haydon had
business with it.

There was in life and land no certainty, Haydon may have mused, miss-

ing land is most revealing. Stockley Donelson, future brother-in-law of Andrew
Jackson, had already been appointed surveyor for Eastern Tennessee and was searching out good land for them all. Stockley's father, John II, was at this time still up in
Kentucky, not yet appointed; the letter also sheds light on surveying practices.
[24] Abernethy, *Three Frontiers*, 66–67, points out that most were there by 1795.
1795.
[25] NCR, XXIV, 483.
[26] Most historians, following Haywood, *C & P*, 124, say the commissioners came in
the fall of 1783; some undoubtedly did, but the bill concerning the soldiers' lands
was not finished until the spring of 1784, NCR, XXIV, 566–568, though Martin had
given his instructions to the surveyors the previous October, *ibid.*, XVI, 912. See also
for discussion, *ibid.*, XVI, 919, Dec. 8, 1783, and *ibid.*, XIX, 938, undated, but indicative of the spring of 1784.

ing the faces of men now dead. On the other hand there were things that went on unchanged by time or distance or revolutions. What, he may have wondered, had he been of a philosophical turn of mind, was the difference between North Carolina the Colony and North Carolina the State? Hundreds of years before in England and later Virginia and then the Carolinas, men had heard the same words that Haydon and other men converging on the new court were hearing now—county, justice of the peace, court, sheriff, bailiff, jury, jurors, whipping post.

The Revolution had changed no names, nor had it changed local government for the southerner. The set-up of county government would in Middle Tennessee be the same as it had been during colonial days in North Carolina.[27] The legislative bodies of both colonial Virginia and North Carolina had formed counties, levied taxes, appointed justices of the peace, decreed the size and shapes of courthouses, levied the poll tax and special taxes as needed such as that for the building of a courthouse; all with no by-your-leave from the citizens living in the newly created county.[28] The voters were allowed to elect, though not to nominate, members of the legislative body, who in turn dictated everything else.

White males over twenty-one, provided they were free men and able to satisfy the property qualifications, had, in addition to voting for members of the colonial legislative bodies, voted also for the lower-ranking officers in the musters and at times chosen their immediate superiors in a military campaign. They had had no direct voice in local government. The Revolution had come and gone; out of it were to come two things dear to the hearts of most borderers—the right of any free man to vote without regard to property qualifications, and separation of church and state; no longer would the German or Scotch-Irish borderer have to pay tax for the upkeep of a church in which he did not believe.[29] There was one other change, dear to the hearts of the few, hated by the many; under colonial land policy no man or company had been allowed to hold giant tracts of land indefi-

[27] Changes were made from time to time in such matters as the fees clerks were to receive, NCR, XXIV, 911, this in 1787, but there was no basic change in the county setup until the Second Constitution of Tennessee.

[28] Laws for the creation of counties varied in minor points; compare Davidson, NCR, XXIV, 540, 617, with Sumner, *ibid.*, 826–828, but in none did the citizens elect county officers.

[29] These reforms came for the most part several years after statehood; in Virginia, for example, Baptists continued to be jailed many years after the Revolution. Kentucky in waiving property qualifications in her first constitution was considered most liberal but Abernethy, *Three Frontiers*, 76–77, points out that this was done because the land titles in Kentucky were in such a mess the actual property owners could not be determined.

nitely, pay no taxes under the excuse the land belonged to the Indians, but at the same time have no settlers. There were in Virginia a few of the more influential who had, during colonial days, slipped around the law, but neither Crown nor colony had consistently followed a policy of encouraging and abetting the land speculator at the expense of the settler.[30] Bad titles were practically unknown.

There were, mostly from Kentucky, with some from the Cumberland, bitter complaints of the new land policy, but there is no record that Haydon Wells or anybody else on the Cumberland complained of the make-up of county court, or marveled at the strangeness of that institution—the newly created county, which, different from most things in life, grew smaller as it grew older, and the more affluent and influential its settlers [31] and the larger their numbers, the more quickly would come the decline in size. Many such as John Rains who had come to the Cumberland from the New River settlements in western Virginia could remember when one county, Augusta, had embraced all of what men were now calling Kentucky. Davidson County, no different from the others, was beginning life with fewer people than most,[32] but better than five thousand square miles of land. Legally the boundaries began on the North Carolina–Virginia line at the point where the Cumberland first crossed it, or several miles north of present-day Celina; it then went south fifty-five miles, turned west to strike the Tennessee River, then followed the river back to the North Carolina–Virginia border.[33] The interesting thing about Davidson County in 1783 was that most if not all of it belonged to the Indians; nobody had yet made any treaty with the Chickasaw, and it was some years before the Cherokee claim to land south of the Cumberland east of a point on the river forty miles above Nashville was relinquished.[34]

[30] Large grants were given, but always on the condition that the grantee must in so many years get settlers, or show cultivation of 3 acres out of every 50. See Abernethy, *Three Frontiers*, 40. If the grantee did not get settlers, his grant reverted to the Crown; see Beverly, *Virginia*, 225–227.

[31] The small counties in the Kentucky Bluegrass not only made for convenience, but multiplied the jobs and appointments.

[32] The actual number of people, both settlers and visitors, in Davidson County or Middle Tennessee as it actually was, is not known.

[33] NCR, XXIV, 540, and *ibid.*, XVI, 912.

[34] This boundary was reaffirmed at the Treaty of Hopewell in 1785, NCR, XVII, 583—forty miles above Nashville. Mrs. Gertrude Morton Parsley, Reference Librarian, State Library Division, Tennessee State Library and Archives, by means of a detail map of the Cumberland located this point in present-day Wilson County, a few miles below the mouth of Cedar Creek. Everything south of the Cumberland above this point belonged to the Cherokee, including most of present-day Wayne County with Stockton's Valley, but Virginia permitted the land to be sold, and even in Tennessee

The lower house of the North Carolina Assembly had, meeting at Hillsborough in April, settled most other matters for the new county, including the appointment of eight justices. Only two of these, James Robertson and Samuel Barton, wounded when hunting his cow, were first settlers on the Cumberland. Three others, Anthony Bledsoe, Daniel Smith, and Thomas Molloy, did not settle until some months after the meeting of the first court, and as James Robertson was in North Carolina, only four justices met to form the new court of Davidson. These were Isaac Bledsoe, who had come out in the spring and would for the next several months live with Kaspar Mansker, Isaac Lindsay and F. Prince, both newcomers, and Samuel Barton.[35] There was nothing unusual about a county court sitting with half the justices it was supposed to have; it was, to begin with, a self-perpetuating body; if members died, moved away, or declined to serve, the remainder of the court could appoint others in their stead.[36]

Even one justice of the peace, or JP as he was later called, was a form of neighborhood father, exercising a very great deal of power. He could "bind over to good behaviour—whore makers, fathers of bastards, cheats, idle vagabonds, night walkers, eavesdroppers, men haunting bawdy houses with women of bad fame, or men keeping such women." He was exempt from military duty, but could perform marriage ceremonies, take a deposition regarding loss or theft that could substitute as a sworn statement in court, and two judges sitting together could hail before them and fine "a single woman with child." [37]

The justices of the peace, meeting together four times a year, formed the county court, and in the early years on the Cumberland this court exercised a very great deal of power, even trying John Montgomery, ex Long Hunter and officer under Clark, for treason against Spain.[38] A superior

---

the boundary was disregarded. Daniel Smith's 1796 map of Carey's Atlas, Clements Library, shows a straight boundary east of the Cumberland, not following the river until near present-day Burnside.

[35] DC, I, 1. See also Ramsey, *Tennessee,* 494.

[36] DC, I, 171. On this occasion Daniel Smith and Isaac Lindsay, who had also been appointed trustees of Nashville, declined to serve. The remaining three trustees—Samuel Barton, Thomas Molloy, and James Shaw, the first two also county justices—appointed Joel Rice and David Hay.

[37] John Haywood, *The Duty and Authority of Justices of the Peace,* Nashville, 1809, pp. 176, 254, 258. Judge Haywood's work was one of the earliest attempts to define the duties of justices of the peace; the whole framework of local government under which the first settlers lived was based on tradition and custom, much of it old in England when Virginia was settled.

[38] DC, I, 5. This was in connection with Colbert's Gang, a colorful bunch of river pirates on the Mississippi, working out of Chickasaw Territory, and troublesome to Spanish as well as to American traders. Montgomery was acquitted.

court,[39] roughly corresponding to today's circuit court, was not organized in Middle Tennessee until 1788 when Judge John McNairy and his young friend Andrew Jackson came.

Every county had to have a clerk to keep the minutes, and enter all records—a stock mark or an inventory—and as each person who entered a record paid a fee, the clerk's office was a most lucrative one.[40] Micah Taul, first clerk of Wayne County, Kentucky, a place of several hundred people but far less wealth than any county in Middle Tennessee, earned around $1,000 a year,[41] an awful lot of money for a sixteen-year-old appointee from the Kentucky Bluegrass when measured in three cents a pound beef and twenty-five cents a gallon whiskey. It is doubtful if Haydon Wells or any of the observers were surprised to hear the clerk's job went, not to one of the first settlers, but to another newcomer, Andrew Ewing. There would have been general approbation when the job of sheriff fell to Daniel Williams,[42] who had come in 1779 with the Buchanans, and had many times shown his courage during an Indian attack, for the job of sheriff was a good one, paying also on a fee basis. The sheriff collected bad debts, and performed all manner of duties from whippings to brandings for all of which the individual must pay a fee.[43]

One of the most lucrative jobs in any new county was that of entry taker, for all men who wanted land had to enter a claim and pay a fee. Most bystanders no doubt saw it as nothing more than natural that this good job should go to a member of the court, Samuel Barton. Once the land claim [44]

[39] NCR, XXIV, 766–767. This was the act of establishment; the court did not function until almost two years later.

[40] Many laws were passed relative to the fees of clerks; the high fees for all needed services had been one of the complaints of the Regulators, but they remained high. NCR, XXIV, 911, states the fees for 1787, much lower than formerly, but even so a clerk was allowed 2 shillings for each "copy sheet" of deposition he recorded; this, around half a long day's labor, was a hardship on a poor farmer, trying to prove land ownership; cases like that of Michael Stoner required many pages of depositions.

[41] RK, XXVII, No. 79, "The Memoirs of Micah Taul" (cited hereafter as Taul, "Memoirs"), 14. He was clerk of both the county or court of pleas and quarter-sessions as it was often known and the district or superior court. It was common in both Kentucky and Tennessee to give several appointments to the same man.

[42] DC, I, 1. See also W, 3XX (11), 2. Daniel was brother of Sampson.

[43] NCR, XXIV, 398–401, is a 1781 law relative to the fees most officers mentioned here should receive; a sheriff for example got 8 shillings for an arrest, and 5 shillings 4 pence for putting a person in the stocks; whippings, etc., paid accordingly, while the collection of debts was done on a percentage basis. Gray, *Bishop*, 164–183, though he was not given the job until 1805, is a good picture of the duties of under-sheriffs or constables such as he.

[44] The highest entry fee found was that in the Cumberland Compact—12 pounds. In general the Revolution brought a decline in entry fees; in 1780, NCR, XXIV, 314–316, the entry fee was 4 pounds, registering the deed 3 pounds. In 1781, *ibid.,*

was entered, the land must be surveyed; Anthony Bledsoe who already had two appointments, was given another, that of surveying at the local level, but as two were needed James Mulherrin who had helped build French Lick Station, got one of these.[45] Surveyed, the landholding in order to be entirely legal, must be recorded with the Registrar of Deeds, also for a fee, to be paid in money. The job of registrar [46] was thus a lucrative one, but neither hazardous nor hard, and went to another member of the court and newcomer, F. Prince.

It is doubtful if Haydon Wells or any other first settler was much given to the use of such words as democracy, liberalism, and equality. Still, there was behind the settlers on the Cumberland quite a long tradition of what we now call democracy, or at least certain aspects of it, for never at any time did anybody make an attempt to equate democracy with economic security. The right of any freeman to vote without regard to property qualifications had not been a part of North Carolina or Virginia law during colonial days, but this right had been exercised on many occasions all along the borders, particularly in organizing military expeditions. Another mark of democracy, widely used, was the petition; [47] in both Virginia and North Carolina it served often as the voice of the voiceless—slaves and women, even the wives and widows of Tories.

The right to express an opinion of any free white male able to vote had

400, the entry fee dropped to 8 shillings, but remained the same regardless of acreage—10,000 or 50.

[45] The surveying fee had also dropped, but chiefly on paper, for the common practice in both Kentucky and Tennessee was to pay the surveyor in land, one-fourth to one-half, depending on quality and acreage; the larger and richer, the smaller the proportion that was demanded. See W, 29S, 63–68, an account concerned chiefly with Col. Henry Rutherford who surveyed for James Robertson, it gives many details of surveyors and surveying practices. See also NCR, XXIV, 316; this 1780 law stipulated 12 pounds as the fee for surveying 300 acres, and 20 shillings for each further 100 acres. In 1781, *ibid.*, 400, the surveying fee dropped to shillings 16 and 2 for the boundaries above.

[46] The registrar was paid by the copy sheet; a man with a smallish boundary of poor land strung along the head of a creek with a dozen corners paid more than a man with a nice square of rich level land with only four corners. All of these jobs could be farmed out, usually to apprentices who worked for nothing but their keep and the experience; see Taul, "Memoirs," 8.

[47] The petition, particularly to the king, had long been used in England, and though it gradually declined in use in the colonies, was still often seen during and immediately after the Revolution, while the petition signed by many male citizens such as the Watauga Petition continued to be used to some extent; see NCR, XIX, 942–943, a British wife petitions for her Tory husband; *ibid.*, 596, Mary Moody, widow, asks for support for her family; *ibid.*, 151, petition of Miss Mary Jones, and *ibid.*, 931–935, "Petition of sundry inhabitants of Hillsborough for Thomas Hunt of tender years—under sentence of death for horse stealing." The petitioners had heard his trial and did not think him guilty.

been taken pretty much for granted during the first three years on the Cumberland. The first known election was held by the Eaton party late in the winter of 1779 when they elected officers before going into camp for the winter.[48] The Cumberland Compact, though devoted chiefly to methods of buying land and in many ways a totalitarian document,[49] still provided that triers, or men who would roughly correspond to justices of the peace, should be chosen by vote in each station. No qualifications for voting were given, and the Compact was open to any free white male willing to sign. There is no record that the provisions for government of this document were ever carried out; the Indians destroyed the planned stations, and the whole thing was soon declared illegal, but democracy prevailed on the Cumberland. The petitions Robertson carried over the mountains were signed by rich and poor alike, and when an informal parley was held, such as that at French Lick in April of 1781, each man gave his opinion.

All white male Cumberland settlers had in the June just passed been asked to vote on a matter that was at times a topic of hot debate. This was the proposed treaty with the Chickasaw; should it be held that year, 1783, in the region of French Lick. The Virginians were eager, hoping for the land the Chickasaw held in what is now West Kentucky, and as much more as they could get. Governor Benjamin Harrison of Virginia had written many times to the three men he had chosen for the job—Isaac Shelby, Joseph Martin, the Indian agent appointed by Patrick Henry, and John Donelson, Sr.

James Robertson was opposed. The reasons he gave were that there was not enough food for so many men as would come to a treaty and there was also the danger the Chickasaw warriors would spy out the locations of the various stations, learn the weakness of the settlement as a whole, and go home only to return as warriors.[50] Robertson, different from a very great many then coming into power, was never a man to put personal glory ahead of general good; but any unbiased observer, knowing the circumstances, would undoubtedly have wondered why James Robertson himself had not been chosen to treat with the Indians. He was actually on the land;

---

[48] W, 32S, 372.

[49] The Cumberland Compact, Putnam, *Tennessee*, 94–100, was totalitarian in that it stipulated the signer agreeing to buy land should have no recourse to any other court, but it was also democratic in that it made use of the recall—both entry takers and triers, these last corresponding to justices of the court, could be recalled by popular vote.

[50] Putnam, *Tennessee*, 182–200, is a full discussion of the pros and cons, and how each station voted.

he had had more experience in dealing with Indians than all three of the men named by Benjamin Harrison, and he would have been a representative of North Carolina. Why, Robertson may have wondered, were Virginians coming to treat on land claimed by North Carolina? In the old days each colony had treated with the Indians and it was not until after the French and Indian War that the southern colonies together had had an Indian Agent. He may have reasoned, too, that Indian treaties were more properly the province of the Continental Congress. He asked for a vote and lost. The voters from the three stations, for no one reported from Mansker's or Mauldin's, were overwhelmingly in favor of the treaty; only the station where Robertson then lived, Freeland's, was opposed. Many of those who voted would have been newcomers and mere visitors able to go home again if things got too bad, but even first settlers at Eaton's were in favor of it, reasoning no doubt that any try at peace was worth the trouble.

All such democratic procedures were finished now. It would be many years before the little man in Kentucky or Tennessee, or the rest of the south for the matter of that, would vote again on any matter save militia officers and representatives to the State and Federal lawmaking agencies and indirectly for President. Men such as Kaspar Mansker and George Freeland, who had built stations, were not in 1783 even allowed to say who should be the constable or colonial version of policeman. County Court appointed these;[51] only Edward Swanson, who had made the exploratory journey with Robertson and returned as a first settler, and appointed at Freeland's, was an old-timer; the names of the other appointees are new, never mentioned by the old ones who wrote or told Mr. Draper of early days and Indians.

Haydon Wells may have wished for a job, an appointment of some kind, but at this time almost nothing[52] went to the men who had come as first settlers. It is possible that most felt the slight but little. They had a far bigger hurt; the catastrophe coming upon them was a tidal wave, making a man forget the rain. As the law now stood in the North Carolina Assem-

[51] DC, I, 3.

[52] Practically all the first settlers named are well represented in county records—serving on grand juries, as appraisers of estates, viewing roads, acting as road supervisors. Amos Eaton, for example, though he twice built a station and was a man of prominence and property, and well connected—his wife a sister of Anthony Bledsoe—is never mentioned in North Carolina Records, but see DC, I, 15, 24, 29, 31, 36, 59, 82, 115. The same is true in varying degrees of Obediah Terrell, Thomas Sharpe Spencer, Humphrey Hogan, and most others as long as they survived. The first Davidson County Grand Jury, not chosen until January 1784, *ibid.*, 4, was made up almost entirely of first settlers—Haydon Wells, John Buchanan, Benjamin Drake, James Mulherrin, William Gower, and others.

bly all would lose, not only the land that many had chosen, but the work of three years; stations, fences, cleared fields would go to some one of the newcomers and they would not even be given land in its place. Back in the old days before the Revolution, men like Holston and Stalnaker had been allowed to keep land they had settled in far places,[53] and any man like John Preston who brought himself, family, and help across the ocean had been allowed to claim the King's Bounty of fifty acres for each soul transported. The trek across country, the building of stations and clearing of fields had taken a greater toll in lives than any trip across the ocean, and had cost a mint of money. But the old days were gone.

There were bright spots, the brightest represented by the business Haydon Wells had before the court that day. He must have puffed a bit with pride, waiting his turn before the four "worshipful justices," sitting with their backs to the fireplace, facing the assembled throng. They were no doubt pleased to grant the request of Haydon Wells. He had come to ask permission [54] to build a water-powered gristmill on Thomas Creek, north of the Cumberland, for no mill dam, ferry, or tavern could be operated without permission from county court.

Tradition relates that the mill Haydon built was a small and crude affair, but even so it represented a victory. Now after the fifth season of growing corn on the Cumberland, there was in spite of Indians, weather, canebrakes, family hogs, weeds, sprouting stumps, floods, squirrels and other wild animals, makeshift fences, and loss of land, at last corn enough to make the building of a water-powered mill practical, proof the land could be kind even to the landless.

Haydon Wells went down in history as the first man to build a mill on the Cumberland. This does not mean that no Cumberland settler had meal or flour before Haydon's mill. All stations had hand mills and horse mills, the stones brought by several first settlers; lacking these a family could make and use a corn pounder or hominy block as did Clark's men. Those able to afford it bought flour from the French traders [55] who continued to come to French Lick after settlement. Still, a water-powered mill was a landmark in the development of the community; not only a sign of perma-

---

[53] Even as late as the Revolution, land in western Virginia was acquired by right of settlement; see Kercheval, *Virginia*, Doddridge, "Notes," 247–251.

[54] DC, I, 2.

[55] Beginning with Martin Chartier in 1693, the Cumberland seems never to have been without traders; but they are usually mentioned only incidentally in connection with something else as Lavinia Craighead, W, 6XX (50), 17, remarked, "The next fall [in 1781 after the Battle of the Bluff] a trader came in and told Gen. Robertson that thirty Indians had been killed."

nence, but in a sense marking the end of the lean years when nobody put up anything but horse mills because there was so little corn to grind. Frederick Stump put up a mill a few months later, and soon Johnnie Boyd [56] was operating a still, even more proof there was plenty of corn.

True, all first settlers without too much money continued to have lean seasons, and hard times were by no means ended for many, but for the settlement as a whole the cornless years were behind. No future traveler, though some complained at having to eat cornbread, ever complained of scant rations after reaching Middle Tennessee.

There had been lean times as indicated by John Cockrill's story of risking his life to get bear meat, but in general the Cumberland Country, compared to the Kentucky Bluegrass, was a land of plenty. In the hard winter of 1779–80 Daniel Smith boarded some days with Kaspar Mansker, and members of his party had a few weeks earlier visited Price's Station up the Cumberland, but there was no complaint of scant rations until Smith reached Kentucky, where he and several other men traveled on the Ohio for ten days,[57] their sole food a quart of rotten corn, per day, per man. This was considerably more than Clark's soldiers had on an Ohio campaign in 1780; each man was given six quarts of rotten, moldy corn; they "might parch, pound, or bake it," but it was all they got; finished with this, the only food they had in the Ohio woods was slippery elm bark which they gnawed "as bad as Elks used to." [58] Colonel Henry Fleming visiting Kentucky in the hard winter, a respected visitor treated to the best, found short rations in most of the stations, and the prisoner Lord Henry Hamilton traveling through Kentucky a few months earlier, almost starved, and had no bread at many meals. Kentucky at that date had had settlers for five years, and supplies were fairly easily obtained by way of the Ohio.

The Cumberland, with fewer settlers and more trouble from the Indians, managed less than four years after settlement to have enough food, in spite of a great influx of visitors—most on the business of setting up the county and running boundaries—in the spring of 1784.[59] And as on any border, plenty of food meant plenty of corn. There were behind Haydon Wells,

[56] Permission was not needed to erect a still, and hence there is no official record, but there is agreement that "Old Johnnie Boyd" was the first; see W, 6XX (49), 4.

[57] THM, I, Smith, "Journal," April 26–June 24.

[58] FQ, II, Clinkenbeard "Interview," 128.

[59] Williams, *Travels*, Lipscomb, "Journal," 278, speaks of those who had lately come, but mentions no scarcity of food; and was able to get supplies to take him back east. Corn must have been fairly plentiful in the winter of 1782–1783; the "Government of Notables" meeting early in 1783, Putnam, *Tennessee*, 186, provided for the payment of guards with corn.

asking for a mill, many frontiers in America; no two had been the same. Reverend Doddridge's picture of a pioneer community in western Virginia during the Revolution in which tea and coffee were unknown, and people ate from woodenware and were disinclined to use pewter because it dulled their hunting knives, for they apparently had no table knives or forks, had little in common with any settlement on the Cumberland where most used pewter, and some had coin silver.[60]

None of the settlers on the Cumberland would seem to have had anything in common with the Pilgrims of New England who had neither rifle nor log house and not one good horse among them.

There was, however, one thing the New England intellectual, the gentleman of Tidewater, the Pennsylvania German, elegant Mr. Polk just come to Nashville, and Haydon Wells, uninfluential settler, all had in common. This was corn. It is impossible to overestimate the importance of corn in the settlement of America. First settlers in James Town had often wasted time in hunting precious minerals, and when tobacco became an important cash crop, many were inclined to neglect the growing of corn for tobacco, so that for many years there had to be laws forcing each planter to grow a certain number of acres of corn to fend off starvation, if not for himself, for often he could afford imported flour, at least for his servants.

Yet, by 1700 the "poorer sort" preferred the pone, though the bread in gentlemen's houses was still commonly of flour. In time even the gentleman settling on the Piedmont or in the Great Valley where flour, no matter how wealthy he might be, was less easily had because he was away from the sea and ships, might eat, if not pone, many foods made of corn. William Byrd found all settlers in the stumpy, new ground fields of the then backwoods of the Piedmont growing corn, and even Dr. Walker, Tidewater descendant, made in 1750 no attempt on the frontier of New River to buy flour, but contented himself with meal and "small hominy."

Corn, too, as horse feed, was, save for woods pasture, their first source of power, and to any first settler meant more than groceries and gasoline do to us today. Corn meant fat hogs, lard for the grease lamp, as well as meat; surplus corn meant whiskey, while the fodder was their only winter forage when new fields were too stumpy for hay, and Indians killed all cattle that wandered far away.

Wheat, too, had many uses, but was not adapted to the new ground field.

[60] This was a rather scarce item in the first years; even the Donelsons, DW, I, 109, list only one half-dozen silver spoons, but as a rule wealthier families—the Bledsoes are good examples—left household goods to the wife, and as nothing had to be sold, there were no detailed inventories.

Corn, unlike the small grains, throve in rich new ground soil; the higher the nitrogen content, the blacker and deeper the humus, the better the corn. Much of the land on the Cumberland was so rich it had to be reduced with corn two or three seasons before any small grain would grow and make grain instead of merely rank grass. Nor could the small grains compete with the heavy growth of sprouts and big weeds such as bull nettles and Spanish needles that sprang to life in every new ground field.

Corn was not only a proud and mighty plant of a growth so rapid it could lift itself above the weeds, but it could be planted with a hoe or grubbing hoe in ground too filled with roots and stumps for a plow to make a planting furrow. Once planted in this fashion in hills four feet apart, and these in the rough field in rows about the same distance between, it could be cultivated with the hoe. Wheat and other small grains, sown broadcast as they were, not only had to have an even seed bed with enough loose dirt to cover the seed with a makeshift toothed harrow or even a length of brush, but once sown could get no further help from the farmer.

Another advantage of corn was that it would grow into a tall but sturdy plant able to hold its ears well out of reach of turkeys or raccoons, but down-hanging and so well wrapped no damage could come from rain or snow and the smaller birds. The man who planted it might be killed by Indians before it was laid by, but late in the winter when the snow was deep his hungry sons could sneak back to the field and find ears of corn, still safely held above the snow. The small grain crops such as wheat were not only at the mercy of every bird that flew or walked, but would, when past their prime, fall down and leave their seed to rot. There was, too, something kind and proud and free about the corn, big stuff a man could walk among, and reach his arms for the ears, six feet above the ground on fourteen-foot stalks. It grew in a wide variety of soils, and would yield at least something for bread on poor ground in a dry year.

Travelers from Europe commented much on the American grain that was "neither sown nor reaped." [61] Corn by the time of the Revolution had, more so than any other crop, left its mark on the speech of the people; by it the farmer away from the sea divided his years; men did not always speak of spring but corn-planting time, followed by the replanting; mid-summer meant the time of laying by; late summer in August brought fodder pulling, and fall, usually November after frost, meant corn gathering.

Stories of two hundred years and more ago, like many of my childhood, or even now among the older people in the hills, were marked in time by

[61] Smythe, *Tour*, I, 294–299.

the growth of corn: "The cornfield beans had not uncrooked . . ." "The corn was in the silk," or knee high, or just up enough "you could follow the rows across the field," or in the milk, or topped. Corn was always there, under all life as was the earth itself. The name corn, instead of maize or Indian corn, showed that it was to the settlers, not one of the cereals, but the cereal; the wheat of the Englishman, oats of the Scotchman.

Men on the Cumberland would have talked of corn gathering and the yields of their different fields when, less than a month after Haydon Wells had got permission to build a mill, there was on November 5th [62] another gathering of men south of the Cumberland. The Chickasaw Treaty, later known as the Treaty of Nashville, though Nashville had not yet come into being, was at last being held. It was, no different from any other Indian treaty, a ceremonious and dignified occasion, but undignified by any dwelling, for it was held, adding insult to injury, on the land James Robertson would move to about a year later, down on Richland Creek, near where it is now crossed by the Charlotte Pike.[63]

They "smoked" together, and then the Red King rose, and speaking through the interpreter Depford, began, "Friends and Brothers"; and all the worry that the Chickasaw did not want to treat was blown away, for the Red King wanted peace with the settlers, and declared the two peoples must not live "like two puppies thrown together and provoked to fight." He finished, "I have in my hands a string of white beads. . . ." It was soon the turn of big John Donelson to rise and speak. He remains, in spite of his journal of the trip down the Tennessee and a few letters, a mystery man, of whom almost nothing is known before the Revolution, and little between his arrival on Cumberland and his death from Indians six years later. He was one of several men who during and shortly after the Revolution leaped into sudden prominence and prosperity, a prosperity that would not have come had there been no revolution. A North Carolina lawmaker under the colonial government went so far as to declare, "this Colonel Donelson has a reputation of being a land jobber and is complained of." [64]

[62] W, 1XX, 65.

[63] There is a Tennessee Historical Commission marker on the site of Robertson's home, Travellers Rest, but we cannot be certain his first forted farm on Richland Creek, described as only a mile from the Cumberland and begun late in 1784, occupied the same site, though it was the same general location. See W, 6XX, 963, and sketch *ibid.*, 1S, 60.

[64] NCR, IX, 1244. This was in connection with the outlawing of Henderson, and Donelson was associated with Henderson; see also, *ibid.*, 1169. Some of Donelson's influence is thought to have come by way of Patrick Henry; Donelson's only sister married a Henry, said to have been a relative of Patrick; there were Henrys on the flotilla; in Kentucky, John Donelson, often spelled Donaldson, was an appraiser for

The colonial government of North Carolina had given Henderson short shrift, outlawing his purchase less than a week after it took place, and different from the state governments that came later, offering no land in return.

Donelson had failed to get land in Kentucky, but he and Benjamin Harrison, governor of Virginia, got along quite well together, as the many letters Harrison wrote concerning the treaty indicate; and only once did Harrison get worried,[65] asking Joseph Martin his opinion of John Donelson, for Harrison had heard that Donelson was interested in buying Indian lands, and men who treated with the Indians, giving them goods bought by hard-pressed state governments,[66] were not supposed to be interested in land for themselves. Everybody wanted the fine Chickasaw lands. Virginia [67] was at this time trying to buy through George Rogers Clark some in Kentucky, now known as the Jackson Purchase, and the company of which Donelson was a member wanted land down on the Tennessee in what is now Alabama, and which the men in their letters referred to as The Bent,[68] a great boundary of rich land no white man was able to settle until after the defeat of the Creeks.

The men listening to the treaty in the chill November weather represented four contestants: the Chickasaw, represented by twenty-two of their Nation—six of these women, twelve warriors, and four chiefs—had no wish to fall out with "their fathers the English for we love them." Still, as they had told Simon Burney,[69] more than a year before, "it is our desire to be at peace with you that our corn may grow and our stocks increase for the benefit of our children hereafter." These were also the desires of the white settlers, a few at least of whom must have been there, though in all the discussion of when and where to hold the treaty, no reference was ever made to settlers on the Cumberland. The third interested contestant, also wanting peace and land, was the soldier of the line, the one with money enough to consider settling, a little back home for a start, but not enough,

---

the estate of John Henry; Hugh Henry executor; see LC, I, 78—August Court of 1783; see also *ibid.*, 8, the July term of 1781, which would indicate Donelson was in Kentucky at that date.

[65] W, IXX, 63. This about a month before the treaty, ". . . look into it and give us your opinion of him."

[66] W, IXX, 55, is a list of articles to be given the Indians at the Treaty of Nashville, and one held at The Long Island of the Holston.

[67] W, IXX, 56.

[68] W, IXX, 71.

[69] W, IXX, 50. This was not a treaty, but more in the nature of a feeler, held July 9, 1782. See also NCR, XVI, 441–442, Benjamin Harrison to Alexander Martin, Oct. 22, 1782.

needing more land, able to move out and pull through a year or two without getting too much in debt, but not able to hold indefinitely a piece of paper promising land. The fourth contestant was the land speculator, hoping for land and more land, able to hold it until the price rose and he could subdivide and sell.

All treaties like all battles hold for both sides some element of victory, some taste of defeat. And so it was with this one. The Chickasaw, though allies of the loser, the English, did not speak humbly, but complained, "The white people have got a very bad trick that when they go a hunting, as there are many that follow it for a livelihood, and find a good piece of ground, and they make a Station Camp on it and the next thing they go to building houses." Still, they wanted peace and were willing enough to yield the ground now claimed by settlers, but stood firm on the land dear to the hearts of the land speculators: "We hold," the Red King said, "the lands from the mouth of Duck River to the mouth of the Tennessee and to the ridge between Cumberland and Tennessee as high up as Duck River as a hunting ground for the support of our women and children, and that is the only manner we know to supply them."

The treaty lasted for some days,[70] but nobody got past Duck River Ridge. Presents were distributed—twelve ruffled shirts, red cloth, linen, blue kerseys for the chiefs; four more shirts, though only two were ruffled, to the interpreter; powder, ball, red cloth, linen, dowlas to the young men, and more dowlas to the Indian women.[71]

This, the treaty of Nashville, paved the way for future treaties, and a lasting peace with the Chickasaw. In August [72] of the following year a Chickasaw chief, Mountain Leader, came with some of his young men to Robertson bringing strings of beads and a rich belt of wampum, but greater than the gifts they bore was their offer of allying themselves with the white man against what was to be the greatest enemy of the settlers on the Cumberland—the Creeks.

However, the very success of the treaty that Robertson had not wanted, was a blow to Robertson's prestige, and a further boon to John Donelson and his relatives. He got from North Carolina, though he was not known there but seemingly through his friendship with Benjamin Harrison and

---

[70] The expenses of the treaty listed, W, 1XX, 55, charges for provisions for 32 people for 20 days, but the body of the treaty, *ibid.*, 65, indicates only 3 days of treating, Nov. 5, 6, 7.

[71] W, 1XX, 55.

[72] This visit is described in Robertson's letter of Nov. 1, 1784, NCR, XVII, 91–92; see also *ibid.*, XIX, 739.

others in Virginia, the very lucrative appointment as surveyor more or less in charge of lands west of the mountains. His son Stockley had the appointment as surveyor for lands in the eastern district of the western lands or what was to be East Tennessee, and as these appointments meant the surveyors would be paid in land, they meant to each a very great deal of land indeed. Young Stockley became the largest landholder in East Tennessee, while the in-laws and connections of John Donelson in time owned not only much of Middle Tennessee, but much land further south, still claimed for many years by Indians.

One other Virginian, Daniel Smith, who had already been appointed a justice of the peace, got a surveying appointment.[73] Daniel Smith, however, though serving Virginia as a Commissioner in 1779–80, was not only an experienced surveyor, possibly the only man in the whole west who could draw a map with any degree of accuracy, but he was also a seasoned borderer, and was not, like John Donelson, the Polks, and others who would soon step into positions of influence and power, unknown to the average borderer. The men who came into power in 1783, their way paved by the success of the treaty in making peace enough at least that some could live there, though the Polks, like the Bentons who also got much land at this time, never moved out until the place was considerably safer, would rule, not only Middle Tennessee for the next sixty years, but at times most of Tennessee, with Jackson,[74] a son-in-law of John Donelson, the treaty maker, becoming President and Jackson men in the White House through succeeding terms.

[73] There were three surveying appointments for general preemptions; Stockley Donelson was given East Tennessee, his father Middle Tennessee, and on his death his son, Capt. John, Jackson's brother-in-law got the appointment, for by North Carolina law a son could heir an appointment of his father; Martin Armstrong and Daniel Smith were in charge of military grants and land got by right of preemption in what is now Middle Tennessee, soon to be Davidson County. See W, 29S, 75, and NCR, XVI, 960.

[74] The pattern is well illustrated in General Jackson's list of officers in 1813 and succeeding campaigns; John Coffee, Colonel of Cavalry, later General, nephew-in-law of Jackson's wife; Stockley Donelson Hays, quartermaster general and nephew-in-law of Jackson's wife; Stockley Donelson Hutchings, quartermaster sergeant, *ibid.* relationship; Dr. William Butler, surgeon, *ibid.* relationship. This group, some of whom later distinguished themselves, was going against the Indians, and it is not recorded that any, including Jackson, had ever fought an Indian. One could fill several pages with positions political and military held by in-laws of Andrew Jackson, land office, justice of the peace, and on into the next generation in the White House; in the meantime the old Indian fighters—Bledsoes, Seviers, Robertsons, Castlemans, etc., are seldom mentioned; most were dead and there were no appointments for their sons; Robertson though not considered too old in 1813 to go off to the Chickasaw was turned down for a military appointment by Jackson on the grounds was too old, A, V, 273–274, Jackson's letter of refusal to Robertson.

Most of these men had along with influence, a good bit of money, or at least ready cash, and by late 1783 money would buy land most any place in Tennessee, regardless of who claimed or lived on it. The original copy of the Chickasaw Treaty was lost,[75] but this never mattered to the men in North Carolina east of the mountains, busy setting up a county, and opening a land office.

The southern end of Davidson County was repudiated when peace was made with the Chickasaw; they claimed everything south of Duck River Ridge; their claim was not denied but back in North Carolina the boundaries of the county were not changed. Instructions for the laying off of the soldiers' lands had been given before the treaty was made,[76] and the sonorous vowels of the Red King were hardly stilled before in faraway Hillsborough the land office was opened. Anybody with money could buy land outside Davidson County, and this meant more of the very land the Chickasaw had refused to part with. It also meant land, some in the eastern boundary of Davidson County, that belonged to the Cherokee, and would continue to belong for many years. Most knowledge of the various Indian tribes, their claims and rights had been swept away by the Revolution. James Robertson was one of the few men experienced in dealing with Indians who had taken the American side of the cause, and he was never given the honor and glory, not to mention the high pay, of treating with the Indians [77] at this time, though the Indians often came to him.

Everybody wanted land. The price was cheap, the same as that for the preemptions offered the settlers; ten pounds per hundred acres in specie, or the specie certificates North Carolina had used to pay for supplies. North Carolina paper money would also be accepted at eight hundred for one. The land office was a howling success, and so great was the tumult of men struggling to get entries recorded no business could be done for some days.[78]

Land warrants flew right and left; anybody with specie or a specie

---

[75] W, 1XX, 76.

[76] NCR, XVI, 912, Oct. 28, 1783.

[77] The lowest pay found for treating was $5 daily, but this in 1804, A, V, 185.

[78] Haywood, *C & P*, 108–109, 129; the expression peculiarly American, "land office business," seems to have come into use at this time, and can still be heard. The land office bill, NCR, XXIV, 478–482, had many safeguards on paper, but they were not enforceable. A further law, *ibid.*, 483, expressly forbade any but soldiers, guards, and others holding preemptions for services, from getting land in the boundary set aside for soldiers, for the space of three years, but much of the best land went to people who were not even citizens of North Carolina. See also, *ibid.*, 565.

certificate was eager to put it in land, for there was always the chance it might buy nothing else, and North Carolina currency was higher than it would ever be again. This new country shaping up into the United States might make its own money, and North Carolina money would then be useless. And so the land went, with much in Davidson County and all out, owned by Chickasaw and Cherokee.

The little man on the frontier, afraid to leave his family to the mercy of the Indians and unable to take the time and money needed for a far trek over the mountains, never had a chance. Even the well-to-do first settlers in Middle Tennessee with no agent to act for them never had a chance. The land office closed,[79] almost before they had time to get there. A landless soldier [80] declared it was done so that no one else might get a warrant, and the speculators could thus get more for their land.

This was the result in many cases where the speculator got his hands on good land, but it seems not to have been a scheme cooked up by the North Carolina Assembly solely for the benefit of the speculators. North Carolina at this time planned [81] a quick cession of her western lands to the United States, but before doing so she at least went through the motions of setting aside good land for her soldiers, and paying the men with land who had supplied the soldiers. The land office was supposed to enable her to "sink her specie," and give the holders of paper money a chance to redeem it. It seems to be true that most were careless, many in high places sworn to guard the public good were greedy, and the voices of the few,[82] who aware of what had happened to the Kentucky Bluegrass were wary of the land office, went unheeded. In any case the public domain went into private hands; land that might have gone to unpaid soldiers or have been set aside for education as was done in the Northwest Territory, went to the speculator who could afford to hold it, without paying taxes,[83] until the title was cleared.

[79] NCR, XXIV, 571.

[80] W, 29S, 75.

[81] NCR, XXIV, 561-563. This the land cession bill was later repealed, but in the meantime there was actually a bill, though it did not get past the House, *ibid.,* XIX, 428, for forming a West Carolina. Ideas of federal power were just being formed, and the North Carolina lawmakers felt that states had many powers later delegated to the federal government.

[82] NCR, XVI, 369, this, part of a long letter, 357-377, of Morris to Martin, July 29, 1782, shows good understanding of what could happen and did.

[83] Andrew Jackson, for example, eager for more land, offered in 1805 $15,000 for 40,000 acres on Duck River, certain he could get it, for the Indian title was "to be lifted" and "it would be subject to taxes," and Jackson had heard the owner could not pay taxes. Facts and figures used by permission of the publisher, Carnegie Insti-

Land on paper was one thing; land surveyed and registered very much another. This meant that somebody would have to go visit the land, Indians or no, to get the work done. Some of the men appointed to various supervisory capacities came out in the fall of 1783, though the land bills were not completed until 1784.[84] Late in the spring of that year the woods of Middle Tennessee were filled with commissioners, surveyors, chain carriers, guards, and hunters; in general the same sort of assemblage that Byrd had had with him in running the line fifty years before. There were differences; this line was the boundary of a county, not a colony, but the biggest difference was that Byrd and all those with him had been paid in cash; all these men were to be paid in land.

The land, once so big, began to look little, that is the good land. There is in the Tennessee Bluegrass only around 5,500 square miles, and like the Kentucky Bluegrass, this has many rough spots, some thin-soiled, rocky, fit for little but cedar forest, and a good bit of river bottom, swampy and subject to overflow. There were in the meantime between seven and twelve thousand [85] North Carolina soldiers, each entitled to at least one square mile of land, with all officers and those with long service records given more.

This probably accounts for the laying off of the biggest grants first, and these chiefly north of the Cumberland in what are now Davidson and Sumner counties—fine rolling fertile land. The great bends of the Cumberland went to such as Daniel Smith, wealthy Robert Hays,[86] friend of William Blount, future Territorial Governor of the "Territory South of the Ohio River." Robert Hays in 1786, not long after settling on the Cumberland, married a daughter of John Donelson; four years later Andrew Jackson married another daughter. Soon, most of the wide acres in the bends of the Cumberland near Nashville, more or less in the center of civilization, and hence safer from the Indians, were owned by kin and in-laws of one family. Few Revolutionary privates appear to have been granted land in this, the choicest region. Even such honored men and

tution of Washington, from *Correspondence of Andrew Jackson*, edited and compiled by John Spencer Bassett, copyrighted by Carnegie Institution of Washington, Washington, D.C., 1926 (cited hereafter as Bassett, *Jackson Correspondence*), I, 114-115, Jackson to John Jackson.

[84] NCR, XXIV, 565-566; see also NCR, XIX, 938.

[85] Hanna, *Scotch-Irish*, I, 5, citing figures, points out the difficulty of arriving at the exact number of men who served from any colony. Terms of enlistment were short, counted separately, and often confused with figures for men enlisted for more than one term.

[86] Hays, for whom Haysborough north of the Cumberland was named, had served in the Revolution with William Blount and came as a young bachelor to Middle Tennessee around 1784; see Thwaites, *Travels*, III, Michaux, "Journal," 93.

ranking officers as Tilman Dixon who early came to his grant and built a station had as a rule to content themselves with land, if not in, at least near the Indian boundaries. The Bledsoes, Isaac and Anthony, got large grants some miles north of the Cumberland and other men with money and hence able to buy acquired large holdings of less desirable lands; among these were the Winchester brothers,[87] George and James.

While some were amassing great boundaries of the best land, the settlers could only look on, watch surveying lines run through their fields, and bisect the stations they had built. The lawmakers in offering them preemptions had stipulated they must vacate all property "owned by the State." Some, such as Humphrey Drake, did and left the country. Most stayed, and a few were affluent and lucky enough to get a guard right or surveying job, on the local level, and hence get land, while others could buy a preemption from a soldier or land speculator.

Their petition had in the spring of 1784 been traveling between the House and the Senate for more than two years. It had been read, reread, amended, reported out of committees, and "laid on the table." Never was it important enough to be made a bill in its own right. Late in the spring of 1784, the Cumberland settler problem was taken out of the final amendment to the bill for relief of the soldiers, and tacked on to the repeal of the land office act, for it was then the Assembly closed the land office and ceded the western lands to the United States. The clause in this bill merely observed that since many of the inhabitants on Cumberland had not yet bought the certificates that would entitle them to preemptions, their time for paying would be extended twelve months.[88] Paying? Many had died in debt.

The North Carolina Assembly had, in the spring of 1784, many land matters to attend to; one was to make a special grant of 25,000 acres to a man who deserved it, General Nathanael Greene, but in spite of the Chickasaw Treaty of the fall before, the Assembly stipulated his land should be laid off on the south bank of the Duck River of the Tennessee.[89]

They also created a seat of government for the new county, Davidson, and at least on paper the cornfields adjacent to French Lick became a town, the act stipulating that the "Town on Cumberland River," [90] should be at "a place called The Bluff near the French Lick—said Lick not to be

[87] George was killed in 1794, but Cragfont, home of James, is now owned by the State of Tennessee. Both were active in the military and political life of Middle Tennessee. See W, 3XX (18), 6, the account of a neighbor, William Martin.
[88] NCR, XXIV, 566.
[89] NCR, XXIV, 569–570.
[90] NCR, XXIV, 616–617.

included in the Town." It was to consist of two hundred one-acre lots, each to be sold for the very high price of four pounds. James Robertson at long last had land—four town lots of his own choosing.

We cannot even be certain why James Robertson was given the lots; different from Daniel Smith, he was not made a director of the town, though he was the only one to get free lots. Free is hardly the word; Robertson had more than earned the lots by all the food and ammunition he had supplied men defending the Cumberland, not to mention the several thousand miles of horseback travel back and forth to see about land, not just for himself, but for all the original settlers.

He had in the spring [91] of 1784 made another trip to North Carolina, carrying still another Petition of the Inhabitants of Cumberland. He probably had some help from his brother Elijah and William Polk [92] who in that year represented the Cumberland settlers in the North Carolina Assembly. Somebody in the spring of 1784 caused the North Carolina lawmakers to change their minds quite suddenly.

One day there was a law promising the settlers on the Cumberland nothing more than the opportunity of paying for their lands. The next thing the House was reporting out of committee and reading a bill for the Relief of Sundry Inhabitants of Davidson County, and by May 10 this bill with its 151 names had already received favorable attention in the Senate.[93] Such was its speedy consideration, the House was able by May 28 to pass and return it to the Senate.[94] There was now no question of its passing, this separate bill that gave the settlers who, in the land office amendment just passed, had been no more than debtors, each 640 acres of free land.

James Robertson started home with the good news. June 16th he was in the mountains alone riding west toward Captain Thomas Amis's, near present-day Rogersville, Tennessee. There, he fell in with a party of travelers on their way to the Cumberland to see about land. He spent the next two weeks in their company, up and down Clinch Mountain, Powell's Mountain, Cumberland Gap, the rivers to cross and the creek bluffs to climb; a route he would by then have known in his sleep. June 20th found

---

[91] DC, I, 10. James Robertson was present for January Court of 1784, but absent, *ibid.*, 18, for the April term.

[92] Robertson's brother Elijah was a settler on the Cumberland and William Polk was a temporary visitor on land business; see NCR, XVII, 264.

[93] NCR, XIX, 572–573, the Committee Report of Mr. Person on "The Bill for the Relief of Sundry Inhabitants of Davidson County."

[94] NCR, XIX, 609; the final reading in the House came May 22; see *ibid.*, 633, 661. The final law, also with list of names, is in NCR, XXIV, 629–630.

Robertson and party only at the Dripping Spring, for they had stopped at settlements near Stanford, Kentucky, and on the way to hunt. Here, Robertson left with a Mr. Cloud, and hurried on, only the two of them, though seventy miles, and that mostly Barrens, lay between them and French Lick.[95]

We can be certain that once in the settlements he spread the news; the Bill for the Relief of Sundry Inhabitants of Davidson County would be made into law by the North Carolina Assembly. The petition upon which the bill was based was not the same Robertson had carried over the mountains in the winter of 1781; the land office had gone first to Hillsborough; there was a county, but the important thing, the list of names, was still there. It is doubtful if the names had changed a great deal save in their arrangement; some of those signing in 1781 may have gone away and their names dropped, but mostly it was a matter of crossing out a signature and writing in a dead man's name.

First on the list of those getting land were the sixty-seven living men who had been there in May of 1780, and one woman—Ann Robertson Johnston—now Ann Cockrill. These were the people who had held the Cumberland, the lucky ones. Next came the sixty-three dead; their heirs were to get 640 acres; this list included William Neely, Nicholas Gentry, James Harrod, Edward Larrimore and others whose inventories have been mentioned. In addition there were nineteen living men who had come a bit later than the others, but these also were to get land. These included John Buchanan, Sr., who had stayed behind in Kentucky for a few months while his sons and the Mulherrins came on to build French Lick Station; the two Gais men up from Natchez, and John Kennedy and John Costillo from Kentucky.

Each of these, the living and the heirs of the dead, was allowed 640 acres of land, "without being required to pay any price to the State for the same, provided that every person receiving such grant shall pay the office and surveyor's fee for the same." It was further ordered that each grant should be made "to each and every one of the before named persons as if they had paid the full price of ten pounds per hundred acres." [96]

It was a great victory from ten pounds per hundred in the early spring to free land before the corn was laid by. The settlers on the Cumberland in Middle Tennessee were in truth the children of fortune, the chosen ones. They of all the first settlers in the old west, Kentucky and East

[95] Williams, *Travels*, Lipscomb, "Journal," 273–277.
[96] NCR, XXIV, 630.

Tennessee, got free land. The word free is the wrong one; almost half had died for it, more than half if the Renfroes and others who got nothing are counted. Kentucky did in later years offer the poor ground in the Barrens, treeless and crawfishy, as a bounty, and for a little while some of the rougher land on the Big South Fork and eastward, but all her good land was taken away from the Daniel Boones and others who had settled and held it. The first settlers of East Tennessee bought their land from the Indians; those who did not buy got nothing; and when their land was ceded with no by-your-leave from the men on it to the United States, they under Sevier revolted, and had for a little while their own "State of Franklin." [97]

Had the settlers of Middle Tennessee been treated in the same fashion, the whole history of our country might have been different. Speculation is a waste of words, but the Indians, notably the Chickamauga and the Creeks, did not yield Middle Tennessee as easily and as quickly as the northern Indians gave up Kentucky. There was in 1784 when the settlers got their land still eleven more years of weekly, often daily Indian attacks and all the biggest battles and the greatest losses still ahead. A few of the men who in 1783–84 got lucrative appointments and choice lands, notably the Bledsoes and Daniel Smith, were experienced borderers and took an active part in both fighting and treating with the Indians. A few others of the Revolutionary soldiers, such as the Winchester brothers, Tilman Dixon, the Douglasses [98] and Edmonsons,[99] are often mentioned in accounts of Indian warfare. But as a rule, the biggest landholders and the most influential men of later years—the Donelsons, Robert Hays, John Coffee, John Overton and others to whom historians give much space—either came too late, or like Andrew Jackson [100] and Captain John Donelson who on the death of his father, the Colonel or Flotilla John, got the

---

[97] The fullest treatment of the "Lost State" is that by Judge Samuel Cole Williams, *History of the Lost State of Franklin*, New York, 1933.

[98] Joseph Bishop came out with Captain William Douglass, father of Elmore, already there, Gray, *Bishop*, 30. Elmore settled in what was to be Smith County and was mentioned by travelers—Rev. Asbury preached in his home in the fall of 1800—and was prominent at the local level.

[99] The Edmonsons, mentioned by Michaux in 1796, formed a large and prosperous family, some settling in what was to be Montgomery County; father and sons had served at Kings Mountain, see Draper, *Kings Mountain*, 407–408.

[100] Jackson did hold appointive jobs in the militia, but none of the correspondents whom Mr. Lyman C. Draper questioned on the matter could remember Jackson as having served on any campaign against the Indians; he was for the frontier an odd sort of man, seemingly unfamiliar with any weapon save the pistol; no chance account speaks of his hunting or taking part in contests of rifle marksmanship; his record in the Revolution was unusual for a boy his age, brief and ending in capture.

same lucrative appointment he had had, were never active in the defense of the community. They had to have James Robertson to attend to such matters as securing the return of a captured child, or planning an invasion after seven years of almost constant suffering from the Indians.

They also had to have men like Kaspar Mansker, John Buchanan, the Eatons and Frederick Stump to build stations where neighboring farmers might sleep, or where they themselves might stay until they built their own. Many of the future leaders of Tennessee and the nation were there or coming shortly after 1784; John Overton, Judge McNairy, Robert Hays, Andrew Jackson, the Polks and Donelsons, but no one of these, though most held military titles, ever actually took part in early Indian warfare; Jackson is reported [101] to have run away from a skirmish in East Tennessee and left a companion to be killed. They were not shirt-tail men, able and unselfish enough to risk their lives as did titleless Thomas Sharpe Spencer or old John Buchanan.

It is possible that Robertson pointed out such ugly facts to somebody with influence at Hillsborough, else the Assembly would never have done such an unheard of thing as giving fine land to an uninfluential hunter of German descent, but this they did. Kaspar Mansker was one of the very few lucky enough to stay on his original choice.[102] Frederick Stump also got to keep his land on White's Creek.

The pattern of land settlement on the Cumberland in Middle Tennessee was infinitely fairer and more honest than that of the Kentucky Bluegrass where neither a poor pioneer such as Edward Larrimore,[103] nor even a good German farmer on the order of Frederick Stump, would ever have had a chance. No one of these had influence, or much money, yet all got land. This mingling of divers people gave Middle Tennessee a rich cultural heritage. Early, the Cumberland settlements felt the influence of independent and fearless first settlers unafraid of Indians, and men who had

[101] Knoxville *Gazette*, Sept. 14, 1793. We have no proof that had Jackson stayed he could have saved his comrade; the men had gone out after horses, seemingly unarmed, for nothing is said of resistance; Jackson's code was not that of the borderer.
[102] Kaspar also got several large parcels of land, as did others of the first settlers, usually as guard rights or on a soldier's warrant. See Davidson County Register Book, I, 222, 223—this 1784. I have avoided the use of this work; the original was burned and this only a remembered copy; surveys for most of the first settlers are given, but the land acquired, not by right of settlement but from some soldier's warrant; many were surveyed by James Mulherrin, authorized by Martin Armstrong.
[103] Edward was killed by Indians before he got his land, and when it did come it was confiscated to pay his debts, DW, I, 44; the same fate, *ibid.*, 61, befell Zachariah White who had come on the exploratory journey, returned as a first settler to be killed at the Battle of the Bluff.

fought in the Revolution. It would know, too, the thrifty ways and farming skills of the many German farmers who settled in the neighborhood of Stump's plantation. All these had, in many respects, even more influence in shaping the economic pattern than the wealthy families of note of which so much has been written—Overtons, Polks, Donelsons, Whites, and others including Andrew Jackson. These, the settlers of wealth and social pretensions, either inherited or acquired, gave Middle Tennessee some reflection of Tidewater at least in the physical manifestations of life—carriages with coachmen, blooded horses, dinings, and winings.

None of these, however, not even Andrew Jackson, could reckon without the strong middle class with which they were surrounded, for Middle Tennessee was not destined to be, any more than colonial Virginia had been, a world of haves and have nots, each pitted against the other as in Kentucky. The differences in patterns of early settlement probably accounted in great measure for the vast difference between the two Bluegrasses. Their soils were similar, both were sought out by pioneers during the Revolution with future settlers coming largely from the older colonies. Each was drained by a tributary of the Ohio, permitted slavery, had the same religions, were but a short distance apart, and early connected by roads.

Yet, nothing could be less similar than their histories. Kentucky Bluegrass settlers tended to build a little world within a world, an island of the Cotton Kingdom of the deeper south without the cotton and not colonial Virginia. In the Kentucky Bluegrass great landholders owned much land and many slaves, and though often denied Tidewater in their blood they compensated for this lack by liberal dosings of it in the physical aspects of their lives. Middle Tennessee was a wider world, and though it held many voices and clashing opinions, it was soon to be the voice of the young United States, ever able to outshout Clay, Webster, and Calhoun, producing three Presidents to Kentucky's none. The Kentucky Bluegrass, personified by Henry Clay, poor Scotch farmer's son, husband of a land speculator's daughter as was Jackson, neither wanted Jackson for president nor Texas as a State, but, romantic as it was and elegant, the opinions of the northern Bluegrass never mattered. Those of the other shaped the nation.

However, in the late summer of 1784 Texas begging for annexation was far away. Could old Jacob Castleman who had helped save the Kentucky settlements, then come to the Cumberland and there lost his life, read here such pretty words as victory and democracy, he would shake his head and go away. He, nor any of his kin, got any free land. They came too late. Neither did John Rains, Edmund Jennings, the Drakes, nor any of the Renfroes.[104]

The tragedy was that many had settled, thinking there would be headrights as in Virginia at times. Peter Renfroe, for example, was one of the few survivors of the Red River massacre in the summer of 1780, and was rather unusual in that he could not sign his name. He figured he was entitled to 820 acres of headrights, having brought no doubt a wife and children. In September of 1780 Peter sold his headrights for an unspecified sum to George Pirtle, who in turn sold them to George Freeland who still had them when killed. Whatever Freeland [105] paid was wasted money, for Peter Renfroe got no land.

The headrights were only one loss among many to George Freeland's widow; the station her husband had helped build, the fields he had cleared, and all other work he had done went to somebody else. It was many years before either Kentucky or Tennessee had a law stipulating the man who lost his land through a bad title should get paid for any of his improvements. John Buchanan, thinking of his dead brother, and all the work he, his father, and brother Samuel had done, the shelter they and the Mulherrins had given, may have felt cheated when looking at such a one as Lardner Clark. He got 320 acres of land for merely guarding the men who ran the boundaries; John Buchanan got only 640 for making it possible for Lardner Clark and others to survive; meantime he had bought all his own ammunition, and everything else needed.

Everybody but Mansker and Stump had to move; and once again it was the first settlers who were the first to build more stations; the Buchanans went out to Mill Creek; the Eatons back to White's Creek,[106] Robertson to Richland Creek, each taking with them several families. Nor was their land, no different from that of the soldiers, entirely free. True, the North Carolina entry fee had declined from four pounds in 1780 to only four shillings in 1783, but they had to pay surveying costs, and in a small holding of 640 acres, this usually amounted to one-third.

Still, the first settlers enjoyed advantages. Some got guard rights, and as

---

[104] William Martin, W, 3XX, 32, stated that at least two of the men came up to Kentucky; most were killed.

[105] DW, I, 155.

[106] Most began clearing land for new stations in 1784, but the Eatons appear to have lived across from the Old French Landing until around 1786; a 1791 court reference, DW, I, 219, speaks of "Heaton's Old Station." See also DC, I, 76.

there was no great influx of settlers, land continued cheap and many, like Edward Swanson, John Buchanan, Mansker, the Stumps,[107] John Boyd, prospered, and as they were on the spot, able to see and sometimes help survey land, they, as a group, suffered less from careless surveying, and sometimes dishonest surveyors, than middle-class farmers who settled later.

A very great many families, including the widows of the Bledsoe brothers, were in the years to come to suffer because of the low quality of the surveying done by unskilled men unaccustomed to the work. The uneven boundaries, no different from those in Kentucky, caused trouble. The North Carolina lawmakers [108] had more or less hoped the land would be laid out in squares, and if not squares, oblongs, and if oblong the length was never to exceed twice the width. This was also the custom in Virginia, and it prevented a man from owning several miles of river bottom and so cutting off access to his neighbors on the hill above, and such a law tended to a more equitable division of bottom lands. Still, it made for most uneven boundaries, and plots of land with square corners and four sides only were in Tennessee as in Kentucky to be the exception rather than the rule, for the surveyors were permitted to use creeks, mountains, and rivers as boundaries, and hence the holdings like the counties are of every conceivable shape.

Uneven boundaries, vague lines, ignorant and dishonest surveyors, the whole complicated by overreaching grabs of land speculators, brought financial ruin and heartbreak to future settlers. Typical is the story of what happened to an ancestor of Booth Tarkington, after the Indian wars were over, but "before the shaking of the earth in 1811. Jesse [Tarkington] went upon David Beatty's land near Nashville where he stayed three or four years. The Indians stole his horses, and David Beatty sold him two. Having then but little means or money left, he sold his lease of land to Beatty and moved down about 17 miles to near where Franklin now is. There father bought land of two men named Murray and Tatum, who had entered it with Revolutionary War land warrants. When my father moved there (about 1801) my mother carried me in her arms and she said I cried all the way. There father cleared up a farm, built houses and a barn, and soon had a very good orchard. . . .

"But in twelve years there came an older overlapping claim to the land

[107] The reconstructed copy of Davidson County Register Book, I, indicates that first settlers did get minor appointments and hence land—James Robertson 2,000 acres on Richland Creek as guard right, 218; De Monbruen and Stump, *ibid.*, 233, 358, but John Rains, 194, bought his.
[108] NCR. XXIV. 567.

than that conveyed by Murray and Tatum to my father, and after a suit at law my father lost the land. Murray and Tatum were insolvent and there was no recourse left. Then father leased land of a William Hadley on which he stayed two years . . . the Creek Indians the second time stole all my father's horses . . . so he bought a three year old colt and did his plowing.

"A number of lawyers such as Messers Haywood, White, and Andrew Jackson made fortunes by the land suits growing out of those claims." [109]

And so they did; it was almost always the middle-class farmer, able to buy land in family-size plots, enough for his own use, who suffered most. If he unknowingly bought from a land speculator, land that still belonged to the Indians, and still unknowing, cleared fields, built houses, barns, and other outbuildings, he would sooner or later learn, if not from the scalping knife at least from officialdom, he could not stay. He lost all his work, and sometimes his life.[110]

In sharp contrast was the speculator who held the Indian lands. Some idea of how the business worked may be gained from the story of a five thousand acre tract of land, today swallowed by Memphis, Tennessee, but in 1796 when Andrew Jackson bought half of it from his good friend John Overton for only $100, still claimed and used by the Chickasaw. As time passed Jackson sold parts, always at a profit; by 1818 he had only a fourth of his original holdings; this he sold for $5,000.[111] He made in the twenty-two years he held the land a profit of $5,525 from investing $100 for one year, for he quickly sold off enough to get back his original investment. The big jump in price came in 1818 when largely through Jackson's own efforts as General and treaty maker, the land was cleared of Indian title. At no time did he or any of the others have to pay taxes. The reasoning was that since the Indian owned the land, the white man holding the warrant should not have to pay taxes.

Taxes also fell heaviest on the small farmer or the man with nothing. First there was the muster; each free man regardless of his property status had to spend at least four days yearly in musters, supplying gun, ammunition and other necessities. A lark for the man with slaves to do his work,

[109] Reprinted by permission of the author from *Life and Times of Edward Swanson* by William Henry McRaven, copyrighted by William Henry McRaven, Nashville, 1937, pp. 113-115. The narrator here is the Rev. Joseph Tarkington, grandfather of Booth Tarkington.
[110] As late as 1809 Return Meigs moved 201 families off Chickasaw lands and 83 off Cherokee, A, V, 262. These people were in double jeopardy—the Indians and the holders of the Indian lands.
[111] THM, I, 192-195.

and an officer into the bargain, but a hardship for the man who worked by day's wages, and had to reckon the cost of powder and ball. Road workings were, in the early years, slightly more equitable; each man had to furnish a hand not only for himself but for all taxable polls; this meant all slaves, usually above sixteen years of age, so that in the matter of roads the man with many wagons and a carriage usually had to contribute more than the man without even a sled.

Special taxes such as a poll tax levied in 1786 for the building of a courthouse in Sumner County [112] fell just as heavily on the man with nothing, as on wealthy Daniel Smith. Even more unfair when viewed through modern eyes was the land tax. The Cumberland settlers were in the matter of this tax as in free land given preferential treatment, for it was 1787 before the North Carolina Assembly laid a tax on her land west of the mountains, and then only one shilling per hundred acres. Low as this was it represented a strain on the poor man struggling to make a living in some rocky cedar glade, paying exactly the same tax acre for acre as did the Donelsons on rich river bottom land with many improvements. Neither mansions nor mills nor any improvement on the land was considered taxable property until Tennessee made her second constitution in 1834–35. During this time rural properties were not taxed according to evaluation. The man with a broken-down gelding paid the same amount of tax on his horseflesh as did Andrew Jackson on a thousand-dollar brood mare; the only exception was in breeding stallions. Much the same situation prevailed up the Cumberland, under first Virginia, and then Kentucky law.[113]

There is no record that much of any one complained about the state of things in Middle Tennessee during the early years. The land tax, low as it was, still worked a hardship on those men who had managed to grab thousands of acres of land clear of Indian title. Kentucky was, during these years, the lodestar for western-bound settlers. Middle Tennessee continued too dangerous. The great inrush of settlers expected by many failed to materialize; the region had in 1795 less than ten thousand white settlers, and possibly one-sixth of these living on land they either had bought or were trying to buy. Speculators who had plunged too heavily were in a fair way of losing their shirts; as early as 1788 John Hadley was offering

---

[112] NCR, XXIV, 826–828, a shilling a poll and 4 pence on each 100 acres of land. Local taxes were levied by the North Carolina Assembly and varied from point to point; interesting is *ibid.*, 940–943, six different tax tables for six different localities; see also NCR, XX, 288.

[113] A résumé of Kentucky taxes during her first years of statehood is found in AMS, Finance, I, 433. Land in Kentucky was divided into three grades and taxed accordingly but improvements were not considered.

50,000 acres of land for sale at the "Nashville Cumberland Settlement, North Carolina." [114] Long lists of land to be sold for unpaid taxes were features of the first Nashville newspapers. Land continued cheap; in the mid-nineties Frederick Stump sold good rich black land on White's Creek for a dollar an acre, and by 1802 unimproved land near Nashville was not bringing more than five dollars an acre, though it is doubtful if there was by this date much good unimproved land in the immediate vicinity of Nashville. Land of course varied widely in quality, with the price also dependent on location and state of title.

Another added fillip was lost land; [115] almost every list of delinquent taxes carried a few items, "location unknown," but still whoever had bought the warrant had to pay taxes if it had been entered as being free of Indian title. By no means all men who managed to get thousands of acres in warrants made fortunes. It is doubtful if John Sevier, for example, who in August of 1795 sent off to North Carolina 150 warrants, each for 640 acres, and hence representing a domain of 150 square miles, made enough out of it all to pay for the fortune he had spent on Indian warfare. They were to begin with laid off near the mouth of Obey's River where most of the land was rough, and not too desirable. In 1798 he sold 28,000 acres at only $250 per thousand acres, a forced sale for he had to pay a debt. The highest price he ever got was when he sold 150 acres for two horses,[116] and if the horses were fairly good this would mean at least a dollar an acre. Meanwhile, he like other men used the warrants as money, loaned or put up as security.

This happened to many of the 151 given to first settlers or their heirs in 1784. Some like Thomas Sharpe Spencer [117] sold at once. In this case the buyer, Ephraim Peyton, in time settled on the land, but often the warrants circulated for years, with many not taken up until well past 1800, and by that late date the acreage called for by the warrant, if it could be had at all, must be found on the rougher lands of the Highland Rim and the Plateau.[118]

---

[114] Kentucky *Gazette*, Feb. 2, 1788.

[115] Tennessee *Gazette*, June 15, 1803, advertised six parcels of land, "the situation of which is unknown," one of 3,000 acres.

[116] THM, V, 179, 255. Bassett, *Jackson Correspondence*, like most other source materials, particularly the accounts of travelers and court minutes, has much on land—price, customers, titles, law suits, etc., etc.; see in particular I, 21-22, 38-39.

[117] DC, I, 33.

[118] Overton County on the Plateau and not formed until 1806 was a last resort for many land warrants from the Revolution, held until this late date, most signed by Willie, half-brother of William, Territorial Governor, Blount. See Register Book, I.

The number of speculators, land warrants in circulation, fortunes made and lost in land were out of all proportion to actual settlement. Still in the late summer of 1784, there was no longer the doubt there had been at times, that the first settlers could hold Middle Tennessee. Daniel Smith and the Bledsoes began stations late in that year, but even without these Haydon Wells, John Buchanan, and the others must have felt a taste of victory. They had corn, a mill, a county, and land.

CHAPTER XIII

SILK HANDKERCHIEFS
AND FEATHER BEDS

THE SETTLERS on the Cumberland who late in 1783 and early 1784 sought out the clerk of new Davidson County to record a stock mark or list an inventory were, except for now and then a fort school, enjoying for the first time in almost four years the benefits of an institution other than the home. Settlers upriver in Kentucky would live, some for more than twenty years, with no institution except the home. Children would get at least the rudiments of an education, religion take root, land be bought and sold, and in general civilization get planted, all with no focal point of life save the home, for throughout these years county court was across the Cumberland and for some almost two hundred miles away.[1]

This though somewhat unusual was not as remarkable then as it would be now. Home was, throughout the English-speaking world, much more important to begin with than it now is, and particularly so in the south. Life revolved about the plantation, not the town. The home was the center of social, cultural, and often for the younger children, educational life; and such manufacturing as was done took place on the plantation. Still, the older portions of the colonial south and especially Tidewater had from earliest days goodly representations of both Church and King,

[1] Kentucky County was created in 1776; this was in 1780 divided into Fayette, Jefferson, and Lincoln counties of Virginia; in 1792, the year the State of Kentucky was formed, a part of present-day Cumberland County became a part of Green County, organized in that year, but for close to twenty years most of the Cumberland Country in Kentucky east of Red River was governed from Stanford, though there were hundreds of families in the region, with many south of the Cumberland. Nashville served as a trade center, and there was little intercourse with Kentucky.

and soon there were small towns with courts, and in time theatres, taverns, institutions of learning, newspapers, a militia as well as representatives of the King's Army.

Even in the Great Valley and later in East Tennessee, the Church as an institution continued to be important, though instead of the Church of England it was the Presbyterian Church. In Augusta County the church, before the formation of county court, constituted in many communities a form of governing body, and even in East Tennessee as early as 1773, some years before Washington County, the first west of the mountains, was organized, there were two Presbyterian congregations. These, wishing to be a part of the larger Church body, sent in 1773 a petition with 130 signatures to the Hanover Presbytery.[2]

Nothing like this happened on the Cumberland in Middle Tennessee. The first recorded minister, Reverend Thomas Craighead, did not come until 1785,[3] and there is no record that anybody petitioned for him. I found no mention of any church building until 1787,[4] and this in the Red River region, close to Kentucky and comparatively safe from Indians, but seemingly unused. As late as 1800 the one church building in Nashville, and the only one south of the river, was still unfinished.[5] Yet, Middle Tennessee was destined to become a center of religious life for all the old southwest, and the newer south. Religion was there, taking firm root all through the first years, but because of the smallness of the population and the Indians ever waiting in ambush, it was practiced in the home with Bible, psalm book, and such sermon books as Watts' *Upon Prayer.*[6]

[2] Summers, *Southwest Virginia,* 138–141, lists the names.
[3] Albert C. Holt, *The Economic and Social Beginnings of Tennessee,* submitted to George Peabody College, 1923, as a dissertation for a Ph.D. and housed in Joint University Libraries, Nashville, 149.
[4] DW, I, 307. Cramer's Meeting House was merely mentioned in a private land transaction, and I found no mention of its use.
[5] Williams, *Travels,* "Journal of Reverend Francis Asbury" (cited hereafter as Asbury, "Journal"), 309, Aug. 19, 1800. The only church building finished and in use in all of Middle Tennessee at the time of Asbury's visit was Drake's Creek Meeting House, south of Mansker's; at least Asbury, *ibid.,* conducted services there.
[6] DW, I, beginning with Nicholas Gentry, 7, who had a Bible, most families had some work of a religious nature. The William Neelys, *ibid.,* 166—4 sermon books (titles of sermon books were seldom listed), Crook's *Confessions,* a *Psalm Book;* the Jacob Castlemans, *ibid.,* 194—*Bible, Hymn Book, Testament.* Montgomery County yielded much the same, Charles Feas, MW, I, 27, 3 *Bibles,* 2 *Testaments,* 3 *sermon books,* and upriver see PW, I, 46, 70, 77. Much insight into the reading habits of Middle Tennessee in 1797 may be gained from the religious works stocked in the store of Gen. James Winchester near present-day Cragfont—6 Whitefield's *Sermons,* 16 *School Bibles with Psalms,* 12 *Testaments,* 18 *Methodist Hymn Books* were only a few of the many items in the long list that also included such secular works as Lord Chesterfield's *Advice.* Items reprinted by permission of Robert T. Quarles, Jr., Presi-

Home was and continued to be for fifteen years, the center of all life, save governmental, and even the first courts, for lack of courthouses, met in private homes, and the jailer's home had to do for jail, or lacking a jailer, that of the sheriff. Early courts [7] were held in Kaspar Mansker's home, and it like Frederick Stump's was a stopping place for travelers, though most any home along a frontier road was a tavern of sorts offering "dry entertainment" to anybody the housewife cared to put up.[8] Frederick Stump's farm was a center of milling and distilling; he had a tavern in his home, and on Sundays and some week days it became a place of worship, open to any minister or group who cared to conduct a service, though it was only to the Moravians that he served free dinners.[9] The James Robertson home down on Richland Creek was a pioneer version of a combination of today's Pentagon and State Department, for here the Chickasaw came to visit and the Creek and Chickamauga to treat,[10] and from it came supplies for the unpaid soldiers.[11] Here, too, could sometimes be found a captive Indian child or so waiting to be exchanged for a white child.[12]

The Robertson farm like most others on the Cumberland was a fort, for all forts on the Cumberland, save Fort Blount, built around 1792,[13] were the homes of men, women, children, and babies, instead of mere living quarters for soldiers. There were more men than women, and many of these were spies and guards, hired by the owners, and any man who would survive had to be both soldier and hunter at times, but living never degenerated into total warfare. True, the Cumberland pioneers, no different from any other people in all the history of the world, were never able to devote themselves entirely to a positive life. It seems to be the nature of life that all of us from the plowed-up earthworm struggling to hide from the sunlight to the nation spending most of its income on preparation for war, must

dent of the Tennessee Historical Society, owner of the Mss bill of Jan. 7, 1797, from Philadelphia, housed in the Archives Division, Tennessee State Library and Archives, Nashville.

[7] W, 29S, 74. This was not county court but a meeting of surveyors and land commissioners, including Daniel Smith who lived at Mansker's for several months in 1784 while his station on Drake's Creek was being built.

[8] Parton, *Jackson*, I, Baily, "Tour 1797," 184.

[9] Williams, *Travels*, Schweinitz, "Report," 511-512.

[10] NCR, XVII, 91-92, and *ibid.*, XIX, 739.

[11] W, 30S, 523, from the account of Thomas Hickman.

[12] A, III, 287. Robertson kept two Creek girls for some time.

[13] Fort Blount, known in its early days as Big Lick Garrison on Cumberland, see Smith, *Description*, 14, was on the northern side of the river, across from the mouth of Flinn's Creek, near the crossing of Tollunteeskee's Trail. See in the Clements Library, Abraham Bradley, Jr., "Map of the United States Exhibiting the Post-Roads, the Situations, Connections and distances of the Post offices, 1804." This work shows Fort Blount.

give much to the negative aspects of life. The Cumberlander had more enemies to contend with than almost any man in the history of our country —corruption in high places, a Federal government that would not only do nothing for him but was at times openly antagonistic, all the usual enemies of the pioneer from sprouting stumps to indebtedness for supplies to carry him through the lean first years, bad titles, and always the Indian.

Still, the fifteen years of forted life and Indian warfare most knew changed their lives far less in all aspects than does the cold war direct our lives. The blood-tested and tagged young city child of today, who lives knowing what road he should take in case of an attack, never permitted to forget the atom bomb, and carefully reared to hate the name of all ideologies his elders believe might limit his job opportunities when he grows up, certainly suffers more emotional scarring and mental terror than did little Polly Dunham of Freeland's Station, showing the scars on her scalp. She knew the taste of victory. She could always boast that though the Indians ringed her head for scalping she still had all her hair. Her mother had, on hearing her screams, rushed out and in spite of being badly wounded, had driven the Indians off with a hoe.[14]

We talk much today of preservation, of survival, and of destroying things that seem to threaten our way of life. The ones writing their memories to Mr. Draper never spoke of survival; they would, I think, have scorned a life that offered nothing more. They were not even determined to destroy the Indian;[15] this came later. They were determined to live, Indians or no. This meant having, or being part of, a home. Fort Loudon, no different from other forts in the old west held by wifeless soldiers, eventually fell, and the woods closed over its site, but any man who built a cabin and cleared a bit of land and brought a wife and children, even though all were killed and the house burned, had made another little hole in the Indian's life pattern and extended the frontier.

It is doubtful if the average pioneer thought of himself as an empire builder. He was determined to live, and regardless of how near or far death waited, the Cumberlander lived until he died. Even the thrifty Scotch or German farmers, so much a part of the scene, showed by the things each left behind him, that the most important thing to do with life was to live it.

Most died, preparing for an earthly future; Jacob Castleman to leave his

[14] W, 32S, 318.
[15] W, 30S, 445–456. This story of John Blair, scalped, shot, trampled upon and left for dead, is the only instance found of a white man who hated all Indians, and of him the narrator remarked, "He dislikes Indians to this day."

flax "unbroke," and young heifers that would in time have made cows; some left "cotton in ye seed," others with unused cloth for the new suit,[16] gears for the new wagon, pewter for new spoons.[17] Most were killed or wounded, not in Indian battles, but while going about the business of their lives: "a woman washing at the spring," "carrying a basket of clothes," [18] "sitting by the fire and singing at the top of his lungs," [19] "with a load of cane on his shoulder for his horse," [20] "he had just had a log rolling," [21] "at the springhouse," [22] "behind a nursery of trees," [23] and "on their way to school." [24] Pages would be required to enumerate the incidents surrounding the deaths, but in them all there is nothing to indicate either men or women neglected their work through fear of Indians. Cautious they were, but clothes got washed, cows milked, children taught, fields cleared and stables built; the forted home made life possible. Life never consisted in hiding behind its walls.

The war whoop sounded often as did the battle shout, and now and again one could have heard the quivering screams of a child's agony as some grim-eyed, gray-faced mother used the shoemaker's awl: "for I have sean my mother bore hundreds of awl holes through the skull of the younger Bolden so as to let the flesh through, [he] and the older son were both shot close by the nipples on the left side and came out thru rite side and behold neither of them dide." [25]

Still, most of the day-to-day sounds, sights, and smells around any forted farm were those of the plantation growing in the woods; cow and horse and sheep bells, the forever ringing axes, thud of maul, tearing sound of white oak under the froe, whoosh of drawing knife, crash of falling tree, sputter and crackle of a limekiln fire, ring of blacksmith hammer, meat frying, whir of spinning wheel, thumpety bang of a loom, whispering scratch of flax or hemp running through the hackle, and through and over and under everything the sound of the human voice. All things indicate that the Cumberland pioneer in the use of his voice was closer akin to the

[16] MW, I, 3.
[17] DW, I, 231–232, sale of the William Neely goods.
[18] W, 32S, 204.
[19] W, 6XX (99), 5–6.
[20] W, 6XX, 69.
[21] W, 31S, 193–194. This was Isaac Bledsoe, ambushed April 2, 1793.
[22] W, 31S, 388.
[23] W, 31S, 388.
[24] W, 30S, 241. These were two young Bledsoe boys, cousins, a son each of Anthony and Isaac.
[25] W, 6XX, 98.

laughing, crying, cursing, storytelling, joking, singing Englishman as portrayed by Smollett and other eighteenth century English novelists than to any group in America today.

On any summer day one could have heard singing, both in the woods around French Lick and behind fort walls; for some a patriotic favorite of the Cumberland, recounting the lack of valor of some men at Point Pleasant; for even in his songs the pioneer was outspoken:

> "And old Andrew Lewis, in his tent he did set
> With his cowards around him, alas he did sweat
> His blankets spread over him, and hearing the guns roar,
> Saying was I at home, I would come here no more." [26]

Old ballads of death and love and hard-hearted maidens have survived until today, and everybody religious or no sang hymns, and Watts [27] was for the borderer ever a favorite:

> "Not all the outward forms on earth
> Nor Rites that God has given
> Nor will of man, nor Blood, nor Birth
> Can raise a soul to Heaven.
>
> The Sov'reign will of God alone
> Creates us heirs of Grace
> Born in the image of his son
> A new peculiar race."

One could have heard the treble voice of a young child sing-songing as he shelled the bread corn: "a b – ab; e b – eb;" until at last triumphant and with no quick peepings, "u b – ub," the first line in Dilworth [28] that so many of them had. Sunday afternoons while many boys played, young

---

[26] Thwaites-Kellogg, *Dunmore's War*, 163, quoting W, 3XX (18), 51.

[27] Isaac Watts, *The Psalms, Hymns, and spiritual Songs of the Old and New Testament Faithfully translated into English metre based on the New England Psalm Book, printed in 1640*, Boston, 1758, p. 357. This was only one of several editions of Watts circulating in America by the time the Cumberland was settled. Beginning with James Smith in 1766 some edition of Watts is mentioned on the Cumberland, for his doctrine of predestination was acceptable to both Baptist and Presbyterian. The Methodist hymn books stocked by Gen. Winchester would on the other hand have leaned heavily on Wesley.

[28] Thomas Dilworth, *A New Guide to the English Tongue*, School Master, Wapping School, June 14, 1740, 1773, Boston edit., p. 2. Even the children of Methodists would through Dilworth, also circulating in numerous editions and stocked by Gen. Winchester, get something of Watts, for Dilworth quoted him much.

Jonathan Ramsey at Eaton's could have been heard, slowly reading from the same book, "The way of man is not as the way of God. The law of God is a joy to me." [29]

Upriver and about four miles from French Lick around Buchanan's Station, still being built in 1785, grown, but unmarried, John Buchanan might have been heard chanting as he struggled with that tricky thing, the double rule of three: "If twenty dogs for thirty groats go forty weeks to grass how many hounds for sixty crowns may winter in that place." [30]

John had by that date lost a brother and a father [31] to the Indians, and the family had for many months been split up with his mother and the Mulherrin women living in Kentucky. They had lost four years' work in the fort they had helped build at French Lick, and the fields they had cleared, but there had been time to make an arithmetic. We know the look and feel of John Buchanan's arithmetic, homemade in 1781, even the smell of the tanned deerskin cover decorated with a cotton flower, but we can only surmise how young John looked. His dress and the way he wore his hair, and the cut of his shirt would have been like those of his father and other farmers of that day, for in matters of dress as well as home life the pioneer showed his determination to live as a civilized man, and this, following the custom of the southern colonies, meant dressing well.

The old colonial laws on dress had never held even in the Great Valley. Dress, much more so then than now, was for men a form of self-expression, but was yielding rather rapidly to what one might call Americanization or standardization. Still, if the group that met in 1775 on the Watauga to listen to Attakullakulla could have been transported unchanged to the first court on Cumberland, the difference would have been in degree rather than in kind.

French Lick and other stations had drawn heavily from East Tennessee in settlers but they had from earliest years a mixing and a mingling of peoples and customs unknown in the Scotch–Irish world of the Holston. Chickasaw brave, Tidewater dandy, seasoned Indian fighter, German farmer, *coureur de bois,* and Spanish trader all added something to the Cumberland, and always, like a gay lady out of sight but obtainable, was the influence of New Orleans.

[29] W, 5S, 73. Quote from Dilworth's *A New Guide to the English Tongue,* Boston, 1773, p. 2.
[30] Quoted by permission of Robert T. Quarles, Jr., President of the Tennessee Historical Society, owner of Mss Book of Arithmetic by John Buchanan, 1781. Housed in the Archives Division, Tennessee State Library and Archives, Nashville (cited hereafter as Buchanan, *Arithmetic*).
[31] Featherstonhaugh, *Excursion,* I, 199–211.

Wigs were going out of fashion, and French Lick like the Holston country was not exactly wig territory, but one might have seen a wig or so,[32] and now and then a head of powdered hair such as little Felix Robertson [33] saw in 1786, but this so unusual he remembered it to his old age.

John Buchanan, born in 1759, probably wore long hair until after his marriage [34] in 1786, for as late as 1788, "It was customary [35] for young people to wear their hair long," and still later Andrew Jackson, not so young, wore his long hair in a circle of eelskin on his first venture into national politics.[36] Still, through these years short hair became more and more common, though it was 1802 before the United States [37] Army decreed that all its members should wear short hair. In time most of the older men compromised and wore a rather short bob as did Washington and other founding fathers. Sevier, Robertson, and other leaders of the old west are so painted.[38]

Sales and inventories, store accounts and tailors' bills as well as chance accounts of Indian warfare such as "a bullet through his hat brim," [39] "the Indians laid hold of his vest," indicate that the working man was decently dressed in hat, coat, vest, shirt, shoes, stockings, and waistcoat, depending on the season and his work. We can be certain Haydon Wells put on his "best bib and tucker" when he appeared in court, but that no blacksmith, not even prosperous Mr. Snyder, would have shaped a horseshoe without the leathern apron, worn by all blacksmiths.[40]

[32] Guild, *Old Times*, 89, described Judge White as wearing a wig as late as 1825.

[33] Robertson, "Memories," Nashville *Journal of Medicine and Surgery*, VIII, 452.

[34] Buchanan, *Arithmetic*. See also Featherstonhaugh, *Excursion*, I, 200-205. John's first wife was Miss Mary Kennedy who died after bearing a son; he then married in 1791 Miss Sally Ridley, whose father Col. Daniel Ridley came in 1790 and built a station about two miles from Buchanan's.

[35] Ramsey, *Tennessee*, 512, quoting Joseph Brown captured in 1788.

[36] Parton, *Jackson*, I, 196.

[37] The battle of General Butler's queue went on for some time; it was 1805 when Jackson and other prominent Cumberlanders petitioned the army concerning Butler, AMS, Class V, I, 173-174.

[38] S. G. Heiskell, *Andrew Jackson and Early Tennessee History*, Nashville, 1918, contains portraits of early leaders of Tennessee, a few such as that of John Coffee with their wives, and all give some indication of hair styles and dress.

[39] W, 6XX (50), 21.

[40] John Neagle's "Pat Lyon at the Forge," though of a later date, around 1826, and from a different section of the country, is I believe quite typical of the dress of the blacksmith, cooper, or cobbler of this period—plain shirt, leathern apron, with breeches and stockings; these though fairly common among workingmen at the settlement of the Cumberland, gradually yielded to trousers. "Pat Lyon" cited by permission of the Department of Fine Arts, Carnegie Institute of Pittsburgh, from *Survey of American Painting*, published and copyrighted Department of Fine Arts, Carnegie Institute, Pittsburgh, 1940 (cited hereafter as Carnegie, *Survey of Painting*), Plate 29, courtesy Museum of Fine Arts, Boston.

Young John Buchanan, prosperous farmer and landowner, soon a major of militia, would as he went about his work in the fields or getting out logs have worn knee breeches, drop-seated, made of coarse linen or even hemp linen in summer and woolen cloth or linsey-woolsey in winter. He had, if not silver, brass or steel knee buckles for Sundays, but for everyday he most probably used garters, strips of red or blue cloth tied at the knees, bringing stockings and breech leg together.[41] Stockings were customarily of linen or woolen thread, hand-knitted, and practically all men wore stockings as they appear in most inventories. John's work shoes would have been rather coarse, possibly even of home make or by a local cobbler, as many families [42] had sides of sole leather, though all sole leather did not go into shoes, but often into harness.

There were flannel shirts for winter, flannel drawers,[43] and plenty of overcoats, but in summer the work shirt like the breeches was most commonly of tow linen, though much work clothing was of hemp linen,[44] particularly that worn by the slave—and Edward Larrimore,[45] forced to sell his all to pay a debt, had a coat, vest, and shirt of hemp linen. The style and fit of the work shirt depended upon the time and skill of the womenfolk; young John Buchanan's probably had buttons but few if any ruffles, while many were cut on the order of the sailor's middy blouse, a thing to be slipped over the head, buttonless and with no collar or only a small square one.[46]

The working man often wore in summer a hat homemade of woven osier twigs, flax, wheat, or oat straw,[47] but not always. The Cumberland pioneer, like the hill farmer one hundred and fifty years later, sometimes wore a felt

[41] Kercheval, *Virginia*, 152.
[42] DW, I, 175, 307; MW, I, 3.
[43] Drawers were less plentiful and appear to have been owned only by the more affluent men. DW, II, 132, John Deadrick had both flannel and nankeen drawers, and earlier, *ibid.*, 7, Ezekial Carruthers had two pair.
[44] Hemp when carefully hackled and well bleached made quite nice-looking cloth; a good example may be seen in the Mountain Life Museum, Levi Jackson Wilderness Road State Park, London, Ky. Pioneer Clinkenbeard in Kentucky, FQ, II, 109, "Interview," wore hemp shirts, and hempen cloth was the first made in their station, *ibid.*, 108, 119.
[45] DW, I, 4.
[46] The Frye and Jefferson Map of 1751, facsimile reproduction, Dumas Malone, Princeton University Press, 1950, shows tobacco hogshead handlers dressed only in breech clouts, and field hands in the deeper south often in summer went without shirts.
[47] Williams, *Smith*, 13, tells of osier twig hats. Richmond Kelly, *The Kelly Clan*, Portland, Ore., 1901, p. 72, though writing of Pulaski County, Ky., past the pioneer period, around 1835, describes homemade hats much like those used earlier; they were "durable and heavy," with wheat straw on the outside and flax straw inside, to make "a double straw hat."

hat, summer as well as winter. John Bond,[48] for example, had when he was killed only an old felt hat, one blanket much worn, and one old coat.

Poor John Bond, however, had the least of any man whose clothing was mentioned at all. The basic outfit of the working man, simple as it was, lent itself to many variations. Instead of a hat, there might be a leather or woolen cap which by 1800 could be had at most any general store.[49] Paid guards, hunters, and even working farmers, when not in the woods where bright clothing was a death trap, more closely resembled the present-day popular conception of a pirate than that of a pioneer. Pigtailed and pantalooned in buckled shoes or boots, they often wore bright satin, velvet, or still brighter "quilted Spanish silk" [50] jackets, and waistcoats, the whole topped off with bright silk handkerchiefs for both cravats and head coverings. Joseph Bishop,[51] visiting the Illinois in 1793, was so dressed, though the Indian with him wore a beaver hat, breech clout, and moccasins.

Leather continued to be worn, and many doubtless dressed as did Terry Poe, who, coming in 1791, wore leather breeches and worsted stockings, but different from most he had "a poultice on his sore toe." [52] Most farmers had at least one pair of leather breeches, though these were always expensive; Mr. McCain's selling in 1789 for the very large sum of two pounds, though his velvet jacket brought only six shillings.[53] Prices of clothing, however, sold in the small world of the middle Cumberland mean little; added to the question of demand, as in the case of ironware, was the problem of proper fit and always the possibility the article was badly worn, and judging from the contrast between the high price of cloth [54] and the small amounts brought by many articles of clothing, the Cumberlander with money to spend avoided secondhand clothing.[55]

Few hunting shirts and no moccasins were found in inventories, though

---

[48] DW, I, 54.

[49] Dr. Daniel Drake wore a wool hat as a boy in Kentucky in the 1790's, Drake, *Letters*, 76. Fur hats are advertised in early *Gazettes*, and are particularly abundant in Coffee Papers, though few listed in the accounts were so expensive as the fur hat Robert Barnett of Lebanon bought from Jackson and Hutchings, Coffee Papers, 1802, for $6. The closest thing found to a coonskin cap was the "raccoon hat" of J. Conrad, MW, I, 3.

[50] W, 3XX, 32.

[51] Gray, *Bishop*, 88–90.

[52] *Ibid.*, 31.

[53] DW, I, 107.

[54] See in particular the account of Col. Thomas Butler, Coffee Papers, rendered Aug. 26, 1804, for purchases made for two years previous.

[55] Court records list the buyers; hence we can know that, DW, II, 7, Andrew Jackson attended the sale of a Davidson County farmer and bought a grubbing hoe for $3 but none of the wide assortment of clothing offered.

they were sometimes mentioned. Hunting shirts were at this time more common among the wealthy; Daniel Smith had one made for him,[56] and wealthy Pleasant Lockett had a hunting shirt, but also a broadcloth coat, much cloth, and other clothing.[57] The less affluent hunted without a special outfit, and made do with what they had. Boots were rather scarce, and I found only one pair of gum boots,[58] but this didn't mean the farmer went with cold wet feet; in winter he greased his work shoes well with tallow, and for extra warmth, lacking boots, he wore two pair of woolen stockings, the second pair footless, often an old pair much worn, pulled down over the shoe and fastened in the manner of a "gaither." [59] Lacking extra woolen stockings, woolen cloth was cut and sewed into the proper shape, or such was the manner in which Mrs. George Madison, north of Nashville, made foot warmers for the frostbitten elder Michaux in January of 1796.[60]

Leggings were fairly common, but much less so than twenty years before, and all found were, when described at all, of cloth instead of leather. They, too, were brightly colored, usually blue, ranging in price [61] from $5.50 to only a few shillings. Leggings were held up by strings fastened to the belt,[62] but cumbersome as they were, had until around the time of the Revolution been almost a must for the man traveling in the woods. There was by the time the Cumberland was settled less need for this protective leg covering. Pantaloons had come into use for the working man. These, reaching to the ankle, were worn by the poor man for the same reason the Virginia soldier wore them—"to save stockings." [63] We see them all through the old west; Pressly Anderson on his way to Kentucky "walked along barefooted with his pantaloons rolled up"; young Daniel Drake got a new pair of fustian,[64] and inventories of most farmers on the Cumberland list at least one pair of pantaloons, "called trousers then." [65]

The overall, also quite well established at the settlement of the Cumberland, was an adaptation of trousers, a working garment with bib and straps, made to be worn without belt or jacket, and, like trousers, issued to

---

[56] THM, I, 62.
[57] DW, II, 17. Lawrence Lollar, another well dressed gentleman, dying around 1791, also had a hunting shirt, *ibid.*, I, 291.
[58] MW, I, 17, but this was 1797.
[59] Drake, *Letters*, 76.
[60] Thwaites, *Travels*, III, Michaux, "Journal," 87.
[61] MW, I, 3; DW, I, 291.
[62] Kercheval, *Virginia*, Doddridge, "Notes," 257.
[63] VS, I, 526.
[64] Drake, *Letters*, 68. P. Anderson, FQ, II, Clinkenbeard "Interview," 98.
[65] RK, XXVII, No. 79, Taul, "Memoirs," 9.

soldiers during the Revolution.[66] One could by the mid-nineties buy them in East Tennessee at the general store, and they, too, were sometimes brightly colored and often made of corduroy.[67] Like other work clothes, they were also made of leather; Captain Budd traveling to Middle Tennessee in the summer of 1784 had new "overalls and mockersons made and that night was afraid to pull them off for fear he could no more put them on again."[68] Dressed deerskin was pleasantly soft to the touch when dry, but unless carefully tanned, would, after being wetted, dry hard and stiff, and throughout the pioneer period, a good bit of tanning was done at home. Ten-year-old John Smith wore in 1795, a pair of new deerskin trousers made entirely by his father, who with his older sons was batching in Stockton's Valley, a few miles north of the mouth of Obey's River. In the fall when the corn crop came in, young John was tolled off to make the two-hundred-mile round trip to Horne's Mill on Dix River near present-day Danville. He, in his old age, remembered little of the trip save his own new trousers and the sight at Crab Orchard of a fiddler in yellow velvet breeches and a gay coat.[69]

The frontier had place both for velvet breeches and home-tanned home-made deerskin trousers, but in general the buckskin-dressed frontiersman was not much in evidence. The only man I met, dressed entirely in buckskins, was the well educated not to say sophisticated Dr. James White who came to Middle Tennessee in 1784, and later spent much of his time at Hickman's Station on Sulphur Creek a few miles west of Nashville. The good doctor at times went on what was then known as a spree; dressed in buckskins he would go marching about with a gourdful of whiskey under his arm, demanding that all grown males drink with him. Major William E. Lewis refused, and was forthwith knocked down and called a "damned aristocratic liar."[70]

---

[66] VS, I, 396, 526. The overall was more popular in the War of 1812; for example, 16 women of Barren and Hardin counties, Ky., who in 1812 donated clothing for the troops sent "eight sets" of overalls, some with shirts and some with jackets, but only one woman sent "2 yearn hunting shirts." See W. Richardson, "Patriotic Females of Kentucky," RK, XXVII, 107–108. The Revolutionary soldier fought in whatever he could get; in Virginia the officers hoped only to get for their men, shirts, jackets, breeches, VS, I, 390.

[67] John Sevier often bought overalls for his workmen during the 1790's; see THM, V, 173, 176.

[68] Williams, *Travels*, Lipscomb, "Journal," 275. One of the stories of my childhood was that of an ancestor, chased when a young boy, by a bear; the "bear" after much excitement turned out to be his dried trousers, one leg clapping against the other as he ran.

[69] Williams, *Smith*, 25.

[70] Nashville *Journal of Medicine and Surgery*, VIII, Robertson, "Memories," 449.

Some early citizens on the Cumberland were no doubt as unsavory in appearance as Tom Johnson found his Danville neighbor Captain Hughes around 1789:

> A dingy hat compound of wool,
>   Closely confined his empty skull
> Beneath short hair in Baptist dock
>   With vermin strung in every lock
> His little eyes both sore and red,
>   Were sunk an inch within his head:
> O'er which a pair of eye-brows rose,
>   Shading the wart upon his nose.
>
> The old blue coat kept for parade
>   Was clean, 'tis true, but badly made;
> His breeches I can't tell whether
>   Deer or cow once owned the leather
> But this I'm sure I know full well,
>   They greasy were and black as Hell.
> His stockings were of sable hue
>   And leathern strings confin'd his shoe.[71]

More than one white-collar worker may have cut no better figure than did an apprentice court clerk in Kentucky's Winchester of 1795, whose "coat was of blue cloth—had been made for a large man, but razeed to come near fitting him, his pantaloons were of the coarsest kind of striped linsey-woolsey—his shirt of about five hundred hemp cloth, shoes he had none—but he wore a pair of moccasons that looked like they had been made of undressed bull's hide." [72]

Such may have been on the Cumberland, but it is doubtful if the court clerk in moccasins was any more typical of the frontier than bachelor merchant John Deadrick [73] who came out around 1789. He had in addition to the usual clothing, a sword, a pistol with holsters, eight pair of silk stockings, and what was less common, several pair of drawers, and a hundred dollar gold watch. There were many men wealthier than he, but

[71] Quoted by permission of the editor and publisher, John Wilson Townsend, from *O Rare Tom Johnson*, Lexington, 1949, a facsimile of an 1821 edition of Johnson's poetry, first published as *The Kentucky Miscellany*, Lexington, 1789, p. 18.

[72] RK, XXVII, No. 79, Taul "Memoirs," 9.

[73] DC, I, 346, and DW, II, 105-106, 132, for inventories and sale.

so fortunate, theirs were not among the early inventories. The Cumberland pioneer could buy around French Lick before the Indian wars were over, velvet, thicksett, Royal Bib, buckram, or a hat lining.[74] He could, still without leaving his community, visit a tailor [75] and a hatter,[76] or order anything he wished from New Orleans or Philadelphia.

The John Deadricks and Dr. Sappingtons were early settlers, but they did not grub the sprouts and fight the Indians. Such a one was Jacob Castleman,[77] who poorer than most for he got neither land nor pay for all the powder and lead, not to mention blood he'd lost in helping win Kentucky and Tennessee, had little more than a change of clothing when he died. He had a coat, jacket, and breeches, but even with only these, a well made shirt, worsted stockings, and buckled shoes, he could have had the neat and thrifty air of a good German farmer.

The three pieces mentioned most likely formed a suit, a good deal like that worn by Andrew Greer when in 1780 he left the battlefield and went to tell the Continental Congress of the victory at Kings Mountain. His suit was the customary homespun wool now a rather faded or "tolerable blue" as it was then known, almost the color of a well worn pair of today's blue jeans. The breeches fastened just below the knee with small buckles covered with the suit material as were the buttons on the vest and the split-tailed long suit coat. The full-skirted and caped greatcoat, the most common overcoat of the day, was also of homespun, but the cloth had gone through a fulling process that matted the fibers and gave a close, felt-like finish. The medium-crowned, wide-brimmed, felt hat has about it the same air of neat respectability and comfort as have the other articles.[78] All bespeak the abundant life of a big man who lived well, but reserved his broadcloth for Sundays. Such would have made the Sunday best for Jacob Castleman and many other thrifty farmers.

John Buchanan, Sr., a tall, spare, blue-eyed man who survived the first bloody years, but after being forced to move was killed down on Mill Creek before the new station was finished, dressed much like Jacob Castleman or Andrew Greer; for he had two coats, two jackets, two pairs of

---

[74] DW, II, 133. This the inventory of merchant Henry Wiggins contains all manner of items for the cobbler—24 pr. shoe buckles, the hatter—hat linings, and numerous bolts of cloth and other items for the tailor.

[75] Judging from the Lanier merchandise of 1787, DW, I, 34, 63, tailoring was even by this date an expanding trade—30 pr. scissors, 6 gross needles, 2 doz. thimbles.

[76] DW, I, 78. A Davidson County hatter of 1788 takes an apprentice.

[77] DW, I, 194.

[78] The Greer clothing, property of the Tennessee Historical Society, may be seen in the Tennessee State Museum, Nashville.

breeches, a greatcoat, and knee and shoe buckles.[79] Most inventories of
first settlers who were farmers give much the same general picture. Lawrence Lollar,[80] another first settler, but killed before he could settle his
land, had all of the old-fashioned stand-bys owned by Buchanan, with
shirts, stockings, and garters, and in addition a pair each of overalls and
trousers, along with various extras such as a silk handkerchief. The handkerchief sold for a dollar; his shoes brought only a shilling, but his overalls
went for two dollars as compared to two dollars, one shilling and six-pence
for a shirt.

In general, the older and wealthier the man, the less inclined he was to
wear either trousers or overalls for these were worn chiefly by the laborer.
Most farmers and professional men would have looked in silhouette little
different from Dr. Sappington in shorts and buckled shoes, and many continued to dress in such fashion all their lives. Micah Taul's father, a Quaker
turned Baptist, who came to Kentucky in 1787 had "a great contempt for
the fashions and innovations of the day. When I can first remember [Mi-
cah was born in 1785] he wore a low-crowned, broad-brimmed hat—and
he wore no other fashion to the day of his death. Nor did he change the
fashion of his coat or waistcoat—perhaps a few years before his death [in
1812] he substituted pantaloons for short breeches." [81] Knee breeches continued to be worn long after the War of 1812; as late as 1833 both Chief
Justice Marshall and Judge Duval of the Supreme Court attended Washington social affairs in the old style of "shorts and knee buckles." [82] Mr.
William Gubbins was admitted to practice at the Davidson County Bar
in the spring of 1785,[83] and was killed by Indians [84] almost a year later.
He might, judging from other inventories, be taken as fairly typical of
what the professional man [85] wore on the Cumberland in the 1780's. Less
elegant than Mr. Deadrick, more affluent than Mr. Castleman, he was probably about average with his one dozen stocks as the neckcloth of the day
was known. Most would have been of good linen, though like all cloth of
the day, homespun; modern usage of the word often indicates coarseness,

[79] DW, I, 69, the John Buchanan inventory.
[80] DW, I, 291.
[81] RK, XXVII, No. 79, Taul, "Memoirs," 9.
[82] Burke, *Emily Donelson*, II, 34–35, quoting Mary Coffee—greatniece-in-law of
A. Jackson—Jan. 27, 1833, to her brother in Alabama.
[83] DC, I, 62.
[84] NCR, XVIII, 609. His inventory DW, I, 59.
[85] See Bassett, *Jackson Correspondence*, I, 41, and note for clothing items of another
lawyer on the Cumberland, ten years later, though A. Jackson could not, in his dress,
compare with Mr. Gubbins.

but material of homespun thread could be anything, even sheer hand-blocked cotton [86] or linen, that made in East Tennessee by tradition so fine a yard web could be pulled through a "finger ring."

Many of the ten shirts owned by Mr. Gubbins were of fine linen, we can be certain, nicely ruffled, though between the snowy stock, fastened with a silver buckle, and any one of his eight vests, all "of different kinds," little of his shirt front was visible. Some of the vests would have been of silk and brightly colored; everything indicates that on the Cumberland the bright silk vest or waistcoat, even for the poor hunter such as Joseph Bishop, was much more common than the hunting shirt. Mr. Gubbins belonged to the old school for he had no trousers, only breeches, five of cloth and one of leather; he also had overalls, and five coats, one of which was claret colored. He had twenty-one pairs of hose, one pair of silver shoe buckles with buckle brush, shoe horn and shoe brushes, though nothing was said of shoes, but gloves were listed.

As Mr. Gubbins went about on business he carried a small pocketknife, a parchment pocketbook, some of his silk and linen handkerchiefs, possibly his powder flask and loaded whip handle, and we can be certain he wore his silver watch chain with its four keys.[87] He had a cotton nightcap, and had prepared himself for the rigors of a frontier boarding house by bringing his own large butter knife and linen and silk napkins. He may have been something of a sportsman for he had a jointed fishing rod, but most of his possessions were those customarily owned by lawyers—two papers of ink powder, several quires of paper with the usual wafer box. He had among "sundry other trifles," many pamphlets and several books, including Blackstone's *Commentaries* and Montesquieu's *Spirit of Laws.*

The outfit of Mr. Gubbins was no better than that of many well-to-do farmers. John Harrison,[88] killed in the early nineties, also had a wide assortment of clothing featuring many silk waistcoats, some of which must have been highly ornamental for they brought around $1.75 each, with breeches going for three dollars and stockings for fifty cents. Joseph Conrad [89] was a working farmer, well-to-do, with land, tools, and horses. His wardrobe indicates in some measure the varied life of a farmer in the outlying regions,

[86] Michaux, *Travels, 1802,* 295, declared the cotton cloth in West Tennessee as Middle Tennessee was then known, to be the finest of any he had seen in the U.S.

[87] In any inventory of a man killed by Indians the fact that the body, even when found, was usually stripped of everything, should be taken into consideration; Mr. Gubbins may have had a watch and numerous other possessions; if on horseback at the time these could have included silver spurs, saddle, and furniture.

[88] DW, I, 312.

[89] MW, I, 3.

for the listing of his inventory was one of the first things attended to by the clerk of newly formed Montgomery County in 1797. His blue cloth leggings brought $5.25; a pair of overalls, $4.50; leather breeches, $4.75 as compared to $3.00, six days' wages, for a pair of silk hose.

His cheaper suits of vest, coat, and breeches sold for as low as $1.75 and none for more than $6.50 with shirts selling accordingly, flannel bringing $1.25. He had many silk handkerchiefs, and not only a greatcoat, but also a surtout, a long and close-fitting garment, more suited to carriage riding in winter than for horseback journeys as was the greatcoat. He probably wore with his surtout, his best beaver hat that with cover sold for $6.00, three less than his silver spurs. His boots sold for $8.50 and these with the spurs, and all secondhand, represented more than four months' wages for a woman worker in Mr. Slater's cotton mill not long opened in New England.[90]

Silver spurs, broadcloth suits, silk hose, and brightly colored waistcoats were ever a part of pioneer life all up and down the Mississippi, thickening of course in the vicinity of New Orleans, but even far up on the Indian-infested Ohio of 1790, Captain Johnston coming down from Pittsburgh was "handsomely dressed in a broadcloth surtout, red vest, fine ruffled shirt and a new pair of boots." [91] Mr. Jacob Skyles, his traveling companion, had a cargo of silks, cambrics, broadcloth, chocolate, sugar, woolen nightcaps, and whiskey. Articles from such cargoes would eventually reach the Cumberland; others came up from New Orleans, and small and easily carried luxury items on the order of silk hose and dress patterns [92] of satin were brought by those such as James Robertson who visited North Carolina and even Philadelphia on business.

Many of these luxury items went to the lady of the household, but the dress of women compared to that of men is almost never mentioned by travelers or incidentally by those giving firsthand accounts of accidents and battles. Women were at such times usually around, but woman's dress during this period was much more standardized than that of men, and there is nothing to indicate that the colonial and pioneer women in America

[90] Clark, *Manufacturers*, 391–394. In 1791 women in the Hartford woolen mills got $1.00 for a fourteen-hour (sometimes longer), six-day week; boys for the same amount of time got $0.42; wages in New England were much lower than in the west at this time.

[91] McClung, *Sketches*, 227.

[92] The word "pattern" as used by the pioneer meant the amount of material needed for a specific thing. Sevier, THM, V, 189, bought July 8, 1796, "6 pair silk stockings and a muslin habit," but in April of 1797 he gave a "muslin pattern to Joanna and a dimity one to Polly."

dressed differently from English women of comparable economic and social conditions. Many men did, and constantly we meet them. No woman could compete with handsome Colonel Tarleton during the Revolution in "jacket and breeches of white linen fitted to his form with the utmost exactness," and boots of russet leather halfway up his legs, "the broad tops of which were turned down, the heels garnished with spurs of an immense size and length of rowel." The whole topped off by "a low-crowned hat, curiously formed from the snow-white feathers of the swan." All this on an unbroken, pawing stallion "with tassels on his Spanish bit" [93] was a sight that Hollywood has never even tried to re-create.

Even the hunter along the Ohio in 1802 "in a waistcoat with sleeves, a pair of pantaloons, and a large red and yellow worsted sash" [94] had a dash and an air of derring-do his wife, doing her housework in a long-tailed, full-skirted two-piece dress, brightened with an apron and almost always set off with a cap, white and lacey for the more affluent, could never match. Thus it is that constantly we meet few women but many men such as Colonel Benjamin Cleveland of East Tennessee who, during the Revolution, wore "two checquered handkerchiefs girted about his middle," [95] and Mr. Marshall in his shirt sleeves with a "red handkerchief on his head." [96]

Fairly typical of the pioneer woman's wardrobe all up and down the river is that of Catharine Lefever, widow of Isaac Lefever, a first settler. It is possible he was one of De Monbreun's hunters, and hence a Frenchman from Vincennes or the Illinois, but the French Catholics were not inclined to give their sons the names of Old Testament characters as were the French Huguenots, nor is it probable a French hunter would have got free land. Isaac was more likely to have been a descendant of Isaac and Catharine Lefever, who in 1712 came with other Huguenots to what is now Lancaster County, Pennsylvania, and there with their German friends who had also come from the Palatinate were among the little band of Pennsylvania gunsmiths who developed the American rifle.

Isaac Lefever was killed by Indians in 1781, leaving his young wife with two baby daughters. Whatever Catharine's national origin, she spoke English, too well in fact, for in 1784 a Davidson County jury that included the great hunter Thomas Spencer found her guilty of slander against another woman. Reparations were set at the very large figure of two hundred

[93] Parton, *Jackson*, I, 83, quoting Mrs. Ellet.
[94] Michaux, *Travels, 1802*, 137.
[95] W, 30S, 11.
[96] McClung, *Sketches*, 232.

pounds, hard money, and she being unable to pay it, the court ordered all her personal possessions sold.[97]

She must have watched with anxious disappointed eyes as all her pretty things were examined and sold, for even her scarlet cloak, that was for a woman what the greatcoat was to a man, brought only thirty-two shillings.[98] Different from the more affluent such as Mrs. James Robertson and the Donelson women, Catharine had no silk or satin dress, but chiefly calico. However, at this date calico was not the cheap mass-produced material of seventy years ago, but like any cotton cloth was more expensive than linen, and Catharine's may have come from France. Twenty years later when cloth was somewhat cheaper, calico still cost a dollar a yard in John Coffee's store at Haysborough, or two days' wages without keep. Yet, Catharine, a poor man's wife, had five calico petticoats, and one of these was red, for the petticoat of that day was not an undergarment but a skirt, gathered and held up with a drawstring, worn with the old-fashioned short gown or with a jacket as a waist. There were six cotton jackets, chiefly of calico, and also two calico gowns, and two robes, one-piece garments which in her case would have been worn instead of dressing gowns as house dresses, enlivened by aprons.

Her husband had been dead for almost three years, but she had as yet no mourning dress, only a black silk shade, black silk handkerchief, and four yards of black silk. While sewing or doing her housework she would have worn one of her two "papered caps," and of course an apron, the choice depending on her work, for she had several, some of gauze and one corded for dress-up, for the dainty apron has been a part of every woman's wardrobe for hundreds of years. Her underclothing consisted of two calico slips, and four others of the cheaper cotton gauze. Like practically all women of that day she sewed, and for this she had a basket, sewing silk and scissors with many short lengths of calico and other cotton cloth, some lace, both silk and cotton, as well as bows, tape, and numerous pieces of ribbon of various widths and styles, some striped, and in addition five yards of silk lace.

Like most other women she at times rode horseback, and for this she had the usual habit,[99] hers striped; with this she doubtless wore her leather

[97] DC, I, 29, 31.
[98] DW, I, 41-43. See also DC, I, 124.
[99] Riding habits had been in high style in England at least since the days of Samuel Pepys who didn't like them at all on the Queen and her ladies. Mrs. John Haggard, killed by Indians in the spring of 1792, had, DW, II, 4, a riding skirt, and much more clothing than Catharine Lefever—eight petticoats.

gloves, though she would also have worn them with her scarlet cloak. Her silk mitts [100] were reserved for summer wear with one of her good calico outfits, her dressed chip hat, her black silk shade, and her fan. On dress-up occasions, calling for the chip hat, she would have worn with her best calico jacket, one of her four pairs of cuffs, her beads, and two rings, and certainly her large brooch, known then as a stomacher. With all these she would have worn her silk stockings, and carried some one of her several silk handkerchiefs, though a large one was often worn scarf-like about the neck. She had cotton stockings, but for kitchen wear probably wore her "old blue" ones.

Snuffboxes were rather rare on the Cumberland,[101] but Catharine had two, though no mention is made of snuff. The stick of twist she had could be used for either chewing or smoking, not uncommon among women of that day; Rachel Jackson was not the only one to smoke a pipe. Catharine may, in attempting to support herself and children after the death of her husband, have sold many of her personal possessions and dower property. She had locket buttons, but no locket; a bedstead, sheet, and blanket, and an old feather bed, things along with a horse and saddle most girls of even rather poor farmers received at marriage, but Catharine had neither horse nor saddle. She did have the minimum toilet articles of a pair of brushes, a looking glass, and one smoothing iron. There were also a pail, small kettle, frying pan, two pair candle snuffers, a nutmeg grater, brass inkstand, and a covered chest. All her possessions brought only forty-six pounds, and she was remanded back to the custody of the sheriff.[102]

Mrs. William Neely whose husband had come with Robertson on the exploratory journey of 1779 and was killed about a year later, continued to keep house for her younger children until she was killed in 1788. Older and more old-fashioned than Catharine Lefever, she had three short gowns, by then going out of style, four petticoats, a cloth cloak, and an "old calico gown." [103] Most of the estate was set aside for the younger children, and it is possible that her best articles of clothing were left for these.

These inventories of middle-class farm wives or even those of somewhat

[100] Plain mitts were used as work gloves, and even to my childhood one of my grandmothers wore them when churning.

[101] No other first settler found had a snuffbox, but wealthier men coming later quite commonly owned them in the early nineties. DW, II, 91, "and some snuff." See also *ibid.*, 177, 178.

[102] Catharine confessed, DC, I, 36; and her daughters, *ibid.*, 59, were ordered bound out to Francis Armstrong to serve as servants until eighteen years old; he was to teach them to read the Bible, DW, I, 96.

[103] DW, I, 166. In connection with Mrs. Neely's death see Ramsey, *Tennessee*, 478.

wealthier women in Davidson County of the mid-nineties give little indication of the "chip bonnets, long silk gloves, most fashionable lace cloaks," [104]
silk garters, white Persian or plain silk shawls, ivory combs, and necklaces
that were a part of every well-to-do, and some not so well-to-do women's
wardrobes. Mrs. James Robertson's reticule and the few articles of clothing [105] we can still see indicate the pioneer woman never let Indians and a
temporary one-room log home interfere with her love of dainty things.

Still, even wealthy women seldom had, during the early years, as various
a wardrobe as their menfolks. A Nashville belle who in her old days wrote
of the Nashville of the early eighteen hundreds when she was a child there,
recalled that during those years even the fashionable ladies had no more
than two "good dresses" [106] of silk or satin, and these sometimes made by
themselves, though by this date ladies' tailors and habit-makers were, judging from the ads in the *Gazette*, quite numerous.

Dress for both men and women was ever important; John Bradford, editor of the Nashville *Gazette*, found space for discussion of women's clothing, not buried as today in a woman's page, for early newspapers were not
much inclined to subdivide humankind, but in the general news. He was
in 1803 much against the fashion of overly long earrings, and advised young
girls to wear strings of pearls in their ears as a substitute, "but a few white
ostrich feathers rising on the head before and a train of silk sweeping on
the ground below, add so much grace to a moving female figure as to attract all eyes with unceasing admiration." [107]

Nashville had before this date become a center of fashionable life for the
old west. The only member of the family for whom fashions were not of

---

[104] In addition to accounts in the Coffee Papers, inventories, and the comments of
travelers early Tenn. *Gazette* ads are revealing; see April 15, 1801, Lark and Robinson,
Taylors, advertise; see also one of the many ads of Bustard and Eastin, Feb. 18,
April 1, 1801.

[105] Several items belonging to Mrs. James Robertson and her sister-in-law Ann
Robertson Cockrill may be seen in the Tennessee State Museum, Nashville. Some
idea of the taste for luxury in the old southwest may be gained from Georges Henri
Victor Collot, French traveler down the Mississippi in 1796. His work, *A Journey
in North America*, tr. J. Christian Bay, English ed. O Lange Firenze, 1924, was
largely concerned with the possibilities of French trade with America; and in II,
201–206, he made long lists of goods—everything from carriages to ladies' ready-made
satin gowns—he felt would sell well in the Mississippi Valley.

[106] Miss Jane H. Thomas, *Old Days in Nashville Tennessee*, Nashville, 1897 (cited
hereafter as Thomas, *Old Days*), wrote that Nashville ladies were never idle; some
could sew and ruffle a man's linen shirt in a day; though a petticoat with double
flounces took longer.

[107] Tenn. *Gazette*, Sept. 7, 1803. There had by this time been an abrupt change in
style; the high waist, etc., etc.

prime importance through these years was the baby, and judging from the several portraits [108] of barefooted babies in simple dresses tied at the neck with a drawstring, dress even among the wealthy was quite simple. Older children as always reflected in their clothing the lives of their parents; chance accounts of Indian warfare indicate boys wore hats, coats, vests as did the older men, made of butternut linsey or tow linen for work or school, with the more expensive fustian or even broadcloth reserved for Sunday best. Trousers through these years appear to have been more commonly worn by boys than men, as during the Revolution we see a "ten year old servant boy, dressed in a leather cap, drab colored coat, turned up, and blue and brown trousers." [109]

In poorer homes or even among the middle class both young boys and girls continued to wear the buttonless one-piece baby garment until three or four years old, and little boys, no different from Dr. Samuel Johnson and other great men before and since, continued to wear dresses until old enough to go to school. Judge Jo Guild, though not a pioneer, settled in an outlying region of Middle Tennessee, shortly after 1800. He, in his old days, declared he had worn the long shirt with a split in the tail or "toga" until old enough to squire the girls to church.[110] This may be something of an exaggeration, but there was undoubtedly much less haste to get the boy into trousers then than now, and the expression "shirttail lad" meant a child older than a baby, about the same as "shaver." Most boys were going to mill, watering the horses, or even guiding them in a stumpy field at plowing time at least by the time they were ten years old, and as all of these jobs were best done in trousers or breeches, it is doubtful if many wore the shirttail as long as Judge Guild, but they did wear dresses and pinafores most of the time for the first several years.[111]

---

[108] Carnegie, *Survey of Painting*, Plate 4, Anonymous, "Baby in Red Chair," thought to have been painted around 1790, shows simple baby dress and bare feet, much the same is seen in *ibid.*, Plate 16, Joseph Blackburn, "Portrait of Mr. and Mrs. Isaac Winslow and Their Children." Here, though of an earlier date, the parents are extremely well dressed, in contrast to the simply dressed bare-footed baby.

[109] NCR, XII, 460.

[110] Guild, *Old Times*, 387, 397.

[111] I found no inventory of a child's clothing on the Cumberland; the worshipful justices were never that hardhearted. The Buchanans, Robertsons, Bledsoes, and other farming families undoubtedly had in dress a good deal in common with that depicted in Carnegie, *Survey of Painting*, Plate 32, Edward Hicks, "The Residence of David Twining in 1787," courtesy The Museum of Modern Art. Here we see the substantial farmer dressed in stockings, breeches, shoes, a suit, and hat, all plain in cut and reminiscent of the Greer suit, but the working man wears trousers and a sleeveless jacket; the grandmother is plainly dressed in white cap and apron. See also Burke, *Emily Donelson*, with portraits done by Ralph E. W. Earl, nephew-

Joseph Bishop's velvet jacket, the cotton flower on John Buchanan's arithmetic, and Catharine Lefever's dressed chip bonnet bespeak, quite as much as do the bars of lead and pounds of powder, the Cumberland pioneer's attitude toward life. He would fight if he had it to do, but mainly he was interested in living, and living was for the average southern colonial something of an art, not a mere breathing, or even a long search for the twin securities of heaven in the one hand and earthly riches in the other.

The furnishings of their homes also indicate this. Even those who came by pack horse had many things in no way connected with the grim business of merely staying alive while changing the hunting grounds of the Indian into a white farming community. A fiddle is a most unhandy thing to carry by pack horse, yet Samuel Buchanan brought one in that fashion, and when he was killed in 1787 David Buchanan paid [112] seven dollars for it, and this a dollar less than Samuel Castleman paid for that of Thomas McCain; [113] somewhat more than the price of a second-rate cow and calf, and the Castlemans were poor.

True, when taken in their totality most of the furnishings of first settlers' homes of which we have record were primarily utilitarian, but never quite completely. One of the barest was that of Cornelius Ruddle. He came with the Buchanans to French Lick late in the fall of 1779. There, in 1782 he met and married "the beauteous Jane Mulherrin," [114] daughter of John Mulherrin who had come with the Buchanans and helped build French Lick Station. Cornelius Ruddle like others who settled there lost four years and more of work, not to mention money gone for ammunition, so that the chances are he was poorer when he died than when he came.

Still, luckier than many, he did get 640 acres of land in 1784, but three years later on a May morning he went hunting, killed two turkeys near his home at Buchanan's Station on Mill Creek, hung them up on a bush out of reach of dogs and foxes, then went looking for more.[115] Lurking Indians, hearing the shot, came searching, found the turkeys, and lay in ambush until he got back.

in-law of A. Jackson; Mr. Earl was neither a pioneer nor a great artist, but the portraits of his in-laws, including Aunt Rachel and Uncle John Donelson, shed much light upon hair styles and ladies' caps and kerchiefs of well-to-do early settlers later in life.

[112] DW, I, 296–297.

[113] DW, I, 107.

[114] Guild, *Old Times*, 317, gives a traditional account of this wedding.

[115] Ramsey, *Tennessee*, 462, conflicts with NCR, XX, 692, A. Bledsoe's letter of 1787 tells of Ruddle's death in May of that year; Ramsey gives the date as 1784. There was in May of 1784 no Buchanan Station yet built on Mill Creek. DW, I, 54, Ruddle's inventory.

He was, thus, when he died little more than a bridegroom starting in life, beginning all over again, clearing fields and laying fence, his first work gone to somebody else. Not all his possessions were sold; his land seems to have been saved for his children, but woe to the wife and children when the head of the house died deeply in debt; all his possessions could then be sold to the highest bidder, or even if alive and the court levied against him, he could like Catharine Lefever have everything sold, save enough to hide his nakedness. This unhappy lot seems not to have befallen the Cornelius Ruddle family.

It is doubtful if at this date the Ruddles had more than a one-room cabin in Buchanan's Station, but a large room, floored, a fireplace in one end, with plenty of space for the three beds they had. Following the custom these beds would have all been in the back, two "corner beds," and the "middle bed." Three beds in one room was not unusual; the pioneer, like the southern colonial behind him, liked big rooms; even huge Cragfont, home of a wealthy family, has fewer rooms than do many tiny middle-class, three-bedroom homes of today, their total floor space not twice as much as the main or "front room" of Tilman Dixon's original log home. Inclination and necessity made a happy combination in the log or stone home where an inside partition was as much trouble as an outside wall, for in thinking of houses, furniture, or anything else made of lumber, it must always be remembered that throughout this period the only sawed lumber to be had was by whipsaw,[116] a slow and expensive process whether done by man or water power.

The Ruddles had one underbed, this a wide and shallow bed, low enough it could be pushed under the big beds during the daytime. This, only one of many contrivances the pioneer used to save space, such as the folding table or quilting frames that when not in use were swung ceilingward. Children could sleep in the underbed but most of these were big enough they could be used for grown-up visitors,[117] though they varied in size. Beds in any pioneer home, save among a few of the wealthy, were the most important and most commonly owned pieces of furniture. All families

---

[116] The circular saw was not known in the United States until around 1815; see Clark, *Manufacturers*, 431.

[117] The underbed of the pioneer was not a substitute for a cradle, but according to Michaux, *Travels, 1802*, 59, most homes in the west contained "four large beds, two of which are very low, are pushed under the others in the daytime, and drawn out of an evening into the middle of the room receive the whole family . . . ." The underbed was the pioneer version of the English trundle bed in which Pepys sometimes slept when traveling, but the term was rarely used on the Cumberland; upriver Isaac Hays, PW, II, 300, had a trundle bed.

whose inventories were studied had beds, up the river in the poorer regions as well as down.

The next most commonly owned piece of furniture was the chest; the Ruddles had only one. Like other families they had a table, but only two chairs. Most families had more chairs, and usually several tables, but the Ruddles were not unusual among first settlers in that they had no form of cupboard, but like many other families they used shelves, set cornerwise and supported by pegs set into the logs.[118] On these were stored when not in use, the family's one half dozen pewter plates, two pewter basins, a pewter dish, four tin cups, one half dozen pewter spoons, two forks, and one half dozen knives. On a lower and sturdier shelf or bench would have stood the two water pails.

There was a washtub, this usually of cedar set ware like the pail, or sometimes the half of an old barrel. When not in use the tub stood outside, usually under a gouged length of sapling gutter to catch rain water, for all woodenware suffered if left dry for too long a time. The family also had two keelers; these were large shallow receptacles of wood, really wooden pans used for cooling milk, washing dishes, catching the drippings from the cheese press, or any one of the many uses to which the housewife must put a shallow pan.

The woodenware like the pewter would have been near the hearth, center in the small home of most activities of the housewife. Here was the Dutch oven or baker as it was usually called; three-legged and with a close-fitting cover, it was about the most important cooking utensil in any pioneer home. Most baking not done directly in the ashes as in the case of potatoes and sometimes hoecake was done in the Dutch oven. The Cumberland settlers, like other southerners, were little inclined to build an oven in the chimney as were the people of New England and Pennsylvania. Even the wealthy continued to favor the big fireplace in the separate kitchen. The Ruddles had, according to the inventory, only one other cooking utensil, and this a frying pan which, when not in use, would have hung on a peg set into the chimney.

The chances are that Jane Ruddle kept the kettles and other utensils, selling only what she wished, but a woman could make do with a Dutch oven that could be used for heating water or boiling meat and beans. It is doubtful if the Ruddle home as yet had a proper stone chimney with chimney piece or mantel, but on the chimney piece or nearby shelf were the

---

[118] W, 5S, 75, ". . . on a little board shelf resting upon a couple of wooden pins inserted in the logs."

small things owned by the Ruddles in smaller amounts than most families. Men at this date were clean shaven, so that Cornelius Ruddle had a razor and a looking glass, a small one, we can be certain, for most, compared to the iron cookware, sold rather cheaply, only a shilling or so. The same shelf would have held the candlestick when not in use, the lead inkstand, knitting needles, bullet molds, and possibly also "Ye book of common prayer."

Somewhere nearby was the box iron and heater. Practically all homes had at least one iron as had Catharine Lefever. The Ruddles had a box iron and with it the heater or chunk of iron to be heated in the coals and then slipped inside the box. In another type of box iron,[119] the box was filled with charcoal or glowing embers, then one ironed away, fumes escaping through the little chimney each had.

The walls of the Ruddle home, though neither plastered nor papered, were far from bare. The family's spare clothing hung about on pegs, or over long poles swung from the ceiling.[120] These, with the shelves and other things to be hung up as were the Ruddle cotton cards, gave the home of any first settler something of a "lived-in" look. Somewhere around was their little spinning wheel, though when in use on winter evenings it had an honored place near the fire, as did their cotton gin. This was the old-style roller gin, in general design not greatly different from a hand-powered wringer in a frame, save that early ones were made entirely of wood with grooved rollers, one larger than the other.[121]

The Ruddles probably kept most of the tools ordinarily left in the barn or farm forge just outside the door or even inside, for though they had five cows and calves, only one horse "fourteen hands high" is mentioned, and the chances are they had no stable, usually the first outbuilding put up. Thus, the saw set, with which Cornelius may have earned extra money by sharpening the saws of his neighbors, was also kept in their home. Hanging on an inside wall, at least until there was a protective porch or barn, would have been the bridle, handsaw, two beaver traps when not in use, while the ever expensive and precious ax was during the nighttime kept within doors in case of an Indian attack.

The Indians, as was their custom when killing a lone man, robbed Cornelius of his knife, gun, shot bag, and anything else he had. Nothing is said

[119] This form of box iron may be seen in Mr. John Lair's Museum at Renfro Valley. The type used by the Ruddles may be seen in the Smithsonian and was stocked by Baynton, Wharton, and Morgan in the Illinois.

[120] Michaux, *Travels, 1802*, 36-37, giving a generalized description of the log home of the west.

[121] Smythe, *Tour*, II, 71, and Anburey, *Travels*, II, 425, are descriptions of the wooden roller cotton gin and methods of ginning in use during the Revolution.

of these things, but during all of pioneer years, the guns, shot bags, powder horns, and wiping tow were, like the man's hat, hung on wall pegs, ready for instant use.

During rainy days and evenings, common on the Cumberland in fall and winter, the Ruddles as they worked in the firelight, she at spinning and he at seeding cotton or whittling, must have talked much of the future. There were first the saddles, one for him and one for her; the trees or wooden parts were made, most probably done by himself, since many, even the Indians, whittled their own saddle trees. The Ruddles also had the expensive saddle irons, that is the rings and buckles for surcingle, girth, and crupper; he now had only to get the leather, take the parts to a saddler and have them made, or let the saddler supply the leather.

They may have talked, too, of their need of another chest, for like many men he was killed, owning a chest lock and key; but the finest thing of all would be the wagon, and for this he had the gears. Jane Ruddle would have listened, talking now and then, head bent over whatever work she did. But the work was never finished for when he died there were 231 pounds of cotton "in ye seed," and 130 pounds of flax. These, plus fifty bushels of "Indian corn" and two sawhorses are all the possessions listed. Proof of their poverty is in the saddle trees; even the bound boy was often given a saddle and horse at the end of his servitude,[122] and practically all inventories of substantial farmers list at least two saddles, one for the husband and one for the wife.

The Ruddle family is an example of a Cumberland pioneer family with the basic essentials and little more, but most of us would be exceeding poor if the head of the house worked for four years with no pay save corn or whatever else the Indians let him grow, with the added possibility that cows, horses, sheep, and hogs once owned may have been stolen and killed by the Indians or strayed out of the country. Yet even the few possessions left indicate a way of life more than a mere eating, sleeping, and working. They wore clean, ironed clothes, for irons and washtubs were practically universal as were the looking glass and razor. They were prepared for writing letters, though the Ruddles were unusual in that they had only one

---

[122] Binding varied: Catharine Lefever's daughters, aged six and four, indigent, and bound as servants, were each to get only a decent suit of clothing, DW, I, 96, but as a rule more fortunate children got more and were taught more. Fairly typical is the indenture of Patrick Murphy, 6 years old when in 1799, MW, I, 31, he did "bind and put himself apprentice unto Hugh McClure, Merchant in Clarksville." He was to be taught in "the trade and majesty of a merchant . . . be educated in arithmetic" and when he was 21 years old he was "to get one full suit of good cloaths which shall be new and one hundred dollars or a horse and saddle . . . ."

book; there may have been a Bible and other books kept for the children.

William Neely, another first settler, was a rather poor man in that he worked at clearing land for Robertson, yet he had a very great deal more of everything, including slaves, than had the Ruddles, nor had he come by pack horse but by flatboat which permitted bringing more. How much he had we do not know, for only a part of his possessions were sold. He was to begin with unusually well supplied with carpentry and farming tools; quite a shelf would have been required to hold all his books that included Gray's works, four sermon books, a psalm book, the ever popular Crook's *Confessions of Faith*, and other works by Joseph Smith.

The Ruddles had nothing of brass, but the Neelys had a "fine brass hatchet," a ten-gallon brass kettle, only one of a great collection of cookware that included many large iron pots, two Dutch ovens, a good deal of tinware, much pewter ware and a spoon mold [123] with fourteen pounds of pewter so that when new spoons were needed they had only to make them. There were fourteen forks, and fire tongs and shovel of iron, this last in the poorer houses often made of wood. The Neelys had in addition to the usual spinning wheel and cotton cards a hemp hatchel and wool cards. Most families in comparable circumstances had more appliances for the manufacture of cloth—looms, sleighs, warping frames, and dye pots are found in many early inventories.[124]

The Buchanans came by pack horse, but managed to bring a great many of the so-called non-essentials, for who is to say what is and is not needful. Samuel Buchanan must at times have found his fiddle a most essential thing; he also had a case of bottles, glass tumblers, a sugar bowl, eight Delft plates, a set of tea ware, a good many books, two quires of writing paper, along with good assortments of tools, table and cook ware, and beds with bedding.

Leaving the merely well-to-do and visiting the wealthier one could by 1790 find most anything from armchairs to framed pictures and watering pots.[125] It would be unsafe to mention any article and say it was not in

---

[123] DW, I, 166—sale, 231-232. A spoon mold belonging to James Robertson may be seen in the Tennessee State Museum at Nashville.

[124] As a rule settlers known to have come by pack horse and killed soon after arrival had only the smaller appliances for clothmaking; looms are not mentioned in either Buchanan inventory, though there were spinning wheels, but Nicholas Gentry, DW, I, 7, killed before he could settle his land, had "one weaving loom." One of the best equipped families was that of William Overall, *ibid.*, II, 17, his sale; see also John Blackamore, *ibid.*, II, 348, and James Dean, *ibid.*, II, 242-244, particularly well equipped, for he had the rare, at least in inventories, warping frame.

[125] DW, I, 249, 255, this partial listing of the 1792 inventory of John Rice, a bachelor merchant in business on the Cumberland at least since 1784 and who in 1786, *ibid.*,

the neighborhood of Nashville by 1790. The detailed will, once common in the south, had gone out of fashion, and when such men as the Bledsoes found themselves dying and solvent, they made the wife the executrix, stipulating only the land, slaves, and stock each child was to receive, leaving the household possessions unlisted.[126]

Household possessions, widely as they varied, still had much in common. The most common of all was the feather bed. Will after will, all up and down the Cumberland, mentions feather beds, just as do the wills of Virginia and the Carolinas and behind these, all of Europe not too poor for feathers. Samuel Pepys took it rather hard when he had to sleep without feathers as did travelers to the Cumberland close to one hundred and fifty years later, for it was only in the poorer inns and overcrowded forts or families that feathers were not to be had.

Major Thomas Hickman,[127] who in the early years served as a guard on the Cumberland, complained neither of Indians nor the forted life, but of the fact that for two years he never slept on a real bed. His was the soldier's makeshift of four poles driven into the ground with more poles or rived boards forming a framework; on these, boards were laid and covered with straw, wild grass, pine boughs or anything else suitable for a mattress. Buffalo robes, bearskins or the cheap blankets used in the Indian trade served for both sheets and blankets.

The makeshift bed took many forms; sometimes it was so fixed in the corner of a cabin that only one stake or crotched stick like that used for an ash hopper was needed; from the one fork two poles led at right angles, each to an opposite wall, and over these the bed was made.[128] Travelers

47, was selling rum, whiskey and sugar, mentions rugs, numerous books, 7 framed pictures, watering pot, and numerous other items, most of which were undoubtedly designed for sale; as early as 1789 settler Eusaubius Bushnell, *ibid.*, 120, had armchairs that brought more than 11 pounds for two, a big dictionary, bed curtains, and other items not found in the average first settler's home. John Deadrick, DW, II, 132, had an unusually fine library, though it is possible most books—8 vols. Hume's *History of England*, $18—only one among many such items—were intended for sale.

[126] A few men, notably John Rice, made their wills several years in advance, but possibly half were killed with no will—at least none was recorded—and many were like that of Thomas Bledsoe, SW, I, 26, oldest son of Anthony—"Verbal will of Thomas Bledsoe mortally wounded by Indians Oct. 3, 1794—all estate to be equally divided between brothers and sisters." James Leeper, not long married to Susan Drake when mortally wounded at the Battle of the Bluff, the man of whom it was said, "could he have had a good surgeon—" willed April 16, 1781, DW, I, 10, that his "Lands entered in Henderson's office" should go to his child; but if his wife were not pregnant, half of the land should go to her, and half to his father; household goods were not listed.

[127] W, 30S, 525.

[128] Kercheval, *Virginia*, Doddridge, "Notes," 271.

sometimes encountered such makeshift beds at out-of-the-way inns, and the Moravian missionaries crossing the Plateau in 1799 found an inn near Southwest Point some miles west of Knoxville where the shelves around the walls served as beds with bearskins the sole bedding.[129] Much sleeping or at least napping and resting on hot days was undoubtedly done on the pallet. Travelers [130] in the southern colonies mentioned the pallet, and generations later we children, on hot summer days, took naps on pallets, sometimes on the floor and sometimes in the yard under the thick shade of the box elder tree, and the baby played on a pallet when he could be persuaded to do so, but for all its uses the pallet was found in no inventory, for it was but, at least for us, an old quilt folded, or two or three stacked for softness.

Still, even with only poles and rived boards the pioneer could have quite a proper bed, for the least important part of the whole was the stead; bed and furniture meant a feather bed with bed linens, coverings, and pillows, or quite commonly a bolster or pillow long as the bed was wide. The only exception I found was Mr. William Gubbins, he of the twenty-one stocks, for he had a mattress, this, considering his wardrobe, most probably hair. Everyone else, from the Donelsons with twenty-nine slaves to Cornelius Ruddle without a saddle, had feather beds, up the river as well as down.

Feathers run through all the stories. As Clark's soldiers in 1779 passed a surrendered and ransacked station in Kentucky, feathers from the ripped beds were scattered all around; [131] McNitt's defeat on the Kentucky Road [132] in 1786 was marked, not only by blood and corpses, but by the feathers all over; and as a child I shivered and shook as a long-ago grandmother on New River—I think it was Keziah Chrisman's mother for Keziah was married there in 1772—in the common predicament of many a wife during the French and Indian War, only a baby for company and a husband gone from home, sat all night long and burned her feather beds and pillows, handful by handful, and so kept an Indian from coming down the chimney.

The warm plump softness of the feather bed preferably came from the goose; little girls were often given a setting of goose eggs as the beginnings of a dower. Once hatched and grown from goslings into geese, they

---

[129] Williams, *Travels*, Schweinitz, "Report," 499–500.
[130] Anburey, *Travels*, II, 329–330. The use of the word here would indicate quilts or some such rather than the heap or bed of straw given by Mr. Webster.
[131] FQ, II, Clinkenbeard "Interview," 106–107.
[132] W, 29S, 110.

could be picked about every seven weeks, a job that required skill and patience as well as strength and fortitude; if unskillfully done the goose might end up with torn skin and the picker with bruises on her arms and face from beating wings. Next to gunpowder, feathers were about the most expensive things on the Cumberland; in 1792 Joseph Bishop [133] sold feathers from the breasts of the swans and wild geese he shot for a dollar a pound in Middle Tennessee, and up the river in Pulaski County, years later, a pound of feathers cost more than a gallon of whiskey.[134]

There was much difference between feather beds; some even used the feathers from chicken breasts and backs, but this was quite scandalous. James Biswell [135] must have been a rather poor man, apparently making his living through trapping. He got no land and had neither horse nor cow, but was in 1785 forced to sell his two pewter plates, a small dish, one little kettle, a kettle pot, one cedar pail, two earthen pans, one half dozen knives and forks, the little spinning wheel, two boxes, and his feather bed and blanket, all for only ten pounds.

His feather bed with only a blanket for furniture was but a poor thing compared to that of William Neely selling for thirty-three hard dollars, with most of the Neely cows bringing less than ten dollars each, and twenty head of hogs only fifteen dollars though several of these may have been suckling pigs.

The feather bed usually weighed between forty and sixty pounds, but much of the price depended on the furniture or bed clothes. Families such as the Donelsons had a wealth of extra sheets and pillows with cases. Mr. Biswell had neither sheet nor pillow, but as a rule sheets, quilts, counterpanes, and other bed linens were abundant but expensive. Mrs. Neely's extra bedtick and one sheet sold for seven dollars or only fifty cents less than the black and white cow, while a coverlid brought three dollars.

Selah Puckett,[136] a widow of Montgomery County many years later, had over and above her bed furniture eight sheets, seven counterpanes, three bed quilts, and two bed blankets. Selah Puckett's sheets sold in 1807 may have been of cotton, but Rachel Jackson's [137] of 1791 were, like other household linens of that day, of linen. It was not until the toothed cotton gin began to be more widely used in the early nineties that cotton

---

[133] Gray, *Bishop*, 55.

[134] PW, I, 31, David Buster's feathers sold for 33⅓ cents a pound, but Zachariah Ford's 1,150 gallons of whiskey, *ibid.*, II, 87, sold for only 27½ cents per gallon.

[135] DW, I, 64.

[136] MW, I, 208.

[137] The Donelson property was not sold, but a valuation was placed upon most items to attain a more equitable division; DW, I, 109, 167, and 199.

cloth grew more common, while the introduction of improved machinery for both spinning and weaving further decreased the price. All through pioneer years the kitchen towel and the best sheets were of coarse or fine linen, with the more time-consuming cotton cloth saved for clothing.

Cloth of any kind continued to be expensive.[138] The cheapest cloth in John Coffee's [139] store at Haysborough sold in 1803 for thirty-five cents or the equivalent of around ten pounds of fresh pork or beef, and this a coarse tow, worn chiefly by slaves or very poor whites. Next cheapest was a muslin for only fifty cents; some grades of calico could be had for as low as a dollar a yard but most cotton goods ranged between this and the $2.37½ that cottonade cost. The farmer's wife at the same time got between fifty and seventy-five cents for her plain linen cloth, and seventy-five for mixed cloth, or linsey-woolsey, a term not used by the pioneer.

Still more expensive than the bed furniture were the bed curtains, and though it was by 1780 no disgrace to sleep in a naked bed and many well-to-do families lived without bed curtains, they were still quite common. The curtains were sometimes sold with the other bedding as "two feather beds with furniture and curtains, $62.00," [140] but usually as in the Cowan [141] sale upriver in Pulaski they were sold separately, a "stand" of red and one of blue each bringing ten dollars, compared to a "fine double blanket" for $8.27, and an "alagant" bedspread for three dollars, quite a lot of money in this neighborhood where all home produce was cheap; sixty head of cattle were valued at only $293.675 and slave children sold for as low as fifty dollars each.

Wooden furniture to serve the prime necessities of life was cheap, and prices indicate that most who came by pack horse used bedsteads, tables, chairs and sometimes chests, produced by local carpenters and cabinet-makers or even homemade. Samuel Buchanan's feather beds with furniture each brought twenty-five dollars, but six chairs only two dollars, less than the cost of one good shirt. In contrast was the flax wheel, a small thing, requiring little wood, but the skill of a wheelwright reflected in the price of three dollars, six pence.

---

[138] The State of Franklin in 1785 made a number of products legal tender; rye whiskey, always more expensive than that of corn, was rated at only 2 shillings, 6 pence per gallon, but woolen cloth was 10 shillings the yard, Ramsey, *Tennessee*, 297.

[139] Coffee Papers, 1802–1804.

[140] DW, II, 272; see also *ibid.*, I, 120.

[141] PW, I, 145–147. These were the effects of Andrew Cowan who like a neighbor, Samuel Newell on the other side of the Cumberland, served as a justice in the first court of Sevier County—Ramsey, *Tennessee*, 669—and like Newell moved to Kentucky after the collapse of the State of Franklin.

Buchanan's split-bottomed chairs were not necessarily rough or ugly; good wood, even cherry and walnut, could in the very early years be had by the landowner for nothing, and the six chairs thus represented only the cost of the labor with froe, drawing knife, and auger. Much furniture, even in later years, was made by journeymen carpenters working without lathes; chair legs and rungs could be whittled and drawn to a semblance of roundness, and with a cunning intermingling [142] of green wood and well seasoned a slat-backed, split-bottomed chair could be made that would last for generations. In the spring when the bark slipped easily, a chair could be even more quickly made by bottoming with hickory bark. Hickory withes could also be shaped into frames for chairs, tables, or even beds, the whole like the split-bottomed chair held together with no bit of metal.

Tradition as well as inventories indicate such furniture served the first needs of the family come by pack horse, instead of the puncheon, for I have neither in the old stories or written form encountered a puncheon bench or table in a private home. A puncheon to begin with was not customarily half a log, but a thick board hewed from the half of a split log and took a deal of work to make. Once made it was too heavy to move with any ease, and the pioneer housewife forced to use one or two rooms for a multitude of activities ranging from sausage-stuffing to cloth-making needed movable furniture.

The pioneer also, in so far as possible, avoided in the very early years the use of furniture that demanded sawed lumber. The skillful worker could with an especially long-bladed froe get boards suitable for table tops, benches, and even chests. Sawed lumber, as late as 1802, was selling [143] for $4.50 a hundred feet, walnut or cherry, down at Natchez, and as freight downriver even to New Orleans was sometimes as low as a cent a pound, this meant a high price around Nashville, and in the early years sawed lumber was almost impossible to get.[144]

The chest was usually the first piece of "good furniture" made of sawed lumber to be had in the average home, and though not so important to the pioneer as to the sailor, a strong chest fastening with lock and key supplied a pressing need for the keeping of the numerous small, but often expensive, articles, not handily hung on pegs or put on shelves. There was

[142] Smith Ross, furniture maker of Pine Knot, Ky., explained to me the cunning craft of making chairs. The Samuel Buchanan chairs were designated as split-bottomed.

[143] Tenn. *Gazette*, Nov. 20, 1802, "Prices Current at Natchez." Later ads in later years revealed no lowering of the price until sawmills became common around 1820.

[144] Mrs. Daniel Smith's letter of 1793, A, V, 293–294, well demonstrates this.

also the problem of safety; families while traveling or during periods of Indian trouble were often forced to share quarters with strangers, some of these the wandering ne'er-do-wells who infested all frontiers, though theft, judging from the court records, was much less common than today.

The poor such as James Biswell had to get along with only a box, most probably of rived lumber, far different from Catharine Lefever's covered chest, or the large red chest and round green box owned by Mr. Gubbins. There had been in the colonies dower chests and wine chests, sugar chests and chests of drawers, all these often painted or highly decorated with inlay and carving. Some of these may have found their way to the Cumberland; there were also trunks and the more expensive portmanteaus with special saddles for carrying which were, until the Revolution, usually imported from England or France.

More common than box, or chest of drawers, was the simple, but good wooden chest with lock and key, such as Samuel Buchanan's that in contrast to the six chairs for two dollars, brought seven, or a chest of William Ramsey,[145] bringing fifteen shillings as compared to four chairs for five.

These two-to-seven-dollar pieces of furniture were large, well proportioned, and made usually of only six pieces of thick board of fine cherry or walnut, perfectly plain, even the battens on the hinged cover were on the underside so that the top might serve as a seat. Many families had at least two, and still others such as the Ruddles and the Thomas Browns had when killed a chest lock with key that would in time have been put into another chest. The chest lock like all imported articles of iron or brass was expensive; Thomas McCain's [146] selling as late as 1789 for eight shillings, or two more than a velvet jacket, and three more than four chairs brought at the William Feas sale.[147]

Once he could lock up his most precious possessions be they promissory notes or rose blankets,[148] the pioneer could get on with another good piece of wooden furniture, this usually a proper bedstead. Though less common than the chest, good bedsteads, well made of seasoned cherry or walnut, either came to Middle Tennessee by flatboat, or like the chests, were made at a very early date, the more probable explanation as at least

[145] DW, I, 176. William Overall's cherry chest sold, *ibid.*, II, 17, in 1794 for $3.12½ but that of black walnut brought $7.13, while a poplar chest, *ibid.*, II, 34, brought only $1.00.

[146] DW, I, 107.

[147] MW, I, 27.

[148] MW, I, 17. Extra bed furniture, towels, tablecloths, etc., were quite common; in addition to the Donelsons and others mentioned in DW, I, see *ibid.*, II, 34, 232, 242–244.

one carpenter took an apprentice boy in 1784. William Gower's [149] two bedsteads sold for three pounds, quite a sum when contrasted to a Buchanan bed appraised at one dollar. John Law's [150] bedsteads brought fifteen shillings each, and William Gubbins, killed in 1786, had a walnut bedstead.

The more expensive of these beds were what we now refer to as tester beds, but most were much like the one that can still be seen in the Tilman Dixon home; uncurtained but massive, well made of cherry or walnut, commodious enough that, with an underbed, they could take care of the whole of a visiting family, and like most furniture made by local craftsmen on the Cumberland, not only built to endure, but of eye-pleasing proportions.

There were short-posted or muley beds, and cheap poplar beds, made without a lathe, though in many of even the walnut or cherry beds the posts are square instead of round, but regardless of wood or workmanship most beds of the day held the sleeper high in the air, well above drafts, and like previous generations of beds had sometimes to be mounted with a footstool, but this left room for storage—underbed, and chamber pot that could be had for 12½ cents.[151] The proper bed, instead of the slats that came later, had, affixed on the inside to head and foot and each side, a stout piece of squared up timber; into these four pieces holes were bored to receive the 110 feet or so of hempen rope [152] that when laced back and forth and tightened with a bed-cord turner formed the counterpart of today's springs; onto this firm but springy framework was often laid a shuck tick, or later straw; one or two feather beds followed, and on these the furniture, the whole topped with a bright coverlid or bedspread.

No family on the Cumberland need be ashamed of a home that had little in the way of furniture save good beds, chests, split-backed chairs and homemade tables. Most had these things, but the heads of many early families were killed before the wife could realize the dream of most wives before and since—"more storage space." Mesdames Ruddle, Castleman, and John Buchanan, all come by pack horse, had neither cupboard, safe, nor dresser. Badly needed articles, for save for the cubbyhole under the stairs, and many of even the double-log homes had no second story, the average

[149] DW, I, 175.
[150] DW, I, 308.
[151] MW, I, 271.
[152] Haywood, *N & A*, 10. This length was arrived at from Haywood's method of measuring a sinkhole, but not all bed cords were the same length, as the varied hole spacings in the old beds indicate; inventories did not specify length, typical, MW, I, 17, "2 bed cords."

pioneer home had no closet space. Attics were, among the Germans,[153] commonly used for the storage of small grains such as rye, and many families kept sweet potatoes and other foods needing warm and dry storage there.

Closets,[154] like partitions, were hard to build when no sawed lumber was to be had, and were practically non-existent. This lack was filled by massive, yet beautifully proportioned presses, cupboards, and safes. Like the chests, made usually by local cabinet-makers or traveling journeymen, these pieces, almost without exception, have no metal save keyholes, and no adornment except now and then a keyhole inlaid with ivory, but even this less for prettiness than for the endurance of ivory against generations of turning keys.

Many homes in the Cumberland Country still use the old pieces; fine examples can be seen in the Tilman Dixon home, and though of a later date, much of the furniture in the Sam Davis home south of Nashville is the same as that owned by the pioneer with a love of fine woods and simple designs, but like most of his furniture, primarily utilitarian. In my childhood we had in the dining room a seven-foot, two-piece cupboard, known as the press. The bottom was in the nature of an oversize washstand on short legs—two doors with wooden knobs opening into wide shelves; above was one drawer, shallow, but wide and long as the press would permit. This lower part was topped with heavy slabs—two—of cherry and could have been used alone as a sideboard, but in our home never was, for like any proper press it had a top part, rising almost to the ceiling, with two plain doors opening onto more wide shelves, and topped by a plain cornice. Each side and door panel was of one plank of cherry wood, the whole held together with dovetailing and wooden pins.

This press like others made by conscientious country carpenters was little different from the cupboards and cupboard-presses owned by John Stewart,[155] William Overall, and many on the Cumberland before 1800. Pioneers coming by pack horse had to have such pieces made, but so great was the demand that merchant Wiggins[156] sold cupboard locks along with butcher knives and hat linings.

[153] Kercheval, *Virginia*, 102.
[154] The word "closet" in the modern meaning was not used by the pioneer; he might use it as a verb, but closet meant a small room, sometimes for sleeping, sometimes the counterpart of today's "den." I found among many early ads for homes none with "closet space."
[155] MW, I, 284. The inventories of the first settlers yield few of the larger pieces; but first and early settlers who lived past 1790 were well supplied. See DW, II, 17, 177, 242–244, 319, 348, for inventories with representations of these larger pieces.
[156] DW, II, 133,—merchant Wiggins died in 1798.

The cabinet-maker able to build a press could, by varying the design, produce a wide assortment of furniture. He could leave out the upper shelves, set in pegs or put a pole across the top, and the housewife could use it for storing clothes instead of folded linens. He could lengthen the top, do away with the bottom entirely and have what we in my childhood still called a wardrobe, a variety of clothespress; walnut, dark and high, like a double coffin stood on end.[157] The bottom of the press could be transformed into a sideboard, a chest of drawers, or a bonnet chest, or, made smaller with a hinged cover opening into a sink-like space, it became the wine chest long known in the southern colonies; the wine chest could in turn be varied to make a sugar chest such as Robert Nelson had.[158]

Coming in two pieces as the cupboard-press did, the thrifty farm wife could get it on the installment plan, or have a cheap one made of poplar,[159] the top without doors and smaller in length and width but not height. This, she would in time put in the kitchen but before the family got around to a separate kitchen she would keep in a corner near the cooking fireplace, for this was the pioneer version of the dresser on which the English housewife had for generations dressed her fowls and meats; it was by 1780 going out of style, and had become more in the nature of a cupboard with storage space for cooking utensils and food. Some such as Leah Lucas,[160] whose husband David was killed at French Lick in 1781, never got past the dresser furniture, but others did. The Vanhook [161] dresser upriver with furniture brought only fifteen dollars, a dollar less than the Cowan corner cupboard without furniture.

Another piece of furniture, primarily for kitchen use, was the safe,[162] more often mentioned in early wills than the dresser. Designed primarily for the keeping of food, rather than cooking utensils, it was little more than a shelved box on legs with doors that had instead of wood for paneling, tin punched with holes, usually in some well known design such as six-pointed stars; other times the panels were of coarse linen affording

[157] The early Cumberlanders were more inclined to say, DW, II, 319, "clothes press." They were usually specific: chest of drawers, *ibid.*, 244; writing desk, MW, I, 117, but John Blackamore's cupboard, bringing $17, DW, II, 348, is not designated as corner or cupboard-press.

[158] MW, I, 284.

[159] Poplar was to the Cumberlander what pine was to the New Englander—second best; kitchen furniture was often made of it. Well-to-do Dr. Sappington, DW, II, 274, with a good bit of silver, both hollow and flat ware, 3 rugs, and 2 walnut folding tables, and a writing desk had also a poplar cupboard and a "poplar kitchen table."

[160] DW, I, 46.

[161] PW, I, 156.

[162] MW, I, 284.

the same protection from flies with circulation of air as did the punched tin.

More versatile than any piece mentioned, but also had at an early date was the corner cupboard or simply cupboard. Different from the cupboard-press and dresser, it did not come in two pieces, but was one heavy, gigantic piece of furniture, usually perfectly plain; sometimes, but not often with a drawer,[163] it consisted almost always of four doors, the upper longer than the lower, both sets opening onto shelves, deep and wide as the interior of the cupboard. Almost always made of cherry or walnut this piece of furniture could be found in any room in the house, and was used for the storage of all things from bottled whiskey to cheese or good linen and best hats.

One should not think of the average pioneer or even those in better than average circumstances as was Tilman Dixon, with a great variety of rooms. It was only such noteworthy places as Cragfont that had drawing rooms; parlors came later, and still later, living rooms—every room in the house was for living. Separate kitchens, as indicated by the ads and still earlier, chance accounts, were like loom houses, wash houses, dairies, and spring houses, among the first things to be built. In the meantime, even the prosperous family with slaves, but no more than four to six big rooms in a big double log house, would have beds, cupboard-presses, chests, corner cupboards, chairs and tables in every room, including the one for eating; I found no early reference to a dining room.

Scattered among these larger pieces of furniture were smaller things, also of local make; folding tables,[164] usually of walnut, were quite common, as were desks; that of William Overall, an early settler in good but not affluent circumstances, sold for $15.00 in 1795. Chests of drawers were rather rare in inventories as were armchairs, but were there as were framed pictures, and an occasional wall, not only plastered but papered, for "hanging paper" was stocked by a Nashville merchant, Mr. Leneer, by 1787,[165] and for how much earlier we do not know.

Even upriver the Cowan family had a seven-dollar mirror, brought most likely from New Orleans or Philadelphia; made for hanging on a wall and finer by far than the shilling looking glass by which Cornelius Ruddle

---

[163] The Tilman Dixon home has a good example of a corner cupboard with a drawer; design is not specified in inventories—DW, II, 17, 92, 242–244, 274.

[164] Valentine Sevier, Dr. Sappington, and many others had folding tables, usually of walnut.

[165] DW, I, 34, 63. The Leneers (spelled in some records Lenear) had also 16 chairs, such an unusually large number that one feels some were stock in trade in 1787.

had shaved, but certainly a small poor thing when compared to those around Nashville in the homes of the wealthy. Middle Tennessee from earliest years attracted monied men; gold and silver coins to the value of thousands of Spanish milled dollars are more common in very early court records involving transactions [166] than later; as early as 1789 Jedidiah Morse [167] wrote that many "opulent" families had gone from Natchez to the Cumberland, and opulent they no doubt were; some who had gone to Natchez before and during the Revolution had as many as two hundred slaves.

Complete inventories of such families are unavailable; it is perfectly possible that with plenty of slaves to do the upriver rowing they brought by 1785 harpsichords, parlor settees, pier glasses, and other furnishings associated with fashionable living on the Cumberland. Andrew Jackson, when still no more than a man on his way up, was by 1804 buying parlor settee and chairs in New Orleans.[168] Wealthier homes, such as those of the Winchesters, Hayes, Lewises, or even that of Judge McNairy who early gave grand balls, would long since have had these things, and with them the draperies, silk rugs, marble mantels, and other accessories that might have been found in most any place in the United States of that day. Most of these were ordered from New Orleans or Philadelphia, but by 1800 Nashville merchants were stocking all manner of things from mahogany framed mirrors and portable writing desks to Queens ware and china.[169]

Contrasted to those of the calmly wealthy as was Tilman Dixon, the furnishings of the fashionable home, drawing as it did inspiration and materials from both New Orleans and Philadelphia and these in turn with goods from the four corners of the world, comprised a medley rather than a symphony of shape, color, and design. The furnishings of such homes were more akin, at least in spirit though of a different style, to the furniture, rugs, draperies, and accessories now in the Hermitage than to the average well-to-do farm home on the Cumberland, such as that of William Overall where each piece of furniture was part and parcel of the Cumber-

---

[166] DW, I, 13, "5156 Spanish milled dollars," *ibid.*, 14, "1300 Spanish milled dollars," "400 Spanish milled dollars." These were cash payments, not debts, the last by Frederick Stump.

[167] Morse, *Geography*, 420–421.

[168] Bassett, *Jackson Correspondence*, I, 96.

[169] The ads of Bustard and Eastin, and Black and Williams, listing numerous items appeared often in early Tenn. *Gazettes*. See in particular issues of Feb. 18, and April 1, 1801; as the years pass clothing becomes constantly more elaborate; and by 1805 Bustard and Eastin have "Ladies fashionable beaver ruffed hats," along with Leghorn bonnets, parasols, cambric, etc., etc.

land—cherry chest or walnut writing desk. There was in the small world of Middle Tennessee that by 1800 had scarcely 30,000 inhabitants, a very great deal of keeping-up-with-the-Joneses; even John Coffee, then a bankrupt bachelor with little need of such, was by 1809 estimating the cost of the china, secretary, and chairs he was buying at one hundred dollars; less certain of the stove, he only "thought" it would cost one hundred dollars.[170]

Other families such as the parents of Sam Davis,[171] wealthy with over a hundred slaves, would live with the old things in wide-porched spacious homes, never know a lack of sugar and enjoy it without a mahogany sugar chest. Fine furniture they might in time buy, but many would continue to use the old big beds, missing the blanket rolls in the solid footboards of shiny mahogany that hurt their eyes and shut off any cooling breeze on a hot summer's night. Many homes all up and down the river still have the early pieces; severely simple with neither inlay, veneer, nor carving, they are totally different from the cupboards, sideboards, bedsteads, and other pieces of New England, and are even more simple than those made on the Virginia Piedmont, for they show little influence of earlier and contemporary American and English furniture makers, and nothing at all of the love of ornamentation characteristic of the German cabinet-makers who made much of the furniture in the American colonies.

The wide-doored presses and big solid corner cupboards of dully gleaming cherry or walnut have a strength and dignity coupled with honest forthrightness with not a little grace that speak of the early substantial farmers on the Cumberland, good people who ate and slept well, rode good horses, sometimes with silver spurs at their heels, but continued all their days to live in good log houses, set in a cluster of outbuildings, but with no parlor. The big rooms of such a home as that of the Conrads, Overalls, Cowans, or Lees upriver spoke of peace and prosperity and solidity. The wide-planked floors of fine-grained woods—ash, maple, beech, oak, and sometimes walnut—were kept bright by many scrubbings, for the pioneer wife had her scouring days,[172] and judging from the washtubs, irons, chance accounts of washing and clothes baskets they were a cleanly people.

[170] Coffee Papers, 1809.

[171] The Sam Davis home, south of Nashville, is not a pioneer home, but in the corded beds, the sugar sack with stave top, the good, expensive, but usually simple furniture of native woods as contrasted to the mahogany and rosewood in the Hermitage there is much that could have been found in many pioneer homes.

[172] W, 3XX (18), 5. William Martin's picture, brief as it is, of Sally Buchanan with her skirts tucked up and surrounded with servant girls, still gives a good idea of scouring day.

Few, if any, upriver and not too many even in Middle Tennessee had silk rugs such as Mr. Gubbins had, but rugs are found quite often in early inventories.[173] Braided, hooked, and woven rugs, or matting, had long been made in the colonies, and these along with dressed bear and deerskins, the pallet or sheepskin in front of the fire for the baby, were found in many homes.

Most homes, of even the poor, held more life and brightness than can be achieved today in the reconstructed cabin that at best is seldom more than a dusty memory where the tangled warp in a half-threaded sleigh hangs crookedly above a broken-down loom, and dull pewter and rusty iron stand in sad lifelessness by a dead hearth fire. The pioneer home was alive—cooking smells, wandering dogs, playing children, working men and women.

There was, even without people, a life and a brightness, impossible to re-create without the smell of new wood and the look of it; the rich, red gleam of cherry in chest, press, or corner cupboard, poplar safe or kitchen cupboard softly yellow from many scrubbings with lye soap or ashes, and further back from the fire, winking in the light and with some brightness even on cloudy days, the high posts of the great beds which, though un-curtained in most homes, were set off by red or blue coverlids, colors mentioned in many early wills. Red cedar churn warming near the hearth, more cedar in the piggen of milk or pail of water, white satiny shine of gouged buckeye in the bread tray, and the winking gleams of curly maple in the chair back were all alive, come out of the land.

Few of the first settlers, come by pack horse, had presses or even chests enough to hold the family linens and clothing, so that the walls of any early home would have been alive with color—woman's scarlet cloak, white ruffled cap, silver spurs, and among these the numerous articles that would in later and more affluent days be left in the loomhouse or the shop —skeins of linen thread or brightly colored wool awaiting needles or weaver's spool, warping frame, wool and cotton cards, flax or hemp hackle.

Sunlight, firelight, flame of candle or grease lamp picked up further bits of brightness from the many small articles owned by most families,[174] all

[173] DW, I, 59, 107, 268, and more common still in DW, II.

[174] Catharine Lefever; the Buchanans, Samuel and John, Valentine Sevier and William Overall had quite a collection among them of tea ware, teapots, spice mortars or mills, nutmeg graters, many materials for writing such as inkstands, as well as candlesticks, snuffers, lamps, lanthorns—W. Overall, DW, I, 283, and though children's possessions were almost never sold and hence seldom mentioned, there were in most homes at least a few toys as the Ruddles, *ibid.*, 54, had a "chile's ball."

these about the room on walls, or shelves, or table—brass inkstand, feather quill, white writing paper, brass star or patch box on the gunstock, conch shell used as a dinner horn, shine of well scrubbed pewter, glint of leather bookbinding, ribbon in the sewing basket.

First settlers such as the Ruddles either left their gourd seed behind or had them all destroyed by Indians, but soon even the wealthier homes around Nashville knew the graceful shape of gourds in all manner of places—big gourds [175] for fat, salt, soft soap, round-sided and softly swelling as the split basket, this last made usually by the same man who bottomed the chair, handy for gathering eggs or carrying on horseback. Here and there were turkey wings [176] used for fanning up the fires and shooing off the flies until the family had a proper fly-shoo of peacock feathers.

First settlers on the Cumberland could from earliest days have about them many small articles—provided they had something to trade. The store, already mentioned up the river in Pulaski County, had in 1801 all manner of things from window latches and snuffer pans to watch seals, teaspoons, and hooks and eyes. Judging from the things come down to us, the Cumberland pioneer liked the severely simple—the grease lamp, pewter pitcher, baby's high chair, and dishes of Queens ware or Delft in brown or gray-white with bands of blue were simple but pleasing in design as the furniture, pottery, and baskets of local make.[177]

The little design or ornamentation in the home furnished almost entirely with local products was reserved chiefly for the gunstock and the things the housewife made, though much of even the cloth, judging from the samples that remain, was more apt to be plain than checked or striped, but often brightly colored; there might be a flower on the bottom of the butter mold, a carved sunburst on the mantel, and a rather intricate design for the coverlid.

Mrs. Henry Hail of Pulaski County has an old bedspread made of

[175] Gourds were used by even the well-to-do; Jesse Morris, DW, II, 272, had an unusually fine assortment of goods including the very scarce "cradle with cloths," but he had a soap gourd, a gourd of hog's fat; there were also powder gourds, MW, I, 55. Gourds, judging from their prices, were prized; "4 large fat gourds," DW, II, 244, brought $1.02 as compared to "6 setting chairs," for $5.01 at the same sale, or a few years earlier "2 cedar piggens," $0.50, *ibid.*, 32.

[176] Jesse Morris, *ibid.*, 272, also had 5. I found nothing to indicate that the ceiling fan, in time common in the better homes of the deeper south, powered by young slave hands and a string, was at this time used on the Cumberland.

[177] China I found not at all among the first settlers; that didn't mean it wasn't there but it was scarce and expensive; near the end of the pioneer period one china bowl and saucers brought $6.50, DW, II, 303; on the other hand most of the first settlers had at least some Delft, or "delph" as the pioneer called it—"8 Delph plates." S. Buchanan, *ibid.*, I, 296, and Dr. Doddridge, Kercheval, *Virginia*, 255, referred to it as delph.

cotton grown, spun, and woven on the Cumberland. The loom was warped, spools filled, but when the weaver sat down to work there was by the loom a draft, showing each thread, for the design was made,[178] not by using several treadles as in the case of the coverlid, but by following the draft and lifting the filler thread at the required places with goose quills. Thus, with goose quill, shuttle, and treadle the design grew. Almost a thousand years before Irish monks had made the same design as a part of the ornamentation of their Book of Kells,[179] and just as one finds the eight-pointed or oval-shaped star on the gunstock of which this was a variation, so does one find the one in Mrs. Hail's bedspread in many places in all the years before and since.

The same thing is true for most of the other designs repeated with scraps of cloth on quilts, with thread in sampler or embroidery, in brass or silver on the gunstock, or even punched in the tin of the safe door. Possibly the best place for seeing most of the designs used by the Cumberland pioneer is in the blue and white tiled floor of the old Senate wing of the Capitol in Washington. These tiles were made in England, and the stars, dogwood flowers, and crosses used were old when the tiles were new.

The pioneer was no blind, unfeeling man. He knew what he had and sometimes what he wanted. One of the things he wanted more than anything was a good home for the center of his world. Some might say that General James Winchester from Maryland was, when he built Cragfont, merely hoping to put up the biggest and the finest home in all the west, but standing in the now ruined doorway looking out over the sweep of country, remembering stone mills by a mill dam once in the stream below, the store where by 1797 one could buy *Lord Chesterfield's Advice* or Gallatin on *Finance*, the home becomes what it once was, the center of a busy world, and looking out across rolling fields and hills, it seems wrong not to give the General or his Lady or both the same awareness of beauty in the view as has the present-day beholder. Why did so many early settlers build on hillsides? Merely to catch the breeze?

Almost none could build a Cragfont. Many struggled for years only to lose land, buildings, stone spring house and all that had made a home. Pioneer William Clinkenbeard in Kentucky, like many who settled the Bluegrass there, never got land he could for a little while call his own. He

---

[178] I am indebted to Mrs. Hail not only for a description of how it was made but for photographs of the spread, an ancient pewter pitcher, and many other items from pioneer days.

[179] Book of Kells or Latin Manuscripts of the New Testament Gospels, a facsimile edition by P. C. Duschnes, New York, 1950-51, 32R.

fought in the Revolution when hardly more than a child, came to Kentucky and there lost everything, even his cow, some of this trouble from Indians, some from men, smarter than he in the ways of depreciated currency. Still, he married and started a home; no pewter, no Queens ware for such as he whose shirts were made of hempen cloth. "My wife and I had neither spoon, dish, knife or anything to do with when we began life; only I had a butcher knife. When old Mr. Strode went in he left a little pot with us, and when he came back he brought out some more with him, and we gave him $4.00 and a punch crown for that we had, and glad to get it. The first dishes we had were trenchers made by one [Enos] Terry in the Station—a turner. He turned dishes and bowls, and being no hunter exchanged them for meat and tallow to us hunters. A parcel of them dishes, new and shining, and set on some clapboards in the corner of the cabin, I felt prouder of in those times than I could be of any dishes to be had now." [180]

[180] FQ, II, Clinkenbeard "Interview," 98. Dr. Doddridge in Kercheval, *Virginia*, 276, also recalled the beauty of ash bowls and the neat, smooth even puncheon floors of his childhood during the Revolution.

CHAPTER XIV

AROUND THE FAMILY HEARTH

HOME WAS the center of the pioneer's world. Center of home for all in the early years when Indian troubles forced most to live in small houses behind picketed walls, was the family hearth, source of warmth, sometimes light, and always food. It is impossible to look at some long since forgotten cooking hearth without wrinkling the nose, reason only half conceding the smells are dead, and remembering that green oak burning, cedar kindling bursting into flame, boiling hominy, steaming sassafras tea, baking cornbread, frying meat, boiling beans, sweet potatoes roasting in the ashes, and boiling meat, smelled then as now.

All these smells like that of new woolen cloth dripping from the dye pot, wet ashes in the hopper, and whiskey fresh from the doubler, the pioneer knew. Along with these were often others that bespoke the wider world—boiling coffee, freshly grated nutmeg, tea, ginger, cinnamon, mace, wines, and even orange juice,[1] for the French traders, carrying all manner of things, were in and out of the region. A man with money could buy flour; by 1786 at least one Nashville merchant[2] was stocked with sugar,

[1] As early as 1776 a French merchant, M. Bomer from the Illinois, on or near the Cumberland, had among an assortment of goods that featured bed clothes and whiskey, orange juice; see I, V, 36.

[2] DW, I, 47, the inventory of James Moore was the first found, but he was not the first merchant; Turnbull and others were mentioned, Haywood, C & P, 130. Other inventories already mentioned yielded no food, but most general stores stocked alcoholic beverages, coffee, tea, sugar, and spices. In addition to the accounts in the Coffee Papers, 1799-1804, early ads are revealing; James Hennen, though a Middle

rum, and whiskey, and judging from the number of sugar bowls in inventories, most had sugar up from New Orleans.

Early tavern rates [3] for Middle Tennessee were not set up for such homely things as cornbread and bear meat, but well before 1790 the worshipful justices were setting the prices for Jamaica Spirits, India rum, brandy, taffia, toddy made with sugar and whiskey, Port, Maderia, Burgundy, Claret, and of course Champagne, retailing at 20 shillings the bottle. True, whiskey was mentioned first; one half pint, the least amount sold in the tavern of that day, was to cost two shillings, with the least amount of toddy sold—one quart—to cost three shillings six pence. Nashville was ever noted for her food and drink. Journalizing travelers to Middle Tennessee, beginning with John Lipscomb in 1784, though often suffering on the journey, mentioned no scarcity of food or forage once Mansker's was reached; even the Dukes of Orleans traveling in 1797 had no complaint of food in Nashville.

Still, imported foods were, even for the well-to-do, a minor item in the economy of any pioneer household. The clothing and furniture of such men as John Deadrick and John Rice came from the four corners of the world, though usually by way of England, France, or Spain. Yet their larders reveal no wine cellars, no stocks of anchovies and smoked oysters, favorite items of the day, but instead such Cumberland products as dried peas and beans, bacon, potatoes, and corn.

There was after 1783 no over-all scarcity of corn, but most settlers, even those coming later,[4] and not hard up for cash, would know days and sometimes weeks when they were glad even to get a little meat. Until the first crop was in, bread corn had to be bought from some established farmer such as Frederick Stump; this meant for the settler in outlying regions, not only money and time, but a long trip through Indian-infested country. Many did like the John Smith family—waited until the corn crop was in. Plenty of corn usually meant plenty of food, for in the early years meat was almost always more easily had than bread. The big game was gone before settlement began, but squirrels, waterfowl, and other small game continued plentiful.[5]

Tennessee version of an apothecary, stocked in 1799 along with drugs, all manner of spices, Castile soap, and "pearl barley"; *Rights of Man or The Nashville Intelligencer*, March 11, 1799. See also in Tenn. *Gazette*, Nov. 20, 1802, Roger B. Sappington—Tamarinds, sugar candy, etc.

[3] DC, I, 26; SC, I, 10.

[4] Gray, *Bishop*, 152-156, gives a good picture of the hard time newcomers had even in the '90's.

[5] Squirrels continued so abundant they were a pest to the sprouting corn and the

The pioneer could, like the Long Hunter, live for a time on meat alone, and he could live on bread alone if he had it to do, but like the rest of the United States and Britain behind him, he wanted and expected to have both. The poverty of the peasant on the Continent, living chiefly on bread, with meat reserved for holidays, and dairy products save cheese practically unknown, was not for America with its rich soil and sparse population. Most Americans were, at this date, of British origin, bringing with them the Britisher's love of meat, and they improved upon even this. Early travelers in both the east and west commented upon the prodigious quantities of meat eaten by Americans.

Bread and meat for everybody, even the slave, was looked upon almost as an inalienable right.[6] The basic diet of the pioneer was, in its overall pattern, not different from that of the rest of the country, though coming from the southern colonies, as most pioneers did, they had behind them a tradition of abundant food and overflowing tables, unknown in the more northerly colonies; meat in New England and even New York was less abundant, and thrifty farmers who sold much cheese had less butter and buttermilk at home than had the butter-producing southerners.

Still, in the first years of settlement, the pioneer never felt too badly off if he had little but bread and meat with of course a few vegetables, dairy products, maple sugar, wild honey, and a little something to trade for a nutmeg now and then or even flour, carried by most French traders. Such a diet was well above that of the slave, often the working man hired with keep as part of his pay,[7] and of course the common soldier.

The daily ration of the Virginia soldier during the Revolution was a pound of flour, slightly less than two pounds of salt or cured meat, but close to three of fresh. He was also given half a gill of salt, a gill of vinegar,

State of Tennessee made "squirrel scalps" legal tender for taxes. Gray, *Bishop*, 41, described a walnut tree in which through the years an estimated 1,500 squirrels were killed.

[6] Mathew Carey, ed. *The* American *Museum or Universal Magazine containing essays on agriculture—commerce—manufactures—politics—morals—and manners*, Philadelphia, Jan. 1787–Dec. 1792 (cited hereafter as American *Museum*), VI, 456. Here, in 1789 the editor was most critical of a lately opened "Bridewell" that served the prisoners no meat at all, only ox-cheek soup on Sundays.

[7] Coffee Papers, "Estimates for Working the Salines." John Coffee's plan for running a saltworks is one of the most revealing business documents of the day—wages, type of work, cost of supplies are all given; food for the woodcutters, kettle attenders and others was to consist of 6,000 pounds of pork, 2,000 of beef, 200 barrels of meal (the barrel of meal or flour was at this time 196 lbs. net), but only 25 of flour. Nothing else is mentioned. The document is undated but appears to have been drawn up in late 1803 or early 1804. His partner in the venture was to be Andrew Jackson who in January of 1804 authorized Coffee by letter, Bassett, *Jackson Correspondence*, I, 80, to buy the works provided the price was right, but the venture got no further.

and a gill of rum or whiskey.[8] This ration was for most Virginia soldiers merely a thing on paper, for many privates went not only barefoot but hungry, while Clark's men, fighting at the behest of Virginia leaders, were lucky to get even half-rotten corn.

Twenty years later the idea of proper food for the common man had not materially changed, but the amount of meat had been cut in half. The American soldier [9] of 1804 was allowed only one and one-fourth pounds of beef or twelve ounces of pork. The flour had been increased to eighteen ounces; rum, whiskey, or brandy was the same, though only two quarts of salt and four of vinegar were allowed to each one hundred men, but no longer did the soldier have to furnish his soap and candles; the army gave four pounds of soap and a pound and a half of candles daily to each one hundred men. This ration, too, existed chiefly on paper; men under Andrew Jackson whether fighting British or Indians quite often had no food at all, and during the War of 1812, hunger was the usual portion of the Kentucky or Tennessee private.[10]

Even the well fed soldier or woodcutter at the saltworks never knew the full joys of corn in all its variations. It is true that the first meal from the first crop in the newly cleared field was, like the first gristmill in the community, a landmark in life, and stories were often told, beginning, "It was before the crop was in," or "before we'd cleared that field." Ten-year-old John Smith riding to mill with the first corn after many months of "wild turkey's breast for bread," [11] felt like any traveler standing in some gap looking down, the hills behind him, smooth going ahead.

Still, no family ever had to wait until the corn was hard to start eating, for the goodness of corn at almost any stage of its growth was only one of its many advantages. The wife of the pioneer farmer growing his first crop of corn would have risked her scalp more times than one to walk out and pinch the young grains in the green ears. When plump and filled with milk it was time for "rosen yers," beloved by most peoples who ever knew corn. Boiled, roasted, or cut off and fried, then seasoned with milk and butter, green corn served both as a vegetable and substitute for bread. It could also be stored for winter use by first boiling, then cutting off the grains and drying on a sheet spread in the sun.[12]

[8] VS, III, 201.
[9] Tenn. *Gazette*, quoting the War Department, Feb. 4, 1804.
[10] Wayne County *Outlook*, 1898, "The Journal of Rhodes Garth." This account of the northern campaigns by a Wayne County soldier speaks more of hunger than of eating; they had almost no whiskey and little food save what was sent from home.
[11] Williams, *Smith*, 24.
[12] A few of the older women in my childhood still dried roasting ears.

The time for pinching was not yet done, even when the last planting for roasting ears was withered in the late-summer drouth. Usually by mid-August and often earlier, the grains, though soft enough to be cut by a hard thumbnail, showed no milk. Then it was time for gritted bread, the first bread many settlers had. During my first year of teaching, this on Cave Creek of the Cumberland, my landlady one day remarked the corn was hard enough for gritting, had a body needed gritted bread. I had heard much of gritted bread, especially during The War when yearly the guerrillas stole the corn as soon as it was hard enough to grind, but I had never eaten gritted bread, and I wondered aloud how it would be.

Next afternoon, walking home from school, the landlady's children hurried, jumping up and down with giggles of anticipation, and soon I learned Mom had a surprise for Teacher. We found it—Mom on the back porch hard at work with corn and gritter. The gritter was much like that used during the Revolution,[13] a heavy piece of rectangular tin punched with a fairly large nail so that small jags stuck out after the fashion of an oversize nutmeg grater. The two longer sides were nailed to a heavy board, the edges close enough together the tin curved up to leave a space between it and the wood, so that as one rubbed the ear of corn back and forth the coarse meal fell through onto the board, held slantwise with one hand, and resting in a long bread tray of gouged buckeye.

Like so many of those "simple" things done in the early days, it looked to be a job for a child, but when I tried it I first gritted a thumb and two knuckle joints, thus ruining a batch of meal with blood; then, fearful for my hand, I produced meal at too slow a rate until Mrs. Blankenship again took over and got enough for the supper's bread in short order. She gritted meal for me all fall, for it was good; baked with buttermilk and eggs, it was a little like spoon bread, but not quite, nutty and sweet, though of course with no sugar, only the taste of the young corn. Poor corn growers had often in the early fall to turn to gritted bread, but others with never empty corncribs had it every fall because they liked it.

Another primitive method of making meal, working best on semi-hard corn, was the corn pounder as the whole device—the wooden mortar and the pounder—was known. The hollowed space in the mortar was larger at the bottom than at the top so that the grains falling back might be forced continually toward the center; the wooden block for pounding might be

---

[13] Kercheval, *Virginia*, Doddridge, "Notes," 274. Dr. Doddridge called it a grater, which it was, but I never heard it called anything but gritter. See illustration, FP, 29, Verhoeff, *Kentucky River*, opposite 138.

powered by hand, but preferably by a long sweep supported by two forked sticks,[14] one shorter than the other, and working on the same principle as the well sweep that can in out-of-the-way regions still be occasionally seen. The corn pounder was sometimes known as a hominy block; the corn was pounded, then sifted, with the fine reserved for bread,[15] the coarse for hominy; though if a family were hungry enough it could do as did Clark's soldiers,[16] pound awhile and boil the whole, both coarse and fine, and eat it in the manner of mush, but some, lacking milk, had, like the soldier, to eat it with nothing or bear's grease.

Much has been written of corn pounders and graters, but much more common on the Cumberland, and also found on all other frontiers, was the hand mill. Many first settlers, among them James Freeland [17] who built the station in which Felix Robertson was born, brought hand millstones. These, though smaller, were much like those used in a horse or water-powered mill. The big difference between the hand mill and the horse mill was that the hand mill worked through the direct application of power to the top stone or runner, and had no gearing. The stones were set into a stout frame of wood pegged and fitted together,[18] with a spout on one side from which would come a slow trickle of meal, if enough hands turned the mill hard enough. There was near the edge of the top stone an iron spike; a powerful long-armed man might seize the spike, and turn the runner while feeding corn into the hole in the middle, but generally it took two to work the thing, one to feed, while the other, using both hands, ran round and round, forcing the feeder to be constantly jumping out of the way. Much more satisfactory was the hand mill that had, instead of a spike, a long stout pole [19] with one end set in a strong crosspiece of wood, and the other end of the crosspiece so fixed that it could revolve around a barn rafter or some solid overhead pole, thus making it possible for two to grind by running round and round.

The hand mill at best seems to have been no more than a temporary device, and as some inventories list only hand millstones, there is the question if even those who brought them, used them. No traveler mentioned one, but travelers, inventories, and chance accounts of Indian warfare, all mention horse mills. These were also a common feature of all frontiers, and

[14] Kercheval, *Virginia*, Doddridge, "Notes," 274-275.
[15] Williams, *Smith*, 46.
[16] I, VIII, 478.
[17] DW, I, 16.
[18] The Mountain Life Museum of the Levi Jackson Wilderness Road State Park has an ancient hand mill in a frame.
[19] Kercheval, *Virginia*, Doddridge, "Notes," 274-275.

used in the Kentucky forts [20] before the Cumberland was settled. The horse mill like the hand mill had the advantage of being a device the settler could use behind fort walls without risking his life from Indians, but it was a much more complicated piece of machinery, for it, like the water mill, was geared up so that the runner stone might revolve at a much greater speed than the horses, or oxen such as Davy Crockett used,[21] walking round and round it. There also had to be a hopper,[22] with a stout overhead framework to hold it, more apparatus for hitching up the horses, and lastly the gearing, sometimes accomplished by means of a narrow circular platform or track, on which the walking horses caused a short log-length to revolve; this in turn was fastened to a pole geared to the runner stone, thus forcing it to turn at the same rate as the rolling log on the platform.

Complicated as it was to build, the advantages of the horse mill over the hand mill were enough, that in the very early years most forts such as Hickman's and Bell's [23] depended upon these, and judging from the number of horse mill bolts and screws offered for sale in Pulaski County in 1801,[24] the horse mill was, in this region at that date, the most common method of making meal. Middle Tennessee was a different story; as early as 1797 the horse mill had so declined in use that Francis Baily [25] had trouble finding meal because the weather had been dry and there was no water in the millraces to turn the mill wheels.

Well before the Indian wars were ended, Middle Tennessee settlers were risking their scalps to go to mill, and the mill, millrace, and millpond became parts of the life of every community as they had been in Europe for preceding generations. Few made a round trip of two hundred miles to mill as did John Smith, but many risked their lives on shorter journeys. One of these was Abraham Mason,[26] who in 1790 had with his wife and ten children settled on Richland Creek near the James Robertson Station. Like most families with no fort of their own, the Masons farmed by day, but spent their nights at the forted station of a neighbor. On the day Mr. Mason went to mill, when night came and found him not home, Mrs. Mason went with the children as usual to Sutes' Station. Her sleep, with

[20] Hamilton, "Journal," 195.

[21] A, V, 41. This, a letter of Davy Crockett describing the death of his niece in a horse mill powered by oxen.

[22] FP, 28, Verhoeff, *Kentucky River*, opposite 139, an illustration of a horse mill in the Kentucky hills; crude, but it appears to have the usual "cogs, Wallower, and trundle head."

[23] W, 30S, 464, and at Bell's, *ibid.*, 255.

[24] PW, I, 3.

[25] Parton, *Jackson*, I, Baily, "Tour 1797," 182–183.

[26] A, III, 90.

no home-coming husband, must have been an uneasy one, for by daylight she was out searching; nine children behind her, and the oldest, a fourteen-year-old boy, in front, carrying the gun. Home, they found father; he had got back from mill after dark, and had decided to chance Indians and sleep there.

Even by this early date, going-to-mill was a chore to be performed by some member of every farm family save that of the miller. However, chore is not the proper name for this pleasant task that usually took most of the day, and sometimes for the boy meant a swim in the millpond, and always news and gossip, particularly at the smaller mills. At these, the wheels did not turn continuously, but as a rule there were mill days, once or twice a week, or in dry weather the miller with a small pond might have to stop grinding for weeks together, and when mill day at last came it was in the nature of a community reunion.

Meal bags are found in many early inventories;[27] corn and meal, wheat and rye, could not be carried in just any old sack. The meal bag was made of the same strong, double-sleighed material as the feather tick, and about fifty-four inches long, big enough to carry two bushels of corn, one in either end, and still leave an empty space in the middle.

Once the housewife had the corn meal she might use it in a number of ways, though, judging from the mention of sifters,[28] she always sifted it first. A stand-by on all borders was mush,[29] made usually with corn meal, but sometimes with rye flour; with milk it continued for generations to be a favorite supper dish of parents for children. Mush for grownups was served only when little else was to be had, for everybody wanted and expected bread and meat three times daily.

The simplest form of bread was that made of meal, salt, and water, and known variously as corn pone, hoecake, or corn dodger. Hoecake is said to have been so named from the custom of the slaves in Virginia,[30] who, given only meal, mixed it with water and baked it on their hoes. Bread could be cooked as corn was sometimes parched, simply by dropping in hot ashes, or the cook, not caring for the taste of ashes, could use a rock sloped toward the fire as did Joseph Bishop.

[27] DW, I, 253. *Ibid.*, II, 272—4 meal bags. MW, I, 17, "2 baggs."
[28] MW, I, 3, 15.
[29] Lord Henry Hamilton, "Journal," 196, ate in the spring of 1779 at Harrodsburg in Kentucky mush and milk for both breakfast and supper, but as a rule mush or bread and milk was supper food for children; there was a superstition as late as the days of a grandmother that meat at night was bad for young children; coming of meat-eating age at night was a landmark in life.
[30] Anburey, *Travels*, II, 335.

Many liked the sweet nutty taste of hoecake, and farm families continued to eat it for generations. Long a favorite in the farm home was the cake baked in front of the fire on a slanted board, usually of carefully smoothed ash, kept for the purpose. The board was sloped toward the fire so that the cake cooked first on top, and no small art was required to turn and get it back onto the sloping board without spilling it into the ashes.

As cooking stoves grew more common, and in remote rural districts this was not until after The War, the hoecake was supplanted by the corn pone, and this, too, made of meal, water, and salt. My grandmother's school first scalded the salted and sifted meal by mixing it with boiling water, then shaped it by hand, and baked it in a heavy iron pan, preferably greased with a meat skin. Another school simply put in cold water, but this was not the true corn pone learned from the Indians, who often cooked the corn quite thoroughly before pounding it into a mushy mass, still to be shaped and baked for bread.

Best beloved and most common of all cornbreads was what we have come to know as cornbread, baked in a Dutch oven covered with coals, leavened, and mixed with eggs and buttermilk. This bread [31] was not radically different from the good unsweetened product one can still find today in Nashville; the big difference was in the meal; meal, often of kiln-dried corn, and produced by high-speed grinding processes, never tastes the same as that from fresh undried corn ground by a slowly turning stone.

The pioneer housewife had no soda or saleratus; instead she used a pinch of lye. Some by tradition made an especial baking lye [32] from corncob ashes, while others boiled down the same lye water they used for soap or hominy, and saved a bit for baking, for lye went not only into the cornbread but the hot biscuit and gingerbread as well. [33]

---

[31] Michaux, *Travels, 1802*, 134, stated the loaves weighed 8-10 pounds and were generally eaten hot; he wrote also of "maize bread," *ibid.*, 54, cooked on a plank, common enough, but he found also, in western Pennsylvania, wheaten bread baked on a board.

[32] Mrs. Henry L. Stacy of West Liberty, Ky., sent me, collected from Mrs. Jeston Gevedon of Grassy Creek—the following recipe: burn corncobs to ashes, put the ashes in water and boil the mixture down to a strong lye. After straining, boil again to a thick paste; put the paste between two metal discs, cover with hot coals and heat (potash was always made by burning lye) until the paste is brittle. Pound to a powder; it was then ready for use.

[33] *American Cookery* by Amelia Simmons, an American Orphan, Hartford, 1792. The 1796 edition (cited hereafter as Simmons, *American Cookery*), 36, directed readers to put two teaspoons of lye in the gingerbread, a common practice; see American *Museum*, VIII, 180. I am indebted to Mrs. Frances Brewer, Director of the Rare Book Room, Detroit Public Library, for the use of the Simmons work, and other

There were many varieties of cornbread, method and mixture depending on the materials at hand. The first settlers when meal was scarce thickened their bread with black walnut meats,[34] and all families had pumpkin bread, usually in the fall when the pumpkins began to get good; there was persimmon bread, descendant of the "prune bread" De Soto's men had eaten two hundred and fifty years before, but possibly the favorite was crackling bread, cornbread or corn pone made rich and crisp and flavorsome with generous handsful of leaf-lard cracklings just before putting the bread to bake.

It was not enough for the first settlers as well as succeeding generations to have some form of cornbread at each meal; they often had, in addition, corn served in some other fashion. A favorite was hominy,[35] still widely eaten. There was small hominy such as that bought by Dr. Thomas Walker on New River in 1750, and made by the John Smith family forty years later in East Tennessee, but my own people seem to have been big hominy people all the way back, and my great-grandmother, Permelia Jane Dick, born in 1819, probably made it as did her great-grandmother on New River in 1750.

Hominy like meal began with good white corn, a thing not always to be had, and many a pioneer housewife sighed because she had to serve bread or mush or hominy that might be any shade from bright orange-yellow to gray-blue; many old-timers remember the speckled corn with its red and blue grains that, save seed carefully as they would, was always mixing with the white. Hominy, or at least my great-grandmother's version, was best when made from undented, flinty corn. She selected the corn, ear by ear, from the crib, saw to it that it was shelled as for meal, that is with small and chaffy grains from both ends nubbed off.

Some used lye water, but she took clean ashes from the hearth, and in most homes woe to anybody who spat in the fireplace; even in that not used for cooking, the ashes were usually saved for lye water. The half bushel or so of hominy corn with plenty of water was put into the big,

---

cookbooks named, each part of a cookbook collection, lately acquired by the library, and at that time uncatalogued.

[34] W, 30S, 282. Smythe, *Tour*, I, 151, described one kind of persimmon bread made with wheat bran.

[35] Hominy is usually considered to be of Indian origin, but Indian hominy, though made of corn beaten was more in the nature of a soup; and the Indian word for hominy, at least in the south, depended on the tribe, and none found bore any relation to the white man's word; see Lawson, *Carolina*, 136, though he gives only two names. Anburey, *Travels*, II, 335, described hominy as broken corn boiled with French beans—a version of what we and many others—though the corn was cut roasting ears—called succotash. My own feeling is that hominy as we now know it was not of Indian origin, but the American adaption of English pilled wheat.

three-legged iron kettle, that usually stood outside under a shed on a semi-permanent rock foundation, then enough ashes were poured in to yellow the corn hulls. The corn was cooked, and only an experienced hominy maker could know exactly the right time to take it off the fire. If cooked too short a time, little flakes of hull would stick and that was disgraceful; but if too long a time or with too many ashes, not only hulls but hearts also would disappear, and hominy without hearts was shapeless and mushy, "an abomination."

The hominy, when boiled exactly the right length of time, was dipped out into a bushel split basket, kept especially for the purpose; smoking hot, it was rushed to the spring branch, where, using the basket as a sieve, the corn was repeatedly rinsed with much rubbing; whatever ashes were left in the corn helped take off the skins and gradually with many rinsings disappeared. If cooked the right amount of time with the right amount of ashes or lye water, the hulls would slip with little trouble, and the whole grains come clean and white and plump.

The hulled corn was put on the fire again, cooked awhile, then "changed," that is dipped out and washed at the spring again, just to make certain hulls and lye were gone. It was put on the fire in fresh water and cooked until the corn grains were tender. Finished, it was known as raw hominy. This, in cold weather, could be kept for some days in the spring house.

Small hominy, or hominy grits, was a somewhat different story, and in general was to the south what groats were to the British generations before, though of more importance to many and eaten in a different fashion, almost always with gravy. Small hominy could be dried and kept for summer use, or grits, the coarser part of sifted pounded corn or coarsely ground meal, could be boiled without pre-cooking. A big difference between big and small hominy was in the nature of the gravy; big hominy was often fried, milk was then poured in, and the whole left to simmer for a time; properly cooked, the grains remained firm and shaped but around them was the milk gravy; grits were usually served with a separate gravy made from ham drippings or bacon grease.

Hominy had by the time the Cumberland was settled long been a stand-by on all frontiers from Pennsylvania southward, and could be made at any season, but the real hominy-making time was the first cold snap of fall that brought hog-killing weather, a great day for the whole family, for no family felt well fed without meat thrice daily, and the favorite meat was that of the hog.

English beef and mutton had in many sections of the south, long since yielded to pork as the preferred meat. William Byrd had complained much of the North Carolinians' love of pork, and described a true Roanoke entertainment as "pork upon pork and pork again upon that." [36] First settlers on the Middle Cumberland were even more dependent upon pork and beef than most first settlers on previous frontiers. Wild meat was scarce.

True, all settlers would now and then have had some wild meat, especially bear, though by 1796 in the neighborhood of present-day Dixon's Springs it sold for ten silver dollars [37] the hundred pounds, an extremely high price when compared to the prices set on meat to be taken instead of tax money by the Sumner County court of nine years before.[38] Wild meat, especially bear and venison, continued to be a fairly staple article of diet for settlers on the Highland Rim east of the Cumberland and in remote valleys up in Kentucky, long after they had disappeared from Middle Tennessee. Travelers [39] found, as late as 1800, bear meat a staple food in out-of-the-way places, and Davy Crockett's bear-hunting adventures took place well after the pioneer period, but chiefly on land, held at this time by the Chickasaw, where white hunters ventured only at the risk of losing their scalps.

The successful hunter coming home like John Cockrill with the bear meat wrapped in the skin, the oil carried in the bear's bladder,[40] could mean, not only much delicious eating, but a bearskin for a coat or rug. The housewife could clarify the oil by boiling it with shaved slippery elm bark,[41] then store it for future use. The bladder itself could serve as an oilcloth for wrapping letters or packages to be carried on horseback, and the spareribs and sides of young bears could be cured with salt and smoking as pork was cured, but no Cumberland inventory revealed wild meat of any kind.

Buffalo meat was even scarcer; only one traveler, and that John Lipscomb coming in 1784, mentioned fresh buffalo meat,[42] and this from an animal killed north of Nashville in what is now the Kentucky Barrens. Now and then in the early nineties hunters found one,[43] but usually down-

---

[36] Byrd, *Writings*, 321.

[37] Gray, *Bishop*, 152.

[38] SC, I, 4.

[39] Williams, *Travels*, Schweinitz, "Report," 504.

[40] Gray, *Bishop*, 112, is an account of running from the Indians with 3 gallons of oil in a bladder.

[41] Mereness, *Travels*, Fleming, "Journal," 640.

[42] Williams, *Travels*, Lipscomb, "Journal," 275.

[43] At least one by the ex Long Hunter John Montgomery, W, 30S, 268. See also *ibid.*, 257–260.

river past Clarksville. Joseph Bishop, big-game hunter coming out in 1791, saw no buffalo until he visited the Illinois, few deer, a good many bear, but chiefly he killed game birds and squirrels, and by 1797 hunting in the whole of Middle Tennessee was so profitless that Bishop put in a crop of corn.[44]

There are from the early stations in Kentucky many stories concerning buffalo meat, made usually into jerk, and the use of buffalo wool that when mixed with the fibers of the bull nettle [45] was often woven into cloth, but nothing was written of such things either by travelers to or settlers in Middle Tennessee; the hunters' paradise had been hunted by too many for too long. A few deer continued to be found; James Biswell [46] had, for example, in 1784 along with some beaver and wolfskins fifty-seven pounds of shaved deerskin, and one in the hair, but this, compared to the old days when hunters would come home with two pack-horse loads, or five hundred pounds, was small indeed.

There were undoubtedly times when the skill of the hunter meant the difference between starvation and a full stomach, but such days were gone around Nashville certainly by 1783. Meat from domesticated animals was the stand-by and on the whole quite plentiful. The soldier was usually less well fed than the prosperous family, yet two of these in the early eighties wrote later that they never ate wild meat at all, but beef, milk, and butter. Both were sentries at French Lick, and when food got low Robertson would bring in a beef from Richland Creek and say, "Divide it out." [47]

The justices of Sumner County court,[48] hoping to feed some troops North Carolina had promised to send, made food legal tender; corn was so plentiful by this date, 1787, it was valued at only two shillings eight pence per bushel; beef was only three pence per pound as was good bear meat without bones—and "prime buffalo meat," like dried beef, was only six, fresh pork four, and venison, of which less than twenty years before hunters had wearied, was a luxury, retailing at nine pence per pound, more expensive than even dried beef.

Beef was throughout the pioneer period and for many years to come, cheaper than pork, but English beef had in its trek from Tidewater to Mid-

[44] Gray, *Bishop*, 155.
[45] W, 29S, 142. The bull nettles that grew six feet high in the virgin soil were picked up in the early spring after they had fallen and somewhat rotted; they were then broken and treated as was flax. See also FQ, II, 114, Clinkenbeard "Interview."
[46] DC, I, 64.
[47] W, 30S, 253.
[48] SC, I, 4.

dle Tennessee undergone many changes; the stand-by of the British soldier or sailor—salt, corned, or pickled beef—is rarely mentioned in the first years, though soon it was being salted and barreled and shipped down-river.[49]

All sources indicate the Cumberlander preferred his beef fresh. This was a logical development in a completely rural region with unusually good grazing grounds, but expensive salt, and no vinegar; items that continued to be imported long after the pioneer years were ended; the cheapest price ever found for salt was $2.50 per bushel, and this not until 1801; in the early years salt cost per pound three to four times the price of beef.[50] Backwoods armies, such as that traveling to the mouth of the Kanawha in 1774, drove their beeves, and travelers often did the same thing; a fashion set by De Soto hundreds of years before.

The pioneer, no different from later generations, never waited until cold weather to enjoy fresh beef. One farmer in the community would kill a beef, stall-fed for a time when at all possible, and divide it out among his neighbors, each taking no more than could be conveniently used, but this no small amount even in hot weather for an average-size family and help could, with no gluttonizing, eat close to twenty-five pounds a day, the amount without bones held sufficient for eight soldiers. The meat finished, another family would kill, and in turn pay back whatever part had been borrowed be it a flank or a hindquarter, taking care to make the payment equal in weight and quality. Judging from the number of scales [51] and steelyards [52] in early inventories, the first settlers, though many might in cloudy weather be forced to guess the time, never guessed on weights. Many also had units of liquid and dry measure, ranging in size from a quart to a half bushel. However, capable as he was of managing, the early settler in any community dealt often with the butcher, for the butchering of beef animals was one of the first industries to disengage itself from the plantation.

[49] "Prices current at Natchez" was a feature in many early Tenn. *Gazettes;* see in particular issues of Sept. 16, 1802, and May 30, 1804; these prices for barreled beef are about the same as those of John Coffee, 3¢ per pound in his "Estimate for working the Salines." Still, in spite of quotations it is doubtful if much meat in brine was shipped from Middle Tennessee until salt got cheaper around 1805, and upriver all meat continued to go to market on the hoof.

[50] DW, I, 107, the sale of the effects of Thomas McCain reveals that 5 bushels of salt in 1789 brought 40 pounds as compared to 33 for a sorrel horse and only one pound, 11 shillings, for a "big cart."

[51] DW, I, 24, and see also *ibid.*, 34, for the inventory of the Leneer brothers, merchants with 6 pr. of small scales.

[52] John Buchanan, DW, I, 69, a first settler, had both steelyards and a half-bushel measure, as had many others, including William Overall, *ibid.*, 283, and James Moore, 47.

John Sevier, though he ate much home-killed meat, visited the Knoxville butcher often in the 1790's, and by 1801 there were butchers [53] in Nashville advertising for stall-fed cattle.

Hog-killing time was and continued to be a part of farm life for both rich and poor all up and down the Cumberland as elsewhere. It is only within the last few years that better roads and local packing plants with freezing facilities have induced most farmers to let somebody else butcher their hogs.

Hogs were in the very early years in Middle Tennessee much less plentiful than cattle, though up the river where the canebrakes were smaller but the oak, chestnut, and beech trees more abundant, just the opposite appears to have been true with hogs so numerous that wills like those in Virginia a hundred years before speak of a "parcel of wild hogs." [54]

Pork continued more expensive than beef, largely because it was the favorite meat; fresh or cured, ham, sausage, smoked bacon or salt jowl, the Cumberlander had a use for it all. The elegant dinings in young Nashville more commonly featured among a variety of other meats a baked ham,[55] instead of the roast of beef found in the better homes in William Byrd's Virginia; and in our world of the upper Cumberland the smokehouse with hams and bacon left from the last hog-killing when the new ones were ready to hang for their March smoking was, like the never empty corncrib, the barrels of whiskey, and the bolts of "extra cloth" a symbol of the good life.

The average family had fresh pork the year around, killing a pig whenever anybody felt the need, but still there was no time quite like hog-killing time; this meant plenty of fresh, juicy pork, cracklen bread, new lard, and sausage strong with red pepper and sage, as well as souse meat and a fresh supply of soap. A few farmers, no different from hill farmers of later years, now and then killed hogs fattened on little save mast, cane roots, and anything else they could find. The meat from such animals, or so I found it years ago, had not the fat, tender lushness of pen-fattened hogs, but was leaner, less tender, and on the whole more in the nature of wild meat.

A few settlers during the first three or four years may have eaten meat from mast-fattened hogs, but certainly such men as Frederick Stump and good farmers like William Hickman who, though a later comer, had by

[53] Tenn. *Gazette*, March 11, 1801.
[54] MW, I, 432, lists a "clan of wild hogs," but this was in Montgomery County and past the pioneer period.
[55] Thomas, *Old Days*, 39.

1790 an eight-hundred bushel corncrib,[56] fattened their meat-hogs as did John Sevier and other farmers of that day. The Sevier hogs were usually put up in October, and though in that large household beeves and hogs were killed at any time with additional meat from the butcher, and some venison, the real butchering-time came after about two months' corn fattening. The Sevier help in December of 1794 killed "eight fattening hogs," after having killed several beeves.[57] This was a rather poor pork year; next season they butchered sixteen hogs on the 15th and 16th of December.[58]

It was a long way from the killing of the hog to the hundred pounds of bacon Mrs. Neely [59] had when killed. Early the Neely household with all help would have had the biggest kettles filled and boiling, hogs knocked in the head, stuck, and swung up by pulleys for proper bleeding—by 1801 pulleys could be bought even upriver near Somerset [60]—and not having a pulley they could heave the rope over the limb of a tree.

We cannot say that Mrs. Neely caught the blood and made a black or blood pudding; this pudding, once so common in Europe, was made by one of my great-great-grandmothers, but gradually disappeared in the plentiful hog country west of the mountains. Blood pudding or no, most of the iron, brass, and woodenware of the family were called into service at hog-killing time. The animals were scalded in a hogshead or poplar trough, scraped, gutted, and allowed to cool. There appears to have been only one important difference between the handling of the pig then and now. The animal was not split down the back and pork chops made. I found no mention of pork chops, and the pioneer treated the carcass as a few families still do in the back hills. The backbone with the tenderloin still in it was chopped out of the ribs, cut into lengths, and usually boiled; sometimes the tenderloin was left with the backbones, other times it was cut out and fried or mixed with the sausage meat.

The middlings, hams, and shoulders were often all cured, that is put down in the big poplar trough with salt, a little saltpeter, and brown or maple sugar. There were no exact rules, but like most other things the curing of meat "all depended." Much depended on the weather; excessive cold that froze the meat was not good; weather too warm was worse and a big shoulder or ham might spoil before it took salt. All activities revolv-

[56] W, 30S, 465.
[57] THM, V, Sevier, "Journal," 173.
[58] THM, V, 191.
[59] DW, I, 166.
[60] PW, I, 3, inventory of John James, storekeeper.

ing about meat were in some homes governed by the moon and signs of the Zodiac, though judging from my own people, the only saying they ever really followed was: "The ox is in the ditch," and in that region of innumerable farming and manufacturing activities made still more complex by the weather, the ox was usually in the ditch. Meat had to be killed on a good hog-killing day, regardless of the sign, and a man behind in his spring plowing and it a rainy March would hang his meat to smoke when it was ready, and so have it out of the way before plowing, even though the moon was on the wane and the meat would shrink excessively.

Smoking was an art for which there was no exact recipe; upriver many preferred a very low fire of green hickory chips, made of rather small limbs with the bark on. One did one thing and the next another; some after curing with smoke, and others before, dipped the meat in boiling water and then ashes to prevent insect trouble, but then it wouldn't get any nice mold. Whatever they did, was an old story by the time the Cumberland was settled; Virginia hams were already famous, and English history does not go behind English bacon.

Good bacon was all during pioneer years the most expensive meat, bringing at times down at Natchez [61] 18½¢ a pound and never less than twelve, in contrast to barreled, salted pork or beef that never brought more than three and often less.[62] Cured meat in some form, usually bacon, formed the basis of the summer's cookery, for the Cumberlander, like the British behind him, liked many of his vegetables—beans, peas, turnips, cabbage, greens or "pot herbs"—cooked with ham hocks, jowl meat or bacon, and cabbage and turnips cooked with fresh pork in winter.

There were, too, sausages of many varieties, and the old wooden sausage cutters and stuffers with their small bits of metal for blades can still be found,[63] though sausage could be made with a knife and a board or even a hatchet. Mrs. Stump and other housewives of Germanic origin would have had a greater variety than Mrs. Robertson, but it is doubtful if in the good hog country of the Cumberland any housewife made as much sausage, which was a way of utilizing scraps, as had either her British or German ancestors. Blood pudding, stuffed into a length of prepared intestine and smoked, was one form of sausage, but possibly the favorite was that

[61] Tenn. *Gazette*, Sept. 16, 1802.
[62] *Ibid.*, May 30, 1804, lists the 196-pound barrel of pork at $7.50; subtracting cost of the barrel, usually $1.00, see Coffee Papers, transportation, and salt would leave less than a cent per pound for the meat.
[63] The Mountain Life Museum has these old-style sausage cutters with stuffing attachment in good condition.

best known in the region today, a raw mixture made less of scraps than of a careful blending of lean and fat, seasoned with sage and red pepper, sometimes smoked and sometimes not, sometimes aged and sometimes not, but always fried and eaten hot, often with gravy and hominy.

The most common sausage made of pre-cooked meat was what some now call headcheese, a thrifty way of utilizing the head and feet; these were cleaned by "swinging," scraping, and scrubbing in lye water, then boiled until tender, the bones taken out, meat cut up, highly seasoned with salt, sage, and red pepper, then while still warm, pressed so that all the grease came out. This sausage was often pickled, but could be sliced, rolled in meal and fried.

The rendering of the lard was another important but often unpleasant chore of hog-killing time; there was for lard as for all animal fats a ready sale and lard in that day of high fat consumption [64] and no synthetics such as margarine was a much more important article both for home consumption and trade, than it is today. It was used in seasoning most foods, save cakes, and large quantities were needed, not only for the biscuit, but for frying—anything from sweet potatoes to cabbage or half-moon pies— and many wills mention lard or fat tubs as well as fat gourds.[65]

Soap making was still another job to be done at hog-killing. The more energetic housewives dumped the intestines into the biggest kettle, covered them with water, and after boiling for some hours, left the kettle to cool overnight, for soap making like other activities connected with hog-killing was done outside; most farms had in time, usually on the spring branch below the spring house, if not a wash house at least a shed and nearby the big kettle. Here, in summer the housewife or her help did the family wash, but it was easier to come to the big kettle and water supply than to move these about; thus, the location of the big kettle or kettles was usually the scene of all manner of activities from soap making to dyeing.

Cool, the gut grease was skimmed off, the kettle emptied and lye water put in. Some boiled this down until it would float an egg, others tested it with a bit of cloth, for the strength and amount of lye "all depended" on

[64] I have no statistics, but all things from travelers to inventories indicate their fat consumption was higher than today. This was true in the hills before World War II —large quantities of lard and fat meat along with butter; that of the Indians appears to have been still higher, for even the meat-loving English, and of course the Jesuits, complained of greasy food. Yet, among all these peoples heart attacks and bad hearts appear to have been extremely rare.

[65] Beginning with Nicholas Gentry, DW, I, 7, killed before he could settle his land, fat tubs are common. Upriver, PW, I, 17 . . . a tub brought 3 shillings as compared to 2 for the Gentry tub. Butter tubs were also common.

how much grease a body had. When the lye was right, the soap grease was put in and the whole boiled until it would coat the paddle, and if cooked right, the mixture when cold would be a soft mass, firm enough to hold its shape when cut; further drying hardened and wrinkled it. Soap was one of those happy things on which it was hard to make a complete failure. Some women [66] boiled the lye water a while, then with no previous cleaning or boiling threw "guts and all" into the soap kettle, and boiled some more; if there was too much grease to mix with the lye it would come to the top and when cool could be skimmed off; if too little, the water and other waste would be on the bottom. There were all kinds and colors of homemade soap, much of it soft and kept in gourds as the listings of soap gourds indicate.

Soap making, lard rendering, not to mention sugar making, and the weekly boiling of the family wash, made at least one big kettle a prime necessity for the farm family, and most first settlers were much better supplied than was the Ruddle household. Samuel Buchanan had a kettle that must have held more than thirty gallons as it brought thirteen dollars compared to a six-gallon pot for four dollars, a Dutch oven and stewpan for seven dollars, and a skillet for two dollars. Kettles came in all shapes and sizes; some such as William Overall [67] had teakettles, William Neely had a ten-gallon brass kettle, but this was above average size for brass. Biggest of all was the iron pot of John Blackamore [68] that sold as late as 1803 for thirty-one dollars. This kettle was most probably a very large sugar-water or salt-boiling kettle, for John Coffee estimated the cost of the salt-boiling kettles he was planning to buy as only eleven dollars each for kettles of twenty-two gallons capacity and weighing 160 pounds.[69]

Ironware for cooking was, compared to tin, earthenware, pewter, and wood, relatively expensive, but much less so than brass, or even a proportionate amount of iron used in nails, horseshoes, or tools. These last were made of bar iron, really a form of refined cast iron wrought with water-powered hammers, and sometimes almost as expensive as steel. Kettles, skillets, and Dutch ovens that sometimes weighed as much as fifty

[66] Drake, *Letters,* 14, is an account of soap making somewhat different from this; Drake's too-little-appreciated work, dealing as it does with a childhood in Kentucky during the 1780's, has a very great deal in it concerning food, clothing, education, and farming activities of the Kentucky farmer-settler, but Drake was from New Jersey, with a different background from most settlers on the Cumberland, and living under very different circumstances—no Indians.

[67] DW, I, 283.

[68] DW, II, 348.

[69] Coffee Papers—"Estimates for working the Salines."

pounds each [70] were all known as castings as they were, with no prior re-fining, cast directly from the melted ore, and were by the early nineties being made in East Tennessee; by 1802 small castings were bringing only ten cents a pound; John Coffee buying wholesale, planned to pay only eight, but at even the higher reckoning the John Blackamore kettle would have weighed 310 pounds and held better than sixty gallons.[71]

Cookware if the housewife had something to trade was never a problem. Joshua Mounts,[72] a pot merchant, peddled his kettles and ovens up and down the Cumberland in 1791, but found the few inhabitants so well supplied he had to try his hand at hunting. In general the ironware used by the pioneer housewife in baking, boiling, and frying is better known than any other facet of pioneer life, chiefly because in the back hills iron cook-ing utensils over an open fire continued to be used until long after The War; even now the swinging crane with hooks, mentioned in early inven-tories,[73] is still used in a few homes on winter days to boil the beans or hog's head. Unable to afford iron, the housewife could always get tin,[74] cheap and plentiful, a skillet selling for as low as twenty-five cents, and five tin cups and a tin coffee pot bringing only two dollars in the late nineties, but the family preferred iron, and usually had it.

The Long Hunter or even the farm wife could, in stirring the pot or lifting meats, use large wooden spoons, or often a pointed stick, but many had flesh forks,[75] which, judging from their price, were heavy, requiring much iron, and wrought at that. The most common tool used in the prep-

[70] John Stewart of Montgomery County, MW, I, 479, had two ovens weighing a total of 90 pounds.

[71] Cheaper iron made large kettles more common in later years; there is in the Mountain Life Museum a sugar-water kettle, as they were usually known, 42 inches across the top, and cast without legs, made to be put on a brick or stone foundation. Such kettles, shallow, this one was only around 18 inches deep, were also used for boiling salt, and at hog-killing time.

[72] Gray, *Bishop*, 44. The Indians lived so far away that when they came to make war they brought their camping outfits, so that any successful foray on a band of Indians yielded kettles; as for example 27 brass kettles and "40 or 50 blankets" were found among the effects of a war party chased out of present-day Smith County; booty was always sold and the proceeds given the soldiers, their only form of pay; this parcel brought $310—W, 1S, 50. Such events account in some measure for the slow pot-sales of Joshua Mounts.

[73] Practically all families had pot hooks, with the more affluent such as Richard Shaffer, DW, I, 311, owning two pair and sometimes more.

[74] DW, I, 45, this the inventory of John Porter who judging from his other effects could afford little else, but many such as the Neelys, *ibid.*, 166, with 6 tin cups had also much copper, pewter and brass.

[75] DW, I, 311. The Richard Shaffer fleshing fork with a camping knife and steel brought a pound, 8 shillings, as compared to 2 pails, 2 piggens, 2 coolers for 16 shil-lings.

aration of meat was the butcher knife; mentioned in many inventories at a wide range of prices, they were also stocked by Mr. Wiggins, and were all in all most versatile tools. One moment in the housewife's hands slicing the bacon, next skinning a beef, and perchance, a week later gone with the head of the house on a war party and scalping an Indian.

"But as he resisted," James Brown wrote, "I got him by the hair of the head with my left hand and him a striving all the time to get hoald of my legs to throw me out of the cannough I made a cut at his head and the skin peeled off a season—and on a third cut brought all the skin from the top of his head, and he sprang up and said, 'Naugh Wai whi.' It is in English, 'That will do.' My reply, 'Inkla,' which is in English, 'No,' I then threw him into the creek and caught him by the feet. . . ." [76]

Scalps and scalpings are often mentioned, but never scalping knives. Another thing never mentioned is the roasting spit. William Byrd, both at home and when visiting wealthy neighbors, often encountered a roast of beef, a reflection of England where the spit of beef or mutton turning on the hearth was ever a part of the good life. Neither travelers nor inventories indicate spits on the hearth as a feature of life on the Cumberland; much roasting, particularly hams and turkeys,[77] was done, but some would have cooked in the ground as did the Long Hunters, and all those with giant Dutch ovens such as John Stewart had roasted in these.

André Michaux complained in 1796 of the widespread use of the frying pan, and intimated it was almost the sole utensil for cooking meat.[78] He visited, but spent little time among the wealthier families, where he might have found a roasted ham or even joint of beef. Meat was certainly boiled with vegetables, and continued to be broiled over the coals; charcoal and ashes were considered healthful even by such men as Daniel Smith and Andrew Jackson.

Plenty of meat, both cured and fresh, and plenty of bread, mush, roasting ears, and hominy meant the end of hunger, but the aim of the Cumberlander in eating was considerably more than the appeasement of hunger. Desserts would have been impossible, hot breads unpalatable, gravy but a poor and watery thing, and in general the family table a sad and dreary place without dairy products. By 1801 and for how much earlier we do not know, Nashville merchants were selling "Loaf sugar and coffee,

[76] W, 6XX, 274.
[77] Roasting for the great wedding feasts of a few years later that featured 20 pigs and 25 turkeys, see Guild, *Old Times,* 351, must have been done in the ground; for not even Col. Archie Overton had 45 big Dutch ovens.
[78] Thwaites, *Travels,* III, Michaux, "Journal," 92–93.

young Hyson, and Hyson skin and Bohea Tea, Pepper, Allspice and Ginger, French Brandy and Spirits, Sherry and Port Wine, Best James River tobacco, and Spanish and American Segars." [79] The hunter could exchange his skins and the farm wife her butter, maple sugar, and linen cloth for "Tamarinds, Sugar Candy, Cloves, Pearl Barley, Windsor shaving soap and English ague and fever drops."

Yet, all of these dainties and drugs together could not rival the place of butter, buttermilk, and milk in the life of the average family. The love of dairy products, brought from Britain, had not been lessened in the fine cattle country of America, but as the frontier moved west had increased in importance. Beverly and Lawson, writing shortly after 1700, mention the abundance of milk and butter in Virginia and North Carolina, and less than thirty years later, Byrd found "seas of milk," in the backwoods of the Piedmont. Later travelers in this same region found the same thing; one in 1774 enjoyed a "splendid breakfast of elegant milk," butter, pumpkin butter, cornbread, and venison in western Virginia.[80] A visitor a few years later, did, like most visiting Englishmen, quarrel at hominy and cornbread, but found the butter around Hillsdale, North Carolina, "exceeding good." [81]

East Tennessee carried on the tradition; cheese and other dairy products are often mentioned, and many must have had spring houses as well stocked as that of a Tory mother, who while preparing a meal in 1780 for a visitor, directed, "Kate, set the table, go down to the spring house and bring up some good cool milk and butter, put on the cheese and meat pie." [82]

The family cow pushing her head through the canebrake or nuzzling her calf penned by the fort walls was ever a part of pioneer life. The Donelsons were one of the few settlers who brought no cows, and in most discussions of food for the settling farm family dairy products should have first place, but it must be remembered that by no means all pioneers were farmers.

Cows, calves, milk, and butter run through numberless stories of Indian warfare. Samuel Barton was shot when he went to see if his cow had calved; Joseph Brown,[83] when wounded, was advised to drink buttermilk;

---

[79] Tenn. *Gazette*, Jan. 18, 1801; Black and Williams also had saddlery, brimstone, Japanned and tin ware, dry goods, cotton and wool cards, etc. Such ads were quite common by this date.

[80] Linn, *Buffalo Valley*, 63.

[81] Smythe, *Tour*, I, 161.

[82] W, 32S, 444.

[83] A, V, 203.

when Hall's Station was attacked in 1787 the daughter of the house carried a piggen of butter to safety.[84] Elder John Smith, remembered of his settling in Stockton's valley in 1795, that "for a while after settling we had no food but milk." [85] Even the soldiers at French Lick in the early eighties had milk and butter,[86] and practically all travelers from Lipscomb in 1784 to the younger Michaux in 1802 mention one or more dairy products.[87] Churns, coolers, piggens, pails, and butter tubs are found in varying quantities in practically all inventories of first settlers who were farmers, and along with these the cows and calves.

Girls and women on the Cumberland, like women on other frontiers, risked death from Indians to milk the cows; men often wove cloth, cooked, sewed leather into breeches, but milking was considered a job strictly for females, even twelve-year-olds such as Mary Stewart down on Mill Creek near Buchanan's Station. One evening in 1787 when Mary's parents were gone from home, and she was left to tend the younger children and milk the cows, but protected by her fourteen-year-old brother, the Indians attacked. Little Peter ran onto the house roof and down the chimney, and though the Indians chased little Nancy and frightened Mary, they did no harm because her brother William killed one.[88]

The chances are that Mary milked into a piggen, red cedar most likely as was the churn. The milk would have been strained through a coarse piece of cloth, then set in a cool place until the cream rose. Mrs. Robertson, the Stump, Buchanan, and Eaton women, and all others who had at times to live crowded into forts felt the lack of many a thing, but one of the worst was that of a good, forever-cool spring house of stone or even logs for temporary use. No proper place for cooling milk in summer meant not only blinky milk unfit to drink, but no sweet cream for the cream jug that most of them had, and neither good butter nor buttermilk could come from milk not properly cooled.

Still, a body could make cheese. The first step was to get the stomach of a freshly killed calf, scour it well with salt, let it drain awhile, then put in fresh salt, and sew it up. The salt-filled stomach was then kept wet overnight in salt water. Next morning the woman extracting rennet for cheese took two quarts of "fresh spring water," and into it put "haw-

[84] W, 31S, 394.
[85] Williams, *Smith*, 22.
[86] W, 30S, 523.
[87] Francis Baily traveling through in 1797, Parton, *Jackson*, I, Baily, "Tour 1797," 183, found milk was a "standing dish," and, *ibid.*, 192, spring houses common. Michaux, *Travels, 1802*, p. 236, also commented on the "milk diet" of the west.
[88] W, 1S, 88–92.

thorne hops, rose leaves, cloves, cinnamon, mace, marjoram, and two large spoonfuls of hops." After boiling the mixture for awhile she cooled it until "milk warm," then poured it into the salted maw or stomach; she added a slice of lemon, sewed the stomach up again, and let it stand for two more days. The resulting liquid was rennet, ready either for mixing with fresh milk, or bottling for future use.[89]

The pioneer housewife could follow the above recipe only in principle, using salt enough to extract the rennet and keep the stomach from putrefying. Her use of spices and sliced lemon all depended; it is doubtful if any family on the Cumberland was ever so remote as not to have nutmeg,[90] and other spices commonly sold such as cloves, and some had rose leaves as soon as the cuttings from "back home" had flowered, but whole lemons were a different story, even among the very wealthy families. Lime juice and orange or lemon juice were brought up from earliest days, but I found no mention of the whole fruit until around 1812.

Once the rennet was extracted, cheese making was fairly simple; the press could be made with a rock-weighted pole, and the same spring house good for cooling milk would do for curing cheese, but cheese, though now and then mentioned in accounts of home cookery, was never of prime importance on the Cumberland. Middle Tennessee did not even supply her own needs, and cheese from New England was in later days, advertised in the Nashville papers.[91]

The trouble with cheese was that, in the making of it, the remaining liquid was whey, not the good, thick buttermilk that came from the churn along with butter. When a body made cheese, there was not even clabber, a thing we children loved as much as did John Lipscomb who made "great slaughter"[92] on it in 1784; carefully lifted from the bottom of the cream crock, eaten with salt and pepper, nothing could be more refreshing on a hot day. And so the Cumberland housewife made butter instead of cheese; and butter early became a surplus product to be sold down the river and always in demand.[93]

[89] *The Art of Cookery by a Lady*, London, 9th edit., 1765 (cited hereafter as *Art of Cookery*), 173.

[90] Nutmegs sold as high as 2 for 35 cents; cinnamon was from $12\frac{1}{2}$ to $16\frac{2}{3}$ cents an ounce; but cloves were 25 cents. See Coffee Papers, 1799–1803.

[91] Nashville *Clarion*, Feb. 12, 1813.

[92] Williams, *Travels*, Lipscomb, "Journal," 275.

[93] Butter prices were, along with beef, pork, and other products, quoted in the newspapers, and merchants often asked for butter; see Nashville *Gazette*, May 30, 1804, and Sept. 16, 1802. Michaux, *Travels, 1802*, 35, found all western farmers with milk and butter, and when in Kentucky, *ibid.*, 236, found much butter being shipped to the West Indies.

In addition to bread, meat, and dairy products the Cumberland settlers produced the usual potatoes and vegetables, though judging from the complaints [94] of travelers and the few times they are mentioned, vegetables were not in the early years grown in such varied abundance as in East Tennessee, and no early writer of the Cumberland gave a long list of commonly grown vegetables as did John Lawson for North Carolina. Most vegetables in use today were grown in the United States long before the Cumberland was settled; the big exception was the tomato; even to the girlhood of my grandmothers the fruit was known as "love apples" and considered poison.

Those most commonly grown on the Cumberland were the old standbys on any frontier—beans, peas, turnips, and cabbage.[95] These like the pumpkins that sometimes reached a weight of 140 pounds,[96] grew well on rich new ground soil, and had the advantage of keeping in such storage as a first settler could provide, though second crops of turnips and cabbage were often started in late summer, and not harvested until late in the fall. Many, particularly the Germans, made their cabbage into kraut, a most useful food to any family before the invention of canning, for it could for long periods be kept in kegs or barrels. They may also have made turnip kraut as did a neighbor of my childhood, quite a good dish, as was also green beans put through a fermentation process, but known as pickled beans instead of bean kraut. More enjoyable than either to the pioneer with neither apples nor pears to store for winter, were raw turnips and cabbage.

Beans and peas were favorites and could be grown among the corn, while those not eaten green were stored; two bushels of peas [97] bringing only $2.50 in 1803 as compared to 83¢ for only one bushel of sweet potatoes; these, sometimes known as "Carolina potatoes," had long been a favorite in the south for roasting in the ashes, frying, or mixing with milk, eggs, and spices to make pie filling. Some families would have used a variety of pea, known as the salat pea, still a few years ago grown in the back

---

[94] Brother Schweinitz in his "Report," Williams, *Travels*, 516, complained of the lack of vegetables, but Robertson's daughter, Lavinia, wrote, W, 6XX (50), 11, that in 1781 when they were so hard pressed by Indians they grew nothing "but cotton and vegetables." Still, no first settler's inventory revealed potatoes or kraut or even dried beans, though these may have been eaten by the widow before the inventory was made; even meat and corn were not always mentioned in the first inventories.

[95] Typical is well-to-do John Deadrick, DW, II, 106—corn, turnips, cabbage, and potatoes. See also, *ibid.*, 242–244, 290.

[96] Nashville *Clarion*, Nov. 19, 1810.

[97] DW, II, 290, 293.

hills from handed-down seed. These, instead of being hulled, were pre-pared and cooked with meat much as were green beans.

These last, boiled with bacon, are still a favorite on the Cumberland, sometimes cooked in an iron pot in much the same manner as Mrs. Jocelyn, south of Nashville, cooked those she served her visitor, Francis Baily, in the summer of 1797.[98] Mr. Baily didn't relish the dish of bacon and beans too well, but I can think of no better eating, if prepared by the old ways handed down. The preparation of a mess of beans was just about as im-portant a job as the making of good butter. Much depended on proper beans; the favorite varieties were cornfield beans—the speckled goose-craws or the brown Octobers—and these must be well plumped out, with a few brown-hulled ones to be shelled, their soft, bright seed to be cooked with the green ones.

Beans for next day were picked late in the afternoon into a basket or a tucked-up apron, and when the early supper was finished, the woman, often a grandmother, if she could see well sat with them in her apron, broke off the ends, pulled off the strings, and broke them into pieces. Next morning they were put into a kettle, iron of course, and cooked during breakfast getting; after breakfast they were taken to the spring house and changed and washed through two or three waters. They were put on the fire again, outside in hot weather, and this time a large chunk of cured hog meat, jowl bacon would do in beans, sliced down to the skin, but the lye-water-scrubbed skin left on was put in. Beans and bacon cooked along till noon; you could eat a few for dinner, but they were better left sim-mering along till supper.

Sometime along before supper some Irish potatoes would be peeled, quartered, and buried in the beans; a little later some roasting ears, and last the okra pods on top. All this with cornbread, sliced cucumbers, pickled beets, red pepper relish, with some fried meat and gravy, and the usual wild honey, preserves, pickles, slaw, and sweet potatoes, baked in the ashes, made quite a good supper.

Dried green beans, known as shuck or fodder beans, needed an even longer cooking but in winter made a fair substitute for fresh green beans, and in drying them in summer the old ones followed much the same re-cipe as that given in a Nashville newspaper of 1811,[99] save they did not put in a teaspoon of sugar. However, the main bean in winter was the dried bean, almost always boiled, for beans boiled with bacon and less

[98] Williams, *Travels*, Baily, "Tour 1797," 409.
[99] Nashville *Clarion*, May 7, 1811.

often ham hocks, were to the Cumberland partly what the baked bean was to New England, though in that country of abundant meat, beans and peas together were never as important as in New England.

Most Cumberland housewives hulled their boiled beans as did my great-grandmother. She first boiled them awhile in weak lye water, then carried them to the spring branch where, like the hominy, they were washed in a basket, until the cold water on the hot swollen beans made the hulls slip with little trouble. Her husband would not have eaten unhulled beans, and certainly she would never have served them. The English cookbook [100] of 1701 directing housewives to hull their beans had not been published when her people came to America, but the old ways lived from mother handed down to daughter.

I have never found anything—food or custom—that I could, with complete confidence, say was purely white American. Most activities from growing corn to building log houses were adaptations of things either learned from the Indians or brought to America. We children ate many clove-studded pickled beets, put soap on felons, and admired the pickled walnuts of a neighbor. The London lady of more than 250 years ago gave recipes [101] for all such things, including how to treat a felon, and though we no longer used the word "sousing" for pickling, we, no different from our neighbors, did refer to the one pickled sausage—headcheese—we had, as souse meat.

Another learning handed down was that of how to pick a mess of salat greens.[102] Known variously as pot herbs, salat, or simply a mess of greens, this dish was not peculiar to the new world, but had long been known in the old, and in writing of wild greens no generalizations can be made for they, too, "all depended." Each woman had her own special mixture, depending on the time in spring, and the location; Mrs. Captain John Donelson remembered their party gathered lamb's-quarters in 1780, but we seldom picked lamb's-quarters, though many of the neighbors did, for it had a long history as a pot herb, and was eaten in America before 1700. Many greens such as plantain were so beloved by the English colonists

[100] Written by a Lady, *The Whole Duty of a Woman*, London, 1701, "boil your beans so the skins will slip off," 202.

[101] *Ibid.*, soap on felon, 75; pickled beets, 265; green pickled walnuts, 260; and another favorite, "pease soup," 147, mentioned by John Lipscomb in 1784.

[102] This word is not in Webster's and as we used it, the meaning was not that given in OU, for salat was not a variation of salad; we had both. Salat or sallet or salet was any green leafy vegetable cooked—salat greens could mean a mixture of wild greens or poke salat, still heard at times; turnip salat meant turnip tops, while salads of various kinds, especially potato, were an old story, but not so old as the other.

they planted the seed in new clearings, but the pot of wild greens simmering over the fire was a great deal more varied than in Europe, for into it went the taste and knowings of many nationalities including those of the Indian; some picked poke with a sparing hand as did the Chickasaw women, forever remembering the root was a deadly poison, while others cut the young thick shoots close to the root in the manner of gathering asparagus; rolled in meal, fried in lots of lard, the shoots were then eaten with a little vinegar as were most wild greens; a Virginia traveler [103] during the Revolution found poke somewhat like "spinage."

Many varieties of wild lettuce and mustard, later prized for greens, not only did not thrive in the woods but were not native to the region, so that the housewife had to depend largely upon plants native to riverbank or woodlands such as poke and crow's foot. One settler [104] remarked that in Kentucky of the early 1780's women followed the cows, and picked whatever they ate because they knew it wasn't poison; but this is doubtless only the tale of a man who knew nothing of wild greens but the eating; it wasn't just what you picked, but the proportion that told the tale; blue root was good, very good, but it needed a bit of dock to balance it off; too much wild lettuce made for bitterness, but none at all gave overmuch dullness; tips of wild grape shoots were good, but not too many.

Much has been written of pot likker, some on the Cumberland cooked their greens with bacon in a kettle, much as green beans were cooked, and the resulting liquid was pot liquor; but our school only boiled the greens in a kettle, and then cooked them in a skillet in which bacon had been cooked, and if you left the bacon with the greens it was still better. Wild greens were, of course, not their only pot herbs; cabbage was often boiled as were turnip greens, kale, mustard, and colewort, great-great-grandmother of present-day collards.

One of their most versatile vegetables was the pumpkin which like the watermelon [105] would grow untended among the corn. Pumpkin could be stored in the fall, down under the fodder bundles, and then served as a vegetable—peeled and boiled, it was then fried—through most of the winter; it could be dried, or, freshly cooked, put into the cornbread batter; cooked with spices and sugar or honey it made a fairly good butter,

[103] Anburey, Travels, II, 376.
[104] FQ, II, Clinkenbeard "Interview," 98.
[105] Old Johnnie Boyd grew watermelons in his corn patch near French Lick Station in 1787, and in that year on a bright moonlight night young bucks guarding the fort, raided the patch and frightened the wits out of some in the Station who thought they were Indians; W, 30S, 251–253. Watermelons, like cucumbers, radishes, celery—grown by Sevier—would, like other vegetables, always eaten fresh, not appear in an inventory.

and when cooked for a long time in a large quantity of water, strained, and the water further reduced by boiling, pumpkin molasses could be had.

It is doubtful if much pumpkin molasses was made on the Cumberland; I found no reference to this form of sweetening, but several to maple sugar and maple sugar-making.[106] Even those families with no sugar bush could have bought maple sugar when they could not afford the more expensive loaf or even brown sugar, for maple sugar usually sold from a third to a fourth of the price of the other,[107] and the making of it was an old story by the time the Cumberland was settled. However, the most common form of sweetening to go with the hot cornbread and butter was undoubtedly honey. De Soto's men, two hundred years before, had found a few wild bees, but by the time the Cumberland was settled so many swarms of "English flies," descendants of those imported by the colonials, had escaped their parent hives that wild bees were abundant all up and down the Cumberland. Up in the Rockcastle Country and in the Big South Fork many rock bluffs still bear the name of Bee Cliff, and the following of wild bees to a rich store of honey, sometimes in a cliff, sometimes in a tree, was a highly specialized form of hunting.[108] Not all had to hunt; in September of 1798 [109] forty swarms settled on Judge McNairy's garden fence, with twenty returning the following fall. Plentiful as were the wild bees, many of the first settlers had bee gums; Samuel Buchanan's [110] three selling for seven dollars in 1788.

Plentiful and cheap as were the substitutes, they were never able to take the place of the sugar brought up from New Orleans at great trouble and expense. The inventory of the first storekeeper found, and this in 1786, stocked sugar,[111] and mention of sugar and sugar bowls and sugar chests along with large amounts in store accounts, all indicate that even the aver-

---

[106] There are several references to making maple sugar on the Cumberland, but each only incidental to the real story—trouble with Indians. Williams, *Travels*, Schweinitz, "Report," 516, deplored the custom in Middle Tennessee of tapping the trees in December. Mereness, *Travels*, Fleming, "Journal," 631–636, gives a detailed description of how maple sugar was made in Kentucky in the spring of 1780, an account which jibes quite well with tradition.

[107] Williams, *Travels*, Schweinitz, "Report," 450, gave only 12½ cents per pound for fresh maple sugar in East Tennessee as the price the maker got; loaf sugar sold for many years past the pioneer period at around 50 cents per pound; see purchases of John Coffee from Jackson—1804–1806, Coffee Papers. Michaux, *Travels, 1802,* 156, commented of Kentucky that "only poor class use maple sugar."

[108] The only bee to follow was the one loaded; some for this purpose put sweetened water or even honey on an open sunny rock to attract the bees; but others used bottled and slightly aged urine.

[109] Williams, *Travels*, Schweinitz, "Report," 512–513.

[110] DW, I, 297. The Castlemans, *ibid.*, 194.

[111] DW, I, 47.

age farmer was willing to trade much bacon, butter, and country cloth
for sugar. Jelly could not be made without sugar, but even far upriver,
jelly and traditional methods of making were old as the settlement of the
country.

In discussing any phase of pioneer life sweeping generalizations are
seldom safe. This is especially true of food; it was only in the first two or
three years when Indian depredations reduced all families in any given
station to an almost hand-to-mouth existence, that all ate pretty much the
same food. Nationality origins, economic status, and family likes and dislikes exercised a certain amount of influence, then as now. It is doubtful
if Mrs. De Monbruen, for example, ever in her life supervised a hominy
making; she probably served her immediate family cornbread only when
flour could not be had from traders; on the other hand, Mrs. Hugh Rogan,
fresh from Northern Ireland, may have served oat cake and rye or even
bean bread. There was also by this date quite a variation in the food habits
of the different regions of America. Tidewater settlers, and particularly the
South Carolinians, who grew it, had developed a great fondness for rice;
and rice was soon a staple [112] to be brought upriver; it continued to be
eaten and even far upriver seems to have been always obtainable, and was
a part of the traditional food habits of many.

One of the hardest things on which to form any kind of general opinion is the place of flour in the diet of the average pioneer Cumberland
family. Michaux,[113] visiting Middle Tennessee in 1796, declared he had no
bread made of flour during the entire time spent in the region. In contrast
were the memories of a soldier who went on the Nickojack Campaign of
1794 and enjoyed the "fine streaked Bacon," [114] and good flour. Francis
Baily, three years later, complained much of cornbread, though neither
he nor the Dukes of Orleans found fault with the fare in Nashville. However, long before this, flour and wheat were occasionally mentioned in
business transactions, and the Hickmans, though not first settlers, had in
1790 sheaves of wheat in the fort yard.[115]

Certain it is that by 1800 a good deal of wheat was grown,[116] flour was

[112] Rice is quoted at only 9 cents per pound in "Prices Current at Nashville," in
the *Nashville Impartial Review*, Jan. 17, 1807; used in Parton, *Jackson*, I, 245. There
is the question, too, of how much the use of rice in the old west depended upon immigrating South Carolinians. Morgan had in the Illinois served rice pudding more
than any other dessert; I, XVI, 481, Morgan to his wife in the fall of 1768.
[113] Thwaites, *Travels*, III, Michaux, "Journal," 88.
[114] W, 32S, 271.
[115] W, 30S, 370.
[116] Flour and wheat, beginning around 1790, are of fairly common mention in court
records, as DW, I, 252 and 308, "wheat in the sheaf."

mentioned along with corn and meal in lists of prices of exported goods, and "superfine boulting clothes" [117] suitable for flour were advertised. Still, flour continued to cost three to four times as much as meal, and field hands and poorly paid workmen seldom had bread made of it.[118] As a rule, flour to the average settler with not much money to spend or produce to trade, was always somewhat scarce for the first few years. He might have an abundance of everything else, including dairy products, but have flour only for Sunday breakfast biscuit, gravy thickening, and pie crust; wheat was not a crop for the new ground.[119]

Cumberland housewives with their varied backgrounds served many forms of wheaten bread, and daintier fare such as waffles, cooked over the fireplace in long-handled irons.[120] There were biscuits of many varieties, some made with liberal amounts of butter and eggs, and lightly sweetened so that they were much like the English biscuit of today; others were more kin of ship's or travelers' biscuit,[121] most designed to prevent hunger rather than tempt the appetite. The North Carolina or beaten biscuit was good hot or cold, but no kin at all of the hot soda biscuit [122] that was in the early years made with buttermilk and lye as was cornbread. Hot breads twice or even thrice daily, an unheard-of luxury in most of Europe where cooking fuel was scarce and dear, were, by the time the Cumberland was settled, an accepted part of life in the south, and cornbread was commonly eaten hot.

Still, the housewife continued to have her baking days when flour was available. Good German housewives such as Mrs. Stump and Mrs. Kapp would have brought with them cakes of dried yeast, made by themselves and thickened with meal for the drying, and for their yeast they would have carried the seed of hop vines to be planted in a corner of the yard

[117] Tenn. *Gazette*, Feb. 18, 1801.

[118] John Coffee in his "Estimates for working the Salines" planned to use only 25 barrels of flour, to 200 of meal and 1,000 of corn.

[119] The Moravian missionaries who in 1799–1800 visited Stump, one of the best farmers in Middle Tennessee, declared, Williams, *Travels*, Schweinitz, "Report," 516, that good mills were rare and little wheat was grown.

[120] Good examples of these may be seen in the Mountain Life Museum. Waffles were old when the Cumberland was settled, and everybody remembered how Jackson ate waffles for breakfast the day he killed Dickinson, but this was past the pioneer period.

[121] Biscuit are quite commonly mentioned in the Draper Manuscripts, usually in connection with Indian troubles; as in 1782, the men had "biscuit in their budjets," or "a goodly quantity of biscuit," W, 28S, 78. These were most probably some variety of ship's or travelers' biscuit.

[122] Hot biscuit like hot cornbread appears to have been one of those things that developed, but by 1812 they were commonly eaten even in Ohio; see *Memorial to the Pioneer Women of the Western Reserve*, Western Reserve Historical Society, Cleveland, 1924, V, 969.

or even by a window. Still, much wheaten and rye bread, roughly denominated as "fermented bread," [123] depended not upon yeast for leavening,
but upon the spontaneous fermentation of wild yeast such as is to be
found in the sourdough pot of the gold miner, the salt-rising bread made
by our grandmothers, or the breads of Amelia Simmons, lady of Boston,
who in 1792 directed her readers to use "emptins," [124] a watery mixture
got by putting a piece of dough into a crock of water and leaving it to
ferment, really a form of sourdough. Another common levening agent was
barm, but as the Cumberlanders were not great brewers it is doubtful if
many housewives used barm.

If flour ran short we can be certain it was saved for gravies, dumplings,
cakes and gingerbread, and pie crust, and most particularly for meat pie.[125]
Most nationality groups have some means of combining various foods,
usually a meat and a cereal or cheese and cereal, to make a whole meal;
and with the British [126] this meant meat pies of every conceivable variety
—tongue, lumber, pigeon, sea, ham, ox cheek, goose—for which only half
a peck or one gallon of flour was required to make the "walls and bottom."

The biggest pie baked in the biggest Dutch oven was a part of pioneer
life much in evidence at wedding feasts and other celebrations. The beauty
of such pies was that they could utilize small or large amounts of almost
any kind of meat, and were in a sense no more than the Long Hunter's pot
of various meats, put into a crust. The American version of sea pie,[127] a
favorite, was a small cheap thing using only a pound and a half of butter
and four pounds of flour in the crust; into the lined oven were placed
split pigeons, turkey, veal, small birds, salt and pepper with slices of salt
pork for seasoning, more flour and a pint and a half of water for gravy.

The Cumberlander was inclined to use squirrel, wild turkey, venison,

[123] Dr. Daniel Drake, *"Notices" Concerning Cincinnati,* Cincinnati, 1810, reprinted
in *Quart. Pub.* Ohio, III, 31.

[124] Amelia Simmons, *American Cookery,* prescribed most of her bread baking to be
done with "emptins;" pp. 43, 48. An early recipe for "making bread without yeast
or barm," much like what we now know as salt-rising bread, was in the American
Museum of 1789, VI, 292–293; the method seemingly unknown in Philadelphia where
yeast and barm were commonly used.

[125] Meat pies are often mentioned in accounts of pioneer living: Kercheval, *Virginia,*
Doddridge, "Notes," 253–255; Drake, *Letters,* 55, and Trabue in W, 32S, 444, but
everything indicates that in the good meat-growing country of the Cumberland
whole turkeys, hams, and pigs replaced the meat pie.

[126] Meat pies are common in English literature from Mother Goose to Dr. Samuel
Johnson who on Sundays commonly dined at home on meat pie; and early English
cookbooks give them much space; see A London Lady, *The Whole Duty of a
Woman,* 20, 26, 84, and *Art of Cookery,* 139, 140, 142, 226, for some interesting
"pyes."

[127] Simmons, *American Cookery,* 23.

beef, chicken, though fowls were far from plentiful in the early years, and any other meat at hand, but instead of the nutmeg and ginger of the London Lady of a hundred years before, the Cumberland housewife used sage and red pepper. The great dinings in young Nashville [128] also featured meat pies, but these were dainty things of individual size at each place.

Some bread in the early years was a mixture of wheat and rye flours, or even rye and corn meal, for the use of rye as a food disappeared rather slowly. Long after rye bread was only a memory of a memory, one of my great-grandfathers insisted on mush for supper in his old days, and this made of rye, which, like wheat for flour, had, because of the method of threshing, to be washed and dried before sending to mill.

Another thing that disappeared was furmenty. The American version was by tradition little more than the boiled grains of wheat served with milk and sugar, and little kin of English furmenty,[129] a dainty fare of currants and many spices partaking more of the nature of a dessert.

Most average farm families during their first few years of settlement would have had to content themselves with a "little sweetening," at the end of each meal—honey or maple molasses,[130] butters and preserves of wild fruits if these could be gathered in spite of Indians, puddings of various varieties such as sweet potato, Indian, or persimmon—all things that called for few or no eggs and little flour.

Given flour enough and a few eggs, which, judging from the scant mention of fowl in the earliest wills, were scarce, the housewife could make many of the favorite pies of today—pumpkin, sweet potato, ever a greater favorite in the south than pumpkin, vinegar, buttermilk, persimmon, and of course cobblers or pan pies of blackberries and whatever wild fruits grew in her neighborhood with cooks on the heads of creeks upriver using huckleberries. One of our favorite pies and an old one by tradi-

---

[128] Thomas, *Old Days*, 39.

[129] *Art of Cookery*, 154. I have at one time or another prepared, particularly while living in the Cumberland National Forest with proper materials and equipment for experimentation, most dishes mentioned in this chapter, and made cheese, soap, souse meat, etc., but I failed in the two simplest—the traditional preparation of furmenty, for I could never, even with a pressure cooker, get the squeak out of wheat, and I have never, though I still practice, been able to roast Irish potatoes in the ashes without getting one side overdone and the other under.

[130] The word "molasses" was used in the same sense we use "syrup" today; Mereness, *Travels*, Fleming, "Journal," 632, "Maple molasses," and Drake, *Letters*, 87, "pumpkin molasses." Sorghum cane from which sorghum molasses was made was introduced by the Department of Agriculture, and not commonly made until about the time of The War, and was unknown to the pioneer.

tion was the half-moon fried pie, good with any filling, highly spiced and sweetened apple butter, blackberry jam, thick peach butter.

The pioneer housewife had these last two not long after settling, but apples on any border were a rarity; the trees matured slowly, and as most everybody moved in 1784, apples were non-existent on the Cumberland for many years,[131] though in later days the more affluent bought both apples and apple butter from New England and Pennsylvania. Peaches matured much more quickly, and were much more common.

If the old stories and brief mentions of desserts give any true picture, the Cumberland housewife when she had the milk, eggs, butter, and flour was in the matter of desserts more nearly English than in any other aspect of food, for most desserts were much less sweet than similar foods today. Custard pie was ever a favorite as was fruit cobbler, this always served with a sweet, frothy sauce, known as "dip," the only remnant of syllabub left to us upriver. The great dinings in early Nashville of course featured syllabub, custards, cakes, and many other delicacies such as calfheel jelly,[132] all long known to the English housewife.

Even upriver the dessert was a must for company. Young Aunt Dolly, living near the village of Monticello, Kentucky, when confronted with unexpected company for dinner on a May Sunday in 1803, had nothing prepared. Her household was a small one with only two slaves—Frank, a gift from her father-in-law to her husband, and Agnes, a part of her dowry; while these two were bustling about, preparing the meal, she went out to the nearby Barrens and picked wild strawberries; when the main course was finished, the table was cleared as was the custom, and the strawberries served in a deep dish with a pitcher of cream and a bowl and

[131] Williams, *Travels*, Lipscomb, "Journal," 279, Aug. 30, 1784, "We got a few apples that was a great rarity." Lipscomb had just returned from a trip through Kentucky, and was then in western Virginia. Other travelers commented on the lack of apples, but possibly the best indication of scarcity in Middle Tennessee was the newspaper ads. The Nashville *Clarion*, Jan. 19, 1813—cider apples; *ibid.*, May 7, 1811, "green apples;" *ibid.*, Feb. 22, "for sale from Pittsburg, apple cider, apple butter." Some apples were grown locally and *ibid.*, Aug. 4, 1812, vinegar was advertised for sale at Franklin, Tenn., which as this town was not on the river would indicate local manufacture.

[132] Jane Thomas, *Old Days*, 39, 101–102, 104; *Art of Cookery*, 286. The same book and others mentioned have many recipes for syllabubs of various kinds, but as these called for large amounts of eggs it is doubtful if the pioneers had them. Another favorite was gingerbread, mentioned often by Jackson and Sevier, with all early cookbooks, including Simmons, *American Cookery*, giving many recipes. Jane Thomas remembered that in her childhood, ginger cookies were sold in Nashville, stamped with a horse.

spoon placed before each person. Old Matthew Lyon, late of Vermont, but then running for Congress from Kentucky, liked the dessert.[133]

The Virginia middle class on the Piedmont during the Revolution after getting up around six and having an eye opener of strong toddy, went out and worked or supervised till ten o'clock, and then sat down to cold meats, cold turkey, fried hominy, toast and "cyder," ham, bread and butter, tea, coffee, and chocolate.[134] The Cumberland farmer soon was having most of this, especially the ham, toddy, bread and butter, but more coffee than chocolate or tea. Walton's tavern [135] at present-day Carthage was in 1797 serving travelers a breakfast of cornbread, rashers of bacon, and coffee. Some farmers would have had by this date a good deal more, or much the same "miserable fare" an English traveler found on the Piedmont, "bacon, eggs, hoecake, peach brandy, and whiskey." Many Cumberlanders preferred such a breakfast to anything else—good fresh eggs, home-cured bacon, hot cornbread with plenty of good butter, gravy, or honey in the comb, all with good coffee and good whiskey, the whole flavored slightly with wood smoke from hardwood embers, was not bad eating. Few farm wives when in a good way of being established served as little as one meat for breakfast; bacon, ham and red gravy, fried chicken, squirrel in season, and fried beef might all be had at once on any table in summer; winter brought fresh pork, more beef, with turkey, sausage, souse meat, cured meats from the last hog-killing for anybody who wanted them, and up-river venison appeared on many tables until well after The War.

Dinner in those households where the menfolks worked in the fields came around one o'clock as contrasted to larger establishments with overseers where all meals were later. The noon meal had about everything served at breakfast with the addition of vegetables, boiled meats, and often beans—green in summer, boiled dried beans in winter. Peas were a favorite food, both green and dried, and there were potatoes, but the Irish potato [136] never was so prominent in the diet of the southern colonial, and later the Cumberlander, as the sweet potato, and with plenty of hominy, potatoes were little needed.

Desserts demanding flour and eggs were not always to be had, but the

[133] RK, XXVII, 18–19.
[134] Anburey, *Travels*, II, 341.
[135] Parton, *Jackson*, I, Baily, "Tour 1797," 186.
[136] There were then as now many superstitions concerning the effects of certain foods. One great-grandmother had, for example, fed Irish potatoes in very small quantities and none at all to the young children; she thought, in common with others, that the eating of Irish potatoes caused stupid lazy children.

farm wife on a substantial plantation could with no notice usually serve up a meal, much like that Mary Slocumb served her unexpected visitor, Colonel Tarleton, when he dropped in on her plantation on the Neuse River in April of 1781. She had boiled ham and greens, turkey and sweet potatoes, boiled beef, sausages, baked fowls, half a dozen different dishes of pickles, stewed fruits and "other condiments," all with peach brandy.[137]

This did not compare with the elegant dinings that came early to the great establishments in Middle Tennessee, but throughout the Cumberland, even in narrow steep-walled valleys there was fertile soil—and this meant good eating. It was good hog and cattle country, and with much unsettled forest land nearby or even owned by the farmer, game continued abundant with pork so plentiful that a long-gone grandmother eager for a quick jelly-making fire or merely in a hurry, would cry, "Nance, run fetch a little salt pork and throw it on and spark it up a little."

Inventories, up the river as well as down, list innumerable articles for cooking, the preparation of food, and for eating, and most had in addition to the usual iron, pewter, earthen and woodenware, brass and tin, several articles—a nutmeg grater or a spider—not absolutely essential, but among them all I found no coffee roaster. This may have been there as in New England, but most housewives parched their coffee in a skillet, and lived without china or silver.

Not all had tablecloths, but these are quite often mentioned. Some doubtless used oilcloth, well established as a style [138] before 1800, but practically all tablecloths, like other household linens, were, during this period, of linen. The Cumberland housewife must have been quite a cleanly soul; no traveler complained of dirt, not even in the very early years. Daniel Smith stopped at Eaton's Station and boarded with Kaspar Mansker in the hard winter of 1779–80, but complained of nothing until he went up to Kentucky, where at The Falls he found a landlady who was a "Xanitippe" [139] of a woman as well as dirty.

It took a deal of scouring and scrubbing to keep the pioneer kitchen and the array of utensils clean. Woodenware alone demanded much labor, and every kitchen, rich or poor, separate or together, used wood for all manner of things—for the dairy, mixing bread and other foods, laundry,

---

[137] Elizabeth Fries Ellet, *Women of the American Revolution*, New York, 1849, I, 351–352.

[138] Ramsey, *Tennessee*, 655, gives the expenditure of the Legislature of the State of Tennessee for an oilcloth table cover at its first meeting in 1796; and the John Coffee store accounts for 1803–1804 have several listings of oilcloth.

[139] THM, I, Smith, "Journal," 63.

and storage of everything from dried beans to whiskey. It was cheap enough that no woman ever need do without an extra churn. At John Law's sale,[140] for example, one iron wedge brought eight shillings, a washing tub, butter tub, and churn together only twelve, while two pails, two piggens, and two coolers sold for only sixteen shillings as compared to five for a pair of shears. The large amount of woodenware needed explains in part the separate kitchen, and also why early, most settlers had spring houses, loom houses, wash houses, smokehouses; the kitchen was already crowded with utensils needed in the preparation of food; it had little space left either for storage or fireside manufacture.

The Cumberland pioneer in some aspects of his life continued for many years to be an English colonial—local government, horse stock, books, and the pattern of his education were, like the pounds and pence with which he reckoned, of British origin. Food habits, even by the time the Cumberland was settled, had become more Americanized than any other aspect of life. It was not only that wheat had for many yielded to corn, roasting to frying, and cold bread to hot, but tea, even on the Virginia Piedmont,[141] was being supplanted by coffee.

The greatest change was in drinking habits. Any early English cookbook gives much space to brewing; the cost of brewed drinks is mentioned more than once as a legitimate part of the cost of rearing a family, and even schoolboys had their beer, ale, or porter. In addition to these, cider, mead, and to a less extent, metheglin, were made and consumed in the English farm home. The brewed or fermented drink was in English economy no luxury; apples, honey, and small grains were to be had at home; it was cheaper to make brews of these and let most of the milk go into cheese, though much butter was made.

This pattern was carried to America, and early writers of the southern colonies mention homemade brews and the attempts of the settlers to brew from corn, persimmons, and such, for small grains were not happy in the sandy lands and warm climate of Tidewater. The Piedmont was, once the land was cleared and reduced somewhat with corn, more suited to the small grains, but brewed drinks had here another factor to contend with that had nothing to do with the soil—the increasing numbers of

[140] MW, I, 308.
[141] Neither Smythe nor Anburey found during the Revolution tea in the average home on the Piedmont and even the upper class used it but little; see Smythe, *Tour*, I, 41–42, but some tea continued to be used; many inventories contained teakettles and tea ware; tea, both Hyson and Bohea, figure quite prominently in the John Coffee store accounts, but it grew increasingly rare.

Scotch and Scotch-Irish. Most English writers of and visitors to northern Ireland or the Scottish Highlands whether Smollett in fiction or Keats, writing a letter more than seventy years later, commented on the widespread manufacture and use of whiskey among the Scotch. It kept the poor Highland cattle herder warm and relieved the grief of the wealthy, and toddy was to the Highland Scot what it would be to the Cumberland farmer a hundred years later.

There were other reasons why whiskey on the Cumberland supplanted brews; corn, as Mr. Chiswell learned, was unsuited to brewing, but by that date some Scotchmen were undoubtedly experimenting with making whiskey from corn, as whiskey was common in western Pennsylvania and Virginia by 1740. As the colonials, and these heavily seasoned with Scotchmen, pushed westward, we hear less and less of brews, and cider, because of the scarcity of apples, was seldom made. Brews and fermented drinks persisted to some extent, and are mentioned in tavern rates for East Tennessee.[142] Metheglin, beer, and ale were doubtless made by many, but even to my mother's childhood metheglin was no more than the memory of a memory. It was cheap to make and could be a by-product of honey storing and straining time, and for its manufacture required only the woodenware any farm household had at hand. The housewife [143] was directed to boil a variety of spices in a small amount of water; this water was then put into honey, and water added until the mixture would float an egg; different from cider, yeast was added to start fermentation, for honey will not, of its own accord, ferment as will sweet things made by man. Metheglin like mead, made in much the same fashion, could be drunk when fresh.

A thrifty family in New England with a market for cheese and not too much good grazing ground, found it cheaper to consume brewed drinks and sell cheese. The Cumberlander seldom worried over what was most profitable, taking instead what he wanted—and this meant whiskey, buttermilk, and coffee. The wealthy of Middle Tennessee were also part of a wider world where wine was and continued to be, a feature of all expensive dinners,[144] and could be more easily had by water from New

[142] Ramsey, *Tennessee*, 669, in tavern rates for Sevier County mention is made of beer, cider, and metheglin.

[143] Written by a Lady, *The Whole Duty of a Woman*, 75.

[144] I found no wine chests among the first settlers, but all tavern rates for Middle Tennessee price wines, and as early as 1790, Andrew Jackson, far from affluent, spent down at Natchez $190 for wines and "sundries," Bassett, *Jackson Correspondence*, I, 8. This was probably his honeymoon, as in January of the next year, 1791, Rachel Donelson Robards was referred to as Rachel Jackson, DW, I, 199, Jan. 28, 1791. The

Orleans than in East Tennessee. Brewed drinks are seldom mentioned on the Cumberland, and I found no inventory with any, though whiskey, beginning around 1795, commonly appeared in most inventories of even the fairly well-to-do and figured in many store accounts.

The distilling of whiskey,[145] like the serving of hot breads, was helped along by an abundance of cheap firewood. The pioneer housewife either was herself, or had someone about her, skilled in building and laying fires, for most families had cranes and hooks but neither dog iron nor fender.[146] These heavy pieces of iron were expensive, and even the housewife with a shovel of iron instead of wood, quite often managed without them.

She could still have a good cooking fire; most depended upon the wood, and in this matter the cook was something of a dictator, and woe to the lazy farm boy who brought in easily cut poplar or pine. Most by tradition wanted the back log of green hardwood—maple, hickory, and chestnut were all acceptable; oak would do but it took a deal of heat from the foresticks to get green oak in a good way of burning. The foresticks must also be of hardwood, preferably seasoned, but not too dry, though in the end it all depended on how much had to be cooked how soon. A new fire was never much good for cooking.

problem of truth is a big one when discussing wine-drinking habits, or any other aspect of life among the wealthy. I found no bottle of wine in any early inventory, and the affluent Donelsons had for silver only one half dozen teaspoons—that is as revealed in this inventory, and no other family at first had any. Still, by 1801, Nashville *Gazette*, June 10, a silversmith had set up shop in the small world of Middle Tennessee that had only around 30,000 people and almost a third of these slaves, and by 1803, Dr. Sappington, DW, II, 274, had a good bit of hollow silverware. Mrs. Henry Hail up near Somerset, Ky., has several sets of flat coin silver, much of it made at a very early date by a maker in Louisville; and even among a branch of my own people, thrifty, bookish, Scotch from South Carolina, there was enough silver that one child's share was half a dozen, heavy, large, tablespoons of coin silver, engraved with the surname of the family.

[145] Everything indicates that for many years Middle Tennessee did not produce enough whiskey for her own needs. It was not until 1794 that whiskey was found in any Middle Tennessee inventory, and then only in small quantities: DW, II, 4, 4 gals. 1 qt.; 34, 7 gals., 5 pints; 272, 20 gals. There were by the middle of 1796, 97 stills in Middle Tennessee, but some distillers like the Rev. Thomas B. Craighead produced only 30 gallons, a few none, with even the larger ones such as Frederick Stump with four producing only around 600 gallons. These facts and figures cited by permission of Mrs. Harriet Owsley, Senior Archivist, Manuscript Section, Tennessee State Library and Archives, Nashville, Tennessee, from the Jacob McGavock Dickinson Papers, Judge John Overton's Record of Distilleries for the years 1795–1802 when he was Supervisor of Internal Revenue for the District of Tennessee, 9–11.

[146] The word *dog iron* can still be heard in the hills, and most firedogs were so listed; Eusaubius Bushnell had in 1789, dog irons, DW, I, 120.

EPILOGUE

THE KETTLE singing from the crane above the glowing hickory embers was like most other aspects of pioneer life, both new and old. Fire and kettles were old in Europe when Martin Chartier visited the Cumberland. The heat of hickory embers had long been known to the American Indian, but was strange to England. The pioneer put the three together.

The first settlers on the Cumberland, like first settlers elsewhere, invented nothing and most certainly not democracy. They pioneered no new system of government or religion or agriculture. Rather the successful pioneer was a master hand at adapting old learnings to a new environment; we see this not only in the physical aspects of his life—log house learned from the Swede; whiskey from the Scotch; corn, moccasins, poplar dugout, from the Indians, but also in the pattern of agriculture, trade, industry, education, speech, and all other aspects of his life so abundantly represented in source materials, my gleanings could not be incorporated into one book. Zachariah White, running from his classroom into mortal combat with Indians in the spring of 1781, taught in a form of fort, unknown in England. Yet, he like all other early teachers on the Cumberland used textbooks of English origin. Most early ministers on the Cumberland, even Asbury, preached at times in the woods, but the basic tenets of their theology were, like the hymns of Watts and Wesley, of European origin.

The new log house in the new ground field was new to the man who cleared the land, but behind him other men on older borders to the east had built cabins and cleared fields. The Cumberland pioneer was merely re-creating a way of life known by that date to many other men; the pattern shaped and changed somewhat by the land, the climate, the river, and the Indians. All these influenced the pattern of his life, but it was not a new pattern.

Mr. Gubbins, admitted to the Davidson County Bar in 1785, dead of Indians less than a year later, was a pioneer lawyer, but in his dress, his Blackstone, his quires of writing paper and packets of ink he was trying to re-create the life of a lawyer he had known in North Carolina Tidewater. He, like most of the other men about him, was still part of the world on the other side of the mountains. General James Winchester, buying Lord Chesterfield, Paine, Dilworth, and Voltaire, stocking them in his store on Bledsoe's Creek, was attempting to re-create a bit of Philadelphia's cultural and educational life on the frontier; and most of this life in turn was owed to England. Basically he was still an English colonial; what we now refer to as the American Way of Life had not, south of New England, begun to develop.

Much has been written of a thing called "the pioneer mind." I found no mind I could hold up and call "the pioneer mind," and no man I could call "the pioneer." The difference between the first settlers on the Cumberland and the rest of the country was one of degree and not of kind. They did not call themselves pioneers; later, other men, viewing them with different eyes, gave the name. The old ones lived to learn they were the last of their generations to plant British culture in the woods. Past the Mississippi the trees thinned, and the settlers who went there were quite often self-consciously American. Whatever the pioneer on the Cumberland was, he was not that. As one delves deeper into the complexities of his social, intellectual, and educational life one realizes more and more that the purely physical aspects of his world were in a sense the least of him. One also realizes there can never be a complete and perfect seeing. We cannot see him as he saw himself; this is not a mere matter of time or change in physical environment. Our eyes, looking at him across the years, must study him through a maze of modern concepts in sociology and psychology, unknown to the pioneer, but thick about us as Cumberland River fog. Our attitudes toward religion, man's relationship to his government and his fellow man are entirely different from those that surrounded the old south from which most pioneers came. Pavlov's dog had not yet salivated, and the Reformation was still a vital force.

INDEX